D0561135

POLITICAL LEADERSHIP IN DEMOCRATIC SOCIETIES

Nelson-Hall Series in Political Science

Consulting Editor: Samuel C. Patterson
The Ohio State University

LIBRARY
I.U.P.
Indiana, PA

321,8
P759L

POLITICAL LEADERSHIP IN DEMOCRATIC SOCIETIES

Anthony Mughan
THE OHIO STATE UNIVERSITY

Samuel C. Patterson
THE OHIO STATE UNIVERSITY

EDITORS

Nelson-Hall Publishers
Chicago

Project Editor: Dorothy Anderson

Cover Painting: *Allies Day, May 1917*; Childe Hassam; National Gallery of Art, Washington, DC; Gift of Ethelyn McKinney in memory of her brother, Glen Ford McKinney.

Library of Congress Cataloging-in-Publication Data

Political leadership in democratic societies / [compiled by] Anthony
   Mughan and Samuel C. Patterson.
         p.   cm.
      Includes bibliographical references and index.
      ISBN 0-8304-1218-2
      1. Democracy.   2. Political leadership.   3. Comparative
government.   I. Mughan, Anthony.   II. Patterson, Samuel Charles. 1931–
JC421.P66   1991   91-2761
321.8—dc20   CIP

Copyright © 1992 by Nelson-Hall Inc.

All rights reserved. No part of this book may be reproduced in any form
without permission in writing from the publisher, except by a reviewer
who wishes to quote brief passages in connection with a review written
for broadcast or for inclusion in a magazine or newspaper. For information
address Nelson-Hall Inc., Publishers, 111 North Canal Street, Chicago,
Illinois 60606.

Manufactured in the United States of America

10   9   8   7   6   5   4   3   2   1

TM The paper used in this book meets the
     minimum requirements of American
     National Standard for Information
     Sciences—Permanence of Paper for
     Printed Library Materials, ANSI
     Z39.48-1984.

A000006351021

Contents

Contents

Preface

This book arose out of a project to offer advanced undergraduate students a course on political leadership from a comparative perspective. We quickly discovered that a suitable text was lacking. A good deal had been written in political science and other disciplines on the concept of leadership, and historically or psychologically oriented biographies of political leaders from various countries abounded, but there was no single volume that looked more generally at *leadership in action*. This was not true of particular countries, of course. We found, for example, an overwhelming abundance of books and scholarly articles on the American presidency and on individual presidents and their relations with Congress, the Supreme Court, and the American public in particular. By and large, however, this literature is remarkable for the narrowness of its focus. The United States has the only fully presidential system of government in the democratic world, but its uniqueness is rarely acknowledged. Writers on the presidency generally show little interest in the nature of executive leadership in democratic societies as a whole and in the generalizability and comparative implications of the American experience. Moreover, where comparative analysis does exist, as, for example, in Richard Rose and Ezra N. Suleiman's *Presidents and Prime Ministers* or Colin Campbell and Margaret Jane Wyszomirski's *Executive Leadership in Anglo-American Systems*, they tend to concentrate on the governmental role of chief executives.

This anthology is intended to make the study of democratic political leadership more accessible to undergraduate students by avoiding the shortcomings in the existing literature. We have selected readings that juxtapose political leadership in a presidential system of government, the United States, with the same phenomenon in parliamentary systems of government, principally Great Britain. Second, the readings do not focus on a single aspect of the phenomenon of political leadership in democratic societies, but seek to reflect its diversity and complexity. In this regard, we identify a number of "ingredients" of leadership and organize the readings around them. Broken down into eight sections after a general discussion of the nature of political leadership, these ingredients are (1) the role of personality and of the socioeconomic and political background of elected political leaders; (2) their attitudes and behavior as they are shaped by both the structure of conflict in society and institutional "rules of the game," which help to shape distinctive patterns and styles of leadership; (3) the two-way linkage between leaders and followers; and (4) the impact of political leaders. In an effort to impose a coherent overview of leadership, we preface each section with a brief introductory essay highlighting the significance of the topic it addresses.

Twenty readings are included in the anthology. To economize on space, we have abridged a number of them, omitted tables, figures, and references to other literature when not absolutely necessary, and generally deleted all footnotes. Our hope and belief is that these measures have in no case impaired the presentation, development, and integrity of the argument. Interested readers can find the full text by referring to the original form of each reading.

Finally, we would like to acknowledge the meticulous copy editing work of the staff at Nelson-Hall and of Jean Berry in particular. Our deepest debt of gratitude, however, is to our wives, Karen and Suzanne respectively, for their support and tolerance of work demands that did not always fit well with the demands of family life.

SECTION I

INTRODUCTION

The Ubiquity of Leadership

The most general characteristic of leadership is its ubiquity. A glance at the world around us suggests that it is an inevitable and probably necessary concomitant of social organization. Wherever individuals come together in pursuit of a common goal, one or a few of their number emerge to focus, channel, and oversee the activities of the larger collectivity. Such individuals commonly are called leaders and, in addition to helping to define collective goals, they usually formulate the strategy for achieving them.

Because individuals tend by and large to pursue their ambitions and aspirations through membership in groups, the division of labor between leaders and led pervades society. Leadership can be found in short-lived as well as long-lived groups and in groups of different size and complexity ranging from nuclear families to nations. It may be found in groups with different goals ranging from the promotion of some highly particularized interest to the social, economic, and political transformation of whole societies. And it may be found in groups that accord deference to their leaders for very different reasons ranging from unquestioned and unquestioning religious belief to stringent performance criteria.

The achievement of political goals is only one of the many ends of group activity in society, which means that leadership in the political sphere is one aspect of a larger phenomenon. Political leadership can be differentiated from leadership in a wide range of social activities,

1

including business, entertainment, fashion, sport, morality, education, religion, and crime. Moreover, political leadership itself assumes a diversity of forms, because the demands it makes of individuals in positions of leadership vary with the cultural, social, economic, and political circumstances in which they operate.

For instance, the skills necessary for the effective leadership of a large, multipurpose organization like a political party are not the same as those necessary to provide similar leadership for a small, single-purpose interest group. At the very least, interest group leaders are not required to possess the electioneering skills essential to compete successfully for public office in democratic political systems. In the same vein, argumentation, persuasion, and the maintenance of popular support are essential ingredients of effective political leadership in democratic societies; but they are less central to the provision of the same brand of leadership in authoritarian societies, in which resort to manipulation and coercion is a readier leadership reaction to disagreement.

The Study of Political Leadership

The study of leadership has a long and venerable tradition in political theory. The early writings on the topic tended to be mainly normative; thinkers were concerned less with the nature of political leadership and more with stipulating the kind of people who should assume the mantle of leadership and the criteria that should guide their behavior in power.

Leadership in the Classics

An example of the concern about who should lead is Plato's *The Republic*, written four centuries before the birth of Christ. Plato's intent in this still influential book was to sketch the ideal state. His assumption was that such a state would be based on the rule of reason. He thought that an understanding of the rational order underlying the scheme of things derives from knowledge, so it followed logically that political leadership was properly the preserve of philosopher–kings: statesmen whose education, training, and temperament conferred on them the right to rule for the individual and common good.

Writing much later, Niccolo Machiavelli typifies the concern with how leaders should behave. In contrast to Plato, Machiavelli based his theory on the assumption that individuals and states are governed by passion, not reason. His book *The Prince* is essentially a prescriptive how-to-rule manual. Its background is the corrupt and war torn Italy of the sixteenth century. Machiavelli's contention is that the provision of effective leadership should prevail over all other considerations, even if this entails resort to ruthless and despotic rule. A leader is justified in using whatever means are necessary to safeguard the state and satisfy the two most universal desires in human nature, the security of property and of life. In such matters, the issue is not whether a prince's actions are virtuous or vicious. Rather, it is whether they are appropriate to the situation at hand and lead quickly and efficiently to success.

Analytical Perspectives on Leadership

In the past one hundred years or so, the industrial and democratic revolutions have had a differential impact worldwide. Societies now vary markedly in their internal complexity and in their social, economic, and political character. As a direct result, more recent leadership theorists have abandoned the traditional, relatively simple normative focus in favor of a more analytical perspective on the nature of the relationship between leaders and followers. The best-known endeavor of this kind is Max Weber's (1947) treatise on the basis of leadership authority over followers.

Starting from the argument that all political leaders seek to legitimize their authority in the eyes of the governed, Weber identifies three types of leadership authority that are distinguished by the source of their legitimacy. These are the *rational–legal*, the *traditional*, and the *charismatic*. The basis of rational–legal authority is the "impersonal order" of norms and regulations defining the status of the person issuing the command. Widespread acceptance of the "sanctity of immemorial traditions" is the foundation of traditional authority. Charismatic authority arises from an individual's personal characteristics—attributes that set the person apart from others and endow him or her with exceptional powers or perhaps even supernatural, superhuman qualities.

The ideas of Plato, Machiavelli, and Weber are testimony to the fact that political leadership has been an important concern of political theory for centuries. However, until very recently, theorizing about and studying political leadership has not enjoyed the same status in modern political science. With a few notable exceptions (see, for example, Edinger 1966; Rustow 1970; and Seligman 1950), neglect was largely the watchword. Paige (1972,6) reviewed the literature and concluded that "aside from specific pioneering insights, the study of political leadership, although intuitively recognized as important by probably all political scientists, has not yet been made a subject of specialized professional concern." He depicted the study of leadership as no more than an emerging field in political science.

The theme of ignorance and neglect was repeated later in the 1970s in a Pulitzer prize-winning book on leadership.

> If we know all too much about our leaders, we know far too little
> about *leadership*. We fail to grasp the essence of leadership that is relevant
> to the modern age and hence we cannot agree even on the standards by
> which to measure, recruit, and reject it. . . . Leadership is one of the most
> observed and least understood phenomena on earth. (Burns 1978, 1–2)

This neglect is perhaps understandable. Political science has concentrated the bulk of its attention on liberal democracies. These are political systems in which governance is generally viewed as a collective
phenomenon, whether by prime ministers and their cabinets or by
presidents in collaboration with Congress and other relevant political
actors. Leadership, in contrast, is generally thought of as the preserve
of a single individual and viewed as the exception rather than the rule
in this type of political system. At best, leadership in democracies became associated with crisis, whether as the result of war (as with Winston Churchill in Britain), economic depression (as with Franklin D.
Roosevelt in the United States), or constitutional collapse (as with
Charles de Gaulle in France). At worst, it became associated with the
collapse of democracy (as with Adolf Hitler in interwar Germany) or
with its institutionalized rejection (as with authoritarian states like
Franco's Spain or totalitarian ones like Stalin's Soviet Union).

In sharp contrast, the 1980s witnessed a reversal of this apparent
assumption that leadership is not characteristic of "normal" democratic
politics. One measure of the newly found importance of leadership for
political scientists has been the outpouring of scholarly literature on it.
This literature ranges widely and is too voluminous to summarize here.
Some of the more notable recent works include Blondel's (1987) ambitious attempt to provide a general framework for the systematic study of
leadership; Gardner's (1989) general treatise on the subject; Willner's
(1984) exploration of the nature of charismatic leadership; Jones' (1989)
collection of essays addressing the question of how leaders interact with,
transform, or are controlled by the organizations they lead; two works
approaching leadership as the art of manipulation (Bailey 1988; Riker
1986); Kellerman's (1986) useful source book on leadership theory; and
Rose and Suleiman's (1980) collection of case studies of executive leadership in presidential and parliamentary systems of government.

Leadership and Power

A perhaps more telling measure of the concept of leadership's contemporary importance is the exhortation that it, and not power, be considered the essence of politics (Tucker, this volume). The study of the pursuit and exercise of power has long been accepted by many as the raw

material of the study of politics. However, for a number of revisionists a leadership-based definition of politics has the advantage of being more inclusive than a power-based one, of explaining relationships between leaders and followers that power cannot. In the words of a converted power advocate:

> Our main hope for disenthralling ourselves from our overemphasis on power lies more in a theoretical, or at least conceptual, effort than in an empirical one. . . . It lies in a more realistic, a more sophisticated understanding of power, and of the often far more consequential exercise of mutual persuasion, exchange, elevation, and transformation—in short, of leadership. (Burns, this volume, p.18)

Not everyone agrees with this definitional separation between power and leadership. Nonetheless, leadership has come to displace power as the conceptual focus for students of the most widely studied leadership institution in the contemporary world, the United States presidency. The tone for the study of the modern presidency was set by Richard Neustadt in his 1960 book *Presidential Power*. The essential argument of this book is that the president cannot command obedience; rather, he can get others to go along with him only through persuasion and bargaining.

Many observers saw in the president's limited power resources the root cause of his inability to provide national leadership (Burns 1963). This equation of power with leadership, however, suffered a serious setback when the "imperial" presidencies of Lyndon B. Johnson and Richard M. Nixon produced the national humiliations of Vietnam and Watergate. It obviously took more than the aggrandizement of power to improve the quality of presidential leadership.

Since leadership is what is commonly sought of presidents and since it is not synonymous with power, it followed all but inevitably that students of the presidency would abandon the power approach in favor of a leadership one. Recent prominent examples of the approach include an edited book evaluation of each president from Franklin Roosevelt to Ronald Reagan from the perspective of their leadership style (Greenstein 1988), another arguing that presidential leadership of Congress exists only "at the margins" (Edwards 1989), another examining the psychology of successful political leadership in the White House (Simonton 1987), and yet another examining its practice (Kellerman 1984).

Moreover, this transition to leadership is evident not only in the United States. The analysis of the political role of the prime minister in parliamentary democracies has traditionally been based on a power approach, where the question has been asked whether the prime minister is really no more than the "first among equals" in the cabinet (Weller 1985). For instance, Kavanagh (1987, 178) made the point that "British political science has little or no literature on political leadership. In Britain, one refers to the office of prime minister and his or her performance rather than national leadership or leaders. Together with King's companion piece in this book, Kavanagh's own essay on the "mobilizing" style of Margaret Thatcher represents a break, albeit a more muted one than in the United States, with the usual power-oriented approach to the study of chief executives.

The Urgency of Political Leadership

The upsurge of interest in the study of political leadership seems to have issued partly from the contemporary urgency of leadership. In the 1970s a crisis of leadership came to be widely perceived. Reeling under the impact of worldwide recession brought on by huge oil price increases in 1974, Western democracies did not generally seem to know how to cope with the situation. They appeared to lack purpose and direction as they passively acceded to the consequent disruption of the international economic system.

Unlike other times of crises in recent memory—such as the Great Depression or World War II—no one emerged during the 1970s with the vision, imagination, and skill to lead the Western world out of the recession. Instead, individual nations turned in on themselves to pursue their own narrow self-interest, and the economic crisis deepened throughout the decade. Under the circumstances, Burns (1978,1) seemed more than justified in claiming that "the crisis of leadership today is the mediocrity or irresponsibility of so many of the men and women in power."

People in leadership positions seemed to have become the prisoners rather than the masters of their institutional and political environment. Over time, consensus had come to be valued more highly than conflict as democratic governments deliberately integrated important societal groups into the policy-making process. Harmony was viewed as a better way of achieving shared goals than was strife, but the price of harmony was inflexibility as these groups avidly protected the interests and privileges of their members.

The consensus turned sour, however, as its original high aspirations gave way to "the lowest common denominator of policies designed to avoid trouble" (Middlemas 1979, 429). The very rigidity of this style of government raised doubts about its ability to cope with the externally induced economic and social problems of the 1970s. In the face of this uncertainty, speculation centered not on the active circumvention or defusion of the crisis, but on whether Western democracies had become ungovernable (Dahrendorf 1980) and, relatedly, on the contribution of this "arteriosclerosis of government" to the long-term decline of nations (Olson 1982).

Political leaders, it seemed, were severely constrained in their actions by the bounds of the established consensus. The radical, reforming impulses of the likes of President Jimmy Carter in the United States, Prime Minister Edward Heath in Britain, and President Francois Mitterand in France came to nothing once they confronted the reality of the entrenched political power of special interests in their respective societies. Creative, adaptive leadership was not seriously entertained as a solution to the ungovernability problem. The assumption seems to have been that individual leadership was a thing of the past, an art form that had become impossible in the era of big government and international interdependence.

An important reason for the focus on leadership in the 1980s was that this assumption was no longer widely shared. The 1980s witnessed the emergence of a number of individual leaders who not only rejected the arteriosclerotic consensus of their respective political systems, but who also met with considerable success in dismantling that consensus. They were able to change the terms of the social, economic, and political debate in their own societies in particular and in the international system in general. The archetypal leader in this mold probably is Mikhail Gorbachev, who became the Soviet Union's top leader in 1985. An inveterate reformer both domestically and internationally, his initiatives threatened fundamental change in the economic, social, and even political structure of the Soviet Union and other Eastern European communist countries, as well as in East–West relations (Lewin 1988).

His best-known democratic counterparts are probably Ronald Reagan, U.S. president from 1980 to 1988, and Margaret Thatcher, British prime minister from 1979 to 1990. The magnitude of their achievements is vividly conveyed in an essay on each of them included in this book (Jones, section IX; King, Section VII). But we should draw attention to the distinctive economic, social, and political doctrines to which they have given their names, Reaganism and Thatcherism. Both leaders are commonly credited with having brought about revolutions in their respective societies (Jenkins 1988; Jones 1988). Even allowing for journalistic exaggeration, the measure of the impact of their leadership is that none of their chief executive predecessors achieved the notoriety of having an "ism" coined from his last name.

The Concept of Political Leadership

Oddly enough, although leadership is a widely researched phenomenon, the literature on the subject does not offer a single, widely accepted definition of the concept (Gibb 1969; Stogdill 1974). Existing studies have made some progress insofar as they have discredited the "great man" theory of leadership. This theory appeared early in the study of leadership. It held that the assumption of a leadership position was dependent on the possession of certain physical or psychological traits. Supposedly important traits included height, weight, intelligence, self-confidence, an urge to dominate, and so on. However, the actual study of individuals in leadership positions produced no universal set of traits common to all of them. Moreover, individuals with the hypothetically relevant traits were all too often found not to be in positions of leadership (Gibb 1969, 216–27).

Leadership as a Relational Phenomenon

Personality factors are insufficient in themselves, however. Leadership cannot inhere in individuals because it is a relational phenomenon. Leaders cannot exist in the absence of followers, and the demand for leadership varies with the situation. In other words, leadership is a pattern involving three essential components: leader(s), followers, and the functional relationship between leaders and followers. It is a function of both the social situation and personality, and of these two in interaction (Gibb 1969, 268–71).

This is the dominant conceptualization of leadership, covering all instances of leadership in principle. Yet it tells us little about any of them in practice. There are as many instances of leadership as there are permutations in the complex relationship between leaders, followers, and varied situations. How do they interact and with what implications for the character of leadership at different points in time and space? Are there regularities in their interaction that, for example, allow us to identify a democratic leadership style?

The central problem with the interactionist approach to the study of leadership is its indeterminacy. It leaves unspecified the pattern of causality in the relationship between leaders, followers, and situation. Two responses to this problem are possible. First, we may seek to impose order on the immensely complex phenomenon that is leadership by formulating a deductive theory. Thus Wildavsky (1989, 89–90) has written: "Theorizing depends on seeing (or imposing) regularities on what may originally appear to be disparate happenings. . . . Without having a theory of interpretation to impose meaning on disparate events, piling up an infinity of 'situations' is bound to prove stultifying." Second, we may proceed inductively, examining political leaders and their relationship to followers in particular situational contexts. In this way, "situation" is, by and large, held constant and so cannot explain variation in leaders, followers, and their interaction. Such explanation can legitimately be sought elsewhere.

This book adopts the second of these responses, largely because it is more suited to our intended audience. We are far from achieving a deductive theory of leadership, but that is no reason why we should not make some headway in better understanding political leadership. Our view is that this is best achieved by an in-depth examination of leadership in practice in different types of societies—democratic or authoritarian, traditional or modern, parliamentary or presidential.

Leadership in Democracies

We have chosen to restrict our focus of attention in this book to liberal democratic societies. This decision was taken on the pragmatic ground that, in overall qualitative and quantitative terms, the best and most comprehensive empirical research on leaders, followers, and their interaction has been done in this type of society. This focus is not meant to imply that the pattern of political leadership in democracies is indistinguishable from the pattern to be found in authoritarian political systems. Indeed, the important differences between them cannot be disputed. In democracies, to the extent that leadership is a mutually constraining partnership between leaders and followers, and to the extent that the authority of leaders is not imposed but founded on freely given and periodically renewed popular consent, one would expect patterns of leadership to differ from such patterns in authoritarian systems. Democratic political leaders are expected to be attentive and responsive to the demands and wants of followers. By contrast, the same relationship in authoritarian political systems is relatively strained and subject to follower dissatisfaction.

This difference, however, is one of degree and not of kind. An important reason for this convergence is that the relationship between leaders and followers is mediated by situation. For instance, under normal circumstances democratic political leaders may be the more attentive to and watchful of the constitutional rights of followers. But adverse circumstances, and particularly a situation in which national security is threatened, can lead them to behave in an authoritarian manner. A well-known example of such behavior is the U.S. government's internment without trial of 70,000 Japanese–American citizens after the Japanese air force bombed Pearl Harbor in 1941.

Relatedly, democratic political leadership is not always the self-less activity that the periodic popular election of office holders might lead us to anticipate. Authoritarian political leadership is widely accepted as involving a strong element of manipulation and self-seeking, if only to retain power. But often democratic politicians are also concerned with reelection or the realization of some other important goal and are not beyond some degree of manipulation to achieve their aims. Riker (1986, ix) has discussed this phenomenon in terms of the "art of political manipulation." His term for it is *heresthetics*. It is about "structuring the world so that you can win." Riker believes that the "novice heresthetician must learn by practice how to go about managing and manipulating and maneuvering to get the decisions he or she wants." He illustrates this art with examples drawn from important episodes in American political history.

Democratic political leadership, in short, is distinctive but not unique so that its study is germane to the study of political leadership generally. If we can come to understand leaders and their relationship to followers in different institutional contexts in democratic societies, then we will have begun to understand leadership wherever it may be found.

The Approach of This Book

To limit our study of political leadership to democracies is a first step in coming to grips with its complexity. Nevertheless, a wide arena with a few boundaries remains. For example, all organizations are political in the sense that they have to choose between competing claims in allocating scarce and valued resources. Even in democratic societies, however, not all organizations are democratic in the sense that the leaders making allocational decisions are accountable to followers through the medium of free and competitive elections. Indeed, a very large literature exists on leadership in organizations in which managers are neither elected by nor answerable to the other employees in the organization (a good summary is Yukl 1989).

Such leadership may reasonably be argued to be political, but it can less credibly be held to be democratic. We therefore ignore it and define political leaders as individuals who hold elective governmental office. Moreover, because democratic governments can be of either the presidential or the parliamentary type, we have selected readings that compare the process of leadership in the two forms of government in the belief that this comparison, by highlighting the effects of institutional context, throws the general phenomenon of democratic political leadership into sharper relief.

In the absence of a satisfactory definition, the nature of political leadership in practice would seem best established by breaking down the overall phenomenon into its important ingredients (Hermann 1986). The structure of this book reflects our view of what these ingredients are. The first of them is a need to know about the leaders themselves. Thus, after the two essays in Section II offering distinctive views of what political leadership is, we deal in Sections III and IV with the role of personality in politics, with the socioeconomic and political backgrounds of leaders, and with the influences on their recruitment and selection.

The second ingredient concerns attitudes and behavior in office. Section V shows that, once elected, political leaders' own views of what constitutes appropriate behavior change as they are socialized into the "rules of the game" and come to share with political opponents both attitudes toward public policies and orientations toward their jobs. Section VI deals with the external constraints on their behavior. These include principally the institutional framework in which leaders have to operate, the structure of the conflict they have to manage, and the nature of the circumstances in which they come to power. Then, in Section VII we look at some case studies of successful political leaders in action—Dwight D. Eisenhower as the hidden-hand president, Margaret Thatcher as the iron-lady prime minister, and Lyndon B. Johnson as the congressional leader par excellence.

The third ingredient is the linkage between leaders and followers and this is the subject matter of Section VIII. Linkage is a two-way process and the readings in this section examine it from both perspectives. On the one hand, we see the differing ways in which British Members of Parliament relate to their constituents and constituencies. On the other, we address the question of the qualities that voters look for in their leaders. The fourth, and final, ingredient involves the political impact of leaders. This impact can range from short term legislative success to long-term change in the way politics are conducted and, focusing on the experience of presidents of the United States, Section IX looks at the conditions allowing chief executives to leave their mark on the political process.

Section II

Two Views of Political Leadership

Introductory Comment

To embark on the study of leadership is to wade into a definitional morass. Definitions and counterdefinitions abound and researchers seem to come no closer to reaching agreement on the meaning of the term. One recent survey of theory and research on the subject, for example, concludes that "there are almost as many definitions of leadership as there are persons who have attempted to define the concept" (Stogdill 1974, 259). A good part of the explanation for this situation, of course, is that the ubiquity of leadership makes it especially difficult to formulate a single definition that captures its essence in the almost infinite number of situations in which leaders and followers find themselves interacting in the modern, complex world.

The numerous definitional attempts that have been made remain at a very high level of generality, taking the line that leadership is the process of mobilizing followers to achieve common goals. In this regard, a general consensus exists on the phenomenon's two basic characteristics. These characteristics are (1) leadership is a relationship between one or more persons who exercise influence and one or more persons who submit to that influence and (2) leadership is a relationship that is best studied within the framework of the dynamics of group interaction. Put another way, leadership is an asymmetric relationship and the degree of asymmetry can change from situation to situation even if the partners to the relationship do not. The theoretical writing on political leadership thus has two foci. On one hand, it speaks to the basis of this asymmetry. On the other, it deals with the different forms the relationship can take in different situations. These foci will now be examined in turn.

Perhaps the most controversial characterization of the relationship between leaders and followers is the one basing it on power. An early political science example of this approach is Janda's (1972, 358) definition of leadership as "a particular type of power relationship characterized by a group member's perception that another group member has the right to prescribe behavior patterns for the former regarding his activity as a group member" (see also Blondel 1987, 2–3).

This power perspective has been criticized on two specific grounds, one normative and the other empirical. The normative criticism is exemplified by the reading by Burns in this section. He starts from the assumption that leadership connotes partnership, a relationship of voluntarily accepted and mutual influence between leaders and followers. The degree of influence of the former over the latter may well be greater, but influence still flows in two directions. Power, in contrast, is a term associated with domination and control, with the imposition of the will of the leader(s) on followers. Thus, Burns (1978, 27) takes the moral position that "an absolute wielder of brutal power" like Adolf Hitler cannot, indeed should not, be called a leader.

The empirical criticism of the power perspective is that it is too all-encompassing and, thus, too static. In trying to provide a single definition for all instances of leader–follower interaction, it implies that a rigid hierarchy of command characterizes all of them; the balance of influence changes in no significant respects across place or time. A great deal of leadership research, however, throws this cast-in-stone image of the leader–follower relationship into serious doubt. One of the better-known examples is Burns' distinction (pages 25–26, this section) between *transactional* and *transformational* leadership. The former is a routine, hierarchical, and mutually beneficial "exchange of valued things," whereas the latter corresponds more to an evenly balanced partnership in which "leaders and followers raise one another to higher levels of motivation and morality."

The tendency to view leadership as a balance of influence between leaders and followers is also apparent in the classification of whole political systems by differences in their style of leadership. These differences correspond roughly to the traditional distinction between democratic and authoritarian political systems, and four distinct styles can be identified. These are (1) a laissez-faire style, in which group goals are achieved through the autonomous orientations and abilities of members; (2) a democratic style, in which the attainment of group goals requires that members be brought to be suitably motivated to achieve them; (3) an authoritarian style, in which leaders prescribe and enforce the conduct to be followed by members in the attainment of group goals; and (4) an autocratic style, in which leaders enjoy absolute and unlimited control over all activities of the group in the pursuit of its goals (Dion 1968).

This example highlights the heuristic utility of the interactionist approach to the study of political leadership. At the same time, however, it suggests the main weakness of the interactionist approach relative to the more static power perspective. That is, to view the interaction between leaders and followers in terms of a balance does not delimit the phenomenon of leadership, because the balance can be ever more finely tuned so that there are as many definitions of it as there are differences of degree in the balance of influence. Political leadership in democratic societies is an illustrative case insofar as it turns out on closer inspection not to be a single point in the balance. Rockman (1984), for example, distinguishes between mechanistic, bargaining, and entrepreneurial strategies in his analysis of presidential leadership in the United States. Broadly speaking, these strategies involve, respectively, accommodation among interest groups, cooptation and incremental redirection, and the "stirring of activist souls" (Rockman, 1984, 223–29).

The larger problem, then, is that different situations could lend themselves to ever-finer distinctions so that leadership would eventually lose its identity as a general phenomenon. The reading by Tucker in this section starts from a recognition of the problems that situation poses for the development of a theory of political leadership and makes the argument that progress is more likely to be made if we ignore leader–follower interaction and focus more modestly on "the question of what it is that leaders do, or try to do, in their capacities as leaders, what functions do they perform in the process of exerting influence upon their followers" (page 36, this section). Tucker explicates this argument in some detail. Readers can decide for themselves whether his neglect of situation affords greater insight into the nature of political leadership in the short term and a more promising path to a theory of political leadership in the long term.

Select Bibliography

Blondel, J. 1987. *Political Leadership: Towards a General Analysis*. London: Sage.
Burns, J.M. 1978. *Leadership*. New York: Harper & Row.

Paige, G.D. 1977. *The Scientific Study of Political Leadership*. New York: Free Press.

Rustow, D.A., ed. 1970. *Philosophers and Kings: Studies in Leadership*. New York: George Braziller.

Stogdill, R.M. 1974. *Handbook of Leadership: A Survey of Theory and Research*. New York: Free Press.

Tucker, R.C. 1981. *Politics as Leadership*. Columbia: University of Missouri Press.

1

The Power of Leadership

James MacGregor Burns

$\mathbf{W}$e search eagerly for leadership yet seek to cage and tame it. We recoil from power yet we are bewitched or titillated by it. We devour books on power—power in the office, power in the bedroom, power in the corridors. Connoisseurs of power purport to teach about it—what it is, how to get it, how to use it, how to "gain total control" over "everything around you." We think up new terms for power: clout, wallop, muscle. We measure the power of the aides of Great Men by the number of yards between their offices and that of Number One. . . .

Why this preoccupation, this near-obsession, with power? In part because we in this century cannot escape the horror of it. Stalin controlled an apparatus that, year after year and in prison after prison, quietly put to death millions of persons, some of them old comrades and leading Bolsheviks, with hardly a ripple of protest from others. Between teatime and dinner Adolf Hitler would decide whether to release a holocaust of terror and death in an easterly or westerly direction, with stupendous impact on the fate of a continent and a world. On smaller planes of horror, American soldiers have slaughtered women and children cow-

From *Leadership*, by James MacGregor Burns (New York: Harper and Row, 1978), pp. 9–28. Copyright © by James MacGregor Burns. Reprinted by permission of Harper and Row Publishers, Inc.

ering in ditches; village tyrants hold serfs and slaves in thrall; revolutionary leaders disperse whole populations into the countryside, where they dig or die; the daughter of Nehru jails her political adversaries—and is jailed in turn. . . .

Sheer evil and brute power always seem more fascinating than complex human relationships. Sinners usually outsell saints, at least in Western cultures, and the ruthless exercise of power somehow seems more realistic, moral influence more naive. Above all, sheer massed power seems to have the most impact on history. Such, at least, is this century's bias. Perhaps I exemplify the problem of this distorted perception in my own intellectual development. Growing up in the aftermath of one world war, taking part in a second, studying the records of these and later wars, I have been struck by the sheer physical impact of men's armaments. Living in the age of political titans, I too have assumed that their actual power equaled their reputed power. As a political scientist I have belonged to a "power school" that analyzed the interrelationships of persons on the basis only of power. Perhaps this was fitting for an era of two world wars and scores of lesser ones, the murder of entire cities, bloody revolutions, the unleashing of the inhuman force of the atom.

I fear, however, that we are paying a steep intellectual and political price for our preoccupation with power. Viewing politics *as* power has blinded us to the role of power *in* politics and hence to the pivotal role of leadership. . . .

Our main hope for disenthralling ourselves from our overemphasis on power lies more in a theoretical, or at least conceptual, effort, than in an empirical one. It lies not only in recognizing that not all human influences are necessarily coercive and exploitative, that not all transactions among persons are mechanical, impersonal, ephemeral. It lies in seeing that the most powerful influences consist of deeply human relationships in which two or more persons *engage* with one another. It lies in a more realistic, a more sophisticated understanding of power, and of the often far more consequential exercise of mutual persuasion, exchange, elevation, and transformation—in short, of leadership. This is not to exorcise power from its pervasive influence in our daily lives; recognizing this kind of power is absolutely indispensable to understanding leadership. But we must recognize the limited reach of "total" or "coercive" power. We must see power—and leadership—as not things but as *relationships*. We must analyze power in a context of human motives and physical constraints. If we can come to grips with these aspects of power, we can hope to comprehend the true nature of leadership—a venture far more intellectually daunting than the study of naked power.

The Two Essentials of Power

We all have *power* to do acts we lack the *motive* to do—to buy a gun and slaughter people, to crush the feelings of loved ones who cannot defend themselves, to drive a car down a crowded city sidewalk, to torture an animal.

We all have the *motives* to do things we do not have the resources to do—to be President or senator, to buy a luxurious yacht, to give away millions to charity, to travel for months on end, to right injustices, to tell off the boss.

The two essentials of power are motive and resource. The two are interrelated. Lacking motive, resource diminishes; lacking resource, motive lies idle. Lacking either one, power collapses. Because both resource and motive are needed, and because both may be in short supply, power is an elusive and limited thing. Human beings, both the agents and the victims of power, for two thousand years or more have tried to penetrate its mysteries, but the nature of power remains elusive. Certainly no one has mastered the secrets of personal power as physicists have penetrated the atom. It is probably just as well.

To understand the nature of leadership requires understanding of the essence of power, for leadership is a special form of power. Forty years ago Bertrand Russell (1938, 1) called power the fundamental concept in social science, "in the same sense in which Energy is a fundamental concept in physics." This is a compelling metaphor, it suggests that the source of power may lie in immense reserves of the wants and needs of the wielders and objects of power, just as the winds and the tides, oil and coal, the atom and the sun have been harnessed to supply physical energy. But it is still only a metaphor.

What is power? The "power of A over B," we are told, "is equal to maximum force which A can induce on B minus the maximum resisting force which B can mobilize in the opposite direction." One wonders about the As and the Bs, the Xs and the Ys, in the equations of power. Are they mere croquet balls, knocking other balls and being knocked, in some game of the gods? Or do these As and Xs and the others have wants and needs, ambitions and aspirations, of their own? And what if a ball does obey a god? . . . Surely this formula is more physics than power. But the formula offers one vital clue to power: power is a *relationship* among persons.

Power, says Max Weber—he uses the term *Macht*—"is the probability that one actor within a social relationship will be in a position to carry out his own will despite resistance, regardless of the basis on which this probability rests (Parsons 1957, 152)." This formula helps the search for power, since it reminds us that there is no certain relationship between what P (power holder) does and how R (power recipient) responds. Those who have pressed a button and found no light turned on, or who have admonished a child with no palpable effect, welcome the factor or probability. But what controls the *degree* of probability? Motive? Intention? Power resources? Skill? Is P acting on his own, or is he the agent of some other power holder? And what if P orders R to do something to someone else—who then is the *real* power recipient? To answer such questions, P and R and all the other croquet players, mallets, and balls must be put into a broader universe of power relationships—that is, viewed as a *collective act*. Power and leadership become part of a system of social causation. . . .

A *psychological* conception of power will help us cut through some of these complexities and provide a basis for understanding the relation of power to leadership. This approach carries on the assumptions above: the power is first of all a *relationship* and not merely an entity to be passed around like a baton or hand grenade; that it involves the *intention* or *purpose* of both power holder and power recipient; and hence that it is *collective*, not merely the behavior of one person. On these assumptions I view the power process as one *in which power holders (P), possessing certain motives and goals, have the capacity to secure changes in the behavior of a respondent (R), human or animal, and in the environment, by utilizing resources in their power base, including factors of skill, relative to the targets of their power-wielding and necessary to secure such changes.* This view of power deals with three elements in the process: the motives and resources of power holders; the motives and resources of power recipients; and the relationship among all these.

The power holder may be the person whose "private motives are displaced onto public objects and rationalized in terms of public interest," to quote Harold Lasswell's classic formula. So accustomed are we to observing persons with power drives or complexes, so sensitive to leaders with the "will to power," so exposed to studies finding the source of the power urge in early deprivation, that we tend to assume the power motive to be exclusively that of seeking to dominate the behavior of others. "But must *all* experiences of power have as their ultimate goal the exercise of power over others?" David McClelland (1975) demands. He and other psychologists find that persons with high need for power ("*n* Power") may derive that need for power not only from deprivation but from other experiences. One study indicated that young men watching a film of John F. Kennedy's Inaugural felt strengthened and inspirited by this exposure to an admired leader. Other persons may draw on internal resources as they grow older and learn to exert power against those who constrain them, like children who self-consciously recognize their exercise of power as they resist their mothers' directives. They find "sources of strength in the self to develop the self."

These and other findings remind us that the power holder has a variety of motives besides that of wielding power over others. They help us correct the traditional picture of single-minded power wielders bent on exerting control over respondents. (Their main motive may be to institute power over *themselves*.) In fact power holders may have as varied motives—of wants, needs, expectations, etc.—as their targets. Some may pursue not power but status, recognition, prestige, and glory, or they may seek power as an intermediate value instrumental to realizing those loftier goals. Some psychologists consider the need to achieve ("*n* Achievement") a powerful motive, especially in western cultures, and one whose results may be prized more as an *attainment* than as a means of social control. Some use power to collect possessions such as paintings, cars, or jewelry; they may collect wives or mistresses less to dominate them than to love or to display them. Others will use power to seek novelty and excitement. Still others may enjoy the exercise of power mainly because it enables them to exhibit—if only to themselves—their skill and knowledge, their ability to stimulate their own capacities and to master their environment. Those skilled in athletics may enjoy riding horseback or skiing as solitary pastimes, with no one but themselves to admire their skills. . . .

Still, there *are* the single-minded power wielders who fit the classical images of Machiavelli or Hobbes or Nietzsche, or at least the portraits of the modern power theorists. They consciously exploit their external resources (economic, social psychological, and institutional) and their "effectance," their training, skill, and competence, to make persons and things do what they want done. The key factor here is indeed "what they want done." The motives of power wielders may or may not coincide with what the respondent wants done; it is P's intention that controls. Power wielders may or may not recognize respondents' wants and needs; if they do, they may recognize them only to the degree necessary to achieve their goals; and if they must make a choice between satisfying their own purposes and satisfying respondents' needs, they will choose the former. Power wielders are not free agents. They are subject—even slaves—to pressures working on them and in them. But once their will and purpose is forged, it may be controlling. If P wants circuses and R wants bread, the power wielder may manipulate popular demand for bread only to the degree that it helps P achieve circuses. At the "naked power" extremity on the continuum of types of power holders are the practitioners of virtually unbridled power—Hitler, Stalin, and the like—subject always, of course, to empowering and constraining circumstances.

The foundation of this kind of control lies in P's "power base" *as it is relevant to those at the receiving end of power.* The composition of the power base will vary from culture to culture, from situation to situation. Some power holders will have such pervasive control over factors influencing behavior that the imbalance between P's and R's power bases, and between the possibility of realizing P's and R's purposes, will be overwhelming. Nazi death camps and communist "re-education" camps are examples of such overwhelming imbalances. A dictator can put respondents physically in such isolation and under such constraint that they cannot even appeal to the dictator's conscience, if he has one, or to sympathetic opinion outside the camp or outside the country, if such exists. More typical, in most cultures, is the less asymmetric relationship in which P's power base supplies P with extensive control over R but leaves R with various resources for resisting. Prisons, armies, authoritarian families, concentration camps such as the United States relocation centers for Japanese–Americans during World War II, exemplify this kind of imbalance. There is a multitude of power balances in villages, tribes, schools, homes, collectives, businesses, trade unions, cities, in which most persons spend most of their lives.

To define power not as a property or entity or possession but as a *relationship* in which two or more persons tap motivational bases in one another and bring varying resources to bear in the process is to perceive power as drawing a vast range of human behavior into its orbit. The arena of power is no longer the exclusive preserve of a power elite or an establishment of persons clothed with legitimacy. Power is ubiquitous; it permeates human relationships. It exists whether or not it is quested for. It is the glory and the burden of most of humanity. A common, highly asymmetric, and sometimes cruel power relation can exist, for example, when one person is in love with another but the other does not reciprocate. . . .

Because power can take such multifarious, ubiquitous, and subtle forms, it is reflected in an infinite number of combinations and particularities in specific contexts. Even so, observers *in* those contexts may perceive their particular "power mix" as the basic and universal type, and they will base elaborate descriptions and theories of power on one model—their own. Even Machiavelli's celebrated portrait of the uses and abuses of power, while relevant to a few other cultures and eras, is essentially culture-bound and irrelevant to a host of other power situations and systems. Thus popular tracts on power—how to win power and influence people—typically are useful only for particular situations and may disable the student of power coping with quite different power constellations.

Still there are ways of breaking power down into certain attributes that allow for some generalization and even theory-building. Robert Dahl's (1968) breakdown of the reach and magnitude of power is useful and parsimonious. One dimension is *distribution*—the concentration and dispersion of power among persons of diverse influence in various political, social, and economic locations such as geographical areas, castes and classes, status positions, skill groups, communications centers, and the like. Another dimension is *scope*—the extent to which power is generalized over a wide range or is specialized. Persons who are relatively powerful in relation to one kind of activity, Dahl notes, may be relatively weak in other power relationships. Still another dimension is *domain*—the number and nature of power respondents influenced by power wielders compared to those who are not. These dimensions are not greatly different from Lasswell and Abraham Kaplan's (1950) conception of the weight, scope and domain of power.

A more common way to organize the data of power is in terms of the *size* and *arena* in which power is exercised. The relation of P and R is, in many studies, typically one of micropower, as Edward Lehman (1969) calls it. Most power relations embrace a multiplicity of power holders; the relation is one among many Ps and many Rs. As power holders and respondents multiply, the number of relationships increases geometrically. Macropower, as Lehman contends, has distinct attributes of its own; the complex relations involved in the aggregate are not simply those of micropower extended to a higher plane. Causal interrelations become vastly more complex as a greater number of power actors and power components comes into play. Paradoxically, we may, with modern techniques of fact-gathering and of empirical analysis, gain a better understanding of mass phenomena of power and leadership than of the more intricate and elusive interactions in micropower situations.

Whatever the dimensions or context, the fundamental process remains the same. *Power wielders draw from their power bases resources relevant to their own motives and the motives and resources of others upon whom they exercise power.* The power base may be narrow and weak, or it may consist of ample and multiple resources useful for vast and long-term exercises of power, but the process is the same. Dominated by personal motives, P draws on supporters, on funds, on ideology, on institutions, on old friendships, on political credits, on status, and on his own skills of calculation, judgment, communication, timing, to mobilize those elements that relate to the motives of the persons P wishes to control—even if in the end P overrides their values and goals—just as P mobilizes machines and fuel and manpower and engineering expertise relevant to the tasks of building dams or clearing forests.

Power shows many faces and takes many forms. It may be as visible as the policeman's badge or billy or as veiled as the politician's whisper in the back room. It may exist as an overwhelming presence or as a potential that can be drawn on at will. It may appear in the form of money, sex appeal, authority, administrative regulation, charisma, munitions, staff resources, instruments for torture. But all these resources must have this in common: *they must be relevant to the motivations of the power recipients.* Even the most fearsome of power devices, such as imprisonment or torture or denial of food or water, may not affect the behavior of a masochist or a martyr. . . .

Leadership and Followership

Leadership is an aspect of power, but it is also a separate and vital process in itself.

Power over other persons, we have noted, is exercised when potential power wielders, motivated to achieve certain goals of their own, marshal in their power base resources (economic, military, institutional, or skill) that enable them to influence the behavior of respondents by activating motives of respondents relevant to those resources and to those goals. This is done in order to realize the purposes of the *power wielders, whether or not these are also the goals of the respondents.* Power wielders also exercise influence by mobilizing their own power base in such a way as to establish direct physical control over others' behavior, as in a war of conquest or through measures of harsh deprivation, but these are highly restricted exercises of power, dependent on certain times, cultures, and personalities, and they are often self-destructive and transitory.

Leadership over human beings is exercised when persons with certain motives and purposes mobilize, in competition or conflict with others, institutional, political, psychological, and other resources so as to arouse, engage, and satisfy the motives of followers. This is done in order to realize goals mutually held by *both* leaders and followers, as in Lenin's calls for peace, bread, and land. In brief, leaders with motive and power bases tap followers' motives in order to realize the purposes of both leaders and followers. Not only must motivation be relevant, as in power generally, but its purposes must be realized and satisfied. Leadership is exercised in a condition of *conflict* or *competition* in which leaders contend in appealing to the motive bases of potential followers. Naked power, on the other hand, admits of no competition or conflict—there is no engagement.

Leaders are a particular kind of power holder. Like power, leadership is relational, collective, and purposeful. Leadership shares with power the central function of achieving purpose. But the reach and domain of leadership are, in the short range at least, more limited than those of power. Leaders do not obliterate followers' motives though they may arouse certain motives and ignore others. They lead other creatures, not things (and lead animals only to the degree that they recognize animal motives—i.e., leading cattle to shelter rather than to slaughter). To control *things*—tools, mineral resources, money, energy—is an act of power, not leadership, for things have no motives. Power wielders may treat people as things. Leaders may not.

All leaders are actual or potential power holders, but not all power holders are leaders.

These definitions of power and of leadership differ from those that others have offered. Lasswell and Kaplan (1950) hold that power must be relevant to people's valued things; I hold that it must be relevant to the *power wielder's* valued things and may be relevant to the *recipient's* needs or values only as necessary to exploit them. Kenneth Janda (1972, 57) defines power as "the ability to cause other persons to adjust their behavior in conformance with communicated behavior patterns." I agree, assuming that those behavior patterns aid the purpose of the power wielder. According to Andrew McFarland (1969, 174), "If the leader causes changes that he intended, he has exercised power; if the leader causes changes that he did not intend or want, he has exercised influence, but not power. . . ." I dispense with the concept of influence as necessary and unparsimonious. For me the leader is a very special, very circumscribed, but potentially the most effective of power holders, judged by the degree of intended "real change" finally achieved. Roderick Bell et al. (1969, 4) contend that power is a relationship rather than an entity—an entity being something that "could be smelled and touched, or stored in a keg"; while I agree that power is a relationship, I contend that the relationship is one in which some entity—part of the "power base"—plays an indispensable part, whether that keg is a keg of beer, of dynamite, or of ink.

The crucial variable, again, is *purpose.* Some define leadership as leaders making followers do what *followers* would not otherwise do, or as leaders making followers do what the *leaders* want them to do; I define leadership as leaders inducing followers to act for certain goals that represent the values and the motivations—the wants and needs, the aspirations and expectations—*of both leaders and followers.* And the genius of leadership lies in the manner in which leaders see and act on their own and their followers' values and motivations.

Leadership, unlike naked power-wielding, is thus inseparable from followers' needs and goals. The essence of the leader-follower relation is the interaction of persons with different levels of motivations and of power potential, including skill, in pursuit of a common or at least joint purpose. That interaction, however, takes two fundamentally different forms. The first I will call *transactional* leadership. . . . Such leadership occurs when one person takes the initiative in making contact with others for the purpose of an exchange of valued things. The exchange could be economic or political or psychological in nature; a swap of goods or of one good for money; a trading of votes between candidate and citizen or between legislators; hospitality to another person in exchange for willingness to listen to one's troubles. Each party to the bargain is conscious of the power resources and attitudes of the other. Each person recognizes the other as a *person*. Their purposes are related, at least to the extent that the purposes stand within the bargaining process and can be advanced by maintaining that process. But beyond this the relationship does not go. The bargainers have no enduring purpose that holds them together; hence they may go their separate ways. A leadership act took place, but it was not one that binds leader and follower together in a mutual and continuing pursuit of a higher purpose.

Contrast this with *transforming* leadership. Such leadership occurs when one or more persons *engage* with others in such a way that leaders and followers raise one another to higher levels of motivation and morality. . . . Their purposes, which might have started out as separate but related, as in the case of transactional leadership, become fused. Power bases are linked not as counterweights but as mutual support for common purpose. Various names are used for such leadership, some of them derisory: elevating, mobilizing, inspiring, exalting, uplifting, preaching, exhorting, evangelizing. The relationship can be moralistic, of course. But transforming leadership ultimately becomes *moral* in that it raises the level of human conduct and ethical aspiration of both leader and led, and thus it has a transforming effect on both. Perhaps the best modern example is Gandhi, who aroused and elevated the hopes and demands of millions of Indians and whose life and personality were enhanced in the process. Transcending leadership is dynamic leadership in the sense that the leaders throw themselves into a relationship with followers who will feel "elevated" by it and often become more active themselves, thereby creating new cadres of leaders. Transcending leadership is *engagé*. Naked power-wielding can be neither transactional nor transforming; only leadership can be.

Leaders and followers may be inseparable in function, but they are not the same. The leader takes the initiative in making the leader-led connection; it is the leader who creates the links that allow communication and exchange to take place. An office seeker does this in accosting a voter on the street, but if the voter espies and accosts the politician, the voter is assuming a leadership function, at least for that brief moment. The leader is more skillful in evaluating followers' motives, anticipating their responses to an initiative, and estimating their power bases, than the reverse. Leaders continue to take the major part in maintaining and effectuating the relationship with followers and will have the major role in ultimately carrying out the combined purpose of leaders and followers.

Finally, and most important by far, leaders address themselves to followers' wants, needs, and other motivations, as well as to their own, and thus they serve as an *independent force in changing the makeup of the followers' motive base through gratifying their motives.*

Certain forms of power and certain forms of leadership are near-extremes on the power continuum. One is the kind of absolute power that, Lord Acton felt, "corrupts absolutely." It also coerces absolutely. The essence of this kind of power is the capacity of power wielders, given the necessary motivation, to override the motive and power bases of their targets. Such power objectifies its victims; it literally turns them into objects. . . . Such power wielders, as well, are objectified and dehumanized. Hitler, according to Richard Hughes (1962, 266), saw the universe as containing no persons other than himself, only "things." The ordinary citizen in Russia, says a Soviet linguist and dissident, does not identify with his government. "With us, it is there, like the wind, like a wall, like the sky. It is something permanent, unchangeable. So the individual acquiesces, does not dream of changing it—except a few, few people. . . ."

At the other extreme is leadership so sensitive to the motives of potential followers that the roles of leader and follower become virtually interdependent. Whether the leadership relationship is transactional or transforming, in it motives, values, and goals of leader and led have merged. It may appear that at the other extreme from the raw power relationship, dramatized in works like Arthur Koestler's *Darkness at Noon* and George Orwell's *1984*, is the extreme of leadership-led merger dramatized in novels about persons utterly dependent on parents, wives, or lovers. Analytically these extreme types of relationships are not very perplexing. To watch one person absolutely dominate another is horrifying; to watch one person disappear, his motives and values submerged into those of another to the point of loss of individuality, is saddening. But puzzling out the nature of these extreme relationships is not intellectually challenging because each in its own way lacks the qualities of complexity and conflict. Submersion of one personality in another is not genuine merger based on mutual respect. Such submersion is an example of brute power subtly applied, perhaps with the acquiescence of the victim.

More complex are relationships that lie between these poles of brute power and wholly reciprocal leadership-followership. Here empirical and theoretical questions still perplex both the analysts and the practitioners of power. One of these concerns the sheer measurement of power (or leadership). Traditionally we measure power resources by calculating each one and adding them up: constituency support plus access to leadership plus financial resources plus skill plus "popularity" plus access to information, etc., all in relation to the strength of opposing forces, similarly computed. But these calculations omit the vital factor of motivation and purpose and hence fall of their own weight. Another controversial measurement device is *reputation*. Researchers seek to learn from informed observers their estimates of the power or leadership role and resources of visible *community* leaders (projecting this into national arenas of power is a formidable task). Major questions arise as to the reliability of the estimates, the degree of agreement between interviewer and interviewee over their definition of power and leadership, the transferability of power from one area of decision-making to another. Another device for studying power and leadership is *linkage theory*, which requires elaborate mapping of communication and other interrelations among power holders in different spheres, such as the economic and the military. The difficulty here is that communication, which may expedite the processes of power and leadership, is not a substitute for them.

My own measurement of power and leadership is simpler in concept but no less demanding of analysis: *power and leadership are measured by the degree of production of intended effects*. This need not be a theoretical exercise. Indeed, in ordinary political life, the power resources and the motivations of presidents and prime ministers and political parties are measured by the extent to which presidential promises and party programs are carried out. Note that the variables are the double ones of *intent* (a function of motivation) and of *capacity* (a function of power base), but the test of the extent and quality of power and leadership is the degree of *actual accomplishment* of the promised change. . . .

2

Politics as Leadership

Robert C. Tucker

Systematic thought about politics began in Greece about two and a half millenia ago, and an academic discipline called *political science* has flourished in various countries for a century or so. Yet there is still no consensus on the essential nature of the discipline's subject. Political scientists are not in general agreement about what it is they are studying. Let us then begin at the beginning: What is politics?

There is a classic answer to this question, and likewise a classic dissent. Both appear in the Platonic dialogues. The answer, advocated in the dialogues by the Sophists, holds that politics is in essence the pursuit and exercise of power—in the interest of those who pursue and exercise it. As Gorgias the rhetorician expounds this position in Plato's dialogue the *Gorgias*, the chief good in human life is power, and statesmen acquire power through the art of persuasion, rhetoric. So, for example, Pericles owed his power over the Athenian city-state to his command of persuasive eloquence. The same theme is argued by another character in the dialogue, Callicles, in a starker way. He declares it a natural law ("Nature's *nomos*") that those with greater power rule the polis for self-

From *Politics as Leadership*, by Robert C. Tucker (Columbia: University of Missouri Press, 1981), pp. 1–30. Reprinted by permission of the University of Missouri Press. Copyright © 1981 by the Curators of the University of Missouri.

seeking purposes, imposing their will upon the weak. Callicles, it has
been observed, was propounding, long in advance, Nietzsche's idea of
the superman imbued with *Wille zur Macht*.

Plato makes Socrates the exponent of the dissenting view. Socrates
does not deny the factual prevalence of politics as the self-interested rule
of the powerful in most times and places. But this merely means that true
statesmanship (*politiké*) is a rare phenomenon on earth. Indeed, Socrates
(1937, 582) says in one place: "I think that I am the only or almost the
only Athenian who practices the true art of politics; I am the only politician of my time." The idea underlying this statement is that statesmanship is an art analogous to gymnastics and medicine, arts that tend to the
body. Just as medicine is the art of tending the body with a view to restor-
ing it to a healthy state, so statesmanship is tendance of the soul, whether
through legislation, which establishes a standard of the soul's health, or
through the administration of justice, which cures diseases of the soul.
Rhetoric, the art of persuasion, is sham politics, rather as cosmetics, the
artful decking out of the body, are sham gymnastics. The true statesman,
possessing knowledge of what is good for man, is a physician of souls. So
runs Plato's argument in the *Gorgias*. Elsewhere, as in the late dialogue
the *Politicus*, he varies the analogy and pictures the statesman as shepherd of the human flock. Statesmanship is the art of tending the flock.

I think it fair to characterize Plato's dissenting view as one that
equates politics with leadership. He does not deny that rulers exercise
power, whether in accordance with law as in the case of the righteous
king or arbitrarily and autocratically as in the case of the tyrant. But he
believes that in essence, ideally, politics has a positive function to perform for the community of citizens in which the ruler exercises power. It
is not the exercise of power for power's sake, nor is it the simulacrum of
statesmanship that the rhetorician may produce by flattering the populace with his art of persuasion. It is an activity with utility for the polis,
the activity of giving direction to the community of citizens in the management of their common affairs, especially with a view to the training
and improvement of their souls. The notion of politics as the directive
function in the state is the crux of Plato's position. In our time we can
hardly rest content with his further thought that the directive function
consists in the moral tendance of citizen's souls. Still, his greatest achievement was to formulate, or at any rate to adumbrate, a leadership approach to the nature of politics as distinct from the power approach that
was widely accepted in his time and is still widely accepted in ours.

The position taken in these pages is in the Platonic tradition. While
recognizing, as any realistic view must, that power considerations bulk
very large in political life, it holds that politics in essence is leadership, or
attempted leadership, of whatever is the prevailing form of political

community. It departs from Plato in advancing this as a descriptive proposition rather than a normative one. Leadership is not an ideal form of political rule; it is what we factually find when we study closely the political process. Consequently . . . political leadership comes in many forms: effective and ineffective; wise, constructive, and beneficial to the political community on some occasions, and unwise, destructive, and disastrous on others. . . .

The Power School

In modern times, the classic answer has generally prevailed over the recurring dissent. From Machiavelli, who produced in *The Prince* a "how-to" manual for the princely power-seeker and power-holder, the concept of politics as power has been a salient strain in political theorizing. In the nineteenth and twentieth centuries it has been, I believe, the dominant school.

Machiavelli's advice to the prince leaves us in no doubt as to what, in the Florentine's view, politics is about. After considering the various kinds of government, he raises the key issues, such as: The Way to Govern Cities or Dominions That, Previous to Being Occupied, Lived Under Their Own Laws; Of New Dominions Which Have Been Acquired by One's Own Arms and Ability; Of Those Who Have Attained the Position of Prince by Villainy; How the Strength of All States Should Be Measured; Of Cruelty and Clemency, and Whether It Is Better to Be Loved or Feared; Whether Fortresses and Other Things Which Princes Often Contrive Are Useful or Injurious; and How a Prince Must Act in Order to Gain Reputation.

Marx, like his master Hegel, was an admiring reader of Machiavelli and may have been especially struck by the statement in chapter nine of *The Prince* that there are "two opposite parties" in every city, "arising from the desire of the populace to avoid the oppression of the great, and the desire of the great to command and oppress the people." The "two opposite parties" resemble the two opposing classes of Marx's class-struggle doctrine. Marx views the state as an agency of the power of a possessing class and politics as the coercive use of state power to protect the possessing class's mode of production and the associate set of property relations. Consistent with this position, revolutionary politics is the deployment of rebellious coercive power to overthrow an existing state order and the socioeconomic structure that it protects. As Marx's disciple Lenin put it, the state is "a special kind of cudgel, *rien de plus*."

From Marx's teaching on politics as class power the influential Italian school of politics as elite power took its rise in Gaetano Mosca and Vilfredo Pareto. The elite theorists could be described as disillusioned

Marxists. Marx envisaged a human future without classes, hence without the state and the politics of power, whereas the elite theorists believe it to be written in the constitution of man and society that there will forever be a diversion between a power-holding minority, the ruling elite, and a majority that submits to the elite's power. The majority submits because of coercion or through acceptance of an ideological "political formula" that masks the situation of elite rule.

Academic political science in mid-twentieth-century America has been strongly under the influence of the power approach to the political process. The elite theory found a well-known application to America in C. Wright Mills's book *The Power Elite* (1956) and other works of its genre. Some theorists, perhaps best typified by Anthony Downs in *An Economic Theory of Democracy* (1957), have sought to construct a politics on the analogy of economics. The postulated wealth-maximizing "economic man" of modern political economy finds his counterpart here in a postulated power-maximizing "political man" single-mindedly seeking to win elections and stay in office through coalition-building in party politics. In this model, the ulterior purposes for which power is desired are of no more interest to the political scientist than those for which economic man desires wealth are to the political economist.

To other power theorists, best instanced by the late Harold Lasswell, the inner sources of the postulated power motivation are of profound importance. Having described politics in an earlier text as "the study of influence and the influential," or "who gets what, when and how." Lasswell went on, in his book *Power and Personality* (1948), to define a politician man (*homo politicus*, to use his own phrase) as one who accentuates power, demands power for the self, accentuates expectations concerning power, and acquires at least a minimum proficiency in the skills of power. This definition of political man as power-seeker was accompanied by the hypothesis that "power is expected to overcome low estimates of the self." By "power" Lasswell meant the capacity of a person to dominate or determine the actions of others. In a forthright later statement of this position, he wrote: "In human affairs the demand to coerce is the phenomenon with which we are most concerned as professional students of politics" (1960, 278). Not all or even most contemporary political scientists would agree with all of these statements, but there might be something approximating a consensus on Lasswell's broader proposition, cited approvingly in a text by Robert Dahl (1963, 5), that politics may be defined as "the study of the shaping and sharing of power."

We have touched very briefly upon some influential versions of the concept of politics as power-seeking. A full and systematic examination of that position is beyond the scope of our study. What can be said by way of general evaluation of it? First, it seems clear that the pursuit of power goes on constantly under all political systems of which we know. To acquire the role of a constituted political leader, in other words, to occupy an official leadership position in a political order, a person normally seeks power by whatever are the prescribed or permitted means and procedures, and once having become a constituted leader he often seeks to enhance his power position. Moreover, the student of political history is likely to find, here and there, some individuals who resemble in their behavior and motivation the power-lusting *homo politicus* that Lasswell has pictured, or the power-maximizing party politician of Downs's theory of democracy.

But all this having been acknowledged, the dissenter has some telling arguments to advance against the view that reduces politics to the seeking and exercise of power. First, some constituted leaders have shown themselves capable, at one time or another, of rising above personal or party power considerations in their political conduct. More important, some persons have been or are now political leaders without possessing power or occupying high political office; some among these have not even aspired to it. They will be called here *nonconstituted leaders.* Examples from recent history might include Mohandas Gandhi, Martin Luther King, Jr., Dr. Albert Schweitzer, Milovan Djilas, Jean Monnet, and Academician Andrei Sakharov, a nonconstituted leader of contemporary Russia. . . .

Finally, and this may be the decisive point, the power approach fails to tell us what political leaders do, or are expected to do, in their capacities as leaders. To define politics as the exercise of power is rather like saying that an airplane pilot manipulates wheels and levers. He certainly does that, but he does it in the process of flying the airplane. The question that the power theorists fail to answer, or to answer satisfactorily, is: What is the equivalent of "flying the airplane" for people of power in political life? Or, to return to the economic analogy favored by political scientists like Downs, economic man maximizes his wealth in the course of providing certain goods or services. What "goods or services" does political man provide in the course of maximizing his power, or with the power that he has maximized? It is not my contention that the power approach has no great relevance to the understanding of politics, but I do think that it is critically inadequate as a basis for such understanding, because it does not reveal what it is that political leaders do or attempt to do with the power that most really do seek and some do exercise.

The power approach is not to be disposed of, however, by such considerations. One who does not accept the view that politics in its essence is the pursuit and the wielding of power must produce an explanation for the tenacity of that view through the centuries, for the fact that so many eminent thinkers, some with practical, political experience, have espoused it. The political theorizing of such figures as Machiavelli, Marx, and Mosca and such political scientists of our time as Lasswell is not to be lightly dismissed on the strength of the arguments that have been adduced here.

But in order to understand why the power approach has recommended itself so strongly to so formidable a collection of minds, we must first outline an acceptable alternative to it.

The Leadership Approach

If the antecedents of the leadership approach go back to Plato, the idea of building a systematic politics upon the foundation of a concept of leadership belongs primarily to the twentieth century. Max Weber pointed the way early in the century. In his essay on "Politics as a Vocation" (1918) he defined politics as "the leadership, or the influencing of the leadership, or a *political* association, hence, today, of a *state*," and added that by a "state" he meant a "human community that (successfully) claims the *monopoly of the legitimate use of physical force* within a given territory." The conception of the state as "a relation of men dominating men" led Weber, however, to a modified version of the power theory—modified in the sense that politics as a discipline became the study of "authority" defined as legitimized domination in its various forms (Gerth and Mills, 1958, 77, 78). No systematic account of politics in terms of leadership emerged.

It is in the recent history of political science that we see the beginning of conscious efforts in this direction. Such efforts have begun, partly, in disillusion with the power approach. James MacGregor Burns (1978, 11), the author of a major attempt at recasting political analysis in leadership terms, formulates this feeling as a confession:

> As a political scientist I have belonged to a "power school" that analyzed the interrelationships of persons on the basis only of power. Perhaps this was fitting for an era of two world wars and revolutions, the unleashing of the inhuman force of the atom. I fear, however, that we are paying a steep intellectual and political price for our preoccupation with power. Viewing politics *as* power has blinded us to the crucial role of power *in* politics and hence to the pivotal role of leadership.

Others might differently explain their sense of the need to take the leadership road in theorizing about politics. The significant fact is that increasing numbers of practitioners of the discipline are showing that they feel such a need. An anthology of articles on political leadership (Paige 1972) was subtitled "Readings for an Emerging Field," and the editor, in a subsequent volume of his own on this subject, summed up the status of the idea of political leadership as follows: "Past neglect. Present emergence. Future potential." "Now," he went on, "we need to ask, 'What is meant by political leadership?' " (Paige 1977, 61).

He thereby called attention to the fact that leadership is an elusive phenomenon and that there is no consensus among political scientists on what it means. Others have stressed the same point. "The precise nature of political leadership is one of the most difficult problems in the domain of politics, or indeed, in social action, yet it is one of the most real phenomena in political and social behavior," wrote the eminent Chicago political scientist Charles E. Merriam in 1945 (Merriam 1945, 107). . . .

Why is it so difficult to bring the phenomenon of leadership into conceptual focus? One part of the answer is that the most readily apparent way of doing so is not, analytically, the most promising path to take. Leadership is a fact of social life in all spheres, not in politics only, and wherever found it appears under the aspect of a relationship between leaders and those whom they lead. Leadership is a process of human interaction in which some individuals exert, or attempt to exert, a determining influence upon others. . . .

Thus, in advocating what he called a "politics by leadership conception," Lester Seligman (1950, 914) wrote that such a conception would concern itself with generalizing concerning four types of relations: "(1) the relations of leaders to led within particular structures, (2) the relationship between leaders of political structures, (3) the relationship between leaders of one structure and the followers of another, and (4) the relationship between leaders and the 'unorganized' or nonaffiliated." Burns (1978, 19), for his part, defines leadership as "leaders inducing followers to act for certain goals that represent the values and the motivations—the wants and needs, the aspirations and expectations—*of both leaders and followers*." This results in the exclusion of dictators from the category of leaders. Adolf Hitler appears, in Burns's (1978, 27) analysis, as "an absolute wielder of brutal power" and, as such, *not* a leader. Although such a line of reasoning reflects our feeling that leadership involves a voluntary response of followers to leaders, it gives rise to serious problems of political analysis. First, we have much evidence that dictators, including such archetypal twentieth-century ones as Hitler and Stalin, had very many willing followers in their time, the first especially in his earlier years of rule in Germany, and the second especially in his war leadership of Russia in 1941–1945. Second, Burns's view bypasses the key question of what it is that leaders do, or how they function as leaders, apart from interacting motivationally with followers. Hence he is blocked off from allowing that the leader–follower relationship covers a

wide spectrum, ranging from dictatorial forms of leadership at one extreme to highly participatory or democratic forms at the other. A leadership approach to politics must not rule out by its terms of reference the
phenomenon of authoritarian or dictatorial leadership. That Hitler and
Stalin were political leaders is no less a fact than that they were absolute
wielders of brutal power.

The upshot is that while leadership is unquestionably a relation between leaders and followers in interaction and may for various purposes
be analyzed as such, a theory of political leadership cannot easily be developed by elaborating the relational aspect. The more fruitful way is to
start with the question of what it is that leaders do, or try to do, in their
capacities as leaders, what functions do they perform in the process of
exerting influence upon their followers? Here I repeat the point already
made in my discussion of the power school, namely, that as political scientists we must specify what sorts of "goods or services" leaders provide in
the exercise of political power. . . .

In *Heroes and Hero-Worship and the Heroic in History* (1841),
Thomas Carlyle proposed that there are certain individuals whose innate
superiority along one or another line stamps them as natural leaders.
Among twentieth-century social psychologists, this became known as the
"great-man" theory of leadership. Experimental research did not bear it
out. It seemed, rather, that the nature of the group's situation determined who of its members would emerge as a group leader. If the group
was in a fighting situation, then someone with martial capability would;
if it was in a situation that called for careful planning, then someone with
the qualities of a planner would; and so on. Eventually this extreme "situ-
ationist" perspective was abandoned in favor of a middle position that
recognizes the existence of certain general leadership qualities—
intelligence, alertness to the needs and motives of others, insight into situations, initiative, persistence, and self-confidence—along with the variability of leadership traits according to the demands of group situations.
More important than that conclusion, however, is an insight that resulted from research on leaders' attributes, namely, that "leadership
flourishes only in a problem situation" (Gibb 1969, 211).

Because the social psychologists frequently work with small experimental groups and can arrange the situations in which leadership
emerges, they have tended to assume that the nature of the problem situation is a "given," self-evident to the group's members. But would this be
true in real-life situations involving large groups, particularly those in
political life? Might it not very often be the case in politics that the problem needs to be specified, the situation interpreted or defined, and that
just this is one of the functions that leadership serves, perhaps the prime
function? With that crucial critical reservation in mind, I will steer in

what follows by the lodestar of Gibb's proposition that leadership flourishes in problem situations.

Leadership as Activity

Let us begin with Plato's view that leadership has a directive function. A leader is one who gives direction to a collective's activities. The collective may be of any size or kind. It may be a small informal group such as a gang of hoodlums. It may be a university, a business corporation, or an army. In these cases we are dealing with criminal, business, educational, and military leadership respectively. If the group in question is a political community, whether a municipality, a province, a nation-state, or an international organization, then we are speaking of political leadership. A political leader is one who gives direction, or meaningfully participates in the giving of direction, to the activities of a political community.

The idea of leadership's directive function is supported by a kind of imagery that leaders in different times and cultures have frequently used in addressing their followers or those who they hoped would become their followers. It is the imagery of the journey or the road, of direction-giving in a literal sense. The leader will say that the group, or the society, is traveling along a certain path but ought to take a different one, or that the group stands at a crossroads beyond which stretch two alternative roads: one that will lead to the desired destination and another that will lead only to grief and trouble. . . .

If political and other groups are in need of direction, this must be because of uncertainty about what courses of collective action are desirable. One might argue that even in ordinary, day-to-day group life, when no great uncertainties exist, groups are in need of being directed. But such routine direction might better be described as *management*, reserving the term *leadership* for the directing of a group at times of choice, change, and decision, times when deliberation and authoritative decision occur, followed by steps to implement decisions reached. In more familiar terms directly applicable to political leadership, political communities confront situations in which policy must be formulated, promulgated, and executed.

To clarify what is meant by a *situation* (which will be used here as synonymous with *problem situation*), imagine that you are on holiday and visiting a foreign city for the first time. One day you leave your hotel in midafternoon to go for a walk. You drift along enjoying the scene. You walk by a river, through a park, and along winding streets. There *is* no situation, only a set of pleasant circumstances, so pleasant in fact that you take no notice of the passage of time. Then, as the sun starts to set, you suddenly recall that you are to meet a friend at your hotel at seven and go to dinner. You look at your watch and see that the time is already 6:45. You say to yourself; "I'm lost and I'm going to be late!" Now you are in a situation, and these words are your diagnosis, your definition, of it. You think of various possible courses of action that might be taken in the situation. You can hail a taxi, try to find a bus going in the direction of the hotel, or phone your friend and change the time of meeting. You choose what seems the best way out, and act accordingly.

Generalizing, we may say that a situation is a set of circumstances that someone endows with meaning because of the way in which they relate to that person's purposes and concerns. In the hypothetical case just mentioned, the circumstances were the distance from the hotel, the ignorance of the way back, and the seven o'clock date; the purpose that caused them to be endowed with meaning was the intention to keep the date. Situations are thus both objective and subjective in character. The circumstances, although they may be misread or incompletely known, are objective facts; they are whatever they are. The meaning with which they are endowed, however, turns on the purposes and concerns of the people involved; it is inescapably subjective. The interpreting of the meaning is, moreover, a mental act. Finally, situations are practical in that circumstances are endowed with meaning in such a way that some action is required in order to meet them. . . .

When an individual defines a situation on his own and acts in it, leadership as an influencing relationship is not involved (except insofar as we wish to consider that each person exercises leadership of himself in life situations as they occur—an idea in the tradition of Plato). The functional need for leadership arises when people form groups for purposive action, and it arises in the group context because of the necessity of coordinated action when circumstances are endowed with meaning in such a way that a *group situation* is defined and action by the group, or on its behalf, takes place. When groups are small, leadership may be informal and shift from one element or individual in the group to another depending upon the character of the situations encountered. When groups are large and organized, there is usually a formal leadership structure. Examples are the high command of an army, the management of a corporation, the officials of a trade union, or the administration of a university. The leadership structure of a political community is its government.

We may divide leadership's directive function into three [interpenetrating] phases. First, leadership has a diagnostic function. Leaders are expected to define the situation authoritatively for the group. Second, they must prescribe a course of group action, or of action on the group's behalf, that will meet the situation as defined. They must formulate a plan of action designed to resolve the problem in a manner that will serve group purposes. These, of course, may in practice be the purposes of some particular element of the group that equates its own aims with those of the group as a whole. Third, leadership has a mobilizing function. Leaders must gain the group's support, or predominant support, for the definition of the group situation that they have advanced and for the plan of action that they have prescribed. We may describe these functions as diagnostic, policy formulating, and policy implementing.

Two familiar historical examples, both involving leadership in international politics, may be cited for purposes of illustration. The circumstances in the first can be stated quite briefly. On 7 December 1941 the Japanese air force carried out a surprise attack and sank most of the U.S. Pacific fleet, which was lying at anchor in Pearl Harbor in Hawaii. The next day Pres. Franklin D. Roosevelt went before Congress, reported these circumstances, plus the further circumstance that the German and Italian governments had declared war on the United States, and defined the situation for the American political community: the nation was at war. The president said in his speech that 7 December 1941 was "a day that will live in infamy." He prescribed a policy response, calling upon Congress to declare war upon Japan, Germany, and Italy. It promptly did so. The entire session lasted, perhaps, no more than forty-five minutes. The meaning that the reported circumstances had for the United States, their impingement upon the country's purposes and concerns, was immediately clear; the country was in danger, it was in a war situation. In this instance, the mobilization of public support for the proposed policy response presented no difficulty. Mobilization meant just that— mobilization for war. Since the nature of the situation and the necessity of the military response were clear to all, the country rapidly mobilized for the long hard war that lay ahead.

The other case occurred in Europe in 1938. It came about as a result of one of a series of aggressive steps taken by Adolf Hitler after he became leader of Germany. Not long after annexing Austria to Germany in early 1938, Hitler started to make menacing noises toward Czechoslovakia. His pretext was that ethnic Germans in a border area of the Czechoslovak republic, the Sudetenland, were being mistreated. Although a small country, Czechoslovakia was then a considerable military power, with a one-and-a-half-million-strong army deployed along a powerful fortified line of defense in hilly terrain and a well-developed defense industry. The peoples of this country had a strong will to defend its independence. It was estimated that even fighting all alone against Germany's army of that time, Czechoslovakia could hold out for three months. Furthermore, she had a treaty of alliance with France, then the strongest land power in Europe, and France was allied with Great Britain, the strongest naval power. Germany was rearming, but this process was not complete and the Nazi amy was not yet up to planned strength.

Hitler's threats and bluster raised the specter of conflict. The circumstances were endowed with grim meaning by the French and the British as well as by the Czechs themselves and the German people. There was the possibility of a new European war involving the fates of all these countries and others as well. From May 1938, and especially from August, when Hitler issued an ultimatum on the Sudeten question, the existence of a most serious problem situation was accepted by all. There was no doubt among the Allies that it was a situation of danger. But along with agreement on that main point, there were important differences among different leaders' diagnoses of the danger and their prescriptions for policy response. There were differences, too, on the German side.

Twenty years earlier, France and Britain had endured a terrible war with Germany. Public opinion in both countries was strongly in favor of preserving peace if at all possible. This concern was on the minds of the constituted leaders of the two governments. Prime Minister Neville Chamberlain of Britain and Premier Édouard Daladier of France, and it was not lost on the minds of others in responsible positions. Under the influence, in part, of the peace-at-almost-any-price sentiment, Chamberlain and Daladier decided to seek a way out by negotiating with Hitler, and they chose to take him at his word when he claimed that his concern was the fate of the Sudeten Germans. As they defined the problem situation, it was one of local conflict that could be regulated by the major powers given a modicum of goodwill and flexibility on all sides.

Winston Churchill and some others, including First Lord of the Admiralty Duff Cooper, diagnosed the situation differently. As they saw it, there was a discrepancy between Hitler's public definition of the situation as one of local conflict over the Sudetenland and his private definition, in other words, his actual diagnosis, of it. In their opinion, Hitler had diagnosed the situation as an opportunity to destroy Czechoslovakia as a major obstacle on his march to mastery of Europe, and he wanted to accomplish this with the help of Britain and France by persuading their fearful leaders to pressure Pres. Eduard Benes of Czechoslovakia into submission to the demand for cession of the Sudetenland to Germany. To Churchill and Duff Cooper, therefore, the situation was not simply that peace was in danger, but that the democratic states were in mortal danger if Hitler succeeded in swallowing up Czechoslovakia. That would gravely weaken the Allies' military position and correspondingly strengthen Hitler's. Consequently, they favored a different policy response from the one that Chamberlain and Daladier were proposing. While not declaring war, they would be supportive of the Czechs and thereby show Hitler that Britain and France were prepared, *if necessary*, to go to war in order to prevent Czechoslovakia from being overrun. In that case, they reasoned, he would draw back. . . .

The rest, of course, is familiar history. Chamberlain and Daladier made a deal with Hitler in Munich and prevailed on Benes to accept it. Hitler proceeded to dismember Czechoslovakia in stages, as Churchill and Duff Cooper had thought he would do, and the Second World War broke out in 1939 under less favorable conditions for the Allies than would have been the case had the leadership of Churchill and Duff Cooper prevailed in the crisis of 1938.

What about Hitler's leadership? We must admit that, given his aggressive purpose, it was brilliant—a historic bluff that worked, a desperate gamble by an evil leader that succeeded owing largely to his shrewd perception of how the constituted leaders of Britain and France were likely to respond to his threats. Had he been mistaken about this, or had Chamberlain for some reason (such as poor health) been compelled to delay his arrival in Germany for the talks that prepared the deal, the bluff might have been foiled—by a group of German military men who defined the crisis situation as such a danger to Germany that they conspired to remove Hitler and his fellow Nazi chieftains from power before he plunged the country into a great war for which, as they knew, it was not yet adequately prepared. According to a later account given by Gen. Franz Halder, who was chief of the German general staff in 1938 and who survived the war,

> By the beginning of September, we had taken the necessary steps to immunize Germany from this madman. At this time the prospect of war filled the great majority of the German people with horror. We did not intend to kill the Nazi leaders—merely to arrest them, establish a military government, and issue a proclamation to the people that we had taken this action only because we were convinced they were being led to certain disaster. (Churchill 1961, 279)

It was decided, Halder went on, to strike at Hitler and other Nazi leaders at 8:00 P.M. on 14 September. But at 4:00 P.M. that day, news arrived that Chamberlain was flying to talk with Hitler at Berchtesgaden. It appeared that Hitler's bluff was working, and the generals abandoned their planned coup. . . .

An inference that we might draw as students of political leadership has to do with an issue raised earlier: Shall we approach leadership as an interactional process, a relation between leaders and followers, or, alternatively, as a kind of activity that leaders seek to perform in their capacities as leaders? Although it is possible and for some purposes necessary to view leadership in relational terms, our second example suggests that we are on stronger analytical ground when we consider leader–follower relations themselves in the context of leadership activity. For a leader's authority as a leader, his or her hold upon the followers' loyalty and willingness to follow, will depend in some measure upon the effectiveness or ineffectiveness of the leadership performance from the followers' point of view. Unless a leader who fails conspicuously in action as a leader manages to conceal the failing from the political community—as some tyrannical leaders have done, at least until their death or overthrow—that leader's authority is likely to suffer as a consequence of the perceived failure, as Chamberlain's did soon after Munich, and as Hitler's did much later. In the final analysis, the strength of leadership as an influencing relation rests upon its effectiveness as activity.

Having set out the rudiments of a leadership approach to politics, we may now return to the question posed earlier about the alternative view that politics is the pursuit of power. If, as was argued, the power approach is critically inadequate as the basis for a general theory of politics, how can we account for its tenacious hold over time upon thoughtful minds, and the fact that no few leading political thinkers have espoused it? The nub of the answer, I believe, is that the purposes and concerns that have historically conferred meaning on circumstances in the minds of constituted political leaders have been, primarily, purposes and concerns connected with power. The situation-defining function of political leadership has been performed mainly from the angle of the question, What does the given set of circumstances confronting this political community signify for its power position in the political world, or for the power position of the ruling element or political party, or for the power position of the leader himself, or for all of these combined? Political leadership, in other words, has largely been leadership *for power*, and theorists have inferred from this fact, understandably but erroneously, that politics is in essence the pursuit of power. Erroneously, because leadership has on occasion been exercised, can be exercised, and conceivably might come in future to be exercised more and more for ends other than power.

Given the heavy accent on power in past and present political history, a political type has crystallized that is above all, as in Lasswell's formula, power-oriented. This type of human being is not the only one in the wide world of politics, but it is a commonly encountered type whose defining characteristic is effectiveness in the process of acquiring political power. We recognize the type in ordinary parlance when we say of so-and-so that he is an extremely able campaigner for office but not particularly good at governing once the sought-for political office has been won. This leader-for-power will be met with in the future, as always in the past, given the lure of power for some who are also well endowed with the skills needed to attain it. There will also, however, be political leaders for whom power is mainly an opportunity to exercise leadership for ends other than power.

But past political theorizing has understandably been responsive to past political realities, among which the power motivation of political leadership has been conspicuous. As a consequence, students of politics were led to the reductionist error of equating politics with pursuit of power. The notion of politics as a leadership process . . . is more promising in the end because it is more comprehensive. It accommodates the large element of truth in the power approach by recognizing that power motivation has not only been a predominant concern in past history but will also probably always be present in one degree or another in the political process. Yet . . . a leadership approach can illuminate areas of potential analysis and open up vistas for political theorizing that are not found in political study as power theorists have pursued it. The conception of politics as leadership involves the recognition that whatever material interests and power interests figure in political life—as some always do—politics is basically a realm of the mind.

SECTION III

PERSONALITY IN LEADERSHIP

Introductory Comment

Students of leadership at one time sought to discover individual traits that could lead to the effective performance of leadership in groups. The search for definitive traits of leaders led to investigation of a wide variety of attributes. Some studies found leaders to be taller and heavier than followers; some research found leaders healthier, less slovenly, more energetic and active, more intelligent. For a time, scholars even sought to discover whether or not leaders had heavier brains than followers—the so-called "brain weight" theory of leadership! But these studies of leaders' traits were inconclusive; no consistent pattern of traits could be found to distinguish leaders from followers (Gibb 1969).

Yet we know very well that leaders can, as individuals, have a tremendous impact on groups, on social life generally, or on the political world. In politics, who could deny the importance of a George Washington, a Winston Churchill, a Charles de Gaulle, or even an Adolf Hitler? Their leadership, shaped partly by their own personality characteristics, was history making. So invariably discussions about political leaders and analyses of their behavior turn, in one way or another, to their personal characteristics, or personalities. Probably talk about personality in leadership has been going on for centuries. But sustained and systematic analyses date from the psychoanalytic theorizing of Sigmund Freud in the early part of this century, and first systematically applied to the study of political leadership by Harold D. Lasswell (1930).

Like leadership, personality is a term of varying definitions (Greenstein 1969, 2–6). For our purposes it will be enough to think of personality as "including any individual psychological variations that influence behavior" (Elms 1976, v). Study of a leader's personality involves reaching beneath obvious attributes such as appearance, rhetorical skills, experience, or ideology to analyze deeper, more complex characteristics of motivation, inner conflicts, early life experiences, or ego defenses.

Questions of leaders' personalities often enter into everyday politics. Presidential politics in the United States has been highly susceptible to considerations of personality. In 1964 the mental fitness of Republican presidential candidate Barry Goldwater became a campaign issue after a highly controversial survey of psychiatrists raised doubt about his psychological suitability to be president. In 1972 Democratic presidential candidate George McGovern chose Missouri Senator Thomas F. Eagleton as his running mate, but Eagleton was forced to withdraw his vice-presidential candidacy when his psychological fitness for the position became a heated issue after the revelation that he had undergone shock therapy following episodes of nervous exhaustion. The Watergate scandal of 1972–73, which precipitated the resignation of President Richard M. Nixon, stimulated both searching reviews of the presidency as an institution and probings of Nixon's personality (Brodie 1981; Mazlish 1972). Moreover, biographies of both Lyndon B. Johnson and Jimmy Carter are partly psychobiographical (Glad 1980; Kearns 1976).

Interest in the political ramifications of personality is by no means limited to American presidents. Fascinating accounts have been written of the political personalities of a few other American political leaders. Among them is a psychobiography of one of the nation's great city bosses, Mayor Anton J. Cermak of Chicago, who was killed in Miami in February 1933 by a bullet intended to assassinate President Franklin D. Roosevelt (Gottfried 1962). Another such account is the story of the life of James Forrestal, the first Secretary of Defense, who committed suicide in May 1949 by jumping from the Sixteenth floor of the Bethesda Naval Hospital, where he was receiving psychiatric treatment (Rogow 1963).

The political personality of Mahatma Gandhi, the great Indian nationalist leader, is anatomized in the Pulitzer prize-winning biography by psychiatrist Erik H. Erikson (1969). A psychobiography of

Gough Whitlam, the extraordinary leader of the Australian Labour Party and prime minister of Australia from 1972 to 1975, focuses primarily on his adult political career (Walter 1980). Kurt Schumacher, leader of the German Social Democratic Party from the end of World War II until his death in 1952, provides the subject for yet another case study in political personality (Edinger 1965). The rich array of psychobiographies underscores the ways in which inner conflicts and personal motivations may help account for the behavior of political leaders.

Lasswell once said that "political science without biography is a form of taxidermy" (quoted in Rogow 1963, ix). Although political biography need not dwell on the psychological characteristics of leaders, psychobiography has become an important analytical approach (see Cocks and Crosby 1987). The most influential and controversial of the growing number of psychobiographies is *Woodrow Wilson and Colonel House* by Alexander L. George and Juliette L. George (1956). Although there is no substitute for reading the book in its entirety, the readings in this section offer a synthesis and something of the flavor of the controversy surrounding the claims in the book.

Woodrow Wilson was president of the United States from 1913 to 1921. Earlier he had been a college professor, president of the American Political Science Association, president of Princeton University, and governor of New Jersey. A Democrat, Wilson championed various liberal reforms which he called the "new freedom." He lead the nation's involvement in World War I when the United States sided with Great Britain and France against Germany. After the war, Wilson fought for American membership in the League of Nations, the predecessor of the present-day United Nations, but Congress refused to go along with him.

In their study of Wilson as a political leader, the Georges came to believe that basic features of his personality influenced how he conducted himself as president. They sought to explain Wilson's adult political behavior in the light of his early life experiences, and particularly of his relationship with his father. The Georges argue that Wilson's compulsive personality—his stubbornness, orderliness, moralism—could be understood in terms of the ways in which his childhood and upbringing shaped his personality. They show how Wilson's personality influenced major decisions in his career, including major defeats as president of Princeton University and then of the country. Alexander George summarizes and elaborates in the first reading the interpretation of Wilson's leadership that he and Juliette George first developed in 1956.

But the Georges' line of analysis has come under attack by Wilson's official biographer, Arthur S. Link (1947, 1956), and by

Edwin A. Weinstein (1981), a neurologist. Link contends that the Georges misread and misinterpreted the historical evidence, especially the facts of Wilson's childhood experiences. Weinstein argues that Wilson's behavior can be explained in terms not of his personality characteristics, but of his medical history—from dyslexia in childhood to a series of strokes in adulthood (Weinstein 1981; and Park 1986). In short, the attack on the Georges' interpretation of Wilson's leadership contends that his behavior as a leader rested on physiological, not psychological, antecedents. In the second reading, Link and Weinstein, joined by clinical psychologist James Anderson, develop their attack.

In the third reading, Juliette and Alexander George respond to their critics. They counter Link's criticism that their historical research was insufficient; they reassert the validity of their line of analysis of Wilson's personality; and they confront claims made by Weinstein, Anderson, and Link about Wilson's physical health.

This spirited exchange illuminates some of the major issues in psychobiography, and it will help you understand the challenges facing scholarly efforts to use leaders' personality to explain their political motivations and behavior.

Select Bibliography

Brodie, F. M. 1981. *Richard Nixon: The Shaping of His Character*. New York: Norton.

Edinger, L. J. 1965. *Kurt Schumacher: A Study in Personality and Political Behavior*. Stanford, CA: Stanford University Press.

Erikson, E. H. 1969. *Gandhi's Truth: On the Origins of Militant Nonviolence*. New York: Norton.

Glad, B. 1980. *Jimmy Carter*. New York: Norton.

Gottfried, A. 1962. *Boss Cermak of Chicago: A Study of Political Leadership*. Seattle: University of Washington Press.

Kearns, D. 1976. *Lyndon Johnson and the American Dream*. New York: Harper & Row.

Rogow, A. A. 1963. *James Forrestal: A Study of Personality, Politics, and Policy*. New York: Macmillan.

Walter J. 1980. *The Leader: A Political Biography of Gough Whitlam*. St. Lucia, Australia: University of Queensland.

Weinstein, E. A. 1981. *Woodrow Wilson: A Medical and Psychological Biography*. Princeton, NJ: Princeton University Press.

3

Woodrow Wilson's Political Personality

Alexander L. George

This paper was written by Professor George in 1960. It became well known among scholars, many of whom have drawn on and cited it. Professor George chose not to publish the paper at the time because he was in the process of refining portions of the argument and developing the technical implications of a number of points the paper raises. For some of these developments, see Alexander L. George, "Power as a Compensatory Value for Political Leaders," Journal of Social Issues 25 *(July 1968): 29–50. In 1971 Fred Greenstein and Michael Lerner persuaded Professor George to approve the delayed publication of his 1960 paper in their* Source Book for the Study of Personality and Politics. *We republish this early paper of George's not only because of its recognized standing among students of personality and politics but also because it continues to be one of the simplest and most fluent general introductory essays available on the use of depth-psychological categories and procedures in analyses of individual political actors. In illustrating his methodological discussion with case materials on Woodrow Wilson, George draws on his and Juliette L. George's* Woodrow Wilson and Colonel

From *A Sourcebook for the Study of Personality and Politics*, edited by F. I. Greenstein and M. Lerner (Chicago: Markham, 1971), pp. 78–98. Reprinted by permission of Alexander L. George.

House: A Personality Study, *one of the most rigorous and convincing of the psychobiographies of political figures. The original title of the paper, "Some Uses of Dynamic Psychology in Political Biography: Case Materials on Woodrow Wilson," has been abbreviated and footnotes eliminated.*

More so than historical writing at large, biography is selective. By choosing a single individual as his concern, the biographer can focus on those aspects of the historical process which interacted most directly with his subject. The nature of this interaction and, particularly, the extent to which it is reciprocal, is one of the central problems of biography. To what extent was the behavior of the subject culturally and situationally determined? To what extent did it reflect the individuality of his personality? Though variously worded by different writers, this twofold task of the biographer is a familiar and perplexing one.

In a brief but acute statement of the problem, the Committee on Historigraphy emphasized that the writing of biography requires both a systematic field theory of personality and hypotheses as to social roles. While agreeing with this twofold emphasis, we have chosen for several reasons to focus attention in the present article upon the need for a systematic approach to personality factors. First, it would appear that historians generally are already more favorably disposed to the cultural approach, and better prepared to employ it, than to a systematic handling of personality components in biography. Second, we wish to show by introducing concrete case materials that a systematic personality approach may be necessary and particularly rewarding in the biographical study of innovating leaders, those who attempt to reinterpret and expand the functions of existing roles or to create new roles. We are particularly interested, that is, in "role-determining" as against "role-determined" leadership. At the same time, we agree that the creation or reinterpretation of leadership roles can only be understood in the context of social-historical dynamics and the institutional setting. The "great leader," as Gerth and Mills (1953, ch. 12) observe, has often been a man who has successfully managed such institutional dynamics and created new roles of leadership.

We shall draw upon our previously reported study of Woodrow Wilson (George and George 1956) in order to demonstrate how the personality component in a biography may be handled in a systematic fashion. And we shall attempt to show that dynamic psychology provides a number of hypotheses which can supplement a cultural or role analysis of Wilson's interest in constitution-writing and which permit the biographer to view the relationship between his "Presbyterian conscience" and his political stubbornness in a new light.

Some Deficiencies of Pyschological Biographies

In the past three or four decades historians have occasionally turned to the new field of dynamic psychology for assistance in this task. At the same time, specialists in psychology, especially psychoanalysts, have themselves occasionally attempted to apply the insights and theories of their practice to historical figures. The results of such efforts, from both sides, to merge history and psychology in the writing of political biography have not been encouraging. Even when their purpose was not to debunk a historical figure, most psychoanalytical biographies suffered from pronounced and basic deficiencies.

Three major deficiencies in this type of biography may be briefly mentioned. In the first place, in varying degrees such biographies exaggerate the purely psychological determinants of the political behavior of their subjects. In the cruder of these studies, the subject is represented as if in the grip of powerful unconscious and irrational drives which dictate his every thought and action. Even in more discriminating analyses, the revelation of human motive resulting from incisive insights into the subject's personality can easily oversimplify the complexity of motivation and political action.

Secondly, in viewing adult character and behavior as the legacy of certain early childhood experiences, psychological biographies often oversimplify the process of personality formation and the intricacy of personality structure and functioning. Such a psychological approach is by today's standards inadequate for it overlooks the relevance of important developments in "ego psychology" in the past few decades. Contemporary students of personality emphasize that in the course of his development the individual develops a variety of defenses against underlying anxieties and hostilities. He may learn ways of curbing and controlling tendencies which handicap him in various situations; and he may even devise *constructive* strategies for harnessing personal needs and motivations and directing them into fruitful channels. In other words, the individual attempts to cope simultaneously with the demands of impulse, conscience and reality in developing a philosophy of life, a system of values, a set of attitudes and interests, and in choosing in various situations from among alternative courses of action.

And, finally, to conclude this brief review of the major deficiencies encountered in psychological biographies, one is struck by the fact that the actions of the subject are often interpreted in ways which seem highly speculative and arbitrary. Few investigators in this field have come to grips with the admittedly difficult problem of making rigorous reconstructions of personality factors and plausible interpretations of their role in behavior from the types of historical materials usually available to the biographer. The result is that the use which the biographer makes of dynamic psychology often appears to consist in little more than borrowing certain terms and hypotheses, and superimposing them, more or less arbitrarily upon a smattering of the available historical materials concerning the subject.

Personality Types: The Problem of Diagnosis and Classification

Typologies of personality or character are provided by most of the various schools of psychoanalysis and dynamic psychology. The depiction of a type is usually on the basis of one or more traits, or behavioral tendencies. Often, the characterization of types also includes some indication of the origins and underlying psychodynamics of that type of behavior, which enhances the usefulness of the typology to the biographer. We do not propose to review these typologies here or to attempt to assess their relative worth to the biographer. Rather we wish to consider the status or nature of these personality types and some of the problems which arise in efforts to utilize them in biography.

Most of the types in question are to be understood as being general constructs, or *ideal types*. Though derived from empirical observation, they abstract and deliberately over simplify reality. Accordingly, their value to the biographer is necessarily limited, since his task is to describe and explain a particular individual in all his concreteness and complexity.

The biographer cannot be satisfied merely to label his subject as constituting an instance of, or bearing a certain resemblance to, a certain personality or character type. To do so oversimplifies the task of making fruitful use of the theories and findings of dynamic psychology and yields results of a limited and disappointing character. Many investigators whose initial attempt to use a personality approach in biography is of this character become disillusioned and abandon the task. They sense that to type their subject, as a "compulsive" for example, tends to caricature him rather than to explain very much of the richness, complexity and variety of his behavior throughout his career.

We are concerned here with a problem not always clearly recognized in the writing of psychological biographies. *Classification* is often confused with *diagnosis*. To tag the subject of the biography with a label or to pigeonhole him in one of a number of existing categories does not in itself provide what the biographer will need most: namely, a discriminating "theory," i.e., a set of assumptions or hypotheses, as to the structure and dynamics of his subject's personality system.

The "diagnosis *vs.* classification" problem also exists in clinical psychiatry where a distinction is sometimes made between the "sponge" and the "file-drawer" clinician. The "sponge"-type clinician attempts to approach his patient with a relatively open mind, trying to derive a theory about that particular patient from an intensive analysis of his behavior and case history. In contrast, the "file-drawer" type of clinician is more inclined to orient himself to the patient on the basis of general theories and past experience. The one attempts to construct a theory about the patient *de nouveau*, a theory that, as a result, may be highly particularistic; the other stresses gaining insight into the patient by making an astute classification of him on the basis of accumulated theory and experience.

The difference between these clinical approaches is mentioned here in order to point up alternative approaches available to the biographer. As will become clear, we are suggesting that though the biographer should indeed be familiar with available personality theories, he should nonetheless approach his subject as does the "sponge"-type clinician and undertake to develop as discriminating and refined a theory as possible of that particular personality.

In attempting to account for the subject's actions throughout his career, the biographer will have to make specific diagnoses of the operative state of his personality system in numerous situations. To this end, the biographer starts with as good a theory of the subject's personality as he can derive from secondary accounts and from a preliminary inspection of historical materials. Then he reviews chronologically, or developmentally, the history of his subject's behavior, attempting to assess the role that situational and personality factors played in specific instances.

In utilizing a preliminary theory of the subject's personality to make specific diagnoses the biographer in a real sense also "tests" that theory. Detailed analysis of the subject's actions in a variety of individual situations provides new insights into the motivational dynamics of the subject's behavior; these insights, in turn, enable the biographer to progressively refine and improve the theory of the subject's personality with which he started. What the biographer hopes to achieve eventually is an account of the subject's personality that gives coherence and depth to the explanation of his behavior in a variety of situations and that illuminates the more subtle patterns that underlie whatever seeming "inconsistencies" of character and behavior he has displayed.

Two Uses of Personality Types in Biography

Despite the general nature of personality and character types, they may be of substantial use to the biographer in several ways. First, knowledge of these types assists the biographer in developing the kind of *preliminary* theory about the personality of his subject to which reference has already been made. Second, familiarity with the psychodynamics of behavior associated with a particular personality or character type provides the biographer with hypotheses for consideration in attempting to account for the actions of his subject, especially those that cannot be easily explained as adequate responses to the situation which confronted him. Let us consider these two general uses in somewhat greater detail.

A major shortcoming in many conventional biographies, including those of Wilson, is that they lack a systematic theory about the subject's personality and motivations. The biographer is usually satisfied to catalogue individual traits exhibited by the subject without exploring their possible interrelationship and their functional significance within the personality as a whole. Various of Wilson's biographers, for example, have called attention to his marked "conscientiousness," "stubbornness," "single-track mind," and various other traits. They have done so, however, without indicating awareness that, according to Freudian theory, these traits are commonly exhibited by "compulsive" persons.

The term "compulsive" today is commonly applied to persons whose lives are regulated by a strict super-ego, or conscience, which dominates their personalities. Perhaps not generally known, however, is the fact that this type of behavior has been carefully studied over a period of many years by many clinicians; as a result, there are a number of detailed analyses and theories of compulsiveness and the compulsive type that attempt to account for the genesis and underlying dynamics of this type of behavior. Later in this paper we shall attempt to show how this rich body of observation and theory can be used by the biographer. It suffices here to observe that biographers of Wilson, being generally unfamiliar with such materials, have not been in a position to assess the significance of individual traits displayed by Wilson in terms of their underlying dynamics.

Occasionally biographers of Wilson have been able, on the basis of an intensive analysis of a particularly well-documented episode in Wilson's career, to infer or to suggest that his choice of action in a particular situation was apparently governed by personal motives other than the aims and values which he was publicly espousing. But generally they have hesitated to make diagnoses of the operative state of Wilson's personality system in specific situations, to explore in any systematic fashion the complexity and deeper levels of his motivation, or to postulate in detail the role of his personality in his political behavior. Therefore, while these biographers have sensed Wilson's personal involvement in politics and called attention to his many contradictions, their portraits of Wilson's personality are inevitably somewhat flat, even though accurately depicting behavioral tendencies at a surface level.

A familiarity with personality and character types identified in the literature of dynamic psychology will assist the biographer to construct a *preliminary* theory, or model, as to the structure and functioning of his subject's personality. For this purpose there are available to the biographer a variety of typologies of personality and character. Some of these are predominantly sociopsychological rather than clinical in their conception and orientation. Not all typologies of personality are comparable, since they have been constructed from different theoretical standpoints, for different purposes and applications. An overlapping can be noted, however, particularly among some of the typologies provided by various schools of psychoanalysis. Thus, for example, the "aggressive" person in Karen Horney's system bears a substantial resemblance to the Freudian concept of the compulsive type. Similarly, Alfred Adler's central emphasis upon the drive to power and superiority as a means of compensation for real or imagined defects finds a place in many other personality theories as well.

Given the variety of alternative typologies available, the biographer must obviously consider a number of them before choosing the type or types that seem most appropriate to his subject and most useful for the specific questions about the subject's motivations and behavior he is trying to clarify.

Personality theorists, Freudian and non-Freudian, have emphasized that the type-constructs formulated by them are not pure types. Rather, they view the personality functioning of an individual as a mixture of several trends, or types, in a more or less dynamic relationship to each other. This observation applies with particular force to Wilson, in whom several diverse trends can be detected. Nonetheless, the present account is limited to discussing the applicability of the compulsive type to Wilson, partly because of limitations of space and partly because we feel that the compulsive component of his personality is particularly important for illuminating the self-defeating aspects of his behavior.

In any case, having found much evidence of compulsiveness and of the compulsive syndrome in the historical accounts of his life and career, we felt justified in adopting as a tentative working theory that Wilson had a compulsive personality.

We then considered this development and behavior in detail from this standpoint, examining the voluminous documentation of his career that is available to the biographer. In doing so, we encountered increasing evidence of behavior on his part that could not easily be subsumed under the simple model of the compulsive type. This forced us to refine and elaborate the theory as to his compulsiveness, and to attempt to state the *conditions* and to characterize the *situations* in which he did and did not behave in a way (for example, stubbornly) that was in accord with the expectations explicit or implicit in the personality model with which we were working.

Gradually, then, the general construct of the compulsive type (which, as already mentioned, is to be taken as an abstraction and deliberate oversimplification of reality) was modified and brought into consonance with the complexities encountered in the individual case at hand. The point was reached when the picture of Wilson's personality that was emerging became too complex to be retained within the bounds of the compulsive model with which we had started. What remained of that model or theory was the notion of an important compulsive component in his personality and functioning. This component, we shall attempt to show, remained of considerable value as an explanatory principle for some of Wilson's political behavior that has puzzled and distressed many of his contemporaries and biographers.

Another major use of typologies and theories of personality to the biographer is that of providing alternative hypotheses for consideration in attempting to account for the actions and behavioral patterns of his subject. Such general hypotheses are not ready-made explanations to be employed arbitrarily or to be superimposed upon the data. Rather, as a statement of the dynamics of behavior and motivation often or typically associated with a certain personality type, they may serve to orient the biographer's effort to explain the actions of his subject. A familiarity with such hypotheses broadens and deepens the biographer's assessment of the aims and values that the subject pursues in a given situation or in a series of situations. Furthermore, it sensitizes him to historical evidence of the possible operation of unconscious or unstated motives he might otherwise overlook.

During the preparation of our study of Wilson we combed the technical literature for hypotheses about the dynamics of motivation and behavior associated with compulsiveness that might illuminate the nature of Wilson's personal involvement in political activities. We hoped to find clues to certain inept and apparently irrational actions on his part and to discover, if possible, a consistent pattern or thread in the various inconsistencies of behavior and character he displayed.

If Wilson is not the simple clinical stereotype of a compulsive, neither can he be regarded as a full-blown neurotic. True, one cannot read, for example, Karen Horney's insightful and penetrating descriptions of neurotic drives and of the neurotic character structure without being struck by the applicablity of much of what she says to Wilson (Horney 1945). But these descriptions are applicable only to a certain point and, upon reflection, one is on balance equally or more impressed with the extent to which Wilson's behavior and career *diverge* from those of her patients. This divergence from the clinical picture concerns precisely the critical question whether the neurotically disposed individual is able to deal adequately with his conflicts and hence retains the ability to function effectively.

For Wilson was, after all, a highly successful person. He was able to overcome a severe disturbance in childhood development; thereafter, not only did he keep fairly well in check the compulsive and neurotic components of his personality but he succeeded in large measure in harnessing them constructively to the achievement of socially productive purposes. To the clinical psychologist, therefore, Wilson is interesting as much because he was able to overcome childhood difficulties and to perform as successfully as he did in public life, as he is because of the pathological pattern of self-defeating behavior he tended to repeat on several occasions during his public career.

Compulsiveness and the Compulsive Type

To indicate briefly what is meant by compulsiveness and the compulsive type of personality is not an easy task since these concepts are employed somewhat differently within the various theoretical schools which comprise dynamic psychology. The point to be made here is that the existence of different theoretical orientations and, particularly, of important lacunae in knowledge and theory within the field of dynamic psychology need not prevent the biographer from making fruitful use of systematic personality theory as a source of hypotheses that serve to orient and give direction to his own research.

In any case, the usefulness of the technical literature to the biographer will be enhanced if the distinction is kept in mind between the question of the *origins* of compulsiveness and compulsive traits, about which there are various views and the *dynamics* of such behavior, about which there is less disagreement. Similarly, the biographer will observe that specialists seem able to agree more readily on a characterization of the quality of compulsive behavior than on a list of specific traits common to all compulsive persons.

In Freudian theory various correlations are predicted between disturbances of different stages in libido development and the emergence of certain adult character traits. Disturbances in one of these stages of development leads, according to the theory, to the presence of orderliness, stinginess, and stubbornness in adult behavior. These are general traits, or broad tendencies, that manifest themselves more specifically in a variety of ways. By combing the technical literature one can easily construct a richer, more elaborate list of traits which together comprise the syndrome or constellation.

Thus, for example, the general trait "orderliness" may manifest itself in (a) "cleanliness" (corporeal, symbolic); (b) "conscientiousness" (single-track mind, concentration, drive, pedantism, reliability, punctuality, punctiliousness and thoroughness); (c) "regularity" (according to spatial and temporal aspects); (d) "plannedness"; (e) "norm conformity."

Most personality and character types are usually described, at least in the first instance, in terms of certain manifest behavioral traits such as those that have been listed. If the description of a type does not link the traits in question with a theory of personality structure and motivational dynamics, the type-construct will obviously be of little value for motivational and situational analysis of an individual's behavior. At the same time, however, it is overly sanguine to expect that relationships between most manifest behavior traits and their inner, subjective functions for the personality will be of a simple one-to-one character. For, as clinical psychologists have particularly emphasized, the same item of manifest behavior may fulfill different funcitons for different personalities or, at different times, for the same individual. Particularly the political and social behavior of an individual, in which the biographer is most interested, is not likely to reflect single motives; it is more likely to be the outcome of a complex interplay of several motives and of efforts on the part of the person to adjust inner needs and strivings to one another as well as to external reality considerations.

A personality type construct is potentially more useful, therefore, if it is associated with a more or less distinctive type of motivational dynamics, whether or not this be invariably accomplished by a set of distinctive behavioral traits. From this standpoint, leaving aside for the present the question of its validity, the Freudian concept of the compulsive type is a particularly rich one in that it includes, in addition to the syndrome of traits already noted, a rather explicit and detailed set of structural-dynamite hypotheses of this kind.

We shall not attempt to recapitulate the rather involved and technical set of structural-dynamic hypotheses associated with the compulsive type in Freudian theory. Of immediate interest here is the fact that orderliness and stubbornness in persons of this type are said to derive in part from a desire for power or domination, which in turn is said to be related to a more basic need for self-esteem, or security. Thus, according to the technical literature compulsives often show a marked interest in imposing orderly systems upon others, an activity from which they derive a sense of power. They also hold fast obstinately to their own way of doing things. They dislike to accommodate themselves to arrangements imposed from without, but expect immediate compliance from other people as soon as they have worked out a definite arrangement, plan or proposal of their own.

In the spheres of activity in which they seek power gratifications, compulsives are sensitive to interference. They may take advice badly (or only under special circumstances). Often they exhibit difficulties in deputing work to others, being convinced at bottom that they can do everything (in this sphere) better than others. This conviction is sometimes exaggerated to the point that they believe they are unique. Negativeness, secretiveness and vindictiveness are traits often displayed by compulsives. (Considerable evidence of most of these traits and tendencies, too, can be found in the historical materials on Wilson, many of them being noted by contemporaries and biographers.) (Link 1947, 1956)

While particularly that aspect of Freudian theory that regards interferences with libido development as the genesis of adult character traits has been criticized, the existence of certain constellations of adult traits, as in this instance, is less controversial and, in fact, appears to enjoy some empirical support.

In revisions and elaborations of Freudian theory somewhat less emphasis is often placed upon specifying a distinctive content of compulsive behavior. Karen Horney, for example, regards compulsiveness as a characteristic quality of all neurotic needs. Thus, the craving for affection, power and prestige, and the ambition, submissiveness and withdrawal which different neurotics manifest all have a desperate, rigid, indiscriminate and insatiable quality, ie., the quality of compulsiveness (Horney, 1937, 1945).

Much of common to various of these formulations has been summarized in Harold D. Lasswell's (1948, 41–49) account of the functional role of the compulsive dynamism in the personality system and of the general character of the circumstances in which it is adopted. Thus, the compulsive dynamism is one of several possible defensive measures a child may adopt as a way out of an acute tension-producing situation that may arise during the course of socialization and learning. Tension is produced when a relatively elaborate set of requirements are imposed upon the child and reinforced by a system of rewards and punishments of a special intensity and applied in such manner so that deprivations and indulgences are balanced. One possible defensive measure against the ensuing tension is the adoption of a blind urge to act with intensity and rigidity, i.e., the dynamism of compulsiveness.

The reasons and conditions for the emergence of compulsiveness are, as has been suggested, somewhat difficult to formulate precisely. However, in making use of available knowledge of the compulsive personality for purposes of political biography, an answer to the causal question is not essential. Whatever creates a given personality dynamism, the dynamism itself—which is what interests the biographer the most—can be fairly readily identified in accounts of the subject's behavior.

In Wilson's case, even the circumstances under which the compulsive dynamism was adopted are richly suggested in materials collected by the official biographer. Thus, accounts of early efforts at the boy's education, in which the father played a leading role, strongly suggest the sort of acute tension-producing situation that we have already noted, is considered by specialists as predisposing to the adoption of the compulsive dynamism. This, however, evidently was not Wilson's initial method of coping with the tension-inducing situation; rather, for quite a while his method of defense took the form of a tendency to withdraw from the situation. For the time being the boy was unable, perhaps out of fear of failure, or unwilling, perhaps out of resentment, to cooperate with his father's effort to advance his intellectual development. Wilson's early "slowness" (which specialists today might well consider a case of reading retardation based on emotional factors) was a matter of considerable concern to his family; it manifested itself most strikingly in his not learning his letters until he was nine and not learning to read readily until the age of eleven.

At about the time the boy showed signs of beginning to cooperate actively with his father's efforts to tutor him and to make prodigious efforts to satisfy the perfectionist demands that the Presbyterian minister levied upon his son. One can only speculate at the reasons for the change at this time; possibly it was connected with the birth of a younger brother when Wilson was ten. (Wilson had two older sisters but no younger brothers or sisters until this time; he himself recalled that he had clung to his mother and was laughed at as a "mama's boy" until he was a great big fellow.)

In any case, it is easy thereafter to find evidence of a compulsive bent to the young adolescent's personality. It requires no great familiarity with the technical literature on such matters to detect indications of compulsiveness in the youth's extreme conscientiousness, the manner in which he drove himself repeatedly to physical breakdowns, and the singlensss of purpose he displayed in applying himself to the task of achieving knowledge and skill in the sphere of competence—politics and oratory—with which he quickly identified his ambitions.

Wilson's Interest in Constitutions

In the remainder of this paper we should like to develop the case, mainly by way of illustrative materials from the study of Wilson, for supplementing cultural and historical components in biography by an intensive and relatively systematic appraisal of personality.

A number of Wilson's biographers, including the official biographer (Baker 1927, I), have been struck by the interest in constitutions he displayed from early youth. Beginning in his fourteenth year he wrote or revised a half dozen constitutions, an activity that culminated in the Covenant of the League of Nations. It is our thesis that this activity on his part reflects the type of interest in order and power that compulsive persons often display. In other words, he was motivated in part (though not exclusively) by a desire to impose orderly systems upon others, deriving therefrom a sense of power or domination.

The historian will quickly object, and rightly so, offering a more obvious counter-hypothesis, which is certainly plausible; namely that Wilson's interest in writing constitutions was culturally determined. After all, it was part of the belief system of the age that progress in human affairs was to be achieved by such instrumentalities as better constitutions, institutional reform, etc. The fact that Wilson wrote or revised many constitutions, therefore, does not necessarily attest to a personal interest in order and power.

Is it possible to demonstrate that Wilson's motivation in the matter did not stem exclusively from identification with a role that was socially approved? Or, is such a question entirely out of the reach of the historian? In the following remarks we shall attempt to show that such questions are capable of being dealt with on the basis of the materials and method of the historian.

First, why Wilson and not someone else? Why, in other words, did the belief system in question impress itself particularly on Wilson? Is it not more than a coincidence that in every club he joined as a youth he seized the earliest opportunity, often making it the first order of business, to revise its constitution in order to transform the club into a miniature House of Commons? Granted that constitution-making was part of the existing cultural and political ethos and that admiration for the British system was already widespread among American students of government, why should the task of revising the constitution and political structure of these groups always fall to Wilson? Why were none of these constitutions revised along desirable lines by others, before Wilson joined the clubs? It would seem that among his contemporaries it was Wilson who found constitution-making a particularly attractive occupation. The readiness with which he accepted for himself a role that was, to be sure, culturally sanctioned makes the inference plausible that personal motives were strongly engaged by the possibility that constitution writing afforded of ordering the relations of his fellow-beings.

Secondly, what evidence can be found of an unconscious motive or need to impose orderly systems upon others? If such a motive exists, we may expect appropriate pleasurable feelings to ensue from its gratification. However, we cannot reasonably expect that the pleasure experienced by the individual in such instances will be fully articulated under ordinary circumstances. Hence, in the type of historical materials on the subject's inner life usually available to the biographer we can expect only episodic and fragmentary evidence of the fact that an activity on his part has satisfied deeply felt personality needs. This is in fact what we find in this case. For example, after rewriting the constitution of the Johns

Hopkins debating society and transforming it into a "House of Commons," Wilson reported to his fiancee the great pleasure he had derived from the project: "It is characteristic of my whole self that I take so much pleasure in these proceedings of this society. . . . I have a sense of power in dealing with men collectively that I do not feel always in dealing with them singly" (Baker 1927, I: 199).

That constitution-writing had a deep personal meaning for Wilson is further suggested by the fact that such activities were always instrumental to his desire to exercise strong leadership. It is rather obvious even from historical accounts that rewriting constitutions was for Wilson a means of restructuring those institutional environments in which *he* wanted to exercise strong leadership. He wished to restructure the political arena in these instances in order to enhance the possibility of influencing and controlling others by means of oratory. This was a skill in which he was already adept as an adolescent and to the perfection of which he assiduously labored for years. In the model House of Commons which Wilson created, and in which as the outstanding debater he usually became "Prime Minister," independent leadership was possible and, as Wilson had foreseen, the skillful, inspirational orator could make his will prevail.

From an early age, then, Wilson's scholarly interest in the workings of American political institutions was an adjunct of his ambition to become a great statesman. He wished to exercise power with great initiative and freedom from crippling controls or interference. The relationship between Wilson's theories of leadership and his own ambitions and changing life situation, which we cannot recapitulate here, is revealing in this respect (George and George 1956, 144–48, 321–22). Suffice it to say that when Wilson's career development is studied from this standpoint considerable light is thrown on the intriguing question of the role of personal motivations in political incentiveness and creativity. Political psychologists have hypothesized that a compulsive interest in order and power is often to be found in strong political leaders who were great institution-builders and who made it their task to transform society. The case study of Wilson lends support to this general hypothesis.

To posit such personal, unconscious components in the political motivation of some leaders by no means excludes the simultaneous operation of cultural determinants. There is no doubt in Wilson's case that his personal interest in order and power was defined and channelized by the culture and political matrix of the times. Moreover, concrete opportunities to rewrite constitutions and to exercise and perfect his talents as orator-leader were provided by existing situations in which he found himself or that he actively sought out.

Thus, the external situation in which the individual exists necessarily defines and delimits the field in which personality develops and in which personality needs and traits find expression. On the other hand, the interaction between the personality of a political leader and the milieu in which he operates may be, in an important sense, a reciprocal one. A leader's basic needs and values, his motives and dispositions, shape his perception of the situations that confront him and influence his definition and evaluation of the choices of actions open to him.

What is gained by attributing motivations of this character to a political leader? In this case, what difference does it make whether Wilson's interest in writing constitutions had the type of personal motivation in question? The postulate of a deep-seated, unconscious interest in imposing orderly systems upon others as a means of achieving a sense of power, we believe, accounts in part (but only in part) for Wilson's peculiar involvement in the League Covenant and in the making of the peace, the many strands of which we have attempted to document in our book. The biographer who is sensitive to the possible role of unconscious motivation is struck, for example, by the fact that it was Wilson's constant concern to reserve himself final authorship of the Covenant, even though none of the ideas that entered into it were original with him, and that he appeared to derive peculiar pleasure from giving his own stamp to the phraseology of the document.

Similarly, the postulate that Wilson derived from constitution-writing gratification of unconscious personal needs for power and domination may account in part (again only in part) for the tenacity with which he resisted efforts by various Senators to rewrite parts of the Covenant, which in some cases amounted merely to an alteration of its wording. Wilson appears to have subconsciously experienced all such efforts as attempts to "interfere" with or "dominate" him in a sphere of competence that he regarded as his own preserve.

Such an interpretation, taken alone, will seem highly speculative. The reader, we hope, will find it more plausible in the context of the theory of Wilson's personality that we have worked out and utilized in detail for purposes of analyzing Wilson's entire development and career. Briefly paraphrased here, the theory is that political leadership was a sphere of competence Wilson carved out for himself (from early adolescence on!) in order to derive therefrom compensation for the damaged self-esteem branded into his spirit as a child. Particularly when performing in his favored role as interpreter and instrument of the moral aspirations of the people, he considered himself as uniquely endowed and virtually infallible. His personality needs were such that in the sphere of competence, which he regarded as peculiarly his own, he had to function "independently" and without "interference" in order to gain the compensatory gratification he sought from the political arena. These we believe to have been the underlying dynamics of his somewhat autocratic style of leadership to which many contemporaries and biographers have called attention.

The Relationship Between Wilson's Morality and His Stubbornness

The extraordinary role of "conscience" and "stubbornness" in Wilson's political behavior has been noted by numerous of his contemporaries and biographers. It has often been said that Wilson's refusal to compromise on certain notable occasions, particularly as President of Princeton and as President of the United States, was a reflection of his "Presbyterian conscience." When great principles were at stake, as on these occasions, he could not bring himself to compromise. In such situations Wilson characteristically portrayed himself as confronted by a choice between dishonorable compromise of principles and an uncompromising struggle for moral political goals. Accordingly, for him, there could be no alternative but to fight for truth and morality against all opposition, whatever the consequences.

No matter that others, including careful historians such as Arthur S. Link (1947, 76), find his characterization of the situation in these terms unconvincing; that in fact Wilson was not really confronted by such an unpleasant either-or choice. The fact remains that *Wilson* saw it thus. However much one may deplore the political consequences of his refusal to compromise, so the argument goes, surely the only valid conclusion that can be drawn is that Wilson was possessed by an unusually strong sense of morality and rectitude that exercised a determining influence upon his political behavior.

It has seemed plausible, therefore, to attribute great importance to the Presbyterian culture in which Wilson was reared and from which, to condense this familiar thesis, he derived his unusual conscience and sense of morality.

Such a thesis must cope with various questions that can be legitimately raised. For example: If Wilson's refusal to compromise in certain instances is simply a matter of his Presbyterian conscience, then what of the numerous instances in which that same conscience was no bar to highly expedient, if not opportunistic, political behavior on his part? Clearly, at the very least a more refined theory as to the nature of the Presbyterian conscience and of its influence on political behavior is needed.

This general question is merely posed here. Instead of pursuing it further on this occasion let us consider, rather, the usefulness of looking at the relationship between Wilson's morality and his political stubborn-

CHAPTER 3: WOODROW WILSON'S POLITICAL PERSONALITY   65

ness in terms of what is known about the dynamics of the compulsive type. To examine the problem of Wilson in these terms is not to deny the importance of his Presbyterian upbringing or related cultural factors. Nor does it thereby ignore the possibility, which need not be explored here, that compulsive personalities are or were frequently to be found among members of the Presbyterian subculture. Indeed, the Presbyterian ethos no doubt provided reinforcement and rationalization for Wilson's stubbornness. We have elsewhere observed that such a creed produces men of conviction who find it possible to cling to their principles no matter what the opposition. The feeling that they are responsible, through their conscience, only to God, gives them a sense of freedom from temporal authority and the opinions of their fellow men.

The problem of Wilson's convictions that he was "right" in refusing to compromise, and was acting in conformity with moral standards, however, is more complex than it appears at first glance, as we will try to show.

The analysis of "stubborn" behavior in compulsive personalities indicates that it is often a form of aggression. Thus aggressive tendencies, usually repressed, find expression in situations that actually comprise, or can be represented by the individual to himself as comprising, struggles on behalf of goals that receive strong endorsement by the conscience. The operative mechanism is referred to as "idealization" and has been described in the following terms: "The realization that an ideal requirement is going to be fulfilled brings to the ego an increase in self-esteem. This may delude it into ignoring the fact that through the idealized actions there is an expression of instincts that ordinarily would have been repressed. . . . the ego relaxes its ordinary testing of reality and of impulses so that instinctual [in this case, aggressive] impulses may emerge relatively uncensored" (Feinchel 1945, 485–86). One is reminded in this connection of Wilson's repeated expressions of his "pleasure" and "delight" at an opportunity for a good fight, on behalf of a good cause, and his highly aggressive outbursts against opponents who blocked his high moral purposes. The instinctual nature of these eruptions is suggested by their extreme and intemperate quality; they were often personally unbecoming as well as politically inexpedient, and on occasion left Wilson shortly thereafter much chagrined at his loss of self-control.

Whatever the satisfactions of an uncompromising fight for what is "right," it may lead the compulsive person into essentially immoral behavior, behavior which strongly conflicts with role requirements and expectations. Given a culture in which political power is shared and in which the rules of the game enjoin compromise among those who participate in making political decisions for the community, to insist stubbornly that others submit to your own conception of what is truth and morality may in fact contravene political morality. The "right" thing for Wilson to do in the critical phases of his struggles at Princeton and with the Senate in the League matter, in terms of the prevailing political mores, was to have worked together with others who legitimately held power in order to advance as far as possible towards desirable political goals.

Wilson was well aware of this requirement. As a historian and astute student of American political institutions, he knew very well that the "right" thing for a statesman to do is to be practical and accomplish what he can. And he had expressed himself often on this very problem. In an address before the McCormick Theological Seminary, in the fall of 1909, for example, he had said: "I have often preached in my political utterances the doctrine of expediency, and I am an unabashed disciple of that doctrine. What I mean to say is, you cannot carry the world forward as fast as a few select individuals think. The individuals who have the vigor to lead must content themselves with a slackened pace and go only so fast as they can be followed. They must not be impractical. They must not be impossible. They must not insist upon getting at once what they know they cannot get" (Baker 1927, II: 307).

However, at several critical junctures in his public career, when he found his righteous purposes blocked by opponents who would not bend to his will, Wilson did not do the "right" thing; he did not compromise or accommodate, even when friends and political associates enjoined him to do so. Rather, he stubbornly persisted in his course and helped bring about his own personal defeat and the defeat of worthwhile measures which he was championing.

It seems, then, that we are confronted here by a form of self-defeating behavior in which the role of "conscience" in political stubbornness is perhaps much more complex than is implied in the familiar thesis of Wilson's "Presbyterian conscience" and his stiff-necked "morality."

But why must stubborn refusal to compromise be pushed to the point of self defeat and the frustration of desirable legislation if not for Wilson's stated reason that he would have found it immoral to compromise great principles? Once again the literature on compulsiveness provides an alternative set of hypotheses with which to assess the available historical data. It is our thesis, which we have tried to document elsewhere, that Wilson's stubborn refusals to compromise in situations where true morality and the requirements of his role demanded accommodation created feelings of guilt within him. He was vaguely disturbed by what he subconsciously sensed to be his own personal involvement in the fights with his opponents. The greater the stubbornness (a form of aggression against his opponents), the greater the inner anxiety at violating the moral injunction to compromise, which was a very real requirement of his political conscience.

This predicament was worked out in the following manner: stubborn refusal to compromise was maintained to the point where Wilson could demonstrate his "moral superiority" over his opponents. This could be achieved by manipulating the situation so that his opponents were also involved in "immoral" behavior, for example, by permitting their dislike of Wilson to warp their political good sense, by conspiring to defeat Wilson despite the merits of the issue at stake, by refusing to support desirable proposals just because he was championing them, etc. Thus, stubbornness was maintained so that, should it not succeed in forcing the capitulation of his opponents, it would provoke his defeat by selfish and immoral opponents. Thereby, he could at least assuage his anxiety and guilt for, whatever his "crime," it was outweighed by the demonstration in defeat of his "moral superiority" over his opponents.

These, we believe, were the underlying dynamics of the search for martyrdom which other writers as well have seen in Wilson's ill-fated Western speaking tour on behalf of the League of Nations. Whether the available historical materials which we have cited in support of this thesis render it sufficiently plausible and convincing must be left to individual judgment. Instead of rephrasing the evidence and reasoning already presented on its behalf in our book, we shall confine ourselves here to noting that the mechanisms described above, as underlying the possible quest for martyrdom, are very well described in the literature on compulsive stubbornness.

> . . . What is usually called stubbornness in the behavior of adult persons is an attempt to use other persons as instruments in the struggle with the super-ego. By provoking people to be unjust, they strive for a feeling of moral superiority which is needed to increase their self-esteem as a counter-balance against the pressure of the super-ego. (Fenichel 1945, 279)
> . . . The stubborn behavior is maintained the more obstinately, the more an inner feeling exists that it is impossible to prove what needs to be proven, and that one is actually in the wrong. . . . The feeling, 'Whatever I do is still less wicked than what has been done to me,' is needed as a weapon against the super-ego and, if successful, may bring relief from feelings of guilt. (Fenichel 1945, 497)

In brief, therefore, the very "morality" in terms of which Wilson could initially legitimize the open expression of pent-up aggression and hostility ensnared him in profoundly immoral political behavior. His repeated protestations as the struggle with his opponents wore on that he had to do what was "right" and what conscience demanded were, in fact, a cloak for activity that was contrary to the requirements of his leadership role and some of the demands of his own conscience. The repeated protestations that he was acting merely as an instrument of the people's will and had no personal stakes in the battle were the external manifestation of desperate efforts to still inner doubts of the purity of his motivation in refusing compromise and to controvert the knowledge that gnawed from within that he was obstructing his own cause. We have here an instance not of stern morality but of a type of rationalization which has been labelled the "moralization" mechanism, i.e., a tendency to interpret things as if they were in accord with ethical standards when they are actually (and subconsciously known to be) in striking contrast to them.

Thus did Wilson go down to tragic defeat. A subtle personal involvement in political struggle prevented him from anchoring his actions in the profound wisdom of the maxim: "There comes a time in the life of every man when he must give up his principles and do what he thinks is right" (Fenichel 1945, 486).

The Self-Defeating Pattern in Wilson's Career

The thesis of a self-defeating dynamism in Wilson's personality gains in plausibility from evidence that it was part of a pattern which tended to repeat itself under similar conditions during his career. A number of Wilson's biographers have noted that Wilson's defeat in the fight for the League fits into a pattern of behavior he had displayed earlier in public life. Thus, after a painstaking analysis of the bitter and unsuccessful struggle Wilson waged with his opponents at Princeton, Professor Link was led to remark that "a political observer, had he studied carefully Wilson's career as president of Princeton University, might have forecast accurately the shape of things to come during the period when Wilson was president of the United States." Calling the former period a microcosm of the latter, Link ascribed to Wilson's uncompromising battles both in the graduate college controversy and in the League of Nations battle with the Senate "the character and proportions of a Greek tragedy" (Link 1947, 90–91).

Similarly, writing many years before, Edmund Wilson, the distinguished man of letters, saw in the same events of Wilson's career evidence of a curious cyclical pattern that can be detected in the lives of other historical figures as well:

> It is possible to observe in certain lives, where conspicuously superior abilities are united with serious deficiencies, not the progress in a career or vocation that carries the talented man to a solid position or a definite goal, but a curve plotted over and over again and always dropping from some flight of achievement to a steep descent into failure. (Wilson 1952, 322)

The type of enigmatic personality described here by a humanist is one which has been of long-standing interest to the clinician as well. Influenced by Freud's earlier description and analysis of neurotic careers, Franz Alexander in 1930 presented what has become a classical psychoanalytical account of this general character type (Alexander 1930, 292–311). In many cases, driven by unconscious motives, persons of this type alternate between committing a transgression and then seeking punishment. Thereby, their careers may exhibit "alternating phases of rise and abrupt collapse," a pattern indicating that "aggressive and self-destructive tendencies" run along together. "The neurotic character," Alexander continues, "has fired the literary imagination since time immemorial. They are nearly all strong individualities who struggle in vain to hold the anti-social tendencies of their nature in check. They are born heroes who are predestined to a tragic fate."

Let us examine more closely the repetitive pattern of behavior that observers working from different standpoints have detected in his career. As President of Princeton, Governor of New Jersey, and President of the United States, Wilson gained impressive early successes only to encounter equally impressive political deadlocks or set-backs later on. He entered each of these offices at a time when reform was the order of the day, and with a substantial fund of goodwill to draw upon. In each case there was an initial period during which the type of strong leadership he exercised in response to his inner needs coincided sufficiently with the type of leadership the external situation required for impressive accomplishment. He drove the faculty and trustees at Princeton to accomplish an unprecedented series of reforms. The New Jersey legislature of 1911 was a triumph of productivity in his hands. Later, he exacted a brilliant performance from the Sixty-Third Congress of the United States.

We are forced to recognize, therefore, that Wilson's personal involvements contributed importantly to the measure of political accomplishment he attained. In each position, however, his compulsive ambition and imperious methods helped in time to generate the type of bitter opposition that blocked further successes and threatened him with serious defeats. Wilson was skillful in the tactics of leadership only so long as it was possible to get exactly what he wanted from the trustees or the legislature. He could be adept and inventive in finding ways of mobilizing potential support. He could be, as in the first year of the Governorship and in the "honeymoon" period of the Presidency, extremely cordial, if firm; gracious, if determined; and generally willing to go through the motions of consulting and granting deference to legislators whose support he needed. It is this phase of his party leadership that excited the admiration of contemporaries, historians, and political scientists alike. It is essential to note, however, that Wilson's skillfulness in these situations always rested somewhat insecurely upon the expectation that he would be able to push through his proposed legislation in essentially unadulterated form. (As Wilson often put it, he was willing to accept alterations of "detail," but not of the "principles" of his legislative proposals.)

Once opposition crystallized in sufficient force to threaten the defeat or marked alteration of his proposed legislation, however, Wilson was faced with a different type of situation. Skillful political behavior—the logic of the situation—now demanded genuine consultation to explore the basis of disagreement and to arrive at mutual concessions, bargains, and formulas that would ensure passage of necessary legislation. In this type of situation Wilson found it difficult to operate on the basis of expediential considerations and at times proved singularly gauche as a politician. Once faced with genuine and effective opposition to a legislative proposal *to which he had committed his leadership aspirations*, Wilson became rigidly stubborn and tried to force through his measure without compromising it. The greater the opposition, the greater his determination not to yield. He must win on his own terms or not at all!

Personally involved in these struggles, Wilson was incapable of realistically assessing the situation and of contriving skillful strategies for dividing the opposition and winning over a sufficient number to his side. Both at Princeton and later in the battle with the Senate over ratification of the treaty, Wilson was incapable of dealing effectively in his own interest with the more moderate of his opponents. In the heat of the battle, he could tolerate no ambiguity and could recognize no legitimate intermediate position. He tended to lump together all of his opponents. In such crises, therefore, his leadership was strongly devisive rather than unifying. He alienated the potential support of moderate elements who strongly sympathized with his general aims but felt some modification of his proposals to be necessary. Instead of modest concessions to win a sufficient number of moderates over, he stubbornly insisted upon his own position and rudely rebuffed their overtures, thus driving them into the arms of his most bitter and extreme opponents. It was his singular ineptness in the art of political accommodation, once the battle was joined, which was at bottom responsible for some of Wilson's major political defeats at Princeton and in the Presidency.

In these situations—when opposition crystallized and threatened to block Wilson's plan—the desire to succeed in achieving a worthwhile goal, in essence if not in exact form, became of less importance than to maintain equilibrium of the personality system. He seems to have experienced opposition to his will in such situations as an unbearable threat to his self-esteem. To compromise in these circumstances was to submit to domination in the very sphere of power and political leadership in which he sought to repair his damaged self-esteem. Opposition to his will, therefore, set into motion disruptive anxieties and brought to the surface long-smouldering aggressive feelings that, as a child, he had not dared to express. The ensuing struggle for his self-esteem led, on the political level, to the type of stubborn, self-defeating behavior and the search for moral superiority over his opponents that we have already described.

4

A Reappraisal of Woodrow Wilson's Political Personality

Edwin A. Weinstein, James William Anderson, and Arthur S. Link

H istorians, biographers, and political scientists, as well as psychiatrists and psychologists, have long been intrigued by Woodrow Wilson's personality and its relationship to the events of his academic, political, and diplomatic careers. Although interpretations have varied, there is universal agreement that Wilson's personality was of major importance in both his successes and failures.

Along with the conventional descriptions of Woodrow Wilson's character by his major biographers, Ray Stannard Baker and Arthur S. Link, there have been two book-length psychoanalytic studies. The first, *Thomas Woodrow Wilson*, by Sigmund Freud and William C. Bullitt, was written during the 1930s but not published until 1967.[1] This study, a biased application of a simplistic and distorted version of psychoanalytic theory, is not regarded either by historians or psychoanalysts as a scholarly contribution. In one review,[2] Link demonstrated that the evidence on which the psychological interpretations are based is wildly inaccurate and at times even fabricated. In another review,[3] the psychoanalyst, Erik

"Woodrow Wilson's Political Personality: A Reappraisal," *Political Science Quarterly* 93 (Winter 1978–79): 585–598. Reprinted by permission.

Editor's note: Because the issues in this debate are complex and intricate, footnotes have been retained for this selection.

H. Erikson, pointed out that the crude psychological propositions used in the book were certainly not the handiwork of Freud; he added, however, that Freud's involvement with the book, no matter how minimal,[4] remains an embarrassment to psychoanalysts.

The second study, *Woodrow Wilson and Colonel House: A Personality Study*, by Alexander L. and Juliette L. George, was published in 1956 and reprinted with a new preface in 1964.[5] In contrast to the Freud-Bullitt book, the Georges' study has received wide acclaim, and political scientists interested in psychology have held it up as a model of a psychodynamically oriented political biography. For example, Bernard Brodie calls the book "the first interpretation of the character of [Wilson] which impressed one as having depth, coherence, and consistency."[6] Fred I. Greenstein and Michael Lerner write that it is "one of the most rigorous and convincing of the psychobiographies of political figures."[7] Elmer E. Cornwell, Jr., in a recent review of books on the presidency characterized *Woodrow Wilson and Colonel House* as "perhaps the best portrait . . . drawn." Their analysis of the impact on the future President of a strict Calvinistic creed and demanding Presbyterian-minister father," Cornwell adds, "remains the most successful 'psychohistorical' treatment of any President."[8]

It is our view, however, that the Georges' book (along with an explanatory article that Alexander George published in 1960), although not deserving of immediate dismissal, as is the Freud-Bullitt work, present an essentially incorrect interpretation of the personality of Woodrow Wilson and its effect on his career.

The style of the book is graceful and concise, and the Georges have an unusual ability to translate psychological concepts into readily grasped, nontechnical language. They are basically sympathetic to Wilson and have great admiration for his achievements. In addition, as Robert C. Tucker has noted in a recent essay on the book,[9] the Georges deserve credit for advancing, through their case study of Wilson, the understanding that a political leader's personality may play a large or even decisive role in determining his conduct in public affairs. The Georges also made a contribution to the development of the methodology of psychobiography. The two authors, in their Research Note and in the 1964 Preface, and Alexander George in the essay of 1960, described the methods they had used while writing the book and their reasons for adopting the methods; they were the first psychobiographers to attempt to conceptualize the process of applying psychology to biography. Finally, some of the book's shortcomings reflect the time in which it was written. Psychological theory has advanced since the mid-1950s, and a great deal of new evidence about Wilson's life has been discovered since the book's original publication in 1956. The Georges, of course, had to work with the psychological theories and the historical sources which were available at the time.[10]

Nonetheless, the Georges' book, in our opinion, suffers from three major deficiencies, which, taken together, result in an inaccurate portrayal of Wilson's personality. The principal failing of the book is that the research on which it rests is inadequate. Second, the Georges fail to recognize the limitations of their psychological model and their theory. Third, they ignore Wilson's neurological disorders as conditions affecting his behavior.

The remainder of this essay will examine in detail two of the topics most crucial to the Georges' interpretation of Wilson's personality— Wilson's childhood and the Princeton graduate college controversy; present data, which though available to them, was not investigated; and comment on their use of psychological theory.

I

The Georges claim that Wilson suffered from a troubled relationship with his father, the Rev. Dr. Joseph Ruggles Wilson, a distinguished southern Presbyterian minister. Although Woodrow Wilson overcame his childhood difficulties to some extent, they state, pathological patterns continued to plague him periodically throughout his political career. The main evidence offered for this view is Wilson's early learning experience. The facts are well-known: Wilson did not learn the alphabet until he was nine and did not read with even minimal facility until he was eleven. He entered school at the age of ten and performed poorly. The explanation offered by the Georges reads:

> Perhaps the Doctor's scorn of fumbling first errors was so painful (or perhaps the mere expectation of such a reaction was so distressing) that the boy renounced the effort altogether. Perhaps, too, failing—refusing—to learn was one way in which the boy dared to express his [unconscious] resentment against his father.[11]

It is improbable that Wilson's slowness in learning to read was due to emotional factors and highly likely that it was a manifestation of developmental dyslexia. Undiagnosed in Wilson's childhood, the condition was well-known to neurologists at the time that the Georges wrote their book. However, a number of psychiatrists and psychologists still believed that the condition was an emotional rather than a neurological problem, and the Georges simply chose an explanation that was currently popular. The condition is a frequent one, occurring in about 10 percent of the school population, significantly more frequently in boys. Research over the past seventy years indicates that developmental dyslexia is caused by a delay in the establishment of the dominance of one cerebral hemisphere—usually the left—for language. One theory is that, with the maturational lag, there is representation of language in both hemispheres and performance suffers in the competition for control of the same function.

The specific evidence that Wilson had developmental dyslexia can be summed up in three groups. First, by his own admission he was a slow reader into adult life. At the Johns Hopkins, the amount of assigned reading was his bane. "Steady reading," he wrote his fiancée, "always demands of me more expenditure of resolution and dogged energy than any other sort of work."[12] Second, difficulties in calculation are commonly associated with developmental dyslexia, and Wilson was extremely poor in arithmetic. Third, when, as a result of a stroke in 1896, he could not write with his right hand, he was able, within a few days and without practice, to write with his left hand in perfectly formed script. This ability strongly suggests that he had mixed cerebral dominance for language.

The reading disability affected Wilson's development and his relationship with his parents, but hardly in the way that the Georges state. It probably made him more dependent on his family. Also, he may have feared that his reading problems indicated that he was stupid or lazy. The condition probably made Dr. Wilson more pedagogic and insistent on drilling his "lazy" son. To judge from Wilson's pleasant memories of having his family read to him, they seem to have been tolerant of his problem. During the Civil War, Dr. Wilson was away from home some of the time serving as a chaplain in the Confederate Army. Much of the reading was done by other family members and, if the Georges' hypothesis were true, Wilson must have been expressing his "unconscious hostility" toward his mother, sisters, and other relatives. We do not have a good record of Wilson's childhood such as might be gained from contemporary letters, diaries, or autobiographies; like any other child, he may have felt insecurities. However, it is certain that they did not come about in the manner postulated by the Georges.

According to the Georges, Wilson's relationship with his father was nothing less than devastating. They say that Wilson's father "ridiculed his intellectual capacities and made him feel mediocre." They add that Wilson had to endure "barbed criticism," "sarcastically made demands" and "aspersions on his moral and intellectual worth," and that Wilson interpreted these criticisms "as humiliating evidence, that, try as he might, he was inadequate." As a result of this treatment, they conclude, Wilson feared that he was "stupid, ugly, worthless and unlovable."[13] The Georges' entire interpretation of Wilson's personality revolves around their portrayal of his relationship with his father. They argue that, because of this relationship, Wilson forever harbored a deep sense of worthlessness and also carried a burden of rage which he later turned against adversaries, such as Dean Andrew F. West and Senator Henry Cabot Lodge of Massachusetts.

The sole evidence for this view of Wilson's relationship with his father, aside from the Georges' interpretation of Wilson's reading disability, consists of comments made to Baker in the mid-1920s. Wilson's daughter, Margaret, talking of Dr. Wilson said: "His idea was that if a lad was of fine tempered steel, the more he was beaten, the better he was."[14] The metaphor, a favorite of both Wilson and his father, may be interpreted in various ways and at several levels of concreteness. Probably Dr. Wilson was boasting about Woodrow. But any interpretation should take into account Margaret Wilson's feelings about her grandfather. Margaret did not know Dr. Wilson well until she was fourteen years old, when, because of his deteriorating health, he came to live with his son in Princeton. Affected by severe cerebral arteriosclerosis, Dr. Wilson had become testy and puerile, and his grandchildren were afraid of him.[15] Margaret Wilson's statement can hardly be regarded as indicative of Wilson's relationship with his father while the boy was growing up.

The other recollection is a more substantial one. Wilson's cousin, Helen Woodrow Bones, told Baker:

> Uncle Joseph was a cruel tease, with a caustic wit and a sharp tongue, and I remember hearing my own family tell indignantly of how Cousin Woodrow suffered under his teasing. He was proud of WW, especially after his son began to show how unusual he was, but only a man as sweet as Cousin Woodrow could have forgotten the severity of the criticism to the value of which he so often paid tribute, in after life.[16]

This recollection, more than fifty years after the alleged events, may or may not have been accurate. However, Helen Bones (who was the first Mrs. Wilson's private secretary from March 1913 until Mrs. Wilson's death in August 1914, served as mistress of the White House until Wilson married again in December 1915, and continued to live off and on with the president and his second wife) was fiercely and passionately devoted to Wilson. She deeply resented any criticism of the man she idolized.[17] She would probably have exaggerated and magnified the importance of such stories about Dr. Wilson's treatment of his son. She most likely heard the stories from her parents, and there is evidence of bad blood between them and Dr. and Mrs. Wilson.

The Georges cite an additional recollection to give an idea of the nature of this teasing. One morning, according to another cousin, Jessie

Bones Brower (Helen Bones's sister), Wilson's father apologized when his son arrived late for breakfast and explained that he had been so greatly excited at the discovery of another hair in his mustache that it had taken him longer to wash and dress. "I remember very distinctly the painful flush that came over the boy's face," the cousin recalled.[18] If this is typical of Dr. Wilson's teasing, it does not sound harsh or excessive and certainly does not suggest the type of father-son relationship that would handicap Wilson for the rest of his life. Wilson's father was a great wit and punster and used his family as an audience, but there is no indication that he was malicious.

Let us grant that these recollections offer some support for the Georges' interpretation. However, they must be weighed against contrary evidence, which is much more substantial. There are many reports from people who knew Wilson and his father well—sources available to the Georges—about the extraordinarily warm relationship that existed between Wilson and his father during Wilson's childhood.[19] They spent a great deal of time together, and Dr. Wilson read to him and talked to him at length. Early in the week, Wilson's father would visit parishioners while they were at work, and he would take his son along to share the experiences. As evidence of Wilson's submissive attitude toward his father, the Georges cite his helping his father, as a young man, with the dull task of writing the minutes of the General Assembly of the southern Presbyterian Church. If one is to judge by the bitter controversy that led to Dr. Wilson's resignation from the Columbia Theological Seminary,[20] the minutes were anything but dull. In pursuit of their theme of Wilson's "unconscious hostility" toward and fear of his father, the Georges go so far as to interpret Wilson's tender care of his father, over the last years of his life, and his singing of the old man's favorite hymns to him, as evidence of Wilson's guilt and submission!

The Georges emphasize that Wilson was extremely dependent on his father until the latter's death. In support of their view, they cite the observation of a Princeton colleague, Winthrop More Daniels, that Wilson was always the pupil of his father. They fail to cite evidence to the contrary, such as that of Bliss Perry, who commented on the comradely relationship between the two men.[21] It is true that Wilson was financially dependent on his father into his late twenties. However, after the death of Wilson's mother in 1888, he, Woodrow Wilson, became the effective head of the family and the one to whom his brother, sisters, and *father* came for advice and support. Yet the Georges maintain that Wilson's early dependence never changed. As further evidence, they cite the famous "my incomparable father" letter written when Wilson was thirty-two and in the first year of his professorship at Wesleyan. The letter reads:

My precious father,

My thoughts are full of you and dear "Dode" [Wilson's younger brother, Joseph] all the time. Tennessee seems so far away for a chap as hungry as I am for a sight of the two men whom I love. As the Christmas recess approaches I realize, as I have so often before, the *pain* there is in a season of holiday and rejoicing away from you. As you know, one of the chief things about which I feel most warranted in rejoicing is that I am your son. I realize the benefit of being your son more and more as my talents and experience grow: I recognize the strength growing in me as of the nature of your strength: I become more and more conscious of the hereditary wealth I possess, the capital of principle, of literary force and skill, of capacity for first-hand thought; and I feel daily more and more bent toward creating in my own children that combined respect and tender devotion for their father that you gave your children for you. Oh, how happy I should be, if I could make them think of me as I think of you! You have given me a love that grows, that is stronger in me now that I am a man than it was when I was a boy, and which will be stronger in me when I am an old man than it is now—a love, in brief, that is rooted and grounded in *reason*, and not in filial instinct merely—a love resting upon abiding foundations of *service*, recognizing you as in a certain very real sense the author of all I have to be grateful for! I bless God for my noble, strong, and saintly mother and for my incomparable father. Ask "Dode" if he does not subscribe? and tell him that I love my brother passionately.

. . . Ellie joins me in unbounded love to you both.

Your devoted son,
Woodrow[22]

Although still an important figure in the southern Presbyterian Church, Dr. Wilson had encountered disappointments in his work and was frequently discouraged and depressed. His career had not advanced, while Woodrow's had, and he had become increasingly identified with and somewhat envious of his son. Wilson, busy in his new position at Wesleyan and involved with writing *The State* (1889), had not written to his father for some time. Could not Wilson, feeling his neglect of his father, now a lonely widower, have written the letter to raise the old man's spirits and self-esteem? And could he not in fact have been expressing his feelings toward his father?

The Georges claim that Dr. Wilson became proud of his son only after the latter began to show how unusual he was. There could be some argument about when Woodrow Wilson began to display extraordinary talent. Probably it was during his senior year at Princeton, when he was managing editor of *The Princetonian* and had an article accepted by a national review. Yet the many letters that Joseph R. Wilson wrote to his son before 1878–79 reveal affection, admiration, pride in his son, and helpful criticism, but never denigration.[23] Wilson dedicated *Congressional Government* to his father. He wrote:

> To his father, the patient guide of his youth, the gracious companion of his manhood, his best instructor and most lenient critic, this book is affectionately dedicate by the author.

Dr. Wilson had a tremendous influence on his son, and probably no boy grows up without some resentment toward his father. However, on the basis of the evidence there is no reason to believe that the dedication of *Congressional Government*[24] was not a valid representation of Wilson's feelings toward his father.

It is almost incredible that a psychobiography tracing the development of Wilson's personality should make so little mention of his mother, Janet, or Jessie, Woodrow Wilson, about whom a great deal was known when the Georges wrote their book. They spend less than half a page on the subject, quoting from the memories of her that Wilson expressed at the time of her death: "As the first shock and the acute pain of the great, the irreparable blow passes off, my heart is filling up with tenderest memories of my sweet mother, memories that seem to hallow my whole life—which seem to explain to me how it came about that I was given the sweetest, most satisfying of wives for my daily companion. My mother, with her sweet womanliness, her purity, her intelligence, prepared me for my wife. I remember how I clung to her (a laughed-at 'mamma's boy') till I was a great big fellow: but love of the best womanhood came to me and entered my heart through her apron-strings."[25]

A discerning reading of all the evidence about Jessie available to the Georges and of the Wilson family correspondence, which was not available to them, would have shown that this description of Wilson's relationship with his mother was far from complete. Jessie Wilson was indeed a saintly, intelligent woman, devoted to her family, and Wilson was a very loving son. But she was extremely overprotective, and the mutual dependence that she fostered was responsible for the relatively late age at which Wilson achieved emotional and heterosexual maturity. Shy, reserved, and deferential to the outgoing Dr. Wilson, she was intensely ambitious for her husband and son. She was also extraordinarily sensitive to what she felt were slights of others; and, when Wilson or his father encountered setbacks, she invariably attributed them to the spite and malice of their opponents. While Wilson's father pointed out his son's faults and tried to temper his impatience and aggressiveness, she was completely uncritical. Much more than Dr. Wilson, she gave Woodrow the feeling that he was not only intellectually, but morally, superior to his colleagues—a trait that contributed to one of Wilson's greatest failings, his overconfidence. Her influence had a great deal to do with Wilson's shyness and uneasiness with people who were not close to him, and his particular dependence on women. Mrs. Wilson was often ill—probably on a psychosomatic basis—and extremely anxious and worrisome about Woodrow's health. Wilson's attitudes toward illness, derived from both parents, had most important consequences for his career. There is also good evidence that Mrs. Wilson suffered from chronic depression; her son later said many times that he had inherited his tendency toward melancholy from his mother's side.

II

No study of Wilson's behavior during the great crisis of his career can be complete without taking into account the effects of the cerebral vascular disease from which he suffered, intermittently, from the age of thirty-nine until his death in 1924. In 1896, Wilson had a stroke which caused a marked weakness of his right hand, and he had recurrences in 1900, 1904, 1906, and 1907. The stroke of 1906 caused not only weakness of his right arm but almost complete blindness of his left eye, a syndrome indicative of an embolus from the left internal carotid artery. Wilson's attempts to adapt to the consequences of the stroke caused changes in his behavior and helped set into motion events relevant to his defeats in the quadrangle plan and graduate college controversies at Princeton. The course of carotid artery disease is very variable, with frequent remissions, and, in the light of today's knowledge, it is not surprising that Wilson was in good health while governor of New Jersey and when he became president of the United States. The disease, however, is ultimately a progressive one and, by the end of World War I, Wilson was showing signs of generalized cerebral involvement. In Paris, he had an attack of influenza, probably a virus encephalopathy, which, superimposed on preexisting brain damage, produced changes in behavior which may have influenced the outcome of the peace negotiations. In October 1919 he had a massive stroke that completely paralyzed the left side of his body and produced mental attitudes and personality changes which were important factors in his failure to obtain ratification of the Treaty of Versailles.[26]

The Georges are not neurologists or psychiatrists, and some of the information on which the above reconstruction is based was not available to them. Yet even lay observers, such as Herbert Hoover, had commented on the changes of Wilson's mental functioning after the Paris illness. Any behavioral scientist should have wondered about the effects of the massive stroke of 1919. Similarly, the Georges ignored Wilson's stroke of 1906 as a factor in his behavior and explained his problems during the quadrangle (or "quad") plan and graduate college controversies as stemming from an emotionally disturbed childhood.

The controversy over the location and character of the graduate college was the most dramatic event of Woodrow Wilson's term as president of Princeton University. A wealthy alumnus, William C. Procter, in 1909 offered to donate $500,000 to help build a graduate college to house graduate students, but he included an important stipulation—that the building be located on the golf course, nearly a mile from the center of the campus. It was the site which the dean of the small existing graduate school, Andrew Fleming West, a close friend of Procter, had selected. West favored an off-campus site so that graduate students might study undisturbed by undergraduates. Wilson consistently argued that they should live close together, in order, as he put it, that the graduate students might energize the intellectual life of the undergraduates.[27] It was the same idea that had led Wilson to institute the preceptorial system and to propose his quadrangle plan. Originally, both West and Wilson had advocated a central location, but West had changed his view. West believed that Wilson had delayed action on the graduate college in favor of his preceptorial and quad plans—which indeed he had—and charged that Wilson had gone back on his promise of support, given in 1906, at the time when West turned down an offer of the presidency of the Massachusetts Institute of Technology. Wilson believed, with ample reason, that West was an intellectual dilettante, who wished to maintain dominion over an elitist world of his own. Some months before the Procter offer, Wilson had reorganized the faculty committee on the graduate school and broken West's absolute control of the policies of the graduate school.

The Georges see the conflict as based on Wilson's perception of West as a father figure. In their view, the situation caused Wilson to give vent to the unconscious hostility which he had felt, but had never been able to release, toward his own father. They regard the issue of the location of the college as merely an excuse for Wilson to release this unconscious hostility by doing battle with West. At some level, they say, West evoked in Wilson the image of his father. Therefore Wilson resisted West "with all the violence he had once felt, but never ventured to express, in response to his father's overwhelming domination." But, they add, Wilson could not confess, even to himself, that he experienced West as "an unbearable threat," and, consequently, he "disguised all his volcanic feelings against West in terms of a great moral crusade in which he championed the 'right.' "[28]

We have already examined the Georges' previous evidence for Wilson's "unconscious hostility" toward his father. Before considering further their interpretation of the graduate college controversy, additional background is necessary. The situation was already a tense one because of the bitter struggle that had occurred over the quadrangle plan. This was a proposal by Wilson to abolish the exclusive undergraduate eating clubs and construct quadrangles, or residential colleges, assignment to which would be made by lot. Opposition, often violent, soon developed and was led by the eastern alumni. The trustees, who had approved the plan "in principle," when Wilson presented it in June 1907, withdrew their support in October. Wilson continued to press for it, and the battle became so acrimonious that a wealthy trustee and generous contributor to the university, M. Taylor Pyne, threatened to withdraw his support if Wilson ever mentioned the quad plan again.[29] Dean West led the minority faction of the faculty who were in opposite, which, to Wilson's great sorrow, included his best friend, John Grier Hibben.

Wilson's illness was an important factor in the defeat of his quad plan and also laid the groundwork for his defeat in the graduate college controversy. In 1906 he was at the height of his popularity and power at Princeton: the curriculum had been reformed, the faculty upgraded, and the preceptorial system successfully launched. Except for an episode of weakness in his right arm lasting several months in 1904, he had been in excellent health during his presidency. The stroke in 1906 was the first one to be recognized as such, and Wilson received a gloomy prognosis. He and his wife were aware that the condition was similar to that which had robbed his father of his mental faculties. Characteristically, Wilson's reaction was to immerse himself in his work. Originally, he had thought that the quad plan would take twenty years; now he thought it immediately attainable. In the interests of his health, he cut down on his social life. He took regular naps, reduced his personal contacts, and, in contrast to his previous habits, now decided to meet members of the Princeton community only on official business. Prior to the formal announcement to the trustees of the plan in June 1907, he had mentioned the idea to only three intimate friends on the faculty and not at all to the alumni. This lack of preparation contrasted markedly with the way he had organized support for the preceptorial system and must be judged an important cause of his failure. Wilson's increased overconfidence was one of a number of behavioral changes that occurred after the stroke in 1906; he became less empathic, more stubborn, and more prone to overgeneralize and personalize his problems.

The question of the site of the graduate college was far more than a pretext for Wilson to destroy West. At stake were Wilson's control of the university and the character of its educational program. It is debatable whether close association between graduates and undergraduates would have yielded the advantage that Wilson envisaged. However, his emphasis on such an association in the preceptorial and quadrangle plans indicates that the issue was important in itself. The Georges' treatment of the graduate college controversy makes it seem that Wilson stood practically alone in pressing his arguments. Actually, many others shared his point of view. Approximately half of the trustees supported Wilson, and the various votes related to the controversy were all close. Although the evidence is not conclusive, it appears that a large majority of the faculty, particularly the professors who were doing most of the graduate instruction, preferred that the college be built in the midst of the campus. In fact, members of the faculty (and of the board of trustees) were constantly pressing Wilson to stand firm and even to remove West or reduce his influence over the graduate program and college.[30]

Wilson's personality and his pattern of behavior under stress had a great deal to do with the events of the controversies over the quad plan and graduate college. But Wilson's aversion to Dean West did not come about because of unconscious feelings toward his father. Wilson detested West because West was the condensed symbol of so many of the social, educational, economic, and political problems that Wilson faced at Princeton. Moreover, Wilson did not "disguise" his feelings toward West. He expressed them quite openly.[31]

It is impossible in a single article to provide detailed analysis of and commentary on an entire book. It must suffice to say that we believe that the Georges' view of the relationship between Wilson and Edward M. House was highly distorted by overreliance on the House diary, which often presents a one-sided and unreliable account of events; that we find their explanation for Wilson's attempts to remain out of World War I almost arcane; and that recent research had considerably revised their explanation for the so-called break between Wilson and House at the Paris Peace Conference.[32]

III

By today's standard, the Georges' use of psychological theory is inadequate. Their formulations have been largely superseded by the views of ego psychology and by considerations of the development of the self and of social roles and interactions. While the Georges cannot be criticized for not anticipating these approaches, it should be pointed out that the works of Harry Stack Sullivan, Karen Horney, and Erich Fromm were available to them. Also, the commonsense view that most children identify with their parents and grow to resemble them does not seem to have played a part in their thinking. By the 1950s, the idea of fixed childhood hostilities, locked deep in the unconscious, impervious to change, and ready to burst forth in pristine fury, was being challenged. For the

Georges to suggest that Wilson simply and directly transferred his hatred of his father to West and Senator Lodge during the fight over the Versailles Treaty is highly mechanistic, reductionistic, and deterministic. The formulation leaves no room for consideration of character development or identity formation.

The authors could have given a more realistic view of Wilson's relationship with his parents had they taken up family values and cultural norms. For example, Wilson's reluctance to express any negative feelings toward members of his family was shared by them and was a facet of their subculture. It is difficult to accept any theory of personality that does not take into consideration a subject's relationship with his mother, particularly Wilson's mother, who instilled so much anxiety in him. Then, the Georges give the impression that all that one has to know about Wilson is that his self-esteem was disastrously low. Yet self-esteem is rarely unitary. One may feel confident in some areas, insecure in others. Wilson was bothered by feelings that he was ugly; he seems to have identified himself in this respect with his rather physically unattractive mother. Yet he rarely had doubts about his intellectual and leadership qualities after reaching maturity.

Even without detailed knowledge of Wilson's childhood, one would assume, from his compulsive personality traits and his need to control his environment, that he had anxieties and insecurities. Yet to translate such insecurities into an insatiable drive for political power is to provide far too simple an explanation for a complex, multidetermined process. Further, the Georges state:

> His [Wilson's] stern Calvinistic conscience forbade an unabashed pursuit of power for personal gratification. He could express his desire for power only insofar as he convincingly rationalized it in terms of altruistic service and fused it with laudable social objectives.[33]

It is true that Wilson often validated pragmatically arrived at decisions in moral terms, but when in the world of human affairs is concern for the public good divorced from personal gratification?

Woodrow Wilson and Colonel House has important implications for writers of psychobiography. They should be aware that personality theories derive, not only from scientific investigations, but also from ideology, the social milieu, and the personal problems of their authors. Theories are dated, as the Georges themselves point out; theories not only change with the years, but proponents of the same theory differ in their interpretations of it. In an interdisciplinary endeavor, more than superficial knowledge of areas outside of one's primary field is necessary. The historian or political scientist should be familiar, not only with psychoanalytic theory, but also with the many aspects of behavioral science, which, in recent years, have so profoundly influenced psychoanalysis. Above all, the psychobiographer should immerse himself in the primary biographical sources, not least of all for the reason that the criteria for clinical evidence may be quite different from those for historical work.[34] The great acclaim accorded the Georges' book may have helped give the impression that psychobiography can be written by furnishing "deep" interpretations of the work of others. No psychobiography is better than the research on which it rests.

NOTES

1. Sigmund Freud and William C. Bullitt, *Thomas Woodrow Wilson* (Boston: Houghton Mifflin, 1967).
2. Arthur S. Link, "The Case for Woodrow Wilson," *Harper's*, April 1967, pp.85–93.
3. Erik H. Erikson, in *The New York Review of Books*, February 9, 1967, pp.3–6; reprinted in *The International Journal of Psychoanalysis* 48(1967):462–468.
4. The degree of Freud's involvement will not be known until the Bullitt Papers at Yale are opened and we can see what Freud actually wrote. It is well known that Freud disliked Americans in general and Wilson in particular, who he thought was the embodiment of the Puritan moralist and was responsible for the breakup of the Austro-Hungarian Empire.
5. Alexander L. George and Juliette L. George, *Woodrow Wilson and Colonel House: A Personality Study* (New York: Dover Publications, Inc., 1964). Although the book includes an analysis of Wilson's relationship with Colonel House, the central concern is to provide a portrait of Wilson's personality and political behavior (see p.xxi), and it is this portrait, not the analysis of the relationship between Wilson and House, that is the focus of the present essay.
6. Bernard Brodie, "A Psychoanalytic Interpretation of Woodrow Wilson," in Bruce Mazlish, ed., *Psychoanalysis and History* (New York: Grossett & Dunlap, 1971). pp. 115–123.
7. Fred I. Greenstein and Michael Lerner, eds., *A Source Book for the Study of Personality and Politics* (Chicago: Markham, 1971), p.77.
8. *The Wilson Quarterly* 1 (Winter 1977):68.
9. Robert C. Tucker. "The Georges' Wilson Reexamined: An Essay on Psychobiography," *American Political Science Review* 71 (June 1977):606–618.
10. However, Alexander George, in an article published ten years ago ("Power as a Compensatory Value for Political Leaders," *Journal of Social Issues* [July 1968]:29–49, still confidently advances the theory that Wilson's damaged self-esteem, caused by his tyrannical and demanding father, was an important factor in propelling him into politics. The first, second, and perhaps the third, volumes of *The Papers of Woodrow Wilson*, which shed much new light on the relationship between Wilson and his father, were available when George's arti-

cle was written. He presumably did not read these volumes; in any event, he did not cite them.

11. George and George, *Woodrow Wilson and Colonel House*, p.7.

12. Wilson to Ellen Louise Axson, March 29, 1884. Arthur S. Link et al., *The Papers of Woodrow Wilson*, 28 vols. to date (Princeton, N.J.: Princeton University Press, 1966–) 3:496; hereinafter cited as *PWW*.

13. George and George, *Woodrow Wilson and Colonel House*, pp.114, 272, 6, 8.

14. Ibid., p.8.

15. Margaret Axson Elliot, *My Aunt Louisa and Woodrow Wilson* (Chapel Hill, N.C.: University of North Carolina Press, 1944), p.122.

16. George and George, *Woodrow Wilson and Colonel House*, p.8.

17. Expressions of her feelings occur again and again in Helen W. Bones to Jessie Bones Brower, February 12 and 23, April 1 and 12, May 3, and June 1, 7, and 18, 1913, Woodrow Wilson Collection, Princeton University Library.

18. George and George, *Woodrow Wilson and Colonel House*, p.8.

19. See for example, Ray Stannard Baker, *Woodrow Wilson, Life and Letters: Youth, 1856–1890* (Garden City, N.Y.: Doubleday, Page and Co., 1927); Josephus Daniels, *The Life of Woodrow Wilson* (Philadelphia: The John C. Winston Co., 1924); William Bayard Hale, *Woodrow Wilson: The Study of his Life* (Garden City, N.Y.: Doubleday, Page and Co., 1912); William Allen White, *Woodrow Wilson* (Boston and New York: Houghton Mifflin, 1924).

20. About this episode, see John M. Mulder, *Woodrow Wilson: The Years of Preparation* (Princeton, N.J.: Princeton University Press, 1978), pp. 15–17.

21. Bliss Perry, *And Gladly Teach* (Boston: Houghton Mifflin, 1935), p.153.

22. Wilson to Joseph Ruggles Wilson, December 16, 1888, *PWW*, 6:30–31.

23. None of these letters was written during Wilson's early childhood; they date from the year 1875, when Wilson was eighteen years old, and they include seventy-six letters written before September 1885, when Wilson began his first teaching job at Bryn Mawr College. They are printed in *PWW*, vols.1–5.

24. *Congressional Government: A Study in American Politics* (Boston: Houghton Mifflin, 1885), p.iii.

Thirty years later, long after his father's death, we hear Wilson saying about his father: "I remember my father as essentially humble and devout before God, spirited and confident before men. A natural leader, with a singular gift of clear, eloquent, convincing speech. Generous, playful, full of high spirits, and yet given to most laborious industry, alike in the use of books and in the administration of church affairs. A man who believed much more in the efficacy of Christian simple and pure living than in dogmatic advice or spiritual conversation,—a robust Christian.

"The description I naturally associate with his name would be something like this:

"Generous, high-spirited, thoughtful, studious, a master of men and of thought, who sought the life of dogma in conduct and preferred a pure life to a pious profession" [c. May 25, 1914].

And again: "As I look back on my boyhood, it seems to me that all the sense I got, I got by association with my father. He was good fun; he was a good comrade; and the experience he had had put a lot of sense in him that I had not been endowed with by birth, at any rate; and by constant association with him, I saw the world and the tasks of the world through his eyes, and because I believed in him I aspired to do and be the thing that he believed in" [May 29, 1914].

25. WW to Ellen A. Wilson, April 18, 1888, *PWW*, 5:719.

26. See Edwin A. Weinstein, "Woodrow Wilson's Neurological Illness," *Journal of American History* 57 (September 1970):324–351. On a basis of new evidence, it is not likely, as was stated in this article, that Wilson had a stroke in Paris.

27. As Wilson put it in an address before the Princeton Club of New York on April 7, 1910: "As I look back upon my own studies as a graduate student, I realize that . . . the intellectual limitations of the men with whom I was associated in the great graduate school I attended, was that their thought was so centered upon special lines of study that they had become impatient of everything that drew them away from them. I have heard these men again and again deplore the necessity they would some day be under of going through the drudgery of teaching stupid undergraduates,—a state of mind and a point of view which utterly unfitted them for the very profession they were approaching. That was due, in my mind, to the dissociation of graduate study in the life of the university from the undergraduate body. Not only that, but I believe that our universities lack the impulse of advanced study, so far as their undergraduates are concerned, largely because their undergraduates are not sufficiently brought into contact with the graduates. You know, gentlemen, that the process of education is a process of contagion. If you want to educate a man, put him in close association with the kind of intellectual fire you wish him to be touched by" (*PWW*, 20:345).

28. George and George, *Woodrow Wilson and Colonel House*, pp.40, 43.

29. Melancthon W. Jacobus to Wilson, November 5, 1907, *PWW*, 17:468–69.

30. Arthur S. Link wishes to state that much new evidence discovered since the publication of his *Wilson: The Road to the White House* in 1947 has convinced him that his treatment of Wilson and West and the graduate college controversy is inadequate and unbalanced.

31. The entire graduate college controversy is amply documented in *PWW*, vols.18–20.

32. The most authoritative study of House at the Paris Peace Conference, Inga Floto, *Colonel House in Paris, A Study of American Policy at the Paris Peace Conference 1919* (Aarhus, Denmark: Univesitetsforlaget, 1973), proves conclusively that the cause of the so-called break between the two men was House's failure to follow Wilson's explicit instructions while the latter was in the United States.

33. George and George, *Woodrow Wilson and Colonel House*, p.117.

34. The best example in the past few years of a psychiatrist's use of primary historical sources is John E. Mack, *A Prince of Our Disorder: The Life of T. E. Lawrence* (Boston: Little, Brown, 1976).

5

Woodrow Wilson and Colonel House: A Rejoinder

Juliette L. George and Alexander L. George

Arthur S. Link of Princeton University has been studying and writing about Woodrow Wilson for some forty years, and he is the editor of *The Papers of Woodrow Wilson*. The thirty-six volumes thus far published in this series are a tribute to his prodigious scholarship. By common consent, Professor Link is the preeminent Wilson scholar of our time. If Link finds serious fault with an interpretation of Wilson, it behooves those who advanced it to reexamine their work in the light of his criticisms. As authors of *Woodrow Wilson and Colonel House: A Personality Study*, we felt placed under such an obligation upon the publication in *Political Science Quarterly* three years ago of an article by Link in collaboration with Edwin A. Weinstein (a psychiatrist and neurologist who has been studying and writing about Wilson for almost fifteen years), and James William Anderson (a clinical psychologist). In their article Weinstein, Anderson, and Link characterized *Woodrow Wilson and Colonel House* as "an essentially incorrect interpretation of the personality of Woodrow Wilson and its effect on his career."[1]

"Woodrow Wilson and Colonel House: A Reply to Weinstein, Anderson, and Link," *Political Science Quarterly* 96 (Winter 1981–82): 641–645. Reprinted by permission.

Editor's note: Because the issues in this debate are complex and intricate, footnotes have been retained for this selection.

Over the past few years, therefore, we have reviewed our work and have incorporated into our research a great deal of manuscript material that has become available since the publication of *Woodrow Wilson and Colonel House* in 1956. This review in the light of all the evidence, old and new, has served to confirm our belief in the validity of the interpretation of Wilson we offered in *Woodrow Wilson and Colonel House.* Indeed, the data now available permit a much fuller delineation of the relationship between Wilson and his father—of the extraordinary bond that existed between them, the very intensity of which, in our view, is related to the intensity of Wilson's early self-doubt, his suffering and need for approval (all of which now also may be more fully documented). We continue to view Wilson as a great tragic figure whose "tragic flaw"—a ruinously self-defeating refusal to compromise with his opponents on certain issues that had become emotionally charged for him—evolved out of low self-estimates that we believe he developed as a child in response to his father's demands.

We consider it unfortunate, moreover, that Weinstein, Anderson, and Link present as though it were an indisputable fact Dr. Weinstein's *hypothesis* that, beginning in 1896, Woodrow Wilson suffered a series of brain-damaging strokes that significantly and adversely affected his political functioning even so early as during his Princeton presidency. That Weinstein's retrospective interpretation of Wilson's medical problems is open to question among qualified medical specialists is obvious from the statement by Michael F. Marmor, M.D., of the Stanford University School of Medicine (see appendix). Of greater concern, however, is the fact that Professor Link has permitted himself to state unequivocally in *The Papers of Woodrow Wilson* that Wilson suffered such strokes. In numerous notes and other editorial apparatus to several volumes of *The Papers*, Link asserts that Wilson had small strokes in 1896 and 1907 and "a major stroke" in 1906.[2] We believe he has thereby compromised the objectivity of that otherwise superb series and therefore compromised its value to historians, both present and future.

Weinstein, Anderson, and Link state in their critique that *Woodrow Wilson and Colonel House*

> suffers from three major deficiencies, which taken together, result in an inaccurate protrayal of Wilson's personality. The principal failing of the book is that the research on which it rests is inadequate. Second, the Georges fail to recognize the limitations of their psychological model and misrepresent evidence to fit their theory. Third, they ignore Wilson's neurological disorders as conditions affecting his behavior.[3]

We shall address these criticisms in turn.

Source Materials for *Woodrow Wilson and Colonel House*

Weinstein, Anderson, and Link disparage our research—*Woodrow Wilson and Colonel House* furnishes " 'deep' interpretations of the work of others."[4] In our book, we characterized our work as "largely a synthesis and reinterpretation of well-known facts of Wilson's career."[5] We did not claim to be historians, nor was it our aim to uncover new data: rather, we hoped to cast a fresh eye on that which was already known. Indeed, we extracted a great deal of useful information from the published literature. To the extent that we could gain access to them at the time we were doing our research, however, we also studied the major primary sources.

The three principal relevant manuscript collections were: the Wilson papers at the Library of Congress, the papers of Ray Stannard Baker at the Library of Congress, and the papers of Colonel House at the Sterling Memorial Library at Yale University. Mrs. Wilson, who was notoriously chary of granting scholars access to the Wilson papers, rejected our periodically renewed requests until our study was almost complete. Then we were allowed to read a series of documents which, Katharine E. Brand (Mrs. Wilson's representative in the Manuscript Division of the Library of Congress) assured us, was all the collection contained for the years of Wilson's childhood and youth. We found little of significance in what we were allowed to see that Baker had not already published.

Miss Brand herself had charge of Baker's papers and she granted us access to them. We studied the Baker's papers, over a period of years, to the great enrichment of our comprehension of Woodrow Wilson. For Baker, with Mrs. Wilson's help, had collected the reminiscences of scores of Wilson's family, friends, and associates. His papers remain an indispensable source for Wilson researchers.

Access to Colonel House's papers was controlled by Charles Seymour, president-emeritus of Yale University. Shortly after Seymour announced that Colonel House's diary would be open to scholars, we applied for, and were granted, permission to read it. It is a source of abiding satisfaction to us that, although we do not consider ourselves historians, we found and published for the first time numerous passages in House's diary (which Seymour had omitted from *The Intimate Papers of Colonel House*) revealing of certain significant aspects of the Colonel's attitude toward Wilson.

Inga Floto, whose book *Colonel House in Paris: A Study of American Policy at the Paris Peace Conference in 1919* Weinstein, Anderson, and Link refer to as "the most authoritative study of House at the Paris Peace Conference," characterizes *Woodrow Wilson and Colonel House* as "epoch making," a " 'coup' from an historian's point of view."[6] We find it awkward to cite her generous praise but consider the disparagement of our research by Weinstein, Anderson, and Link justification for doing so. *Woodrow Wilson and Colonel House*, Floto writes, is "the first attempt at a consistent utilization of House's voluminous diary in its full, chronological scope," and she credits us with having made available material of "decisive importance."[7]

Weinstein, Anderson, and Link make no reference whatever to our use of primary source materials, let alone to the fact that we unearthed new data. We consider this an unfair omission and their criticism of our research unjustified.

Woodrow Wilson's Personality

We turn now to the second of our "principal failings": ". . . the Georges fail to recognize the limitations of their psychological model and misrepresent evidence to fit their theory."[8] It seems to us that we were not only aware but scrupulous to convey to readers an awareness that what we were presenting for their consideration is an interpretation of Wilson based on certain hypotheses, which we articulated and invited them to examine on the basis of data, which we also presented. We explicitly stated in our book that the validity of our interpretations is necessarily a matter of opinion:

> No incontrovertible proof can be offered. Nor can any one incident be relied upon to sustain this or any other theory of Wilson's motivation. It is only when the man's career is viewed as a whole that a repetition of certain similar behavior is discernable. Let the reader consider whether these patterns of behavior become more consistently comprehensible in terms of the explanations herein offered than in terms of other explanations. That will be the best test of their usefulness.[9]

Weinstein, Anderson, and Link evince no such restraint in the presentation of their hypotheses. Consider, for example, the way they conclude their statement concerning Wilson's inability to read until he was eleven, which they attribute to developmental dyslexia, physiologically determined, and which we, on the other hand, suggest in *Woodrow Wilson and Colonel House* may have derived from feelings of inadequacy and been an unconscious expression of resentment of his father's perfectionist demands.[10] Say Weinstein, Anderson, and Link: "We do not have a good record of Wilson's childhood such as might be gained from contemporary letters, diaries, or autobiographies; like any other child, he may have felt insecurities. However, it is certain that they did not come about in the manner postulated by the Georges."[11] Whence, in the absence of adequate data, these author's certainty? Is peremptory assertion a substitute for reasoned argument? So apparently Weinstein, Anderson, and Link think; for so many of their interpretations and medical diagnoses are couched in categorical language—language that we consider inappropriate to the speculative nature of their enterprise.

The Dyslexia Hypothesis

Let us get down to specific cases: we do not think our hypothesis about Wilson's delayed acquisition of reading skills can be thus handily dispatched. Nor do we consider it irrelevant that Link's present certainty about the cause of Wilson's reading problem follows decades of his failing to recognize that a problem requiring explanation even existed. In *Wilson: The Road to the White House*, published in 1947, he did not even refer to Wilson's early learning difficulties and wrote that "Wilson's boyhood was notable, if for nothing else, because of his normal development."[12] (This notwithstanding that years before, Baker, whose work Link cites, has specifically drawn attention to Wilson's early slow development.)[13]

Twenty years later, in 1967—long after we, in *Woodrow Wilson and Colonel House*, had again drawn attention to the data of Wilson's early learning problems and he himself had mentioned in passing that Wilson "was a late starter"—Link was still arguing that "all evidence indicates that Wilson had a normal boyhood, at least as normal as was possible for boys growing up in the South during the Civil War and Reconstruction."[14]

By 1968, Link was at least referring, however doubtfully, to the "family tradition" which "may or may not be correct" according to which Wilson "did not learn to read until he was nine." (Actually the data indicate he had learned only his letters when he was nine. He could not read until he was eleven.) To be sure, Link was now willing to acknowledge that the boy "seems to have suffered from insecurity on account of his inability to achieve as rapidly as he thought he should," but he was quick to pronounce it "normal insecurity." His personal advantages and precocity aside," Link wrote, "Wilson seems to have been a remarkably normal person during the first forty years of his life. His childhood was serene. . . ."[15]

The article in *Political Science Quarterly* by Weinstein, Anderson, and Link provides gratifying indication that Link has at last taken notice of what he joins his colleagues in correctly describing as the "well-known" facts of Wilson's boyhood learning difficulties. However, the diagnosis he joins them in offering—developmental dyslexia—seems to us to collapse under scrutiny.

Weinstein, Anderson, and Link speak of developmental dyslexia as if it were a now thoroughly understood disability of established etiology.

Undiagnosed in Wilson's childhood, the condition was well-known to neurologists at the time that the Georges wrote their book. However, a number of psychiatrists and psychologists still believed that the condition was an emotional rather than a neurological problem, and the Georges simply chose an explanation that was currently popular. The condition is a frequent one, occurring in about 10 percent of the school population, significantly more frequently in boys. Research over the past seventy years indicates that developmental dyslexia is caused by a delay in the establishment of the dominance of one cerebral hemisphere—usually the left—for language.[16]

A far less confident tone about the nature of reading disabilities and various types of dyslexia is taken by several of the experts who participated in the conference on dyslexia conducted in 1977 by the National Institute of Mental Health. For example, Michael Rutter, a British psychiatrist, contends that the term "dyslexia" has not yet been even satisfactorily defined and that "the presumption of a neurological basis is just that—namely a presumption." He considers it "meaningless" at this time to attempt any estimate of the prevalence of dyslexia.[17] While there is great interest in the hypothesis that a delay in the acquisition of left-hemisphere dominance may be associated with some cases of reading difficulty, Rutter believes that "the evidence on this point remains inconclusive." John Hughes of the Department of Neurology, University of Illinois School of Medicine, writes: "Satz (1976) has summarized the data relating cerebral dominance and dyslexia and has claimed that information is still lacking on this crucial issue." As for the etiology of reading disorders, a number of eminent psychiatrists *continue* to believe that emotional factors are the basis for some of them.[18]

Our purpose in citing the continuing perplexities of specialists in dyslexia research is to counter the impression that readers might well gain from Weinstein, Anderson, and Link that medical research has solved the mystery of reading disabilities and that psychological explanations have been eliminated for all varieties. According to Rutter the very concept of developmental dyslexia "constitutes a hypothesis—the hypothesis that within the large overall group of disabled readers there is a subgroup with a distinct constitutionally determined condition."[19] Very well. Weinstein, Anderson, and Link claim that "Tommy" Wilson was such an intrinsically impaired child. What is their evidence?

"Specific evidence" of developmental dyslexia, Weinstein, Anderson and Link claim, is that Wilson "was a slow reader into adult life. At the Johns Hopkins, the amount of assigned reading was his bane. 'Steady reading,' he wrote his fiancee, 'always demands of me more expenditure of resolution and dogged energy than any other sort of work.' "[20]

The sentence from Wilson's letter to his fiancee, Ellen Axson, that

Weinstein, Anderson, and Link quote in support of their thesis is incorrectly cited as having been written on 29 March 1884. This is an error of some consequence, since its correct date, 29 *November* 1884, places it within the period that Wilson was making a heroic effort to toil through the reading required to obtaining a Ph.D. It was an effort he detested, which only weeks before he had decided to abandon on the grounds, he had written Ellen Axson, that "a forced march through fourteen thousand pages of dry reading" would jeopardize his health. "I am quite sure that I shall profit much more substantially from a line of reading of my own choosing, in the lines of my own original work. . . ."[21]

Nonetheless, in those days, as in these, a degree made a man more marketable. Wilson, avid to equip himself for a job that would give him the wherewithal to marry, reluctantly embarked on the hateful "forced march" shortly after he had renounced it. The drudgery was all but unbearable. His letters to Ellen Axson during these weeks and until mid-February, 1885, chronicle his growing distress. He is tempted "to throw down these heavy volumes and run out into the glories of the open air." He berates himself for not accepting the necessity of complying with the requirements. Try as he will to submit, "I often grow savagely out of humour with my present state of pupilage. . . ."[22]

Reading for the Ph.D. was not the full measure of his problem. "I am handicapped for my degree," he wrote to a friend, "because of the extra work with which I was indiscreet enough to saddle myself." He had committed himself to collaborate on a history of political economy with one of his professors. "I am to wade—am wading, indeed—through innumerable American text writers," he continued, "for the purpose of writing . . . about one-third of the projected treatise." As for the degree, "It's this year or never."[23] The burden proved too great and, finally, on 19 February 1885, he wrote to his fiancée: "I have given up—this time conclusively—the struggle for the degree. . . . Cramming kills me; reading in development of a subject improves and invigorates me."[24]

Is the sentence that Weinstein, Anderson, and Link pluck from one of the letters Wilson wrote in the midst of the struggle described above credible evidence of developmental dyslexia? That construction of it strikes us as tortured. It seems to us much more likely that Wilson's statement indicates his distress at the *kind* of reading that was being demanded of him and the crushing amount of it.

If the record suggested that Wilson was generally a reluctant reader, slow because the very act of reading was difficult for him, the case for Weinstein, Anderson, and Link's hypothesis of developmental dyslexia would gain some ground. The record fails them, however. One has but to look through the diary he kept during the summer after his freshman year at Princeton to see that he was in fact an omnivorous reader, provided only that he had a taste for the matter at hand: Macaulay, Shakespeare, Gibbon, Plutarch, Pepys, Dickens, novels, magazines, encyclopedia articles—all passed under his frequently enthusiastic but, by preference, unhurried scrutiny.[25] The argument may be summed up in a simple statistic: that it takes no less than thirty pages of quite fine print in the index to the first twelve volumes of *The Papers of Woodrow Wilson* to cover the subject category, "Woodrow Wilson—Reading."[26]

Weinstein, Anderson, and Link claim two other "groups" of "specific" evidence that Wilson had developmental dyslexia": he was "extremely poor in arithmetic," an ineptitude commonly associated with developmental dyslexia; and he quickly "and without practice" mastered writing with his left hand when in 1896 (as the result of a stroke, they say, an assertion about which more later) he was unable to write with his right hand. This ability "strongly suggests that he had mixed cerebral dominance for language."[27]

We question that the dyslexia hypothesis finds support from these "groups" of evidence. Being "extremely poor in arithmetic" can have a score of explanations other than developmental dyslexia; moreover, whatever his difficulties with arithmetic, Wilson's capabilities ranged from keeping meticulous personal financial records to overseeing the formulation of national economic policy and the negotiation of intricate international economic questions. As for his lefthanded writing, given Wilson's considerable artistic talents and his intense perseverence, it is not surprising that he succeeded in acquiring that skill. It was not the easy accomplishment that Weinstein, Anderson, and Link suggest, however. We know from Stockton Axson's account that Wilson set about the task with "customary determination."[28] We know from Wilson himself that he practiced "laboriously," notwithstanding which writing with his left hand remained "clumsy and uncertain," "awkward," "tedious," "a painfully slow process"—"it takes me half an hour to [write] one of these pages."[29] In short, Wilson does not seem to have been naturally ambidextrous. Even with practice, writing with his left hand seems to have remained an uncomfortable occasional necessity rather than an easy alternative to the use of his clearly preferred right hand.

The dyslexia hypothesis suffers further when one considers two aspects of dyslexia about which the experts generally agree: that it is strongly associated with disordered handwriting and with persistently atrocious spelling.[30] Wilson's handwriting—as surely Weinstein, Anderson, and Link would agree—is a very model of beautiful penmanship. Even his check registers look like copperplate. And he was an excellent speller. His errors were few and far between.

For the purpose of pursuing our critics' train of thought, however, let us grant for a moment that "Tommy" Wilson suffered from some inborn defect, that it was indeed developmental dyslexia that impeded his learning to read. What would the psychological consequences of such a disability have been, both upon the boy and his parents? The literature on dyslexia is clear that every poor reader, no matter what the cause of his problem, is predisposed to feeling inadequate, "bad," or "stupid."[31]

Weinstein, Anderson, and Link give passing recognition to the fact that "the reading disability affected Wilson's development and his relationship with his parents," but they immediately add "but hardly in the way that the Georges state." How, then, *was* the boy affected? "It probably made him more dependent on his family," they say. They acknowledge that "he may have feared that his reading problems indicated that he was stupid or lazy" and that "the condition probably made Dr. Wilson more pedagogic and insistent on drilling his 'lazy' son." Having edged up to the dread explanation, Weinstein, Anderson, and Link hurry away and remove Dr. Wilson with them: during the Civil War he was sometimes away from home; other family members read to Wilson and he enjoyed that; and the data are lacking, but whatever insecurities Wilson might have felt "it is certain that they did not come about in the manner postulated by the Georges."[32]

This account by Weinstein, Anderson, and Link leaves some nagging loose ends that not only deserve but demand consideration. What would the effect be on a boy to fear that he was stupid or lazy—and, by the way, there is no "may have" about it: years later when he was president, Wilson often reminisced about his boyhood with his physician and friend, Cary Grayson, and Grayson recalls that "he often spoke of himself as being a lazy boy."[33] What attitudes toward himself would his father's "insistent drilling" have engendered—his father, a master of the English language, a brilliant expositor of Calvinist doctrine, which says nothing about developmental dyslexia but a great deal about wickedness and sin and dereliction of duty? Would this devoted father, a man of his times, not have had an especially poignant stake in the intellectual progress of this, his third child but first son, and been frustrated and disappointed at the boy's poor performance? And would "Tommy's self-concept not almost inevitably have suffered? Would he not have felt humiliated, unworthy, inadequate? In short, would this family situation not have fostered the ripening in a boy's heart of those low estimates of himself that these authors deny existed? It seems to us they overlook the ample evidence that this was the case and refuse to draw the conclusion obvious even from their prettified account of the family interaction.

Woodrow Wilson and His Father

For the sake of evaluating Weinstein, Anderson, and Link's thesis on its own ground, we have thus far omitted the ingredient of Dr. Wilson's propensity for sarcasm and severe criticism and how these are likely to have impinged upon his son's development. "The Georges claim that Wilson suffered from a troubled relationship with his father." write Weinstein, Anderson, and Link, and they reject the idea.[34] Having attempted to subtract Wilson's reading problem as indication of father-son stress, they try to belittle the significance of the testimony of young family members that Joseph R. Wilson, a man of many virtues to be sure, was also a sarcastic tease.

The evidence cannot be so handily dispatched, however. And now there is a good deal more of it than was available at the time we were writing *Woodrow Wilson and Colonel House*. There is, for example, an unpublished manuscript by Dr. Stockton Axson, the much younger brother of the first Mrs. Wilson, who lived with the Woodrow Wilsons for a number of years. Axson was not only Woodrow Wilson's devoted friend for over forty years; he was also a great favorite of Wilson's father. The two were fast friends to the day Joseph Ruggles Wilson died, and Stockton Axson thought the old minister a great man. Yet he wrote at length of the forbidding side of Dr. Joseph Wilson and of how, when displeased, his humor "bubbled *hot*" in "scalding sarcasms" which could be "really withering." He had in him, Axson tells us, "a certain savage humor which caused him to say sometimes cruel things even to those who loved him and whom he loved." Notwithstanding his qualities of greatness, he was a "ruthless sort of man," Axson wrote, "a man with a distinct streak of perversity in him," In his sarcasm, he reminded Axson of Jonathan Swift.[35]

The sarcasm, the mordant wit, the cruel teasing, the relentless drilling to which he subjected his son obviously constituted only one facet of Dr. Joseph Wilson's personality. We do not for a moment deny—nor did we in *Woodrow Wilson and Colonel House*—that there is rich and persuasive evidence of the comradship between Wilson and his father, of abiding love, and of the transmission from father to son of moral values and of a range of skills and perceptions that fostered the greatness of Woodrow Wilson.[36] Recognizing and giving full weight to this evidence, however, does not necessitate refusing to recognize, as we think our critics refuse to do, that *all* facets of Joseph Wilson entered into his interaction with his son and that the syndrome we tried to trace in *Woodrow Wilson and Colonel House* also had important consequences. Weinstein, Anderson, and Link write as though they consider it beyond the realm of possibility that the demanding father may have generated in his sensitive son feelings of inadequacy and also of unconscious resentment. Is it likely that the boy never inwardly rebelled at the stern religious teachings graven into his soul? Did Woodrow Wilson enjoy some divine dispensation from experiencing conflicting emotions about a beloved parent? Is it really unthinkable to Weinstein, Anderson, and Link that Wilson may have had to deal with ambivalence?

There is the briefest intimation—half a sentence—that such questions crossed our critics' minds. "Dr. Wilson had a tremendous influence on his son," they write, "and probably no boy grows up without *some* resentment toward his father,"[37] Weinstein, Anderson, and Link write as though any unconscious resentment Wilson felt toward his father was of minor dimensions and without significant repercussions for the understanding of his political behavior. They write as though his early learning difficulties neither resulted from nor led to psychological problems that importantly affected his development. They leave unmentioned and show no sign of having considered the implications of many self-revealing statements Wilson made in private conversations or of dozens of self-characterizations to be found in his letters, in his diaries, and sometimes even in his public utterances which bespeak great inner turmoil.

Wilson's Enduring Anxieties

We shall cite just one such statement to convey the flavor of the evidence. In 1884, at age twenty-eight—long before any of the "strokes" that Weinstein, Anderson, and Link claim altered his personality—Wilson wrote to his fiancée:

> It isn't pleasant or convenient to have strong passions: and it is particularly hard in my case to have to deal with unamiable feelings; because the only whip with which I can subdue them is the whip of hard study and that lacerates *me* as often as it conquers my crooked dispositions. I hope that none of my friends—and much more none of my enemies!—will ever find out *how much it costs me to give up my own way.* I have the uncomfortable feeling that I am carrying a volcano about with me.[38]

In other letters to Ellen Axson Wilson he refers to himself as " a man of sensitive, restless, overwrought disposition," He speaks of his "sombre, morbid nature," his "fears," "anxieties," "morose moods," of "my poor, mixed inexplicable nature." "Deep perturbations are natural to me, deep disturbances of spirit." He writes of "my natural self-distrust," of having "never been sanguine," of often falling when irritated into "the stern, indignant, defiant humour, the scarcely suppressed belligerent temper for which there are abundant materials in my disposition." "I have to guard my emotions from painful overflow," he confides.[39]

Such feelings, so persistently and intensely expressed, require explanation. Weinstein, Anderson, and Link offer none. We believe that these emotions were related to his ceaseless effort to maintain his self-esteem;

that for Wilson carving out a sphere of competence in public life and striving for high achievement were a means of overcoming feelings of unimportance, or moral inferiority, of weakness, of mediocrity, of intellectual inadequacy; that in certain crucial situations in his public career, Wilson's self-defeating stubbornness and unwillingness to defer (or at least make expedient gestures of deference) to men whose cooperation was essential to the accomplishment of his goals were irrational manifestations of underlying low self-estimates against which he had constantly to struggle. It remains our conviction that the hypotheses advanced in *Woodrow Wilson and Colonel House*, applied to the vast body of data concerning Woodrow Wilson, have consistent explanatory power.[40]

Woodrow Wilson's Medical Problems

The third "principal failing" of *Woodrow Wilson and Colonel House*, according to Weinstein, Anderson, and Link, is that we "ignore Wilson's neurological disorders as conditions affecting his behavior." Undaunted by the virtual absence of medical records for this period of Wilson's life, they assert unequivocally that he suffered strokes in 1896, 1900, 1904, 1906, and 1907. They say that "by the end of World War I, Wilson was showing signs of generalized cerebral involvement." They state further that an episode of illness (which Weinstein had earlier diagnosed as a stroke) in April 1919 while he was negotiating the Versailles Peace Treaty in Paris was not only influenza but "probably a virus encephalopathy, which, superimposed on pre-existing brain damage, produced changes in behavior which may have influenced the outcome of the peace negotiations." The massive stroke of October 1919 which, as is well known, paralyzed Wilson's left side also, according to Weinstein, Anderson, and Link, resulted in personality changes "which were important factors in his failure to obtain ratification of the Treaty of Versailles."[41]

It is certainly the case that we did not think that brain damage became a factor to consider in Wilson's political behavior until the autumn of 1919. While doing our research for *Woodrow Wilson and Colonel House*, we were alert to the possibility that personality changes affecting his handling of the League controversy in the Senate may have followed the catastrophic stroke of October 2. There was indeed evidence that he was given to outbursts of tears and temper. His pathetic hope that the Democratic convention might renominate him and that he could win a third term in 1920 suggested impairment of his judgment of the political realities. A moving memorandum by Katharine E. Brand detailing Woodrow Wilson's last years made it clear that in many ways he was but a shadow of his former self. Nonetheless it was our conclusion then and it is our conclusion now that his behavior on the League issue remained intact. Whatever the nature of the brain damage he sustained in the fall of 1919, it altered neither his grasp of his problem with the Senate nor his strategy to deal with it. He had struck his unyielding position long before October 1919—a position that anguished practically everyone who cared personally about him or supported U.S. entry into the League of Nations. Wilson's conduct in this respect after the stroke was entirely consistent with his behavior before it. Both before and after, ample warnings were conveyed to him of the all but inevitable consequences of his refusal at every turn to compromise. Both before and after the stroke, he rejected these warnings, using the same arguments against compromise and co-gently communicating them from his sickbed. The stroke seemed not to modify his behavior one whit in this respect.

Of course, it is possible to argue that he *would* have changed his position had he not been stricken. One can only speculate. Our own guess, given his history, is that he would not have yielded, that his stubbornness was in the deepest sense an expression of the integrity of his functioning on the public issue of supreme value to him. To the day he died, he expressed the conviction that history would vindicate him. To those who knew and loved him best, his refusal to compromise was a source of sorrow rather than of surprise. A sense of some terrible inner logic to his self-defeating behavior in terms of stable, persistent characteristics that they had long since recognized pervades their narratives.

His implacable enemy, Senator Henry Cabot Lodge, too, sensed that Wilson was held to his course by some invincible inner compulsion. The leading opponent of Senate ratification of the Treaty as submitted by Wilson, Lodge based his strategy upon a shrewd assessment of Wilson's personality. He calculated that Wilson would never agree to accept even minor reservations, that rather than compromise with the Senate and particularly with him (Lodge), Wilson would allow the treaty—League of Nations and all—to be defeated.[42]

The drama unfolded quite as Lodge had foreseen. His tactical finesse in maneuvering Wilson from one excruciating refusal to compromise to another testifies to his deadly insight into the tragic flaw in Wilson's character. He was not confounded by any perplexing "changes" in Wilson. His success at predicting Wilson's reactions suggests their constancy through all the vicissitudes of Wilson's health.

There was a time when Link recognized the relationship between Wilson's character and the recurrent defeats he suffered. In his book, *Wilson: The Road to the White House,* Link wrote:

> The Princeton period was the microcosm of a later macrocosm, and a polit-
> ical observer, had he studied carefully Wilson's career as president of Prin-
> ceton University, might have forecast accurately the shape of things to

come during the period when Wilson was president of the United States. What striking similarities there are between the Princeteon and the national periods.!⁴³

Link's comment pertained to the quad and graduate school controversies that fractured the Princeton community in 1907 and continued to reverberate bitterly for years after Wilson's resignation from the Princeton presidency in 1910. The quad controversy revolved about Wilson's plan to build quadrangles in which upper and lower classmen, some graduate students, and unmarried preceptors would live and eat together thereby, Wilson argued, stimulating intellectual exchange outside of the classroom. Opponents, among whom were wealthy alumni on whose contributions any construction would depend, viewed the plan as a threat to the eating clubs to which many were sentimentally attached and as having high-handedly been presented to the Board of Trustees before discussion with faculty and alumni. Moreover, they regarded Wilson's quad plan as a brazen attempt to divert attention and resources from the long-planned development of the graduate college under the leadership of its dean, Andrew Fleming West. In 1906, at Wilson's own behest, West had declined an invitation to become president of the Massachusetts Institute of Technology in favor of remaining at Princeton in order to put the graduate college into operation. A bitter dispute erupted between Wilson and his supporters and West and his supporters which crystallized around the ostensible issue of where the proposed graduate college should be located. Various concessions to Wilson's views were offered including substantial reform of the eating clubs, stripping Dean West of much of his authority, and compromising on the site issue. Wilson refused them all.

Writing in *Wilson: The Road to the White House* about what he then considered Wilson's unreasonable behavior, Link said: "The vagaries of his mind during this period are unfathomable." At that time he found the most striking fact about the whole Princeton controversy "the absence of any clear-cut issue" and that Wilson had shifted from one issue to another so that "it was almost impossible to tell where he really stood."⁴⁴ He attributed Wilson's difficulties at Princeton and later in his career explicitly to his *character* rather than to the logic of the situations he confronted:

> Wilson was a headstrong and determined man who was usually able to rationalize his actions in terms of the moral law and to identify his position with the divine will. . . . The time came at Princeton, Trenton, and Washington when Wilson did not command the support of the groups to whom he was responsible. Naturally, he was not able to change his character even had he wanted to change it, with the result that controversy and disastrous defeat occurred in varying degrees in all three cases.⁴⁵

Link now holds a different view of the Princeton imbroglio, as he indicates in a footnote to the article by Weinstein, Anderson, and Link: "Arthur S. Link wishes to state that much new evidence discovered since the publication of his *Wilson: The Road to the White House* in 1947 has convinced him that his treatment of Wilson and West and the graduate college controversy is inadequate and unbalanced."[46]

The account of the Princeton controversy given by Weinstein, Anderson, and Link suggests that Wilson's actions in fact derived from a reasonable assessment of the situation rather than from characterological idiosyncrasies. If this is indeed Link's current interpretation, it collides with the simultaneous claim that "changes" in Wilson's behavior due to brain damage from the alleged strokes of 1896, 1900, 1904, 1906, and 1907 impaired his performance and played a critical role in his defeat. To us it seems that to the extent that they consider Wilson's refusal to compromise in the quad and graduate college battles a reasonable defense of his principles, they reduce the grounds for arguing the significance of the alleged personality and behavioral changes in consequence of the alleged strokes.

Wilson's Behavior in Paris

If in their article Professor Link repudiates the interpretive structure of *Wilson: The Road to the White House*, Dr. Weinstein also discloses a significant change of view involving one of his key diagnoses: that of Wilson's brief illness in Paris in April 1919. In his widely read and widely quoted article, "Woodrow Wilson's Neurological Illness," published in 1970, Weinstein stated that the most likely cause of Wilson's illness during the Peace Conference was a "cerebral vascular occlusion (blood clot in the brain)"—in short, a stroke. He construed certain aspects of Wilson's behavior during and after his illness as evidence of the kind of behavioral change that would confirm brain damage caused by a stroke. Weinstein described the "cerebral vascular occlusion" as "a lesion in the right cerebral hemisphere extending to include deeper structures in the limbic-reticular system. With the history of lesions of the left side of the brain, indicated by the attacks of right-sided paresthesia and left monocular blindness from 1896 to 1908, he now had evidence of bilateral damage, a condition affecting emotional and social behavior more severely than a unilateral lesion."[47]

This medical description was so precise and authoritative in tone that few laymen would dare to take issue with it. The problem is that the major evidence on which it relied—the allegedly strange changes in Wilson's behavior—is tittle-tattle which has gained momentum and grown in absurdity in its passage from one source to another. The historical record, as we shall shortly attempt to show, provides a background against which Wilson's "strange behavior," viewed in context, seems reasonable and rational.

The speculative nature of Weinstein's diagnoses is revealed by the fact that in the article by Weinstein, Anderson, and Link the minutely described stroke of his earlier article is withdrawn. A footnote states that new evidence indicates that it is not likely to have occurred after all.[48] Now readers are informed that Wilson had an attack of influenza in Paris in April 1919 (as most historians have thought all along). A crucial aspect of the brain-damage thesis is salvaged, however, for Weinstein, Anderson, and Link also say that it was not merely influenza but "probably a virus encephalopathy." In short, as a result of one disease or another, according to Weinstein, Woodrow Wilson sustained brain damage in April 1919 that significantly affected his judgment in the conduct of the negotiations. In both articles "strange" changes of behavior are cited as evidence of altered brain function.[49]

Let us examine some of this allegedly irrational behavior: one manifestation cited by Weinstein in his earlier article (which presumably constitutes part of the documentation of the "changes in behavior" alleged by Weinstein, Anderson, and Link) was Wilson's instruction to his personal staff in Paris that they use official limousines only for official business. Irwin "Ike" Hoover, White House head usher who served as chief of Wilson's household staff in Paris, is the source of this tale, which he recorded in his book, *42 Years in the White House*. This gentlemen, as his letters to his wife indicate, had grown accustomed to taking joyrides practically every day—sometimes two and three times a day. ("It is fine to order up a big limousine, say 'to the hotel' and off it goes," he wrote to his wife. "Come out, say 'home' and you are on the way back." Of the scores of letters he wrote home, there is scarcely a handful—except when he was at sea enroute to or from the conference—in which he did not articulate his use or nonuse of the limousines for the particular day covered. "Ike" missed his family—and also his Dodge automobile to which he referred affectionately in several letters.)[50] Other staff members fell into the same habit of rushing for the cars the moment the president and Mrs. Wilson went out.

One day during his illness in April 1919 the president sent for one member of his staff after the other and found that they were all out in the cars. This angered him and he ordered the staff to curtail use of the cars for personal pleasure.[51] We see nothing "strange" or "irrational" in Wilson's crackdown— unless it be that he did not sooner lose his temper at Hoover's profligate abuse of privilege.

On the basis of "Ike" Hoover's account, Weinstein also accepted as "markedly irrational behavior" after his April 1919 illness that Wilson

was concerned that the French servants in the house the French government had placed at his disposal were spies. The fact is that many Americans at the conference were worried about spies. Joseph Grew, secretary
of the American commission, issued directives warning of the need for
the secure handling of confidential papers, for burning trash, for being
alert to the possibility that telephones were being tapped, and that
French employees might be spying for their government. During the very
week of Wilson's illness, Dr. Grayson wrote in his diary that one of the
servants who claimed not to speak English had been found to know English fluently and that the French government was engaged in spying on
the president. Mrs. Wilson's secretary, Edith Benham, noted in her diary
on 29 March 1919 that conversations at meals had to be restrained because "Colonel House says there are spies here in the house who report
everything to the Foreign Office." Colonel House noted in his diary at the
beginning of the conference that the private wire between his study and
Wilson's "is constantly 'covered' to see that it is not tapped."[52]

It seems to us grotesque that Wilson's concern for security at the
conference should be interpreted by Weinstein and others as evidence of
brain damage. Was Joseph Grew also brain damaged? And Dr. Grayson,
Colonel House, and Miss Benham too?

The Question of Strokes

And what about the earlier episodes of illness in 1896, 1900, 1904, 1906,
and 1907 which Weinstein, Anderson, and Link state were strokes, the
one in 1906 being "the first one to be recognized as such"?[53] By all accounts, Wilson's illness in 1906 was the most serious of his prepresidential
years. One spring morning in that year, he awakened unable to see out of
his left eye. He immediately consulted two eminent Philadelphia specialists (an ophthalmologist and an internist). The medical records, unfortunately, are missing. Surviving letters and later reminiscences, however,
indicate that Wilson was told that a burst blood vessel had caused a hemorrhage in the eye, that he had arteriosclerosis and high blood pressure,
and that he needed prolonged rest. Wilson obediently delegated his duties to Princeton colleagues, spent a quiet summer in England and, with
medical approval, resumed his work in the fall.

Nowhere could we find evidence that this illness had been diagnosed as a stoke or "recognized as such." We wrote to Weinstein and
asked when Wilson's illness in 1906 was recognized as a stroke and by
whom. In his reply. Weinstein cited sources that simply contain no mention of a stroke.[54] He further wrote in this letter that Wilson's ophthalmologist and internist knew that he had arteriosclerosis and high blood pressure and that strokes are very common in these conditions; and that they

may not have told Wilson in so many words that he had had a stroke but used a euphemism instead. Such speculation on Weinstein's part consisting of what he thinks must have been in other people's minds strikes us as utterly inadequate justification for the unqualified claim by Weinstein, Anderson, and Link that the 1906 illness was a stroke "recognized as such," much less for Link's assertion in *The Papers of Woodrow Wilson* that it was "a major stroke."

Of course the question to which all the foregoing discussion leads is: how would competent, independent medical authority evaluate Woodrow Wilson's illnesses throughout his career and Weinstein's diagnoses of them? For a response to this question, we turned to Michael F. Marmor, M.D., associate professor of ophthalmology at the Stanford University School of Medicine. We placed at Marmor's disposal all the data in our possession relating to Wilson's health[55] and made available to him the relevant volume of *The Papers of Woodrow Wilson* as well as the source materials cited by Weinstein in his various articles.

Marmor embodied the results of his review in a letter to us dated 18 May 1981 (see appendix for the text). The letter speaks for itself and we need only note here Marmor's main conclusions: that in the absence of documented findings or medical records, Weinstein's analysis is necessarily speculative; that his own reading of the evidence leads him to question both the medical interpretations of Weinstein and the propriety of presenting such views as historical fact.

As a matter of fact, questions about the validity of Weinstein's diagnoses have been raised previously and were brought to the attention of both Link and Weinstein a decade ago. In 1971, Robert T. Monroe, M.D., an internist long associated with the Harvard University School of Medicine, wrote four pages of comments on Weinstein's article, "Woodrow Wilson's Neurological Illness," which had been published the preceding year. He detailed the medical grounds for doubting Weinstein's interpretations and expressed his overall evaluation as follows: "Professor Weinstein seeks to prove that Wilson 'had a long history of cerebral vascular disease,' and that it 'was associated with alterations in behavior and personality.' In my view he has failed on both counts." Weinstein dismissed Monroe's comments as uninformed, and the following year, volume sixteen of *The Papers of Woodrow Wilson* appeared with the statement in the preface that Wilson's illness in 1906 was "a major stroke."[56]

Implications for *The Papers of Woodrow Wilson*

In conclusion, we should like to say a few words about *The Papers of Woodrow Wilson*, of which Professor Link is editor. The publication of Wilson's papers is one of the major projects in historiography in our time.

These volumes are meant to preserve for posterity a true and unbiased record concerning Woodrow Wilson. Scholars today consult *The Papers of Woodrow Wilson* on the assumption—an assumption upon which they ought to be able to rely—that the facts stated in the informational notes to various documents are true and accurate. Scholars will continue to consult *The Papers of Woodrow Wilson* on this assumption for many generations to come. As we noted at the beginning of this article, the editorial matter of several volumes of *The Papers* contains (in prefaces and in numerous notes as well as in listings in various indices) unqualified allusions to Wilson's so-called strokes between the years 1896 and 1907. (The volumes covering the period of the Paris Peace Conference into which Wilson's illness of April 1919 falls have not yet been published.) We believe that these allusions have prejudiced the objectivity of *The Papers of Woodrow Wilson* and have already misled a number of writers.[57] We also believe that those in charge of the project have a reverence for the truth and a fidelity to their scholarly duties. We suggest that a reconsideration and emendation of the editorial matter that elevates Dr. Weinstein's controversial medical hypotheses to the status of historical fact is in order.

Postscript

A book by Edwin A. Weinstein, *Woodrow Wilson: A Medical and Psychological Biography*, has appeared since this article was completed. We can only note here that Weinstein persists in presenting, as if it were indisputable fact, his theory that Wilson suffered a series of disabling strokes dating back to 1896. The book contains numerous statements implying the existence of medical data and opinion which, so far as we know, simply are not available in the historical record.[58] An even more serious concern is that Weinstein has omitted data of critical diagnostic significance, thus precluding an objective evaluation of his hypotheses by his medical peers. His account of Wilson's episode of visual loss in 1906 is an important case in point.

In describing the 1906 episode, Weinstein writes that Mrs. Wilson "searched for evidence that would bear out the Doctor's opinion that her husband's stroke had been brought on by strain and overwork." He also writes that the Princeton trustees "agreed that the stroke had been caused by overwork." However, we know of no evidence (and Weinstein offers none) that Wilson's doctors, Mrs. Wilson, or the Princeton trustees stated, implied, or even believed that Wilson had suffered a stroke.

Weinstein titles his chapter about the 1906 episode, "A Major Stroke and its Consequences," and he begins with a general description of carotid occlusive disease. In this disorder, blood clots or arteriosclerotic plaques in the neck may fragment and form emboli that lodge in smaller arteries such as those within the eye. He then writes that Wilson's ophthalmologist (Dr. George E. de Schweinitz) "told him that he had sustained a blood clot in the eye," the obvious implication being that "clot" refers to an embolus from the carotid. We believe this is a misleading description because important evidence has been omitted. What de Schweinitz actually told Wilson is not known. It can only be inferred from letters written by Wilson and Mrs. Wilson at the time, and from the later recollections of such knowledgeable people as John Grier Hibben (who had accompanied Wilson to Dr. de Schweinitz's office), Stockton Axson, Drs. Cary Grayson and E. P. Davis, and Eleanor Wilson McAdoo. *All* of these sources say that Wilson's loss of vision was caused by a hemorrhage or burst blood vessel within his eye. Yet Weinstein omits any mention of hemorrhage in his book, even though the distinction between hemorrhage and embolic clot is critical, because bleeding within the eye is *not* characteristic of carotid occlusive disease and indeed militates against that diagnosis. Weinstein's only cited source for the word "clot" is a letter from Ellen Axson Wilson to a cousin in which she says: "Two weeks ago yesterday Woodrow waked up perfectly blind in one eye!—it turned out from the bursting of a blood vessel in it. . . . The clot in the eye is being absorbed with extraordinary rapidity." The word "clot" in the context of Mrs. Wilson's letter seems clearly to refer to a coagulum from the burst blood vessel rather than to an embolus.

We (Michael F. Marmor, Juliette L. George, and Alexander L. George) hope to comment more fully on Weinstein's book elsewhere.

Appendix

May 18, 1981

Dr. and Mrs. Alexander George
Department of Political Science
Stanford University
Stanford, California 94305

Dear Dr. and Mrs. George:

I have reviewed at length the medical and historical source material which bears upon the possibility that Woodrow Wilson had neurologic disease. I am preparing a comprehensive analysis of this material for publication and this letter represents a summary of my impressions and conclusions. You have my permission to quote from this letter, with the proviso that statements should not be taken out of context or used without sufficient material to provide a balanced picture of my views.

Let me say at the outset that the medical analysis of historical figures is by nature a speculative process. In the absence of documented findings or medical records, one must rely upon guesswork and judgment to analyze lay descriptions of disease. Physicians are trained to consider all of the rare and unlikely disease which might afflict their patients, lest one be missed. However, in looking back over history, the approach should probably be the opposite: given the symptoms, search for the most common and likely causes. Under these constraints, historical diagnoses will rarely have the certainty of scientific fact, and should in general be considered hypothesis.

In a series of articles, psychiatrist Edwin Weinstein has argued that Wilson suffered from serious cerebrovascular disease over a period of nearly thirty years, and that discrete strokes accounted for behavioral changes at several critical junctures in Wilson's professional life. This view has been accepted by the eminent historian Arthur Link, who has referred to these "strokes" without qualification in the current edition of *The Papers of Woodrow Wilson*. My own reading of the evidence leads me to question both the medical interpretations of Dr. Weinstein, and the propriety of presenting such views as historical fact.

Weinstein's thesis is that Wilson suffered for many years from cerebrovascular disease, primarily carotid artery insufficiency, and had discrete strokes which influenced his professional behavior. Weinstein contends cerebrovascular disease first became manifest as disability of the right arm, resulting from one or more small strokes in 1896. The strongest and most direct evidence for stroke is considered to be Wilson's episode of left visual loss in 1906, which Weinstein describes as diagnostic of left carotid occlusive disease. Finally the illness which Wilson suffered during the 1919 Peace Conference is viewed as viral encephalopathy superimposed on preexisting brain damage. Each of these points merits careful analysis.

Wilson had difficulty with his right hand and arm for more than twenty years, and referred on numerous occasions to "writer's cramp" which was apparently diagnosed as a "neuritis." The precise symptoms are not spelled out, but the hand and arm were often painful, especially while writing. These symptoms began long before the alleged stroke of 1896, and references to this complaint can be found in the Wilson papers as far back as 1884. There are no references to suggest a sudden onset of symptoms (as from a stroke) in either 1884 or 1896, and the symptoms are too chronic to call them a result of transient ischemic attacks. Furthermore, Wilson also had occasional discomfort and pain in this *left* arm.

"Writer's cramp" is poorly understood as a clinical entity. Some cases may have an organic basis from pathology such as arthritic joint damage or inflammation of the nerves, but many are thought to represent an occupational neurosis. Characteristically the patient has difficulty writing more than a few words, but lacks any major disability for other activities. This fits the descriptions of Wilson's disorder, and there is evidence that even during his severe periods of disability he was able to write brief ledger entries with his right hand which rules out any serious paralysis or limitation of movement. To accept this condition as writer's cramp (even without a precise definition of that term) seems perfectly reasonable in view of the nature and duration of the symptoms, whereas to fit these symptoms into a stroke syndrome places them in the category of unusual manifestations.

The 1906 episode is interpreted by Weinstein as direct evidence for cerebrovascular disease, since right-sided weakness and left-sided blindness are often associated with insufficiency or occlusion of the left carotid artery. However, the ocular findings in Wilson's case argue *against* a diagnosis of carotid occlusion. Wilson awoke one morning aware of poor vision in his left eye, which numerous sources indicate was found to result from bursting of a blood vessel and hemorrhage inside the eye. The fact of the matter is that retinal hemorrhage is *not* a sign of carotid occlusive disease. Carotid disease most characteristically leads to occlusion of the retinal arteries which causes a loss of vision but produces a very different picture (without hemorrhage) inside the eye. Arterial occlusion would not have been described in the language used by Wilson and his family members.

Wilson's doctors noted signs of arteriosclerosis and mild hypertension, and there seems little doubt that he had systemic vascular disease. The most likely cause for Wilson's eye disease would be a retinal vein occlusion, which is often associated with hypertensive vascular disease, and which produces diffuse hemorrhages in the retina. Other possibilities include hemorrhagic macular degeneration. The point to emphasize is that these ocular hemorrhages occur frequently as isolated events; they give evidence of generalized vascular pathology but they do not constitute strokes or carry any direct implication of cerebral ischemia or symptomatology.

There are other reasons to doubt a stroke in 1906. The stroke would have affected the left cerebral hemisphere which has major control over language and speech, yet Wilson clearly suffered no impairment in these areas. Weinstein implies that a stroke caused personality changes that affected Wilson's subsequent activities, but the literature on strokes is quite clear in emphasizing that personality changes are not a characteristic of the stroke syndrome in the absence of cognitive changes or dementia. Weinstein carefully qualifies his argument to state that Wilson's behavioral changes in 1906 were an adaption to his illness and could result from stress as well as brain damage. Considering that Wilson had indeed suffered an ocular hemorrhage, and that he was working with intensity as president of Princeton University, why should it be necessary to invoke strokes or cerebral pathology to account for his actions?

Similar problems arise in analyzing the illness that began on April 3, 1919, during the Peace Conference. Weinstein initially concluded that Wilson had suffered a stroke to explain his behavior during the conference, but the tenuousness of the stroke hypothesis is shown by Weinstein's shift to a diagnosis of viral encephalopathy when new evidence made it clear that Wilson had had respiratory disease. I fail to see the need for postulating any diagnoses beyond severe influenza to account for Wilson's behavior.

Wilson was ill with respiratory symptoms and high fever, and there are surely few of us who cannot attest to the debilitating effect of severe flu. Wilson was confined to bed for five days but was incapacitated only on the first day, after which he resumed conferring and decision making from his bedroom. The term "viral encephalopathy" may apply to a broad range of symptoms, from minimal headache and irritability, to severe somnolence, convulsions, and death. Wilson clearly did not have the latter, and some would argue that the former are in fact a routine component of the flu syndrome. Wilson's activities for the remainder of April 1919 seem quite consistent with a history of severe but uncomplicated influenza, and I should think the burden of proof would be to show otherwise.

Wilson probably had systemic vascular disease for a good part of his life, and there is no question that he ultimately suffered a severe stroke in the fall of 1919. Neither of these observations, however, can be construed as evidence for multiple strokes or for significant neurologic dysfunction during the earlier years of his career. Chronic vascular disease may cause subtle changes in mentation, ultimately resulting in dementia. Could Wilson have had very mild degrees of change accumulating over the years? Certainly this is possible, but how does one distinguish this type of subtle degeneration from other aspects of maturation and aging which are evident in everyone? This man actively ran one of the major universities in the United States, campaigned articulately for the presidency, and was clearly a lucid and powerful thinker in political affairs up to the moment of his serious stoke in 1919.

The interpretations which I have chosen to emphasize focus upon common and ordinary conditions, rather than the unusual or the extreme. I think the odds favor such an interpretation, but these views are admittedly hypothetical and open to review or criticism by others. I hope that my arguments will, at least, raise reasonable doubts about the stroke theory and return it to a position of hypothesis rather than fact in historical source material.

With warm regards,

(Signed) Michael F. Marmor, M.D.
Associate Professor
Division of Ophthalmology
Chief, Ophthalmology Section
Veterans Administration Medical Center
Palo Alto, California

NOTES

1. See Edwin A. Weinstein, James William Anderson, and Arthur S. Link, "Woodrow Wilson's Political Personality: A Reappraisal," *Political Science Quarterly* 93 (Winter 1978–79): 586: and Alexander L. Geroge and Juliette L. George *Woodrow Wilson and Colonel House: A Personal-*

ity Study (New York: John Day Company, 1956; Dover Publications, 1964). We are exiled in good company. Some years ago Arthur Link wrote of Ray Stannard Baker that his eight-volume *Woodrow Wilson: Life and Letters* (Garden City, N.Y.: Doubleday, Page and Co., 1927–1939) suffered from Baker's having "to a large degree imposed his own personality profile upon Wilson." Moreover, claims Link (without justification, in our opinion), Baker portrayed Wilson "as being mainly feminine in personality, if not virtually a sexual neuter." This of the man in whose early volumes Woodrow Wilson fairly springs to life. Baker's prodigious research resulted in the collection of that rich raw data upon which Link's own work—and that of every other Wilson scholar—heavily rests. See Arthur S. Link, ed., *Woodrow Wilson: A Profile* (New York: Hill and Wang, 1968), pp. vii–viii.

2. We shall here cite two of the two dozen instances we have thus far found in Arthur S. Link et al., eds., *The Papers of Woodrow Wilson*, 36 vols. to date (Princeton, N.J.: Princeton University Press, 1966–). Of Wilson's illness in May 1906, it is stated in the introduction to vol. 16: "Years of excessive work take their toll in late May 1906, when Wilson suffers a major stroke that seems for a moment to threaten his life. . . ." (p. vii). In December 1907, Moses Taylor Pyne, a Princeton trustee, wrote to Wilson saying he was sorry to learn "that you were suffering from an attack of Neuritis" (ibid., vol. 17, p. 549). Link's editorial footnote to the word "Neuritis" reads: "In fact, Wilson had unquestionably suffered a slight "stroke" (Ibid., p. 550).

3. Weinstein, Anderson, and Link, "A Reappraisal," p. 587.

4. Ibid., p. 598.

5. George and George, *Woodrow Wilson and Colonel House*, p.323.

6. Inga Floto, *Colonel House in Paris: A Study of American Policy at the Paris Peace Conference 1919* (Aarhus, Denmark: Universitetsforlaget, 1973; Princeton, N.J.: Princeton University Press, 1980); Weinstein, Anderson, and Link, "A Reappraisal," p. 597.

7. Floto, *Colonel House in Paris*, pp. 13, 20, 21. We cite Floto solely on the question of our research and do not mean to suggest that she endorses our interpretation of the House-Wilson relationship. To be sure, she credits us with "elucidating the 'mechanism' " of the friendship in an "unassailable" fashion, but she is critical of our analysis of the "break." Her book is an important contribution to a continuing discussion among historians. We think, however, that the assertion by Weinstein, Anderson, and Link that Floto "proves conclusively that the cause of the so-called break between the two men was House's failure to follow Wilson's explicit instructions while the latter was in the United States" ("A Reappraisal," p. 597) is an oversimplification.

8. Weinstein, Anderson and Link, "A Reappraisal," p. 587.

9. George and George, *Woodrow Wilson and Colonel House*, p. 12. See also ibid., p. 114.

10. See ibid., p. 7.

11. Weinstein, Anderson, and Link, "A Reappraisal," pp. 588–89.

12. Arthur S. Link, *Wilson: The Road to the White House* (Princeton, N.J.: Princeton University Press. 1947), p. 2.

13. Baker, *Life and Letters*, vol. 1, pp. 36–37.

14. George and George, *Woodrow Wilson and Colonel House*, p. 7; and Arthur S. Link, "The Case for Woodrow Wilson," *Harper's Magazine* 234 (April 1967): 91. In anticipation of the argument that Wilson did poorly because his schooling was disrupted in consequence of the disrupted times, let us point out that "Tommy was *conspicuously* poor student compared to his peers. According to Baker, "Tommy" Wilson's school work was decidedly below average" and his teacher complained to Dr. Joseph Wilson that "Tommy" was at the foot of his class not for want of ability but because he would not study (Baker, *Life and Letters*, vol. 1, p. 42; also the Papers of Ray Stannard Baker, Series IB, Box 3, "Memo for the Augusta Period," Library of Congress, Washington, D.C., p. 10). Link had referred to Wilson as a "late starter" in *Woodrow Wilson: A Brief Biography* (Cleveland, Ohio: World Publishing Co., 1963), p. 18.

15. Link, *A Profile*, pp. xiv–xv.

16. Weinstein, Anderson, and Link, "A Reappraisal," p. 588.

17. Michael Rutter, "Prevalence and Types of Dyslexia," in *Dyslexia: An Appraisal of Current Knowledge*, eds. A. L. Benton and D. Pearl (New York: Oxford University Press, 1978), pp. 5, 24. The chapters in this book were written for the National Institute of Mental Health conference.

18. Ibid., p. 9; John R. Hughes, "Electroencephalographic and Neurophysiological Studies in Dyslexia," p. 234 and O. Spreen, "The Dyslexias: A Discussion of Neurobehavioral Research," pp. 178–79, both in *Dyslexia*, Benton and Pearl; also see Leon Eisenberg, "Psychiatric Aspects of Language Disability," in *Reading Perception and Language: Papers from the World Congress of Dyslexia*, eds. D. D. Duane and M. B. Rawson (Baltimore, Md: York Press, 1975), p. 225.

19. Rutter, "Prevalence and Types of Dyslexia," p. 24.

20. Weinstein, Anderson, and Link, "A Reappraisal," p. 588.

21. Wilson to Ellen Axson, 8 November 1884, *Papers of Woodrow Wilson*, vol. 3, p. 415.

22. Wilson to Ellen Axson, 20 January 1885, ibid., p. 623; 13 February 1885, ibid., vol. 4, pp. 244–45.

23. Wilson to Heath Dabney, 14 February 1885, ibid., vol. 4, pp. 248–49.

24. Wilson to Ellen Axson, 19 February 1885, ibid., p. 269.

25. See ibid., vol. 1, pp. 83–128, and 132 ff. for a still earlier diary and "Commonplace Book" in which Wilson recorded his enjoyment of reading. See also Wilson to his sister, Annie Howe, on 19 April 1876 in which he reports "employing most of the last week in reading" and finding "a great deal of enjoyment" in it (ibid., p. 128).

26. See ibid., vol. 13, pp. 267–97.

27. Weinstein, Anderson, and Link, "A Reappraisal," p. 588.

28. "Material on Woodrow Wilson Prepared by Dr. Stockton Axson with Occasional Assistance of Admiral Cary T. Grayson," a memoir owned personally by Professor Link. See chapter entitled "Health and Recreations," p. 15. We wish to thank Professor Link for granting us access to this manuscript.

29. Wilson to Dr. Azel W. Hazen, 29 March 1897, *Papers of Woodrow Wilson*, vol. 10, p. 201. Wilson to Ellen Axson Wilson, 17, 21, and 23 June 1896, and 3 July, 18 August 1896, ibid., vol. 9, pp. 519, 523, 527, 532, 573. Also see Wilson to Ellen Axson Wilson, 29 June 1908, ibid., vol. 18, p. 345.

30. Macdonald Critchley, *The Dyslexic Child* (Springfield, Ill.: Charles C. Thomas, Publisher.

31. Eisenberg, "Psychiatric Aspects of Language Disability," p. 220. See also D. Duane, "Summary of the World Congress on Dyslexia," in *Reading, Perception and Language*, Duane and Rawson, p. 5; and Critchley, *The Dyslexic Child*, p. 97.

32. Weinstein, Anderson, and Link, "A Reappraisal," pp. 588–89.

33. "Memorandum of Interviews with Dr. Cary T. Grayson on February 18, 19, 1926 at Washington," Papers of Ray Standard Baker, Box 109.

34. Weinstein, Anderson, and Link. "A Reappraisal," p. 587. Space limitations preclude further discussion of Wilson's childhood and relationship with his father. For relevant data, See George and George, *Woodrow Wilson and Colonel House*, pp. 6–13, 31–32, 271–72; see also George and George. *"Woodrow Wilson and Colonel House: A Reply to Weinstein, Anderson and Link"* (Paper delivered at the 1981 meeting of the International Society of Political Psychology, Mannheim, Germany, June 1981), pp. 10–78. We hope to publish elsewhere a fuller account, made possible by the data now available, about Wilson's father as his relentlessly driving (as well as wonderfully incisive) critic; and of Wilson's longing to do—as he put it—"immortal work," work of such noble service to humanity that to further it he felt morally justified to indulge his aggressions against those who stood in his way in that sphere of authority in which he sought compensatory gratifications.

One interesting vein of data—a good deal of which Professor Link, unfortunately, has omitted from *The Papers of Woodrow Wilson*—is contained in letters to Wilson from his parents about their difficulties in raising Wilson's much younger brother Joseph R. Wilson, Jr. ("Josie"), ten years Wilson's junior. Dr. and Mrs. Wilson complain to the now studious and increasingly successful "Woodrow" that "Josie" is "lazy"—even as Wilson himself, as a boy, had been made to feel. They disparage "Josie's" nascent competences, express concern about his lack of will to study, seek Wilson's advice about what to "do" about the hapless boy (as, when Wilson was a lad, his father had conferred with the family's distinguished elders about what to "do" about *his* poor performance in school). They poke fun at "Josie," squelch his wish to play, disparage his popularity with his fellows, express surprise and amusement at his accomplishments. In short, years after publication of our book, further documentation has emerged of a parental style that includes the seriously ego-damaging characteristics which we—on the basis of practically no evidence, according to Weinstein, Anderson, and Link, were able to describe in *Woodrow Wilson and Colonel House.*

35. "Material on Woodrow Wilson Prepared by Dr. Stockton Axson," chapter entitled "Woodrow Wilson and His Father," pp. 5, 8, 15–16; chapter entitled "Dr. Joseph R. Wilson," pp. 1, 2, 9. 12–13; chapter entitled "The Personality of Woodrow Wilson," Part II, p. 24; and untitled chapter, pp. 4–5.

36. George and George, *Woodrow Wilson and Colonel House,* pp. 3, 12–13.

37. Weinstein, Anderson, and Link, "A Reappraisal," p. 592 (emphasis added).

38. Wilson to Ellen Axson, 7 December 1884, *Papers of Woodrow Wilson,* vol. 3, p. 522 (emphasis added).

39. See in ibid. Wilson to Ellen Axson (Wilson), 17 February 1885 (vol. 4, p. 263), 13 March 1892 (vol. 7, p. 483), 20 July 1908 (vol. 18, p.. 372), 9 August 1902 (vol. 14, p. 68), 23 February 1900 (vol. 11, p. 436), 28 January 1895 (vol. 9, p. 137), 20 March 1885 (vol. 4, p. 389), and 29 August 1902 (vol. 14, p. 118).

40. See also Alexander L. George, "Power as a Compensatory Value for Political Leaders," *Journal of Social Issues* 24 (July 1968): 29–49.

41. Weinstein, Anderson, and Link, "A Reappraisal," pp. 587, 594. It is useful throughout this discussion to bear in mind Dr. Weinstein's criteria for accepting impaired brain function as an etiological or causal agent in political behavior. He stated them in his article, "Woodrow Wilson's Neurological Illness," *Journal of American History* 57 (1970), as follows: "First, the appearance of clinical evidence of brain damage should coincide with behavioral change. Second, the behavioral change should involve some impairment in performance. Third, it should be possible to classify actions in the political field into behavioral syndromes known to be associated with certain types of brain damage" (p. 325).

42. See Henry Cabot Lodge, *The Senate and the League of Nations* (New York: Charles Scribner's Sons, 1925). Wilson, Lodge wrote, "was simply an element to be calmly and coolly considered in a great problem of international politics" (p. 226). It was "of vital moment to me" to make "a correct analysis of Mr. Wilson's probable attitude" (p. 219; see also pp. 212–13). Lodge's insight was based upon years of hostile but astute observation stretching back to the beginning of Wilson's administration—a period during which, if we understand Weinstein, Anderson, and Link correctly, they believe Wilson to have been relatively free of manifestations of the brain damage from which they say he suffered.

43. Link, *The Road to the White House,* p. 90.

44. Ibid., pp. 76, 78.

45. Ibid., pp. vii–ix.

46. Weinstein, Anderson, and Link, "A Reappraisal," p. 596, n. 30.

47. Weinstein, "Woodrow Wilson's Neurological Illness," pp. 341–42.

48. Weinstein, Anderson, and Link, "A Reappraisal," p. 594, n. 26. We wished to include as part of the data we were assembling for independent medical review the "new evidence" that led Dr. Weinstein to abandon his "stroke" diagnosis. For over a year and a half, however, we were unable to gain access to it. Both Professor Link and Dr. Weinstein stated in reply to our several requests that they were bound by a promise to confidentiality not to reveal it. We were especially interested to know how the new evidence related to Dr. Weinstein's current diagnosis of "virus encephalopathy," upon which the hypothesis that Wilson sustained brain damage in Paris must now rest. We therefore wrote Dr. Weinstein and asked whether the new evidence proved or suggested the diagnosis of virus encephalopathy. In a letter dated 12, September 1979, he replied that the confidential data did not go beyond confirming the diagnosis of influenza.

On 22 October 1980, Professor Link wrote to us that he had been released from the pledge of confidentiality and he granted us access to the diary of Dr. Cary T. Grayson, Wilson's physician throughout his presidency. We thank him for this courtesy.

49. Weinstein, Anderson, and Link make repeated references to physiologically induced behavior and personality changes in Wilson without delineating the characteristic behavior patterns, the underlying personality, upon which the alleged changes impinged. Changes, after all, are comprehensible only in terms of that which preexists. Did the postulated brain damage accentuate certain aspects of a well-established behavior system or did it, in these authors' view, cause quite alien behavior to become manifest?

50. Papers of Irwin Hoover, Box 2, Library of Congress.

51. Diary of Cary T. Grayson, 5 April 1919, Gilbert Close to Arthur Walworth, 7, May 1951, Papers of Arthur Walworth, Yale University Library, New Haven, Conn.

52. Memoranda nos. 29, 32, 47 from Secretary of the American Commission to Negotiate Peace to members of the commission and their staffs, Papers of Tasker H. Bliss, Container 286, Library of Congress; Diary of Cary T. Grayson, 8 April 1919; Diary of Edith Benham Helm, 29 March 1919, Library of Congress; Diary of Edward M. House, 7 January 1919, Yale University Library.

53. Weinstein, Anderson, and Link, "A Reappraisal," p. 596.

54. Alexander L. George and Juliette L. George to Edwin A. Weinstein, M.D., 19 July 1979 and his reply 12 September 1979. Dr. Weinstein cited Baker, Mrs. Wilson, Stockton Axson, and Moses Taylor Pyne. In a subsequent letter (3 October 1979), Dr. Weinstein said he had no other sources.

55. This included the diary of Dr. Cary T. Grayson as well as our

correspondence with both Professor Link and Dr. Weinstein concerning the data upon which they relied for the preparation of their article and, most particularly, for Dr. Weinstein's diagnoses of Wilson's illnesses in 1906 and in Paris in April 1919. Professor Link informed us (letter dated 1 March 1979) that he had no medical records concerning Wilson that have not already been published in the *Papers of Woodrow Wilson* or are not available in the Wilson papers at the Library of Congress.

56. See the Papers of Arthur Walworth, Yale University, for Dr. Monroe's comments and Dr. Weinstein's reaction to them.

57. See, for example, John Mulder, *Woodrow Wilson: The Years of Preparation* (Princeton, N.J.: Princeton University Press, 1978), pp. 143, 145, and 147 for unequivocal references to Wilson's "stroke" of 1896 and its supposed effect on his thinking: see also his account of Wilson's illness in 1906 in which the stroke hypothesis also appears (pp. 185–86). There are numerous other references to the effects of Wilson's alleged strokes on his thinking and behavior.

58. Edwin A. Weinstein, *Woodrow Wilson: A Medical and Psychological Biography* (Princeton, N.J.: Princeton University Press, 1981), pp. 165–167. See also Ellen Axson Wilson to Mary Hoyt, 12 June [1906], *Papers of Woodrow Wilson*, vol. 16, p. 423; Wilson to Nicholas Murray Butler, 1 June 1906, ibid., p. 413; "Memorandum of Interviews with Grayson," Papers of Ray Stannard Baker, Box 109, p. 3; ibid., Box 5, Notebook XXII, pp. 56–57; Cary T. Grayson, *Woodrow Wilson: An Intimate Memoir* (New York: Holt, Rinehart and Winston, 1960 and 1977), p. 81; Stockton Axson, "Material on Woodrow Wilson," chapter entitled "Health and Recreations," p. 23, and chapter entitled "The Physical Man," p. 10. In the Papers of Ray Stannard Baker, see conversation with John Grier Hibben, 18 June 1925, Box 111; conversation with E. P. Davis, M.D., 12 November 1925, Box 106; E. P. Davis, "Memoranda Concerning Woodrow Wilson"; and Gilbert Close to Ray Stannard Baker, 26 September 1925, Box 103. See also Eleanor Wilson McAdoo, *The Priceless Gift* (New York: McGraw-Hill Book Company, 1962), p. 241. It is interesting to note that Weinstein himself, in his article "Woodrow Wilson's Neurological Illness," stated: "De Schweinitz found that the blindness had been caused by the bursting of a blood vessel in the eye" (p. 334). De Schweinitz's finding of a burst blood vessel is also reported in a footnote in *The Papers of Woodrow Wilson*, vol. 16, p. 412, n.1.

59. See Michael F. Marmor, MD, "Wilson, Strokes, and Zebras," *New England Journal of Medicine* 307:528–565 (26 August 1982); Michael F. Marmor, "A Bad Case of History," *The Sciences* 22:36–38 (January–February 1983); Juliette L. George, Michael F. Marmor, and Alexander L. George, "Issues in Wilson Scholarship: References to Early 'Strokes' in the *Papers of Woodrow Wilson*," *Journal of American History* 70:845–853 (March 1984); Arthur S. Link, David W. Hirst, John W. Davidson, and John E. Little, ibid., 945–956; Juliette L. George, Michael F. Marmor, and Alexander L. George, ibid., 71:198–212; Michael F. Marmor, "The Eyes of Woodrow Wilson," *Ophthalmology* 92:454–465 (March 1985).

Section IV

Recruitment and Selection of Political Leaders

Introductory Comment

Personality characteristics come into play in understanding the ambitions that people have to become political leaders. Harold D. Lasswell theorized that some people seek out political offices because they suffer from low self-esteem. These individuals, Lasswell thought, displace private motives—their low sense of self-worth—on public objects (e.g., political office) and rationalize doing so in terms of public interests (Lasswell 1930). He was convinced that ambition for power is rooted in personality. The Georges analyze Woodrow Wilson's yearning for leadership positions in these compensatory terms. But personality characteristics cannot explain everything. Scores of people plagued by low self-esteem do not seek public office, and most ambitious politicians show little sign of low esteem.

The recruitment and selection of political leaders is highly dependent upon the *opportunity structure*. Many people may yearn for public offices that simply are not available. For example, at a particular time only 535 people can serve as members of the U.S. Congress—435 representatives and 100 senators. The opportunity to capture congressional office depends on the raw number of seats available, but it also depends upon the term of the office and the turnover of incumbents.

One scholar estimated that in a political "generation" of twelve years there were about 611 chances to be one of the 435 members of the U.S. House (Schlesinger 1966, 41). The opportunity rate for service in the British House of Commons is lower, largely because of the longer term of MPs. But the actual odds of attaining a legislative seat are higher in Britain on a per capita basis than in the United States because Britain's population is much smaller (Loewenberg and Patterson 1979, 84–86).

Embedded in the structure of opportunity for parliamentary seats, cabinet posts, party officialdom, and other public offices are a variety of channels, or *pathways*, to these offices. These pathways reflect characteristic career patterns in which one office leads to another, which in turn leads to another. In some political systems, pathways to high political offices are very well established and well worn. In Britain, for instance, prime ministers and their cabinets are drawn overwhelmingly from the membership of the House of Commons. In the United States, national political leaders often have served an apprenticeship as state governor or state legislator.

Recruitment pathways can vary substantially between political parties, and they may differ in the extent to which the selection of candidates rests in the hands of the national or constituency party. One scholar found pathways to parliament in Britain much more influenced by the constituency party organizations, and much less affected by the national parties, than had been assumed conventionally (Ranney 1965). By the same token, the recruitment of cabinet officers in democratic societies exhibits a variety of distinctive "roads to power." For cabinet ministers, one pathway to leadership travels through the political party structure, in which individuals work their way up the party hierarchy. Another pathway threads its way through the system of parliamentary committees. Yet another channel runs through the civil service producing what one scholar calls, for France, "mandarin ascent" (Dogan 1989).

Educational institutions may have a crucial role in channeling individuals to power, especially to high political offices. For example, the Oxford and Cambridge universities in Britain, the *grandes ecoles* in France, or even the Ivy League universities in the United States provide a disproportionate share of their nation's political leadership (Guttsman 1965; Suleiman 1978).

Only the properly qualified may travel very far along these pathways to political leadership. In every country there are laws and rules regulating eligibility for public office. Accordingly, *qualification* is a vital feature of leadership recruitment. In the United States a person must be at least twenty-five years old to serve in the House of Representatives and thirty-five years old to be president. Other countries have some age requirement for eligibility to serve in parliament. Similarly, citizenship is often a basic qualification. In Eastern Europe and the Soviet Union, membership of the Communist party was often a required qualification for top leadership. Only peers of the realm may sit in the British House of Lords. Members of the German upper house, the Bundesrat, must be state government officials.

Skill and experience are important qualifications for political leadership, and these are often determined more or less automatically. Entry into the civil service in Western democracies is typically meritocratic and involves competitive examination, with appointments to office automatically going to those with the highest scores. Perhaps a more pervasive automatic qualifier is that of *seniority*, by which top posts go to those with the longest service and greatest experience.

Qualification for political leadership may be derived from particular occupational experiences. This may, of course, develop in the office experiences—local or other subnational public or party offices— that leaders accumulate as they go up the political ladder. But some private occupations lend themselves better than others to political careers. In Western democracies, legal training and experience often provide the credentials needed for leadership ascent, reflecting particularly valued skills. In many countries lawyers are greatly overrepresented in political leadership groups, and this is nowhere better illustrated than by the United States, where large proportions of legislators and top civil servants, and almost all judges, are lawyers. So central have lawyers been to leadership recruitment in the United States that it has been possible to speak of a "convergence" between the legal profession and politics as a vocation (Eulau and Sprague 1964).

Although some groups, like lawyers, are immensely overrepresented among political leaders, others are dramatically underrepresented. Notably, manual workers, or working-class people, are seldom present in any numbers in the leadership; even Communist parties in Western democracies tend to be led by people from middle-class backgrounds. In the United States, where a significant socialist party does not exist, working-class people are less apparent in the leadership than in European countries. Similarly, political leadership everywhere tends to be male dominated. Although women are better represented in the leadership corps of some countries than in others, and some like Prime Minister Margaret Thatcher in Britain reach top leadership, generally women are underrepresented.

Political leadership positions are attained by active mechanisms of recruitment and selection and not merely the inexorable forces of opportunity structure, pathways to power, and credentialization. In every democratic society, individuals are recruited for candidacies and actively selected for offices. In the United States, with its loosely organized party system, candidates can be "self-starters," launching their own candidacies. But even in the United States a considerable proportion of candidate recruitment is carried on by party organizations and leaders who ferret out promising contenders, endorse primary contestants, develop slates of candidates, and make nominations in caucuses and conventions (Crotty 1986).

Active recruitment of political leaders is so pervasive and important that the term *selectorates* is used to identify individuals, groups, or organizations having a central role in selecting political leaders. Selectorates may be large or small, unified or diverse. In the United States political leaders are selected in a highly diversified fashion, involving multiple levels of leadership and a wide variety of actors. In other democratic societies political leaders are selected in a more centralized and homogeneous way, as in parliamentary democracies where prime ministers are chosen by the senior members of their own party in parliament in "the secret garden of politics" (Gallagher and Marsh 1988).

In the readings in this section, we illustrate some of the most important features of recruitment and selection. In the first reading, Martin Burch and Michael Moran examine changes in the composition of the British parliament and cabinet over a period of nearly four decades. Their analysis underscores important differences between the Conservative and Labour parties. They show the changing impact of elite university education on the recruitment of Conservative politicians. And they illustrate the interesting tendency of Labour MPs to be recruited from middle-class, rather than working class, backgrounds, a process known as *embourgeoisement* to denote a tendency for a group to have become more bourgeois.

In the second reading Pippa Norris charts the extent to which women have been recruited to the political leaderships of Western democratic societies. She demonstrates the wide variation across democracies in the representation of women in parliaments. And she shows that among various factors influencing the recruitment of women to parliaments by far the most important is the electoral rules: proportional representation as it is widely practiced by continental Europeans produces more women in leadership than the single member district, plurality vote systems so familiar to Anglo-Americans.

Finally, in the third reading, presidential and prime ministerial selection is analyzed by Hugh Heclo. He explains how the British system of leadership recruitment tends to stress "apprenticeship," while U.S. leadership selection is more "entrepreneurial." Accordingly, prime ministers may be recruited in such a way as to emphasize the requirements of governing, while presidential recruitment may overemphasize running for office at the expense of skill in governing. At the same time, Heclo's analysis suggests ways in which prime ministerial selection may in some ways become "presidentialized."

Select Bibliography

Aberbach, J. K., R. D. Putnam, and B. A. Rockman. 1981. *Bureaucrats and Politicians in Western Democracies.* Cambridge: Harvard University Press.

Blondel, J. 1980. *World Leaders: Heads of Government in the Postware Period.* Beverly Hills, CA: Sage.

Darcy, R., S. Welch, and J. Clark. 1987. *Women, Elections, and Representation.* New York: Longman.

Dogan, Mattei, ed. 1989. *Pathways to Power: Selecting Rulers in Pluralist Democracies.* Boulder, CO: Westview Press.

Eulau, H., and M. M. Czudnowski, eds. 1976. *Elite Recruitment in Democratic Polities.* Beverly Hills, CA: Sage.

Gallagher, M., and M. Marsh, eds. 1988. *Candidate Selection in Comparative Perspective.* Beverly Hills, CA: Sage.

Schlesinger, J. A. 1966. *Ambition and Politics: Political Careers in the United States.* Chicago, IL.: Rand McNally.

6

The Changing British Political Elite

Martin Burch and Michael Moran

T he recruitment of political leadership in Britain has been marked by contradictory forces. On the one hand, powerful democratic influences have long been at work. As the first industrial nation, Britain developed large and confident middle and working classes who soon made their mark in the political arena. On the other hand, a tradition of deference, and a politically astute upper class, ensured that aristocratic influence persisted into the age of mass parties and a democratic franchise. Over twenty years ago Guttsman (1965) documented the glacially slow erosion of aristocratic prominence and the rise of "new men. Since then, examination of the social structure of the elite in Parliament and in Cabinet has been spasmodic (Johnson 1973)." In the meantime, great social and political changes have taken place. The culture of deference has weakened. Determined efforts have been made to promote upward social mobility. Economic growth has created mass affluence and, until recently, full employment. It is now exactly forty years—the conventional span of a generation—since the passage of the 1944 Education Act, a measure designed to promote social mobility and equality of opportu-

"The Changing British Political Elite, 1945–1983: MPs and Cabinet Ministers," *Parliamentary Affairs*, 38 (Winter 1985): 1–15. Copyright © by Oxford University Press. Reprinted by permission of Oxford University Press.

nity. This is therefore a fitting moment to examine how far the slow broadening of the elite documented by Guttsman has continued or how far, alternatively, social changes and policy reforms have produced more radical developments.

Our examination is confined to MPs and Cabinet ministers. Of course political elites transcend these two groups, but Parliaments and Cabinets undoubtedly contain important segments of elites. What is more, since we possess evidence about the social profile of the parliamentary leadership going back to the beginning of the century, a study of this group in the 1980s allows us to examine long-term changes in that profile.

The study of the social origins, education and career patterns of political elites is part of the classical tradition of political sociology. In the last decade, however, such studies have fallen widely out of favour. The reasons are encapsulated in three particularly damaging criticisms. First, it has been pointed out that there rarely exist any well-thought-out theoretical justifications for studying elite backgrounds. Second, it has been shown that it is quite wrong to assume the existence of any simple correlation between elite ideology and social origins—by assuming, for instance, that those risen from the working class are especially likely to support left-wing ideologies. Finally, it has been observed that the majority of social background studies usually only investigate a narrow range of variables, typically concerning education and occupation. The choice of variables is, moreover, often dictated by what is conventionally included in standard directories like *Who's Who* rather than by any reasoned criteria of relevance.

These powerful arguments have punctured the inflated intellectual pretensions of elite studies. They should not, however, be allowed totally to displace investigations of elite backgrounds which, once their limitations are recognised, can helpfully illuminate important aspects of leadership recruitment. Studies of the backgrounds of successive leadership cohorts are especially revealing. To hold political office is to have access to valued social goods, just as surely as property ownership confers valued social goods on the wealthy. The "goods" of political office include status, a measure of fame, the opportunity to exercise power and, often, a substantial income. Studies of the changing composition of leadership groups give us some sense of how these valued social goods are being distributed, in exactly the same way as studies of successive generations of millionaires reveal the relative importance of inheritance and achievement in the distribution of wealth.

Of course, longitudinal studies of successive generations can only be carried out at the price of relying heavily on material drawn from standard directories. This makes the available evidence limited and imperfect. The alternative to this limited and imperfect evidence is, however, often no evidence at all. The standard techniques used to gather information about the population at large—such as social surveys and census returns—are rarely appropriate when studying contemporary elites, and are even less rarely appropriate in longitudinal studies, when many of the subjects are dead. The evidence from directories is second best, but it is a good deal more revealing than no evidence at all.

Directory entries for elites in Britain provide one particular item of information which has been widely used, and wisely criticised. Just under five per cent of Britons are educated at public (i.e. private) schools, most of whose pupils pay sizable fees. The proportion of a particular cohort educated at such schools is commonly taken as a measure of how far members of the cohort have privileged social origins. The validity of this measure is known to be suspect. Classification of an institution as a public school usually depends on membership of the "Headmasters' Conference," the representative association for fee-paying schools; but members of the Conference range from the most socially exclusive institutions, like Eton, to modest schools drawing day-pupils from the local community. Even for fee-paying pupils, attendance at an HMC school is therefore an imperfect measure of privileged origins, while a minority of public school pupils are scholarship-holders, exempted in whole or part from payment of fees. A public school education is thus not an infallible sign of a materially privileged background.

These facts do not, however, destroy the usefulness of evidence about education; they only mean that it must be used with care. The comparatively indiscriminate category of "public school" can be refined by examining the representation of particular sub-groups, such as those from the elite schools like Eton and Harrow. Nor should the significance of scholarship pupils from humble backgrounds be overstated: survey evidence has shown only one in every thousand in a public school to be the child of an unskilled manual worker (Noble 1975). The study of elite origins and education, while fraught with difficulties, is therefore not redundant. Indeed, in both academic enquiry and in everyday argument about British politics assumptions and assertions are constantly made about how elites are recruited. This study is a partial test of the accuracy of such assumptions and assertions. Before we turn to the evidence, however, it is necessary to sketch the two most influential views of how elites are recruited.

Two very different interpretations of the changing shape of elite recruitment have dominated post-war discussions of the subject in Britain. The first, most commonly voiced by left-wing radicals and by some social scientists, is usually labelled "closure" theory (Heath 1981). This asserts that, whatever the opportunities for upward social mobility in society at large, at the very top powerful social mechanisms close off access to elite positions, reserving leadership posts for a small minority disproportionately drawn from families of those already enjoying privilege. On this view, elites in Britain are largely self-recruiting. Little impact is to be expected from social change or policy reform.

By contrast, the official ideology of some of the most powerful institutions in Britain denies the existence of "closure." On this second view, elite recruitment has become increasingly meritocratic. Consequently, access to elite positions is open to individuals of ability from a wide range of social backgrounds. There also exists a less optimistic interpretation of the working of meritocracy, best called the "convergence" view (Johnson 1973). According to this account, the increasing emphasis on meritocratic criteria is making the parliamentary leaderships of both major parties more alike. Politics is being dominated by individuals who are 'professionals' in a double sense: in the sense that they have a life-long commitment to a specialist career in politics; and in the sense that they are drawn from the professional middle classes, and have acquired the conventional marks of merit by success in formal education. In the process of convergence, social groups at the extremes are being excluded from leadership: those of aristocratic backgrounds are being squeezed out of the Conservative Party, those of working class background from the top of the Labour Party.

We now turn to the evidence. As we shall show, the complex evolution during the post-war years of that crucial part of the political elite represented by MPs and Cabinet ministers does not fit any single interpretation.

Members of Parliament

Evidence about the characteristics of Labour and Conservative MPs, 1945–83 [will be presented]. (We have ignored the other small parties.) For the period up to October 1974 we draw on data produced by Mellors (1978), and for the 1979 and 1983 Parliaments we use material extracted from a number of standard directories. Since Mellors exhaustively examines the 1945–74 period, we focus chiefly on the last decade, using his evidence to provide a standard by which to measure the extent of recent change. . . .

We use data on educational background and a variety of selected social characteristics for all MPs, but in the case of the Conservative Party we have made only limited use of information on occupational background. This is because past figures and presently available data on occupation are unreliable. Many MPs claim a multiplicity of previous employments without indicating which might be primary. Uncertainty also surrounds the definition of a "professional" occupation. These problems make occupational statistics slippery and uncertain. Even in the case of the Labour Party, where the evidence is more straightforward, they have to be used with caution.

The Conservative Party

Between 1945 and October 1974 the Conservative benches were remarkably stable in their social composition. The most striking sign of stability was revealed by the extent to which Conservative MPs were predominantly drawn from public school and, to a slightly lesser extent, Oxford and Cambridge (shorthand: Oxbridge). . . . In percentage terms, the public school element remained in the mid to upper seventies for most of the period, while Oxbridge graduates ranged between 50% and 57% of all MPs. There is also evidence of a marginal increase in the public school and Oxbridge proportions in the years the party lost elections—especially 1964, 1966 and February 1974—suggesting that MPs from these backgrounds tended to be concentrated in its safer seats.

Beneath this persistent pattern of public school/Oxbridge domination, some marginal changes were nevertheless taking place. There was a slight drop in the number of old Etonians, a trend clearest among new MPs from 1966 onwards. This perhaps also indicated a decline in the aristocratic element within the party. It was paralleled by a small but fairly consistent rise in the proportion of MPs who had been educated at state secondary schools *and* non-Oxbridge universities: the figure rose from 6% of all Conservative MPs in 1950 to nearly 12% in October 1974. Apart from these changes, the most notable alteration lay in the more or less persistent rise in the number of MPs with local government experience, from just over 14% in 1945 to 31% in October 1974. This change is evidently linked to the rise of "career" politicians in the party recently documented by King (1981).

Throughout the 29 years following the Second World War Conservative MPs thus conformed to a narrow and exclusive pattern of recruitment based on public schools and Oxbridge. The 1979 and 1983 figures, however, show a decisive change from this established pattern. With hindsight, we can now see that some of the changes were germinating as long ago as 1970.

Five main alterations [occur]. First, there is a decrease in MPs drawn from an Oxbridge background. In 1979 the overall total for Oxbridge fell below 50% for the first time since 1945, while in 1983 fully 54% of all Conservative MPs were non-Oxbridge. Second, there is a decline in public school recruitment, resulting in a drop to 64% of all MPs in 1983. The full measure of this change is more clearly revealed by figures for new MPs: among this group the public school intake fell to just over 53% in 1979 and to 47% in 1983. [There was also] a substantial fall in new Conservatives with a public school *and* Oxbridge background, to one quarter of those newly elected in 1983. The third change is an increase in those MPs who were both educated at state secondary schools and who took their first degrees at non-Oxbridge universities: among the new intake in 1983 these were more numerous than those with a traditional "patrician" public school/Oxbridge background. A fourth change is the continued decline in the number of Old Etonians, to an all-time low in 1983 of just over 12% of all Conservative MPs and 6% of the new recruits. A fifth and final change—in some ways the obverse of Eton's decline—is the rise, especially amongst new MPs, of those with only elementary and secondary education.

These five changes, of which the first three are the most important, suggest that in terms of educational background the Conservative Party has become more open and less exclusive in its sources of recruitment. The significance of these developments lies in the way they break with a stable pattern maintained throughout the post-war period until 1970 and only marginally altered between then and the end of the decade.

Some features of the 1979 and 1983 intakes nevertheless marked a continued process of evolution rather than a break with the past. The rise in the numbers of MPs with local government experience continued, reaching 38% of all Conservative MPs in 1983 and over half of those newly elected in that year. The trend toward younger newly elected Conservative MPs has also continued: only 46% were over forty years old in 1983, whereas over 60% were over forty in 1966.

Of course it may be that the changes in Conservative recruitment described here reflect the size of recent Conservative victories, especially in 1983. It is possible that the traditional pattern of recruitment still continues in safe seats. To test this proposition we compare . . . some key educational characteristics of four groups: all new MPs returned, those returned for seats other than the most marginal (a majority of 5% plus), those from seats fulfilling a modest criterion of safety (a majority of 10% plus) and those from very safe seats (15% plus majorities). If the changes in the whole group of new MPs described earlier is merely the result of the Conservatives' huge majority, we ought to find that the less marginal the seat, the more "traditional" the educational background of the new MP. This is plainly not so. The most instructive figures . . . cover MPs in safe Conservative seats. The 32 MPs in this category have virtually invulnerable majorities. It used to be the case that such seats were dominated by well-connected patricians who were able to use the security of a safe constituency to build careers on the front benches. This is no longer the case: this group contains exactly the same proportion of public school/Oxbridge products as among MPs as a whole, while the proportions of Old

Etonians and public school products are almost identical in the two groups. If anything, new MPs in the safest seats have by one measure more modest backgrounds than do new members as a whole, because a markedly higher proportion have only the barest minimum (elementary-/secondary) of state education.

In summary, we have identified a marked shift in the social character of the Conservative Party in Parliament. This shift, moreover, is not a product of the possibly transitory Conservative majority in 1983; it reflects deeper and more enduring developments in the party.

The Labour Party

The most important change in the social composition of Labour Members during the three decades after 1945 is well documented, notably by Mellors (1978). It consisted in the decline in the proportion of manual workers from just over a quarter (in 1945) to less than an eighth in 1974. . . . This went with a fall in the proportion of MPs who had only elementary and secondary education, to less than half the 1945 level, and a marked increase in the proportion of university-educated MPs. At the same time there was a fairly steady, though less substantial, rise in the proportion drawn from Oxbridge, while the proportion of MPs educated at state secondary school and non-Oxbridge universities more than doubled. There also occurred a persistent rise in the proportion of MPs drawn from the professions, notably from teaching and lecturing.

Labour maintained a fairly steady representation of MPs with local government experience, ranging from a low of 39% in 1959 to a high of just over 46% in February 1974. These developments are further confirmed [for] new intakes, but here trends are less obvious than in the case of the Conservatives. There is some evidence of a falling-off of new MPs drawn from the professions (especially teaching) in February 1974, only to be followed in October 1974 by a reassertion of professional recruitment. Overall, the picture that emerges is of a party gradually shaking off its working-class roots and developing a more formally educated and professionally employed personnel. The Parliamentary Labour Party became increasingly white collar and university educated and more solidly middle class.

The data for 1979 and 1983 suggest a marginal alteration in this pattern. The figures are, however, open to a variety of interpretations, especially because in these two elections the numbers of Labour MPs reached their lowest level since 1935. The figures for all Labour MPs . . . show a rise in the proportion of manual workers within the parliamentary party and, especially in 1983, a clear fall in the Oxbridge and public school contingents. These developments may indicate a return to the party's immediate post-war state, a view which finds some support in the data on new MPs. . . . Here a word of caution is necessary. In both instances the number of new MPs is very small, at 40 and 34 respectively, so generalisations are difficult. Moreover, as we shall see, in some cases the data on 1979 and 1982 are contradictory.

With this caution in mind, we may note amongst new Labour MPs a marked decrease in the Oxbridge and teacher/lecturer proportions, as well as an increase in the number of manual worker recruits to a level (20%) closer to the pattern up to 1964. There is also a clear rise in the proportion with local government experience, to an all time high of over 64% in 1983. The other figures are less certain, with those with elementary and secondary education only rising to 40% in 1979 then falling back to half that in 1983. There is also a large drop in state secondary non-Oxbridge university recruits in 1983, a fall in public school *and* Oxbridge Members in 1979, and a marked decline in those with professional occupations in 1983. But none of these developments are confirmed over both election intakes.

Overall, the figures for the Labour Party are less clear-cut than are those for the Conservatives. The trend toward an increasingly middle-class, white-collar, professional party does, however, appear to have slowed down in 1979 and by 1983 may even have been reversed. The truth is that it is too early to be certain.

Cabinets

Few people serve in Cabinets: since 1955 only 77 individuals have been Conservative Cabinet ministers, while the total for the Labour Party is only 56. Detailed analysis of such small groups is plainly difficult. Although we will glance at the characteristics of new Cabinet entrants since 1970, most of our discussion focuses on Cabinet membership over the last three decades. Guttsman's (1965) earlier work provides an analysis of selected social and educational characteristics of all Cabinet members for the period 1916–1955. This data . . . provides a set of benchmarks for measuring long-term changes in the characteristics of individuals recruited to Cabinets.

Conservative Cabinets

The most striking social feature of the modern Conservative leadership is, of course, the fact that the two most recent Conservative Prime Ministers have been grammar school/Oxford educated meritocrats of modest social origins. It is often said that Mr. Heath and Mrs. Thatcher are indicative of a more general rise of lower-middle-class meritocrats in the party, and indeed we found some support for this view when examining MPs.

. . . The accuracy of this belief [can be tested] as it applies to the very top positions. The figures show that, while important long-term social change is indeed happening, the characteristics of the two most recent leaders are not an accurate guide to either the scale or the direction of that wider change. There has been no remarkable advance in Conservative Cabinets by state school educated meritocrats. On the contrary, products of the public schools were actually more common in 1955–84 than in 1916–55. Nor is there any sign of a significant advance by self-made men from the humblest social backgrounds: the proportion of Cabinet ministers born to working-class families, and the proportion with only an elementary or secondary education, actually fell slightly in the 1955–84 period compared with the earlier decades. Neither the state school meritocrat nor the spectacularly self-made man have become more common. There has been one important social change, reflecting a trend already identified by Guttsman, a continuing decline in the proportions of Cabinet ministers drawn from the very highest ranks of society. [There are] two important signs of this development: the fall in the proportion of ministers with aristocratic backgrounds and the decline of the two most socially exclusive public schools, Eton and Harrow, as suppliers of Cabinet personnel.

The advantage of amalgamating all evidence for 1955–84 is that it provides numbers large enough to give some confidence when it comes to statistical analysis; the disadvantage is that it may conceal trends within the years in question. We have checked for this possibility by examining new entrants to Cabinet since 1970 (they number 34). In important respects this group shows no great change from the past: over 80% were public school educated and three quarters went to Oxbridge. However, the two changes already noted have persisted: aristocrats continue to fall (only 15% of post-1970 entrants have such backgrounds); and there has occurred a further sharp fall in the proportions of Etonians and Harrovians to 15%, whereas [in the period] 1916–1955 the two schools supplied nearly half of all Conservative Cabinet ministers.

Given the small numbers involved, it is not easy to assess the significance of these trends. One way of exploring the matter more deeply is to look beyond the Cabinet to more junior ranks in the present government. In Britain it is rare for individuals to attain Cabinet rank without serving in some more junior ministerial position, except when a party takes office after a long period in opposition. We looked at non-Cabinet members of the administration formed in June 1983 who were aged 45 or less on appointment, reasoning that it is this group which contains the brightest prospects for further advancement. The evidence suggests that not only is there no great social transformation in prospect, but that some of the social changes recorded in the Cabinet figures might well be partly reversed in the future. Of the 29 members of the government outside the Cabinet under the age of 45, over a third (10) are from aristocratic backgrounds; over 80% (24) are public school educated; and nearly a quarter (7) are Old Etonians. The only significant departure from past patterns is that only a little more than half (15) are Oxbridge educated.

The evidence for the Conservative Party may thus be summarised as follows. Long-term change in the social composition of the Conservative leadership is modest. Mr. Heath and Mrs. Thatcher are atypical, not signs of the rise of meritocrats from humble origins. Change has not, contrary to common belief, made the party leadership more socially diverse. Conservative Cabinets are in one important sense becoming more, not less, homogeneous. The party is not recruiting a larger proportion of humbly born meritocrats into its leadership, but there has been a marked drop in the representation of those drawn from the very apex of the social structure—as shown by the decline in aristocratic numbers and in those from the most prestigious public schools. Conservative Cabinets, far from becoming more socially diverse, have thus become more homogeneously middle-class.

Labour Cabinets

Analysing Labour Cabinets is difficult both because numbers are small and because Labour has not now supplied any Cabinet ministers since the late 1970s. In the meantime, the party has undergone significant changes in both ideology and organisation. It would be dangerous, therefore, to assume that past trends will simply be extrapolated into the future.

Past trends are nevertheless clear. . . . Labour Cabinets before 1955 were very different socially from those of their Conservative opponents: just over half of Labour Cabinet members had only the legal minimum of education; over a half had not been to university; barely more than a quarter had a public school education; and likewise only just over a quarter had been to Oxbridge. Most distinctive of all, 55% had been born the children of working-class parents.

It is commonly asserted that the subsequent history of Labour's parliamentary leadership has involved social embourgeoisement, the dominion of Labour Cabinets by middle-class cohorts increasingly resembling those on the Conservative side. The evidence only partly supports this assertion. It is true that if we compare the post-1955 period with the preceding forty years there is evidence of a growing middle-class contingent. Though Labour Cabinets have remained socially and educationally distinct from those formed by Conservative Prime Ministers, it is nevertheless the case that there has been a sharp rise in the proportion educated to university level, including a marked increase in the Oxbridge contingent. . . . These figures also reflect a changing balance in favour of those who have practised a middle-class profession, at the expense of those who were at some stage of their adult lives manual workers. There is even a discernible rise in the numbers educated at public schools. But these figures do not tell the whole story, for two reasons: they fail to reveal one significant way in which the elitism of Labour Cabinets has actually declined and they exaggerate the extent to which those of working-class backgrounds have been displaced. We deal with each of these points in turn.

. . . Early Labour Cabinets contained a significant sprinkling of aristocrats and—not an identical group—Etonians and Harrovians. This was partly due to a lack of faith in native working-class talent among Labour leaders like Ramsay MacDonald. This upper-class group has been in decline and by the 1970s had nearly reached a point of extinction. New entrants to Labour Cabinets after 1970 (admittedly only numbering 19) contained not a single product of Eton or Harrow nor a single aristocrat. The proportion of the 1970s entrants educated at a public school (at just over a fifth) was smaller even than in the period 1916–55.

One reason for the decline of the high-born is that the education system began to produce able meritocrats of modest social origins. This phenomenon also explains why the decline of working-class recruits in the upper reaches of the party is less sharp than is commonly believed.

. . When we follow Guttsman's original practice of identifying working-class background by parental occupation, the shift away from the working class, though marked, still leaves a sizable contigent of working-class origins. There is indeed evidence of some recent reversal even in the identifiable modest trend toward social embourgeoisement: of the 19 fresh Labour Cabinet entrants in 1974–79, eight were children of manual workers.

The most striking long term alteration at the top of the Labour Party is not so much in class composition as in mode of social ascent. In the period examined by Guttsman the majority of Labour Cabinet ministers experienced intra-generational social mobility: they entered adult life in the working class, and then rose out of it through a career in the Labour movement. In our period, a substantial number of Cabinet ministers were likewise born to the working class, but rose through education from the working class, capping this success with a political career.

The recruitment patterns in the Conservative and Labour Parties are different. The changes over time experienced in both parties have likewise differed. To this extent no single theoretical interpretation—

whether it consists of closure theory, or of the assertion that there is a process of convergence toward meritocrats selection—can make sense of what is happening at the top of British politics.

The nearest closure theory comes to reality is in the case of Conservative Cabinets. Though the decline of the old ruling class first documented by Guttsman has continued, the social mechanisms restricting the range of recruitment remain strong. Their strength is even greater than is suggested by mere statistics, such as those documenting public school dominance. The Conservative Party is undoubtedly meritocratic by aspiration: it would like to draw its leaders widely from many social groups in order to be led by the most able. The fact that recruitment outcomes defy these meritocratic aspirations argues for the existence of powerful, deeply-rooted mechanisms closing off the top of the Conservative Party to those not born to privilege.

Yet the party is plainly not immune to change. There is occurring a very slow 'flattening' of the social profile of Conservative Cabinets. Among the wider group of Conservative MPs, change in the post-war years has been even more pronounced. It has accelerated dramatically since the end of the 1970s and has revealed a marked decline in public school and Oxbridge dominance. There are two ways of interpreting the importance of these latter changes. They may token a significant shift in the pattern of recruitment at the top of the party. Cabinets, of course, generally reflect the social composition of a parliamentary party of a decade or more ago. In the next ten or fifteen years, therefore, it is possible that a future Conservative Cabinet will begin to reflect the social patterns evident among new MPs in recent years. Alternatively, the forces of closure may triumph. Cabinets are not a representative sample of the backbenches. The recruitment process may still favour those with advantaged social backgrounds, as it has so often done in the past. This would appear to be the case if we look at those younger, non-Cabinet ministers who are the most likely source of future Conservative Cabinet members, though admittedly very few of them were recruited to Parliament in 1979 and 1983.

If the more meritocratic pattern of recruitment amongst Conservative MPs continues, and if the exclusive pattern at the very top of the party remains, then the leadership will not only become increasingly unrepresentative of its parliamentary supporters but will also be forced to draw ministerial recruits from an ever-decreasing section of the parliamentary party. This would suggest that, if only as a consequence of the force of numbers, there must in time be some dilution in the establishment make-up of Conservative Cabinets. Only the next decade will tell whether this expectation is to be fulfilled.

The future pattern of recruitment at the top of the Labour Party is even less clear. Indeed, it is not at all certain whether Labour will continue to occupy a major place in British politics. If its electoral decline continues, then the social characteristics of the party's leaders will cease to be of much interest to anyone other than specialist scholars of the Labour movement.

It seemed until about a decade ago that Labour was succumbing to mechanisms of closure, with a formally meritocratic ideology producing a party dominated at the top by university-educated middle-class professionals. The notion that working-class recruits are being excluded from the top of the party now has to be modified. For the first time in half a century Labour has a leader of impeccable working class origins in Mr. Kinnock. This leader, furthermore, illustrates a facet of recruitment too easily neglected. As the university-educated son of a labourer, he typifies the extraordinary number of Labour MPs who are socially mobile, through education, out of the working class. Of all Labour members returned in 1979, for instance, over half were the children of manual workers; and while the same Parliament contained only 19 MPs who had worked as miners, it contained 35 more who were the children of miners. In short, even in the 1970s Labour provided a relatively open channel for those of working-class origins to enter the political elite. We have seen some signs that the party has also arrested the decline in numbers of MPs with adult experience as manual workers. The long-term significance of these developments nevertheless remains unclear. The great defeats of 1979 and 1983, together with their organisational and ideological consequences, plainly altered the party. Even more than in the case of the Conservatives, the future social shape of the Labour leadership in Parliament and Cabinet is not clear. The patterns of the past are reducible to no single theoretical stereotype; the patterns of the future are likely to be similarly complicated.

7

Electoral Systems and the Parliamentary Recruitment of Women

Pippa Norris

Comparative studies of political leadership confirm that, with notable exceptions like Margaret Thatcher, Benazir Bhutto, and Cory Aquino, the higher echelons of political power worldwide are dominated by men. This proposition has held up remarkably well no matter whether the country was conventionally classified as developed or underdeveloped, democratic or dictatorial, capitalist or communist. By the late 1980s, however, the universal validity of this generalization had become questionable. While there were still few women in the U.S. Congress, the Japanese Shugi-In, the Australian House of Representatives, and the British House of Commons, they had made significant breakthroughs in the Norwegian Storting, the New Zealand House of Representatives, the West German Bundestag, and the Dutch Tweede Kamer.

Why is this? In democratic societies, institutional factors, notably electoral laws, have long been identified as a critical factor in determining women's access to parliamentary office. The conventional wisdom is that women tend to be more successful under electoral systems using proportional representation (PR) with multi-member constituencies than under majoritarian systems with single-member districts. "It is the unanimous finding of all those studies which have been explicitly concerned with the linkages between women's legislative representation and the nature of electoral system that systems of proportional representation ap-

Prepared especially for this anthology.

pear to favor higher levels of female representation" (Castles 1981, 22). Nevertheless, our understanding of this relationship remains largely speculative. Few systematic, cross-national studies have explored which specific aspects of proportional electoral systems, whether ballot structure, district magnitude, or degree of proportionality, increase parliamentary access for women representatives.

Moreover, the conventional wisdom about the importance of institutional factors has not gone unchallenged. Critics point out that there is as much variation in the recruitment of women between certain countries using proportional electoral systems (such as Belgium and Norway) as between proportional and majoritarian systems (such as New Zealand and Italy) (Hain 1986). The working of electoral systems, it seems, may be highly conditioned by the national context in which they are situated, including the social environment, historical traditions, and cultural milieu.

The aim of this chapter is to reexamine the effect of electoral systems on the legislative recruitment of women in the twenty-five democratic societies. The chapter starts with a broad international overview to see where women have been most, and least, successful in gaining access to parliament. Next is an assessment of the importance of different types of electoral system, including district magnitude, degree of proportionality, and ballot structure to the explanation of the variation in this phenomenon between democratic societies. Finally, the impact of electoral systems relative to socioeconomic and cultural variables is analyzed. The chapter concludes by discussing the role of electoral reform in increasing the number of women parliamentarians.

Women in Parliaments

To establish how women fare in gaining access to parliaments internationally, the outcomes of national elections to the lower house or to unicameral parliaments in the 144 countries for which information is available from the Inter-Parliamentary Union can be compared. This comparison has to be treated with some caution, however. It takes no account of whether parliaments are effective and powerful legislative assemblies or merely symbolic bodies, it tells us nothing about the role of women in other formal and informal political arenas, and it does not distinguish between democratic and nondemocratic countries.

Legislative office continues to be dominated by men: In June 1987, women represented on average about one in ten (9.7 %) of all members of the lower houses of parliament in these 144 countries. But this global figure disguises striking contrasts between, and within, regions. In Eastern Europe and the Soviet Union of the 1980s, women did relatively well, constituting an average one in four elected members, owing mainly to the

Figure 7.1 Number of Women in Parliament in 25 Developed Democracies

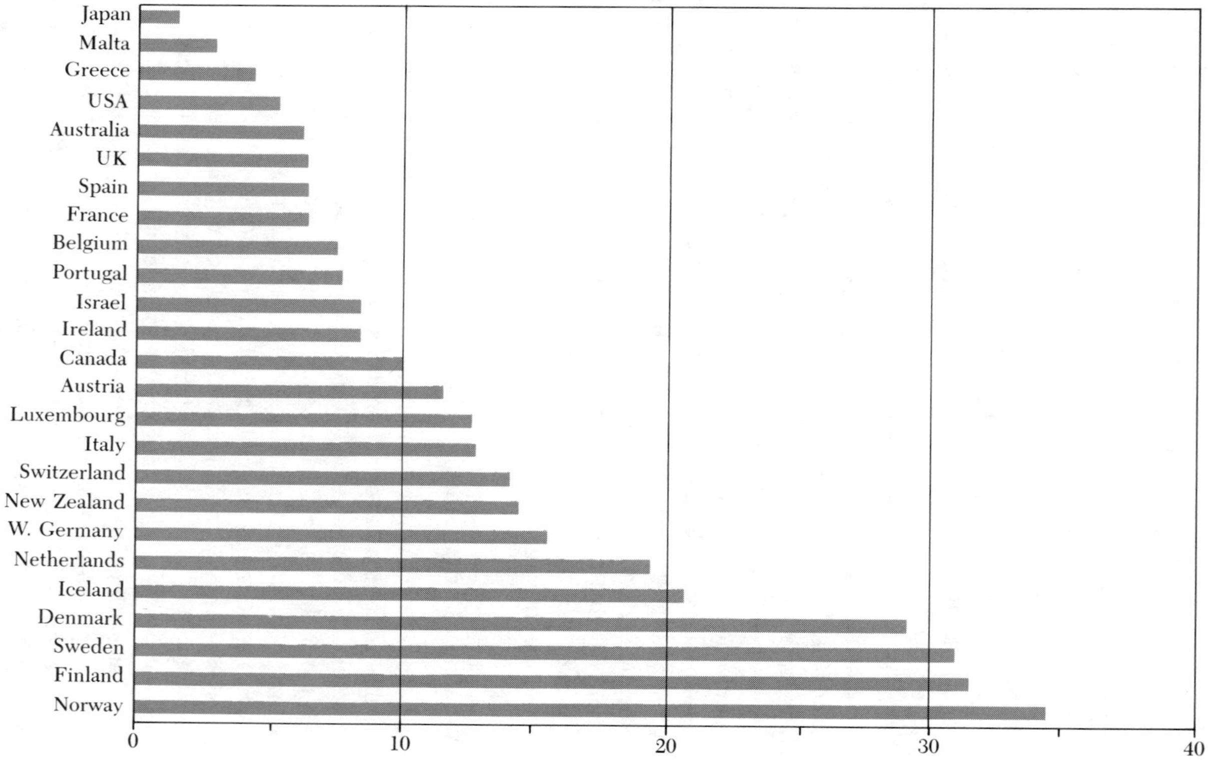

Communist party's use of positive quotas (Browning 1987). They have been even more successful, however, in the Scandinavian countries where they comprise almost a third (29 %) of elected representatives. But the same is not true of their performance in other western European democracies, in the developed Pacific and in North America (see figure 7.1). Some of these differences have increased over time. Since the early 1970s, for example, women have been elected in increasing numbers to the parliaments of the Netherlands, West Germany, and New Zealand, while their number has changed only minimally in Australia, Japan, the United States, and the United Kingdom.

Electoral Systems and the Recruitment of Women

Electoral systems vary widely across a range of factors, including differences in electoral formula, the size of the legislature, suffrage and registration requirements, the structure of party competition, districting procedures, campaign finance laws, and the number of parties. Three principal features of electoral systems should be important for cross-national differences in the parliamentary recruitment of women. These are ballot structure (whether party list or single candidate), district magnitude (the number of seats per district), and degree of proportionality (the allocation of votes to seats).

Electoral systems for the lower national legislatures can be classified into four principal types: plurality (e.g., UK), majority (e.g., Australia), semi-proportional (e.g., Japan), and proportional (e.g., Netherlands) (Bogdanor 1983). Proportional systems can be further divided according to whether the list is national, regional, or local; whether the allocation of seats is national or regional; and whether the choice of candidates is closed, flexible, open, or free. Highly proportional party list systems with large districts should provide the most favorable conditions for the election of women.

Ballot structure is commonly held to have a direct impact on the opportunities for the nomination of women. The logic of choice argument is that in single member constituencies where local parties can pick only one standard bearer, the selection committee may hesitate to choose a candidate representing an electoral risk. Hence, women may be disadvantaged, as may ethnic, regional, or racial minorities who do not conform to the standard candidate model. But there is a different logic of choice in systems where voters are presented with national or regional party lists. Where parties offer a choice among many candidates, it is unlikely that votes will be lost as a result of having women on the list. Indeed, their absence may cause offense by advertising a party's prejudices, thereby narrowing its electoral appeal.

The liberal elite thesis suggests that party list systems give greater control to national and regional party leaders who, tending to have less conservative attitudes toward gender roles, are more likely than are local party activists to promote women. The related affirmative action argument suggests that national or regional party lists permit both the employment of selection quotas and positive training mechanisms, establishing a minimum proportion of women candidates. But where selection is at the discretion of a local constituency party, there are few effective mechanisms for bringing about the nomination of more women. Quotas are impossible to enforce where only one candidate is to be selected by each local party. The British Labour party, for example, has mandated that if any women apply for a seat, at least one of them has to be short-listed for interview by the constituency party. But the national party executive is unable to insist on the selection of a woman because this would conflict with the principle of local autonomy.

Proportionality may also have an indirect effect on the opportunities for women. Greater proportionality increases legislative turnover so that aspirants to legislative office, including women, ethnic, linguistic, or regional minorities, have more opportunities to seek nomination. Proportionality also serves to enhance both party competition and the number of parties represented in parliament, thereby increasing the potential for candidates of whatever stripe to enter politics through diverse channels.

The thesis that electoral systems differ in the opportunities they provide for the nomination and election of women receives its support from three primary sources of evidence: comparisons within countries, comparisons over time, and comparisons across countries. Some countries employ a mixed electoral system, using both majoritarian and proportional methods in the same contest or in elections to different levels of office. Australia is a good example. It uses the alternative majoritarian vote in its 148 single-member electoral divisions for the House of Representatives and multi-member state-level districts with proportional quotas for the Senate. In 1987, 6.1 percent of the House members and 22.4 percent of the senators elected were women. In Japan, with its single nontransferable vote for the House of Representatives and its district party list system for the upper House of Councillors (Shangi-In), 1.4 percent of the House members and 8.8 percent of the councillors elected in 1986 were women.

Similar evidence is available in countries that have changed their electoral systems at some point in time; the recruitment of women to parliament has varied accordingly. The classic case is France. Between 1945 and 1956, and again in 1986, proportional representation was used to assign seats for the National Assembly. But from 1958 to 1981, and again in

1988, members were elected by the single-member, first-ballot majority system, with a runoff plurality ballot. With the exception of 1981 and 1988, more women were elected under proportional representation than under the majoritarian system (Beckwith 1990). Although no more than a minority of all elections during this period, these two exceptions are important for cautioning that the effects of electoral systems are not determinate.

The most systematic evidence is cross-national. The direct elections to the European Parliament allow the comparison of the twelve member states of the European Community in a simultaneous cross-national campaign employing different electoral systems. National governments are free to determine their electoral arrangements for the European Parliament, and the basic electoral system used in eleven of the twelve member states is proportional representation. Party lists with a single national constituency are used in eight countries. The exceptions are Belgium and Italy with regional lists, Ireland and Northern Ireland with a system of single transferable votes in multiple constituencies, and Britain with a simple majority vote in single member seats.

The June 1989 elections confirm that the five countries with the highest proportion of women Members of the European Parliament (MEPs) employed national party list systems. The proportions elected to the national and European parliaments being highly correlated (r = .63), where women are strongly represented nationally, such as in Denmark and the Netherlands, women have also generally done well in elections to the European Parliament. Yet, there are exceptions to this pattern, the most striking of which is France.

In the national elections of June 1988, using a first ballot majority and second ballot plurality system, thirty-three women (5.7%) were elected to the National Assembly. In the 1989 election of members of the European Parliament, eighteen women (22%) were elected when a national party list was used.

Still, it cannot be assumed that there is an invariable relationship between electoral arrangements and the success of women in getting elected to the European Parliament. In Ireland, where the single transferable vote method of proportional representation was used, only one woman (7%) was elected. Similarly, only one woman (4%) was elected in Greece under a national party list system. In contrast, more women were successful in Britain (eleven out of seventy-eight MEPs or 14%) where the traditional single-member plurality system was used. The evidence about the impact of voting systems from the European elections, therefore, is persuasive but inconclusive.

In the twenty-five developed democracies enumerated in figure 7.1, electoral systems can be classified into the four categories mentioned earlier: proportional party lists, semi-proportional, majority, and plurality systems. Table 7.1 confirms that in recent years, countries with plurality and majority systems, including Britain, the United States, Australia, and France, had the lowest proportion of women in parliament. In contrast, the recruitment of women is strongest in countries that use party lists in large districts, including Scandinavia, the Netherlands, West Germany, Switzerland, and Italy. The percentage of women

Table 7.1 Women in Parliamentary Office in Developed Democracies in the 1980s

Country	No. of Women	Index of Proportionality	Ballot Structure[a]
Proportional Party Lists			
Norway	34	91	Reg. List
Sweden	31	98	Reg. List
Finland	31	95	Reg. List
Denmark	31	97	Reg. List
Iceland	21	96	Reg. List
Netherlands	21	96	Nat. List
West Germany	15	98	Reg. List/Plur.
Switzerland	14	96	Reg. List
Italy	13	95	Reg. List
Luxembourg	12	90	Reg. List
Austria	11	99	Reg. List
Israel	8	94	Nat. List
Portugal	8	93	Reg. List
Belgium	8	91	Reg. List
Greece	4	88	Reg. List
Spain	6	83	Reg. List
Semi-Proprotional Systems			
Ireland	8	96	STV
Malta	3	94	STV
Japan	1	91	SNTV
Majority Systems			
France	6	79	2nd Ballot
Australia	6	87	Alternative Vote
Plurality Systems			
New Zealand	14	80	SMDP
Canada	13	88	SMDP
United States	6	94	SMDP
UK	6	85	SMDP

[a]Reg. List = Regional List; Nat. List = National List; Plur. = Plurality;
STV = Single Transferable Vote; SNTV = Single Non-Transferable Vote;
SMDP = Single-Member District Plurality

elected to office and the proportionality of the electoral system are highly correlated ($r = .54$).

Again, however, the relationship is not determinate. Under the single member plurality systems of Canada and New Zealand, women did as well or better than in half the countries using party list PR. Variations in the parliamentary recruitment of women, in other words, are as great *within* categories as *between* them. We are therefore forced to conclude that the difference between electoral systems is one of degree, rather than kind. Proportional representation may facilitate the nomination and election of women politicians, but its actual effect depends on how electoral laws interact with the wider political, social, and cultural context.

The Cultural and Socioeconomic Context

The question which remains concerns the importance of electoral systems compared relative to other cross-national differences. One cross-national study showed that the PR party list system is the most significant predictor of the recruitment of women to parliaments, proving more important than variables like the proportion of women in the paid workforce, the proportion of women graduates, the strength of right-wing parties, and the strength of Catholicism (Rule 1987; see also Norris 1985).

Cultural and socioeconomic factors appear to remain significant, however. The countries with the highest proportion of women in office share a Nordic heritage, while women have usually fared poorly in Anglo-American countries. Cultural attitudes, in other words, could influence the three obstacles that women must surmount if they are to win legislative office: they must be willing to stand, they must be judged suitable nominees by the party, and they must be supported by voters. We need to examine whether there is a negative relationship between traditional cultural attitudes, common in Catholic countries, and the proportion of women elected to office.

A range of socioeconomic factors might facilitate the entry of women into legislatures. Legislators themselves tend to be drawn disproportionately from high status, well-educated backgrounds. Educational qualifications may make a candidate more attractive to party leaders, as well as providing candidates with confidence, personal skills, and political information. Accordingly, as more women obtain higher educational qualifications, the pool of potential female candidates should grow. In addition, female participation in politics is greatest among women working outside the home, since they develop stronger feelings of political efficacy, interest, and competence. Work may also offer women an organizational basis for political activism through trade union groups and business networks in the community. As more women enter the labor force, a larger pool of motivated and well-connected candidates should be willing to stand for public office.

The political context of the party system may also be relevant insofar as Social Democratic and Communist parties have generally provided more recruitment opportunities for women than Christian Democrats, Conservatives, Liberals, and other parties of the right. The partisan strength of left-wing parties can be measured by taking their annual average proportion of seats in the national legislature since 1960. The proportionality of the electoral system can be measured using the Index of Proportionality developed by Rose (1983). In addition, countries can be classified according to whether their electoral system is proportional (party list) or majoritarian (including semi-proportional, plurality, and majoritarian systems).

Entering these variables into a stepwise regression analysis confirmed previous findings that the proportionality of the electoral system is the strongest predictor of women's recruitment to legislative office. But both the partisan strength of left-wing parties and Catholicism also proved significant. The socioeconomic variables, in contrast, had no impact. The overall conclusion, therefore, is that the proportionality of the electoral system is closely associated with the number of women entering parliament, although the electoral law's effects are modified by the broader political and cultural context.

Conclusions: Electoral Reform

Electoral reform has been advocated for Britain and the United States in the belief that PR would increase the number of women and other minority group members in legislative office. Careful analysis, however, reveals that the effect of electoral systems depends upon the interaction of electoral methods and political, cultural, and social conditions. Electoral reform is no mechanical panacea. The Scandinavian experience shows that where parties are receptive to providing opportunities for women through their use of positive quotas, party list systems of proportional representation can facilitate the entry of women into parliament. But in certain countries, like New Zealand and Canada, more women have been elected to office in single-member districts than in societies like Israel with its national party list system. Proportional representation, in other words, may be significant as an enabling condition, but is by itself neither necessary nor sufficient for the recruitment of more women to parliament.

8

Presidential and Prime Ministerial Selection

Hugh Heclo

Amerian presidents and British prime ministers have often been compared in analyses of the presidency, not least by writers who are critical of the selection process in the United States. Lord Bryce (1893, Ch. 8), in a chapter entitled "Why Great Men Are Not Chosen President," argued that the method of choice naturally tends to exclude "great" men from reaching the top. To support this view, he cited seven or eight prime ministers and only four presidents whom he considered "of the first rank," along with eight presidents and six prime ministers who were "personally insignificant." Building on Bryce's analysis, Ostrogorski (1964) pointed out that even Gladstone would have been excluded from the presidency by residency requirements.

By and large, such comparisons have suffered from oversimplifications imported to confirm a distaste for the noisiness, disorganization, and vulgarity of the method of selection used in the United States. Worse, the actual operation of political recruitment in the United States is usually contrasted with the ideal operation of the British system, to the inevitable disadvantage of the former.

This is an updated version of a chapter originally published in *Perspectives on Presidential Selection*, edited by D. R. Matthews (Washington, DC: Brookings Institution, 1973), pp. 19–48. Reprinted by permission of the Brookings Institution.

Despite its possible abuses, the comparative technique remains of great value. Viewed as a special case of political socialization and recruitment, presidential selection is susceptible to comparison in very broad terms with the process of executive selection in parliamentary systems such as Great Britain. This is in no way to discount social and political differences between the two nations. The formal institutional differences are well known: unitary, parliamentary government with well-organized national parties in Britain, versus federal, presidential government with poorly organized parties in the United States. The challenge is to make such familiar institutional factors speak to the more informal processes, and in particular to the political recruitment of executive leadership. While the essence of parliamentary government is the election of the executive from within the legislature, the essence of presidential government is his choice by a separate, mass electorate. What is not clear is the relationship between such institutional differences in election and the less formal processes of executive selection. Far from overlooking political differences, a comparative approach offers the only means of distinguishing unique from more general phenomena. Like depth perception in optics, political depth perception often depends on a set of partly contrasting, partly overlapping images. Investigation from this bifocal perspective leads one to revise a number of accepted stereotypes concerning the selection of presidents and prime ministers, and hopefully to a clearer view of each.

In this discussion, the American and British selection processes will be compared in five categories: recruitment continuity and timing, selection sites, mobility patterns, selection criteria, and public accountability. We will conclude by considering the relation between selection processes and subsequent behavior in office. Inasmuch as the United States has no party leaders in the British sense of the term, the comparison will be based on the population of presidential nominees and British party leaders—who are, roughly speaking, nominees to the prime ministership.

The discussion will be limited to changes in party leadership since 1900, a period especially significant in British politics since it marks the time of changes in Conservative party selection procedures, the last stages of relevant Liberal party selections, and the beginning of Labour party selections. The leader of the Labour party was selected by majority vote of the parliamentary Labour party until 1980. In that year, under pressure from the left wing of the labor movement, the selection process was broadened to give special weight to Labour politicians outside Parliament. Labour party leaders are now nominated by the parliamentary Labour party but elected in a special delegate conference where (voting separately) trade unions are allocated 40 percent of the votes and Labour

MPs and local constituency organizations each control 30 percent of the votes. Until 1965, the Conservative leaders were selected through a less formal process of "emergence" with the blessing of party elders; in 1965, a new procedure was instituted by which the leader is chosen by the parliamentary party. These more formal arrangements were elaborated in 1975 to require annual election of the party leader and to strengthen the hand of rank-and-file Conservative MPs (victory on the first ballot can occur only with an extraordinary majority extending to a 15 percent lead from all MPs eligible to vote). Throughout the twentieth century, selection of presidential nominees by both parties in the United States has been through nominating conventions of state and local party representatives. Since the end of the 1960s, presidential primary elections and caucuses in the various states have loomed much more important than state party organizations in shaping convention outcomes. Thus the tendency in both countries during this century has been toward a more open selection process, but British procedures compared to American always have been and are more restricted to an inner circle of party politicians.

Selection versus Election

In both Britain and the United States the key locus of choice for the office of prime minister or president is in the preelection selection process. Though more dramatic and publicized, election itself is far less important—in the sense of the number of alternatives eliminated—than selection, when one from a large number of potential candidates is designated. Selection creates the voters' options; elections simply register a choice between A, B, or sometimes C. The distinction is worth emphasizing. By "selection" I mean the initial picking out from a group (the Latin seligere, to separate by culling out); "election" will refer to the effective choosing by vote for office (eligere, to choose). Election is thus a clearly delimited public act, defined procedurally by voting, while selection is a vaguer form of choice that may be carried out by a variety of procedures; selection results in nomination to office, election in the holding of office. One of the most common confusions in the popular conceptions of the presidency and prime ministership is the identification of the election, and its attendant campaign activity, with the prior selection process. The result is usually overemphasis on or misidentification of the differences between the two recruitment patterns.

This distinction may, for example, elucidate the question of continuity in leadership. The British system is usually considered conducive to stability of party leadership, while the United States, with its constitutionally required quadrennial elections, is considered subject to greater fluctuations. This view is difficult to substantiate. Since 1900, there have been twenty-four general elections in Britain and twenty-two in the United States, and a total of seventeen prime ministers and sixteen presidents. Average presidential tenure from 1901 to 1988 has been 5.9 years (5.4 years if Franklin D. Roosevelt is excluded), that of prime ministers slightly over five (exactly 5.0 if Thatcher is excluded). During the same time, there have been twenty-eight changes of party leadership in Britain (twelve for the Conservatives and sixteen for Labor). If one regards the choice of a presidential nominee as roughly equivalent to the choice of a party leader, there were twenty-four changes of U.S. party leadership (thirteen for Republicans and eleven for Democrats). Judging from these crude statistics one could argue that the continuity of executive leadership and of those selected for potential leadership has been not less but greater in the United States than in Britain.

What is the source of the common belief to the contrary? The answer probably lies in the differing relation of the selection process to elections. The difference between the two nations lies not in the absolute length of tenure but in the timing of selection. Selection in the United States is directly and inextricably tied to forthcoming elections, and candidates are chosen for their actual or predicted election performance. As Bryce (1893, 80) put it, "Now to a party it is more important that its nominee should be a good candidate than that he should turn out a good President." The preoccupation with "election success" in the American selection process—and the basis for the assumed longevity of British political leadership—is suggested by surveying the candidates who have been defeated in elections. Since 1900, only six defeated presidential candidates have been renominated. By contrast, the beneficiary of selection in Britain seems relatively impervious to electoral defeat. During this century, in the Conservative and Labour parties, there have been no fewer than sixteen occasions (eight in each party) on which the designated leaders have continued to lead their parties after electoral defeats. This is not to say that pressures have not arisen following such defeats: Arthur Balfour was virtually pushed out in 1911, but only after three lost elections; Stanley Baldwin had to fight to regain control after the 1923 and 1929 defeats; and Sir Alec Douglas-Home's position was greatly weakened after the electoral defeat of 1964. But these cases stand out precisely because of their exceptional nature. Paradoxically, although the American presidential nominee may be far less a party leader than the British prime-minister-designate, he is in effect held far more accountable for electoral defeats.

There appears to be a tendency in recent years for selection of British party leaders to be more directly related to election results than earlier in this century. As Conservative leader, Edward Heath survived one electoral defeat in February 1974 but could not survive a second in October.

To the surprise of party elders, Margaret Thatcher won the leadership in 1975 on the second ballot of the newly reformed selection process. Similarly, changes in Labour party leadership in 1980 and again in 1983 were related to electoral defeats for the party in the immediately preceding months. Still, there is a substantial difference between the two countries. Leadership selection in Britain is not the inescapable prologue to an election campaign that it is in the United States. A good indicator of the difference is found in the assumptions of election analysts in the two nations. Theodore White's (1965) analysis of the 1964 American election, for example, devotes more than half its content to the preelection selection process in each party, while the standard study of the 1964 British general election devotes two paragraphs to the nine-month struggle over the Conservative leadership in 1963 and only three sentences to the Labour party's selection of Hugh Gaitskell's successor in the same year (Butler and King 1965). By the same token, Labour's young leader Neil Kinnock survived the party's 1987 general election defeat with little difficulty, while Michael Dukakis's defeat in 1988 led to his being treated as virtually a nonperson in Democratic party circles.

These differences derive from the nature of government institutions and party organization. While parties supply the personnel for selection, government institutions determine how this personnel will be structured; personnel and structure together define the nature of the selection process. British politicians are selecting the leader of a legislative party for purposes of continuous daily combat in Parliament. U.S. political activists are selecting a candidate for a one-shot election campaign aimed at capturing the nation's highest executive office. British leaders can hope to acquire the executive power as well, but structure dictates that presidential candidates can never be what their British counterparts must always be—a true leader of legislative partisans.

The Locus of Selection

One can scarcely conceive of a modern political system that does not require some sort of preelection winnowing, no matter how inchoate the process. The central characteristic of the executive recruit is that of a "group actor"; designation of a nominee to the highest political office in both Britain and the United States occurs through, and by virtue of, participation in limited political groups. Although designation to the British prime ministership may be far less formal than nomination for the American presidency, identifiable selection procedures in the two countries can be compared in terms of these differing group structures and personnel.

The most important group is of course the political party. No person in either nation during this century has attained nomination to the top office without a clear profession of party allegiance. Even the seeming exceptions only serve to emphasize the point. Both Wendell Willkie in 1940 and Dwight Eisenhower in 1952 were required to confirm their party credentials before nomination; the one recent attempt at a non-party draft—Democratic Senator Claude Pepper's proposal in July 1948 that Eisenhower be adopted as a national candidate and that Democrats confine themselves to subnational elections—was stillborn. In Britain, Winston Churchill suffered several decades of suspicion for his "ratting and reratting" on the Conservative party; the collapse of David Lloyd George's coalition government in 1921 left him a leader without a party, while the creation of a National Government under Ramsay MacDonald in 1931 temporarily left Labour as a party without a leader. By the Second World War, Churchill had learned enough of the importance of party allegiance, even at the height of a struggle for national survival, to insist upon eventually taking up the leadership of the Conservative party (Churchill 1949).

The parties in each nation shape themselves to the structures of government, both in central institutions and in national-local divisions of power. The well-worn distinction between the unitary British state with a parliamentary-cabinet government and the federal United States with separated powers remains the most useful shorthand expression for the extremely complex differences. Such institutional differences will be of concern here only insofar as they are molding forces through which the party groups operate to select national leaders.

At risk of oversimplification, one may say that the central-local party structure in the United States is characterized by a disparate confederacy of state and local party organizations and activists, which intermittently coalesce for the specific purpose of nominating a presidential candidate. One of the oldest observations on the subject remains valid: the central task at the nominating convention is the search for an election "winner," for it is only through striving for such victory that the heterogeneous party can be brought together. In the past twenty years—with state primaries, caucuses, and candidate organizations increasingly replacing party leaders and their organizations as nominating devices—the attention to selecting an electoral "winner" has become even more intense. But the meaning of that term has undergone a subtle change. Old-style party bosses and other leading politicians in control of the nomination process generally looked for a winner *prospectively*, that is, someone who could carry the party slate to victory in the coming general election. In the post-1960s process, the preoccupation with selecting a winner has become more a *retrospective* conclusion based on a string of results in state primaries and caucuses. The problem is that the political activists participating in these grass-roots selection processes may be a poor proxy for the general electorate; candidates are typically expected to pass muster on the particular policies and ideological issues of concern to local activists with less attention to future electability. The national nominating convention is an extreme device used to meet extreme party decentralization, a contrivance which has since its beginning been a consequence rather than a cause of the incoherent nature of America's national parties. The intimate tie between selection and election is thus due not to the unique nature of the presidency but to the decentralization of the parties, which find that the selection of a national election winner is the one common cause in which they can at least temporarily unite.

In Britain, on the other hand, the parties are more continuously unified national organizations, without a regular timetable for choosing party leaders and potential prime ministers. When the succession in party leadership has been disputed, local party organizations have made their voices heard, but usually in the negative form of complaints and grumbles rather than in the expression of positive preferences. The unified national party selectorate thus aims not so much to create party unity, as in the United States, as to preserve it.

On those rare occasions when strong central party leadership has been absent, the British selection process has fleetingly resembled the American. This was demonstrated in 1963 and again in the early 1980s. Prior to 1963 the Conservative party had been cited as the model of coherent party organization, with a smoothly operating, emergence style of leadership recruitment. From the moment of the surprise announcement of Prime Minister Harold Macmillan's serious illness and impending retirement, the usually stolid Conservative party conference of local constituency organizations began to resemble an inchoate national nominating convention, with all the attendant intrigues, gossip mongering, and deals. The "candidate" whom many considered the most likely successful election performer, Lord Hailsham, was given warm and rousing receptions. The maneuvering became, as in the United States, heated, public, and exaggerated. *The Times* wrote disdainfully: "The atmosphere there is unhealthy. With all the hob-nobbing in hotel rooms, the gossip, and rumours, the conference is resembling an American nomination convention. The Cabinet is said to have one candidate, the Parlimentary party another, and the constituency associations a third." The point worth noting is the ease with which the question of selection came to dominate an assembly of localists who suddenly felt that they might be allowed to have a say in the designation of the next leader. While the 1963 Conservative controversy demonstrated that a swing in the American direction is possible, its denouement was equally revealing: the choice of a new leader fell neither to the party conference nor to the local constituency organizations. After the hyperthyroid interlude of the conference, a "process of consultation," managed by Macmillan from his hospital room, led to the selection of the modest Alec Douglas-Home (King 1966). By expanding the post-1980 "selectorate" to include local party organizations and trade union constituencies, the Labor party's reformed selection process has pushed relationships in a somewhat more American direction. The 1981 contest for deputy leader thus produced a raucous struggle between the right and left wings of the labor movement (represented by Denis Healey and Tony Benn respectively), and the 1983 selection of Neil Kinnock over Roy Hattersley produced a similarly lengthy scrambling after votes of party activists that resembled some aspects of a presidential primary.

Important consequences for executive selection flow from national differences in party structure and centralization. Selection in the United States depends on creating from the large number of local supporters those confederal alliances necessary to dominate the nominating convention. Yet if the fragmentation is greater in the United States, so too is the room for maneuver, both in the number of potential candidates and in their strategies. The very diversity of party groups in the United States provides a combinatorial richness and a range of choice far wider than that produced through the British party structure. One can predict with a high probability that the British leader selected will be an experienced party leader with long membership in Parliament and a long career of ascent through junior ministerial, ministerial, and cabinet positions. Of the American candidate one can say only that the nominee will be a politician who, through one means or another, will have succeeded in gaining national attention through the mass media. This emphasis on shifting media attention, as opposed to prior national prominence, has been especially evident since the candidacy of John F. Kennedy in the late 1950s. Those who seriously enter into contention sometimes lack long party backgrounds, legislative experience, or tenure in a national executive office. The strategic environment of both selection and election is a jungle of voting blocs, interest groups, local activists, financial backers, and public relations campaigns. Strategies may range from hoping to win by popular acclaim by running first and hardest in primaries to waiting quietly for a brokered convention.

The breadth of competition in the American system is indicated by the number of contenders for office. While the United States since 1900 has held fewer national elections than Britain and has experienced slightly longer executive tenure and fewer changes in party leadership, it has had approximately 50 percent more contenders under serious consideration for selection. A review of the literature suggests that for the twenty-eight British changes in party leadership roughly forty-five contenders have been considered, while for the twenty-four changes of presidential nominees there have been sixty-eight contenders.[1] This is not to claim an innate superiority for the American process. However, on the assumption that there is a reservoir of political talent spread throughout the political system, the American selection process casts the net somewhat more widely than the British.

The overall differences may be summarized by saying that the selection process in Britain is an apprenticeship system, as contrasted with the entrepreneurial system of recruitment in the United States. Apprenticeship may be understood in its usual meaning of learning a craft, the result of which is gradual advancement into professional ranks under the watchful eye of established masters. "Entrepreneur" has a rather precise meaning in economics that may also be enlightening in politics: one who creates new combinations in the means of production and credit. The entrepreneur's creativity is characterized by innovative rearrangements and the calling forth of new resources rather than by simple management of existing combinations; his is not usually a permanent profession, but consists of a temporary, ad hoc manipulation of the forces at hand. Although the flux and combinatorial richness of the American selection process suggest the label entrepreneurial, this is not to say that the entrepreneur is an independent, freestanding capitalist. New combinations may be created, and usually are, by those who are part of a system drawing upon political credit and capital other than their own (Schumpeter 1961). The distinction between the apprenticeship and entrepreneurial systems is highlighted by a look at the place of political experience in the two nations' selection processes.

Political Experience and Mobility Patterns

Probably the most common generalization is the claim that the prime ministerial system excels because it requires greater governmental experience in the eventual nominee. Bryce (1893, 85), for example, compared the "natural selection" of the English Parliament with the "artificial selection" of American politics.

There can be no doubt that greater parliamentary experience is required by a nonfederal system of unified executive and legislative powers than by the American system. The British selection process appears "natural" in the sense that it provides for apprenticeship from parliamentary ranks to cabinet office. Of the twenty-two British party leaders of this century (through 1988), all had parliamentary experience before their selection, for an average 20.6 years (454 years in toto). Of the thirty-one different U.S. presidential nominees during this period, only fourteen had had any legislative experience, with an average congressional tenure of 10.7 years (150 years in toto). The facile conclusion that British leaders exhibit more experience in government has always been only a short step away.

   Mere membership in Parliament, however, is a poor indicator of real experience in governing, especially in view of the limited legislative role of twentieth century Parliaments as compared with both earlier periods of British history and with the continuously powerful role of Congress. For a more accurate measure of substantive experience in governing, one might look not at the bare number of years a person has sat in Parliament but at the government responsibilities exercised. Such an analysis shows that the relation is the opposite of what is usually assumed. On these terms the government experience of presidential nominees is not inferior to that of British party leaders. A survey of tenure in offices above the menial level of parliamentary private secretary shows that the average experience of British party leaders at the time of their selection was 7.7 years, with a high of 20 years for Churchill in 1940 and none at all for both Ramsey MacDonald in 1924 and Neil Kinnock in 1983. Rather than being less experienced, presidential nominees at the time of their selection had spent an average of 10.3 years in government offices apart from Congress. (This also disregards Eisenhower's career, which, if not formally political, was also not without experience in a significant area of public affairs.) Moreover, in the postwar period legislative experience has become the rule not the exception in the United States (as in the cases of Nixon, Kennedy, Goldwater, Johnson, Humphrey, McGovern, Ford, Mondale and Bush).

   The important distinction between the two nations, however, rests not in the length but in the variety of government experience of designated leaders. With few exceptions, potential prime ministers have advanced along the single route from junior minister to minister, from minister to major cabinet figure, but even this rule has not, on occasion, prevented party leadership, and thus potential national leadership, from falling to relatively inexperienced people. MacDonald and Kinnock have not been the only leaders with meager executive experience in national government. Bonar Law had had three years in an executive government position when he was selected party leader in 1911, and Clement Attlee had had two years at the time of his selection in 1935. In the most recent period the British political career route has obviously not lost its narrowly parliamentary focus, but the path to the top can no longer be counted on to provide future leaders an incubation period in senior ministerial positions. Three of Britain's last four prime ministers (Wilson, Heath, and Thatcher) have reached their positions without passing through any of the three senior ministries that have traditionally been regarded as grooming grounds for future prime ministers (Foreign Office, Treasury, and Home Office). Indeed, the most recent party leaders are noteworthy for their meager experience in any Cabinet positions whatsoever prior to their selection as leader (four years Cabinet experience for Thatcher, two for Michael Foot, and none for Kinnock).

In the United States, without a direct legislative-executive link, the presidential selection process has brought forth a set of men with an astonishing range of political experience. More than half the presidential nominees have, for example, had some experience in nonelective government office, while in Britain only Neville Chamberlain, Gaitskell, and Harold Wilson meet the criterion. Two-thirds of presidential nominees have had subnational government experience, in contrast with Chamberlain and the three Labour leaders (MacDonald, Lansbury, and Atlee) who served on local government councils. Nowhere in Britain is there evidence of anything like the wide catchment drawn upon in the United States. Besides legislators, one finds governors (e.g., Wilson, Smith, Franklin D. Roosevelt, Dewey, Carter, Reagan, Dukakis), men of administrative and/or judicial experience (e.g., Theodore Roosevelt, Alton Parker, William Taft, Herbert Hoover) as well as the occasional nonprofessional politician (Charles Evans Hughes, Wendell Willkie, Dwight Eisenhower).

The evidence suggests that those selected for the presidency are not less politically experienced, but that they are less restricted than British leaders to one level—the national—and to one institution—the legislature (Kane 1968; Butler and Butler 1986). One can of course argue that the offices in the two nations are by nature different, and that many of the offices held by presidential nominees cannot be equated with British cabinet posts as sources of relevant political experience. On the other hand, one may rightfully view state and local political experience as good preparation for sensitive leadership and point to the parochialism found in the rarified atmosphere of political capitals in general and Whitehall in particular. At a time when central government is increasingly criticized for its lack of perspective and responsiveness, alternative career routes and varying political experience can be valuable assets to a political system.

The difference in recruitment in apprenticeship and entrepreneur systems is not simply a question of the distinction between ascription and achievement typically used to describe mobility patterns. Neither nation yields more than a few instances of leaders who have been successfully designated by their predecessors; Balfour and Sir Anthony Eden in Britain and William H. Taft and Nixon in the United States would be the prime examples. More useful is the distinction between sponsored and contested mobility (Turner 1960). Roughly speaking, the British apprentice moves upward by ingratiating himself with his guild masters; the American entrepreneur moves through a wide-ranging series of contests against other largely isolated contenders attempting to arrange their own combinations of political resources. For purposes of his own advancement, the apprentice's constituency is largely internal; the scrutineers in his selectorate are his own political superiors in Parliament, while the American entrepreneur looks far more to an outside constituency of disparate political forces whose self-interest must be mobilized on his behalf. The apprentice's guild operates smoothly by retaining its exclusiveness, but the entrepreneur thrives as his market for potential support becomes more extensive. Thus, though the wide-ranging selection process typically serves as a centripetal force in the decentralized American system, it can easily prove centrifugal in a tightly centralized party structure such as Britain's. After the trauma of 1963, the Conservative party was not long in establishing a formal selection procedure which explicitly lays responsibility on the parliamentary party and seeks to quarantine the disruptive forces of selection.

Selection Criteria and Personality

We have already touched briefly on the question of selection criteria. One can reasonably expect that the more unified and closed selectorate of national politicians in Britain will emphasize somewhat different criteria than the participants in the diffuse U.S. system.

The issue of electoral appeal has already been mentioned. In trying to mobilize the self-interest of many decentralized power centers, the American entrepreneur must appeal to others first and foremost as an election winner. Increasingly over recent decades this has meant going beyond the promise of helping the tickets of state and local party leaders. Candidates must now prevail in a gamut of election contests, appealing both to general party voters in state primaries and to the more fervent and ideological activists who turn out at caucuses. Intense mass media attention magnifies the marginal results into dramas of surging or collapsing momentum. In Britain electoral criteria are also at work in the selection process, regardless of what champions of the more "natural" British ideal may say. Thus during the 1963 selection controversy, the joint chairman of the Conservative party, and many others, backed Lord Hailsham because they saw him as likely to win the election. The point is that this admittedly important consideration was only one of the criteria that the British guild selectorate can be expected to use. The background against which the apprentice is evaluated includes not only an indefinite future election but also many years' performance as a parliamentary and cabinet colleague. Although a nominating convention in the United States may register the entrepreneur's ability to "deal with" others, it presumes a great deal on the perspicacity of local primary voters to expect them to judge a man on his ability to cooperate and work well with party colleagues.

The fact that selection in the British apprenticeship system seeks to preserve rather than to create internal party unity suggests a concern for more cooperative and less openly combative qualities in struggling for leadership within the party. A capacity to advance without rocking the boat typically takes precedence over a flair for self-advertisement. In the U.S. the reverse tends to hold true, and qualities of being a good team player count for comparatively little. Although individual classifications are disputable, recruits can be grouped into certain categories.

In Great Britain, of twenty-two party leaders selected this century:

- nine, or 41 percent, were strong contenders who won a factional fight (Lloyd George, Baldwin, MacDonald, Gaitskell, Macmillan, Wilson, Heath, Thatcher, Kinnock);
- four, or 18 percent, were compromise candidates between stronger candidates (Campbell-Bannerman, Law, Home, Foot);
- nine, or 41 percent, emerged without a factional fight (Balfour, Asquith, Austen Chamberlain, Lansbury, Neville Chamberlain, Churchill, Attlee, Eden, Callaghan).

In the United States, of thirty-three presidential nominations (involving thirty different nominees and excluding second-term nominations of sitting presidents):

- twenty-four, or 73 percent, involved strong contenders who won a factional fight (Parker, Theodore Roosevelt, Wilson, Cox, Franklin D. Roosevelt, Willkie, Dewey [1944, 1948], Truman, Eisenhower, Stevenson [1952, 1956], Kennedy, Johnson [as Vice-President], Goldwater, Nixon [1968], Humphrey, McGovern, Carter, Ford, Reagan, Mondale, Bush, Dukakis);
- two, or 6 percent, produced compromise candidates between strong candidates (Harding, Davis);
- seven, or 21 percent, emerged without a factional fight (Taft [1908], Hughes, Coolidge, Hoover, Landon, Smith, Nixon [1960][2]).

The politician who waits to emerge "peacefully" or serves as a compromise between factious contenders is rewarded more frequently in Britain than in the United States. In both nations there is a contemporary tendency toward an increase in the number of contested selections, but Britain has not gone as far in this direction as the United States.

Perhaps the most frequently cited difference is the part played by personality in the two nations. Selection of prime ministers is said to be less personality-oriented than the selection of presidents, with less concentration on the would-be leader's public image, its packaging, and marketing. When arguments are advanced that prime ministers are becoming increasingly like presidents, the discussion typically centers on the growing force of the leader's personality as opposed to the supposedly greater concern for self-restraint and "character" prevailing in the past.

Again, such distinctions tend to confuse electoral campaign publicity with the more vital preelection selection process. There can be no question that the appeal of a prospective candidate's public image is an important factor in the search for an American presidential nominee. One of the first professional publicity buildups in a selection struggle was given to Wendell Willkie before the 1940 Republican convention—with the now-familiar coterie of public relations experts, family magazine profiles, and intimate portraits of the "real" man. This treatment has been used as a tool of persuasion by prospective nominees ever since. Yet compared with the selling job done on behalf of the "Princeton schoolmaster" by Colonel George Harvey of *Harper's Weekly,* and with William Randolph Hearst's efforts to make Alfred M. Landon the "best-loved family man in America," these later developments amounted to a difference of technique rather than of kind. Since then, of course, personality packaging by media consultants has become a very expensive art form.

Attention to personal images, however, is hardly peculiar to the United States. Thus one of the important factors weakening Home's position among party leaders in 1965, and strengthening Wilson's among his own supporters, was Home's consistently low public-image rating. The last poll before Home's resignation showed him trailing Wilson in every favorable characteristic about which opinions were asked ("tough, sincere, straightforward, progressive"). Even more disturbing was the fact that among Conservative supporters Home badly trailed Wilson's ratings for toughness, being in touch with ordinary people, speaking ability, and capacity to deal with the unions. Six months after succeeding Home, Edward Heath was still trailing Wilson among the general population, but among Conservative supporters was rated second only in his capacity to deal with the unions.

Parliament's near-monopoly as the locus of selection ensures that personality issues will actually play a greater part in Britain than in the United States. In the hothouse atmosphere of Parliament, assessments of working relationships established over the decades are prolific and inescapable. The result in Britain is likely to be an extremely intimate and pervasive attention to the nuances of personality in a selection process aiming to preserve intraparty unity and interparty conflict. Such assessments have a long history. The Conservative party in 1911 chose as its leader the little-known Bonar Law, rather than either of the two leading and more illustrious contenders, Austen Chamberlain and Walter Long, because Long and Chamberlain so detested each other that they threatened to split the party in a fight for the leadership. Chamberlain summed up the feeling when he said of Long, "I made a step toward him and had it on my lips to tell him he was a cad and to slap him across the face" (quoted in Blake 1955, 78). In comparison with the "pompous," "vain," and "weak" Chamberlain, and the verbose and inepetuous Long—and these were the terms of analysis used at the time—Bonar Law was characterized as firm, modest, and straightforward. In the end, rather than give ascendancy to an archenemy, Long and Chamberlain both withdrew in Law's favor.

For much the same reasons, Baldwin was chosen as leader in 1923 over the much more formally qualified Lord Curzon. According to one close observer, this selection, now widely given as an example of the disqualification of peers from the leadership, was in fact "made mainly on the issue of the personal acceptability of the two candidates" (Amery 1948, 22). Compared to the brilliant, experienced, but also imperious and arrogant Curzon, Baldwin was a modest but agreeable colleague to promote.

The cases could be multiplied at length—William Harcourt, Lloyd George, Macmillan, Herbert Morrison, Attlee, George Brown, and others providing examples of the strong part played by intimate assessments of personal qualities. To be selected it is not necessary that an MP rank high in public opinion polls or be personally likeable. Margaret Thatcher was neither in 1975. Nor is it even essential that a candidate's political views be widely shared in the parliamentary party. One estimate is that only a small minority (10–25 percent) of Conservative MPs held what could be called Thatcherite views on public policy at the time of Mrs. Thatcher's selection (Crewe and Searing 1988, 371). In 1975 Mrs. Thatcher benefited from a series of accidents and her own boldness. The withdrawal of Keith Joseph and Edward du Cann for personal reasons as well as inept campaigning by William Whitelaw opened the field to a more junior person. Capitalizing on the widespread desire to dump Heath as leader, Thatcher boldly canvassed for votes to assure a first ballot defeat of Heath. The expectation of many MPs that preferred candidates would enter on the second ballot was thwarted by the momentum of Thatcher's victory over Heath and the leadership fell to her (Cosgrove 1978).

The important criteria have more to do with a candidate's reliability and trustworthiness as a colleague and his or her combat effectiveness in attacking the opposing party. These are the warp and woof of parliamentary life, and daily experience puts MPs in a good position to make these personal assessments.

U.S. political entrepreneurs are relatively free—within the constraints of media exposés (cf. Gary Hart)—to trade in transitory images manipulated in a mass selectorate. By comparison, the British apprentice depends directly on continued esteem and respect from that small group with whom he is serving his apprenticeship. This in turn raises the question of the democratic accountability of the two systems.

Public Participation and Democratic Responsiveness

The more public nature of selection in the American system is often considered a counter to its admitted disadvantages, while the lack of public participation in Britain is the one drawback commonly cited in the British system. And yet it would be unjustified to assume that a less public process is necessarily less democratic; the essential issue is the extent to which public accountability effectively enters into the selection of presidential and prime-ministerial candidates.

Evidence of a sort is provided by the proposition of contested selections in each country, on the shaky assumption that a contest is more likely to be sensitive to changing public concerns than selection by some form of prior understanding in the selectorate. By this standard, the British in fact appear more openly competitive, for while about one-half of American convention selections have gone uncontested, only about one-third of the British selections discussed in this study have occurred without a plurality of candidates appealing to various elements of the party. This difference is explained of course by the large number of incumbent presidents renominated, without which the proportion of uncontested selections in the United States drops to 23 percent. In such cases "selection" is a misnomer for the perfunctory formalities of renomination wrought by the regular election cycle. Still, the near certainty during this century of an incumbent president's renomination and of the inside track to nomination provided sitting vice-presidents should not be neglected by advocates of popular participation.

There are no statistics on the numbers of people consulted during the selection process in each country, but if one counts the number who indicate a preference through the medium of American primaries (some 35 million voters in 1988), British experience clearly can offer nothing comparable. During this century the U.S. linkage between election campaigns and the selection process has been vastly strengthened by the growing importance of primaries.

Again, we should beware of the facile conclusion that the use of presidential primaries in the United States automatically ensures a more "democratic" selection process. While the direct public impact in Britain is minimal, the direct public voice expressed in United States primary elections has by no means determined the selection of candidates. For most of this century American candidates who relied largely on a strategy of primaries and popular acclaim were notably unsuccessful in finally gaining nomination; more often than not, those most successful in primaries have not been selected. In 1912, for example, Theodore Roosevelt won 221 of the 388 delegates elected by primaries to the Republican convention, and Robert M. LaFollette won substantially more states than Taft—all to no avail. On the Democratic side in the same year, Champ Clark had won as many contests as Woodrow Wilson and had 413 delegates to Wilson's 274 by the start of the convention. To take a more recent example, in 1952 Estes Kefauver beat President Harry S. Truman in the New Hampshire primary, won eight other primaries, and had the largest number of pledged delegates at the convention's opening, only to lose to Stevenson. Historically speaking campaigns that most successfully used primaries in the selection process (such as Roosevelt's in 1932 and John F. Kennedy's in 1960) relied on primary results, not to win delegates as such, but to influence state and local party leaders who were doing the selecting. Arnold Rose (1967), for example, contrasts Kennedy's strategy of appealing to the general public, as an instrumental device in seeking the support of party delegates, with Lyndon B. Johnson's and Stuart Symington's use of the "British technique" of endorsement by party elders. Thus in 1960, the importance of the West Virginia primary lay not in the state's convention votes but in its demonstration to party leaders that Kennedy could overcome the religious issue.

All of this changed after 1972. The number of primaries expanded from an earlier average of seventeen states to thirty-six states by 1988, and the proportion of convention delegates selected by primaries grew from less than one-half to upwards of three-quarters. Not surprisingly, since 1972 no contender winning the most primary votes has failed to win his party's presidential nomination. However, because of bandwagon effects and the fact that delegates are allocated by state and not share of total primary votes, the correspondence between public support in primaries and convention delegate strength is by no means always exact. Thus Carter won only 39 percent of primary votes but garnered 74 percent of delegate votes on the first ballot at the 1976 convention; in 1984 Mondale got 38 percent of primary votes to Hart's 36 percent but won 56 percent of convention votes. Still, the correspondence today is closer than it ever was before 1972. In 1968 Humphrey contested no primaries but won on the first ballot with 67 percent of convention votes!

When the indirect role of the public in selection processes is taken into account, however, the British system is by no means unresponsive to democratic influences. By-elections have always served as a means of gauging public support, and particularly within the past twenty years public opinion polls have periodically come into play in the deliberations surrounding the choice of new leaders. In the spring of 1931, Baldwin came under heavy pressure to resign the Conservative leadership because of negative reports concerning opinion at Central Office and among local party supporters. The Conservative leader fought back through the indirect use of public preferences. At first Baldwin considered standing for election himself, but eventually gave explicit backing to Alfred Duff Cooper in the St. George's by-election; success in this test of public approval was decisive in Baldwin's retaining the leadership (Middlemas and Barnes 1969, ch. 22). The events surrounding Home's resignation as Conservative leader in July 1965 show a similar indirect responsiveness to public opinion. After the 1964 Conservative election defeat, reports from the constituencies showed a recurring and rising tide of local discontent. In March 1965, an unexpected Conservative by-election defeat at Roxburgh intensified the discontent and, since it took place next door to Home's own constituency, was interpreted as a blow to his leadership. A further report from National Opinion Polls on July 15 showed Labour's lead increasing and Home trailing even further behind Wilson than before. Amid reports of mounting discontent, and "shaken by the opinion poll," Home retired to his country estate and emerged a few days later to announce his resignation as leader (Butler and King 1967, 51).

Although indicators of public preference can be an important force in undermining the position of incumbent leaders, public opinion in Britain is denied the decisive role in positively designating the candidate that characterizes the post-Sixties U.S. selection process. After Home's resignation, the Conservative leadership went to Heath, who, until his selection, had at best been a distant second choice for succession among both the general public and Conservative supporters. After his selection, the polls shifted to show that Heath was preferred by a wide margin. The same sequence—the choice of a leader who lagged in the polls before being selected—occurred in the Labour party during 1963 on the occasion of Harold Wilson's selection as successor to Gaitskell and in 1975 with Thatcher's unexpected victory over Heath. In the face of such mercurial public guidance, it is not surprising that even those most concerned with the election potential of British contenders for party leadership should hesitate to base their judgments directly on public opinion polls.

The fact that the U.S. system offers vastly greater opportunities for mass participation in the selection process does not necessarily mean democratic accountability is greater than in Britain. It may in fact be less. The decentralization, diversity, and fluidity of the American selectorate make it virtually impossible for anyone to know whom to hold responsible for the resulting leadership choices. Political entrepreneurs find countless opportunities to mobilize or manufacture indications of public support as they compete for precious media attention. Composition of the selectorate shifts from one unrepresentative state (e.g., Iowa) to another (e.g., New Hampshire), and from one year to another. Turnout in primaries and caucuses rarely exceeds 40 percent, and those who participate tend to be divided into two unrepresentative groups: those who are unusually attentive and self-consciously independent on the one hand and those who are unusually well-organized around certain interests on the other (Shafer 1988, 961). In short, selection politics in the United States zigs and zags across two years of transitory issues, interest coalitions, fields of candidates, and media coverage. By contrast, British assessment of public preference (through by-elections, polls, and reports from constituency parties) takes a more limited but coherent form at the hand of several hundred politicians who can be expected actually to know the candidates being considered. And unlike the United States, as just noted, assessments of public support can be used outside the general election cycle to topple British leaders who seem to have lost touch.

Behavioral Links

I have tried to show that through a comparative approach some aspects of what might otherwise be thought unique in American presidential selection can also be found in Britain. The predominant place of the party as the group within which claims to leadership are advanced, the extended political experience required of nominees, the attention paid to questions of personality and public support are all tendencies that may be observed in both countries. At the same time, American selection has been distinguished by its very intimate ties to electoral criteria, by the incoherence of party leadership, by its extended areas of recruitment, and by the recent development of a more fluid, mass participatory process. One system has been described as apprenticeship, the other as entrepreneurial.

This is, however, only one point of departure for a discussion of executive selection in the two countries. Probably the greatest gap in the study of executive recruitment is the failure to establish any reliable connection between different selection processes and subsequent behavior in office. The question is of course not the effect of idiosyncratic recruitment experiences on a particular individual, but rather the possibly consistent effects of broadly differing selection processes.

One significant difference between entrepreneurial and apprenticeship systems would appear to be the greater unpredictability in the behavioral characteristics of presidential candidates. Because of the extremely close linkage between selection and election criteria, choices made through the American system seem more likely than the British to result in the emergence of relatively unknown quantities—persons whose appeal rests in their supposed electoral strength and whose operational character apart from this strength is often disregarded. Examples are the 1976 candidacy of Jimmy Carter and more recently the candidacy of Gary Hart. Of course British leaders have also been chosen with an eye to winning elections, and the cattishness of personality clashes in the House of Commons would seem to know no bounds. But at least the British system ensures that those doing the selecting will know a great deal, perhaps more than they would want to know, about the people under consideration. Given the conventional wisdom about a more personality-oriented (as opposed to party or programmatic) politics in the United States, it is paradoxical that so little will often be known about the candidates being selected. What is likely to prevail, both before and during the general election campaign, is a series of campaign images carefully managed for mass consumption and assessed largely in terms of a preoccupation with electoral horse races.

Perhaps the feature most amenable to analysis is leadership style. The nature and constraints of group interaction leading to selection for leadership may well play a crucial part in socializing the future executive. Learning takes place in both entrepreneurial and apprenticeship systems, the difference being in the type of behavior that is rewarded in the climb to the top of the heap.

Although it is unlikely that any one presidential or prime-ministerial "type" is shaped by selection processes, the route to office is likely to teach presidents, as opposed to prime ministers, to pay greater attention to immediate public preferences and responses in calculating their actions. The difference may easily be exaggerated; no British prime minister has ever deliberately sought public disfavor. But reading the polls can become a habit, and a president who has risen to power by passing a series of short-term, public approval tests, rather than by maintaining good long-term relationships as an apprentice, may well have a more consistently populist perspective than is likely in prime ministers.

By the same token, it seems reasonable to suppose that upon entering office a president will have learned a version of political individualism quite different from a prime minister's collegial perspective. The future prime minister has advanced through a muted struggle requiring cooperation with sponsors and colleagues; his or her fate has been inextricably tied to the collective fate of his selectorate, both in government and opposition. In contrast a modern president will normally have climbed to the highest office through a lone struggle with other political entrepreneurs trying to mold temporary winning alliances in a disorganized party. A president is likely to be predisposed by the real-life recruitment struggle to view his actions and those of his staff as independently justified and legitimate rather than as requiring agreement of colleagues or party. This perspective goes beyond a simple lack of rapport with Congress, which in a system of separated executive and legislative powers is natural enough. By the time of his arrival in office, a newly elected president has undergone one of the most unusual learning experiences in the world. He is likely to have absorbed not simply an individualistic but a tribunal perspective—a psychological terrain in which the outstanding features are the all-powerful but indeterminate people and himself as their chosen leader.

By the same token, the president, unlike the prime minister, will have learned to seek assistance from widely dispersed circles of political and social leadership rather than exclusively from the legislative and civil service fields. Yet no matter what staff is assembled in the executive branch, they will be seen most readily as individualistic cadres rather than as a working collectivity. While more limited in who can be appointed to top positions, a prime minister can be surer of having a united group which is able to work together. In the United States, staff allegiance, responsibility, and consequently fates will be individual and contingent upon electoral success. The legal security of his position means that a president will need be much less concerned than a prime minister with intrigues in cabinet, legislature, and party, but he can also for this reason allow himself to be isolated from these vital sources of information and feedback. As long as he is in office, his party's selection process is virtually terminated; there remains only his towering position and the vague, all-powerful voting public. Likewise, the defeated candidate's army of supporters fades away; he is nothing like a party leader in the British sense of the term. No shadow cabinet position unites the leader and his colleagues in the new tasks of opposition. Nothing remains. If the presidency is a lonely office, the defeated candidate is surely the world's loneliest non-office holder. The successful candidate remains supreme with his associates, but they are his placemen and beyond the court there is little but the election and the nothingless attached to electoral defeat.

The behavioral inheritances from the selection process suggest no absolute standards on which to judge one nation's recruitment procedure "better" than that of another. At a minimum, however, the requirements for selection should be consistent with the requirements for governing. Given the separation of national institutions, the federal diffusion of power, and the regularly recurring congressional and presidential elections, entrepreneurial lessons are probably as appropriate and important to the president of the United States as are the collegial skills acquired by a British prime minister. There is much force in the argument that the selection process socializes the future president in ways in which he would in any event be driven by formal constitutional structure. Yet this should not obscure the fact that selection in the United States is heavily weighted toward electoral rather than other performance criteria. In

Britain the successful apprentice has advanced through exactly the working relationships by which he will one day govern; this may not always help win the election, but it should help him or her in office. In the United States, the selection coalition that was sufficient to win nomination and the electoral skills that were sufficient to win office will not necessarily be sufficient to govern.

If the president's problems involved simply building rather than also using a winning coalition, or if the likelihood of popular acclaim were a touchstone of sensible action, there would be little problem. If policy were susceptible to single, neat, decisive outcomes, the electoral entrepreneurship might suffice. But life is not that simple. The temporary, if dramatic, creation of unity in American presidential selection offers little guidance for the preservation of unity and even less preparation on how to work through the political maze that is Washington. By fleetingly raising public expectations concerning the leader's unifying and governing powers, the selection process in the United States may actually make credible government all the more difficult. In popular conception the president is a "winner" selected to "run" the government; in reality he will often be pulling levers and pushing buttons with only a slight chance of provoking a sustained response from the government machine.

NOTES

1. Serious contenders in Britain are counted as those who have received backing for the leadership from some segment of party opinion; in the United States, they are those who have received at least 10 percent of the votes in national conventions or have made significant primary challenges and been eliminated before the convention, such as Willkie in 1944, Kefauver in 1956, Humphrey in 1972, and Bush in 1980.

2. The proportions do not change greatly whether one includes or excludes those selections that have occurred automatically through succeeding vice-presidents. Five nominees came to office as succeeding vice-presidents and later won nomination to a full term (Theodore Roosevelt, Coolidge, Truman, Johnson, Ford). It is only in the postwar period that qualifications for the presidency have played any significant role in vice-presidential selection. Experts disagree on whether the modern vice-presidency can be counted on to produce a qualified successor in case of presidential death or disability (Twentieth Century Fund 1988).

Section V

Socialization and Integration of Political Leaders

Introductory Comment

The study of leadership recruitment emphasizes the kinds of people that become political leaders and how they are selected. But there is life after political recruitment. Those chosen to be party leaders, members of parliament, cabinet officers, or presidents then learn how to play their roles, how to perform their tasks, how to interact with other leaders, which strategies work best, and how to symbolize their office. The process through which individuals acquire political orientations, values, cognitions, and beliefs is called *socialization*. It is true that political socialization has been studied most extensively as a phenomenon of childhood when political learning is at an early, formative stage; however, political socialization takes place over the whole life cycle. Adults, including political leaders, experience political learning, often based, to be sure, on socialization earlier in life (Sigel, 1989).

To the extent that political leaders of a country share similar socialization and political experiences they are, as a group, very likely to show signs, to one degree or another, of *integration*. They reflect considerable cohesiveness or consensus regarding both key social, political, or economic values and the fundamental rules of the game, or norms, on the basis of which they will operate. The extent to which a group of political leaders in a country are, or can be expected to be, integrated is a matter of empirical inquiry and, perhaps, debate.

The socialization of political leaders, often referred to as *elite socialization*, has not been studied extensively. It certainly is possible that childhood experiences affect the perspectives and behavior of leaders. Because the general values of a society are diffused and transmitted widely in early life experience, leaders will come to a particular public office already versed in the basic rules of the game. A study of new members of the California legislature showed, for example, that freshmen had been well-versed in the rules of the game and representational roles before they entered the legislature (Bell and Price 1975). Even so, the California legislature is an institutional environment in which new members learn a great deal from veterans about public policy and political strategy (Muir 1982). At the same time, California is not necessarily typical; elite socialization experiences may vary across countries and perhaps among leaders within countries (Asher 1973).

Education is a powerful socializing experience for political leaders in all countries. Britain is a good case in point—a society in which the particular educational experience provided in the public (really private) schools and the elite universities. Putnam (1976) has observed that "many of the distinctive features of British elite culture can be detected in vitro in the public school experience: a reliance on internalized norms rather than on codified rules to govern the exercise of power, a preference for amateur generalists rather than technically trained specialists, a finely tuned sensitivity to emergent consensus, a gradualist approach to problems of social change." Elite education in Britain, moreover, increases "the homogeneity and integration of the British elite, for common educational experiences and long-standing ties of friendship and trust increase the ability of an elite to cooperate effectively" (p. 96).

Post-recruitment socialization is most effective in highly institutionalized environments. For instance, observers have commented on the rapidity with which firebrand Labour MPs were absorbed into the British House of Commons and on the remarkable reeducation of Communist party deputies in Italy and France (di Palma 1977, 132–84). More marked, perhaps, is the committee system of the U.S. Congress, especially in the highly integrated committees—such as the House Appropriations Committee—where senior members inculcate in freshmen a strong set of norms about committee goals and practices (Fenno 1966).

The political leadership of democratic societies has a tendency to be cohesive or consensual about the fundamentals—the rules of the game; basic social, political, and economic goals; ideological sophistication; understandings about heading off or managing conflict. One scholar has said that "the problem of integration is the basic one of how any political system holds itself together" (Fenno 1966, 191). Integration is a matter of degree. Of course, political elites may be divided by partisan loyalties, among other things, and may engage in competition among themselves in a variety of ways.

The leadership of parties in power may exhibit marked integration, some minimal level of which is essential to survival. Elite integration varies in size and shape, from the mutually supportive environment of consociational leadership in the Netherlands, to the integrative implications of "ministerial responsibility" in Britain, to the more complex, factionalized politics of parliamentary and cabinet leadership in Japan (Baerwald 1974; Dogan 1975; Lijphart 1968).

Elite integration seems surely to foster and buttress stable politics and effective rule. But there is a persistent tension between consensus and conflict in democratic societies. The integration of a political leadership may mean oligarchy and even tyranny. Unsurprisingly, this tension stimulates an ongoing debate—the elitist—pluralist controversy— between those who claim that the leadership is a highly consensual power elite, or ruling class, and those who claim that pluralist leadership can thrive within the bosom of wide agreement over fundamental values and rules of the game. This elitist-pluralist debate shows up most prominently in research on political leadership in local communities, the so-called community-power studies (Polsby 1980; Waste 1986).

We illustrate these themes in the readings that follow. Donald D. Searing begins with a wide-ranging analysis of the socialization of political leaders in Great Britain. He compares British MPs with parliamentary candidates, attentive publics, and citizens generally to show a high degree of consensus about the rules of the game among leaders. He charts how the rules of the game can "deradicalize" politicians of both Left and Right, but he also shows the extent of conflict between Labour and Conservative MPs over deliberative versus representational norms.

Chong Lim Kim and Samuel C. Patterson, in the second reading, directly address the issue of the integration of political leadership. Their analysis of parliamentarians in six countries shows a rather high level of heterogeneity, not homogeneity, in the background characteristics of these leaders; these are not socially homogeneous groups of leaders. But these MPs do widely share recruitment experiences, and they show quite high levels of consensus regarding the role of the representative and freedom of deliberation. Moreover, Kim and Patterson underscore important value differences between Western democratic leaders and MPs in Third World countries only beginning to institutionalize democratic leadership.

The U.S. House Appropriations Committee in its modern heyday of the late 1950s and early 1960s is the best-documented highly integrated group of political leaders. Richard F. Fenno, Jr., describes how this small group of congressional leaders achieved a high level of consensus and explains the effects that integration had on the committee's legislative power.

Select Bibliography

Burns, J. M. 1978. *Leadership.* New York: Harper and Row.

Clarke, H. D., and M. M. Czudnowski, eds. 1987. *Political Elites in Anglo-American Democracies.* DeKalb: Northern Illinois University Press.

Czudnowski, M. M., ed. 1982. *Does Who Governs Matter?* DeKalb: Northern Illinois University Press.

Czudnowski, M. M., ed. 1983. *Political Elites and Social Change.* DeKalb: Northern Illinois University Press.

Dogan, M., ed. 1975. *The Mandarins of Western Europe.* Beverly Hills, CA: Sage.

Higley, J., D. Deacon, and D. Smart. 1979. *Elites in Australia.* London: Routledge & Kegan Paul.

Putnam, R. D. 1973. *The Beliefs of Politicians.* New Haven, CT: Yale University Press.

9

The Socialization of British Political Leaders

Donald D. Searing

![W]hen streams of research are isolated from one another by methodological style and ideological character, the fact that they share similar explanatory principles is easily overlooked. Thus, since the 1950s many quantitative and "pluralistic" American studies have argued that political leaders are more likely than the public to support procedural rules of the game (McClosky and Brill 1983; Searing 1982). And since at least the 1930s, many qualitative and "left-wing" European commentaries have argued that, in matters of socio-economic policy, members of parliaments become more moderate than their parties' activists (Miliband 1973, Parkin 1971). These important claims are embedded in two partial theories which have previously been treated as unrelated, the theories of institutional support and of deradicalization. And yet, different as these theories may be in many respects, they are driven by similar socialization principles which accompany movement from one role in the political system to another. Such socialization principles are a conservative force inculcating both institutional support in procedural rules of the game and deradicalization in orientations towards public policy (Dawson, Prewitt, and Dawson 1977).

"A Theory of Political Socialization: Institutional Support and Deradicalization in Britain," *British Journal of Political Science* 16 (1986):341–376. Copyright © by Cambridge University Press. Reprinted by permission of Cambridge University Press.

Moreover, the coincidence of these principles invites a synthesis of the previously unrelated, partial theories. Following A. N. Whitehead's advice to "seek simplicity and distrust it," this article will construct a single parsimonious socialization theory that encompasses consequences for institutional support and for deradicalization. After setting out the theory and the methods used to investigate it, I examine its fit with British data on general publics, attentive publics, parliamentary candidates and Members of Parliament. . . . I conclude by giving distrust its due and exploring the main exogenous variables that pull against the theory and confound its results.

Theory and Method

Theories of institutional support and deradicalization are loosely articulated and include a rag-bag of independent variables besides socialization. Still, it is a central theme of both types of theories that socialization into political roles builds support for established patterns of power. The same theme is found in many theories of general political socializaiton which address the consequences of socialization into such political roles as voter, activist or politician. This conjunction between the particular and the general suggests that the particular accounts of institutional support and deradicalization might be linked, and the dynamics of each better understood, by bringing them under the general socialization perspective. To do so, I have sought to crystalize and to state systematically a central proposition from each in such a way that its derivation from the more general socialization perspective will be convincing. The new synthesized socialization theory consists of four simple, interrelated propositions, the first of which is the most general:

P1. *The greater the involvement in a political collectivity, the greater the support for the central views of that collectivity.*

The political collectivities referred to include political systems, parliaments and political parties. The central views referred to include basic political orientations such as freedom of speech or policy beliefs about particular topics such as taxation; they can in fact include any beliefs regarded as very important by a collectivity's members. Thus, beneath its clumsy systematic structure, this proposition has the ring of plain common sense. Its simple claim is that collectivities tend to protect their established procedures and outlooks by teaching them to those who become involved in their affairs—and the greater the involvement, the more effective the teaching.

This teaching relies upon processes of political learning, the learning of any politically relevant belief, and upon political socialization proper, the learning of beliefs that integrate individuals into a well-developed structure of roles. It is also important to emphasize that P1, and the propositions to follow as well, should be interpreted as probabilistic rather than universal. They certainly do not hold in all times and places, nor for all members of a collectivity at any one time and place. Moreover, the proposition points to relative positions of one group compared to another rather than to the content of any given group's ideology. In other words, as the world turns, the relative positions of groups ordered by degrees of political involvement are expected to remain the same even if all slide ideologically to right or left.

Having set out the general socialization proposition, we now turn to institutional support and deradicalization, which can be cast as applications to particular types of attitudes and types of collectivities. Political rules of the game are the types of attitudes, the central views, of primary interests in research on institutional support. This research has found that many such procedural rules are not well-recognized by the public. At the same time, it has been argued that support for these principles can be generated by political involvement and particularly by the sorts of socialization processes that, in the words of a senior member of the British House of Commons, "make a politician conscious of the fact that there's more to be done than winning one round of the battle, that there's a permanence of the fabric that can be damaged if one doesn't honour the sort of unwritten principles." Differences in types of collectivities are not stressed in accounts of institutional support, partly because the focus is on consequences rather than processes of socialization, and partly because all relevant collectivities are believed to teach much the same constitutional message (support for procedural rules of the game), the main difference being that some teach this message more fully and effectively than others. Hence:

P2. *The greater the political involvement, the greater the support for political rules of the game.*

To clarify the argument before it becomes more complicated, it can be depicted in graphs of the sort by which the study's data will subsequently be displayed. Thus, figure 9.1 orders by degree of political involvement on the horizontal axis general publics, attentive publics, activists, candidates and Members of Parliament. P2's prediction about the relationship between degrees of political involvement and support for political rules of the game is described in the upper half of figure 9.1. The claim is that this relationship will be monotonic, that the dependent variable will never decrease as the independent variable increases across the spectrum from general public to Members of Parliament. Figure 9.1 predicts a sharp rise between the attentive public on the one hand and the

Figure 9.1 Two Theories of Normal Socialization: Institutional Support and Deradicalization

(a) Institutional Support

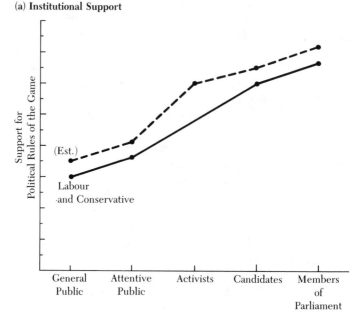

(b) Deradicalization

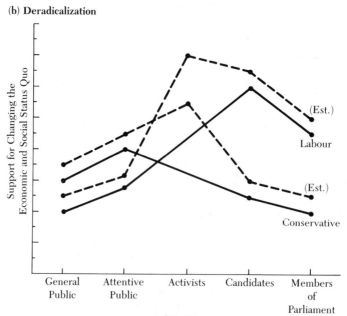

activists and candidates on the other because those who actively participate in political collectivities are much more likely than the public to encounter the full range of norms. The broken line in figure 9.1 has been
added as an illustration of what the shape of the prediction might look
like were it to include the activists, a group for which we do not have data
for our tests. The solid line represents the actual prediction that will be
tested against the evidence.

Deradicalization arguments focus, of course, on different types of
attitudes: beliefs about the substance of economic and social policy. And
the nature of the collectivities involved is more problematic. Those encountered across figure 9.1's steps of political involvement include: (1)
the political system: (2) extra-parliamentary parties: (3) parliament and
parliamentary parties. By contrast with the assumption that all are
teaching much the same message about political rules of the game, accounts of deradicalization argue that in matters of public policy somewhat different messages are taught in different collectivities such that:

P3. *The relationship between political involvement and support for
changing the economic and social status quo is curvilinear.*

The curve begins its rise as the general public is exposed to haphazard political learning in the political system. As we move across the attentive public and into the ranks of the activists, however, extra-parliamentary parties assume a growing importance. Their views tend to be more
radical than those usually imparted by the wider political system on the
one side and by parliament and the parliamentary parties on the other.
And, since neither the attentive public nor the candidates are as preoccupied as the activists are with the extra-parliamentary parties, it is the activists' views that are expected to be the most extreme. This is represented
in the lower half of figure 9.1 where the vertical axis has now become
support for changing the economic and social status quo. Rising along
this axis, the illustrative broken lines predict that the peak of fundamentalism in each party is typically to be found among the activists (Welch
and Studlar 1983; Whiteley 1981).

At this point, the slope turns downwards in figure 9.1 because further political involvement draws individuals towards parliament, where
central policy attitudes tend to be less extreme than those found in the
party machines outside. These attitudes are noticed by candidates who,
through anticipatory socialization, are experimenting with views of the
group to which they aspire, and they are internalized by MPs who,
through socialization in a well-developed role structure, are learning the
message of moderation. Furthermore, inter-party differences, which are
not an issue in research on institutional support, are prominent here. One
such difference is the comparatively steep climb figure 9.1 predicts for

the Labour side between the attentive public and the activists. Another is the smaller range of variation on the Conservative side and the placement of candidates closer to MPs. Underlying these projections is the assumption that, compared to Labour, Conservative leaders have created greater consensus and less alienation between their troops inside and outside Westminster.

Our socialization theory of institutional support and deradicalization can be completed with a fourth proposition connecting the second and third by a link between institutional support and deradicalization. Although this link is found in theories of deradicalization, its present source is Balfour's comment, "Our whole political machinery presupposes a people so fundamentally at one that they can safely afford to bicker." P4 arises from concern for democracy when politicians bicker very cautiously and when consensus flows freely between procedural questions and policy agendas:

P4. *There is a direct, positive and reciprocal relationship between support for political rules of the game and support for the economic and social status quo.*

Commitment to procedural rules is not inevitably associated with loyalty to existing economic and social arrangements. Logically, political rules of the game need not tether the status quo, nor vice versa. Nevertheless, historically and psychologically one apparently leads to the other via socialization, particularly among national politicians who guard the rules and guide the policies. Thus, many rules of the game have important consequences for what is and is not accomplished: they seem to fix boundaries upon behaviour and channel policy change into reformist rather than revolutionary programmes. When the Parliamentary Labour party, for instance, has been Her Majesty's Loyal Opposition, it has generally accepted the Conservative Government's right to govern and to defend the economic and social status quo. Its opposition has been "opposition up to a point" (Punnett 1973). From the other end of the proposition, political moderates rarely attack procedural rules, for, unlike radical colleagues, they seldom find such norms inconvenient. Since their policy aims can be accomplished within existing procedural frameworks, it is less costly for them to accept the cues and endorse the rules of the game.

To investigate the theory's fit with the data, a great deal of data are required. I examine survey responses collected during 1972 and 1973 from British Members of Parliament, candidates, attentive publics and general publics. Members of Parliament ($N = 521$) were interviewed by means of taperecorded discussions. They also filled in printed forms and returned a mailback questionnaire. A response rate of 83 percent applies to backbenchers, members of the government and opposition spokesmen alike. At the same time, a sample of candidates was drawn from the activist stratum's upper layers. It is composed of 107 individuals (response rate 90 percent) who stood and came closest to winning in the 1970 general election but who had never themselves been MPs. The attitudes of attentive publics and general publics are drawn from an opinion survey, also administered at the same time, with a probability sample of 2,500 British adults. The attentive publics are those respondents (16 percent) who scored highest on a Likert-type item about interest in politics. The general publics include all the rest who, responding to a standard party identification question, indicated that they regarded themselves as Labour or Conservative.

These four groups are located at different steps on the scale of political involvement, and data for each of the four will be compared for each party. Two distinct attitude measures are involved. Specific views about procedural rules of the game and about economic and social policies are assessed by Likert-type scales offering four responses. Political values such as "free enterprise" or "economic equality" are measured by a technique derived from the work of Milton Rokeach which requests respondents to rank-order items from an inventory of political ideals (Searing 1978). The institutional support proposition (P2) will be examined first. Then we shall consider P3 which deals with deradicalization. The "Balfour connection," P4, which ties these two together, will conclude the tests and prepare the way for considering the variables that most frequently meddle with the theory and muddle its consequences.

Institutional Support

The theory of institutional support claims that a consensus behind political rules of the game, behind constitutional and procedural conventions, is essential for democracy's survival. The link to socialization enters with the assumption that there is no reason to expect people to support the rules of the game unless they learn to believe in them.

In most countries, the concept of "rules of the game" is broader than the concept of "constitutional norms." In Britain, however, the two concepts are more closely related, because British constitutional norms cover so much more ground than do the constitutions of other nations (Johnson 1977). . . . It proved possible to reduce the multiple indicators in the interview and questionnaire data to a single, composite variable for each constitutional norm. Each norm was then cross-tabulated with all of the others, thereby producing a matrix that revealed two internally coherent but opposed interpretations of rules of the game, two views of the British Constitution that are quite incompatible: every significant correlation between core norms in one and either core or cluster norms in the other is a negative relationship.

It has long been recognized that the British Constitution embodies two principles. The first concerns direction and deliberation. It forces attention on consultation among leading actors at Westminster and is built around the topics of "Parliamentarism," "flexible tactics" and "adaptation." The second focuses on responsiveness and representation for both individuals and groups and revolves around another core triad of topics: "role of the electorate," "individual responsibility" and "vigorous and critical opposition." Nevertheless, standard accounts of rules of the game have underestimated the empirical opposition between these two principles. Together they create an axis that divides procedural views into two configurations that can be characterized as *deliberative* and *representational* interpretations of the British Constitution. Indeed, the first principal component produced by a factor analysis of these data is plainly the deliberation–representation dimension.

Moreover, the split between the two interpretations of rules of the game has much to do with partisanship. Approximately two-thirds of the Conservative MPs and candidates consistently approve at least five out of six norms from the deliberative interpretation, while a similar proportion of Labour MPs and candidates likewise supports representational norms. But Conservative MPs are joined by only 38 percent of Labour respondents: and only 16 percent from their own ranks cross over to endorse the full-blown representational viewpoint. Since socialization mainly teaches norms that are central in a collectivity, we shall investigate the relationship between political involvement and support for political rules of the game first for Conservatives on the deliberative interpretation and then for Labour on the representational.

Deliberative Rules of the Game

At the core of the deliberative interpretation are "parliamentarism," "flexible tactics" and "adaptation: accept limitations." Parliamentarism portrays Parliament as a deliberative assembly for reconciling conflicting opinions and discovering the common interest. Consistency and responsible policy are expected to prevail even when elite deliberation uncovers common interests that prove unpopular. Flexible tactics denotes a very English approach to compromise, which commends it as a constructive process of fitting together different views rather than turning everything upside down. Adaptation is the view that half a loaf is better than none and that prudence requires sensitivity to prevailing climates of opinion.

. . . Endorsements for parliamentarism, flexible tactics and adaptation are plotted against degrees of political involvement. And the pattern is nearly exactly as predicted by P2: the greater the involvement in political life, the greater the support for political rules of the game. As the degrees of political involvement increase from the Conservative general public to the attentive public to candidates to MPs, the dependent variable never decreases. And, consistent with the considerable gap posited between publics and politicians, the sharpest rise is between the Conservative attentive public and the candidates.

The secondary or cluster norms associated with deliberative rules of the game are "concession," "trust in politicians" and the "supremacy of parliament." Concession involves giving political opponents their due through concrete political deals. Representative systems also require considerable trust in politicians, since without such trust it is difficult to see how representatives could compromise. The last secondary norm, parliamentary supremacy, fortifies and legitimizes the deliberative process by claiming that no authority can legitimately challenge or override any law passed by Parliament. . . .Support for these three secondary or cluster norms is distributed in the same pattern as the others. With the exception of concession, between the general and attentive publics, endorsements never decline as we ascend the steps of political involvement. Instead, they increase dramatically from the bottom to the top of the scale. The gap between the Conservative public on one side and the politicians on the other is highlighted by responses to supremacy of Parliament, the norm regarded as the constitution's keystone. It is remarkable that more politicians do not endorse it, suggesting that their constitutional bona fides should not be exaggerated; but more remarkable still is the finding that less than 50 percent of the general public is on the same side of the field.

Representational Rules of the Game

"Role of the electorate," "vigorous opposition" and "individual responsibility" constitute the core norms of the representational interpretation favoured by Labour. That the electorate's views should be "heard up here" and have a significant impact upon public policy is a basic principle of the contemporary constitution. Vigorous opposition is a check against corruption and incompetent administration and is also the system's principal safety valve for protecting minority rights and expressing the electorate's discontent. These representational themes are armed with the weapons of individual responsibility, the doctrine that makes ministers answerable to the House of Commons for their department's work. This norm, which was not included in the public opinion survey, helps to ensure ministerial attentiveness to the electorate's representatives.

As regards Labour endorsements of the representational interpretation, [the analysis showed] the expected increase between the general public and the better-informed attentive public. It also [showed] another steep increase in support for these rules of the game between Labour's attentive public and its candidates, who participate in extra-parliamentary party organizations and look towards Westminster. But the next step, service as an MP at Westminster, reverses the trend: support for the role of the electorate and for individual responsibility norms actually declines with this further increase on the political involvement scale. Why? The answer, I believe, is that representational themes in the constitution are more recent, more partisan and more "radical" than deliberative doctrines—and that this is an example of deradicalization at work on procedural rules of the game, in the same way it is alleged to work on matters of economic and social policy.

The secondary or cluster norms of the representational interpretation include "freedom," "functional representation" and "trust in citizens." Freedom of speech is a constitutional norm because the constitution's democratic and parliamentary characteristics would make little sense without it. Functional representation suggests that representation should be developed through contacts between the executive and organizations like trade unions, professional associations and churches. Trust in citizens, the third cluster norm, has importance for representative government because, just as politicians cannot work together without mutual trust, so citizens are unlikely to join in political activity with people they believe to be untrustworthy.

. . . The pattern for these three secondary norms is the same as for the role of the electorate and individual responsibility: a steady increase in endorsement from Labour's general public to candidates, broken by a decline in support at the next level of political involvement, the Parliamentary Labour party. Thus, the pattern of Labour's support for representational rules becomes in the end curvilinear as a result of stronger countervailing cues among MPs than among candidates. Moreover, compared to Conservatives, Labour produces steeper slopes on average between the attentive public and the candidates, and even steeper ones between the general public and the attentive public. This again may reflect a partisanship that boosts support for doctrines that best fit party ideology.

Overall, the data on rules of the game are consistent with P2. But is a parsimonious socialization theory by itself a convincing explanation? Exogenous variables are certainly involved as well, selection effects being the most obvious, and we shall bring them into focus after examining deradicalization and the Balfour connection.

Deradicalization

The deradicalization proposition (P3) suggests that the relationship between political involvement and support for changing the economic and social status quo is curvilinear. This focuses attention on the concept of an economic and social status quo in terms of which both radicalism and moderation are defined. For Britain, it is widely accepted that the economic status quo is the mixed economy and the social status quo the welfare state. In the Labour party, the winds of radicalism blow from the left and seek to transform the mixed economy into public ownership and the welfare state into genuine economic and social equality. Radicalism in the Conservative party, by contrast, comes from the right and exerts pressure to roll back the mixed economy towards free enterprise and the welfare state towards *laissez-faire*. In both parties, moderation involves resisting these forces, defending the mixed economy and welfare state and insisting on improvement through reform rather than radical change. Since different aspects of the mixed economy and welfare state are at the heart of orthodoxy and controversy in each party, different measures are needed for each, and each side will be examined separately. . . .

Labour: Inequality and Radical Transformation

Like other European socialist parties, Labour originally set out to transform the distribution of power, income and status: and, as in most of the others, the Parliamentary Labour party was soon accused by left-wing activists of abandoning revolutionary tactics, re-interpreting egalitarian goals, collaborating with established elite groups and accommodating itself to the status quo. . . . For each group on the political involvement scale, the proportion of respondents ranking socialism first, second or third increased steadily from Labour's general public to its attentive public to its candidates and, contrary to the accusations, continued to rise from the candidates to the Members of Parliament.

Still, the principal complaint is not that Members of Parliament have abandoned socialist goals but that they have reinterpreted them, that the Parliamentary Labour party has been less concerned with economic equality than with social equality, especially equality of opportunity. This is reflected in . . . the ranking of "economic equality," which follows the predicted curvilinear pattern: endorsements rise steadily to a peak among Labour's parliamentary candidates and then decline among the party's MPs. By contrast, "social equality," widely interpreted by MPs are equality of opportunity, draws greater support from the party at Westminster. Social equality, economic equality, socialism and "participatory democracy" are all important values in the Labour party; and support for them increases from Labour's general public to the attentive public to the candidates. With the two most radical ideals, however, economic equality and participatory democracy, Labour's MPs pull back to produce the curvilinear pattern predicted by P3.

Accounts of deradicalization also claim that Labour MPs support moderate reforms to improve the mixed economy and welfare state but shun more radical strategies. Consistent with this argument, support for comprehensive schools, seen as a moderate innovation at the time of the study, and opposition to selective schooling, by then as much a part of the ethos at Westminster as it was a dogma in the party outside, rises to a peak among the candidates and hardly falls back at all among MPs. In contrast, the educational issue, . . . "university for all" is much more radical. This item proposes making a university education available to everyone who wishes to attend, regardless of previous performance in school. And here the MPs pull away: only 45 percent of them endorse this option as compared to 70 percent of Labour's attentive public and 74 percent of its candidates. In the same vein, the two partisan worlds react quite differently to the proposal "taxation to equality," i.e., to tax the rich as much as necessary to create economic equality. Here the MPs withdraw just as they did on open university admissions. Both these radical items generate the expected pattern which, after a comparatively slight but steady rise from the general public to the attentive public to the candidates, carries the MPs back down to a level of support below that even of the party's general public.

The item . . . "perceive class conflict" directs our attention to views of society and established institutions. Perceptions of class conflict rise between Labour's attentive public and candidates and then decline in the parliamentary party. The same configuration is produced by responses to the "believe men equal" item which is based upon rejection of a claim about natural inequality. The [sizeable gap] here between the publics and the candidates reflects an ideological sensitivity that is more likely to be provided by role socialization in partisan collectivities than by the haphazard political learning of those less involved in political affairs. The left also regards the British monarchy as the chief symbol of many of the traditions and social structures it would like to dismantle. [The issue] "accept criticism of Queen" offers an opportunity to express dissatisfaction with the Royal Family. And the line here rises even more steeply than the others, up to 94 percent among the candidates before declining to 76 percent among the MPs.

Thus, the Labour data are consistent with the deradicalization proposition and indeed with Michels 1962 celebrated analysis of the German Social Democratic party from which much deradicalization theory has been generated. We shall now examine the model's applicability to the Conservative party, for if the theory of deradicalization is well founded it should apply to parties of the right as well as the left.

Conservatives: Laissez-Faire and Authority

Between the wars, the leadership of the Conservative Parliamentary party departed from the previous generation's *laissez-faire* doctrines: and the crushing electoral defeat of 1945 led the Conservative leadership to accept that the economy must not only be managed but mixed, between public and private sectors (Beer 1965, 313–17). Yet Conservative activists in the party outside Westminster did not reorient themselves on the norms of "free-enterprise," "property" and "capitalism" as readily as the MPs did. The results of this "cultural lag" in the extra-parliamentary party can be seen in [the] curvilinear patterns similar to those found for Labour beliefs. Support for free enterprise and property climbs to a summit among the Conservative attentive public and then declines for candidates and MPs. With capitalism, this peak is reached at the top rather than the bottom of the activist stratum, among the candidates.

None the less, the apogee of fundamentalist opinion in the Conservative party will usually be found among attentive publics rather than among candidates (in contrast to the Labour side). Deradicalization theory predicts that the true apogee will be found in the same place in both parties: among the activists whose views are unmeasured here. The contrast with the Labour party can be attributed largely to the success of Conservative leaders in building a consensus that makes the move from the extra-parliamentary party to Westminster seem more desirable than doctrinally dangerous. This in turn facilitates anticipatory socialization for candidates, who look to Westminster for cues, not just to the party in the country.

As they did with the mixed economy, Conservative Members of Parliament tend to accept the welfare state's existing arrangements. By 1950, R. A. Butler's efforts at re-educating the parliamentary party had persuaded it of "the need in our modern democracy to associate the Tory party with progressive and humane causes (Butler 1971, 28–29). Given that "social progress" would be expected to be a source of unease in the extra-parliamentary party, and under Butler's sponsorship a component of the new orthodoxy at Westminster, the pattern should not increase from the Conservative general public to attentive public but should rather decrease and then ascend into the ante-rooms and corridors of Westminster, which is indeed the path it takes. . . .

Although not necessarily incompatible with social progress and the welfare state, values like "meritocracy," "efficiency" and "self-discipline" can have harsh consequences if applied immoderately. The Conservative party generally endorses these values, but [the analysis of the data] demonstrates that support for them is stronger among extra-parliamentary partisans than among MPs. In the same vein, Conservatives also recommend the razor of selectivity to slow down growth in spending on social services and to minimize the egalitarian consequences of these policies; and the "selectivity" item follows the same curvilinear pattern, with support cresting in the attentive public and with a comparatively restricted range of variation.

Finally, "order" and "authority" have always been fundamental Tory doctrines (Blake 1970). Such beliefs are encased in debates on crime and morality, policy areas where, during the post-war period, the status quo also came to be dominated by progressive positions. At the time of the interviews, this progressive consensus was threatened by cries for longer prison sentences and more rigorous parole procedures and for reintroducing capital punishment. The item . . . "harsher punishments" draws the only set of reactionary responses whose pattern is not curvilinear and whose highest point occurs in the Conservative general public rather than among those more involved with the extra-parliamentary party. The familiar picture reappears with the next item, which proposes to "reintroduce the death penalty" for the murder of police officers. These attitudes towards authority are part of the Conservative preference for an ordered, hierarchical society, an image symbolized best for many Conservatives by the Royal Family. And rejection without reservation of "criticism of the Queen" rises from the Conservative general to the attentive public and then again slips down among the candidates and further on down among Members of Parliament.

[The data analyzed here] shows that the deradicalization proposition (P3) applies to the Labour party and also the Conservative party where the curvilinear arc pulls from the right rather than the left. And yet socialization cannot be the only factor at work, for socialization is a conservative force—and the 1970s was a decade of radicalization driven by exogenous variables that need to be taken into account. But first, proposition four.

The Balfour Connection

The theory's fourth and final proposition (P4) submits that there is a direct, positive and reciprocal relationship between support for rules of the game and support for the economic and social status quo. This proposition applies primarily, of course, to socialization in parliaments, for it is mainly in these collectivities that both types of support are likely to be established as central views. Moreover, the projected positive relationship is not simply an artefact of each variable being promoted by role socialization. There are direct independent connections between these two sets of beliefs, and the flow of influence is reciprocal.

Thus, attachment to political rules of the game promotes an acceptance of the economic and social status quo because the rules frequently favour existing policies and arrangements. The proposition is probabilistic rather than universal and refers to general outlooks across sets of rules and policies. Constitutional moderates are rarely socio-economic radicals. And support for a few politically expedient doctrines does not make a constitutional moderate: the supremacy of parliament, for example, has long been supported by constitutional radicals in both major parties, who believe it would facilitate the implementation of their policies against a national consensus. Conversely, attachment to the economic and social status quo promotes acceptance of the political rules of the game because policies characterized by moderation and incrementalism are usually accomplished best by working within the system. Again, there are exceptions, but again it is the general outlooks that are important. The SDP and the Liberals, for example, are socio-economic moderates and general constitutional defenders, notwithstanding that they propose changes in particular procedural rules that they believe are biased against them. Given the reciprocal nature of the relationship, it cannot be analysed conclusively. Nevertheless, it does suggest a consequence worth investigating: that the strongest commitments to rules of the game should be found in political groups with the strongest commitments to the economic and social status quo.

The most valuable support for political rules of the game is support for those rules that are liked best by one's political opponents. In our study, this would be Labour support for the deliberative norms and Conservative support for the representational. These data [were assembled] for each parliamentary party's ideological groups, . : . ranked from high to low according to their relative outlooks on defending the mixed economy and welfare state. These groups attract their members by ideological affinity and exist to study issues from a particular perspective or to pursue political goals and to guide party policy towards ideals that group members would like to see put into practice. The "High" ranking is assigned to the moderate social democrats on the Labour side and to members of Pressure for Economic and Social Toryism (PEST) on the Conservative. The Fabian Society and the Bow Group hold the "Intermediate" rank. And the "Low" support level for existing economic and social arrangements is represented by the Tribune Group and the Monday Club.

For each group within each party there are two [criteria]: the percentage of the group's members that approves all three core norms of the constitutional interpretation preferred by their political opponents [and] the percentage that approves at least five of the interpretation's six core plus cluster norms. These data show plainly that the strongest endorsements for procedural rules of the game are indeed found in groups that also have the strongest commitments to the economic and social status quo. The only exception to the pattern is in Labour's column for core and cluster norms. But even here approval for the rules of the game most preferred by political opponents is four times as strong among both the High and Intermediate supporters of the status quo as it is in the Low group.

The flow of influence is reciprocal: lack of support for the economic and social status quo can also undermine support for constitutional norms. Those who stand to lose or win the most find it most difficult to endorse such norms and, as the political struggle intensifies, they lose their taste for rules that hinder their campaign. It is not at all surprising, therefore, that the decade of the 1970s, which saw so much heated radicalism in attitudes towards the mixed economy and welfare state, was also a decade of constitutional improprieties (Searing 1982). These improprieties are a tribute to the strength of the forces that can counteract the conservative consequences of the political socialization of politicians, and are a further reminder that the theory we have reconstructed in, so to speak, an empty room actually operates in a very full and complicated world.

Exogenous Variables

Our parsimonious socialization theory of institutional support and deradicalization has both plausibility and a reasonable fit with the data. Nevertheless, we must distrust it, for while the parsimony facilitates the mapping of socialization's normal consequences, it locks out many other important variables that potentially contradict the theory or confound its results.

In particular, two types of exogenous variables are so frequently and successfully meddlesome that it is unwise to consider parsimonious socialization theories without giving them their due: "selection effects" and "ideological interventions." Thus, since each group, beginning with the attentive public, is drawn from the previous group, selection or recruitment effects are the most obvious missing variables that might work in the same direction as socialization to produce the patterns observed [to this point]. . . .

Selection or Socialization?

When the distinctive attitudes of a political group are attributed to socialization, a criticism is frequently voiced that these distinctive attitudes may be due instead to recruitment, that is to say, to the criteria by which members of the group were selected. If, for example, MPs seem more power-oriented than candidates, is this because they have absorbed the orientation at Westminster (socialization) or because the more power-oriented candidates were selected for the better seats and were therefore more likely to become MPs (recruitment)? Actually, either socialization or selection variables, or both, may be working at each step on the scale of political involvement. The problem, therefore, is to estimate for each step, each type of attitude and each political party, how much of the observed differences are attributable to one set of variables and how much to the other. . . .

To estimate the mix between selection and socialization effects, it is necessary to reconstruct a picture of the views of the attentive public before it emerged from the general public. This postulated distinctive subgroup within the general public can be reconstructed by matching its background characteristics against those of the present attentive public. And, to retain full information, this is accomplished by weighting the general public according to the attentive public's distributions for age and level of education. Level of education is important here, because the attentive public is better educated than the general public, and because this variable is the most likely background factor involved in political learning prior to emergence from the general public. There are now three groups: general public, matched general public and attentive public. . . . The matched group is the key. *Correspondence between the views of the matched group and those of the attentive public suggests selection, for the attentive public's views would apparently not have changed since it emerged, whereas correspondence between the views of the matched group and those of the general public suggests socialization, for the attentive public's views, now different, were in the past apparently akin to those of the general public.*

In the same way, candidates' distributions on age and education were used to create from the attentive public a matched attentive public, i.e., matched to the candidates' background profile. . . .

We shall use group means $(\bar{X})$ . . . to compare attitude distributions among groups. . . . [These] are calculated for each group and for the matched general public that stands between them. If the matched general public's mean resembles that of the attentive public, this is evidence for selection, since the attentive public did not apparently go on to acquire new views of its own. If, conversely, the matched general public's mean is closer to that of the general public, . . . this is evidence for socialization, since the attentive public has apparently undergone attitude change since being recruited. . . .

Overall, socialization proves more important than selection, but selection is prominent and occasionally predominant for particular stages, types of attitudes and political parties. . . .

The picture changes at the next step on the scale of political involvement, the transition from interest to activity, from attentive publics to candidates. . . . Selection effects and socialization effects are evenly balanced in two cases (Conservatives on political rules of the game, Labour on the economic and social status quo), while socialization predominates in the others where the means of the matched attentive public incline to the left. Plainly, members of the attentive public who make the leap from interest to involvement are sometimes better informed about rules of the game or more fundamentalist than those they leave behind.

The relative significance of the exogenous selection effects increases further at the next highest level of political involvement, the step from candidates to Members of Parliament. . . . And, again, the results differ dramatically by party and type of attitude. Conservatives' means show no selection effects whatsoever for either the economic and social status quo or for political rules of the game. But Labour displays balanced selection and socialization effects for its policy views. Despite Whiteley's finding that the ideology of Labour candidates is unrelated to the "winability" of the seats for which they are selected, selection factors are apparently driven by some policy outlooks in some times and places. Furthermore, although . . . confidence is smaller here, Labour displays predominant selection effects for its beliefs about political rules of the game. It is perhaps surprising to find that even constitutional outlooks may be factors in candidate selection on the Labour side. And yet this pattern, too, is compatible with the stereotypes of the time: Conservatives selecting by "character," Labour by "principles."

In sum, socialization factors dominate the table, but selection factors are important as well. Their significance increases with increases in political involvement, and they are considerably more salient on the Labour side than on the Conservative.

Ideological Interventions

Ideological interventions constitute an equally significant type of exogenous variable. But unlike selection effects their aim is typically in one direction: to counteract moderation. In fact, as the interviews for the present study were being conducted, these countervailing forces were working to confound socialization's consequences and turn Britain's parliamentary parties away from the economic and social status quo. The decade of the 1970s offers a showcase of variables that can neutralize and even override socialization's usual effects.

The ideological interventions of this decade must be analysed as nominal variables. And at present there is no technique for comparing their strength, as in the case of selection effects, to that of socialization. What these dramatic and well-publicized interventions do provide, however, is a remarkable opportunity to penetrate this type of variable's shell and to detect its inner workings, the dynamics through which the normal consequences of political socialization can be resisted. Three components are involved: changes in events, reactions to these events, and actions that affect politicians' outlooks. The events include dramatic changes in economy, polity or society. Reactions to these events are distributed in either period or generational effects. And the individuals who react may be found in external organizations, internal factions or leadership positions. The final step occurs when these individuals organize ideological interventions aimed at radicalizing the parliamentary party. Strategies available to them include manipulating recruitment criteria, forcing moderates to retire, or resocializing sitting MPs.

The events that triggered these forces in Britain were similar for both the Labour and Conservative parties: in the background an ailing economy and social tensions; in the foreground a decade of disdain by party leaders towards fundamentalist purgatives for Britain's problems. There were, however, differences in the key groups who reacted to these events. On the Labour side it was party activists and to a lesser extent the trade-union leaders. On the Conservative side, it was the top leadership and to a lesser extent the activists. There were also differences in strategies. The Labour radicals paid relatively more attention to recruitment and retirement, while the Conservatives concentrated on modifying the views of existing members.

Harold Wilson's Governments of 1964–70 had ignored conference decisions and failed to make Britain more equal. This led to disillusionment within the extra-parliamentary party and to the suspicion that, after six years of social democratic Labour governments, capitalism was actually stronger than before. When the party returned to office in 1974–79, it proved again to be cautious, pragmatic and "Croslandlike" and continued to follow the trails of revisionism. The critical reaction to these events, the second component of ideological intervention variables, came from a generation of young, middle-class graduates who were replacing working-class activists in leadership positions in the constituency parties.

Trade-union support was won over because just as new middle-class radicals had entered the extra-parliamentary party during the late 1960s and early 1970s, so new left-wing union leaders had risen to the top of some of the larger unions at this time. Like the activists, these leaders were discontented with recent Labour Government. And, prodded by the activists, they won in 1979 the battle for mandatory reselection of MPs. This meant that, during each Parliament, each sitting Labour MP would be evaluated by his constituency party against other possible candidates. An opportunity had been created for radical activists to force moderate MPs to retire and to replace them with fundamentalists. By constantly hounding the revisionist leadership (the Leader and Deputy Leader were shouted down at the 1976 Party Conference), and by increasing the sanctions and rewards available to constituency associations, the insurgents also hoped to retard the effects of socialization in the

House of Commons which, they believed, systematically dampened the zeal of left-wing MPs.

What were the results? By the middle of the decade, observers began to note that Labour selection conferences were choosing more left-wing candidates. By the end of the decade, it was quite clear that this had been effective in counteracting some of socialization's conservative consequences and shifting the balance in the Parliamentary Labour Party to the left. There was a stampede to join the Tribune Group; and many formerly moderate MPs began to take unilateralism and the extension of nationalization more seriously than they had before.

On the other side of the House, the Conservative party's radical turn to market approaches after 1974 took place against a background of concern about economic decline, electoral defeats and disappointment with Heath's performance as Prime Minister. Mrs. Thatcher's election to the leadership of the party in 1975 was a reaction to this discontent. She and her chief supporters soon surrounded themselves with intellectual advisers who depreciated the progressive Disraelian approach to Conservatism and identified the key problem of the twentieth century as socialist collectivism. Heath had set out to stop the slide to the left and had failed. The new leadership would pursue the fundamentalist trail and would not turn back.

At the same time, there was an increase in the proportion of university graduates among new party members, just as in the Labour party. Compared to the Conservative activists they replaced, these newcomers were said to be more interested in discussing policies and less deferential to conservative MPs. And one explanation for the party's lurch to the right is that the leadership was pushed by the *laissez-faire* Conservatism of this new and more articulate generation. Some reject this account as a major factor in the radicalization, but pressures from such activists certainly played a part, as did leadership concerns over disaffection among the party's traditional middle-class supporters. With the approval of their right-wing admirers in the extra parliamentary party, Mrs. Thatcher and Sir Keith Joseph contributed the third component of ideological intervention: they acted to re-educate the parliamentary party and to strengthen the hand of the right in the party in the country.

The chief strategy towards the parliamentary party was a mixture of reason and patronage. In 1974 Sir Keith Joseph announced that he had recently been converted to "Conservatism" and founded the Centre for Policy Studies which would become a research body for generating policy proposals and promoting market liberalism. The next year, after her election as leader, Mrs. Thatcher began articulating Conservative principles in a way that made it clear that she too was calling for a return to what she believed was genuine Conservatism. Progressive Conservatives complained that she "worshipped at the shrine of Hayek" and had become "the prisoner of Chicago," but many were not unresponsive to the winds of change (Behrens 1980, 60–62).

By the end of the decade, the result of these activities was a shift in orthodoxy within the parliamentary party, a change from progressive Conservatism to neo-liberal aims. And, despite the pressures of role socialization, which many observers predicted would pull the party back to its usual course, the first Thatcher Government of 1979–83 held to the basic goals. Although there were modifications in targets and techniques, the radical break with the trend of economic policy since the late 1950s was plain.

In sum, the dynamics of the ideological interventions in the Labour party were typical in that party activists were the principal disgruntled actors, but unusual in that some of their leaders had been trained in the social sciences, knew what "socialization" meant and knew what they proposed to do about it. Their main strategy was to bypass its operations. Through reselection, they would get rid of MPs who had succumbed. Through selection, they would recruit a new generation of committed socialists. By contrast, the Conservative party provides a vivid example of another important category of this nominal variable. Here leading figures in the parliamentary party became the radicals and then worked from the top down, a testimony to the significance of strong leadership on the Conservative side and an illustration of the fact that political actors can be active rather than passive participants in their own socialization.

Conclusion

Political socialization is a prominent theme in theories of institutional support and deredicalization. Its consequences are said to buttress existing institutions by encouraging defenders and retraining insurgents. As a Labour MP, a former rebel, put it: "I think instead of me turning this place inside out, they turned me inside out a little."

Because many accounts of institutional support and deradicalization rely upon similar socialization principles, it has been possible to synthesize their central elements into a more general theory which begins with the proposition that the greater the involvement in a political collectivity, the greater the support for the central views of that collectivity. Reaching across a spectrum of involvement that extends from general publics to Members of Parliament, the institutional support proposition applies this thesis as follows: the greater the political involvement, the greater the support for procedural rules of the game. . . . British data on attitudes about two sets of rules with constitutional status, deliberative and representational norms, are for the most part consistent with the prediction. And the transition between interest and involvement, between attentive publics and candidates, proves to be a very important one. This is a step from political learning to political socialization in collectivities where even part-time activity can produce dramatic results in teaching new norms and reinforcing or elaborating those already held.

Accounts of deradicalization apply the same thesis to another set of beliefs, those about major aspects of economic and social policy. Thus, Labour's left-wing critics argue that the socialization of politicians protects privilege. Their opposite numbers on the Conservative side complain that the centre slides ever leftwards. Behind each of these attacks lies the same half-articulated theory: involvement in extra-parliamentary activity encourages fundamentalism, whereas work at Westminster encourages moderation, and therefore the relationship between political involvement and support for changing the economic and social status quo is curvilinear. This too is generally supported by the distribution of attitudes in both parties. The full curvilinear picture is evident in nearly every case, with either attentive publics or candidates taking the most extreme positions on policy matters and Members of Parliament doing the most backtracking. In the same vein, the evidence is more indirect but is nevertheless consistent again for our theory's fourth and final proposition which links institutional support and deradicalization by suggesting that the connection between them is direct, positive and reciprocal.

10

The Political Integration of Parliamentary Elites

Chong Lim Kim and Samuel C. Patterson

A subtle and yet simple argument is conventionally advanced about the role of political elites in the development of political systems. Shorn of all its qualifications and complexities, the argument is reduced to this: the establishment of viable national political institutions and the emergence of effective governmental performance depend in some important measure upon the cohesiveness, homogeneity, and unity exhibited by the political leadership of a nation. For Mosca (1939, 109-19), (1963, 146), the effectiveness of the governing stratum hinged on the recruitment of its members from among the dominant social types. Keller stresses cohesiveness regarding values as the key to the effectiveness of "strategic elites," asserting that "as societies become more differentiated a considerable degree of cohesion and consensus is needed at the top." Lasswell (and Kaplan 1950, 97) believed that the evidence from the experience of industrialized societies supported an "agglutination hypothesis"—that elites would tend to show broad commonalities with respect to values." Field and Higley (1980, 119) go so far as to assert that "the presence of a consensual unified elite is necessary for institutional stability and, hence, for all the better features of political rule." Most suc-

"Parliamentary Elite Integration in Six Nations," *Comparative Politics* 20 (July 1988):379–399. Reprinted by permission of the publisher.

cinct is perhaps Putnam's (1976, 128) dictum: "The argument that elite integration fosters political stability and effectiveness is very prevalent and very persuasive."

If the theory of elite integration, in its boldest form, is roughly correct, then we would surely expect political elites in industrialized societies to exhibit a greater degree of coherence, homogeneity, and unity than comparable elites in less advanced countries. Indeed, either directly or indirectly, analyses of the role of elite integration in political development adumbrate this general expectation. This consanguinity between elite integration and political development has been described eloquently by Putnam (1976, 124):

> Typically, elites are fragmented by the onset of socio-economic modernization. Population growth and economic development foster a division of labor and produce a highly differentiated elite structure. New members . . . are added to the elite. Within the traditional elite itself, integration declines, as its members are differentially affected by social and economic change. Moreover, in the postcolonial epoch through which most of today's poorer nations are passing, centrifugal conflicts along generational cultural lines threaten the fragile unity achieved during the struggle for independence. At the same time, increasing education, urbanization, commercialization, the spread of mass media, and the growth of new political movements are all mobilizing masses of ordinary citizens into unaccustomed political participation, releasing new energies and new pressures. In this situation political development is a contrapuntal interplay of increasing differentiation, which weakens established institutions and increases the complexity of political demands, and increasing integration, which creates new institutions and legitimates a single set of rules for allocating authority. Much depends on the emergence of strong and unified national leadership, but as the record of instability, coups, and political decay in much of the Third World suggests, elite integration is exceedingly difficult to achieve.

Elite integration, a property of the relevant political group, is a matter of degree. Elites may be more integrated in some respects than in others, and the crucial issue for elite performance may reside in the particular dimensions on which consensus is strongest. And, in any event, although Mosca and other elite theorists treated the unity of the political elites as a matter of stipulation, the cohesiveness or fragmentation of elites "should be a matter for empirical investigation rather than definitional fiat" (Putnam 1976, 107).

Political integration is a concept which has enjoyed a wide and very diverse usage. It is used to characterize broad features of national societies such as the transformation of multitribal communities into modern states, the establishment of effective governing authority over a territory, the linking of government and citizens, the process of forming a widely shared value consensus, and the capacity of a people to organize themselves politically.

The integration of a national community or an elite group is an emergent property of a collectivity. As such, integration will not be directly observable but rather must be inferred from observation of factors indicating its extent. For elite groups, Putnam identifies six such "integrative factors," or "dimensions of integration": social homogeneity, recruitment patterns, personal interaction, value consensus, group solidarity, and institutional context. Among these factors, social homogeneity, recruitment patterns, and value consensus are commonly taken to have special significance in elite analysis.

An elite group may be said to be integrated if its members share common social origins, educational and career experiences, and recruitment. Putnam (1976, 109) suggests that "the relative social homogeneity of national elites and of specific subelites could be easily compared by measuring the internal variance in their social profiles." We intend to do just this for parliamentary elites in six nations, three European democracies and three Third World nations. Social homogeneity may be "neither a necessary nor a sufficient condition for elite integration," but there certainly is a very marked tendency for elite members to share common experiences in their social and political backgrounds. Such common experiences facilitate interpersonal interaction within a political elite and have direct and indirect effects upon coherence and cohesiveness of values shared by elite members.

Moreover, an elite may be said to be integrated if its members share basic values. For Putnam (1976, 115), value consensus is "perhaps the most central dimension of elite integration. . . ." Although countless studies of elite social backgrounds have generally demonstrated a very high degree of homogeneity in social origins, status, and careers, elite value consensus has not been investigated very extensively. Cross-nationally comparable evidence about elite integration is still rather rare. In this study we assess three crucial dimensions of elite integration: homogeneity in social backgrounds and careers, common experience in recruitment, and value consensus.

Parliamentary Elites in Six Nations: Data and Measurement

Extensive data were gathered through interviews with members of parliament—one significant kind of national political leadership—in six nations, Belgium, Switzerland, Italy, Kenya, South Korea, and Turkey. If the assumptions and expectations from the theory of elite integration are supported by the data collected from such a diverse collection of nations, then they will have a much firmer footing than is possible based upon existing research.

Three nations—Kenya, South Korea, and Turkey—are located at different corners of the world, one in East Africa, another in the Far East, and still another in the Middle East. They differ significantly in their cultural patterns and in the political contexts in which their parliamentary bodies function. They also differ in their parliamentary history, party system, constitutional framework, and electoral system. The Turkish parliament, originating in the mid 1870s, has the longest lineage of the three. But in its modern form the Turkish parliament, called the Grand National Assembly, began in 1920 during the war for independence. The Korean National Assembly or *Kukhoe* was established in 1948, following the nation's first popular election. In Kenya, where there was some experience with a colonial assembly prior to independence, the new National Assembly was created in 1960 closely based on the Westminster model. By contrast, the parliaments of the European democracies—Belgium, Italy, and Switzerland—all have long histories, with their origins in the twelfth century. . . .

Although a brief discussion of the six parliaments will not do full justice to the rich complexity of these institutions, we need nevertheless to say something about the basic character of each parliament. Of the three Third World parliaments, two are unicameral and one bicameral; two are post-World War II creations, and one dates from the 1920s. The present Kenyan National Assembly dates from 1964, when a constitution creating a unicameral parliament was adopted. Twelve of its 170 members are hand-picked by the president; the remaining 158 are chosen from single-member districts. The operation of the National Assembly follows British practice, but of course there is no opposition party to occupy benches opposite the government. The National Assembly's work is almost completely controlled by the government, but backbenchers often participate vigorously in debates and vote against government-sponsored bills. In the main, however, the National Assembly occupies a secondary role in public policymaking in a system in which major political decisions are made by the president and the executive (Barkan and Okumo 1979).

The National Assembly of South Korea was created just after World War II, but its makeup was altered several times when new constitutions were adopted. At the time of the interviews, two-thirds of the 219 assemblymen were popularly elected, and the remainder were appointed by the president. While the government controlled a comfortable two-thirds of the seats, a third of the members represented various opposition parties. The Korean National Assembly shows a relatively high degree of professionalization, with well-organized committees and a large number of professional staffs. Although it is true that the president's control of the assembly is very substantial, the Korean parliament nevertheless has a role in the shaping of legislation and a significant function in constituency representation (Kim and Pai 1981).

The Turkish parliament has been in existence longer than the legislatures of most other developing nations (Kalaycioglu 1980). It is bicameral, including a 450 member assembly and a 150 member senate. Since 1961, members of both houses have been popularly elected, the deputies from sixty-seven multimember constituencies. In contrast to Kenya and Korea, where the chief executive is elected separately from the assembly, the Grand National Assembly and the Senate together select the president of the nation in Turkey. The president in turn appoints a prime minister, who must win the approval of the assembly for himself and his cabinet. Although the constitution gives all lawmaking power to parliament, as in most countries the initiation of legislation is, in fact, in the hands of the government.

The three European parliaments are historically and constitutionally less diverse than the assemblies of the three Third World nations. All are bicameral systems; all have common historical roots; all function in stable, relatively small, culturally similar environments. The Italian parliament is made up of a Chamber of Deputies of 630 members and a Senate of 315 members. Members are elected for a term of five years (except former presidents of the republic and five notables chosen by the president who serve in the senate for life). Christian Democrats, Communists, and Socialists make up the preponderance of the membership of the two houses. The Italian parliament experienced important changes in the 1970s, acquiring a degree of autonomy from the executive which it had not enjoyed in earlier decades (Manzella 1977).

The Swiss Federal Assembly consists of a National Council (*Nationalrat*) of 200 members and a Council of States (*Ständerat*) of forty-four members. Most are elected for terms of four years, with members of the Council of States representing the cantons (one of which, Glarus, elects its members for only a three-year term). The Swiss parliament operates on the basis of highly consensual norms which make it one of the world's least conflictual legislative bodies. Moreover, in Switzerland there is a very strong interpenetration of major private interest groups and parliamentary political parties, producing a "two-tiered" system of representation (Kerr 1981).

Last but not least, the parliament of Belgium resides in a constitutional monarchy. Its House of Representatives consists of 212 members; its Senate, 181 members. All serve four-year terms, although some senators are elected by provincial councils or are coopted rather than directly elected. In contrast to the consensuality of the Swiss parliament, Belgian parliamentary politics reflect the cleavage-prone tendencies of the nation's politics outside the halls of the legislature. The interesting feature of this parliamentary body is how it copes with socioeconomic, ethnoreligious, and linguistic cleavages (Debuyst 1966).

How homogeneous are members of these varied parliamentary groups in regard to their social origins, backgrounds, and recruitment experiences? And how consensual are they in regard to key political values? In order to answer these questions one needs to devise the measures of homogeneity and consensus. A modified fragmentation formula, originally suggested by Rae and Taylor (1970, 30-33), is employed to measure the homogeneity in social origins, backgrounds, and recruitment. In theory, the Rae formula yields scores ranging from 0 to 1, with a high score indicating greater fragmentation. However, the theoretical unity of 1 is attained only when the number of categories used in the calculation approaches infinity. Consequently, when different background characteristics are coded in different numbers of categories, it is not possible to compare the scores across items. The Rae formula is modified to overcome this problem of comparable measurement as follows: homogeneity score (H) = 1 − F′, where F′ is the adjusted fragmentation score. F′ is defined: F′ = F/Fmax, where F is Rae's fragmentation score and Fmax the maximum score an index can attain given its number of categories. Since homogeneity is what we are interested in, not fragmentation, we simply take the complement of F′, namely H = 1− F′.

The measure of consensus is similarly derived. For ordinal data we use the consensus formula of the following form:

$$C = 1 - \frac{2 \sum_{i=1}^{n} di}{n-1}$$

where C is the consensus score; d is the difference on alternative, defined as equal to the cumulative relative frequency, CF if CF = 1/2 and 1 − CF if otherwise; and n is the number of alternatives. The scores range from 1 (perfect consensus) to 0 (perfect dissensus) (Rae and Taylor 1970, 126). For the survey items measured at the nominal level we take the complement of the Rae fragmentation formula with an appropriate adjustment.

Elite Homogeneity: Social Background and Career

Five principal background and career attributes are scrutinized in order to discern the extent of homogeneity among the members of the six parliaments: their social origins as indexed by the status of their fathers' occu-

Table 10.1   Homogeneity in MPs' Social Origins, Education, and Careers

Characteristics	Belgium	Italy	Switzerland	Kenya	Korea	Turkey
	Homogeneity Scores for:					
Father's occupation	.031	.107	.149	.234	.173	.098
Own occupation	.174	.571	.404	.081	.032	.110
Education	.106	n.a.	.154	.204	.279	.426
Office-holding	.176	.099	.091	.823	.800	.557
Legislative experience	.024	.131	.069	.409	.083	.119
Mean Score	.102	.227	.173	.350	.275	.262
Number of Cases	150	180	235	28	119	104

pations, their educational attainment, their own occupations, their political apprenticeship and the length of their parliamentary service. In table 10.1 we report the homogeneity scores for each attribute across the six nations.

Contrary to the often asserted proposition that elites are drawn as a rule from a dominant and privileged social type, the evidence shows that the parliamentary elites arise from quite diverse social strata. They are, as a group, more heterogeneous than homogeneous. The heterogeneity of the parliamentary elites may be a special case, reflecting the unique character of the institution in which they serve. Parliaments are principally representative bodies, members of which are usually chosen in popular election. In this important respect, they are distinguishable from other types of political elites, bureaucrats, military officers, and judges. Due to the lack of comparable data, we cannot make a direct comparison with other elite groups in each nation. However, the low homogeneity that we discovered in the six nations is suggestive of the hypothesis that parliamentary elites are everywhere significantly more heterogeneous in their social composition than are other elite groups.

Nonetheless, there exists systematic variation in heterogeneity across the nations. With the single exception of members' own occupational experiences, the elites of the Third World parliaments, Kenya, Korea, and Turkey, show a consistently greater degree of homogeneity than do the legislative elites of Belgium, Italy, and Switzerland. A close examination of more detailed breakdowns of the occupational status of the members' father reveals essentially the same conclusion: the Third World elites originate from a narrower range of social classes than do the European elites.

Members of the Third World parliaments exhibit a remarkably high achievement in their formal education, markedly higher than their European counterparts. The percentages of members with a college or postgraduate degree are 95.7 percent in Korea and 77.9 percent in Turkey. By contrast, similar percentages are 54.7 percent for Belgium and

67.6 percent for Switzerland. The difference between the two groups of parliamentary elites indicates something important about the political opportunity structure of the Third World nations and the role of formal education in it. First, opportunities for higher education in these nations are limited to those few who have the advantage of high family status. Second, formal education, especially the attainment of an advanced degree from a prestigious school in the country or abroad, is a crucially important factor in both social and political mobility. Although one cannot infer from the homogeneity scores alone which social class is dominant in the parliaments, it is possible to look at the frequency tables to resolve the question. The results show that parliamentary membership of the Third World nations is practically a monopoly of the well-educated offspring of the upper crust of the society. In the European democracies we see more of the self-made politicians—those who have achieved an elite status without the benefit of a good formal education and a good family background. The homogeneity of the Third World elites is the product of the relatively restricted mobility of these societies.

In their political experiences the Third World elites are more homogeneous than their European colleagues. Fewer of them ever held public offices before they entered the legislature. By contrast, European elites had extensive and varied career experiences, often rising step-by-step through complex and diverse pathways of offices. Pathways to the Third World parliaments are simple and involve neither an extended period of political training nor apprenticeship. For European elites, it is a quite different story. A parliamentary career is often a denouement or a well-deserved achievement after a long and arduous political apprenticeship. Once elected, the European elites tend to remain in their legislatures longer than the Third World elites. Over one-half of the Third World elites are freshman legislators, while among the European elites a smaller number are serving their first term: a high of 24 percent in Belgium and a low of 1 percent in Italy. The rates of membership turnover in the Third World parliaments are significantly higher than in European nations, which impedes their effort to professionalize their representative bodies. The members of the Third World legislatures are highly homogeneous, and this is because they all share a common characteristic, namely their political inexperience.

The European parliamentary elites show a greater homogeneity in one important respect, in their occupational experiences. Most of them are in the highest status professions: law, government service, business management, and university teaching. Nearly two-thirds held such high status professions before their entry into parliamentary service. Only a few of the Third World elites were trained in similar professions. In industrialized European Democracies, career mobility, it might be argued, is largely determined by achievement criteria. The fact that a clear majority of the European elites attained their current status of eminence only after they had demonstrated their ability in a variety of professional pursuits is testimony to the operation of achievement standards in these societies. For the Third World elites, professional distinctions are of no major importance. What is important, however, to a successful political career is ascriptive qualities of a candidate such as family, clan, tribal, and regional ties.

Heterogeneity rather than homogeneity characterizes legislative elites everywhere, probably due to the representational character of the institution. None of the six parliamentary elites shows a high mean score, which suggests that they are all heterogeneous groups in social composition. However, systematic differences exist between European and Third World elites. The European elites are more heterogeneous in their social composition. Belgium, Italy, and Switzerland are all industrially advanced democracies with a high degree of structural differentiation. Their political systems are more complex and yet more institutionalized as compared to the Third World systems. The social composition of elites is likely to reflect the general characteristics of the political system in which they govern. The elites which function in a highly differentiated system are more likely to represent all elements of the population, resulting in heterogeneous elites. In developing nations of the Third World, where structural differentiation is comparatively low and where channels of political mobility are restricted to the privileged few, political elites are unlikely to be broadly representative in their social composition. As their heterogeneity indicates, parliamentary elites are quite permeable groups, although the degree of permeability varies from nation to nation. Compared to other types of governmental elites, membership in parliament appears to be more permeable everywhere, and in European parliaments more so than in the Third World assemblies.

Homogeneity: Recruitment Experiences

How much do parliamentary elites share similar experiences in recruitment? We focus upon that part of the recruitment process most immediate to their entry into parliamentary service. This involves an examination in some detail of "the selection phase" of recruitment. Three variables are important at the selection phase: career paths, sponsorship, and political ambition.

Career Paths

For the purpose of a parsimonious characterization of career paths, a typology has been constructed based on two variables: previous experience in office holding and length of parliamentary service. Four distinct types of political careers . . . emerge: the amateurs, the arrivistes, the parliamentarians, and the careerists.

For the amateurs, politics is a wholly new venture. Before they attained their current legislative seats, they had no significant involvement in politics. Nor did they ever hold a public office at any level. What distinguishes the amateurs from other politicians is their total lack of previous political experience. The arrivistes all have extended periods of political apprenticeship in government, political parties, or interest groups. As a rule, they all began their political careers early in life, most with their initial involvement in low-level offices. As they rise step-by-step up the political ladder, their political skills and organizational acumen are tested and hardened. Membership in parliament represents, for many of the arrivistes, a culmination of their careers after long years of hard work and apprenticeship. The presence of a significant number of arrivistes signifies that pathways to parliament are highly institutionalized, for in this situation few will achieve elite status without climbing a well-defined career ladder. Conversely, if amateurs fill a chamber, it indicates relatively unstructured pathways.

The third career type, the parliamentarians, refers to those members who began their political careers in the legislature and remained in it ever since, accumulating long years of legislative service. Although parliamentarians do not have a long period of political apprenticeship outside the legislature, they do have a long apprenticeship within it. These veteran legislators with their seniority and inside knowledge of the rules and procedures of parliament are the likely candidates to defend the power and autonomy of the institution in relation to the government. The last career type is labeled "the careerists." For these elites, politics is both a way of life and a vocation. They all have very extensive political experience both inside and outside parliament. Practically, their whole life is devoted to political activism. Along the way, they have also acquired rich and varied political skills. The careerists are distinguishable from the arrivistes in that the latter are the recent arrivals to parliament, whereas the careerists have already put in several terms of legislative service. The dominance of the careerists in a parliament indicates both its institutionalization and professionalization.

The data on career paths are summarized in table 10.2. Pathways to parliament are fairly well structured everywhere. No systematic cross-national variations are noticed. In the Third World parliaments the two career types, the arrivistes and the careerists, are most common, accounting for more than two-thirds of membership in each nation. The same is true in the three European parliaments. Even fewer amateurs and parliamentarians are present in these legislative bodies.

Table 10.2   Career Types in Six Parliaments (in percentages)

Career Types	Belgium	Italy	Switzerland	Kenya	Korea	Turkey
Amateur	3	1	4	7	6	16
Arriviste	19	0	37	46	34	42
Parliamentarian	2	16	2	22	2	5
Careerist	76	83	55	25	58	37
Homogeneity Score	.499	.414	.261	.107	.275	.119
Number of Cases	150	180	235	28	119	104

In the European democracies the most dominant career type is that of the careerists, which contrasts starkly the European elites with their Third World colleagues. The careerists account for 76 percent of the Belgian elites, 83 percent of the Italians, and 55 percent of the Swiss members. There are some careerists in the Third World legislatures, but they are significantly less numerous. There is, therefore, evidence to conclude that European parliamentary elites are more professionalized as a group than are the Third World elites.

The high degree of professionalization of the European elites is also indicated by their relatively high homogeneity scores reported in table 10.2. The scores for Belgium and Italy are several times greater than the scores for the Third World nations. The Swiss elites are a small exception with a score of .261, which is still more than twice as great as the scores for Kenya (.107) and Turkey (.119) and is nearly the same as the score for Korea (.275). The general pattern, however, seems clear enough: the European elites must pass through well-ordered career steps and thus more homogeneous pathways to parliament.

Sponsorship

Instigation and sponsorship are important at the selection phase of recruitment. Political parties, factions, interest groups, primary groups, and kinship and tribal associations all perform roles as recruiting agents. . . . It is possible to distinguish the members who had the advantages of sponsorship from others without it, that is, the "self-starters." Sponsorship may affect a politician's behavior, for it places him in a nexus of loyalty and obligation from which a self-starter is free. The data on sponsorship . . . show no clearly interpretable pattern, although a marked variation by country is observable. In some parliaments (Turkey, Belgium, and Switzerland) the self-starters comprise a majority. In other parliaments political sponsorship is highly salient. There is little to distinguish between the European elites and the Third World elites in their use of sponsorship. However, the two groups of elites differ significantly in one respect. When we examine the more detailed data on the types of recruiting agents most active in each nation, we find that parties, interest groups, and party factions are the most active in the European societies. In the Third World nations "communal" or "particularistic" groups are most active as recruiting agents, including kinship and tribal associations, primary groups, and organizations based on parochial interests.

Ambition

Serving in a parliament may be a terminal office for some members, but for others with progressive ambition it is merely a stepping-stone to a higher office. An analysis of members' ambitions reveals something important about the ways in which parliamentary careers are connected to other parts of the political system.

A majority of members of the six nations harbor ambitions beyond their current office. In the Third World parliaments more than one-half show progressive ambition. The ambitions of the European parliamentary elites run even higher: those with progressive ambition are 83 percent in Belgium, 62 percent in Italy, and 82 percent in Switzerland. It is clear that the European elites generally have a better idea as to how far and to which office they could go from parliament and possess a well worked out plan to attain their career goals. In comparison, the Third World elites appear uncertain as to where their legislative service will ultimately lead them. During the interviews we found many hesitant to give us a decisive response because they were themselves unclear about their ultimate career goals. This uncertainty seems to stem from two sources. The first is a relatively low institutionalization of the political career structures in these nations: that is, the interconnections of various career paths are not sharply enough defined to be predictable. The second source is the risk and uncertainty associated with a political career due to the chronic instability of the political system in these nations.

The target offices to which the Third World elites direct their ambitions include cabinet posts, top offices in political parties, administrative appointments, and top management positions in large public enterprises. In both Kenya and Korea members most favored cabinet posts. In Turkey administrative appointments and party offices attract many members' aspirations. Such cross-national differences are indicative of varying opportunity structures and configurations of power in the societies we studied.

The European elites share more common experiences in recruitment than do their Third World colleagues, which make them more homogeneous as an elite group. One sees a clearer structure in the career paths of the European members, in their sponsorship, and in their politi-

Table 10.3   Parliamentary Elite Consensus on Key Values in Six Nations

Values	Belgium	Italy	Switzerland	Kenya	Korea	Turkey
			Consensus Scores for:			
Purposive role perception	.049	.058	.042	.220	.181	.115
Representative focus	.002	.004	.001	.126	.026	.592
Perception of issues	.099	.181	.168	.209	.075	.140
Views on sources conflict	.480	.390	.550	.105	.624	.192
Views on role specialization	.480	.570	.670	.501	.467	.634
Views on right to dissent	.555	.550	.538	.430	.590	.720
Views on economic equity	n.a.	.615	.550	.453	.380	.473
Views on the necessity for social change	n.a.	n.a.	n.a.	.290	.640	.160
Number of Cases	150	180	235	28	119	104

cal ambitions. All of this suggests a well-ordered political world in which they pursue their careers.

Elite Consensus on Key Political Values

The critical test of elite cohesion and unity is the degree to which elite members agree on fundamental political values. An integrated elite shares similar beliefs and attitudes, which enables it to act effectively as a unified group. Thus, elite consensus on key values is a matter of considerable import. We have selected for analysis five broad value realms which seem to us, prima facie, crucial to the performance of parliamentary functions: members' perception of legislative roles, their perception of the priority issues, their beliefs and attitudes toward political conflict, their attitudes toward procedural norms, and their stance on policy issues, that is, the right to dissent, economic equity, and social change. The results of analysis are summarized by nation and by value item in table 10.3.

Purposive and Representational Roles

One important aspect of the system of legislative roles is the question of what functions each member regards as the most important part of his job. Wahlke and his associates (1962, 245–66) called it the "purposive role." Members of the six parliaments were asked: "How would you describe the job of being a legislator, and what are the most important things you do here?" Responses were very diverse and varied. In Kenya, members regard both constituency service and lawmaking as their most important roles. Korean members list lawmaking, representation of broad public interests, and the exercise of oversight power as their most important roles. For the Turkish members, lawmaking and mobilizing popular support for national goals are the most important. Among the European elites, there exists much less consensus on purposive roles: the average consensus score for the three European nations is as much as four times lower than that for the Third World nations. The lack of agreement among the European elites reflects the general character of representational politics in these industrialized democracies. Because of the complexity of their political systems and the democratic requirement for their responsive leadership, they have to perform a diversity of roles.

Members' choice of their representational focus may differ. Who should be represented in parliament? The parliamentary elites were asked to rate the relative importance of groups most relevant to their representational activity. The list of groups includes their political party, their faction, their district constituents, interest groups, ethnic and religious groups, and subcultural groups. Generally, there is little consensus on representational focus in all parliaments. One notable exception, however, is discovered in Turkey. The Turkish elites exhibit a remarkable degree of consensus, with a score of .592, while the scores for other nations are all well below the level of .100. In Turkey there is a unique constitutional prescription that obligates members to represent the general interest of the "whole nation." For all practical purposes, this prohibits them from an open advocacy of any form of parochial or specialized interests. In consequence, a predominant majority of the Turkish deputies chose their "nation" as their principal representational focus.

The groups that members represent are of two types, distinguishable in their degree of organization: politically organized and unorganized constituencies. Politically organized constituencies include political parties, factions, trade unions, and other special interest groups. Some constituencies are ill-defined and politically unorganized entities: district and tribal groups, subcultures, and the nation as a whole. The European elites almost always choose politically organized groups for their representational focus. In a marked contrast, the Third World elites tend to assert that they represent the vague and amorphous interests of politically unorganized constituencies.

Perceived Priority of Issues

A basic agreement on the priority of key issues is a matter vitally important to elite unity and cohesion. Asked what issues or problems they see as the most important ones requiring their closest attention and action, the parliamentary elites agreed little among themselves. The consensus scores are uniformly low in all parliaments. More than any other governmental bodies, the legislature is always a body of many voices. It is a unique arena where divergent policy priorities advocated by different social groups can legitimately compete. Reflective of complex social interests, members are likely to bring to their job conflicting policy priorities and thus a low consensus on issue priorities. In spite of many important differences which divide the European and the Third World parliaments, they show no significant difference in issue priorities.

Beneath the diversity in issue priority, there is still some limited consensus. Members of the Third World parliaments give high priority to the problems relating to constituency services. In Kenya, a preponderant number of its members regard allocation of pork barrels as the single most important issue: they appear solely preoccupied with their job of getting a fair share of porks to their districts. The priority issues that the Turkish members mention most frequently are industrialization, education, and welfare policies. For the Korean elites, three issues are given highest priorities: democratic reforms, income inequities, and the dominance of the executive power. It is, however, important to note that what limited consensus exists in the three parliaments is built upon different issues.

The issue of constituency service does not figure prominently in the perceptions of the European elites. The difference is indeed striking, for virtually every member of the Third World parliaments dares not slight his duty of constituency service. The fact that the European elites tend to downgrade their constituency service may be attributable to two factors. First, most European parties are centrally organized, which means that a candidate's electoral success depends heavily on the support of his party. Second, the electoral systems used in Europe— generally the list system of proportional representation—attenuate legislator-constituency ties.

Beliefs about Political Conflict

Putnam (1973, 93–156) has persuasively argued that beliefs about the nature of conflict constitute an important part of a politician's "world view." As cognitive predispositions, these beliefs affect the ways in which politicians perceive issues and seek solutions to problems. Do parliamentary elites see conflict as something solvable through pragmatic bargaining and compromise? Or do they see it as a matter to be resolved by a total elimination of their opposition? In the interview we asked members to identify major sources of political conflict. The results show that the Third World elites have more fatalistic beliefs about conflict than do their European colleagues. Many Third World elites believe that conflicts arise because of human nature, historical legacy, or ethnic and tribal rifts—sources of conflict not easily amenable to human control. In contrast, the European elites identify economic cleavages, that is, class conflicts, as the principal sources of political conflict.

The European elites exhibit a highly unified belief on conflict. Their consensus scores are significantly higher (between .390 and .550) than the ones for the Kenyan and Turkish elites (.105 and .192, respectively). The exception to this is South Korea, a special case that merits a brief comment. The Korean elites show the highest agreement on conflict (.624). A closer scrutiny of the data from Korea reveals that the agreement is built upon a widely shared belief that much of political conflict derives from the way political institutions are organized. More specifically, they attribute conflict to the party system as it is, the structure of partisan factions, the lopsided relation between the legislature and the executive, and policy differences. To a much less extent, they believe conflicts arise from sources beyond human control, such as human nature and subcultural cleavages. In this respect, the Korean elites stand apart from their Third World colleagues. They hold strong beliefs that conflicts are solvable by human intelligence and hard work, and especially by institutional reforms. In fact, the Korean constitutional framework has been changed eight times since 1948, each time effecting a major restructuring of the National Assembly.

Attitudes on Specialization

Characteristically, all institutions have a body of rules and norms to facilitate their operations, and parliaments are no exception. One such rule pertains to the division of labor, that is, the norm of specialization. Members of the six parliaments all agree, regardless of their varying stages of development, on the necessity and desirability of specialization. The consensus scores are uniformly high in all parliaments, ranging from .467 to .670.

Evidently, the norm of specialization is universal in legislatures. It serves as a common principle for organizing legislative activities in both developed and developing societies. Specialization is an organizational imperative, especially in a collective body like parliament, because individual members possess neither enough information nor technical expertise to make intelligent decisions on all relevant issues. Legislators everywhere seem to recognize this, all agreeing to the importance of specialization.

Policy Consensus

Three broad policy areas are examined: the right to dissent, distributive policies, and social change. The issue of political dissent provokes strong emotions in many Third World nations because it is intimately connected to the important issue of democratic reforms. On the other hand, the modernizing elites of these nations see the freedom of dissent as destructive of their priority goals of socioeconomic development. In industrialized democracies the right to dissent is a part of their fundamental political principles, and therefore we expect to find a unified belief among the European elites. The issue of income equity is salient in all modern societies as familiar struggles over distributive policies amply demonstrate. The developmental strategies that the Third World nations choose vary significantly by country. In some the government pursues a strategy of growth involving a reasonably equitable distribution of benefits and costs across the population, and in others a strategy that favors industrial sectors at the expense of social equity. The goal of achieving quick capital accumulation and a high growth rate often clashes with the objective of ensuring an equitable distribution. Thus, the question of which developmental strategies members support is a matter of considerable policy importance in the Third World nations. Likewise, class conflicts, the result of economic inequities which accumulated over the long history of industrialized democracies, pose as serious a problem as does the issue of distribution for the Third World nations. Of special relevance to the Third World elites is the issue of planned social change. What are their attitudes on social change, and how much consensus is there on the rate of change?

Operational measures of elite attitudes on the three policy issues are constructed from a large battery of survey items. Indexes have been formed to indicate members' beliefs about political dissent, distributive policies, and social change. The consensus scores are computed from these indexes and are reported in table 10.3.

The right to dissent, an essential requirement of any democratic process, is universally supported by members of all six parliaments. A predominant majority affirm the crucial importance of political dissent (notice the uniformly high consensus scores across the six nations). It is evident that legislators everywhere outside Communist systems take the right to dissent as critically important. Our finding contradicts the conventional wisdom that sees the legislatures of the Third World as the bastions of conservative political forces, closely tied to vested interests and the status quo. Huntington (1968, 388), Packenham (1970, 578), and others have propounded this view, asserting that these legislative bodies are fundamentally resistant to policies for social and political change including democratic reforms. Evidence from the six nation data lends no support for the Huntington-Packenham thesis. If anything, the data suggest that the parliamentary elites as a group represent the more progressive and democratic elements among all institutional elites in the Third World nations.

On the issue of distributive equity, there exists a high degree of consensus in all six parliaments. However, this consensus converges on different beliefs and attitudes in each nation. In Kenya and Korea, most members believe that inequality in income is inevitable at the early stage of economic development and that the equity issue is necessarily one that can be tackled only after a nation achieves a high level of affluence. So they support a developmental strategy which concentrates on growth rates in capital intensive industrial sectors, favoring the interests of the educated middle class, landowners, industrial capitalists, technocrats, and owners of import-export businesses. The consensus among the Turkish elites is formed on a different mix of attitudes: a majority of 68 percent believe that equity must be achieved at any cost, even if it means a lower growth rate. Similar beliefs are expressed by members of both the Italian and Swiss elites. Not only do they regard equity as the single most important issue, but they also show a wide agreement that policies should be formulated to reduce economic inequities. The Italian elites exhibit the highest consensus (.615), indicating their strong feelings about the compelling necessity of economic equality. This may be a reflection of the magnitude of economic disparities existing in that society.

The issue of planned social change is particularly salient in the Third World nations. In Kenya and Turkey the elites are divided on this issue. Forty-nine percent of the Turkish elites support programs for rapid social change, while 35 percent are strongly opposed to them. Similarly, 25 percent of the Kenyan elites support rapid changes, and 53 percent oppose these policies. In spite of the fact that these Third World nations are undergoing a process of massive social and economic transformation, their legislative elites fail to present a unified view on this important policy issue.

The Korean elites are an exception, exhibiting a high consensus (.640). Their agreement on social change is, however, based on an interesting mix of both progressive and conservative attitudes. They hold progressive attitudes in regard to economic change, reflecting the nation's single-minded drive for rapid economic growth. They strongly favor policies for the reorganization of key economic institutions to improve their efficiency, the importation of scientific management skills, and the adoption of new and innovative technologies. At the same time, the Korean elites present a unified opposition to a rapid social change which might destroy what they consider their valued traditions and cultural heritages. While they all hold progressive beliefs in economic policies, they are also ultraconservative in their attitudes toward cultural changes.

In summing up, we note the following major findings. First, the amount of consensus shared among legislative elites varies significantly across value realms. There exists a consistently high consensus on both issues of role specialization and the right of dissent, but the degree of consensus on other values is quite low. Second, consensus is often built upon different bases in different parliaments. For example, members of the three Third World legislators all show high consensus on the equity issue. But the consensus in both Kenya and Korea is formed on the belief that inequities are inevitable and that governments should not pursue a vigorous policy of distribution, at least not at this early stage of their nation's development. By contrast, the consensus among the Turkish and the European elites is directed to an active government role in distributive policy. Third, the total amount of consensus over the entire range of value realms examined is uniformly modest in all parliaments. A significant fact is that the Third World parliaments are just as consensual (or dissensual) as the European parliaments. Contrary to the proposition that parliamentary members of established European democracies share greater consensus in their fundamental political beliefs and on the basic rules of the game than do the Third World members, our comparative data show equally modest consensus for both groups of legislative elites. Finally, the presumption that sharing of similar recruitment experiences would lead to a high degree of agreement on key political values proved to be difficult to sustain. European elites share more similarities in their recruitment experiences than do the Third World elites yet do not agree among themselves any more than do legislative elites of the Third World nations.

Summary and Implications

The received theorizing about political elite integration does not appear to be very adequate. Our investigation of parliamentary elites in six nations demonstrates that in regard to social background, recruitment experience, and political values there is very considerable diversity within these six parliamentary groups. In these nations, members of parliament are, to be sure, drawn largely from among those with high socioeconomic status. Nevertheless, the heterogeneity of these elites, in relative terms, is impressive. Although we do find some differences between the European and the Third World elites, their social origins and backgrounds are diverse. By no means are the elites in the advanced democracies more homogeneous than those in the less developed nations. Only in their somewhat greater degree of career professionalization do the elites in the European parliaments appear more homogeneous. Moreover, heterogeneity is the order of the day when it comes to most of the value orientations of these elite groups. It is in regard to role specialization and the right of dissent that we find a marked consensus in these elites, a consensus which appears as pungent within the elites of the Third World as in the European elites.

Theory about political elitism which puts heavy stock in elite cohesiveness on a variety of attributes probably has overstated its case. Elites may, in fact, be made up of rather diverse collections of people. By the same token, theory about political development which rests upon speculation about differential elite integration in less developed as opposed to developed systems seems to need considerable revision. Tidy expectations about differences in elite cohesiveness between these two broad categories of political systems are not borne out by careful research.

Diversity in the social origins, career experiences, and beliefs within a political elite may be vital to its capacity to be responsive to the needs, demands, and expectations of a nation's people. Such diversity may be particularly invaluable in a parliamentary elite, intended to serve a representative function in the political system. So it may well be that a degree of heterogeneity, not homogeneity, in a political elite best serves the process of political development. Despite very great differences among the six systems we have analyzed in political culture, structure, and process, and more particularly despite important differences in their mechanisms for recruiting members of parliament, these systems all exhibit impressive levels of elite diversity. We would expect this diversity to be strongest in the parliamentary elites; a greater degree of homogeneity may characterize other elites of these nations— military, industrial, and bureaucratic.

Patterns of rule differ among political systems in vitally important ways. We by no means wish to imply that the performance of governing elites is not variable in ways which can distinguish crucially between freedom and slavery. At the same time, practices in the exercise of political power have been, and are, diffused. Almost all countries in the world, for instance, have a representative assembly of some kind. It seems that the human species has only discovered a relatively limited number of ways to govern itself. A representative body with constituent ties is one such way of governing. How parliamentary elites should function has been diffused throughout the world from the experience of ancient times, from the explicit inventions which roughly emanated from the twelfth century in Europe, and from colonial borrowings or from admiration of British, French, and American practices in the nineteenth and twentieth centuries. We note the ramifications of such diffusion in the remarkable similarity of high consensus in all six parliamentary elites in value orientations having to do with specialization of the representative role and political dissent. A capacity to develop some complexity of the representative role and a minimal tolerance for political argument, disagreement, even dissent—these are essential ingredients of any institution aiming to perform a representative function. So there is a profound sense in which parliamentary elites, in less developed as well as in developed systems, share diversity in values, but also share a functionally essential consensus about the values that make a representative institution possible.

11

The Integration of Leadership Groups: The House Appropriations Committee

Richard F. Fenno, Jr.

Studies of Congress by political scientists have produced a time-tested consensus on the very considerable power and autonomy of congressional committees. Because of these two related characteristics, it makes empirical and analytical sense to treat the congressional committee as a discrete unit for analysis. This paper conceives of the committee as a political system (or, more accurately as a political sub-system) faced with a number of basic problems which it must solve in order to achieve its goals and maintain itself. Generally speaking these functional problems pertain to the environmental and the internal relations of the committee. This study is concerned almost exclusively with the internal problems of the committee and particularly with the problem of self-integration. It describes how one congressional committee—the Committee on Appropriations of the House of Representatives—has dealt with this problem in the period 1947–1961. Its purpose is to add to our understanding of appropriations politics in Congress and to suggest the usefulness of this type of analysis for studying the activities of any congressional committee.

The necessity for integration in any social system arises from the differ-

"The House Appropriations Committee as a Political System: The Problem of Integration," *American Political Science Review* 56 (June 1962): 310–324. Copyright © 1962 by the American Political Science Association. Reprinted by permission of the American Political Science Association.

entiation among its various elements. Most importantly there is a differentiation among subgroups and among individual positions, together with the
roles that flow therefrom. A committee faces the problem, how shall these
diverse elements be made to mesh together or function in support of one another? No political system (or sub-system) is perfectly integrated; yet no political system can survive without some minimum degree of integration
among its differentiated parts. Committee integration is defined as the degree to which there is a working together or a meshing together or mutual
support among its roles and subgroups. Conversely, it is also defined as the
degree to which a committee is able to minimize conflict among its roles and
its subgroups, by heading off or resolving the conflicts that arise. A concomitant of integration is the existence of a fairly consistent set of norms, widely
agreed upon and widely followed by the members. Another concomitant of
integration is the existence of control mechanism (i.e., socialization and
sanctioning mechanisms) capable of maintaining reasonable conformity to
norms. In other words, the more highly integrated a committee, the smaller
will be the gap between expected and actual behavior.

This study is concerned with integration both as a structural characteristic of, and as a functional problem for, the Appropriations Committee. First, certain basic characteristics of the Committee need description,
to help explain the integration of its parts. Second comes a partial description of the degree to which and the ways in which the Committee achieves
integration. No attempt is made to state this in quantitative terms, but the
object is to examine the meshing together or the minimization of conflict
among certain subgroups and among certain key roles. Also, important
control mechanisms are described. The study concludes with some comments on the consequences of Committee integration for appropriations
politics and on the usefulness of further congressional committee analysis
in terms of functional problems such as this one.

The House Appropriations Committee

Five important characteristics of the Appropriations Committee which
help explain Committee integration are (1) the existence of a well-
articulated and deeply rooted consensus on Committee goals or tasks; (2)
the nature of the Committee's subject matter; (3) the legislative orientation of its members; (4) the attractiveness of the Committee for its members; and (5) the stability of Committee membership.

Consensus

The Appropriations Committee sees its tasks as taking form within the
broad guidelines set by its parent body, the House of Representatives. For

it is the primary condition of the Committee's existence that it was created by the House for the purpose of assisting the House in the performance of House legislative tasks dealing with appropriations. Committee members agree that their fundamental duty is to serve the House in the manner and with the substantive results that the House prescribes. Given, however, the imprecision of House expectations and the permissiveness of House surveillance, the Committee must elaborate for itself a definition of tasks plus a supporting set of perceptions (of itself and of others) explicit enough to furnish day-to-day guidance.

The Committee's view begins with the preeminence of the House—often mistakenly attributed to the Constitution ("all bills for raising revenue," Art. I, sec. 7) but nevertheless firmly sanctioned by custom—in appropriations affairs.

It moves easily to the conviction that, as the efficient part of the House in this matter, the Constitution has endowed it with special obligations and special prerogatives. It ends in the view that the Committee on Appropriations, far from being merely one among many units in a complicated legislative-executive system, is *the* most important, most responsible unit in the whole appropriations process. Hand in hand with the consensus on their primacy goes a consensus that all of their House-prescribed tasks can be fulfilled by superimposing upon them one single, paramount task—*to guard the Federal Treasury:* Committee members state their goals in the essentially negative terms of guardianship—screening requests for money, checking against ill-advised expenditures, and protecting the taxpayer's dollar. In the language of the Committee's official history, the job of each member is, "constantly and courageously to protect the Federal Treasury against thousands of appeals and imperative demands for unnecessary, unwise, and excessive expenditures."

To buttress its self-image as guardian of public funds the Committee elaborates a set of perceptions about other participants in the appropriations process to which most members hold most of the time. Each executive official, for example, is seen to be interested in the expansion of his own particular program. Each one asks, therefore, for more money than he really needs, in view of the total picture, to run an adequate program. This and other Committee perceptions—of the Budget Bureau, of the Senate, and of their fellow Representatives—help to shape and support the Committee members in their belief that most budget estimates can, should, and must be reduced and that, since no one else can be relied upon, the House Committee must do the job. To the consensus on the main task of protecting the Treasury is added, therefore, a consensus on the instrumental task of *cutting whatever budget estimates are submitted.*

As an immediate goal, Committee members agree that they must strike a highly critical, aggressive posture toward budget requests, and that they should, on principle, reduce them. In the words of the Committee's veterans: "There has never been a budget submitted to the Congress that couldn't be cut." "There isn't a budget that can't be cut 10 percent immediately." "I've been on the Committee for seventeen years. No subcommittee of which I have been a member has ever reported out a bill without a cut in the budget. I'm proud of that record." The aim of budget-cutting is strongly internalized for the Committee member. "It's a tradition in the Appropriations Committee to cut." "You're grounded in it. . . .It's ingrained in you from the time you get on the Committee." For the purposes of a larger study, the appropriations case histories of thirty-seven executive bureaus have been examined for a twelve year period, 1947–1959. Of 443 separate bureau estimates, the Committee reduced 77.2 percent (342) of them.

It is a mark of the intensity and self-consciousness of the Committee consensus on budget-cutting that it is couched in a distinctive vocabulary. The workaday lingo of the Committee member is replete with negative verbs, undesirable objects of attention, and effective instruments of action. Agency budgets are said to be filled with "fat," "padding," "grease," "pork," "oleaginous substance," "water," "oil," "cushions," "avoirdupois," "waste tissue," and "soft spots." The action verbs most commonly used are "cut," "carve," "slice," "prune," "whittle," "squeeze," "wring," "trim," "lop off," "chop," "slash," "pare," "shave," "fry," and "whack." The tools of the trade are appropriately referred to as "knife," "blade," "meat axe," "scalpel," "meat cleaver," "hatchet," "shears," "wringer," and "fine-tooth comb." Members are hailed by their fellows as being "pretty sharp with the knife." Agencies may "have the meat axe thrown at them." Executives are urged to put their agencies "on a fat boy's diet." Budgets are praised when they are "cut to the bone." And members agree that, "You can always get a little more fat out of a piece of pork if you fry it a little longer and a little harder."

To the major task of protecting the Treasury and the instrumental task of cutting budget estimates, each Committee member adds, usually by way of exception, a third task—*serving the constituency to which he owes his election.* This creates no problem for him when, as is sometimes the case, he can serve his district best by cutting the budget requests of a federal agency whose program is in conflict with the demands of his constituency. Normally, however, members find that their most common role-conflict is between a Committee-oriented budget-reducing role and a constituency oriented budget-increasing role. Committee ideology resolves the conflict by assigning top, long-run priority to the budget-cutting task and making of the constituency service a permissible, short-run exception. No member is expected to commit electoral suicide; but no member is expected to allow his district's desire for federal funds to dominate his Committee behavior.

Subject Matter

Appropriations Committee integration is facilitated by the subject matter with which the group deals. The Committee makes decisions on the same controversial issues as do the committees handling substantive legislation. But a money decision—however vitally it affects national policy—is, or at least seems to be, less directly a policy decision. Since they deal immediately with dollars and cents, it is easy for the members to hold to the idea that they are not dealing with programmatic questions, that theirs is a "business" rather than a "policy" committee. The subject matter, furthermore, keeps Committee members relatively free agents, which promotes intra-Committee maneuvering and, hence, conflict avoidance. Members do not commit themselves to their constituents in terms of precise money amounts, and no dollar sum is sacred— it can always be adjusted without conceding that a principle has been breached. By contrast, members of committees dealing directly with controversial issues are often pressured into taking concrete stands on these issues; consequently, they may come to their committee work with fixed and hardened attitudes. This leads to unavoidable, head-on intra-committee conflict and renders integrative mechanisms relatively ineffective.

The fact of an annual appropriations process means the Committee members repeat the same operations with respect to the same subject matters year after year—and frequently more than once in a given year. Substantive and procedural repetition promotes familiarity with key problems and provides ample opportunity to test and confirm the most satisfactory methods of dealing with them. And the absolute necessity that appropriations bills to ultimately pass gives urgency to the search for such methods. Furthermore, the House rule that no member of the Committee can serve on another standing committee is a deterrent against a fragmentation of Committee member activity which could be a source of difficulty in holding the group together. If a committee has developed (as this one has) a number of norms designed to foster integration, repeated and concentrated exposure to them increases the likelihood that they will be understood, accepted and followed.

Legislative Orientation

The recruitment of members for the Appropriations Committee produces a group of individuals with an orientation especially conducive to Committee integration. Those who make the selection pay special attention to the characteristics which Masters (1961, 345–357) has described as those of the "responsible legislator"—approval of and conformity to the norms of the legislative process and of the House of Representatives.

Key selectors speak of wanting, for the Appropriations Committee, "the kind of man you can deal with" or "a fellow who is well-balanced and won't go off half-cocked on things." A Northern liberal Democrat felt that he had been chosen over eight competitors because, "I had made a lot of friends and was known as a nice guy"—especially, he noted, among Southern Congressmen. Another Democrat explained, "I got the blessing of the Speaker and the leadership. It's personal friendships. I had done a lot of things for them in the past, and when I went to them and asked them, they gave it to me." A Republican chosen for the Committee in his first term recalled,

> The Chairman [Rep. Taber] I guess did some checking around in my area. After all, I was new and he didn't know me. People told me that they were called to see if I was—well, unstable or apt to go off on tangents . . . to see whether or not I had any preconceived notions about things and would not be flexible—whether I would oppose things even though it was obvious.

A key criterion in each of the cases mentioned was a demonstrable record of, or an assumed predisposition toward, legislative give-and-take.

The 106 Appropriations Committee members serving between 1947 and 1961 spent an average of 3.6 years on other House committees before coming to the Committee. Only 17 of the 106 were selected as first term Congressmen. A House apprenticeship (which Appropriations maintains more successfully than all committees save Ways and Means and Rules) provides the time in which legislative reputations can be established by the member and an assessment of that reputation in terms of Appropriations Committee requirements can be made. Moreover, the mere fact that a member survives for a couple of terms is some indication of an electoral situation conducive to his "responsible" legislative behavior. The optimum bet for the Committee is a member from a sufficiently safe district to permit him freedom of maneuver inside the House without fear of reprisal at the polls. The degree of responsiveness to House norms which the Committee selectors value may be the product of a safe district as well as an individual temperament.

Attractiveness

A fourth factor is the extraordinarily high degree of attractiveness which the Committee holds for its members—as measured by the low rate of departure from it. Committee members do not leave it for service on other committees. To the contrary, they are attracted to it from nearly every other committee. Of the 106 members in the 1947–1961 period, only two men left the Committee voluntarily; and neither of them initiated the move. Committee attractiveness is a measure of its capacity to satisfy individual member needs—for power, prestige, recognition, respect, self-esteem, friendship, etc. Such satisfaction in turn increases the likelihood that members will behave in such a way as to hold the group together.

The most frequently mentioned source of Committee attractiveness is its power—based on its control of financial resources. "Where the money is, that's where the power is," sums up the feeling of the members. They prize their ability to reward or punish so many other participants in the political process—executive officials, fellow Congressmen, constituents, and other clientele groups. In the eyes of its own members, the Committee is either the most powerful in the House or it is on a par with Ways and Means or, less frequently, on a par with Ways and Means and Rules. The second important ingredient in member satisfaction is the government-wide scope of Committee activity. The ordinary Congressman may feel that he has too little knowledge of and too little control over his environment. Membership on this Committee compensates for this feeling of helplessness by the wider contacts, the greater amount of information, and the sense of being "in the middle of things" which are consequent, if not to subcommittee activity, at least to the full Committee's overview of the federal government.

Thirdly, Committee attractiveness is heightened by the group's recognizable and distinctive political style—one that is, moreover, highly valued in American political culture. The style is that of *hard work;* and the Committee's self-image is that of "the hardest working Committee in Congress." His willingness to work is the Committee member's badge of identification, and it is proudly worn. It colors his perceptions of others and their perceptions of him. It is a cherished axiom of all members that, "This Committee is no place for a man who doesn't work. They have to be hard working. It's a way of life. It isn't just a job; it's a way of life."

The mere existence of some identifiable and valued style or "way of life" is a cohesive force for a group. But the particular style of hard work is one which increases group morale and group identification twice over. Hard work means a long, dull, and tedious application to detail, via the technique of "dig, dig, dig, day after day behind closed doors"—in an estimated 460 subcommittee and full Committee meetings a year. And virtually all of these meetings are in executive session. By adopting the style of hard work, the Committee discourages highly individualized forms of legislative behavior, which could be disruptive within the Committee. It rewards its members with power, but it is power based rather on work inside the Committee than on the political glamour of activities carried on in the limelight of the mass media. Prolonged daily work together encourages sentiments of mutual regard, sympathy, and solidarity. This *esprit* is, in turn, functional for integration on the Committee. A Republican leader summed up,

> I think it's more closely knit than any other committee. Yet it's the biggest committee, and you'd think it would be the reverse. I know on my subcommittee, you sit together day after day. You get better acquainted. You have sympathy when other fellows go off to play golf. There's a lot of *esprit de corps* in the Committee.

The strong attraction which members have for the Committee increases the influence which the Committee and its norms exercise on all of them. It increases the susceptibility of the newcomer to Committee socialization and of the veteran to Committee sanctions applicable against deviant behavior.

Membership Stability

Members of the Appropriations Committee are strongly attracted to it: they also have, which bears out their selection as "responsible legislators," a strong attraction for a career in the House of Representatives. The fifty members of the Committee in 1961 had served an average of 13.1 years in the House. These twin attractions produce a noteworthy stability of Committee membership. In the period from the 80th to the 87th Congress, 35.7 percent of the Committee's membership remained constant. That is to say, fifteen of the forty-two members on the Committee in March, 1947, were still on the Committee in March, 1961. The fifty members of the Committee in 1961 averaged 9.3 years of prior service on that Committee. In no single year during the last fourteen has the Committee had to absorb an influx of new members totalling more than one-quarter of its membership. At all times, in other words, at least three-fourths of the members have had previous Committee experience. This extraordinary stability of personnel extends into the staff as well. As of June 1961, its fifteen professionals had served an average of 10.7 years with the Committee.

The opportunity exists, therefore, for the development of a stable leadership group, a set of traditional norms for the regulation of internal Committee behavior, and informal techniques of personal accommodation. Time is provided in which new members can learn and internalize Committee norms before they attain high seniority rankings. The Committee does not suffer from the potentially disruptive consequences of rapid changeovers in its leadership group, nor of sudden impositions of new sets of norms governing internal Committee behavior.

The Role of Subgroups

If one considers the main activity of a political system to be decision making, the acid test of its internal integration is its capacity to make collective decisions without flying apart in the process. Analysis of Committee integration should focus directly, therefore, upon its subgroups and the roles of its members. Two kinds of subgroups are of central importance—subcommittees and majority or minority party groups. The roles which are most relevant derive from: (1) positions which each member holds by virtue of his subgroup attachments, e.g., as subcommittee member, majority (or minority) party member; (2) positions which relate to full Committee membership, e.g., Committee member, and the seniority rankings of veteran, man of moderate experience, and newcomer; (3) positions which relate to both subgroup and full Committee membership, e.g., Chairman of the Committee, ranking minority member of the Committee, subcommittee chairman, ranking subcommittee member. Clusters of norms state the expectations about subgroup and role behavior. The description which follows treats the ways in which these norms and their associated behaviors mesh and clash. It treats, also, the internal control mechanisms by which behavior is brought into reasonable conformity with expectations.

Subgroup Integration

The day-to-day work of the Committee is carried on in its subcommittees, each of which is given jurisdiction over a number of related governmental units. The number of subcommittees is determined by the Committee Chairman and has varied recently from a low of nine in 1949 to a high of fifteen in 1959. The present total of fourteen reflects, as always, a set of strategic and personal judgments by the Chairman balanced against the limitations placed on him by Committee tradition and member wishes. The Chairman also determines subcommittee jurisdiction, appoints subcommittee chairmen, and selects the majority party members of each group. The ranking minority member of the Committee exercises similar control over subcommittee assignments on his side of the aisle.

Each subcommittee holds hearings on the budget estimates of the agencies assigned to it, meets in executive session to decide what figures and what language to recommend to the full Committee (to "mark up" the bill), defends its recommendations before the full Committee, writes the Committee's report to the House, dominates the debate on the floor, and bargains for the House in conference committee. Within its jurisdiction, each subcommittee functions independently of the others and guards its autonomy jealously. The Chairman and ranking minority member of the full Committee have, as we shall see, certain opportunities to oversee and dip into the operations of all subcommittees. But their intervention is expected to be minimal. Moreover, they themselves operate importantly within the subcommittee framework by sitting as chairman or ranking minority member of the subcommittee in which they are most interested. Each subcommittee, under the guidance of its chairman, transacts its business in considerable isolation from every other one. One subcommittee chairman exclaimed,

> Why, you'd be branded an impostor if you went into one of those other subcommittee meetings. The only time I go is by appointment, by arrangement with the chairman at a special time. I'm as much a stranger in another subcommittee as I would be in the legislative Committee on Post Office and Civil Service. Each one does its work apart from all others.

All members of all subcommittees are expected to behave in similar fashion in the role of subcommittee member. Three main norms define this role; to the extent that they are observed, they promote harmony and reduce conflict among subcommittees. Subcommittee autonomy gives to the House norm of *specialization* an intensified application on the Appropriations Committee. Each member is expected to play the role of specialist in the activities of one subcommittee. He will sit on from one to four subcommittees, but normally will specialize in the work, or a portion of the work, of only one. Except for the Chairman, ranking minority member and their confidants, a Committee member's time, energy, contacts and experience are devoted to his subcommittees. Specialization is, therefore, among the earliest and most compelling of the Committee norms to which a newcomer is exposed. Within the Committee, respect, deference, and power are earned through subcommittee activity and, hence to a degree, through specialization. Specialization is valued further because it is well suited to the task of guarding the Treasury. Only by specializing, Committee members believe, can they unearth the volume of factual information necessary for the intelligent screening of budget requests. Since "the facts" are acquired only through industry, an effective specialist will, perforce, adopt and promote the Committee's style of hard work.

Committee-wide acceptance of specialization is an integrative force in decision making because it helps support a second norm— *reciprocity.* The stage at which a subcommittee makes its recommendations is a potential point of internal friction. Conflict among subcommittees (or between one subcommittee and the rest of the Committee) is minimized by the deference traditionally accorded to the recommendation of the subcommittee which has specialized in the area, has worked hard, and has "the facts," "It's a matter of 'You respect my work and I'll respect yours.' " "It's frowned upon if you offer an amendment in the full Committee if you aren't on the subcommittee. It's considered presumptuous to pose as an expert if you aren't on the subcommittee." Though records of full Committee decisions are not available, members agree that subcommittee recommendations are "very rarely changed," "almost always approved," "changed one time in fifty," "very seldom changed," etc.

No subcommittee is likely to keep the deference of the full Committee for long unless its recommendations have widespread support among its own members. To this end, a third norm—*subcommittee unity*—is expected to be observed by subcommittee members. Unity means a willingness to support (or not to oppose) the recommendations of one's own subcommittee. Reciprocity and unity are closely dependent upon one another. Reciprocity is difficult to maintain when subcommittees themselves are badly divided; and unity has little appeal unless reciprocity will subsequently be observed. The norm of reciprocity functions to minimize inter-subcommittee conflict. The norm of unity functions to minimize intra-subcommittee conflict. Both are deemed essential to subcommittee influence.

One payoff for the original selection of "responsible legislators" is their special willingness to compromise in pursuit of subcommittee unity. The impulse to this end is registered most strongly at the time when the subcommittee meets in executive session to mark up the bill. Two ranking minority members explained this aspect of markup procedure in their subcommittees:

> If there's agreement, we go right along. If there's a lot of controversy we put the item aside and go on. Then, after a day or two, we may have a list of ten controversial items. We give and take and pound them down till we get agreement.
> We have a unanimous agreement on everything. If a fellow enters an objection and we can't talk him out of it—and sometimes we can get him to go along—that's it. We put it in there.

Once the bargain is struck, the subcommittee is expected to "stick together."

It is, of course, easier to achieve unity among the five, seven, or nine members of a subcommittee than among the fifty members of the full Committee. But members are expected wherever possible to observe the norm of unity in the full Committee as well. That is, they should not only defer to the recommendations of the subcommittee involved, but they should support (or not oppose) that recommendation when it reaches the floor in the form of a Committee decision. On the floor, Committee members believe their power and prestige depend largely on the degree to which the norm of reciprocity and unity continue to be observed. Members warn each other that if they go to the floor in disarray they will be "rolled," "jumped," or "run over" by the membership. It is a cardinal maxim among Committee members that, "You can't turn an appropriations bill loose on the floor." Two senior subcommittee chairmen explain:

> We iron out our differences in Committee. We argue it out and usually have a meeting of the minds, a composite view of the Committee. . . . If we went on the floor in wide disagreement, they would say, "If you can't agree after listening to the testimony and discussing it, how can we understand it? We'll just vote on the basis of who we like the best."
>
> I tell them [the full Committee] we should have a united front. If there are any objections or changes, we ought to hear it now, and not wash our dirty linen out on the floor. If we don't have a bill that we can all agree on and support, we ought not to report it out. To do that is like throwing a piece of meat to a bunch of hungry animals.

One of the most functional Committee practices supporting the norm of unity is the tradition against minority reports in the subcommittee and in the full Committee. It is symptomatic of Committee integration that custom should proscribe the use of the most formal and irrevocable symbol of congressional committee disunity—the minority report. A few have been written—but only 9 out of a possible 141 during the eleven years, 1947–1957. That is to say, 95 percent of all original appropriations bills in this period were reported out without dissent. The technique of "reserving" is the Committee member's equivalent for the registering of dissent. In subcommittee or Committee, when a member reserves, he goes on record informally by informing his colleagues that he reserves the right to disagree on a specified item later on in the proceedings. He may seek a change or support a change in that particular item in full Committee or on the floor. But he does not publicize his dissent. The subcommittee or the full Committee can then make an unopposed recommendation. The individual retains some freedom of maneuver without firm commitment. Often a member reserves on an appropriations item but takes no further action. A member explained how the procedure operates in subcommittee:

> If there's something I feel too strongly about, and just can't go along, I'll say, "Mr. Chairman, we can have a unanimous report, but I reserve the

right to bring this up in full Committee. I feel duty bound to make a play for it and see if I can't sell it to the other members." But if I don't say anything, or don't reserve this right, and then I bring it up in full Committee, they'll say. "Who are you trying to embarrass? You're a member of the team, aren't you? That's not the way to get along."

Disagreement cannot, of course, be eliminated from the Committee. But the Committee has accepted a method for ventilating it which produces a minimum of internal disruption. And members believe that the greater their internal unity, the greater the likelihood that their recommendations will pass the House.

The degree to which the role of the subcommittee member can be so played and subcommittee conflict thereby minimized depends upon the minimization of conflict between the majority and minority party subgroups. Nothing would be more disruptive to the Committee's work than bitter and extended partisan controversy. It is, therefore, important to Appropriations Committee integration that a fourth norm—*minimal partisanship*—should be observed by members of both party contingents. Nearly every respondent emphasized, with approval, that "very little" or "not much" partisanship prevailed on the Committee. One subcommittee chairman stated flatly, "My job is to keep down partisanship." A ranking minority member said, "You might think that we Republicans would defend the Administration and the budget, but we don't." Majority and minority party ratios are constant and do not change (i.e., in 1958) to reflect changes in the strength of the controlling party. The Committee operates with a completely nonpartisan professional staff, which does not change in tune with shifts in party control. Requests for studies by the Committee's investigating staff must be made by the Chairman and ranking minority member of the full committee and by the Chairman and ranking minority member of the subcommittee involved. Subcommittees can produce recommendations without dissent and the full Committee can adopt reports without dissent precisely because party conflict is (during the period 1947–1961) the exception rather than the rule.

The Committee is in no sense immune from the temperature of party conflict, but it does have a relatively high specific heat. Intense party strife or a strongly taken presidential position will get reflected in subcommittee and in Committee recommendations. Sharp divisions in party policy were carried, with disruptive impact, into some areas of Committee activity during the 80th Congress and subsequently, by way of reaction, into the 81st Congress. During the Eisenhower years, extraordinary presidential pleas, especially concerning foreign aid, were given special heed by the Republican members of the Committee. Partisanship is normally generated from the environment and not from within the Committee's party groups. Partisanship is, therefore, likely to be least evident in subcommittee activity, stronger in the full Committee, and most potent at the floor stage. Studies which have focused on roll-call analysis have stressed the influence of party in legislative decision making. In the appropriations process, at any rate, the floor stage probably represents party influence at its maximum. Our examination, by interview, of decision making at the subcommittee and full Committee level would stress the influence of Committee-oriented norms—the strength of which tends to vary inversely with that of party bonds. In the secrecy and intimacy of the subcommittee and full Committee hearing rooms, the member finds it easy to compromise on questions of more or less, to take money from one program and give it to another and, in general, to avoid yes-or-no type party stands. These decisions, taken in response to the integrative norms of the Committee, are the most important ones in the entire appropriations process.

Role Integration

The roles of subcommittee member and party member are common to all. Other more specific decision-making positions are allocated among the members. Different positions produce different roles, and in an integrated system these too must fit together. Integration, in other words, must be achieved through the complementarity or reciprocity of roles as well as through a similarity of roles. This may mean a pattern in which expectations are so different that there is very little contact between individuals; or it may mean a pattern in which contacts require the working out of an involved system of exchange of obligations and rewards. In either case, the desired result is the minimization of conflict among prominent Committee roles. Two crucial instances of role reciprocity on the Committee involve the seniority positions of old-timer and newcomer and the leadership positions of Chairman and ranking minority member, on both the full Committee and on each subcommittee.

The differentiation between senior and junior members is the broadest definition of who shall and who shall not actively participate in Committee decisions. Of a junior member, it will be said "Oh, he doesn't count—what I mean is, he hasn't been on the Committee long enough." He is not expected to and ordinarily does not have much influence. His role is that of apprentice. He is expected to learn the business and the norms of the Committee by applying himself to his work. He is expected to acquiesce in an arrangement which gives most influence (except in affairs involving him locally) to the veterans of the group. Newcomers will be advised to "follow the chairman until you get your bearings. For the first two years, follow the chairman. He knows." "Work hard, keep quiet, and attend the Committee sessions. We don't want to listen to some new person coming in here." And newcomers perceive their role in identical terms: "You have to sit in the back seat and edge up little by little." "You just go to subcommittee meetings and assimilate the routine. The new members are made to feel welcome, but you have a lot of rope-learning to do before you carry much weight."

At every stage of Committee work, this differentiation prevails. There is remarkable agreement on the radically different sets of expectations involved. During the hearings, the view of the elders is that, "Newcomers . . . don't know what the score is and they don't have enough information to ask intelligent questions." A newcomer described his behavior in typically similar terms: "I attended all the hearings and studied and collected information that I can use next year. I'm just marking time now." During the crucial subcommittee markup, the newcomer will have little opportunity to speak—save in locally important matters. A subcommittee chairman stated the norm from his viewpoint this way: "When we get a compromise, nobody's going to break that up. If someone tries, we sit on him fast. We don't want young people who throw bricks or slow things down." And a newcomer reciprocated, describing his markup conduct: "I'm not provocative. I'm in there for information. They're the experts in the field. I go along." In full Committee, on the floor, and in conference committee, the Committee's senior members take the lead and the junior members are expected to follow. The apprentice role is common to all new members of the House. But it is wrong to assume that each Committee will give it the same emphasis. Some pay it scant heed. The Appropriations Committee makes it a cornerstone of its internal structure.

Among the Committee's veterans, the key roles are those of Committee Chairman and ranking minority member, and their counterparts in every subcommittee. It is a measure of Committee integration and the low degree of partisanship that considerable reciprocity obtains between these roles. Their partisan status nevertheless sets limits to the degree of possible integration. The Chairman is given certain authority which he and only he can exercise. But save in times of extreme party controversy, the expectation is that the consultation and cooperation between the Chairman and ranking minority member shall lubricate the Committee's entire work. For example, by Committee tradition, its Chairman and ranking minority member are both *ex officio* voting members of each subcommittee and of every conference committee. The two of them thus have joint access at every stage of the internal process. A subcommittee chairman, too, is expected to discuss matters of scheduling and agenda with his opposite minority number. He is expected to work with him during the markup session and to give him (and, normally, only him) an opportunity to read and comment on the subcommittee report. A ranking minority member described his subcommittee markup procedure approvingly:

> Frequently the chairman has a figure which he states. Sometimes he will have no figure, and he'll turn to me and say, "_____, what do you think?" Maybe I'll have a figure. It's very flexible. Everyone has a chance to say what he thinks, and we'll move it around. Sometimes it takes a long time. . . .He's a rabid partisan on the floor, but he is a very fair man in the subcommittee.

Where influence is shared, an important exchange of rewards occurs. The chairman gains support for his leadership and the ranking minority member gains intra-Committee power. The Committee as a whole insures against the possibility of drastic change in its internal structure by giving to its key minority members a stake in its operation. Chairman and ranking minority members will, in the course of time, exchange positions; and it is expected that such a switch will produce no form of retribution nor any drastic change in the functioning of the Committee. Reciprocity of roles, in this case, promotes continued integration. A ranking minority member testified to one successful arrangement when he took the floor in the 83d Congress to say:

> The gentleman and I have been seesawing back and forth on this Committee for some time. He was Chairman in the 80th Congress. I had the privilege of serving as Chairman in the 81st and 82nd Congress. Now he is back in the saddle. I can say that he has never failed to give me his utmost cooperation, and I have tried to give him the same cooperation during his service as Chairman of this Committee. We seldom disagree, but we have found out that we can disagree without being disagreeable. Consequently, we have unusual harmony on this Committee.

Reciprocity between Chairman and ranking minority members on the Appropriations Committee is to some incalculable degree a function of the stability of membership which allows a pair of particular individuals to work out the kind of personal accommodation described above. The close working relationship of Clarence Cannon and John Taber, whose service on the Committee totals sixty-eight years and who have been changing places as Chairman and ranking minority member for nineteen years, highlights and sustains a pattern of majority-minority reciprocity throughout the group.

Internal Control Mechanisms

The expectations which apply to subcommittee, to party, to veterans and to newcomers, to chairmen and to ranking minority members prescribe highly integrative behaviors. We have concentrated on these expectations, and have both illustrated and assumed the close correlation between expected and actual behavior. This does not mean that all the norms of the Committee have been canvassed. Nor does it mean that deviation from the integrative norms does not occur. It does. From what can be gathered, however, from piecing together a study of the public record on appropriations from 1947 to 1961 with interview materials, the Committee has been markedly successful in maintaining a stable internal structure over time. As might be expected, therefore, changes and threats of change have been generated more from the environment—when outsiders consider the Committee as unresponsive—than from inside the subsystem itself. One source of internal stability, and an added reason for assuming a correlation between expected and actual behavior, is the existence of what appear to be reasonably effective internal control mechanisms. Two of these are the socialization process applied to newcomers and the sanctioning mechanisms applicable to all Committee members.

Socialization is in part a training in perception. Before members of a group can be expected to behave in accordance with its norms, they must learn to see and interpret the world around them with reasonable similarity. The socialization of the Committee newcomer during his term or two of apprenticeship serves to bring his perceptions and his attitudes sufficiently into line with those of the other members to serve as a basis for Committee integration. The Committee, as we have seen, is chosen from Congressmen whose political flexibility connotes an aptitude for learning new lessons of power. Furthermore, the high degree of satisfaction of its members with the group increases their susceptibility to its processes of learning and training.

For example, one half of the Committee's Democrats are Northerners and Westerners from urban constituencies, whose voting records are just as "liberal" on behalf of domestic social welfare programs as non-Committee Democrats from like constituencies. They come to the Committee favorably disposed toward the high level of federal spending necessary to support such programs, and with no sense of urgency about the Committee's tasks of guarding the Treasury or reducing budget estimates. Given the criteria governing their selection, however, they come without rigid preconceptions and with a built-in responsiveness to the socialization processes of any legislative group of which they are members. It is crucial to Committee integration that they learn to temper their potentially disruptive welfare state ideology with a conservative's concern for saving money. They must change their perceptions and attitudes sufficiently to view the Committee's tasks in nearly the same terms as their more conservative Southern Democratic and Republican colleagues. What their elders perceive as reality (i.e., the disposition of executives to ask for more money than is necessary) they, too, must see as reality. A subcommittee chairman explained:

> When you have sat on the Committee, you see that these bureaus are always asking for more money—always up, never down. They want to build up their organization. You reach the point—I have—where it sickens you, where you rebel against it. Year after year, they want more money. They say, "Only $50,000 this year"; but you know the pattern. Next year they'll be back for $100,000, then $200,000. The younger members haven't been on the Committee long enough, haven't had the experience to know this.

The younger men, in this case the younger liberals, do learn from their Committtee experience. Within one or two terms, they are differentiating between themselves and the "wild-eyed spenders" or the "free spenders"in the House. "Some of these guys would spend you through the roof," exclaimed one liberal of moderate seniority. Repeated exposure to Committee work and to fellow members has altered their perceptions and their attitudes in money matters. Half a dozen Northern Democrats of low or moderate seniority agreed with one of their number who said: "Yes, it's true. I can see it myself. I suppose I came here a flaming liberal; but as the years go by I get more conservative. You just hate like hell to spend all this money. . . . You come to the point where you say, 'By God, this is enough jobs.' " These men will remain more inclined toward spending than their Committee colleagues, but their perceptions, and hence their attitudes, have been brought close enough to the others to support a consensus on tasks. They are responsive to appeals on budget-cutting grounds that would not have registered earlier and which remain meaningless to liberals outside the Committee. In cases, therefore, where Committee selection does not and cannot initially produce individuals with a predisposition toward protecting the Treasury, the same result is achieved by socialization.

Socialization is a training in behavior as well as in perception. For the newcomer, conformity to norms in specific situations is ensured through the appropriate application, by the Committee veterans, of rewards and punishments. For the Committee member who serves his apprenticeship creditably, the passage of time holds the promise that he will inherit a position of influence. He may, as an incentive, be given some small reward early in his Committee career. One man, in his second year, had been assigned the task of specializing in one particular program. However narrow the scope of his specialization, it had placed him on the road to influence within the Committee. He explained with evident pleasure:

> The first year, you let things go by. You can't participate. But you learn by watching the others operate. The next year, you know what you're interested in and when to step in. . . . For instance, I've become an expert on the _____ program. The chairman said to me, "This is something you ought to get interested in." I did, and now I'm the expert on the Committee. Whatever I say on that, the other members listen to me and do what I want.

At some later date, provided he continues to observe Committee norms, he will be granted additional influence, perhaps through a prominent floor role. A model Committee man of moderate seniority who had just attained to this stage of accomplishment, and who had suffered through several political campaigns back home fending off charges that he was a do-nothing Congressman, spoke about the rewards he was beginning to reap.

> When you perform well on the floor when you bring out a bill, and members know that you know the bill, you develop prestige with other members of Congress. They come over and ask you what you think, because they know you've studied it. You begin to get a reputation beyond your subcommittee. And you get inner satisfaction, too. You don't feel that you're down here doing nothing.

The first taste of influence which comes to men on this Committee is compensation for the frustrations of apprenticeship. Committee integration in general, and the meshing of roles between elders and newcomers in particular, rest on the fact that conformity to role expectations over time does guarantee to the young positive rewards—the very kind of rewards of power, prestige, and personal satisfaction which led most of them to seek Committee membership in the first place.

The important function of apprenticeship is that it provides the necessary time during which socialization can go forward. And teaching proceeds with the aid of punishments as well as rewards. Should a new member inadvertently or deliberately run afoul of Committee norms during his apprenticeship, he will find himself confronted with negative sanctions ranging in subtlety from "jaundiced eyes" to a changed subcommittee assignment. Several members, for example, recalled their earliest encounter with the norm of unity and the tradition against minority reports. One remembered his attempt to file a minority report.

> The Chairman was pretty upset about it. It's just a tradition, I guess, not to have minority reports. I didn't know it was a tradition. When I said I was going to write a minority report, some eyebrows were raised. The Chairman said it just wasn't the thing to do. Nothing more was said about it. But it wasn't a very popular thing to do, I guess.

He added that he had not filed one since.

Some younger members have congenital difficulty in observing the norms of the apprentice's role. In the 86th Congress, these types tended to come from the Republican minority. The minority newcomers (described by one of the men who selected them as "eight young, energetic, fighting conservatives") were a group of economy-minded individuals some of whom chafed against any barrier which kept them from immediate influence on Committee policy. Their reaction was quite different from that of the young Democrats, whose difficulty was in learning to become economy-minded, but who did not actively resent their lack of influence. One freshman, who felt that, "The appropriations system is lousy, inadequate, and old fashioned," recalled that he had spoken out in full Committee against the recommendations of a subcommittee of which he was not a member. Having failed, he continued to oppose the recommendation during floor debate. By speaking up, speaking in relation to the work of another subcommittee and by opposing a Committee recommendation, he had violated the particular norms of his apprentice role as well [as] the generally applicable norms of reciprocity and unity. He explained what he had learned, but remained only partially socialized:

> They want to wash their dirty linen in the Committee and they want no opposition afterward. They let me say my piece in Committee. . . . But I just couldn't keep quiet. I said some things on the floor, and I found out that's about all they would take. . . . If you don't get along with your Committee and have their support, you don't get anything accomplished around here. . . . I'm trying to be a loyal, cooperative member of the Committee. You hate to be a stinker; but I'm still picking at the little things because I can't work on the big things. There's nothing for the new men to do, so they have to find places to needle in order to take some part in it.

Another freshman, who had deliberately violated apprenticeship norms by trying to ask "as many questions as the chairman" during subcommittee hearings, reported a story of unremitting counteraction against his deviation:

> In the hearings, I have to wait sometimes nine or ten hours for a chance; and he hopes I'll get tired and stay home. I've had to wait till some pretty unreasonable hours. Once I've gotten the floor, though, I've been able to make a good case. Sometimes I've been the only person there. . . . He's all powerful. He's got all the power. He wouldn't think of taking me on a trip with him when he goes to hold hearings. Last year, he went to _____. He wouldn't give me a nudge there. And in the hearings, when I'm questioning a witness, he'll keep butting in so that my case won't appear to be too rosy.

Carried on over a period of two years, this behavior resulted in considerable personal friction between a Committee elder and the newcomer. Other members of his subcommittee pointedly gave him a great lack of support for his nonconformity. "They tried to slow him down and tone him down a little" not because he and his subcommittee chairman disagreed, but on the grounds that the Committee has developed accepted ways of disagreeing which minimize, rather than exacerbate, interpersonal friction.

One internal threat to Committee integration comes from new members who from untutored perceptions, from ignorance of norms, or from dissatisfaction with the apprentice role may not act in accordance with Committee expectations. The seriousness of his threat is minimized, however, by the fact that the deviant newcomer does not possess sufficient resources to affect adversely the operation of the system. Even if he does not respond immediately to application of sanctions, he can be held in check and subjected to an extended and (given the frequency of interaction among members) intensive period of socialization. The success of Committee socialization is indicated by the fact that whereas wholesale criticism of Committee operations was frequently voiced among junior members, it had disappeared among the men of moderate experience. And what these middle seniority members now accept as the facts of Committee life, the veterans vigorously assert and defend as the essentials of a smoothly functioning system. Satisfaction with the Committee's internal structure increases with length of Committee service.

An important reason for changing member attitudes is that those who have attained leadership positions have learned, as newcomers characteristically have not, that their conformity to Committee norms is the ultimate source of their influence inside the group. Freshman members do not as readily perceive the degree to which interpersonal influence is rooted in obedience to group norms. They seem to convert their own sense of powerlessness into the view that the Committee's leaders possess by virtue of their positions, arbitrary, absolute, and awesome power. Typically, they say: "If you're a subcommittee chairman, it's your Committee." "The Chairman runs the show. He gets what he wants. He decides what he wants and gets it through." Older members of the Committee, however, view the power of the leaders as a highly contingent and revocable grant, tendered by the Committee for so long and only so long as their leaders abide by Committee expectations. In commenting on internal influence, their typical reaction is: "Of course, the Committee wouldn't follow him if it didn't want to. He has a great deal of respect. He's an able man, a hard-working man." "He knows the bill backwards and forwards. He works hard, awfully hard, and the members know it." Committee leaders have an imposing set of formal prerogatives. But they can capitalize on them only if they command the respect, confidence, and deference of their colleagues.

It is basic to Committee integration that members who have the greatest power to change the system evidence the least disposition to do so. Despite their institutional conservatism, however, Committee elders do occasionally violate the norms applicable to them and hence represent a potential threat to successful integration. Excessive deviation from Committee expectations by some leaders will bring counter-measures by other leaders. Thus, for example, the Chairman and his subcommittee chairmen exercise reciprocal controls over one another's behavior. The Chairman has the authority to appoint the chairman and members of each subcommittee and fix its jurisdiction. "He runs the Committee. He has a lot of power," agrees one subcommittee chairman. "But it's all done on the basis of personal friendship. If he tries to get too big, the members can whack him down by majority vote."

In the 84th Congress, Chairman Cannon attempted an unusually broad reorganization of subcommittee jurisdictions. The subcommittee chairman most adversely affected rallied his senior colleagues against the Chairman's action—on the ground that it was an excessive violation of role expectations and threatening to subcommittee autonomy. Faced with the prospect of a negative Committee vote, the Chairman was forced to act in closer conformity to the expectations of the other leaders. As one participant described the episode,

> Mr. Cannon, for reasons of his own, tried to bust up one of the subcommittees. We didn't like that. . . . He was breaking up the whole Committee. A couple of weeks later, a few of the senior members got together and worked out a compromise. By that time, he had seen a few things, so we went to him and talked to him and worked it out.

On the subcommittees, too, it is the veterans of both parties who will levy sanctions against an offending chairman. It is they who speak of "cutting down to size" and "trimming the whiskers" of leaders who become "too cocky," "too stubborn" or who "do things wrong too often." Committee integration is underwritten by the fact that no member high or low is permanently immune from the operation of its sanctioning mechanisms.

The Impact of Committee Integration

Data concerning internal committee activity can be organized and presented in various ways. One way is to use key functional problems like integration as the focal points for descriptive analysis. On the basis of our analysis (and without, for the time being, having devised any precise measure of integration), we are led to the summary observation that the House Appropriations Committee appears to be a well-integrated, if not an extremely well-integrated, committee. The question arises as to whether anything can be gained from this study other than a description of one property of one political subsystem. If it is reasonable to assume that the internal life of a congressional committee affects all legislative activity involving that committee, and if it is reasonable to assume that the analysis of a committee's internal relationships will produce useful knowledge about legislative behavior, some broader implications for this study are indicated.

In the first place, the success of the House Appropriations Committee in solving the problem of integration probably does have important consequences for the appropriations process. Some of the possible relationships can be stated as hypotheses and tested; others can be suggested as possible guides to understanding. All of them require further research. Of primary interest is the relationship between integration and the power of the Committee. There is little doubt about the fact of Committee power. Of the 443 separate case histories of bureau appropriations examined, the House accepted Committee recommendations in 387, or 87.4 percent of them; and in 159, or 33.6 percent of the cases, the House Committee's original recommendations on money amounts were the exact ones enacted into law. . . . House Committee integration may be a key factor in producing House victories in conference committee. This relationship, too, might be tested. Integration appears to help provide the House conferees with a feeling of confidence and superiority which is one of their important advantages in the mix of psychological factors affecting conference deliberations.

Another suggested consequence of high integration is that party groups have a relatively small influence upon appropriations decisions. It suggests, too, that Committee-oriented behavior should be duly emphasized in any analysis of congressional oversight of administrative activity by this Committee. Successful integration promotes the achievement of the Committee's goals, and doubtless helps account for the fairly consistent production of budget-cutting decisions. Another consequence will be found in the strategies adopted by people seeking favorable Committee decisions. For example, the characteristic lines of contact from executive officials to the Committee will run to the chairman and the ranking minority member (and to the professional staff man) of the single subcommittee handling their agency's appropriations. The ways in which the Committee achieves integration may even affect the success or failure of a bureau in getting its appropriations. Committee members, for instance, will react more favorably toward an administrator who conforms to their self-image of the hard-working master-of-detail than to one who does not—and Committee response to individual administrators bulks large in their determinations.

Finally, the internal integration of this Committee helps to explain the extraordinary stability, since 1920, of appropriations procedures—in the fact of repeated proposals to change them through omnibus appropriations, legislative budgets, new budgetary forms, item veto, Treasury borrowing, etc. Integration is a stabilizing force, and the stability of the House Appropriations Committee has been a force for stabilization throughout the entire process. It was, for example, the disagreement between Cannon and Taber which led to the indecisiveness reflected in the short-lived experiment with a single appropriations bill. One need only examine the conditions most likely to decrease Committee integration to ascertain some of the critical factors for producing changes in the appropriations process. A description of integration is also an excellent baseline from which to analyze changes in internal structure.

All of these are speculative propositions which call for further research. But they suggest, as a second implication, that committee integration does have important consequences for legislative activity and, hence, that it is a key variable in the study of legislative politics. It would seem, therefore, to be a fruitful focal point for the study of other congressional committees. Comparative committee analysis could usefully be devoted to (1) factors which tend to increase or decrease integration; (2) the degree to which integration is achieved; and (3) the consequences of varying degrees of integration for committee behavior and influence. If analyses of committee integration are of any value, they should encourage the analysis and the classification of congressional committees along functional lines. And they should lead to the discussion of interrelated problems of committee survival. Functional classifications of committees (i.e., well or poorly integrated) derived from a large number of descriptive analyses of several functional problems may prove helpful in constructing more general propositions about the legislative process.

SECTION VI

PATTERNS OF
LEADERSHIP

Introductory Comment

We have portrayed leadership as a relationship between leaders and followers mediated by the situation in which both find themselves. A leader in one situation may not enjoy the same position in another, though. Individuals suited to the prosecution of a war may not be equally suited to the prosecution of peace and may, in consequence, lose their position as leader once they have brought a war to a successful conclusion. Winston Churchill, for example, was highly esteemed and widely supported as Britain's wartime prime minister, but his Conservative government was voted out of office in the first general election held after the end of World War II.

Examples like this generate a sense of frustration because they give rise to the impression that leadership situations are unlimited in number and variety and thus hardly amenable to generalization. This problem should not be overstated, however. Searing's argument that political leaders are socialized into certain rules of the game and behavior patterns suggests that leaders are not autonomous, self-regulating individuals so that their relationship to followers cannot be altogether unpatterned. Indeed, what makes leadership and followership possible is the stable pattern of mutual expectations that informs the interaction of the partners to the relationship. The content of these expectations will vary from one situation to another depending on the basis of leadership authority. On the one hand, a leader whose authority is accepted as deriving directly from some higher deity will deem himself accountable for his actions to that deity rather than to his followers. A leader whose authority has continuously to be renewed through the secular mechanism of popular endorsement in elections, on the other hand, will deem himself accountable to his followers.

Democratic political systems are especially notable for the constraints they place on the autonomy of political leaders. This is largely because democracy is a system of government explicitly designed to prevent arbitrary rule by persons in positions of power and authority. Constitutionalism, or the notion that the law is above politics, together with the accountability of leaders to followers in regular, free, and competitive elections set boundaries on leadership autonomy that officeholders are well-advised to heed if they do not want to lose their position in the short term or destabilize the shared expectations that underpin the democratic ethos in the long term.

To argue that leadership constraint is institutionalized in democratic systems of government is not to claim that individuals do not matter, that the office shapes the leader to such an extent that one incumbent will behave much like—and have much the same impact as—another. Its more modest claim is that leadership behavior becomes less dependent on the personal characteristics and beliefs of incumbents of leadership positions. The fact that democratic political leaders operate within a set of cultural, historical, institutional, and constitutional constraints means that leadership is patterned to a greater degree than it is in systems of government where such constraints operate less powerfully and, as a result, "personal rule" is more commonly the norm.

The three readings in this section of the book examine some of the more important influences structuring the patterns of leadership to be found in democratic political systems.

The first of them is institutional context. A staple of comparative political analysis is the question of the effect on government of parliamentary and presidential constitutions. In constitutional theory, the difference is marked. Government in parliamentary political systems is a collective enterprise, the responsibility of a cabinet in which the prime minister is merely "the first amongst equals." The separation of powers and the popular election of the president, by contrast, ostensibly make for a greater degree of personal leadership in U.S.-style presidential systems of government. Richard Neustadt takes issue with this portrayal of the contrasting leadership roles of the British prime minister and U.S. president. Instead, he argues, the similarities in the pattern of chief executive leadership in the two countries are greater than the constitutional/ institutional differences between them would lead us to expect. Rather than being at its opposite poles, "they are somewhat differently located near the center of a spectrum stretching between ideal types, from collective leadership to one-man rule" (page 243, this section).

A second important influence on the pattern of democratic political leadership is the structure of conflict in society. Arend Lijphart starts from the observation that the presence of deep and cumulative political cleavages in a society is incompatible with the bargaining and compromise normally associated with effective and stable democratic government. A number of societies exhibiting such cleavage structures have nonetheless exhibited a high degree of democratic stability and Lijphart attributes their success to the purposive actions of political leaders. Rising above the divisions in society, the leaders of the cleavage groupings deliberately negotiate and accommodate their differences to avoid the immobilism and instability threatened by subcultural differences. The result is a highly structured "consociational" system, which entails "government by elite cartel designed to turn a democracy with a fragmented political culture into a stable democracy" (page 266, this section).

The final reading in this section examines the method French political leaders developed to cope with the crises resulting from endemic governmental immobilism and instability. This method, designated "heroic leadership" by Stanley Hoffmann, involved essentially delegating the responsibility for dealing with the crisis to a single individual and then returning him to political obscurity once the crisis had passed. The last "heroic leader" was Charles de Gaulle. He refused to play by the traditional rules of the game, however, and demanded as his price for solving the Algerian crisis the establishment of the Fifth Republic. De Gaulle's substantial political achievements have commonly been attributed to charisma, but a more convincing explanation is political circumstance, or situation. Charlot's (1971, 43–52) analysis of public opinion poll data, for example, shows that "the popularity of General de Gaulle before he returned to power varied with the political situation; the rise in his popularity at the beginning of 1958 is due less to his charisma than to the failure of the Fifth Republic." Even in democracies, in other words, the institutionalized constraints on political leaders become weaker in times of crisis.

Select Bibliography

Blondel, J. 1980. *World Leaders*. London: Sage.
Charlot, J. 1971. *The Gaullist Phenomenon*. London: Allen & Unwin.

Lijphart, A. 1977. *Democracy in Plural Societies.* New Haven, CT: Yale University Press.

Macridis, R. C., and B. E. Brown. 1960. *De Gaulle's Republic: The Quest for Unity.* Homewood, IL: Dorsey.

Nordlinger, E. 1972. *Conflict Regulation in Divided Societies.* Cambridge, MA: Harvard Center for International Affairs.

Rose, R., and E. N. Suleiman, eds. 1980. *Presidents and Prime Ministers.* Washington, DC: American Enterprise Institute.

12

White House and Whitehall

Richard E. Neustadt

"Cabinet government," so called, as practiced currently in the United Kingdom, differs in innumerable ways, some obvious, some subtle, from "presidential government" in the United States. To ask what one can learn about our own machine by viewing theirs—which is the question posed for me this morning—may seem far-fetched, considering those differences. But actually the question is a good one. For the differences are matters of degree and not of kind.

Despite surface appearances these two machines, the British and American, are not now at opposite poles. Rather they are somewhat differently located near the centre of a spectrum stretching between ideal types, from collective leadership to one-man rule. Accordingly, a look down Whitehall's corridors of power should suggest a lot of things worth noticing in Washington. At any rate, that is the premise of this paper.

For a president-watcher, who tries to understand the inner politics of our machine and its effects on policy by climbing inside now and then and learning on the job, it is no easy matter to attempt comparison with the internal life of Whitehall. How is one to get a comparable look? Those

Abridged from a paper presented at the 1965 Annual Meeting of the American Political Science Association, Washington, DC, Sept. 8-11, 1965. Used by permission of the American Political Science Association.

who govern Britain mostly keep their secrets to themselves. They rarely have incentive to do otherwise, which is among the differences between us. Least of all are they inclined to satisfy curiosities of *academics*, especially not English academics. But even we colonials, persistent though we are and mattering as little as we do, find ourselves all too frequently treated like Englishmen and kept at bay by those three magic words, "Official Secrets Act." Why not? Nothing in the British constitution says that anyone outside of Whitehall needs an inside view. Quite the reverse. If academics knew, then journalists might learn, and even the backbenchers might find out. God forbid! That could destroy the constitution. Governing is *meant* to be a mystery.

And so it is, not only in the spoken words of those who do it but also, with rare exceptions, in the written words of journalists and scholars. Only in the memoirs of participants does one get glimpses now and then of operational reality. And even the most "indiscreet" of recent memoirs veil the essence of the modern system: the relations between ministers and civil servants in the making of a government decision (Dalton 1962; Bridges, 1964). Former civil servants have at least as great a stake as former ministers in shielding those relationships: the stake of loyalty to their own professional successors in the governing of Britain. What could matter more than that?

For four years I have made a hobby of attempting to poke holes in their defences, and to take a closer look than either interviews or books afford. Partly this has been a "busman's holiday": having roamed one set of corridors I find it irresistable to look around another set. Partly, though, I have been tempted by the thought which prompted those who organised this panel: namely, that comparison of likenesses and differences would add a new dimension to president-watching.

To test that proposition I have taken every look at Whitehall I could manage by a whole variety of means. Happily for me, White House assignments have contributed to this endeavour. In 1961 when I enjoyed the hospitality of Nuffield College and began my inquiries in Whitehall, the vague status of sometime-Kennedy-consultant opened many doors. It helps to be an object of curiosity. It also helps to have been an official, even in another government: one then "talks shop." In 1963 President Kennedy asked me for a confidential report on the evolution of the Skybolt crisis in both governments. Prime Minister Macmillan co-operated. I learned a lot. In 1964 President Johnson asked me to help facilitate communications between governments in preparation for his first meeting with Harold Wilson as prime minister. Wilson then had just come into office. Whitehall was in transition. Again, I learned a lot. Each time I go to London now I learn a little more.

If this strikes you as a hard way, or an odd way, to do "research," I should simply say that I have found no better way to study bureaucratic politics. While the specifics of official business remain classified, perceptions of behavior in the doing of the business become grist for our academic mill. I shall draw on such perceptions in this paper. You will understand, of course, that I am still a novice Whitehall-ogist. It would take ten years of such "research" before I came to trust my own perceptions. This, perforce, is but an interim report on insufficient evidence from an unfinished study.

What I shall do. . . is to raise two simple points of difference between their machine and ours, with an eye to implications for the study of *our* system:

First, we have counterparts for their top civil servants—but not in our own civil service.

Second, we have counterparts for their cabinet ministers—but not exclusively or even mainly in our cabinet.

If I state these two correctly, . . . it follows that in our conventional comparisons we students all too often have been victims of semantics. Accordingly, in our proposals for reform-by-analogy (a favourite sport of this association since its founding) we all too often have confused function with form. I find no functions in the British system for which ours lacks at least nascent counterparts. But it is rare when institutions with the same names in both systems do the same work for precisely the same purpose. We make ourselves much trouble, analytically, by letting nomenclature dictate our analogies. Hopefully, this paper offers something of an antidote.

For the most important things that I bring back from my excursioning in Whitehall are a question and a caution. The question: what is our functional equivalent? The caution: never base analysis on nomenclature. With these I make my case for a comparative approach to American studies. These seem to be embarrassingly obvious. But that is not the way it works in practice. By way of illustration let me take in turn those "simple" points of difference between Whitehall and Washington.

I

"Why are your officials so passionate?" I once was asked in England by a bright young Treasury official just back from Washington. I inquired with whom he had been working there; his answer "Your chaps at the Budget Bureau."

To an American those "chaps" appear to be among the most dispassionate of Washingtonians. Indeed, the budget staff traditionally prides itself on being cool, collected, and above the struggle, distant from emotions churning in the breasts of importunate agency officials. Yet to my

English friend, "They took themselves so seriously . . . seemed to be crusaders for the policy positions they thought made sense . . . seemed to feel that it was up to them to save the day." If this is how the Budget Bureau stuck him, imagine how he would have felt about some circles in our Air Force, or the European Bureau of the State Department, or the Office of Economic Opportunity, or the Forest Service, for that matter, or the Bureau of Reclamation, or the National Institutes of Health!

His question is worth pondering, though that is not my purpose here (Neustadt 1965). I give it you gratis to pursue on your own time. What I should rather do is to pursue two further questions which his inquiry suggests. First, out of what frame of reference was he asking? And second, is it sensible of him (and most of us) to talk of our own budgeteers as though they were his counterparts? I ask because I think that we are very far from candid with ourselves about the way we get *his* work done in *our* system.

This young man was a principal-with-prospects at the Treasury. By definition, then, he was a man of the administrative class, elite corps of the British civil service. More importantly, he was also apprentice member of the favoured few, elite-of-the-elite, who climb the ladder *in* the Treasury. With skill and luck and approbation from his seniors he might someday rise to be a mandarin. And meanwhile he would probably serve soon as personal assistant to a cabinet minister. In short, he had the frame of reference which befits a man whose career ladder rises up the central pillar of the whole Whitehall machine toward the heights where dwell the seniors of all seniors, moulders of ministers, heads of the civil service, knights in office, lords thereafter: permanent secretaries of the cabinet and Treasury.

English civil servants of this sort, together with their Foreign Office counterparts, comprise the inner corps of "officials," civilian careerists, whose senior members govern the United Kingdom in collaboration with their ministerial superiors the front bench politicians, leaders of the parliamentary party which commands a House majority for the time being. Theirs is an intimate collaboration grounded in the interests and traditions of both sides. Indeed it binds them into a society for mutual benefit: what they succeed in sharing with each other they need share with almost no one else, and governing in England is a virtual duopoly.

This is the product of a tacit treaty, an implicit bargain, expressed in self-restraints which are observed on either side. The senior civil servants neither stall nor buck decisions of the government once taken in due form by their political masters. "Due form" means consultation, among other things, but having been consulted these officials act without public complaint or private evasion, even though they may have fought what they are doing up to the last moment of decision. They also try to assure comparable discipline in lower official ranks, and to squeeze out the juniors who do not take kindly to it. The senior politicians, for their part—with rare and transient exceptions—return the favour in full measure.

The politicians rarely meddle with official recruitment or promotion; by and large, officialdom administers itself. They preserve the anonymity of civil servants both in parliament and in the press. Officials never testify on anything except "accounts," and nobody reveals their roles in shaping public policy. Ministers take kudos for themselves, likewise the heat. They also take upon themselves protection for the status of officialdom in the society: honours fall like gentle rain at stated intervals. They even let careerists run their private offices, and treat their personal assistants of the moments (detailed from civil service ranks) as confidentially as our department heads treat trusted aides imported from outside. More importantly, the politicans *lean* on their officials. They *expect* to be advised. Most importantly, they very often do what they are told, and follow the advice that they receive.

This is an advantageous bargain for both sides. It relieves the politicians of a difficult and chancy search for "loyal" advisers and administrators. These are there, in place, ready to hand. And it relieves officials of concern for their security in terms both of profession and of person. No wonder our careerists appear "passionate" to one of theirs; they have nothing at stake [in Britain] except policy!

So a Treasury-type has everything to gain by a dispassionate stance, and nothing to lose except arguments. Since he is an elitist, ranking intellectually and morally with the best in Britain, this is no trifling loss. If parliamentary parties were less disciplined than they are now, or if he had backbenchers who identified with him, he could afford to carry arguments outside official channels, as his predecessors sometimes did a century ago, and *military* officers still do, on occasion. But party discipline calls forth its counterpart in his own ranks. And party politicians on back benches have no natural affinities for *civil* servants—quite the contrary. He really has no recourse but to lose his arguments with grace and wait in patience for another day, another set of ministers. After all, he stays, they go. And while he stays he shares the fascinating game of power, stretching his own mind and talents in the service of a reasonably grateful country.

The Treasury-type is a disciplined man, but a man fulfilled, not frustrated. His discipline is what he pays for power. Not every temperament can take it; if he rises in the Treasury he probably can. Others are weeded out. But there is more to this than a cold compromise for power's sake. Those who rise and find fulfillment in their work do so in part because they are deliberately exposed at mid-career to the constraints, the miseries, the hazards which afflict the human beings who wield power on the political side. They know the lot of ministers from observation at first hand. Exposure makes for empathy and for perspective. It also makes for comfort with the civil servant's lot. Whitehall's elitists gain all three while relatively young. It leaves them a bit weary with the weight of human folly, but it rids them of self-righteousness, the bane of *our* careerists—which is, of course, endemic among budgeteers.

A Treasury-type gains this exposure through that interesting device, the tour of duty in a minister's private office as his personal assistant ("dogsbody" is their term for it). The private secretary, so called, now serves his master-of-the-moment as a confidential aide, minding his business, doing his chores, sharing his woes, offering a crying towel, bracing him for bad days in the House, briefing him for bad days in the office. Etcetera. Remarkably, by our standards, the civil service has pre-empted such assignments for its own. (Do not confuse these with mere *parliamentary* private secretaries.) Still more remarkably, the politicians feel themselves well served and rarely dream of looking elsewhere for the service. I know an instance where a minister confided in his private secretary a secret he told no one else save the prime minister, not even his permanent secretary, the career head of department, "lest it embarrass him to know." The permanent secretary was the private secretary's boss in career terms. Yet the secret was kept as a matter of course. This, I am assured, is not untypical: "ministerial secrets" are all in a day's work for dogsbodies.

Accordingly, the one-time private secretary who has risen in due course to be a permanent secretary of a department knows far more of what it feels like to perform as politician than his opposite number, the department's minister, can ever hope to fathom in reverse. A William Armstrong, for example, now joint head of the Treasury, whose opposite number is the chancellor of the exchequer, spent years as private secretary to a previous chancellor who was among the ablest men in cabinets of his time. Consider the ramifications of that! And draw the contrast with our own careerists!

Our budgeteers imagine they are the nearest thing to Treasury civil servants. For this no one can blame them. Much of our literature suggests that if they are not quite the same as yet, a little gimmickry could make them so. Many of our colleagues in this association have bemused themselves for years with plans to borrow nomenclature and procedures from the British side, on the unstated premise that function follows form. But it does not.

Functionally, our counterparts for British Treasury-types are *non*-careerists holding jobs infused with presidential interest or concern—"in-and-outers" from the law firms, banking, business, academia, foundations, or occasionally journalism, or the entourages of successful governors and senators—along with up-and-outers (sometimes up-and-downers) who relinquish, or at least risk, civil service status in the process. Here is the elite-of-the-elite, the upper-crust of *our* "administrative class." These are the men who serve alongside our equivalents for ministers and share in governing. One finds them in the White House and in the *appointive* jobs across the street at the Executive Office Building. One finds them also on the seventh floor of State, and on the third and fourth floors of the Pentagon: these places among others. If they have not arrived as yet, they probably are trying to get in (or up). If they have gone already, they are likely to be back.

Let me take some names at random to suggest the types. First, the prototype of all: Averell Harriman. Second, a handful of the currently employed: David Bell, both Bundys (by their different routes), Wilbur Cohen, Harry McPherson, Paul Nitze. Third, a few fresh "outers" almost certain to be back, somehow, sometime: Kermit Gordon, Theodore Sorensen, Lee White. Fourth, a long-time "outer" who is never back but always in: Clark Clifford. Three of these men got their start as government careerists, two as academics, one in banking, two in law, and two on Capitol Hill. The numbers are but accidents of random choice; the spread is meaningful.

The jobs done by such men as these have no precise equivalents in England; our machinery is too different. For example, McGeorge Bundy as the President's Assistant for National Security Affairs is something more than principal private secretary to the prime minister (reserved for rising Treasury-types), a dogsbody-writ-large, and something different from the secretary of the cabinet (top of the tree for them), a post "tradition" turns into an almost constitutional position, certainly what we call an "institutional" one. Yet the men in those positions see a Bundy as their sort of public servant. They are higher on the ladder than my young friend with the question; they do not take budgeteers to be their counterparts: they know a senior civil servant when they see one.

A Bundy *is* one in their eyes—and they are right. For so he is in American practice. I mention Bundy whom they actually know. But if they knew a Sorensen, a Moyers, or the like, I have no doubt that they would see them much the same.

Every detail of our practice is un-English, yet the general outline fits. One of our men appears on television: another testifies against a bill; a third and fourth engage in semi-public argument; a fifth man feeds a press campaign to change the president's mind; a sixth disputes a cabinet member's views in open meeting; a seventh overturns an inter-agency agreement. So it goes, to the perpetual surprise (and sometimes envy?) of the disciplined duopolists in Britain. Yet by *our* lights, according to *our* standards, under *our* conditions, such activities may be as "disciplined" as theirs, and as responsive to political leadership. The ablest of our in-and-outers frequently display equivalent restraint and equal comprehension in the face of the dilemmas which confront our presidential counterparts for cabinet politicians.

The elite of our officialdom is not careerist in the British sense (although, of course, our in-and-outers have careers): why should it be? Neither is the president with his department heads. They too are in-and-outers. We forget that the duopoly which governs Britain is composed of *two* career systems, official and political. Most ministers who will take office through the next decade are on the scene and well identified in Westminster. The permanent secretaries who will serve with them are on the Whitehall ladders now: a mere outsider can spot some of them. Contrast our situation—even the directorships of old-line bureaus remain problematical. Who is to succeed J. Edgar Hoover?

We have only two sets of true careerists in our system. One consists of senators and congressmen in relatively safe seats, waiting their turn for chairmanships. The other consists of military officers and civil employees who are essentially technicians manning every sort of speciality (including "management") in the executive establishment. Between these two we leave a lot of room for in-and-outers. We are fortunate to do so. Nothing else could serve as well to keep the two apart. And *their* duopoly would be productive not of governance but of its feudal substitute, piecemeal administration. We can only hope to govern in our system by and through the presidency. In-and-outers are a saving grace for presidents.

II

Since 1959, English commentators frequently have wondered to each other if their government was being "presidentialised." In part this stemmed from electoral considerations following the "personality contest" between Harold Macmillan and Hugh Gaitskell at that year's general election. In part it stemmed from operational considerations in the wake of Macmillan's active premiership—reinforced this past year by the sight of still another activist in office, Harold Wilson.

Despite their differences of style, personality, and party, both Macmillan and Wilson patently conceived the cabinet room in Downing Street to be the PM's office, not a mere board room. Both evidently acted on the premise that the PM's personal judgement ought, if possible, to rule the day. Both reached out for the power of personal decision on the issues of the day. Macmillan did so through off-stage manoeuver, while avowing his fidelity to cabinet consensus as befits a man beset by the conventions of committee government. With perhaps a bit more candor, Wilson does the same. But what alerts the commentators is that both have done it. Hence discussion about trends toward presidential government.

Yet between these two prime ministers there was another for a year, Sir Alec Douglas-Home. And by no stretch of the imagination could his conduct of the office have been characterized as presidential. On the contrary, by all accounts he was a classic "chairman of the board," who resolutely pushed impending issues *out* of Number 10, for initiative elsewhere by others. He managed, it is said, to get a lot of gardening done while he resided there. I once asked a close observer what became of the initiatives, the steering, the manoeuvring, which Home refused to take upon himself. He replied:

> When ministers discovered that he really wouldn't do it, they began to huddle with each other, little groups of major figures. You would get from them enough agreement or accommodation to produce the main lines of a government position, something they could try to steer through cabinet. Or if you didn't get it, there was nothing to be done. That's how it began to work, outside of Number 10, around it.

That is how it would be working now, had there been a slight shi⌃ in the popular vote of 1964.

The British system, then, has *not* been presidentialised, or nu⌐ at least in operational terms. For as we learned with Eisenhower, the initiatives a president must take to form "the main lines of a government position" cannot be kept outside the White House precincts. Toss them out and either they bounce back or they do not get taken. A president may delegate to White House aides, . . . but only as he demonstrates consistently, day-in-and-out, that they command his ear and hold his confidence. Let him take to his bed behind an oxygen tent and they can only go through motions. Eisenhower's White House was a far cry from 10 Downing Street in the regime of Douglas-Home. That remains the distance Britain's system has to travel towards a presidential status for prime ministers.

But even though the system did not make an activist of Douglas-Home, his predecessor and successor obviously relished the part. The system may not have required it but they pursued it, and the system bore the weight of their activity. In externals Number 10 looks no more like the White House under Wilson than it did a year ago. But in essence Wilson comes as close to being "president" as the conventions of his system allow. He evidently knows it and likes it. So, I take it, did Macmillan.

How close can such men come? How nearly can they assert "presidential" leadership inside a cabinet system? Without endeavouring to answer in the abstract, let me record some impressions of concrete performances.

First, consider Britain's bid for Common Market membership four years ago, which presaged an enormous (if abortive) shift in public policy, to say nothing of Tory party policy. By all accounts this "turn to Europe" was Macmillan's own. The timing and the impetus were his, and I am told that his intention was to go whole-hog, both economically and politically. As such this was among the great strategic choices in the peacetime politics of Britain. But it never was a government decision. For those, by British definition, come in cabinet. Macmillan never put the issue there in terms like these. Instead he tried to sneak past opposition there—and on back benches and in constituencies—by disguising his strategic choice as a commercial deal. The cabinet dealt with issues of negotiation, *en principe* and later in detail, for making Britain part of Europe's economic union without giving up its Commonwealth connections (or farm subsidies). One minister explained to me:

> Timing is everything. First we have to get into the Common Market as a matter of business, good for our economy. Then we can begin to look at the political side. . . . Appetites grow with eating. We couldn't hold the Cabinet, much less our back-benchers, if we put this forward now in broader terms. . . .

Accordingly, the move toward Europe had to be played out in its ostensible terms, as a detailed negotiation of commercial character. This took two years, and while the tactic served its purpose within Tory ranks these were the years when France escaped from the Algerian war. By the time negotiations neared their end, Charles de Gaulle was riding high at home. Macmillan tiptoed past his own internal obstacles, but took so long about it that his path was blocked by an external one, the veto of de Gaulle.

Second, take the Nassau Pact of 1962, which calmed the Skybolt crisis between Washington and London even as it gave de Gaulle excuses for that veto. Macmillan was his own negotiator at the Nassau conference. He decided on the spot to drop his claim for Skybolt missiles and to press the substitution of Polaris weaponry. He wrung what seemed to him an advantageous compromise along those lines from President Kennedy. Then and only then did he "submit" its terms to the full cabinet for decision (by return cable), noting the concurrence of three potent ministers who had accompanied him: the foreign, commonwealth, and defence secretaries. With the president waiting, the cabinet "decided" (unenthusiastically by all accounts) to bless this virtual *fait accompli*. What else was there to do? The answer, nothing—and no doubt Macmillan knew it.

Third, consider how the Labour government reversed its preelection stand on Nassau's terms. Within six weeks of taking office Wilson and his colleagues became champions of the Polaris programme they had scorned in opposition. Their backbenchers wheeled around behind them almost to a man. It is no secret that the PM was the source of this reversal, also its tactician. So far as I can find, it was his own choice, his initiative, his management, from first to last. He got it done in quick time, yet he did it by manoeuvring on tiptoe like Macmillan in the Common Market case (with just a touch of shot-gun like Macmillan in the Nassau case). When Wilson let Polaris reach the cabinet for "decision" leading ministers, both "right" and "left" already were committed individually through things they had been led to say or do in one another's presence at informal working sessions. By that time also, Wilson had pretested backbench sentiment, "prematurely" voicing to an acquiescent House what would become the rationale for cabinet action: keeping on with weapons whose production had already passed a "point of no return."

Superficially, such instances as these seem strikingly *un*presidential. In our accustomed vision, presidents do not tiptoe around their cabinets, they instruct, inform, or ignore them. They do not engineer *faits accomplis* to force decisions from them, for the cabinet does not make decisions, *presidents* decide. A Kennedy after Birmingham, a Johnson after Selma, deciding on their civil rights bills, or a Johnson after Pleiku, ordering the bombers north, or Johnson last December, taking off our pressure for the multilateral force, or Kennedy confronting Moscow over Cuba with advisers all around him but decisions in his hands—what contrasts these suggest with the manoeuvers of a Wilson or Macmillan!

The contrasts are but heightened by a glance at their work forces: presidents with 20-odd high-powered personal assistants, and 1,000 civil servants in their Executive Office—prime ministers with but four such assistants in their private office (three of them on detail from departments) and a handful more in Cabinet Office which by definition is not "theirs" alone. Differences of work place heighten the effect still more: 10 Downing Street is literally a house, comparing rather poorly with the White House before Teddy Roosevelt's time. The modern White House is a palace, as Denis Brogan (1964, 5–6) keeps reminding us, a physically-cramped version of the Hofburg, or the Tuileries.

Yet beneath these contrasts, despite them, belying them, Americans are bound to glimpse a long-familiar pattern in the conduct of an activist prime minister. It is the pattern of a president manoeuvring around or through the power men in his administration *and* in Congress. Once this is seen all contrasts become superficial. Underneath our images of presidents-in-boots, astride decisions, are the half-observed realities of presidents-in-sneakers, stirrups in hand, trying to induce particular department heads, or congressmen, or senators to climb aboard.

Anyone who has an independent power base is likelier than not to get "prime ministerial" treatment from a president. Even his own appointees are to be wooed, not spurred, in the degree that they have their own attributes of power: expertise, or prestige, or a statute under foot. As Theodore Sorensen (1963, 79–80) reported while he still was at the White House:

> In choosing between conflicting advice, the President is also choosing between conflicting advisers. . . . He will be slow to overrule a Cabinet officer whose pride or prestige has been committed, not only to save the officer's personal prestige but to maintain his utility. . . . Whenever any President overrules any Secretary he runs the risk of that Secretary grumbling, privately, if not publicly, to the Congress, or to the Press (or to his diary), or dragging his feet on implementation, or, at the very worst, resigning with a blast at the President.

But it is men of Congress more than departmental men who regularly get from Pennsylvania Avenue the treatment given cabinet ministers from Downing Street. Power in the Senate is particularly courted. A Lyndon Johnson when he served there, or a Vandenberg in Truman's time, or nowadays an Anderson, a Russell, even Mansfield, even Fulbright—to say nothing of Dirksen—are accorded many of the same attentions which a Wilson has to offer a George Brown.

The conventions of "bipartisanship" in foreign relations, established under Truman and sustained by Eisenhower, have been extended under Kennedy and Johnson to broad sectors of the home front, civil rights especially. These never were so much a matter of engaging oppositions in White House undertakings as of linking to the White House men from either party who had influence to spare. Mutuality of deference between presidents and leaders of congressional opinion, rather than between the formal party leaderships, always has been of the essence "bipartisanship" in practice. And men who really lead opinion on the Hill gain privileged access to executive decisions as their customary share of "mutual deference." "Congress" may not participate in such decisions, but these men often do: witness Dirksen in the framing of our recent Civil Rights Acts, or a spectrum of senators from Russell to Mansfield in the framing of particular approaches to Vietnam. Eleven years ago, Eisenhower seems to have kept our armed forces out of there when a projected intervention at the time of Dien Bien Phu won no support from Senate influentials. Johnson now manoeuvers to maintain support from "right" to "left" within their ranks.

If one seeks our counterparts for Wilson or Macmillan as cabinet tacticians one need look no farther than Kennedy or Johnson manoeuvring among the influentials both downtown *and* on the Hill (and in state capitals, steel companies, trade unions, for that matter). Macmillan's caution on the Common Market will suggest the tortuous, slow course of J. F. Kennedy toward fundamental changes in our fiscal policy, which brought him only to the point of trying for a tax cut by the start of his fourth year. Macmillan's *fait accompli* on Polaris brings to mind the South-East Asia resolution Johnson got from Congress after there had been some shooting in the Tonkin Gulf—and all its predecessors back to 1955 when Eisenhower pioneered this technique for extracting a "blank check."

Wilson's quiet, quick arrangement for the Labour party to adopt Polaris has a lot in common with the Johnson coup a year ago on aid to education, where a shift in rationale took all sorts of opponents off the hook.

British government may not be presidential but our government is more prime ministerial than we incline to think. Unhappily for thought, we too have something called a cabinet. But that pallid institution is in no sense the equivalent of theirs. Our equivalent is rather an informal, shifting aggregation of key individuals, the influentials at both ends of Pennsylvania Avenue. Some of them may sit in what we call the cabinet as department heads; others sit in back rows there, as senior White House aides; still others have no place there. Collectively these men share no responsibility nor any meeting ground. Individually, however, each is linked to all the others through the person of the president (supported by his telephone). And all to some degree are serviced—also monitored—by one group or another on the White House staff. The "Bundy Office," and the former "Sorensen Shop," which one might best describe now as the Moyers sphere of influence," together with the staff of legislative liaisoners captained until lately by Lawerence O'Brien—these groups although not tightly interlocked provide a common reference point for influentials everywhere: "This is the White House calling. . . ." While we lack an institutionalised cabinet along British lines, we are evolving an equivalent of Cabinet Office. The O'Brien operation is its newest element, with no precursors worthy of the name in any regime earlier than Eisenhower's. Whether it survives, and how and why, without O'Brien become questions of the day for presidency-watchers. Doctoral candidates take note!

The functional equivalence between British cabinet and our set of influentials—whether secretaries, senators, White House staffers, congressmen, or others—is rendered plain by noting that for most intents and purposes their cabinet members do the work of our congressional committees, our floor leaderships, and our front-offices downtown, all combined. The combination makes for superficial smoothness; Whitehall seems a quiet place. But once again appearances deceive. Beneath the surface this combine called "cabinet" wrestles with divergencies of interest, of perspective, of procedure, personality, much like those we are used to witnessing above ground in the dealings of our separated institutions. Not only is the hidden struggle reminiscent of our open one, but also the results are often similar: "bold, new ventures" actually undertaken are often few and far between: Whitehall dispenses with the grunts and groans of Washington, but both can labour mightily to bring forth mice.

It is unfashionable just now to speak of "stalemate" or of "deadlock" in our government, although these terms were all the rage two years ago and will be so again, no doubt, whenever Johnson's coattails shrink. But British government is no less prone to deadlock than our own. Indeed I am inclined to think their tendencies in that direction more pronounced than ours. A keen observer of their system, veteran of some seven years at cabinet meetings, put it to me in these terms:

> The obverse of our show of monolithic unity behind a government position when we have one is slowness, ponderousness, deviousness, in approaching a position, getting it taken, getting a "sense of the meeting." Nothing in our system is harder to do, especially if press leaks are at risk. You Americans don't seem to understand that.

In the Common Market case, to cite but one example, the three months from October to December 1962 were taken up at Brussels, where negotiations centered, by a virtual filibuster from the British delegation. This drove some of the Europeans wild and had them muttering about "perfidious Albion." But London's delegates were not engaged in tactical manoeuvring at Brussels. All they were doing there was to buy time for tactical manoeuvring back home, around the cabinet table. The three months were required to induce two senior ministers to swallow agricultural concessions every student of the subject knew their government would have to make. But Britain could not move until those influential "members of the government" had choked them down. The time-lag seemed enormous from the vantage point of Brussels. Significantly it seemed short indeed to Londoners. By Whitehall standards this was rapid motion.

One of the checks and balances in Britain's system lies between the PM and his colleagues as a group. This is the check that operated here. A sensible prime minister, attuned to his own power stakes, is scrupulous about the forms of collective action: over-reaching risks rejection; a show of arbitrariness risks collegial reaction; if they should band together his associates could pull him down. Accordingly, the man who lives at Number 10 does well to avoid policy departures like the plague, unless, until, and if, he sees a reasonable prospect for obtaining that "sense of the meeting." He is not without resources to induce the prospect, and he is at liberty to ride events which suit his causes. But these things take time—and timing. A power-wise prime minister adjusts his pace accordingly. So Macmillan did in 1962.

Ministerial prerogatives are not the only source of stalemate or slow motion in this system. If members of the cabinet were not also heads of great departments, then the leader of their party in the Commons and the country might be less inclined to honour their pretensions in the government. A second, reinforcing check and balance of the system lies between him and the senior civil servants. To quote again, from the same source:

> The PM has it easier with ministers than with the civil servants. The ranks of civil servants do not work for him. They have to be brought along. They are loyal to a "government decision" but that takes the form of action in Cabinet, where the great machines are represented by their ministers.

The civil servants can be his allies, of course, if their perceptions of the public interest square with his and all he needs is to bring ministers along. Something of this sort seems to have been a factor in the Labour government's acceptance of Polaris: Foreign Office and Defense officials urged their masters on; Treasury officials remained neutral. The PM who first manages to tie the civil servants tighter to his office than to their own ministries will presidentialise the British system beyond anything our system knows. But that day is not yet. For obvious reasons it may never come.

So a British premier facing cabinet is in somewhat the position of our president confronting the executive departments and Congress combined. Our man, compared to theirs, is freer to take initiatives and to announce them *in advance* of acquiescence from all sides. With us, indeed, initiatives in public are a step toward obtaining acquiescence, or at least toward wearing down the opposition. It is different in Downing Street. With us, also the diplomatic and defence spheres yield our man authority for binding judgments on behalf of the whole government. Although he rarely gets unquestioning obedience and often pays a price, his personal choices are authoritative, for he himself is heir to royal prerogatives. In Britain these adhere to cabinet members as a group, not the prime minister alone. Unless they stop him he can take over diplomacy, as Neville Chamberlain did so disastrously, and others since, or he can even run a war like Winston Churchill. But Chamberlain had to change foreign secretaries in the process, and Churchill took precautions, making himself minister of defence.

Still, despite all differences, a president like a prime minister lives daily under the constraint that he must bring along *his* "colleagues" and get action from *their* liege men at both ends of the Avenue. A sensible prime minister is always counting noses in cabinet. A sensible president is always checking off his list of "influentials." The PM is not yet a president. The president, however, is a sort of super prime minister. This is what comes of comparative inquiry!

13

Consociational Democracy

Arend Lijphart

Types of Western Democratic Systems

In Gabriel A. Almond's (1956) famous typology of political systems, he distinguishes three types of Western democratic systems: Anglo-American political systems (exemplified by Britain and the United States), Continental European political systems (France, Germany, and Italy), and a third category consisting of the Scandinavian and Low Countries. The third type is not given a distinct label and is not described in detail: Almond (1956, 329-93, 405) merely states that the countries belonging to this type "combine some of the features of the Continental European and the Anglo-American" political systems, and "stand somewhere in between the Continental pattern and the Anglo-American." Almond's threefold typology has been highly influential in the comparative analysis of democratic politics, although, like any provocative and insightful idea, it has also been criticized. This research note will discuss the concept of "consociational democracy" in a constructive attempt to refine and elaborate Almond's typology of democracies.

The typology derives its theoretical significance from the relation-

World Politics, 21, no. 2 (Jan. 1969): 207-225. Copyright © 1969 by Princeton University Press. Reprinted with permission.

259

ship it establishes between political culture and social structure on the one hand and political stability on the other hand. The Anglo-American systems have a "homogeneous, secular political culture" and a "highly differentiated" role structure, in which governmental agencies, parties, interest groups, and the communication media have specialized functions and are autonomous, although interdependent. In contrast, the Continental European democracies are characterized by a "fragmentation of political culture" with separate "political sub-cultures." Their roles "are embedded in the sub-cultures and tend to constitute separate sub-systems of roles" (Almond 1956, 398-99, 405-7). The terms "Anglo-American" and "Continental European" are used for convenience only and do not imply that geographical location is an additional criterion distinguishing the two types of democratic systems. This point deserves special emphasis because some of Almond's critics have misinterpreted it. For instance, Arthur L. Kalleberg (1966, 73-74) states that the two types "are based on criteria of geographic location and area," and that "Almond does not come out and specify that these *are* his criteria of classification; we have to infer them from the titles and descriptions he gives of each of his groups of states." Actually, Almond (1956, 392) does indicate clearly what his criteria are, and he also specifically rejects the criterion of geography or region as irrelevant, because it is not based "on the properties of the political systems."

Political culture and social structure are empirically related to political stability. The Anglo-American democracies display a high degree of stability and effectiveness. The Continental European systems, on the other hand, tend to be unstable; they are characterized by political immobilism, which is "a consequence of the [fragmented] condition of the political culture." Furthermore, there is the "ever-present threat of what is often called the 'Caesaristic' breakthrough" and even the danger of a lapse into totalitarianism as a result of this immobilism (Almond 1956, 408).

The theoretical basis of Almond's typology is the "overlapping memberships" proposition, . . . [which] states that the psychological cross-pressures resulting from membership in different groups with diverse interests and outlooks lead to moderate attitudes. These groups may be formally organized groups or merely unorganized, categoric, and . . . "potential" groups. Cross-pressures operate not only at the mass but also at the elite level: the leaders of social groups with heterogeneous and overlapping memberships will tend to find it necessary to adopt moderate positions. When, on the other hand, a society is divided by sharp cleavages with no or very few overlapping memberships and loyalties— in other words, when the political culture is deeply fragmented—the pressures toward moderate middle-of-the-road attitudes are absent. Political stability depends on moderation and, therefore, also on overlapping memberships. Truman (1951, 508–511) states this proposition as follows: "In the long run a complex society may experience revolution, degeneration, and decay. If it maintains its stability, however, it may do so in large measure because of the fact of multiple memberships." Bentley (1955, 208) calls compromise "the very process itself of the criss-cross groups in action." And Lipset (1960, 88–99) argues that "the chances for stable democracy are enhanced to the extent that groups and individuals have a number of crosscutting, politically relevant affiliations." Sometimes Almond himself explicitly adopts the terminology of these propositions: for instance, he describes the French Fourth Republic as being divided into "three main ideological families or subcultures," which means that the people of France were "exposed to few of the kinds of 'cross-pressures' that moderate [their] rigid political attitudes," while, on the other hand, he characterizes the United States and Britain as having an "overlapping pattern" of membership (Almond and Powell 1966, 122, 163; Almond and Verba 1963, 134).

In his later writings, Almond maintains both the threefold typology of Western democracies and the criteria on which it is based, although the terms that he uses vary considerably. In an article published in 1963, for instance, he distinguishes between "stable democracies" and "immobilist democracies." The latter are characterized by "fragmentation, both in a cultural and structural sense" and by the absence of "consensus on governmental structure and process" (i.e. the Continental European systems). The former group is divided into two sub-classes: one includes Great Britain, the United States, and the Old Commonwealth democracies (i.e. the Anglo-American systems), and the other "the stable multiparty democracies of the European continent—the Scandivanian and Low Countries and Switzerland" (Almond 1963, 9–10). And in *Comparative Politics: A Developmental Approach*, published in 1966, a distinction is drawn between modern democratic systems with "high subsystem autonomy" (the Anglo-American democracies) and those with "limited subsystem autonomy" and fragmentation of political culture (the Continental European democracies). The third type is not included in this classification (Almond and Powell 1966, 259).

In what respects are Switzerland, Scandinavia, and the Low Countries "in between" the Anglo-American and Continental European democracies? Here, too, Almond consistently uses the two criteria of role structure and political culture. A differentiated role structure (or a high degree of subsystem autonomy) is related to the performance of the political aggregation function in a society. The best aggregators are parties in two-party systems like the Anglo-American democracies, but the larger the number and the smaller the size of the parties in a system, the less effectively the aggregation function will be performed; in the Continental European multi-party systems only a minimum of aggregation takes place. The "working multi-party systems" of the Scandinavian and Low Countries differ from the French-Italian "crisis" systems in that some, though not all, of their parties are "broadly aggregative." Almond (1958, 275–77) gives the Scandinavian Socialist parties and the Belgian Catholic and Socialist parties as examples. This criterion does not distinguish adequately between the two types of democracies, however: if one calls the Belgian Catholic party broadly aggregative, the Italian Christian Democrats surely also have to be regarded as such. On the other hand, none of the Dutch and Swiss parties can be called broadly aggregative.

Instead of using the extent of aggregation performed by political parties as the operational indicator of the degree of subsystem autonomy, it is more satisfactory to examine the system's role structure directly. Like the Anglo-American countries, the Scandinavian states have a high degree of subsystem autonomy. But one finds a severely limited subsystem autonomy and considerable interpenetration of parties, interest groups, and the media of communication in the Low Countries, Switzerland, and also in Austria. In fact, subsystem autonomy is at least as limited in these countries as in the Continental European systems. According to the criterion of role structure, therefore, one arrives at a dichotomous rather than a threefold typology: the Scandinavian states must be grouped with the Anglo-American systems, and the other "in-between" states with the Continental European systems.

The application of the second criterion—political culture—leads to a similar result. Almond (1960, 42) writes that the political culture in the Scandinavian and Low Countries is "more homogeneous and fusional of secular and traditional elements" than that in the Continental European systems. This is clearly true for the Scandinavian countries, which are, in fact, quite homogeneous and do not differ significantly from the homogeneous Anglo-American systems. But again, the other "in-between" countries are at least as fragmented into political subcultures—the *familles spirituelles* of Belgium and Luxembourg, the *zuilen* of the Netherlands, and the *Lager* of Austria—as the Continental European states. Therefore, on the basis of the two criteria of political culture and role structure, the Western democracies can be satisfactorily classified into two broad but clearly bounded categories: (1) the Anglo-American, Old Commonwealth, and Scandinavian states: (2) the other European democracies, including France, Italy, Weimar Germany, the Low Countries, Austria, and Switzerland.

Fragmented but Stable Democracies

The second category of the above twofold typology is too broad, however, because it includes both highly stable systems (e.g., Switzerland

and Holland) and highly unstable ones (e.g., Weimar Germany and the French Third and Fourth Republics). The political stability of a system can apparently not be predicted solely on the basis of the two variables of political culture and role structure. According to the theory of crosscutting cleavages, one would expect the Low Countries, Switzerland, and Austria, with subcultures divided from each other by mutually reinforcing cleavages, to exhibit great immobilism and instability. But they do not. These deviant cases of fragmented but stable democracies will be called "consociational democracies." In general, deviant case analysis can lead to the discovery of additional relevant variables, and in this particular instance, a third variable can account for the stability of the consociational democracies: the behavior of the political elites. The leaders of the rival subcultures may engage in competitive behavior and thus further aggravate mutual tensions and political instability, but they may also make *deliberate efforts to counteract the immobilizing and unstabilizing effects of cultural fragmentation*. As a result of such overarching cooperation at the elite level, a country can, as Claude Ake (1967, 113) states, "achieve a degree of political stability quite out of proportion to its social homogeneity."

The clearest examples are the experiences of democratic Austria after the First World War and of pre-democratic Belgium in the early nineteenth century. The fragmented and unstable Austrian First Republic of the interwar years was transformed into the still fragmented but stable Second Republic after the Second World War by means of a consociational solution. As Frederick C. Engelmann (1962, 651–52) states, "the central socio-political fact in the life of post-1918 Austria [was that] the Republic had developed under conditions of cleavage so deep as to leave it with a high potential for—and a sporadic actuality of—civil war." The instability caused by the deep cleavage and antagonism between the Catholic and Socialist *Lager* (subcultures) spelled the end of democracy and the establishment of a dictatorship. The leaders of the rival subcultures were anxious not to repeat the sorry experience of the First Republic, and decided to join in a grand coalition after the Second World War. . . . Otto Kirchheimer (1957, 137) also attributes the consociational pattern of Austria's post-1945 politics (until early 1966) to "the republic's historical record of political frustration and abiding suspicion." Val R. Lorwin (1965, 4) describes how the potential instability caused by subcultural cleavage was deliberately avoided at the time of the birth of independent Belgium: the Catholic and Liberal leaders had learned "the great lesson of mutual tolerance from the catastrophic experience of the Brabant Revolution of 1789, when the civil strife of their predecessors had so soon laid the country open to easy Habsburg reconquest. It was a remarkable and *self-conscious 'union of the oppositions'* that made the revolution of 1830, wrote the Constitution of 1831, and headed the government in its critical years."

The grand coalition cabinet is the most typical and obvious, but not the only possible, consociational solution for a fragmented system. The essential characteristic of consociational democracy is not so much any particular institutional arrangement as the deliberate joint effort by the elites to stabilize the system. Instead of the term "grand coalition" with its rather narrow connotation, one could speak of universal participation, or as Ralf Dahrendorf (1967, 276) does, of a "cartel of elites." A grand coalition cabinet as in Austria represents the most comprehensive form of the cartel of elites, but one finds a variety of other devices in the other Western consociational democracies and, outside Western Europe, in the consociational politics of Lebanon, Uruguay (until early 1967), and Colombia. Even in Austria, not the cabinet itself but the small extra-constitutional "coalition committee," on which the top Socialist and Catholic leaders were equally represented, made the crucial decisions. In the Swiss system of government, which is a hybrid of the presidential and the parliamentary patterns, all four major parties are represented on the multi-member executive. In Uruguay's (now defunct) governmental system, fashioned after the Swiss model, there was *coparticipación* of the two parties on the executive.

In the Colombian and Lebanese presidential systems, such a sharing of the top executive post is not possible because the presidency is held by one person. The alternative solution provided by the Lebanese National Pact of 1943 is that the President of the Republic must be a Maronite and the President of the Council a Sunni, thus guaranteeing representation to the country's two major religious groups. In Colombia, the Liberal and Conservative parties agreed in 1958 to join in a consociational arrangement in order to deliver the country from its recurrent civil wars and dictatorships. The agreement stipulated that the presidency would be alternated for four-year terms between the two parties and that there would be equal representation (*paridad*) on all lower levels of government. In the Low Countries, the cabinets are usually broadly based coalitions, but not all major subcultures are permanently represented. The typical consociational devices in these democracies are the advisory councils and committees, which, in spite of their very limited formal powers, often have decisive influence. These councils and committees may be permanent organs, such as the powerful Social and Economic Council of the Netherlands—a perfect example of a cartel of economic elites—or *ad hoc* bodies, such as the cartels of top party leaders that negotiated the "school pacts" in Holland in 1917 and in Belgium in 1958.

The desire to avoid political competition may be so strong that the cartel of elites may decide to extend the consociational principle to the electoral level in order to prevent the passions aroused by elections from upsetting the carefully constructed, and possibly fragile, system of cooperation. This may apply to a single election or to a number of successive elections. The *paridad* and *alternación* principles in Colombia entail a controlled democracy for a period of sixteen years, during which the efficacy of the right to vote is severely restricted. Another example is the Dutch parliamentary election of 1917, in which all of the parties agreed not to contest the seats held by incumbents in order to safeguard the passage of a set of crucial constitutional amendments; these amendments, negotiated by cartels of top party leaders, contained the terms of the settlement of the sensitive issues of universal suffrage and state aid to church schools. A parallel agreement on the suffrage was adopted in Belgium in 1919 without holding the constitutionally prescribed election at all.

Consociational democracy violates the principle of majority rule, but it does not deviate very much from normative democratic theory. Most democratic constitutions prescribe majority rule for the normal transaction of business when the stakes are not too high, but extraordinary majorities or several successive majorities for the most important decisions, such as changes in the constitution. In fragmented systems, many other decisions in addition to constituent ones are perceived as involving high stakes, and therefore require more than simple majority rule. Similarly, majority rule does not suffice in times of grave crisis in even the most homogeneous and consensual of democracies. Great Britain and Sweden, both highly homogeneous countries, resorted to grand coalition cabinets during the Second World War. . . . And just as the formation of a national unity government is the appropriate response to an external emergency, so the formation of a grand coalition cabinet or an alternative form of elite cartel is the appropriate response to the internal crisis of fragmentation into hostile subcultures.

Furthermore, the concept of consociational democracy is also in agreement with the empirical "size principle.". . . This principle, based on game-theoretic assumptions, states: "In social situations similar to *n*-person, zero-sum games with side-payments [private agreements about the division of the payoff], participants create coalitions just as large as they believe will ensure winning and no larger." The tendency will be toward a "minimum winning coalition," which in a democracy will be a coalition with bare majority support—but only under the conditions specified in the size principle. The most important condition is the zero-sum assumption: "only the direct conflicts among participants are included and common advantages are ignored" (Riker 1962, 29, 32–33). Common advantages will be completely ignored only in two diametrically opposite kinds of situations: (1) when the participants in the "game" do not perceive any common advantages, and when, consequently, they are likely to engage in unlimited warfare; and (2) when they are in such firm agreement on their common advantages that they can take them for granted. In the latter case, politics literally becomes a game. In other words, the zero-sum condition and the size principle apply only to societies with completely homogeneous political cultures and to societies with completely fragmented cultures. To the extent that political cultures deviate from these two extreme conditions, pressures will exist to fashion coalitions and other forms of cooperation that are more inclusive than the bare "minimum winning coalition" and that may be all-inclusive grand coalitions.

Almond (1956, 398–99) aptly uses the metaphor of the game in characterizing the Anglo-American systems: "Because the political culture tends to be homogeneous and pragmatic, [the political process] takes on some of the atmosphere of a game. A game is a good game when the outcome is in doubt and when the stakes are not too high. When the stakes are too high, the tone changes from excitement to anxiety." Political contests in severely fragmented societies are indeed not likely to be "good games." But the anxieties and hostilities attending the political process may be countered by removing its competitive features as much as possible. In consociational democracies, politics is treated not as a game but as a serious business.

Factors Conducive to Consociational Democracy

Consociational democracy means government by elite cartel designed to turn a democracy with a fragmented political culture into a stable democracy. Efforts at consociationalism are not necessarily successful, of course: consociational designs failed in Cyprus and Nigeria, and Uruguay abandoned its Swiss-style consociational system. Successful consociational democracy requires: (1) That the elites have the ability to accommodate the divergent interests and demands of the subcultures. (2) This requires that they have the ability to transcend cleavages and to join in a common effort with the elites of rival subcultures. (3) This in turn depends on their commitment to the maintenance of the system and to the improvement of its cohesion and stability. (4) Finally, all of the above requirements are based on the assumption that the elites understand the perils of political fragmentation. These four requirements are logically implied by the concept of consociational democracy as defined in this paper. Under what conditions are they likely to be fulfilled? An examination of the successful consociational democracies in the Low Countries, Switzerland, Austria, and Lebanon suggests a number of conditions favorable to the establishment and the persistence of this type of democracy. These have to do with inter-subcultural relations at the elite level, inter-subcultural relations at the mass level, and elite-mass relations within each of the subcultures.

Relations among the Elites of the Subcultures

It is easier to assess the probability of continued success of an already established consociational democracy than to predict the chance of success that a fragmented system would have if it were to attempt consociationalism. In an existing consociational democracy, an investigation of the institutional arrangements and the operational code of inter-elite accommodation can throw light on the question of how thorough a commitment to cooperation they represent and how effective they have been in solving the problems caused by fragmentation. *The length of time a consociational democracy has been in operation* is also a factor of importance. As inter-elite cooperation becomes habitual and does not represent a deliberate departure from competitive responses to political challenges, consociational norms become more firmly established. . . .

There are three factors that appear to be strongly conducive to the establishment or maintenance of cooperation among elites in a fragmented system. The most striking of these is the existence of *external threats* to the country. In all of the consociational democracies, the cartel of elites was either initiated or greatly strengthened during periods of international crisis, especially the First and Second World Wars. During the First World War, the comprehensive settlement of the conflict among Holland's political subcultures firmly established the pattern of consociational democracy. "Unionism"—i.e., Catholic-Liberal grand coalitions—began during Belgium's struggle for independence in the early nineteenth century, but lapsed when the country appeared to be out of danger. As a result of the First World War, unionism was resumed and the Socialist leaders were soon admitted to the governing cartel. The Second World War marked the beginning of consociational democracy in Lebanon: the National Pact—the Islamo-Christian accord that provided the basis for consociational government for the country—was concluded in 1943. In Switzerland, consociational democracy developed more gradually, but reached its culmination with the admission of the Socialists to the grand coalition of the Federal Council, also in 1943. The Austrian grand coalition was formed soon after the Second World War, when the country was occupied by the allied forces. In all cases, the external threats impressed on the elites the need for internal unity and cooperation. External threats can also strengthen the ties among the subcultures at the mass level and the ties between leaders and followers within the subcultures.

A second factor favorable to consociational democracy, in the sense that it helps the elites to recognize the necessity of cooperation, is a *multiple balance of power among the subcultures* instead of either a dual balance of power or a clear hegemony by one subculture. When one group is in the majority, its leaders may attempt to dominate rather than cooperate with the rival minority. Similarly, in a society with two evenly matched subcultures, the leaders of both may hope to achieve their aims by domination rather than cooperation, if they expect to win a majority at the polls. . . . When political parties in a fragmented society are the organized manifestations of political subcultures, a multiparty system is more conducive to consociational democracy and therefore to stability than a two-party system. This proposition is at odds with the generally high esteem accorded to two-party systems. In an already homogeneous system, two-party systems may be more effective, but a moderate multiparty system, in which no party is close to a majority, appears preferable in a consociational democracy. The Netherlands, Switzerland, and Lebanon have the advantage that their subcultures are all minority groups. In the Austrian two-party system, consociational politics did work, but with considerable strain. . . . The internal balance of power in Belgium has complicated the country's consociational politics in two ways. The Catholic, Socialist, and Liberal subcultures are minorities, but the Catholics are close to majority status. The Catholic party actually won a legislative majority in 1950, and attempted to settle the sensitive royal question by majority rule. This led to a short civil war, followed by a return to consociational government. Moreover, the Belgian situation is complicated as a result of the linguistic cleavage, which cuts across the three spiritual families. The linguistic balance of power is a dual balance in which the Walloons fear the numerical majority of the Flemings, while the Flemings resent the economic and social superiority of the Walloons.

Consociational democracy presupposes not only a willingness on the part of elites to cooperate but also a capability to solve the political problems of their countries. Fragmented societies have a tendency to immobilism, which consociational politics is designed to avoid. Nevertheless, decision-making that entails accommodation among all subcultures is a difficult process, and consociational democracies are always threatened by a degree of immobilism. Consequently, a third favorable factor to inter-elite cooperation is a *relatively low total load on the decision-making apparatus.* The stability of Lebanon is partly due to its productive economy and the social equilibrium it has maintained so far, but it may not be able to continue its successful consociational politics when the burdens on the system increase. Michael C. Hudson (1967, 836) argues that the Lebanese political system is "attuned to incessant adjustment among primordial groups rather than policy planning and execution." As a result, its "apparent stability . . . is deceptively precarious: social mobilization appears to be overloading the circuits of the Lebanese political system." In general, the size factor is important in this respect: the political burdens that large states have to shoulder tend to be disproportionately heavier than those of small countries. Ernest S. Griffith (1956) argues that "democracy is more likely to survive, other things being equal, in small states. Such states are more manageable. . . ." In particular, small states are more likely to escape the onerous burdens entailed by an active foreign policy. . . .

Inter-Subcultural Relations at the Mass Level

The political cultures of the countries belonging to Almond's Continental European type and to the consociational type are all fragmented, but the consociational countries have even clearer boundaries among their subcultures. Such *distinct lines of cleavage* appear to be conducive to consociational democracy and political stability. The explanation is that subcultures with widely divergent outlooks and interests may coexist without necessarily being in conflict; conflict arises only when they are in contact with each other. As Quincy Wright states: "Ideologies accepted by different groups within a society may be inconsistent without creating tension; but if . . . the groups with inconsistent ideologies are in close contact . . . the tension will be great. . . ." This argument appears to be a direct refutation of the overlapping memberships proposition, but by adding two amendments to this proposition the discrepancy can be resolved. In the first place, the basic explanatory element in the concept of consociational democracy is that political elites may take joint actions to counter the effects of cultural fragmentation. This means that the overlapping-memberships proposition may become a self-denying hypothesis under certain conditions. Secondly, the view that any severe discontinuity in overlapping patterns of membership and allegiance is a danger to political stability needs to be restated in more refined form. A distinction has to be made between essentially homogeneous political cultures, where increased contacts are likely to lead to an increase in mutual understanding and further homogenization, and essentially heterogeneous cultures, where close contacts are likely to lead to strain and hostility. This is the distinction that Walker Connor (1967, 49–50) makes when he argues that "increased contacts help to dissolve regional cultural distinctions within a state such as the United States. Yet, if one is dealing not with minor variations of the same culture, but with two quite distinct and self-differentiating cultures, are not increased contacts between the two apt to increase antagonisms?" This proposition can be refined further by stating both the degree of homogeneity and the extent of mutual contacts in terms of continua rather than dichotomies. In order to safeguard political stability, the volume and intensity of contacts must not exceed the commensurate degree of homogeneity. Karl W. Deutsch (1954, 39) states that stability depends on a "balance between transaction and integration" because "the number of opportunities for possible violent conflict will increase with the volume and range of mutual transactions." Hence, it may be desirable to keep transactions among antagonistic subcultures in a divided society—or, similarly, among different nationalities in a multinational state—to a minimum.

Elite-Mass Relations within the Subcultures

Distinct lines of cleavage among the subcultures are also conducive to consociational democracy because they are likely to be concomitant with a high degree of *internal political cohesion of the subcultures.* This is vital to the success of consociational democracy. The elites have to cooperate and compromise with each other without losing the allegiance and support of their own rank and file. When the subcultures are cohesive political blocs, such support is more likely to be forthcoming. As Hans Daalder (1966, 69) states, what is important is not only "the extent to which party leaders are more tolerant than their followers" but also the extent to which they "are yet able to carry them along."

A second way in which distinct cleavages have a favorable effect on elite-mass relations in a consociational democracy is that they make it more likely that the parties and interest groups will be the organized representatives of the political subcultures. If this is the case, the political parties may not be the best aggregators, but there is at least an *adequate articulation of the interests of the subcultures.* Aggregation of the clearly articulated interests can then be performed by the cartel of elites. In Belgium, the three principal parties represent the Catholic, Socialist, and Liberal spiritual families, but the linguistic cleavage does not coincide with the cleavages dividing the spiritual families, and all three parties have both Flemings and Walloons among their followers. Lorwin (1966, 174) describes the situation as follows: "The sentimental and practical interests of the two linguistic communities are not effectively organized, and the geographical regions have no administrative or formal political existence. There are no recognized representatives qualified to formulate demands, to negotiate, and to fulfill commitments." The religious and class issues have been effectively articulated by the political parties and have by and large been resolved, but the linguistic issue has not been clearly articulated and remains intractable. In Switzerland, the parties also represent the religious-ideological groups rather than the linguistic communities, but much of the country's decentralized political life takes place at the cantonal level, and most of the cantons are linguistically homogeneous.

A final factor which favors consociational democracy is *widespread approval of the principle of government by elite cartel.* This is a very obvious factor, but it is of considerable importance and deserves to be mentioned briefly. For example, Switzerland has a long and strong tradition of grand coalition executives, and this has immeasurably strengthened Swiss consociational democracy. On the other hand, the grand coalition in Austria was under constant attack by critics who alleged that the absence of a British-style opposition made Austrian politics "undemocratic.". . .

Centripetal and Centrifugal Democracies

An examination of the other two types of the threefold typology of democracies in the light of the distinguishing characteristics of consociational democracy can contribute to the clarification and refinement of all three types and their prerequisites. In order to avoid any unintended geographical connotation, we shall refer to the homogeneous and stable democracies as the *centripetal* (instead of the Anglo-American) democracies, and to the fragmented and unstable ones as the *centrifugal* (instead of the Continental European) democracies. The centrifugal democracies include the French Third and Fourth Republics, Italy, Weimar Germany, the Austrian First Republic, and the short-lived Spanish Republic of the early 1930's. The major examples of centripetal democracy are Great Britain, the Old Commonwealth countries, the United States, Ireland, the Scandinavian states, and the postwar Bonn Republic in Germany.

The French Fourth Republic is often regarded as the outstanding example of unstable, ineffective, and immobilist democracy, but the explanation of its political instability in terms of cultural fragmentation has been criticized on two grounds. In the first place, Eric A. Nordlinger (1965, 143) rejects the argument that the "ideological inundation of French politics" and its "fragmented party system" were responsible for its chronic instability; he states that this explanation conveniently overlooks "the way in which the game of politics is actually played in France. Although ideologism pervades the parties' electoral and propaganda efforts, this public ideological posturing of French politicians does not prevent them from playing out their game of compromise in the Assembly and its *couloirs.* In fact, the political class thinks of compromise as a positive principle of action, with parliamentary activity largely revolving around nonideological squabbles. . . ." The elites of the center parties that supported the Republic fulfilled to some extent all of the logical prerequisites for consociational democracy except the most important one: they lacked the ability to forge effective and lasting solutions to pressing political problems. They indeed played a nonideological game, . . . but [were] not constructively pragmatic. To turn a centrifugal into a consociational democracy, true statemanship is required. Moreover, it is incorrect to assume that, because the elites were not divided by irreconcilable ideological differences, mass politics was not ideologically fragmented either.

The second criticism of the cultural fragmentation thesis alleges, on the basis of independent evidence, that not only at the elite level but also at the mass level, ideology played a negligible role in France. Philip E. Converse and Georges Dupeux (1962) demonstrate that the French electorate was not highly politicized and felt little allegiance to the political parties. But the lack of stable partisan attachments does not necessarily indicate that the political culture was not fragmented. Duncan MacRae (1967, 333) argues persuasively that political divisions did extend to the electorate as a whole in spite of the apparent "lack of involvement of the average voter." Even though political allegiances were diffuse, there were "relatively fixed and non-overlapping *social* groupings" to which "separate leaders and separate media of communication had access." The combination of fragmentation into subcultures and low politicization can in turn be explained by the negative French attitude toward authority. Stanley Hoffmann (1963, 8) speaks of "potential insurrection against authority," and Michel Crozier (1964, 220) observes that this attitude makes it "impossible for an individual of the group to become its leader." Strong cohesion within the subcultures was mentioned earlier as a factor conducive to consociational democracy; the lack of it in France can explain both that the French people were fragmented but at the same time not politically involved, and that the political elites did not have the advantage of strong support from the rank and file for constructive cooperation.

On the other hand, the example of France also serves to make clear that the lack of problem-solving ability as a cause of political instability must not be overstated. After all, as Maurice Duverger (1964, 77) points out, in spite of all of the Fourth Republic's flaws and weaknesses, it "would have continued to exist if it had not been for the Algerian war." The critical factor was the too-heavy burden of an essentially external problem on the political system. Similarly, the fragmented Weimar Republic might have survived, too, if it had not been for the unusually difficult problems it was faced with.

Germany's experience with democracy also appears to throw some doubt on our threefold typology and the theory on which it is based. Weimar Germany was a centrifugal democracy but the Bonn Republic can be grouped with the centripetal democracies. In explaining this extraordinary shift, we have to keep in mind that cultural fragmentation must be measured on a continuum rather than as a dichotomy, as we have done so far. The degree of homogeneity of a political culture can change, although great changes at a rapid pace can normally not be expected. Three reasons can plausibly account for the change from the fragmented political culture of the unstable Weimar Republic to the much more homogeneous culture of the Bonn Republic: (1) the traumatic experiences of totalitarianism, war, defeat, and occupation; (2) "conscious manipulative change of fundamental political attitudes," which, as Verba (1965, 133) states, added up to a "remaking of political culture"; (3) the loss of the eastern territories, which meant that, as Lipset (1963, 292) argues, "the greater homogeneity of western Germany now became a national homogeneity."

The degree of competitive or cooperative behavior by elites must also be seen as a continuum. Among the consociational democracies, some are more consociational than others; and many centripetal democracies have some consociational features. The phenomenon of wartime grand coalition cabinets has already been mentioned. The temporary Christian Democratic-Socialist grand coalition under Chancellor Kiesinger falls in the same category. In fact, the stability of the centripetal democracies depends not only on their essentially homogeneous political cultures but also on consociational devices, to the extent that a certain degree of heterogeneity exists. The alternation of English-speaking and French-speaking leaders of the Liberal party in Canada may be compared with the Colombian device of *alternación*. In the United States, where, as Dahl (1966, 358) states, "the South has for nearly two centuries formed a distinctive regional subculture," cultural fragmentation led to secession and civil war. After the Civil War, a consociational arrangement developed that gave to the South a high degree of autonomy and to the Southern leaders—by such means as chairmanships of key Congressional committees and the filibuster—a crucial position in federal decision-making. This example also shows that, while consociational solutions may increase political cohesion, they also have a definite tendency to lead to a certain degree of immobilism.

Even in Denmark, which is among the most homogeneous of the centripetal democracies, one finds considerable consociationalism. This does not appear in grand coalition cabinets—in fact, Denmark is known for its long periods of government by minority cabinets—but in the far-reaching search for compromise in the legislature. The rule of the game prescribes that the top leaders of all four major parties do their utmost to reach a consensus. This is *glidningspolitik*, . . . or the "politics of smoothness"—an apt characterization of consociational politics.

14

Heroic Leadership in Modern France

Stanley Hoffmann

I. Introduction

This chapter presents only a few suggestions for the study of political leadership in one country—France. . . .

My use of the word "heroic" is a probably vain attempt to avoid the heady, if largely sterile, discussions provoked by the word "charismatic." "Heroism" is a relative notion: a man who is a hero to my neighbor may be a calamity to me. Maybe it would have been preferable to speak about crisis leadership in France—the point being that whereas there are frequent crises which produce leaders whose behavior will be discussed here, not all of these act heroically. However, in some French emergencies the crisis leader makes no pretense of being unusual. What concerns us here are crisis leaders who either see themselves or are seen by the public as different from the norm—whether their ultimate accomplishments vindicate this view or not. Specifically I will concentrate on three figures and assume for brevity's sake that their exploits as well as the context in which they operated are familiar: Marshal Philippe Pétain, Pierre Mendès-France, and Charles de Gaulle. I will, in the next section,

From *Decline or Renewal? France Since the 1930s*, by Stanley Hoffmann (New York: Viking Penguin, 1974), pp. 63–110. Copyright © 1960, 1974 by Stanley Hoffmann. All rights reserved. Reprinted by permission of Viking Penguin.

present a very general framework for an analysis of their statecraft. The nature, functions, and limits of French crisis leaders can best be understood by reference to the style of authority prevalent in French society in general, and in the French polity in particular, as well as by reference to the political system whose crisis brings them forth. In the following section I will put some flesh on these bones [by describing] with more detail the style of "heroic" leaders, how they conceive of, establish, and maintain their authority; then I will discuss the substance of their statecraft, the kinds of tasks undertaken by them, and their performance in carrying out those tasks.

II. Heroic Leadership in France: A Framework

The general framework for our investigation is provided by recent studies of the French style of authority. Here the pioneer is Michel Crozier (1964), whose extraordinarily rich and provocative work offers a sweeping interpretation of authority relations in France's bureaucracy, industrial organization, education, and political system, in both their structural aspects (how are such relations arranged) and cultural aspects (what are the values served by those arrangements). . . .

Crozier's model is that of a system of authority relations in which each stratum, as he calls it, is isolated from other strata and governed by impersonal rules decreed by a superior authority entitled to set such rules but severely limited in scope and means. Within each stratum there is a fierce insistence on equality that the impersonality of the rule guarantees. The joint activities of the members of the stratum are primarily negative, i.e., aimed at preventing two kinds of encroachments: from outside, to protect the stratum against excessive or arbitrary acts of external authorities; and from inside, to deny any members the possibility of taking over the leadership of the group. Such a structure of authority relations results in a society both centralized and hierarchical: centralized, since decisions are referred to high echelons; hierarchical, since every stratum is concerned with and dedicated to the preservation of its own peculiar rank and status. Yet centralization goes along with strict limitations on the superior's rule-making power, constantly held in check by the ruled, and within each rank there is a fierce resistance to privilege and inequality. This structure also results for the individual in a kind of double bookkeeping: he complies with the rules (explicit and assumed) of the social units he lives and works in, as long as they are not arbitrary; yet his private beliefs remain unaffected by, and often are quite contrary to, his public behavior.

The values served by such an arrangement are many. One is what Crozier has called "l'horreur du face-à-face": a dislike of the form of freedom known as participation (also a dislike of the *face-à-face* of totalitarianism, which abolishes all freedom and turns all life into public life); a desire to avoid direct, interpersonal conflict, which might result in permanent entanglement or personal dependence; a preference for independence, for as broad as possible a sphere of uninvaded private thought and action. Defense of the private sphere provides the main, almost the only excuse for occasional joint action; perpetuation of it is assured by the paucity of communications among categories, as well as by the combined effects of decision-making from above and restraints on the decision-makers' sphere of action. Another value served is what one might call a preference for homeorhetic change. The word "homeostasis" implies a return to the *status quo ante* after each crisis is over; it does not apply to the French example, which is not that of a stagnant society. The word "homeorhesis" implies the acceptance of change *and* a return to equilibrium after change. It therefore better fits the French polity, where there is a pervasive dislike for change that disturbs the existing hierarchy of ranks and statuses and the existing leveling within each stratum, a willingness instead to tolerate either the *status quo* or, if it is untenable and provokes excessive strains, change that affects the whole society yet preserves the delicate harmony of hierarchy with equalitarianism. What is resisted is change at the end of which certain groups find themselves in a situation more disadvantageous than the one they held before or than the one they had been led to expect as the outcome of the change. Homeorhesis means, to be precise, a refusal to retrogress or a resentment at failing to progress during a process of change that improves the lot of others: it is the rejection of absolute or relative *déclassement*. It is based on the fear of insecurity (Waddington 1966).

The matrix for this extraordinary set of arrangements and values is France's school system. Its historical origins are preindustrial, a blend of feudal remnants and rebellion against feudalism. They have worked as a corset within which French industrialization has been forced and contorted. Modern France, from the Revolution to World War II, perfectly blended the style summarized above and a socioeconomic system which slowed down industrialization and preserved a peculiar "balance": this blend produced what I have called the stalemate society. As Crozier (1964) has shown, the French style of authority produces an alternation of routine and crisis. The absence of face-to-face relations, the distance between strata, the concept of a higher authority unsharing and bound by impersonal rules—all these condemn such authority to abstraction and rigidity. In ordinary circumstances, the disadvantages are reduced by informal, "parallel," under-the-counter relations that violate the sacrosanct equality within each stratum and fill the gap that exists between above and below, but this is at best a palliative, especially since the violation is covert, the link suspect. Subordinates' resistance to their superiors and the superiors' inability to innovate result in short circuits, i.e., crises when the "rules of the game" either fail to prevent a deterioration of the subjects' status, contribute to a loss of status, or seem to impinge on their independence. Then, the normal rules of the game are suspended and changes are introduced.

Thanks to Crozier (1964) we have a convincing model of routine authority as well as change. But the model of crisis authority is barely sketched in. Just as routine authority is an odd mix of opposites (hierarchy and equality, dependence on and distrust of superior authority), crisis authority is a blend of extremes. On one hand, it represents the collapse of the norm—both in a substantive sense, since it introduces total change into a previously immobile system, and in a procedural sense, since it corresponds to a collapse of the "delicate balance of terror" which exists in routine authority relations. It bespeaks a sudden willingness of the strata to find a way out of crisis, a relief from stress, a blank check given to a superior no longer bound by restraints and bullied by resistance. Crisis authority reasserts personal authority—one might almost say reasserts aristocratic values, as opposed to the antiaristocratic value of distrust and drive for impersonality.

On the other hand, crisis authority performs a *function* for the system, rather than a *change* of system. The way change is thereby introduced often still conforms to the basic value of France's style of authority—the avoidance of face-to-face relations and the preference for homeorhetic change—as if the authorities to whom power had been given by and for the crisis understood exactly the nature, conditions, and limits of the power delegated. The structure and values of French authority relations are so firm that a crisis leader's attempt to change its style would end in fiasco. Thus crisis leadership in France has two aspects. It has a cataclysmic side, which sets it off from crisis leadership in, say, the United States or Britain. In those two countries, a crisis is usually just a particularly strong challenge that can be handled by the normal procedures of authority; in France, those procedures are suspended and crisis leadership becomes not only a response to the challenge but a sort of revenge against the normal procedures. And it has a functional side—which sets it off from the leadership of totalitarian countries, for there is an aspect of continuity or even complicity. During routine periods, the "parallel relations" (so largely personal) adumbrate (and help avoid) the relations that exist in a crisis: they are the shadow of crisis authority in the impersonal light of routine authority patterns. Even when the shadow takes over, the limits voluntarily observed by or forced upon crisis leaders are a glimmer of, and a promise of return to, that impersonal light in temporary eclipse. A country whose language has no equivalents for the words "statecraft" and "leadership" but contains such cold and static abstractions as *le Pouvoir* and *l'Etat* will be tempted to see in grand leadership a kind of heroic exercise in self-expression, a holiday from rules and routine, an exalting spectacle. Yet the distrust of arbitrariness which the vocabulary suggests reminds the leader of the spectators' determination to stop the show if it threatens to turn the audience into stage props. Crisis leadership represents, in this sense, a return to the highly personalized authority to which the French are subjected in their early childhood: at home and in the first grades at school, parents and teachers are face-to-face superiors, as well as makers or transmitters of impersonal rules that apply to them as well as to the child. Crisis leadership, in order to be effective, must be more than the temporary triumph of the "parallel" procedures that normally exist behind the legal façade: it must avoid arbitrariness and somehow turn the heroic show into the impersonal rules of "total" but harmonious change, just as the personal dependence of the early family and school years turns into the system of depersonalized hierarchy and rule-surrounded independence later on. Thus the function crisis leadership performs is double: it is both the agent of social change *in* the system, and the preserver *of* the system against the mortal threat of destruction by immobility or a change of system.

. . . These very general considerations apply to French political life; the alternation of representative regimes and saviors ("techniques of evasion" from a citizen's "participant" culture) represents, in the political sphere, oscillation from routine to crisis (Almond and Verba 1963). But in order to understand heroic leadership, one has to take into account several specific factors of national political life.

First, there are factors distinctive to the *style of political authority*. Some of the features Crozier analyzed in general terms are accentuated in the political sphere. The negative and brittle character of associations, the difficulty in cooperating and reaching compromises that do more than confirm respective statuses are usual features of French political parties (with the partial exception of the extreme left). Especially true of French parties and interest groups is a tendency to try to obtain what they want by blackmailing higher authority. Hence the resort to a frequently "revolutionary" vocabulary that conceals far more limited intentions yet reveals a general attitude toward change (all or nothing) and authority (defiance and dependence). The lack of communication between strata, the distance between each stratum and higher authority, are characteristic of a political regime in which the citizens elect representatives who tend to behave as a caste of sovereign *camarades*.

But French history and the divergences among Frenchmen concerning political legitimacy have also introduced three features that are *peculiar* to the political sphere. The most obvious is addiction not merely to revolutionary talk, but to violence. In other words, the degree of willingness to observe the rules of the game when the results fail to give satisfaction is low. Also, the centralizing efforts of the *ancien régime*, the work and ideology of the Revolution, and the mistakes made by the post-1815 monarchies injected into the whole political sphere a special kind of equalitarianism. Crozier is concerned only with equality within each stratum (otherwise determined to preserve its rank privileges). But authority patterns in the political sphere are distinguished by national equalitarianism, that is, an insistence by most of the population on, and the superior authority's somewhat grudging acceptance of, the dogma of equality before the law, irrespective of social privileges. Hence the existence of *le Peuple*, which does not mean the "presence" of the people as participating citizens in a democratic civic culture, but suggests an aspect of universal suffrage that is important even for elites and leaders fundamentally hostile to what Tocqueville called democracy: that it is impossible to act in the political sphere as if the various strata were completely isolated from each other and political decisions involved only certain select groups of society (this is why one finds a plebiscitarian component even in the most antipopular movements). The third feature is a nostalgia for unanimity and consensus—a by-product of equalitarianism, a reaction against the curse of violence.

All those features point in the same direction: to the fragility of "routine authority." It is challenged, pressured, milked by groups that offer more stress than support, more resistance than service; exercised over citizens used to violence, distrustful of privileges for the neighbor, and yet reluctant or unable to handle their own problems; torn between expectations of over-all equalitarianism or unanimity that render the continual resort to "parallel relations" illegitimate, and demands for special protection and favors that make them indispensable. "Routine authority" is bound to be excessively abstract, unimaginative, distant, and sclerotic. In other words, the "revenge" aspect of heroic leadership is bound to be especially important. . . .

One must take into account the *nature of the political system* itself. Limiting ourselves to the Third and Fourth Republics, we can fill in the framework in the following fashion. Certain features reinforce the conclusions derived from our study of the style of political authority. The institutional setup of the parliamentary Republics afflicted "routine authority" with a kind of anemia that went far beyond the general weakness described in Crozier's model. The reason for this was to be found in the ideological divisiveness of French political life. Given the framework of the French style of authority, French parliamentarianism was probably the only way of insuring the peaceful coexistence of clashing ideologies. Nevertheless, the number and nature of the parties (shaped either for the mere occupation of power or for sterile opposition); a deliberative rather than representative Parliament concerned with general principles rather than reform; impotent cabinets; the need to govern *au centre* almost all the time; multiple brakes and no motor—all this made "routine authority" almost a caricature of Crozier's model.

The structure of the two Republics allows one to present what the French would call a *portrait-robot* of the kind of leader who would succeed best in a system of that sort. One could call him the nondirective leader, the perfect broker, and compare him usefully not to executive leaders in other political systems, but to successful legislative leaders in a highly decentralized assembly such as the United States Senate. What he needs is a certain indifference to policy outcomes, resignation to letting events impose decisions which can then be "sold" as inevitable (instead of risking trouble by suggesting decisions which anticipate events), a Byzantine respect for ritual, inexhaustible patience for bargaining with a wide variety of groups, scrupulous observance of the dogma of equality among members of Parliament and of the sacrosanct distance between them and the electorate (that is, no appeal to the people above the heads of the parliamentarians)—to make sure that, should he be overthrown, he would not be ostracized later. He needs, finally, the art of manipulating the "parallel relations," knowing how to use the key men who, behind the façade of impersonal equality, nevertheless have their hands on the levers of influence. Smooth unobtrusiveness, self-effacing procedural skill, flexibility, what the French call *astuce*—these are the functional requirements of "routine authority": we recognize men like Camille Chautemps, Henri Queuille, Edgar Faure (until he asserted himself and dissolved the Assembly in 1955) and even Briand or Blum.

However, the institutional setup and political formula of the Republics also presented features that gave to their routine authority a resilience that somewhat alters the routine-and-crisis pattern suggested by Crozier. Routine authority, despite its tendency toward paralysis, nevertheless functioned, and the two parliamentary Republics showed a remarkable aptitude for self-preservation. The colorful deadlock of parliaments and cabinets should make us forget neither the bureaucracy, grinding out impersonal rules at a distance from the public and also taking part in the game of parallel relations, nor the consensus on which the Republics rested. Among social groups and political forces, beneath all the ideological differences about the ideal society and the best regime, there was a broad consensus favoring a limited state, congruent with the prevailing style of authority; *in most circumstances*, a career bureaucracy together with a parliamentary system more adept at checking than at moving that bureaucracy corresponded exactly to what was desired. Legitimacy was conditional; to most social or political groups and forces the regime was acceptable as long as its activities left intact their sphere of independence while settling conflicts to their satisfaction. And this was precisely what happened most of the time. The political formula produced a political class diverse enough to appease the characteristic equalitarianism of the political sphere; the setup admirably divorced equalitarianism from social reform and thus pleased most groups and parties, at the same time condemning those that wanted change to play the homeorhetic game, i.e., to ask for all or nothing (thus usually playing into the hands of those who wanted nothing). As a result, the political system was informed with a sense of legitimacy that disappeared only in major crises where the conditions for legitimacy ceased to be met.

In certain kinds of emergencies the system was even capable of injecting into "routine authority" a certain amount of efficiency for a while. This temporary closing of the ranks was essentially defensive: the Third Republic managed to defend itself against attacks from outside authorities threatening the regime. Two kinds of techniques were used. One was attrition: attracting the enemy into the game—into Parliament—where he would spend and waste his energies and means of action; this was a gentle death, and it worked against most antiparliamentary movements. The other technique, used against both antiparliamentary movements and against foreign powers or domestic forces of subversion that operated outside the political sphere, was to get everyone to agree to back a trusted parliamentarian and burden him with the responsibility of eliminating the threat: René Waldeck-Rousseau, Georges Clemenceau, Raymond Poincaré, Gaston Doumergue, Édouard Daladier, Guy Mollet received such temporary delegations of effectiveness.

When less extraordinary threats or strains, instead of being resolved by the political system, resulted in deadlocks among the parliamentarians, hence in the fall of the government, the system resorted to the "cabinet crisis," a mechanism of considerable interest. . . . It was part and parcel of "routine authority" insofar as it aimed at and usually succeeded in avoiding the switch to crisis leadership, followed ritual rules that reflected the structure of the parliamentary game, and resulted in frustrating foes and defusing threats rather than giving a new impulse to society. Yet the cabinet crisis was in a small way a kind of crisis leadership, insofar as it resulted in a (temporary) resolution of deadlock and achieved this largely through "parallel relations."

I seem to have derailed from the track of heroic leadership onto the sidetrack of routine authority. But it remains true that heroic leadership can only be understood by reference to its counterpart. The nature, resilience, and deep roots of routine authority in France explain in particular the following propositions.

Within the parliamentary regime there was occasional room for limited executive authority, as long as its temporary trustee respected the style and rituals of parliamentarism. But any attempt to act "heroically" within the confines of the regime was bound to fail: the hero would be stifled and his leadership could unfold only when the formal procedures had collapsed altogether. . . . Nothing has been more enlightening than what happened to de Gaulle and Mendès-France's attempts to combine a style of heroic leadership with opposition to and within the Republic: both the RPF and the Radical party turned from vehicles for their leaders' return to power into splintering, fiercely negative organizations, leading a short, nasty, and brutish life, torn between job-seekers ready to be absorbed in the "system" and hyperbolic champions of *la politique du pire*, reduced to proving their existence through their capacity to destroy.

The tension between routine and crisis authority is greater in the political sphere than in the rest of French society. The resilience of routine political authority explains why resort to a different kind of leadership is postponed until a situation breeds something like a national sense of emergency, a conviction that there is no other alternative. This, and the peculiar weakness of normal leadership, explains why heroic leadership is met with chiliastic hopes that facilitate change. It is worth noting that the emergency of 1940, the greatest in modern French history, engendered not just one but two rival heroic leaders. This kind of charged atmosphere and these large hopes induce a violently emotional repudiation of routine authority. Yet this very repudiation condemns the heroic leader to a perpetual quest for a legitimacy of his own, and makes his singularity a prison.

Insofar as the political system merely exaggerated features of the national style of authority and represented the wishes of most social "consensus groups" and most political forces, heroic leadership, although free from the special limits imposed by the "games, poisons, and delights of the system," still had to pay heed to the inherent limitations of that style, those desires, and those wishes.

If we try to define the relations between French heroic leadership and the style of authority and the political system, we come to the notion of a vicious circle in French heroic leadership, for it perpetuates the style and preserves within the political system a tension between two extreme types of authority, which fight yet need each other.

Heroic leadership is the statecraft of an "outsider" who cleans Augeas's stables so that Augeas does not have to do what he hates above all—getting involved, alienating what he considers his right to privacy, to independence, to (vigilant) absence. Heroic leadership arrives when change can no longer be delayed. But what it provides is direction without mobilization, and the citizens who are led respond with support yet without participation. The unwritten contract of French patterns of authority is respected, the bonds and trust of democracy *à l'anglo-saxonne* and the bondage and terror of totalitarianism are avoided. Heroic leadership is indeed a *spectacle*—the leader has the double prestige of rebellion and prowess: he reasserts individual exploits after and against the impersonal, anonymous grayness of routine authority.

Yet the spectacle itself is part of the whole drama of French authority, for the leader performs in a way that perpetuates nonparticipation—he turns the show into a monologue addressed to the whole people, instead of channeling the structured participation of his supporters in either totalitarian or democratic "face-to-face" organizations, and his "personal power" confirms his adversaries in their own purely *negative* associations and in their distrust of strong leadership. As Pitts (1963, 243) has incisively suggested, "prowess is created by the recognition of the spectator as much as by the actions of the hero." Equality—that constant value—is preserved, since the hero addresses himself to all the spectators indiscriminately; independence—the ultimate value—is preserved, since prowess is a mode of "seduction," not participation: heroic leadership is a thing to be admired (passively) or imitated (individually). To be sure, it establishes a theatrical *face-à-face* between the leader and his people; yet it perpetuates *la peur du face-à-face*, if by *face-à-face* we mean the direct bargaining and involvement of democracy. De Gaulle did not try to organize a political force of his own until after his resignation in 1946 (even then he called it a Rally, not a party); and Mendès-France's battle to gain control of the Radical party began only after he had been overthrown in February 1955.

At first sight, it seems as if each heroic leader, although unable to break the pattern of distance and noninvolvement, should at least be able to violate the other chief value—the preference for homeorhetic change—since there are no brakes on him. The authority patterns of heroic leadership seem a triumph of *le bon plaisir*, manifest both in the mass (or mock) equalitarianism of the *spectacle* and in the important extralegal systems of parallel personal relations behind the scenes, where the decisions are made. Yet brakes exist, for leadership (like power) is not merely an attribute, it is a relationship. There is no effective leadership without support. And support is facilitated when the forms of impersonality and the *respect des droits acquis*—i.e., respect for the hierarchy of ranks and statuses—are observed. Here is where the bureaucracy comes in again: preserver of the basic trend behind the wild zigzags on the parliamentary fever chart, it is also the regulator and routinizer of heroic leadership. One cannot contrast a representative and an administrative tradition in French political history (Wahl 1958), because the administrative reality behind the changing political façade is permanent. What varies is the way the administration operates. In "representative" periods—which are the routine—it receives some impulses and is submitted to stringent checks from a distrustful and stalemated political class. In "savior" periods, some of the checks are lifted and the impulse is invigorated (yet still tends to translate itself into general rules). Support would disappear and heroic leadership would be pitifully checkmated if the leader forgot the formidable capacity of opposition of the various "strata" to schemes that promote the "wrong" kind of change: French society dispenses its antidotes to totalitarianism along with its resistance to voluntary participation. This explains why, behind the proud façade of rule by fiat and self inspiration, the heroic leader is often as frustrated as his despised "routine" predecessors, obliged to coax, bargain, and compromise, to rule by "equivocation, prevarication, and slow elimination of every alternative" (Williams 1964, 443). . . . The vigilance of the "strata" also explains why a revolt against heroic leadership can occur. In May 1968, de Gaulle faced a revolt by groups worried about their status and protesting against the current mixture of public *immobilisme* and detrimental state interference. In April 1969, even his mild reformism appeared threatening to many.

This impression of a vicious circle is reinforced if one considers the relations between heroic leadership and the political system. The drama of French heroic leadership lies in its symbiotic relation to the political system it denounces. . . . This drama takes the form of a quest for legitimacy. Both Pétain and de Gaulle were determined to be properly christened by the Republics they intended to lay to rest—and the wretched parliamentarians were willing to sprinkle the water on their assassins' brows. The parliamentarians endorsed charisma both because by preserving "the silken thread of legality" (Aron 1965) they wanted to remind the heroic leaders of their limits and because they saw them as protection against others who would be less respectful of the French way of authority: the advocates of a single party on the Nazi mold in July 1940, or the paratroopers in May 1958. Regarding the heroic leaders, their insistence on receiving a proper delegation was, *nolens volens*, recognition of the essential legitimacy of the fallen regimes—as if the new legitimacy they wanted as a direct verdict of the nation would be incomplete without legality, i.e., without the endorsement of the previous regime. Even the de Gaulle of the Resistance years, eager though he was to make a clean break with the fallen Third Republic, ended by reviving its parties in order to gain a full measure of internal and international legitimacy.

A second, and more important, aspect of the symbiosis between the new regime established by the heroic leader and its routine predecessor is that the former is plagued by being basically uninstitutionalizable. It is hard to overcome the contradiction between regular leadership and heroic leadership: the heroic leader comes from the depths of history to give a solo performance of patriotic prowess—and insures by his acts that regular leadership after him may well, in reaction against him, not be leadership at all. Both the Vichy regime and de Gaulle's Fifth Republic were marked by a permanent concern about legitimacy: neither the endorsement of the prior regime nor the plebiscites of the crowds seemed to suffice. De Gaulle's fatal referendum of April 1969 was at least as much an attempt to rekindle the legitimacy which the events of May 1968 had doused, as an attempt to gain approval for specific reforms. Characteristically, legislative elections, however triumphal, do not end the quest for the Grail. Both Pétain and de Gaulle tried to find security and solace in arguments that nonetheless underlined the fragility of the construct: one was that the leader had a "historical" legitimacy deriving from his past deeds, another that the services rendered by the new regime gave it legitimacy (in other words, legitimacy is once again conditional).

To the problem of legitimacy we may add that of transition: of how to move back from heroism to routine. By 1943, Pétain, having reached the end of the frayed rope that had tightened around his neck, wanted to give power back to the very Parliament that had blessed him and that he had disgraced. De Gaulle's first exercise of power ended in his resignation, and there was a total restoration of the "routine" political system. In his second regime, he tried to build something that would preclude any return to the old routine, especially through the procedure of popular election for the President, and the transition to Pompidou, in 1969, was assured with remarkable smoothness. Yet it is still far from clear whether his system will not some day turn out to be a façade behind which a new restoration will triumph, or will not be dismantled by opponents victorious after long frustration. For the Fifth Republic to depart from the traditional pattern, what is required is something like a realization of Gaston Defferre's concept of 1965, . . . the President as leader of a majority party or majority coalition. But the prerequisite is an end to splintering, and though Pompidou won with such a formula four years after Defferre's fiasco, France is still far from accepting this unanimously. De Gaulle's conception was simple, fierce, and self-fulfilling: since French parties are hopelessly splintered and condemned to behaving like "delinquent peer groups," the President must be "the nation's man." This would not really end the oscillation from parliamentary regime to "savior," but it would institutionalize the savior. The trouble was that treating the parties as delinquents helped to keep them that way—negative associations concerned with winning power and excluding others from it—and the regime's parliamentary features offered enough chances for deadlock to justify fear of either an "escalation" into dictatorship or a return to routine impotence. If the party system deteriorates (i.e., if the

Gaullist coalition explodes) or fails to reform further (i.e., if the Left fails to match the considerable transformation and regrouping on the Right), or if on the contrary a united Left, under Communist guidance, successfully challenges the constitutional system and cripples its Presidency; if finding a "nation's man" at regular intervals is impossible (the notion of criteria for charisma is somewhat elusive!), then all the provisions of the Constitution will be useless to stop the Presidency from fading back into the blurred blandness of Third and Fourth Republic premiers. De Gaulle, who in 1962 believed that the popular election of the President was a sure deterrent to such a decline, in December 1965 proclaimed almost desperately that constitutions were mere "envelopes" and that the condition of the political parties made him, de Gaulle, a continuing "national necessity." But the heroic leader cannot become immortal, and all "heroic" regimes recurrently tamper with their constitutions so as to ease a transition back to "normalcy." It had been the case with both Napoleons. The Fifth Republic had three constitutional referendums under de Gaulle, in 1958, 1962, and 1969.

The return to normalcy has now, for the first time, been less than tragic. The two Napoleons ended in national disaster, Pétain's regime in the horrors of insurrection and invasion, but de Gaulle's regime broke out of the vicious circle. Still, as the momentous year from May 1968 to April 1969 showed, the difficulty remained: heroic leadership in France is connected too closely with a cataclysmic sense of emergency and with the notion of "total" transformation to handle a process of gradual evolution easily and well.

III. The Style of Heroic Leadership

My preceding remarks offer a very rough indication of what heroic leadership is like in France. Here I want to sketch in more detail some of the main features of its style.

When I say that the heroic leader is, with reference to "routine authority," the outsider, I mean this in two different ways. He tends to be a man who has not played the political game, either because he has had little contact with it (an indispensable factor if the crisis that brings him to power amounts to the collapse, and not merely the stalemate, of the regime) or because he has shown impatience with its rituals and rules. He is thus in strong contrast to, say, a Roosevelt or even Churchill. Pétain and de Gaulle fitted the first category: although both had had governmental experience before June 1940, this merely heightened their sense of power and their distaste for the crippling conditions imposed by the Third Republic on its exercise. The second category includes Clemenceau, who was called to head the war government of 1917 precisely for the qualities that had made him obnoxious to his colleagues in peacetime, and Mendès-France, who had been a sharp and intransigent (if loyal) censor of the Fourth Republic until the Dien Bien Phu emergency brought him to power.

Moreover, the heroic leader has been a rebel against the prevalent order of things or the prevalent ideas. When those ideas are believed or proven to be bankrupt and the order breaks down, he has the kind of prestige that best fits in with French notions of authority—prestige that comes from defiance, from nonconformity, from not having participated in the errors of the evil way. His personality and behavior have shown that he has the necessary ingredients for heroic leadership; he has maintained his independence from superior authority, he has said no, he has been right when such authority was wrong, and he usually suffered for it, either through setbacks to his career or through temporary withdrawals from the public scene.

And yet there is a difference between being "out" and being an adventurer, between defiance and nihilism, between being outside routine authority and being outside the over-all pattern of French authority. The French turn to heroic leaders when there is no "normal" alternative, but their selection of a hero is not haphazard. Clemenceau had been in the wilderness through much of his career—yet he was a former Premier and tested leader. Mendès-France had resigned with éclat from de Gaulle's cabinet in 1945 and mercilessly denounced the colonial and economic policies of de Gaulle's successors—yet he was in many ways a devoted servant of the parliamentary Republic and Radical party. Pétain's military career before 1914 had suffered from his advocacy of a defensive strategy at a time when the high command was wedded to the offensive—yet he had become one of the military glories, a minister, and ambassador of the Republic. De Gaulle's career had known rough days for reasons inversely symmetrical to Pétain's—yet he too had tried to gain influence through the ordinary channels, not in plots against them. True, the temporary two-star general of 1940 literally stepped out of France's institutions and exerted a brand of heroic leadership—pure, unbound, and self-made—that is unique in French history; but his success in rallying the Free French and the Resistance around himself was due not just to his character and his statecraft. The rebel hero was not n'importe qui; he had served (however briefly) in the cabinet and had had a distinguished (if difficult) career. He was admirable, but he was also respectable. . . .

With respect to heroic leaders' beliefs, we find some interesting features that contrast with those of the "routine leaders." To begin with, there are areas of unshakable dogmatism: a conviction of possessing certain truths, the triumph of which is the condition of France's salvation and the purpose of one's leadership. Indeed, it is worth scrutinizing the words of leaders like Pétain, Mendès-France, and de Gaulle for their references to perdition and salvation, for expressions of their therapeutic approach—France being a beloved patient badly treated by puny quacks but at last to be cured by a doctor who knows exactly what is wrong and what is to be done. To be sure, each leader had his own dogmas, and each one was capable (or had to show himself capable) of flexibility in action. Yet Pétain's austere doctrine of authoritarian regeneration through suffering and the restoration of rural values, de Gaulle's doctrine of a strong state engaged in a permanent struggle for greatness on the world scene, Mendès-France's doctrine on the primacy of economics—all contrast with the skepticism of many parliamentary premiers and the willingness of many other leaders with principles and ideals to set them aside when they came to power.

Partly because of their previous experience of having been right and unrecognized, the heroic leaders' image of themselves is a peculiar blend of self-orientation and identification with a cause. Self-orientation is hardly limited to heroic leaders—French politicians' capacity to project their personality onto the center of the stage and to discuss issues in terms of the issues' effect on their own psyches is remarkable. But there is a difference between the narcissism of Édouard Herriot or Léon Blum and the vanity displayed by heroic leaders. The vanity of Pétain, de Gaulle, or Mendès-France was not narcissistic but active and self-transcending; each one saw himself as the carrier of a message greater than himself. Mendès-France, the least vain of the three, had serene confidence in his own ability; Pétain "gave his person to France in order to alleviate her misery"; de Gaulle turned himself into a "somewhat fabulous character" whom he discussed in the third person, who was clearly the agent of destiny and whose moves had to be carefully thought through precisely because they shaped France's fate.

This self-perception accompanies a coldly or caustically harsh perception of the nonheroes: in all three cases, there is an undeniable sense of superiority. Mendès-France once confided to the deputies that France had been unlucky in some of her leaders before him. Pétain's treatment of his opponents, his indifference to the personal fate of his followers, his obvious lack of sympathy for individual members of the elites he was trying to shore up collectively were not just symptoms of that "shipwreck," old age. And de Gaulle's way of using his own followers as instruments or treating them as part of the "heavy dough" he had to knead—a "king in exile" attitude detected by one of his superiors at an early age—the haughtiness that froze the ardor of so many *résistants* when they met him for the first time needs no elaboration. We have here a clue to their personalities, too: nongregarious men who exhibit in different degrees that melancholy so well described by de Gaulle, the most self-analytic and gifted of them; a propensity to solitude in the midst of action, as well as proud and bitter solace once duty has been performed. After all, it is perhaps fitting that heroic leadership should be exercised by men who are loners by personality as well as origin.

The political behavior of heroic leaders seems to display a permanent contradiction. There is, on one hand, the aspect of revenge I have often mentioned—the repudiation of and reprisals for the routine pattern and its servants. On the other hand, there is a nostalgia for unanimity and reconciliation. This nostalgia is in a way related to the revenge, since the routine pattern is blamed for being divisive and for not having represented the "latent" general will, but it is partly contradicted by the exclusion of the "old regime" from unanimity. The drive for consensus, however vague, mystical or personal, is indispensable for marshaling support, since the heroic leaders shun the structured support provided by the ordinary means (parties and established interest groups) and would be at sea if faced merely with the hostility of discarded *notables*. The drive for punishment is also necessary; it gives the leader's most enthusiastic supporters a sense of accomplishment (as well as jobs), and it provides him with an argument whenever support wanes: "Do you want a return to the old mess?" Thus heroic leadership always seems to have two faces: a sectarian one and a Rousseauistic one, with the leader in a position comparable to Rousseau's legislator. In Vichy, the sectarian face was particularly evident, yet Vichy too had its myth of latent unanimity: it supposedly was reasserting "natural" community structures that had been hidden but never erased by the defunct Republican superstructures. De Gaulle's regime offered the clearest image of the two faces—constant flaying of the "parties of the past" and celebration of the "will of the nation," which they had not heeded. Mendès-France was not in a position to "punish" the political forces that had fought him, yet there was an element of vindictiveness in his relations with the MRP and with right-wing Radicals, and in order to get the indispensable support of the leaders of parties and interest groups, he too resorted to the myth of unanimity, thus putting (unsuccessfully) popular pressure on a restive Assembly.

Heroic leaders also tend to behave in a way that constitutes a pointed reversal of routine authority, even when punishment or revenge is ruled out. Whereas the life of the ordinary Premier is absorbed by a kind of pure game of politics—a perpetual process, engaged in by professional players—the heroic leader tries to make the public (presumably fed up with such politics) believe that he is not playing politics: the others are politicians, he is a statesman. (Vichy's official designation was *l'État français*, and de Gaulle's first decision upon his arrival in liberated Paris was to "put the State back in its center, which was of course the Ministry of War," before meeting the Resistance leaders in the Hôtel-de-Ville

[Passeron 1966, 234]). Ordinary politics means a method rather than a set of goals, a procedure for making (or avoiding) decisions rather than the decisions themselves; the leader who aims at goals and lives for decisions denies that his policies are politics. To a social scientist, politics means difficult choices among values and difficult confrontations of ideas; the heroic leader, even when he proclaims that to govern is to choose, tends to propose to the public that *his* policies are a suprapolitical course of action dictated not by necessity, but by the higher good of the country. De Gaulle's "in the interest of France," Vichy's "eternal truths," even Mendès-France's *dossier*—facts and statistics leading to necessary conclusions—constitute three very different approaches to "depoliticization"; in reverse order an economist's version, a mystical (yet basically right-wing) one, and an astutely political one. Politics also means bargaining and the public banter of horse trading. The heroic leader tried to maintain a façade of rigorous hostility to such debasing procedures, although a great deal of private trading goes on behind the scenes. Pétain liked to announce "his" decision in trenchant terms and terse decrees when the incessant clashes of personal cliques and clans had temporarily halted. De Gaulle's disdain for negotiation, his preference for unilateral offers (and vetoes) to which others must adjust and which preserved the appearance of sovereignty, marked his handling of the Algerian war, indeed of all foreign policy; his transfiguration of bargaining into "arbitration," and even his paradoxical attempt to institute "participation" in *his* way, marked his handling of domestic affairs. Mendès-France, true enough, had to bargain more than he originally wanted to, and more still as his time in office ran out, but it cramped his style and proved the incompatibility between the "system" and his leadership. Routine authority is legitimate because of what it *is*, the heroic leader is legitimate because of what he *does*.

As one punster has put it, the style of such leadership is Caesarean. For ordinary premiers, politics is a French garden of rules and regulations where they move with caution; but the heroic leader, even when he observes the unwritten rules of French authority, refuses to be bound by the "ordinary" rules of the political system. . . .

Ordinary politics all too often mean the demise of responsibility: responsibility is dismembered and buried by the too numerous occupants of power, is repudiated by temporary leaders with a variety of reasons for wanting to appear as merely the executors of collective compromises or as the foster parents of "other people's children." The heroic leader seizes responsibility as a sword, instead of hiding behind the shield of committee procedures; he puts the spotlight on his acts and claims personal authorship even for measures actually instituted below him. Sometimes, these claims are pathetic and even repulsive, as with many of Pétain's punitive "decisions," actually initiated by his entourage or forced upon him by the Germans. Sometimes there is an aspect of deliberate and (again) spectacular provocation, as when de Gaulle personally took responsibility for vetoing Britain's entry into EEC instead of letting Macmillan's application get lost in the procedural side streets at Brussels, when he turned against Israel in 1967, when he called for a free Québec, and when he defied the rebellious French on May 30, 1968. The heroic leader tends to thirst for responsibility, just as the routine leader longs for absolution: Pétain's proud statement to his judges and de Gaulle's claim to all the social and economic reforms of the Liberation are cases in point. Ordinary men doubt and change their minds. The heroic leader acts as if he never hesitated and, when he writes—as de Gaulle did so abundantly—erases all trace of the roads he once thought of taking but did not, or took but abandoned.

Ordinary politics take place in a fishbowl, and the ratio of words to deeds is extraordinarily high. Heroic leaders certainly do not shun words, but the flow of explanations and justifications is thinner, and above all they depend to a high degree on secrecy and surprise. Secrecy and surprise are necessary ingredients of the spectacle, components of prowess, ways of renewing the alertness and applause of a people whose support is needed but whose participation is unwelcome. Moreover, the obstacles found *below* the political surface, where the relevant "strata" resist change, oblige the heroic leader to resort to concealment and cunning, for he has to preserve the myth according to which past inefficiency was due only to the rules of the political game (the myth of heroic omnipotence), and he must be able to conclude deals and make retreats behind the scenes which, if public, would make the Emperor look naked—i.e., he must disguise the reality of his limitations. Mendès-France's steeplechase suspense in dealing with Indochina, Tunisia, and the European Defense Community (EDC) was both functional in the short run and dysfunctional (rather early) *à la longue*, in that it infuriated the parliamentarians, who were made to look silly. Because they had to fight heavy odds in constraining situations where candor could have been fatal, Pétain and de Gaulle resorted to ambiguity, cunning, and deviousness, often deceiving every group in turn. But when similar constraints confronted routine leaders, they usually could not even resort to that black magic: cunning may well be a resource of the weak, but the parliamentary premiers were *too* weak, and when they tried it they often could not control events. (One thinks of the sequels to Faure's devious dealings over Morocco in the summer of 1955—leading far more rapidly to independence than he had wished—or of Mollet's Suez operation in 1956.) Routine authority is characterized best either by blustering statements in sad contrast to the outcomes ("No German guns pointed at Strasbourg,"

"French Algeria forever," etc.) or by plaintive confessions of impotence ("We are condemned to live together," "My subordinates did not obey my orders"). Heroic leadership—and this speaks volumes for the tragic circumstances in which the French turn to it and for the limits within which the hero must operate—is characterized best by Mendès-France's month-long self-ultimatum for a Geneva settlement, and by de Gaulle's dazzling first words to the Algerian crowd: *"Je vous ai compris."*

A third aspect of the heroic leader's conduct concerns his behavior toward the citizenry as a whole, his quest for effusive unanimity, not revenge. Here we find one, but only one, feature common to our three statesmen. It is what might be called their constant call to collective prowess. Heroic leadership offers the spectacle of the hero defying the Gods, and it mobilizes the spectators' enthusiasm by presenting the performance as a national undertaking. So, to rally support, the hero makes a conscious attempt to promote the audience's identification with the character on the stage, thus wrapping his legitimacy in their complicity. This identification *ipso facto* evades the problem of organizing and channeling support: simply, each citizen is asked to feel like a hero. . . .

In the Fifth Republic, although the population was kept in a state of mental and emotional alert by de Gaulle's incomparable sense of personal drama—well-spaced and well-prepared public announcements, trips sublime or familiar, recurrent crises—there was always an effort to present his actions as the reaching toward and the unfolding of a "great undertaking," a *grande affaire,* a "national ambition." Here, the simile most congruent with the General's own idea of himself (or at least—given the man's complexity—his public version of his self-image) would be that of a modern Moses guiding his flock toward a (very misty) Promised Land. . . .

. . . [For] Mendès-France, the problem of legitimacy was simplified by his being a regular Premier. [He] could be satisfied with (and indeed democratically believed in) the self-evident eloquence of deeds. But Pétain and de Gaulle needed and wanted more. Conditional legitimacy based on achievements past and present is fragile—hence the effort to give it deeper roots by digging, so to speak, into the national psyche. Their style of heroic leadership represents a return to the mold of the *ancien régime,* adapted to modern circumstances. . . . Here, too, we find a sense of distance between the leader and the led. The two military men, like the Radical politician, were singularly unbending and ungregarious characters. But whereas Mendès-France struggled somewhat against this, Pétain and de Gaulle cultivated it. . . . In both cases, there was a repudiation of familiarity, a cult of separateness from the herd, which somehow recalls the distance between the subjects and the King. Mendès-France wanted his popularity to be based merely on respect for things well done, although his precarious position required him to whip up respect by means of drama; Pétain wanted from the French the dependent love and anxious trust of children; and de Gaulle, cynical or contemptuous of love, preferred consent based less on reason than on awe. Mendès-France tried to mitigate the sense of personal separateness and the budding personality cult that grew around him by stressing his team. Pétain and de Gaulle tried to compensate the personal distance that removed them from the crowd with dips into the crowd and receiving delegations from the crowd, thus paying homage to the requirement of equalitarianism. But, as in the *bande*, "where," as Pitts (1966, 243) has described it, "all members are equal in their common subordination to the leader," this merely confirmed the purely personal, uninstitutionalized nature of leadership and the abyss between Him and Them: it was paternalism on a grand scale. . . .

The natural milieu of French heroic leadership has always been monarchic: the two Napoleons established empires. Pétain transferred and transformed his 1917 technique of command by personal presence and appeal into a pseudomonarchy—with the cramped ceremonial of Vichy's Hôtel du Parc and the pomp of provincial tours, masses in cathedrals, dedications of symbolic trees, pictures of the Leader in every home, schoolchildren's letters to "le Maréchal" and food packages from him. De Gaulle (who inclined toward Louis XIV rather than Saint Louis) had his rites of press conferences, parades, receptions, and motorcades. They all cultivated mystery and cunning, in the best imitation of *le secret du roi*.

This half-instinctive, half-deliberate re-creation of an old tradition shows once again the two aspects of heroic leadership: repudiating one set of rules on behalf of personality, and framing personal power in a reassuring alternate set. Heroic leadership is original insofar as it accepts, develops, and exploits the plebiscitary implications latent in the *ancien régime* (a regime that once engaged in battle against the political power of the feudal elites, just as the heroic leaders battle the political power of "routine authorities").

A clue to the endurance of the classical style is provided by the two leaders' rhetoric. . . . Pétain (who rarely wrote the first drafts of his speeches) prescribed for himself a codelike simplicity and directness of style that seemed to dismiss all the impurities and excrescences grafted on the French language in the nineteenth and twentieth centuries; stark formulas worthy of medals and frontispieces were his form of eloquence—and, in a highly word-conscious nation, not the least of his appeals. De Gaulle's range was greater; where Pétain liked his sentences short and striking, de Gaulle indulged in long and complex phrases, as if to display his incredible memory—indeed, as his age increased, so did the length of his phrases (Cotteret and Moreau 1969). Yet he, too, [was] addicted in other respects to Chateaubriand's precept of "leading the French through dreams. . . ." His fondness for archaic words and sentences that often seem translated from Latin gave an early seventeenth-century flavor to speeches that were (therefore) almost impossible to translate well. The fact that both men were educated by the Jesuits, steeped in classics, and worked on literary projects partly explains this, but only partly: de Gaulle's speeches as a statesman differed in style from his prewar writings; the older he became, the heavier the classic patina.

. . . What modern heroic leadership needs is not only the techniques of undifferentiated unanimity, which are within the realm of means, but also a grandiose sense of purpose. The heroic leader, to use Max Weber's distinction, must be both statesman and prophet; his dogmas serve him well, and if his dogmas are too sketchy or too dry, he must somehow wrap them in a prophetic vision. The classicism of the statesman must be united with a prophetic romanticism. The literary style, to be most effective, should convey all the allusions and associations of France's golden classic age; the modern heroic leader must rule by the romantic resonance of his language as well as by the weight of deeds. Even Mendès-France, least romantic of men, communicated a vision of economic progress, social change, efficiency, and fraternal "concert" that, in the cesspool climate of 1954, attracted those perpetual seekers after romantic causes, the young and the intellectuals. Even Pétain, flayer of ideology and foe of romantic disorder, tried to be a quaint sort of prophet: the prophet of a return to *"une francité archaïque,"* (Plumyène 1964), the awakener of a romanticism of youth camps, physical fitness, folkloric revival, imperial duty, and agrarian utopia. And what was wartime Gaullism if not a prophecy of resurrection, a romanticism of patriotic exploits, an adventure against a formidable foe in order to save French honor, an epic of an unknown leader "too poor to bend," spiting the Allies in order to save France's future? If the second coming of Gaullism saw the prevalence of statecraft over prophecy, of stately prose over epic poetry, the prestige of the *Rex* of the 1960s still rested fundamentally on the myth and mystique of the *Dux* of 1940. And de Gaulle's foreign policy served a vision sufficiently sweeping and remote to be termed a prophecy. . . .

IV. The Impact and Future of Heroic Leadership

Heroic leadership alone can succeed in injecting massive doses of innovation into a national system that is suspicious of change and ordinarily combines tolerance for individual experimentation with social conformity. But since the conversion to change requires a mobilization of national energies, a reawakening of the general will, a call to national identity, heroic leadership serves also to maintain the system. When routine leaders can no longer preserve it or make change acceptable, heroic leadership saves the society by adapting it, perpetuates society by renewing it. Yet heroic leadership's importance should not conceal its disadvantages. The features of the national system that heroic leadership sustains may themselves deserve to be jettisoned, whether a style of authority that impedes participation and restrains economic and social progress, or a style of behavior on the world stage that prolongs the game of national units proud of cultivating their differences. Even if one accepts these features, there are flaws in heroic leadership of the French polity that one cannot help noting: the plague of impermanence, which drives heroic leaders into an endless and often reckless gamble for legitimacy; the rallying of support through magic rather than reason, the manipulation of frequently infantile needs for dependency, a civic culture in which mass hypnosis replaces organized citizenship; the tendency of a brand of leadership that represents the authoritarian pole of the national style to slide into tyranny or to glide from the search for unanimity into the imposition of conformity—even if the French body politic produces its own antidotes.

Good democrats would like to celebrate at last the demise of French heroic leadership. Yet to replace it requires the demise of the entire national style of authority. For heroic leadership preserves that style not only by periodically saving it from paralysis, but also, more perversely, through its own tendency to violate the rules of homeorhesis (not, as in the case of routine authority, out of anomie or neglect, but out of activism and excess)—at which point, more or less cataclysmically, a swing back to routine authority takes place. De Gaulle has written that when the traditional leadership of the old elites vanishes, the "man of character" becomes the only alternative to anonymity. Whether a "man of character" can be found every seven years, and not only in emergencies, or whether the anonymous elites of routine French politics will resume their role remains to be seen. Even if a synthesis between the two kinds of authority should be achieved in the political system, this would not be the end of the story. For if the style of authority is unchanged in society (and in the civil service), occasional short circuits may occur comparable to that of 1968, which even a regime less personal than de Gaulle's and less impotent than the parliamentary Republics may find hard to handle. The mere synthesis of two kinds of political authority will not suffice to transform the style of authority outside political life; to do that, France's political leaders must deliberately and daringly experiment with institutional innovation in key sectors of society—education, business, the civil service, local government.

Let us look back at our three leaders: Mendès-France, Pétain, de Gaulle. We can finally (as usual) point to some fine paradoxes. In an age in which economic progress has become a primary concern of the French, the leader who made it the cornerstone of his program owes most of his diminished appeal to the memory of the spectacle he once gave. The leader most apparently concerned with stabilizing what he saw as the essence of France and with safeguarding the existence of the French, is the one who most adventurously strayed from what her "essence" allowed and what her (if not their) existence required. The leader apparently most suspicious of dogmas, most "existentialistically" engaged in recurrent self-definition through action, without attachment to old forms of shibboleths or any other limits than the "realities" of the "situation," has been the one most aware of the unwritten rules even heroic leadership must respect to be successful—at least up to 1968, but again in the way in which he made his exit. French heroic leadership is like French classical theater: it never ceases being dramatic, yet the drama must follow rules. Whether such leadership is closer to the august and candid characters of Corneille, or to the devious and driven characters of Racine, is up to the reader to decide.

SECTION VII

LEADERSHIP
STYLE

Introductory Comment

We have seen that the autonomy of political leaders is constrained by the cultural, societal, institutional, and constitutional context in which they operate. Institutional and constitutional constraints are especially strong in democracies and they serve to impose certain uniformities of behavior on incumbents of the same leadership position. Broad patterns of leadership thus become identifiable. Whoever he or she may be or whatever his or her party, for example, the U.S. president is obliged by public expectation and constitutional dictate to forge a cooperative, rather than confrontational, working relationship with Congress if the country is to be governed effectively. Similarly, the British prime minister must cooperate with his or her Cabinet if the unity of the majority party that is so essential to the efficient functioning of parliamentary government is to be maintained. The examples are endless, but the larger point is simple: leaders may shape their political environment, but are more certainly shaped by it.

Taken to extremes, this observation would imply that incumbents of a particular leadership position will behave indistinguishably. All modern presidents, for example, would have the same relationship with Congress. But even the most cursory review of recent political history belies this claim. In point of fact, the political environment in which democratic political leaders operate is better thought of as establishing the boundaries of permissible political action and, within these boundaries, individual incumbents enjoy considerable latitude in defining their own job description. All British prime ministers, for example, will shunt aside their Cabinet only at great personal political risk, but not all of them will feel equally bound by its collective, egalitarian ethos.

This self-defined job description will be reflected in the individual's leadership style. In his study of Prime Minister Thatcher, King (page 320, this section) defines style in terms of the leader's "characteristic working methods." As Barber (1968, 52) emphasizes in his definition of style as "a collection of habitual action patterns in meeting role demands," these "methods" are shaped in part by the demands of the job. But that is not all. Role demands themselves reflect in good part the incumbent's personal conception of the kind of behavior that is appropriate to the role. Different individuals, in other words, can fill the same role in markedly dissimilar ways if they do not have the same conception of the behavior, or orientation, appropriate to it.

One of the better-known examples of the variability, and importance, of role orientations focuses on elected representatives in U.S. state legislatures (Wahlke et al. 1962). Asking how legislators represent their constituents, the authors identify three distinct role orientations, or leadership styles. First is the "trustee," the representative who sees himself as a free agent, required to make decisions according to principles, conviction, and desire. Second is the "delegate," who rejects acting on the basis of his independent judgment in favor of consulting his constituents, accepting their instructions and even subordinating his own judgment to their instructions. Finally comes the "politico." His leadership style is structured by a dynamic mixture of trustee and delegate role orientations.

A second example is the numerous schemes for classifying U.S. presidents on the basis of their leadership style. The more traditional of these are dichotomous and basically divide presidents into those who choose to exercise only the powers that are explicitly granted to the chief executive in the Constitution and those who seek to expand his remit by aggressively appropriating those powers that are not constitutionally reserved for the other branches of the government. Koenig (1968, 10–12), for example, labels these different leadership styles "literalist" and "strong." The former are "respectful, even deferential, to Congress," while the latter, in the words of President Theodore Roosevelt, "do anything that the needs of the nation demanded unless such action was forbidden by the Constitution or by the laws." Using much the same criteria to make much the same distinction, Hargrove

(1966) contrasts "presidents of restraint" and "presidents of action." Kavanagh (1987) has recently introduced this tradition into the study of British prime ministers with his distinction between their "mobilizing" and "reconciling" leadership styles.

A more elaborate and sophisticated analysis of this type has conscripted personality to complement role orientation to understand better the different leadership styles of U.S. presidents. In an influential and controversial book, Barber (1977) added to the "active/passive" role orientation of presidents a "positive/negative" satisfaction dimension. This results in the identification of four types of president. Briefly, the active-positive president "sees himself as developing over time toward relatively well-defined personal goals—growing toward his image of himself as he might yet be. There is an emphasis on rational mastery" (Barber 1977, 12).

For the active-negative president, in contrast, "the activity has a compulsive quality, as if the man were trying to make up for something or to escape from anxiety into hard work" (Barber 1977, 12). The passive-positive president also lacks self-confidence and is "the receptive, compliant, other-directed character whose life is a search for affection as a reward for being agreeable and cooperative and personally assertive" (Barber 1977, 13). Finally, passive-negative presidents "are in politics because they think they ought to be. . . . Their tendency is to withdraw, to escape from the conflict and uncertainty of politics by emphasizing vague principles (especially prohibitions) and procedural arrangements. They become guardians of the right and proper way, above the sordid politicking of lesser men" (Barber 1977, 13).

Barber's thesis is not beyond criticism (see, for example, George 1974). It achieved instant popularity, however, if only because it predicted the troubles into which the Nixon presidency would eventually run as the result of his perseverance in trying to cover up the Watergate break-in. Moreover, in classifying Lyndon Johnson along with Nixon as an active-negative president, it also apparently helped to explain why Johnson failed to extricate America from a war in Vietnam that, like Watergate later, did so much political harm to the president and the nation. Many eyes turned wistfully to the passive-negative, and highly popular, presidency of Dwight D. Eisenhower in the 1950s.

The readings in this section of the book have been selected as particularly insightful case studies of the characteristic working methods of three important political leaders, one a U.S. president, another a British prime minister, and the third a spectacularly successful leader of the U.S. Senate. As such, they provide fascinating insights into how personality, situation, and ideology combine to produce the distinctive styles of three successful political leaders.

Greenstein's article is part of his larger, revisionist appraisal of Eisenhower as president. Arguing essentially that appearance gave a misleading impression of substance, he makes the case that Eisenhower was an activist and rejects the passive-negative classification commonly associated with him. Evans and Novak's analysis of Lyndon Johnson's working methods provides food for thought about whether his presidential failings could have been foreseen or whether his style was highly suited to his role as Senate majority leader but less suited to the different role demands of the presidency. Finally, in light of King's analysis of Margaret Thatcher's leadership style, readers might like to ask whether Barber's typology transcends contextual differences unrelated to personality or ideology to be useful for the study of prime ministerial character as well. Few would doubt that Mrs. Thatcher would qualify as an activist political leader, but the classification of her as negative or positive might arouse more debate.

Select Bibliography

Barber, J. D. 1977. *The Presidential Character: Predicting Performance in the White House*, 2d ed. Englewood Cliffs, NJ: Prentice-Hall.

George, A. L. 1974. "Assessing Presidential Character." *World Politics* 26:234–82.

Geyelin, P. 1966. *LBJ and the World*. New York: Praeger.

Ripley, R. B. 1969. *Majority Party Leadership in Congress*. Boston, MA: Little, Brown.

Stoessinger, J. G. 1979. *Crusaders and Pragmatists: Movers of Modern American Foreign Policy*. New York: Norton.

Young, H. 1989. *One of Us: A Biography of Margaret Thatcher*. London: Macmillan.

15

Eisenhower's Leadership Style

Fred I. Greenstein

isenhower, like Truman, had a desk ornament bearing a motto epitomizing his view of leadership. Rather than "The buck stops here," Eisenhower's declared *"Suaviter in modo, fortiter in re"* (Gently in manner, strong in deed). The motto nicely captures the essence of Eisenhower's approach to leadership, a repertoire of six strategies that enabled him to exercise power without seeming to flex his muscles. The strategies, which were characteristic of Eisenhower the man, enabled him to balance the contradictory expectations that a president be a national unifier yet nevertheless engage in the divisive exercise of political leadership.

For covertly exercising the prime-ministerial side of the chief executive's job Eisenhower employed five strategies: hidden-hand leadership; instrumental use of language; the complementary strategies of refusing in public to "engage in personalities" but nevertheless privately basing actions on personality analyses; and the selective practice of delegation. Together these enabled him to use a sixth strategy that helped make him a

From *The Hidden Presidency*, by Fred I. Greenstein (New York: Basic Books, 1982), pp. 57–99. Copyright © 1982 by Basic Books, Inc. Reprinted by permission of Basic Books, Inc.

Editors' note: Many of the direct quotations in this chapter come from President Eisenhower's private papers and, for simplicity, are not referenced. Precise references are available in the orginal.

credible chief of state—building a public support that transcended many of the nation's social and political divisions.

The individual strategies were not uniquely Eisenhower's. Any single act or utterance of Eisenhower was likely to include more than one strategy, and the six strategies did not exhaust his repertoire. But he fit them together in a way that made his presidential leadership distinctive.

Hidden-Hand Leadership

Presidents often find it necessary to maneuver in secrecy. Presidents who seek to establish a professional reputation with other leaders as skilled, tough operators, and who want to be recognized by historians as "presidential activists," however, sometimes deliberately stimulate accounts of their tour de force exercises of personal influence. Kennedy used this tactic in his bravura 1962 assault on the steel industry that forced a price increase recision. In 1964 Johnson encouraged publicity about his personal mediation of an impending railroad strike, an around-the-clock exercise in which he virtually locked union and management negotiators in the White-House cabinet room. Carter's intense personal participation in negotiation in the Camp David accords between Egypt and Israel is another example of publicized presidential activism.

Although Eisenhower cultivated the reputation of being above political machination, he was an activist. However, in part because he chose not to publicize his activities and in part because his activities did not always fit the popular conception of an activist, he was not considered one. Commentators usually associate activism with efforts to effect major innovations (usually liberal) in public policy. Eisenhower sought, at least in domestic policy, to restrain policy change, but he was active in doing so. He worked hard, considered it his reponsibility to shape public policy, and followed through on his initiatives.

A president who seeks influence and cultivates a reputation for not intervening in day-to-day policy-making will necessarily hide his hand more often than one who seeks recognition as an effective political operator. Eisenhower often camouflaged his participation not only in political activity generally falling outside popularly conceived bounds of presidential leadership, but also in more commonplace political leadership. In either case sometimes he used hidden-hand strategy to conceal his activities from all nonassociates; sometimes it suited his purposes to target his hidden-hand leadership so that selective nonassociates would be made aware of his actions.

An example of simple hidden-hand leadership—one that is a paradigm of Eisenhower influence attempts and has been kept completely secret—was his 1954 effort to influence Senate Democratic Leader Lyndon Johnson, an act which, if exposed, would have been controversial in any administration. Believing that Johnson was straying from the course of "fine conservative government," the president used a wealthy Johnson supporter to coerce him. Employing an intermediary, who concealed from the Johnson backer that Eisenhower had initiated the scheme to influence Johnson, Eisenhower "laundered" his own participation in the exercise. Mrs. Whitman took notes on Eisenhower's telephone conversation to Treasury Secretary George Humphrey, during which he told Humphrey to call Texas oil multi-millionaire Sid Richardson, who Eisenhower noted "was really the angel for Johnson when he came in." The telephone log summarizing their conversation records these instructions:

> Ask [Richardson] . . . what it is that Tex wants. We help out in drought, take tidelands matter on their side, and tax bill. But question is, how much influence has Sid got with Johnson? He tells Sid he's supporting us, then comes up here and disproves it (yesterday for instance). Perhaps Sid could get him on the right channel, or threaten to get [Texas Governor Allen] Shivers in a primary and beat him for Senate.

Because Richardson was an old friend of Eisenhower's—they met in 1941—Eisenhower and Humphrey agreed that the latter should talk to Richardson so "it can't be said that DDE is taking advantage of a long-time friendship."

Clearly Eisenhower's efforts to influence Johnson required such discretion. Eisenhower, however, also concealed his involvement in conventional politicking that would not have been controversial if he had been prepared to be viewed as a political professional. In 1957, for example, he sent a letter to Secretary of the Treasury Robert Anderson. Anderson, a Texas lawyer, whom Eisenhower frequently mentioned to associates as the man he felt best equipped to succeed him, had served as Secretary of the Navy, and Deputy Assistant Secretary of Defense, and had just assumed the Treasury secretaryship. Throughout this period, although ostensibly not a political operative, at Eisenhower's behest, Anderson drew on his long personal friendship with Lyndon Johnson to serve as private administration conduit to and pulse taker of the mercurial Senate Democratic leader by maintaining virtually daily contact with Johnson. This role extended into that of a general behind-the-scenes political aide.

Eisenhower's letter to Anderson contained a detailed set of procedural suggestions for managing congressional relations. The suggestions were originally drafted by Henry Cabot Lodge, who had been a two-term senator and an active figure in securing Eisenhower's nomination.

From his post as United Nations ambassador, Lodge regularly and also without publicity advised Eisenhower on strategy and tactics for domestic politics. Eisenhower had originally offered Lodge the job that Sherman Adams was to fill. When Lodge stated his preference for the United Nations position, Eisenhower agreed but stipulated that Lodge should advise him privately on domestic matters. (The two exchanged about 150 letters on this topic during Eisenhower's presidency.)

In his letter to Anderson, the "apolitical" Eisenhower passed on Lodge's suggestions. They included such standard fare as insisting that department secretaries establish personal friendships with the congressional chairmen whose committees supervised agency operations and also ingratiate themselves with the chairmen's wives; that they grant all favors requested by friendly congressmen immediately if possible, and if not possible, explain why, stressing their desire to be helpful wherever feasible; and that they pay verbal deference to congressional authority when testifying on Capitol Hill but frame their approach to Congress on the premise that congressmen would prefer to be led than to lead.

This not very novel codification of ways to influence Congress would have elicited only modest interest had it leaked from the Kennedy or Johnson White House. In the Jimmy Carter years its release might even have been a reassuring sign that the president was learning the rules of the Washington game. But such directives were inappropriate for a president who avoided being linked with political operations. Consequently, in sending the Lodge memorandum, along with a comment on it by General Persons, Eisenhower instructed Anderson to study the documents carefully, and after doing so, "I request that you personally destroy them both. I am particularly anxious that no word of any concerted effort along this line ever reach the outside because a leak would tend to destroy the value of the effort." Eisenhower noted, however, that Anderson was free to communicate the contents to his staff, but with a key qualification, "[A]s your own ideas." . . .

Hidden-hand leadership, whether simple or targeted, by an ostensibly nonpolitical president can, however, cut two ways. While it may permit the president to achieve what would be a controversial outcome without backlash, it also has intrinsic limitations in situations where the object of influence can best be persuaded if he thinks the action urged on him is one the president wants him to take.

The strategy failed . . . when Eisenhower attempted to exercise influence indirectly within his official family. His efforts . . . were unsuccessful . . . [when] Eisenhower tried indirectly to dissuade Nixon from running for vice-president in 1956. . . .

In February 1956, before Eisenhower had announced his own candidacy, he suggested to Nixon that his chance of becoming a winning Republican presidential candidate in 1960 would be greater if, rather than running for a second vice-presidential term, he establish independent status as secretary of a major cabinet department, adding with matter-of-fact detachment, "if we can count on my living five years." Recapping this conversation to party chairman Leonard Hall, Eisenhower talked about another reason for removing Nixon from the ticket; to get a stronger running mate and groom an alternate 1960 candidate for the presidency. Robert Anderson, as usual, was his first choice. He also was fascinated with the notion that it might be possible to crack the New Deal coalition by enlisting a conservative Democrat and Roman Catholic, Ohio Senator Frank Lausche.

Although Eisenhower preferred an alternative to Nixon as a running mate, he made clear to an aide that he felt "there is nothing to be gained politically by ditching him." Hall, in a massive underestimation of Nixon's tenacity, assured Eisenhower that it would be "the easiest thing to get Nixon out of the picture willingly." Eisenhower replied, "Well, all right, you see him and talk to him, but be very, very gentle." Hall's mission, of course, failed.

Unwilling to depart from his strategic rule of avoiding visible wire-pulling within the party and unwilling to instruct Nixon not to run, Eisenhower succumbed to the pressures of Nixon's many party supporters and to the impact of the write-in votes Nixon garnered in the early primaries. He announced in March that the team would again be "Ike and Dick." Eisenhower deliberately traded one desired result, dropping Nixon, for others, such as preserving his politics-free image and avoiding a factional squabble. And in doing so, he failed to accomplish his goal of obtaining a preferable second-term running mate. . . .

Instrumental Use of Language

Eisenhower found it natural to express himself straightforwardly and incisively, arraying facts and rigorously justifying his policies and actions. He could do this by using precisely etched prose and he took pride in his capacity to do so. He was, however, also willing to replace clear, reasoned discourse with alternative ways of expressing himself when they better served his purposes. Neither pride in ability nor his natural predilection for clarity kept him from deliberately turning to language that was emotive and inspirational or purposely ambiguous. Verbal expression was his instrument; he refused to indulge his obvious pleasure in analytic thought and clear expression as an end in itself.

I say that clear expression was natural to him because it is the manner he adopted in private circumstances. . . .

His dictated list of editorial changes on the first draft of his 1954

State of the Union message shows Eisenhower's work as a word clarifier and also as a stylist striving for public effect. As one of the rare editing efforts in which he explained the reasons for his changes, the list illustrates how in his writing, as in other endeavors, he formulated abstract rules for many of his operating procedures. In the course of transmitting four general and thirty-eight specific instructions for change, he tightened the prose by telling the speech writer that "sections need to be more distinctly marked" and admonished: "Do not be afraid to say 'I come to so-and-so'. . . . You cannot take the human mind from subject to subject . . . quickly!" And, almost nigglingly, he had the assertion "confidence had developed" changed to "constantly developing confidence" to indicate "continuing action."

Eisenhower also conveyed instructions designed, in a latter-day phrase, to make the speech play better in Peoria. He instructed the speech writer to eliminate such technical language as "substantial reductions in the size and cost of Federal Government" and "deficit spending" on the grounds that the "man we are trying to reach" better understands the phrases "purchasing power of the dollar" and stability "in the size of his market basket." The changes advanced his aim of expanding his party's base to encompass the upper blue-collar and lower white-collar nucleus of the Democratic party's coalition.

In addition to using words as instruments for communicating substance and emotions, Eisenhower also sometimes employed them in a fashion similar to his hidden-hand strategy—to create smoke screens for his actions in his role as covert prime minister. Some of his utterances served to obscure sensitive subjects from public view; others conveyed deliberately ambiguous messages that left him freedom of action. Deliberate use of ambiguity and evasiveness were, of course, not unique to Eisenhower. What distinguished him from other politicians was the ability to leave the impression that such utterances were guileless.

His press conferences furnish a good perspective on his use of language to convey ambiguity. The most instructive are those for which transcripts have been kept of the preliminary briefings so that a record is available of what he chose to say and why. But the entire body of his official exchanges with the press reveals his use of ambiguity and other verbal strategies. Some of his press conference practices contributed to the impression that he simply was uninformed, when in fact he was choosing to be ambiguous. He was more disposed than other presidents simply to say that he was not aware of certain issues, including some that had received wide press attention. He also often directed questioners to one of his associates for an answer, suggesting that the issue on which he was being queried was not of sufficient magnitude or "ripeness" to warrant presidential attention. "Well, this is the first I've heard of that," and "You'd better take that up with Secretary X" are common assertions in his press conferences.

The texts of the preliminary briefings make it clear, however, that in claiming ignorance he often was following a practice he used as early as his first press conference on becoming European theater commander in June 1942, which the *New York Times* described as an "excellent demonstration of the art of being jovially outspoken without saying much of anything." Even then he was sufficiently self-conscious about ways that a leader can use his mode of expression as a tactic to advise others—such as his embarrassingly outspoken subordinate commander, George S. Patton, Jr.—on verbal comportment. Quoting "an old proverb . . .: 'Keep silent and appear stupid; open your mouth and remove all doubt,'" he advised Patton that "a certain sphynx-like quality will do a lot toward enhancing one's reputations.". . .

Intentional evasiveness was a standard Eisenhower press conference tactic. Sometimes, as in a March 16, 1955, press conference, he mixed vagueness with ambiguity studiously designed to have different effects on different audiences. The issue was whether, under what circumstances, and with what kinds of weapons the United States would defend Quemoy and Matsu. In his previous news conference, Eisenhower had warned that in the event of a "general war" in Asia the United States was prepared to use tactical nuclear weapons. Just before the following week's conference, the State Department conveyed through Hagerty the urgent request that the president not discuss this delicate matter further. Eisenhower reports that he replied. "Don't worry, Jim, if that question comes up, I'll just confuse them."

Joseph C. Harsch of the *Christian Science Monitor* raised the question, asking, "If we got into an issue with the Chinese, say, over Matsu and Quemoy, that we wanted to keep limited, do you conceive us using [atomic weapons] in that situation or not?" Eisenhower responded:

> Well, Mr. Harsch, I must confess I cannot answer that question in advance. The only thing I know about war are two things: the most unpredictable factor in war is human nature in its day-by-day manifestation; but the only unchanging factor in war is human nature. And the next thing is that every war is going to astonish you in the way it occurred, and in the way it is carried out. So that for a man to predict, particularly if he has the responsibility for making the decision, to predict what he is going to use, how he is going to do it, would I think exhibit his ignorance of war; that is what I believe. So I think you just have to wait; and that is the kind of prayerful decision that may some day face a president.

The vagueness and ambiguity in this response was contrived to serve several ends. It allowed Eisenhower to sidestep a potentially divisive encounter with right wing "China Firster" Republicans, which would have destroyed his ability to pass such high priority programs as the annual foreign aid appropriation. It also conveyed an ambiguous warning message to the PRC, which would have been delighted to occupy Quemoy and Matsu, a matter alluded to in his letter to Gruenther a month earlier. Finally, for the American public, the message was a reassuring reminder that any decision taken would reflect the professional judgment of a president who understood the nature of war. Eisenhower and Hagerty recognized that Eisenhower's style in press conferences was well received by the general public, even if it left the impression among Washington cognoscenti that he was obtuse. They, after all, introduced the practice of releasing tapes and kinescopes of presidential news conferences to the public.

Eisenhower preferred to persuade other leaders through reasoned discourse, but did so only with those of his counterparts who he thought had the capacity and motivation to be influenced by rational argument. . . .

If [some] would listen to reason, this was not true of [all] right-wing Republican legislators. In ironing out differences of opinion with the deeply emotional conservatives and nationalists in his own party, Eisenhower often met them on their own narrowly defined terms rather than seeking to convert them to his more comprehensive view of contemporary issues. When, for example, referring to the planned trial of an American soldier who had killed a Japanese woman, Taft's successor, William Knowland, rumbled in the Legislative Leadership meeting that he would not want a son of his to be tried by a Japanese court, Eisenhower did not take the time to discuss the importance of adhering to the Status of Forces Treaty. He allowed the aide conducting the briefing to placate Knowland by simply noting that in such cases Japanese courts settled for a fine and an apology: an army court martial would yield a long prison sentence.

Needless to say there is nothing unique, in or out of politics, about adjusting one's discourse to circumstances. What distinguishes Eisenhower's is its remarkably wide range—from highly cognitive, to emotional, through deliberately obfuscated uses of language—the self-consciousness with which he changed gears, and, above all, his ability to keep discrepancies in his expressive modes from coming across as inconsistency. He accomplished this largely by using cool reasoning in private contexts and benign, if not bumbling sounding, discourse in public.

"I Do Not Engage in Personalities"

This was Eisenhower's curiously phrased way of asserting his strategy of not criticizing others personally, no matter how strong the provocation. . . .

Eisenhower's fullest statement of the reasons for his rule not to engage in personalities and its basic rationale is in a March 9, 1954, letter to his businessman friend, Paul Helms.

> For the past thirteen years I have occupied posts around which there focused sufficient public interest that they were considered news sources of greater or lesser importance. . . . Out of all those experiences, I developed a practice which, so far as I know, I have never violated. That practice is to avoid public mention of any name *unless it can be done with favorable intent and connotation;* reserve all criticism for the private conference; speak only good in public. (Eisenhower's emphasis)

Then, stating the psychological basis for the practice, he observed:

> This is not namby-pamby. It certainly is not Pollyanna-ish. It is just sheer common sense. A leader's job is to get others to go along with him in the promotion of something. To do this he needs their goodwill. To destroy goodwill, it is only necessary to criticize publicly. This creates in the criticized one a subconscious desire to "get even." Such effects can last for a very long period.

When Eisenhower told Helms he reserved personality "criticism for the private conference," he did not go on to suggest the almost clinical objectivity with which he could analyze and think about the problems of dealing with people who hampered him but whom he refused publicly to criticize. There is no better illustration of how his private and public assertions diverged than the contrast between a 1953 exchange with persistent journalists who sought to foster a confrontation between Eisenhower and Senator Taft and a diary entry he made a month later. Taft, in a speech of May 26, 1953, concerning the stalemated Korean truce negotiations, asserted that if the negotiating team meeting in Korea could not agree on a militarily secure truce line, the United States should "let England and our allies know that we are withdrawing from all further peace negotiations in Korea" because we "might as well . . . reserve to ourselves a completely free hand."

This was typical of the kind of emotional statement by Taft that Eisenhower deplored. . . .

The White House withheld comment on Taft's speech, but Senator John Sparkman, the 1952 Democratic vice-presidential candidate, called the speech a "diametric contradiction" of Eisenhower's policy, and the senior Democratic foreign policy spokesman, Senator Walter George, said that Taft was advocating "the road that leads directly to complete isolation and a third world war." In Eisenhower's May 28 press conference, Richard Wilson of Cowles Publications, attempted in an extended colloquy to smoke Eisenhower out. Did he, or did he not agree with the senator? Eisenhower avoided "engaging in personalities" with Taft by being persistently elusive, insisting that Taft's remarks had been misinterpreted by the reporters.

Wilson persisted, "if I read his speech correctly—in fact, that is what he said exactly." No doubt Taft was referring to the possibility that lack of cooperation by the *Chinese* could force the United States to withdraw from negotiations, Eisenhower speculated. Yes, Wilson replied, but he took Taft's position to be that disagreement between the United States and Great Britain might also be cause for withdrawing.

> Eisenhower: There is something confusing here. I don't believe I had better answer it. I don't understand what could be meant by such a thing. Look—suppose all of us here are friends, and we are trying to get somebody out on the street to agree to something and he disagrees, does that mean we all suddenly here become enemies and break up? I don't understand that!

Straining for precision, Wilson received permission to read directly from Taft's speech, which contained the blanket assertion, "I think we should do our best now to negotiate this truce, and if we fail, then let England and our other allies know that we are withdrawing from all further peace negotiations in Korea." Eisenhower again offered an interpretation of Taft's meaning: it might be that the United States *and* its allies would at some point agree that the negotiations had become fruitless and withdraw from them. "As I say," Eisenhower concluded, "there is some idea there that I am not grasping, and I don't think it is fair to ask me to try to comment on it when I don't."

Eisenhower relentlessly refused to grasp an idea that would force him to disagree publicly with Taft. . . .

Action Based on Personality Analysis

World War II presented Eisenhower with a classic leadership dilemma: how to maximize the effectiveness of subordinates who have some personal qualities that make them well suited for the tasks that need to be performed, but who also have flaws that can undermine their performance. The man who was in the best position to evaluate Eisenhower's wartime leadership, European command Chief of Staff, General W. Bedell Smith, once described how Eisenhower dealt with this complication by assessing each subordinate's qualities in terms of assets and liabilities and shaping his job so that it exploited the former and minimized the impact of the latter. . . .

Personality assessment was virtually a reflexive act for Eisenhower. This propensity is most extensively documented during the war years when he kept up a regular flow of letters to his immediate superior, General George Marshall, explaining his thinking and actions. The comments on Patton alone are voluminous: For example,

> I doubt that I would ever consider Patton for an army group commander or for any higher position, but as an army commander under a man who is sound and solid, and who has enough sense to use Patton's good qualities without becoming blinded by his love of showmanship and histrionics, he should do as fine a job as he did in Sicily. . . .

Without a Marshall to report to while president, examples of Eisenhower's use of personality analysis in determining how to respond to people and how to employ them tend to be preserved only in fragmentary form. These include his diary notes on Taft; a comment warning his press aide Hagerty that it would be difficult to persuade Agriculture Secretary Ezra Taft Benson to retract an error because he is a "stubborn man and I don't suppose we can get him to do that"; and his warning to the Republican party chairman to be "very, very gentle" with Nixon in discussing his political ambitions. . . .

In congressional relations, because the committee and leadership way stations are controlled by semiautonomous individuals, each with his own idiosyncrasies, personality analysis played a particularly key role. . . .

Eisenhower's sensitivity to personalities enabled him to identify and therefore bypass blocks in his channels for influencing Congress. One frequent block was Taft's successor as Senate Republican leader, William F. Knowland. Eisenhower recorded in a diary reflection on how great a loss Taft's death in the summer of 1953 had been: "Knowland means to be helpful and loyal, but he is cumbersome. He does not have the sharp mind and the great experience that Taft did. Consequently, he does not command the respect in the Senate that Taft enjoyed." He was regularly irritated by Knowland's simplistic views as well as clumsy leadership. (He told a friend that "Knowland has no foreign policy except to develop high blood pressure whenever he mentions the words 'Red China.' ") But he successfully concealed his distaste from Knowland, who in his Columbia Oral History interview made only the conventional observations that Eisenhower was a nonpolitical leader, "sincere" and "without guile." . . .

Eisenhower's analyses of the personalities of members of his official family also were of the greatest importance, particularly in determining the extent and nature of the authority he delegated to subordinates. The

thumbnail sketches he made in his private diary four months after taking
office of two occupants of major cabinet posts, the secretary of state and
the secretary of defense, not only illustrate his characterizations of subordinates but also provide insight into his practice of selective delegation.

Of John Foster Dulles, Eisenhower wrote,

> I still think of him, as I always have, as an intensive student of foreign af-
> fairs. He is well informed and, in this subject at least, is deserving, I think
> of his reputation as a "wise" man. . . . [But] he is not particularly persua-
> sive in presentation and, at times, seems to have a curious lack of under-
> standing as to how his words and manner may affect another personality.

Of Charles Wilson, whose confirmation hearings had been flawed by the
first of many verbal faux pas, he observed, "Mr. Wilson is prone to lecture, rather than to answer, when asked a question. This not only annoys
many members of Congress, but it gives them unlooked for opportunities
to discover flaws in reasoning and argument." But neither man's defects
incapacitated him from Eisenhower's standpoint, because he was able to
devise ways to use their strengths and neutralize their weaknesses.

Delegation Selectively Practiced

Eisenhower's wartime experience of commanding a vast intricate organization and his extensive staff experience in the army, an institution with
an explicitly elaborate organizational structure, undoubtedly account
for the self-consciousness and subtlety with which he approached delegation of authority. First, he was highly attentive to the general need for
delegation, if the head of a complex organization is not to be inundated
with details. Secondly, he took care not to delegate in a fashion that
would dilute his own ability to keep the actions of his associates in line
with his own policies, adjusting the degree of his supervision both to the
abilities of his associates and to the extent he believed his own participation in a policy area was necessary. Finally, he was highly sensitive to a
side effect of delegation, that of sharing credit with subordinates for popular policies, but also (especially important for a president who emphasized his role as chief of state) diffusing blame for unpopular policies
throughout the administration rather than allowing himself as chief executive to be the main recipient of blame.

Taking stock of the leadership principles he had practiced and commenting on a *Life* editorial praising his presidency but asking whether he
had sometimes been "too easy a boss," Eisenhower stated his view on the
general need to delegate in a 1960 letter to Henry Luce. Eisenhower's
comments were straightforward extensions of his prepresidential admin-

istrative rhetoric and action, exemplified both by his tribute in *Crusade in Europe* (Eisenhower 1948) to General Marshall's advancement of subordinates who had the capacity to make decisions without constantly referring back to higher authority, and the instruction he gave to his principal aides in June 1942 on assuming American command in Europe that they were "free to solve their own problems wherever possible and not to get in the habit of passing the buck up." Eisenhower pointed out to Luce that "the government of the United States has become too big, too complex, and too pervasive in its influence on all our lives for one individual to pretend to direct the details of its important and critical programming. Competent assistants are mandatory: without them the executive branch would bog down." Moreover, wholehearted support of subordinates could not be won by "desk pounding":

> To command the loyalties and dedication and best efforts of capable and outstanding individuals requires patience, understanding, a readiness to delegate, and an acceptance of responsibility for any honest errors—real or apparent—those associates and subordinates might make. . . . Principal subordinates must have confidence that they and their positions are widely respected, and the chief must do his part in assuring that this is so.

Eisenhower handled delegation selectively to be sure his policies were satisfactorily carried out. One kind of selective delegation he practiced before and during his presidency consisted of assigning a clearly defined mission to an able subordinate who, in effect, would become more of a deputy than a delegate. . . .

Robert Anderson, as we may infer from Eisenhower's willingness to support him as a successor, also fell in the category of a deeply respected subordinate. During the time he was Treasury secretary, beginning in 1957, Anderson was used as a delegate rather than a deputy and presided over issues of great complexity about which Eisenhower was not minutely informed; he felt as though Eisenhower had given him virtual carte blanche. Anderson, who was also closely associated with Lyndon Johnson during his presidency, compares the two presidents:

> President Eisenhower's background in history was a military one. He came up through all of his life in the atmosphere of having staffs, delegating large amounts of responsibility, assuming large responsibility delegated to him, but having a very tight staff operation. For example, when I was in the Treasury, I have no recollection of the President ever calling me to suggest a policy or anything of the sort. It was always the other way around. . . . On the other hand . . . President Johnson . . . grew up as a congressman. . . .
> He was not surrounded by either large staffs or where he could say,

"I'm going to delegate these responsibilities," because *he* was the congress-man, *he* was the senator, *he* was the majority leader. . . . So I think, in President Johnson's administration, there was more of a personalized pres-idency, a president who by his very nature became more involved in more details, in more operations, and in more procedural matters, than in the days of President Eisenhower.

Not all of Eisenhower's subordinates, however, were extended the same freedom of action that Anderson enjoyed. Although some were left largely to their own devices, others would periodically experience Eisenho-wer's direct intervention in their activities. As one might expect both from Eisenhower's expert knowledge of national security issues and from his pri-vate characterization of Charles Wilson, the first Eisenhower defense sec-retary had little policy-making leeway. Much of the time Eisenhower treated Wilson neither as a deputy nor as a delegate, but rather as little more than an expediter of detailed presidential instructions.

In his diary entry on the former General Motors chief, Eisenhower observed: "In his field, he is a really competent man. He is careful and positive, and I have no slightest doubt that, assisted by the team of civil-ian and military men he has selected, he will produce the maximum secu-rity for this country at minimum or near minimum cost." The last six words indicate the principal reason the top executive of the nation's larg-est corporation had been chosen for the Defense Department. Eisenho-wer did not need a military expert to head a department he knew inside out and to determine overall policy: in this sphere, the president's own background and skills scarcely could be equaled. Thus, following the ap-proach described by Bedell Smith, the "tool" Eisenhower chose to head the largest government department was a man with a record for effi-ciently managing the nation's largest corporation. Wilson's duties, how-ever, were limited mainly to internal management—making the depart-ment function in a businesslike manner—while Eisenhower and those closest to him in the national security policy-making community were re-sponsible for establishing defense policy.

Eisenhower is often quoted as having expressed impatience at Wilson's proclivity to bring problems to the White House that might have been settled by Wilson himself: "Charlie, you run defense. We both can't do it, and I won't do it. I was elected to worry about a lot of other things than the day-to-day operations of a department" (Gellhoed 1979, 19). It may be true that Eisenhower had to press Wilson to be more independent in the managerial aspects of Defense Department leadership, but it is clear that on major policy issues—ranging from levels of funding to over-all strategic stance—Eisenhower personally made defense policy and in doing so entered deeply into organizational and managerial issues. . . .

Eisenhower delegated to Secretary of State Dulles substantial power, but with Dulles, unlike any other cabinet member, he entered into a collegial working relationship. Although most accounts of United States foreign policy between 1953 and 1958 take it for granted that Dulles was the senior colleague (Etheridge 1978, 79, 82), the reverse was true. The two men were in daily touch even when Dulles was out of the country on his many missions as presidential emissary. If they could not talk by telephone because Dulles was overseas, they exchanged coded cables. Eisenhower often accepted Dulles's advice. They jointly perfected policies, but Eisenhower made the final decisions and Dulles executed them. . . .

Their response to the downing of a British plane and two American search planes off Hainan in June 1954 illustrates the dynamics of the collaboration. Dulles, on learning of these events, called the White House. Eisenhower asked Dulles how he suggested handling the matter. Dulles's reply was that if the president approved, he would issue "a protest against further barbarities in attempting to shoot down rescue-type planes." Eisenhower not only already knew of the incident but also had already discussed making a protest with the congressional leaders who agreed that this should be done. He told Dulles he had asked the leaders to keep the information secret until there had been consultation within the administration and instructed him to send a message to British Foreign Secretary Anthony Eden urging that the British simultaneously release a strong statement. This would increase the impact of the American statement and avoid possible Anglo-American friction. Dulles agreed with this tactic. The two concluded that Dulles, after clearing the policy with Eden, would make the public statement and Eisenhower would delay any comments of his own.

This episode reveals genuine consultation. It also shows that before hearing from Dulles, Eisenhower had already established a course of diplomatic action. Moreover, Eisenhower determined the tactic that was pursued, but Dulles, in implementing Eisenhower's instructions, was the publicly visible actor. . . .

Dulles was [also an] object of animosity that in another presidency would have been directed toward the chief executive. Other Eisenhower associates performed the same function—consciously or unconsciously—in their own spheres. Farmers who rankled at the moves toward decreasing subsidization of agriculture blamed the zealous Mormon elder, Ezra Taft Benson, who served as Agriculture secretary for eight years—not Eisenhower. Many of the inevitable irritations produced by White House nay-saying found their target in the staff chief, Sherman Adams. There is no evidence that Eisenhower chose these people because they would be ready targets for critics. Adams and Dulles in fact were succeeded by men

of gentle personality. Nevertheless, Eisenhower's underlining [italics] in
the following passage describing Lyndon Johnson's presidential style in
Arthur Krock's memoirs, shows his awareness of how a subordinate's tendency to garner criticism could protect his leader's public support:

> *Partly because of his incessant ubiquity, Johnson, as much as any president*
> *in our history, has closely identified himself and his office with the disas-*
> *ters, foreign and domestic, economic and social, into which the United*
> *States has become more and more deeply involved in his time.* This . . . is
> to a considerable degree the consequence of his innate trait of craftiness.
> But it also is the product of an evasive or soaring loquacity which induces
> him to utter and write paragraphs when sentences would cover the point or
> event, and to allow his promises to run far beyond the clear limits of attain-
> ment. *Another source of this close identification with all acts, policies and*
> *thorny situations is a passion to control every function of government,*
> *though subordinates are always available in profusion to take the gaff,* or
> without diminishing him, the credit. (Eisenhower's emphasis)

The strong personal loyalty engendered in Eisenhower's team players accounted for their willingness to accept criticism for policies that
were in fact the president's and that did not arise from their own delegated authority.

Building Public Support

In examining Eisenhower's strategies it is no surprise to find him under-
scoring Arthur Krock's diagnosis that Lyndon Johnson's presidency had
ended so painfully because Johnson dissipated public support, among
other ways, by identifying "himself and his office with . . . disasters" and
"with all acts, policies and thorny situations" despite the availability of
subordinates "to take the gaff." In his own presidency, Eisenhower had
been helped by gaff-taking subordinates and had even occasionally simu-
lated acts of delegation to deflect controversy. More generally, by keeping the controversial political side of the presidential role largely covert
(without, however, abdicating it) and casting himself as an uncontrover-
sial head of state, he maintained an extraordinary level of public support.
    This high level is well known: his 64 percent average approval rate
in the Gallup polls throughout his eight years; always more approval
than disapproval in the monthly Gallup polls asking, "How good a job do
you think President X is doing?"; and his two landslide elections. The nature of this support—why people liked him—is less precisely documented. One valuable source of evidence, however, is available in the
reports that citizens gave of why they liked or disliked each candidate in

the pioneering 1952 and 1956 electoral surveys conducted by Angus Campbell and his University of Michigan associates.

In 1952 Eisenhower, who had been wooed by both parties since World War II because of a powerful public appeal that regularly put him at or near the top of Gallup's annual "most admired American" poll, was mentioned far more often for his human qualities (for example, warmth and sincerity) than for his experience, beliefs, or leadership skills. In 1956, after four years of acquiring governing experience and giving the public an opportunity to reach conclusions about the merits (or lack thereof) of his policies and skills, he was again mentioned more often for what he was as a person than for what he had done or could do as a president. But there was a difference between public responses to him in the 1952 and 1956 polls that puzzled the Michigan voting analysts: references to why Eisenhower was liked were even *more* lopsidedly personal and less political and governmental in 1956 than in 1952 (Campbell et al. 1960, ch. 3). While this difference might have seemed to belie common sense, we can readily see that it follows from his leadership style of refusing to be identified with "disasters" and "thorny situations."

Partisan Democrats would have had less difficulty explaining the findings than did the studiously nonpartisan University of Michigan scholars. They would readily have granted that Eisenhower had maintained his popularity by accentuating the chief of state role. Liberal columnist Marquis Childs, for example, described him as a "captive hero," a term borrowed from an ancient practice in which the powers that be in a country legitimized their political control by capturing a king who served as a reassuring but impotent figurehead (Childs 1958).

As we have seen Eisenhower *did* exercise political leadership. If his economics tended to be laissez-faire, his politics were decidedly though covertly interventionist. Much of his intervention, however, was geared to preventing conflicts before they occurred, or resolving them without associating the mechanics of their resolution with the president and presidency. [An] example of Eisenhower's hidden-hand interventions bears directly on why it was possible for him to remain popular and to accentuate his apolitical image while in office. The first is the 1953 leak directed to the Chinese Communists to stimulate them to reach a truce agreement. An Eisenhower who was still presiding over a stalemated war of attrition in Korea would neither have been popular nor viewed so often as "good" on purely personal grounds. . . .

Apart from maintaining support by quietly eliminating irritants that eventually would have tarnished his popularity, Eisenhower was intensely preoccupied with and worked intensely at "public relations," a phrase he used freely to describe actions not only during his nominating campaign and presidency (Kelly 1960), but also during his prepresidential years. . . .

Professional public relations men were among the first civilians to gather in the loyal network of businessmen that formed around Eisenhower and participated actively in drafting him to run for the presidency. Notable among them were William E. Robinson who, after years as an advertising and sales executive at the *New York Herald Tribune*, went on to head his own public relations firm, and Sigurd S. Larmon of Young & Rubicam. When Eisenhower acceded to a presidential candidacy, his campaign for nomination and election made innovative use of spot radio and television commercials. He and his associates also made a consistent effort to improve his ability to "come across" to the American people. His whistle-stop campaign covered more miles than Adlai Stevenson's. And he flexibly experimented with prepared and outlined speeches delivered informally from notes, submitting himself to the guidance of professionals. He used actor and television producer Robert Montgomery to advise him on the mechanics of delivering speeches and experimenting with other ways of reaching the public.

Eisenhower prepared his speeches with an understanding of his public image and endeavored to enhance and maintain it. . . .

Many of Eisenhower's presidential utterances directly play on the public image of the military hero who is a soldier of peace. On one occasion he compared the primitive rifle in use when he was a lieutenant before America's entry in World War I with the devastating weapons that had emerged from World War II in order to dramatize the overriding urgency of avoiding nuclear war. He went on, using the homely language of a sincere, humane soldier of peace, to reassure his audience. Granting that the problems of nuclear stalemate have no "easy answer" and that many contemporary problems "have no answer at all, at least in the complete sense," he compared the government's responsibility of "doing our best" with "what the ordinary American family does."

> It has the problems of meeting the payments on the mortgage, paying for the family car, educating the children, laying aside some money for use in case of unexpected illness. It meets these problems courageously. It doesn't get panicky. It solves these problems with what I would call courage and faith, but above all by cooperation, by discussing the problem among the different members of the family and then saying: this is what we can do, this is what we will do, and reaching a satisfactory answer.

These homilies served to introduce a plain speaking but thoughtful exposition of the basic lines of foreign and domestic policy, including warnings against excessive fears of internal Communist subversion and a penultimate pitch for his legislative program. His concluding remarks voiced the sturdy patriotism and piety of a turn-of-the-century midwestern family, using a figure of speech that echoed the daily Bible readings of his own childhood:

> I don't mean to say, and no one can say to you, that there are no dangers. Of course there are risks, if we are not vigilant. But we do not have to be hysterical. We can be vigilant. We can be Americans. We can stand up and hold up our heads and say: America is the greatest force that God has ever allowed to exist on his footstool. . . .

Whatever intellectuals may have thought of such remarks, they were unquestionably reassuring to the bulk of citizens. After, as before taking office, Eisenhower's seemingly effortless facility in winning public confidence never stopped him from also working to find additional ways to enhance his support. This accounts for the great care he took in preparing speeches, planning campaigns, and working at the task of exhibiting the buoyant, optimistic side of his personality. Nor did he let his team approach to leadership vitiate his attention to maintaining personal support. He was fully aware that his popularity was essential to his ability to exercise influence over other leaders. As he once noted, "one man can do a lot . . . he can especially do a lot at any particular given moment, if at that moment he happens to be ranking high in public estimation. By this I mean he is dwelling in the ivory tower and not in the dog house."

16

Margaret Thatcher: The Style of a Prime Minister

Anthony King

Margaret Thatcher is a person who arouses strong feelings, within her own party and in other parties, among the general public, not least among her own cabinet colleagues. Precisely for this reason, dispassionate accounts of her premiership are rare. The desire to praise Thatcher, or to bury her, typically overwhelms the desire to understand how one person, at one time, does one job. This chapter does not seek to judge Margaret Thatcher, to say whether her influence on Britain has been for good or ill, nor does it seek, in the style of the armchair psychoanalyst, to plumb the depths of "the Thatcher personality." Rather, it seeks to describe Thatcher's characteristic working methods as prime minister and political leader. There are all sorts of ways of being prime minister. What is Thatcher's way? Given the goals she sets herself, how does she set about achieving them? In the final analysis, are *her* means well adapted to *her* ends?

An Unusual Prime Minister

Fully to appreciate her premiership, it is essential to recognize that Margaret Thatcher is a very unusual prime minister, in two crucial but little-

From *The British Prime Minister*, edited by Anthony King (Durham, NC: Duke University, 1985), pp. 96–140. Copyright © 1985 by Anthony King. Reprinted by permission of Duke University Press.

noticed respects. The first is that she is, and always has been, in a minority inside her own party and her own government. The reason is simple. Thatcher holds strong views, especially on economic policy. But she was elected leader of the Conservative party in February 1975 not because she held those views, but largely despite the fact that she held them. A majority of Conservative MPs in the winter of 1974–75 were determined to unseat the then party leader, Edward Heath, and Thatcher was the only one of Heath's former cabinet colleagues with the courage and determination to stand against him. The relatively small number of Tory MPs who shared Thatcher's economic views undoubtedly voted for her, but so did a far larger number of Tory members who saw her chiefly as the instrument of Edward Heath's political destruction. . . . Thatcher, in other words, was not elected primarily as a Thatcherite. To this day, while most Conservative MPs broadly sympathise with the prime minister's aims and are prepared to stand by her publicly, it is doubtful whether more than two or three dozen of them fully share her monetarist convictions. Most prime ministers represent a broad consensus of opinion, or at least majority opinion, within their party. Thatcher is considerably more isolated.

The second way in which Thatcher is unusual is related to the first. Most British prime ministers have a few overarching policy aims, such as the maintenance of world peace or the restoration of full employment, and most of them are in sympathy with the general purposes of their party. Otherwise, the goals of most incumbents of Number 10 are much more narrowly political. They want to remain in Number 10 and/or keep their cabinet united and/or hold their party together and/or win the next election. They do not, in the majority of cases, have important policy aims peculiar to themselves. To be sure, the appeasement policy of the late 1930s was Neville Chamberlain's personal policy, and both Harold Macmillan and Edward Heath were personally committed to the Common Market; but examples like these spring to mind precisely because they are so unusual. And even commitments like Chamberlain's to appeasement and Heath's to the Common Market were in a single field of policy. They did not encompass the whole range.

Margaret Thatcher is different. She is probably unique among twentieth century British prime ministers in having a policy agenda—a set of views and a set of priorities—that is peculiarly her own and is in no way merely an emanation of her government or party. She feels strongly about the substance of policy. She has policy aims in a large number of fields—taxation, public spending, privatisation, law and order, the welfare state, relations with the Soviet Union, defence, the Common Market, and so on—and, even when she does not have fully fledged aims, she certainly, much more often than not, has opinions. Moreover, these aims and opinions are *hers*. Harold Wilson, to take the extreme case, sought to be little more than the Labour party writ large; wherever was the balance of forces within the Labour party, there was Wilson. Thatcher, by contrast, is by no means just the Conservative party writ large. Victory for her party is not synonymous with victory for her; she has a clear, and personal, sense of the direction in which she wishes to lead the party. She describes herself, rightly, as a "conviction politician," but she is also a "substance politician," someone more concerned with arriving at the right outcome than with how that outcome is reached. If she often seeks to impose her point of view, it is because she actually has a point of view—and because her point of view matters more to her than preserving party unity or enjoying a quiet life. To repeat: this makes Thatcher unusual, probably unique, among prime ministers of this century.

If Margaret Thatcher is unusual in being in a minority in her own party, and in the strength and range of her substantive political opinions, she resembles more closely her predecessors in Downing Street in having had a number of formative political experiences. In Harold Macmillan's case, they were the carnage of the First World War and the depression of the 1930s. In Harold Wilson's case, they were the Bevanite controversies of the 1950s and Hugh Gaitskell's aggressive style of Labour party leadership. Thatcher's formative experiences all occurred during the premiership of Edward Heath. There were three of them, and it is important to take careful note of each.

The first related to the famous U-turns in the economic policy of the Heath government that took place in 1971 and 1972. The Conservatives under Heath had been returned to power pledged to roll back the economic power of the state, to give private enterprise its head, to give free rein to market forces, not to bale out private companies that got themselves into difficulties and, above all, not to try to control wages ("We utterly reject," the 1970 Conservative manifesto had declared, "the philosophy of compulsory wage control"). But, within little more than two years of taking office, the Heath administration had effectively abandoned all of these commitments. The Rolls-Royce aeroengine company had been nationalised, the 1972 Industry Act had given the government sweeping new powers to assist private industry, and towards the end of 1972 the government, contrary to its pledges, had introduced the most draconian incomes policy in Britain's peacetime history. The economic wisdom of these changes of policy could be, and still can be, debated (though Margaret Thatcher was subsequently to form her own views); but of their political consequences there could be no doubt. By making Heath appear feeble and vacillating, and by demoralising many of his followers, they seriously weakened his position as party leader. Furthermore, they did not lead to victory at the next election. Far from it: the

Conservatives not only lost the February 1974 election but suffered one of the most dramatic reversals in British electoral history. Thatcher drew the obvious inference. Determination might not bring success; but lack of determination was almost certain to result in failure. If she ever became prime minister, there would be no U-turns (or at least no U-turns that could plausibly be described as such).

Secondly, Thatcher observed that Heath paid a heavy price for permitting himself to become isolated from his followers in the House of Commons. Heath enjoyed the company of a few close intimates, normally cabinet colleagues, with whom he discussed policy and when in power arranged cabinet agendas and conclusions; but he was otherwise an aloof man, with little small talk and, so far as anyone could tell, no interest whatever in his fellow Tory MPs, let alone their wives and families. He was the opposite of gregarious, and almost every Conservative MP still loves to tell the story of how Ted Heath snubbed him socially, or failed to remember his name, or by his mere presence caused a promising conversation to come juddering to a halt. The result was that, while Heath had a small circle of intimates, he lacked a larger circle of friendly acquaintances, politicians who might stand by him—or at least be loath to desert him—in some hour of need. More important, Heath apparently did not realise that, in addition to being friendly with his supporters, it was in his interest to listen to what they had to say. They, too, were members of parliament. They, too, had opinions. They wanted to be listened to, strongly believed that they were entitled to be listened to. Any leader who failed to listen to them ran the serious risk of forfeiting their support as Heath ultimately did after the election defeats in 1974. Thatcher observed all this, and learned. From the moment she succeeded Heath as party leader, she operated on the principle: "They elected you. They can un-elect you. Never lose touch with them."

Margaret Thatcher's third formative experience arose out of the miners' strike of the winter of 1973–74. Heath had taken on the miners—only one of a number of trade unions with formidable political muscle—and had lost. Not only had he lost in the sense that the miners eventually secured almost all of the pay rise that they had been demanding; not only had he lost in the sense that the miners' victory destroyed his incomes policy; but, as a direct consequence of the miners' strike and the early election that he called in an effort to counter it, he had lost the premiership itself, to be followed a year later by his loss of the party leadership. However, unintentionally, however inadvertently, Heath had found himself pursuing a policy of confrontation. He had paid for this policy with his political life. Thatcher was determined not to repeat the experience. We shall describe in more detail later in the chapter the impact that the miners' strike, and other incidents like it, had on her thinking. . . .

Three Premierships, Not One

In the aftermath of the Falklands campaign and the Conservatives' easy victory in the June 1983 general election, it is tempting to see Margaret Thatcher's first term of office as an undifferentiated whole, with the prime minister as dominant from the beginning as she was to become later. To do so, however, would be to extrapolate her triumphant present (as it seemed in the autumn of 1983) back into her more troubled past. In fact, Thatcher's first term 1979–83 fell into three distinct phases. Her leadership style proved more successful in some of them than others.

The first phase lasted from her election victory in May 1979 until roughly the autumn of 1981 and is a period of her life that the prime minister would probably prefer to forget. It was during this phase that she attracted such unflattering nicknames as "Attila the Hen" and (worse) "the Immaculate Misconception." Apart from Lord Carrington's successful negotiation of a satisfactory settlement in Rhodesia, almost nothing seemed to go right for her and her administration (and even the Rhodesian settlement was condemned as a sell-out by a substantial section of Tory backbench opinion). The government had been elected to cut taxes and interest rates, to slash public expenditure, to cut government borrowing, to reduce the rate of growth of money supply and, above all, to bring down the rate of inflation. Instead, between 1979 and the late months of 1981, taxation increased both absolutely and as a proportion of gross domestic product (GDP), interest rates soared to record levels, public expenditure (like taxation) rose in both absolute and proportional terms, public sector borrowing went up instead of down, the rate of growth of money supply hugely exceeded the government's targets, and the rate of inflation, far from falling in the first instance, actually doubled in the course of Thatcher's first year in office, from 11 to 22 percent. On top of all this, Britain's rate of economic growth fell to zero (and in some months was actually negative), bankruptcies in the private sector multiplied while the government poured huge sums of money into public sector industries such as coal, steel and cars (British Leyland); and unemployment rose seemingly inexorably, from 5 percent of the labour force in June 1979, Thatcher's first full month in office, to 12 percent in the period October–December 1981 (Riddell 1983). . . .

Hardly surprisingly under the circumstances, the government's economic difficulties were accompanied by—some would say partly caused by—deep divisions in the cabinet. On coming to office, the new prime minister had had little choice but to appoint a cabinet in which her own staunchest supporters—those who shared both her economic views and her determination to put them into effect—were in a small minority. To have appointed a purely Thatcherite administration at the outset would have transformed many senior Conservatives, holdovers from the Heath era, from half-hearted friends into whole-hearted enemies, and would also have sown doubt and suspicion among those Tory MPs—probably a majority—who, while perfectly willing to give the Thatcher experiment a reasonable chance to succeed, were by no means persuaded that it actually would. In any case, few Thatcherites by 1979 had acquired the requisite experience and authority for cabinet office.

Conscious of her minority position, the new prime minister set about constructing her administration in an unusually collegial manner. William Whitelaw, Lord Carrington, and Humphrey Atkins, the outgoing chief whip, were closeted with her as names and offices were traded, and on one or two key appointments the prime minister permitted herself to be overruled. Certainly Whitelaw and Carrington, men of the old regime, scarcely concealed their disapproval of the new economic doctrines and of many of the young meritocrats who espoused them, while Atkins played a role peculiar to the Tory party, influencing junior appointments in a way unknown on the Labour side. More than that, cabinet ministers were left free to choose some of their own subordinates, with the result that here too a number of Thatcherites were vetoed. The most that the prime minister could do at this stage was ensure that, in a cabinet of 22, four of her strongest supporters—Sir Geoffrey Howe, John Biffen, Sir Keith Joseph and John Nott—were given the four most important economic posts, chancellor of the exchequer, chief secretary to the treasury, secretary of state for industry and secretary of state for trade.

The upshot, in this first phase of the government, was that the cabinet was deeply divided on almost every aspect of economic policy and that the prime minister frequently failed to get her way. She and her loyal group of economic ministers succeeded in controlling financial policy in the narrow sense—taxation and interest rates—but they were defeated again and again over such matters as public spending cuts and state subsidies to the nationalised industries; and the man she had reluctantly appointed secretary of state for employment, James Prior, thwarted her every attempt to persuade the cabinet to introduce measures to curb trade unions tougher than those envisaged in the party's manifesto. The avowedly Thatcherite 1981 budget was unacceptable to many ministers. When it was revealed to the cabinet on the morning of budget day, it provoked immediate criticism from ministers and then open dissent in the lobbies later in the day. The 1981 revolt continued throughout the summer, with even Lord Thorneycroft, Thatcher's own choice as party chairman, siding with the dissidents. She removed him before the October party conference, where it was reckoned that his known scepticism would have a detrimental effect on the party's morale.

Cabinet meetings during this period were often fraught, personal relations between Thatcher and several of her senior ministers were not good, and accounts, often detailed, of the cabinet's internal dissensions appeared frequently in the press. . . . [And] even without Lord Thorneycroft, the party conference of October 1981 probably marked the nadir of Thatcher's first term of office. . . .

In fact, however, although few noticed it at the time, a second, more confident phase of Margaret Thatcher's premiership had already begun. It lasted from the autumn of 1981 until April of the following year. During this phase, although unemployment continued to rise, several other economic indicators began to look healthier. Public spending and the money supply were gradually brought under control, interest rates started to come down, and, best of all, the rate of inflation, having peaked at 22 percent in April and May 1980, fell steadily until it reached 12 percent in the spring of 1981. Single-figure inflation was confidently—and, as it turned out, accurately—predicted for 1982.

At the same time, the prime minister began gradually to win the economic argument inside the government. In one sense, she, Howe, Biffen and the others had never really been threatened; there was no way in which hard-pressed ministers in non-economic departments like Agriculture, Education, Defence and the Foreign Office could devise a plausible alternative economic strategy, let alone impose it on a reluctant prime minister and chancellor of the exchequer. But, in another sense, the very existence of a plausible alternative strategy, wherever it came from, would have provided the Tory dissidents with a rallying ground and might well have put the Thatcherites on the defensive, forcing them to make concessions. In the event, however, no such alternative strategy ever materialised. The "wets" as the Thatcherites dubbed their critics, exploiting a convenient public-school term of abuse, could do little more than resist this or that spending cut ad hoc and go round the country making unhappy-sounding speeches. No one ever showed how higher public spending, or a more relaxed approach to the money supply, could create more jobs without at the same time sucking in large quantities of imports and refuelling inflation. The view gradually gained ground that, however unsatisfactory the government's existing policy might be, there was no real alternative to it and that, whatever else Thatcher was doing, she at least deserved credit for educating the British public into the hard facts of economic life. The longer the Thatcherites stuck to their economic guns, the harder it became to dislodge them—and the smaller the number of Tory MPs who even wanted to try.

Thatcher further strengthened her position at the beginning of phase two of the administration by promoting several of her own people within the government and by demoting or sacking several of the wets. . . .

But the main changes came in September 1981. They brought

about—as they were intended to—a major shift in the balance of power within the cabinet. The prime minister dropped three well-known wets, Sir Ian Gilmour, Lord Soames and Mark Carlisle, and brought into the cabinet three men on whom she could rely, Norman Tebbit, Nigel Lawson and Cecil Parkinson. Equally important, James Prior was shifted from a post where he could get in the prime minister's way on economic matters, Employment, to a post where he could not, Northern Ireland. Prior's eventual acceptance of Northern Ireland, although he had told everyone within earshot that he was extremely reluctant to move, substantially weakened his position. Having been one of Thatcher's more resourceful opponents, he suddenly looked like somebody who could be pushed around. Taken together, the effect of the 1981 cabinet changes was partly numerical; the Thatcherites' strength in the cabinet increased from four to seven, with all of the important economic posts in Thatcherite hands. But it was also moral; the changes signalled that the prime minister was ready to punish dissenters and that there was to be no fundamental shift in economic policy.

The departure of Lord Carrington, the foreign secretary, some months later tilted the balance in the cabinet still further in Thatcher's direction. Carrington had never openly opposed the prime minister on domestic matters, but then he had never actively supported her either. Indeed the Thatcherites from the beginning had regarded him with special suspicion. He had never knocked on doors or had to deal with constituency mail. He had held a "coalface" cabinet appointment only once, and then very briefly at the start of 1974, when as energy secretary he had been instrumental in persuading Heath to take on the miners and to call the disastrous February 1974 general election. Moreover, in Thatcherite eyes, he did not know how the House of Commons worked—he had never been an MP—and cared even less. . . .

The position in the government in the early months of 1982 was thus one of uneasy compromise. The civil war of 1979–81 was over. The Thatcherites and the surviving wets had tacitly agreed that they could live together, and talk of replacing the prime minister before the next election, of which there had been so much only a few months earlier, largely subsided. All the same, Thatcher's own position was still in no sense commanding. She was forced to yield to her critics' demand, following the unpopular 1981 budget, that major issues of economic policy be discussed in the full cabinet; and scepticism about both her and her policies was ready to resurface at any moment. At the end of this second phase of her administration, Margaret Thatcher, although she had made progress, was still a prime minister on trial.

Then the Falklands war—the Argentine invasion, Thatcher's resolute response, Britain's victory—changed everything. It proved what some had doubted, that she was capable of performing effectively under the most extreme pressure. It vindicated her posture as a leader who could be counted on to take hard decisions and see them through to success. It made her for the time being a national hero. The result was that she had, for the first time, an opportunity to take charge of the whole government and bend it to her will. . . . Following the Falklands, Thatcher could still on occasion be defeated in cabinet, but her position of overall dominance was never again in doubt. No one questioned her authority. She was respected as she had never been respected before. Her air was one of supreme confidence and success. This third phase of the Thatcher premiership was to last up to and beyond the 1983 election.

Popular Responses

One important element affecting any prime minister's influence is his own standing, and his government's standing, in the eyes of the general public. Other things being equal, the greater a prime minister's public prestige—or, more precisely, the greater a prime minister's public prestige is thought to be by his cabinet colleagues—the greater is likely to be his capacity to bend those colleagues to his will (always assuming that he has a will). A prime minister thought to be leading his party to electoral disaster is likely to find that his colleagues increasingly question his judgement and are reluctant to acknowledge his authority. By contrast, a prime minister believed to be an election winner will almost certainly find that outside prestige can be translated into inside influence. Every prime minister's standing with the general public is a factor operating constantly in the background, setting the tone and defining the limits of what the politicians in his immediate environment are prepared to do for him—or to him.

Given the importance of public prestige, . . . [it is pertinent that] the three [usual] indicators of the prime minister's and the government's standing [the percentage of voters saying that they were satisfied with Thatcher as prime minister, that they would vote Conservative and that they approved of the government's record to date], although separate in theory and to some extent in fact, track broadly together (Butler and Butler 1986, 263–64). Someone satisfied with the prime minister is more likely to favour the prime minister's party; someone who approves of the government's record is more likely to be satisfied with the prime minister; and so on. Nevertheless, as can be seen, Thatcher's personal standing was somewhat higher than that of her party and government during most of her first year in Number 10 and again after Britain's victory in the Falklands.

[This pattern corresponds closely with] the three phases of the

Thatcher premiership that we have just been describing. In phase one, especially from the spring of 1980 onwards, the standings of prime minister, party and government alike—none of which had ever been very high by the standards of the 1950s and early 1960s—declined steadily and at times sharply until, in the last months of 1981, they hit an all-time low. This was the period when the government was failing to achieve any of its economic objectives and when dissension in the government and the Tory party was rife. Then, in phase two, Thatcher's own standing, and those of her party and government, improved to a limited degree (though the position just before the Falklands invasion was no better than it had been a year before). Finally, in phase three, following the invasion, the war and the British victory, the standings of prime minister, Conservative party and government all but took off, soaring to heights never reached even in the aftermath of the 1979 election victory. The events in the South Atlantic, together with the government's increasing success in the battle against inflation, transformed Thatcher's and the government's standing in the eyes of the public. That fact in itself helped to consolidate Thatcher's position within her administration.

The sheer scale of the shifts in public attitudes towards Thatcher— from . . . a satisfaction rating of 46 percent in October 1979 to one of 24 percent in October 1981 to one of 52 percent only nine months later in July 1982—is mainly the result of external events (the state of the economy, foreign affairs, etc.); but it probably owes something, too, to the unusual clarity of Thatcher's public image and to the profoundly divergent responses her image evokes. . . .

[Opinion poll data] testify, if testimony were needed, to the strength of [this] image. . . . When compared with other [leading] politicians, she was almost invariably placed either towards the top or near the bottom of the range; she was seldom placed anywhere in the middle. Fully 67 percent of Gallup's respondents thought she had a "strong forceful personality"; a miniscule 2 percent thought she was "weak." Far more people, 43 percent, thought she was a "good speaker" than thought the same of anyone else; only 6 percent thought she was a "poor speaker" (compared with the 43 percent who thought the same of [the Labor party leader] Michael Foot).

But, although Thatcher's image was strong, it was by no means overwhelmingly favourable. On the contrary, if she elicited an unusually large number of positive responses, she also elicited an unusually large number of negative ones. . . . Thatcher's personal and political style produces sharply different reactions in different people. . . . In 1983 more people said of Thatcher than of any other prominent politician that she "put the country's interests ahead of politics"; but at the same time more people said of her than of any other politician that she was "too much of a politician." Similarly, she scored high on both sincerity and lack of sincerity, on being in touch with the people and not being in touch with them, on having the qualities of a good prime minister and on not having them. People are in no doubt where they stand on Margaret Thatcher; but they do not all stand in the same place. . . .

One further point concerning Thatcher's standing with the public should be made. It is widely believed, in other countries as well as in Britain, that Thatcher is an unusually popular prime minister and that her popularity with the public is an important source of her authority within the government. This belief is certainly correct, but only of the post-Falklands period. Before the Falklands war, Thatcher was not only unpopular in an absolute sense . . . , she was in fact very nearly the most unpopular prime minister in modern British history (Butler and Butler 1986, 263–64). . . .

. . .Only Heath among postwar prime ministers has had a lower overall satisfaction rating than Thatcher; but Thatcher's low overall rating conceals the remarkable surge of public support for her that took place during and after the Falklands war. Before the war, the prime minister's ministerial and parliamentary colleagues saw her as someone who might well drag them down to defeat at the next election; after the war, they saw her as someone who would almost certainly lead them to victory. The gain to her authority was immense. "Thatcher *victrix*" is a post-Falklands phenomenon.

The Prime Minister as Leader

So much for the record of Margaret Thatcher's first term. The question now arises: how has she comported herself as prime minister, both during the three phases of her first term, and in general? Is there anything distinctive about the way in which this individual does this job? It turns out that indeed there is.

All British prime ministers, like all American presidents and German chancellors, are conventionally described as "political leaders" the clear implication being that their task consists of determining the direction in which their government shall go and then of persuading their governmental colleagues to follow them. The image conjured up is of a scout master leading a troop, or a choir master leading a choir. Leaders lead. A leader who did not lead would be a contradiction in terms.

This image, however, is in fact false to the way in which most British prime ministers comport themselves most of the time. There are two reasons for this. The first has already been referred to: most British prime ministers are not in the position of having a large number of aims, personal to themselves, across a wide range of fields. Their preferences are very largely those of their party and the majority of their cabinet colleagues. Thus, Attlee did not "lead" his government on the issue of giving independence to India: that was the direction in which the Labour party and the postwar Labour government wanted to go anyway. Likewise, the Conservatives in the 1950s were not "led" by Churchill, Eden or Macmillan to cut taxes and relax the controls on British industry: party, government and the mood of the time were at one. Acts of genuine leadership, in which prime ministers try to steer their cabinets in directions in which they might not otherwise go, stand out precisely because of their comparative rarity. Such an act of leadership was Macmillan's over Europe in the early 1960s, when he set about persuading the Tory party and the cabinet, against all their instincts, that Britain should seek to join the EEC; another, more negative in character, was Harold Wilson's leadership of his first government in resisting, for as long as he could, the devaluation of sterling. But such episodes are not the norm. Heath's cabinet was so united that it did not require leadership in this sense. Wilson was usually content to count heads round the cabinet table. Callaghan in his cabinet took the occasional initiative—for example, over educational standards—but generally concerned himself, inside the administration, with keeping his colleagues out of trouble and refereeing intra-cabinet disputes. . . .

The second reason why British prime ministers are leaders who so seldom lead relates to their position within their own governments. British prime ministers cannot take many decisions entirely on their own; most of the time, they have to carry their cabinets—or at least their senior colleagues—with them. Moreover, they do not enjoy security of tenure; in the back of their own minds, and everybody else's, is the thought that a prime minister who loses his party's confidence, or seems to be about to lead his party to defeat, can be got rid of (however difficult it may be to get rid of him in practice). It follows that a prime minister who takes a personal policy initiative in cabinet, and who sees that initiative rebuffed by the cabinet, suffers not one defeat but two. He *both* fails to achieve that specific policy objective *and*, simultaneously, suffers a diminution of his authority as prime minister, by however small an amount on any single occasion. Each defeat makes another defeat more likely. Each is a demonstration of the prime minister's political vulnerability. Not surprisingly, most prime ministers take few policy initiatives of this kind; and, when they do, they usually make sure in advance that they can count on their colleagues' backing.

Not so Thatcher. Indeed it would be hard to imagine a prime ministerial style more different from that of the majority of her predecessors than Margaret Thatcher's. She is in politics, as she often says, not "to be" but "to do," not to preside over Britain's economic decline but to try to

reverse that decline. She is by temperament and political instinct an activist. However, she found herself in a minority in her own cabinet in her
first two or three years in Number 10—and was still in a minority, though
a considerably larger one, even after the 1983 general election. After all,
as we saw earlier, she was elected Conservative leader, not because of her
economic views but, if anything, in spite of them. She therefore had no
choice, given her aims and determination, but to lead in an unusually
forthright, assertive manner. Partly this was a matter of her personality;
she is a forthright and assertive person. But it was at least as much a matter of the objective situation in which she found herself. She was forced to
behave like an outsider for the simple reason that she was one.

Her approach manifested itself most strikingly at meetings of ministers. Most prime ministers tend to play a waiting game in cabinet and
cabinet committees. They encourage the minister or ministers most centrally concerned with an issue to introduce the discussion and then intervene themselves only at a fairly late stage. The aim is to see whether a
consensus emerges around the table. If one does, that settles the matter
unless the prime minister has some particular reason for expressing a contrary view. If no consensus emerges, even amongst the more important
ministers present, then the prime minister may well come in and try to
steer the final decision in one direction or another. Prime ministers may,
of course, influence the discussion by the order in which they ask ministers to speak, by the tenor of the questions they ask, and so on; and they
may well have nobbled one or more of their cabinet colleagues beforehand. But typically, except on a few major issues about which they feel
strongly, their approach tends to be cautious and circumspect. Thatcher,
by all accounts, operates in a totally different manner. She states her
views at the outset, or lets them be known. Often, unusual in a prime
minister, she thinks aloud. She interrupts ministers with whom she dis-
agrees and insists on standing and fighting her corner. Unlike most prime
ministers, she does not merely chair cabinet discussions: she is an active
participant in them. More often than not, she dominates them (Wapshott
and Brock 1983, 192–93, 204–5 and 207).

This technique must ensure that the prime minister frequently gets
her way when she would otherwise not have done: other things being
equal, most ministers would much rather be on the prime minister's side
than anywhere else. But it also ensures that she is frequently defeated in
cabinet—and is seen to be defeated. Indeed Thatcher probably finds herself on the losing side of arguments in the cabinet more often than any
other prime minister in this century. In February 1980, during the national steel strike of that year, she failed in an attempt to persuade Prior
to bring in a one-clause bill to ban secondary picketing. In November of
the same year the cabinet forced Thatcher and Howe to raise taxes by

refusing to accept public spending cuts on anything like the scale they were demanding. . . . In mid–1981, as we saw earlier, she was forced to yield to cabinet pressure for full-dress discussions on economic policy. In July 1982, even after the Falklands victory, the wets overcame prime ministerial objections to a £500 million package for aiding the jobless. A few weeks later, after what was said to be "a monumental row" in the cabinet, the Central Policy Review Staff's controversial report on the national health service was shelved. None of these events, however, caused the prime minister in any way to alter her style.

This unusual insistence on being the active leader of the government—on leading it, as it were, from outside rather than inside—manifests itself in another, rather curious way: in the prime minister's penchant for talking about the government as though she were not a member of it. The customary pronoun used by prime ministers when speaking about their own government is "we"; Thatcher's pronoun is usually "we" but often "they." "They" are making life difficult for her; "they" are having to be persuaded; "they" are too concerned with defending the interests of their own departments. The language is not typically British. It is more like that used by American presidents when speaking about Congress. It is significant that the prime minister thinks in this way of her own cabinet as being, in effect, another branch of government. And, just as American presidents have to put up with hostility from Congress, so Thatcher has to put up with her not always amenable cabinet colleagues.

Respecting Power, Weighing It

Margaret Thatcher thus leads from the front. She stamps her foot, she raises her voice. For a British prime minister, she is extraordinarily assertive. Given this element in her style, it might be supposed that Thatcher was a rash politician, given to rushing in, acting on impulse, taking uncalculated risks. But nothing could be further from the truth. Thatcher is in fact a remarkably cautious politician. Not only is she cautious, but she respects power and has an unusually well-developed capacity for weighing it, for seeing who has it and who has not, for calculating who can damage her and who cannot. She is often described as an emotional person; in her ability to weigh power, she is more like a precision instrument.

One obvious illustration of this point is her handling of cabinet appointments. She probably hoped from the beginning to be able to reduce the proportion of non-Thatcherites in her administration. Certainly the behaviour of several of them—Sir Ian Gilmour in February 1980 delivered a scarcely-veiled public attack on the government's economic policies under the guise of a lecture on "Conservatism"—irritated her intensely. But some of those who were wet in the political sense were not at all wet in the temperamental sense: if sacked from the government, they could, and would, mount a formidable campaign against her policies from the back benches. She was therefore careful to pick off only those whom she calculated would not make a nuisance of themselves. . . .

[She] thus sacked ministers, not according to how much they disagreed with her but according to how weak they were—and how strong she was (Wapshott and Brock 1983, 206). There were two other men in the cabinet whom she would probably have loved to get rid of, James Prior and Peter Walker, both of whom did little to conceal their distaste for monetarist economics or their dislike of her personally; but, if either of them went, they would certainly not go quietly and would become a focus for discontent amongst Conservative MPs. So they stayed. Even so, the prime minister, carefully taking the measure of each, neutralised Prior by sending him to Northern Ireland and Walker by relegating him to relatively minor posts, first at Agriculture, then at Energy. . . .

Thatcher's careful handling of her cabinet changes is well known. Less widely appreciated is the extreme circumspection that she and her government have shown in their dealings with powerful trade unions. The lessons of Heath's confrontation with the miners in the winter of 1973–74 were not merely learnt; they were studied carefully. Before being ousted as party leader, Heath had commissioned a report from Lord Carrington concerning the ability of a Conservative government, or any government, to resist the claims of militant trade unions that were in a position to disrupt the whole of the country's economic and physical life. Heath had in mind the miners, but also such groups as the power workers, gas workers and railwaymen. Carrington's conclusions, leaked to the press in 1978, were bleak. Once the miners had gone on strike, the Heath government had been defeated not because it was ill-organised or inept but quite simply because the miners had more power than the government did. A government's only recourse in such a conflict would be to the use of troops, and Britain did not have enough troops, nor did they have the requisite skills. In any case, the use of troops would do irrevocable damage to the fabric of the country's social and political life. The conclusions to be drawn were obvious: . . . avoid confrontations with powerful unions at almost any cost; if a powerful union makes menacing noises, buy it off as quickly and as unobtrusively as possible. Such an approach would be dependent on the government not having an incomes policy; but the Conservatives did not want to have an incomes policy in any case, on other grounds.

. . . In dealing with public sector pay during its full term, the Thatcher government consistently conceded much larger increases to militant groups of workers possessing industrial muscle than to groups that were either less militant or possessed less muscle. . . .

[This strategy] refutes the suggestion . . . that Margaret Thatcher is some sort of latter-day Lord Cardigan, eager to lead political charges of the Light Brigade. She is not. She is someone who prefers to fight another day, who is always ready to compromise (though only when she believes that there is no alternative). Those who overlook Thatcher's sensitivity to power—her respect for it, and her ability to weigh it—overlook an essential element in her prime ministerial style.

People, Not Organizations

A different element in her style, consistent with her respect for power but not in any way stemming from it, is her approach to techniques of decisionmaking. Most politicians, like most business managers, probably fall into three rough categories. The first consists of those who, confronted with a new situation or problem, instinctively think in terms of an organisational response—the setting up of a new committee, the merging of two departments, the creation of a specialist policy unit. The second consists of those who, possibly for reasons of personality or simply because they are unaccustomed to working in large organisations, are more people-centred. Their response to a new situation or problem is to think in terms of individuals: who would be good at dealing with this new situation or problem? The third category, considerably rarer than either of the others, consists of people capable of thinking both organisationally and in human terms at the same time.

Few politicians fall into this last category, but Edward Heath provided an unusually clear instance of the first. Hence his wholesale reorganisation of government departments and his creation of new institutions like the Central Policy Review Staff. Margaret Thatcher, by contrast, provides a striking instance of the second category. Hers is an almost exclusively people-centred style of government. Her interest in the structure of government is minimal. She is unconcerned with nuts and bolts, and organisation charts bore her. Instead, she feels at home working with, through—and, if need be, around—individual human beings. Faced with a new problem or determined to embark on a new initiative, she asks, not "How can I organise this work so that it will be done effectively?" but rather "Who can I get to help me? Who would be the best person to turn to?" Weighing people, like weighing power, is central to the way she does her job.

Against this background, one of the first decisions—or, rather, non-decisions—of her administration may seem curious. On entering Downing Street in May 1979, she brought with her only a handful of her own people. She behaved as though she were perfectly content to operate for the most part through the established institutions of government—the civil service, the cabinet and cabinet committees. . . . At the end of her first term, fewer of Thatcher's own people, as distinct from permanent civil servants, were working at Number 10 than had worked there in the time of either Harold Wilson or James Callaghan. . . . Her advisers . . . were keen that she should expand her personal operation at Number 10 and establish a genuine "prime minister's department"; but there is no evidence that she more than toyed with these ideas (Greenaway 1984).

Given her intention to be an activist prime minister, given that she found herself in a minority in her own government and given that senior officials were well known not to be enthusiastic about the main lines of her policy, Thatcher's failure to build up her own staff at Number 10 is, on the face of it, puzzling. A person in this position might have been expected to surround herself with like-minded people whom she could trust; she might have been expected to create a prime minister's department which could serve as a counterweight to all the other departmental interests in Whitehall. Paradoxically, however, it was almost certainly her very "people-centredness" that caused her not to behave in this way. In the first place, it was not her instinct to think in terms of institutional solutions to substantive problems. In the second, and more important, all of her previous experience had taught her that, if she knew her own mind and were determined and forceful enough, she could attain her objectives through the medium of face-to-face argument and persuasion. She was easily her own best advocate and also her own chief of staff. She had no need of hordes of assistants and intermediaries. On the contrary, they might have the effect of diluting the direct force of her own strong personality and of coming between her and the substance of the arguments. In the end, she had mastered the civil servants in the Department of Education and Science in this way, and her campaign for the Tory leadership, however much help she received from supporters . . . had been esstially a one-woman affair. In Downing Street, as in opposition, she wanted to ensure that *she* was in control.

This determination to be at the centre of things, to direct rather than merely supervise, has influenced her operating style in other ways. Thatcher in no sense "abolished cabinet government," at least during her first term. As we have seen, she was frequently defeated in cabinet; and, even on the Falklands, in the words of one cabinet minister, "She had to carry us on every major decision. That task force would never have sailed without cabinet approval" (quoted in Hennessy 1983, 4). Nevertheless, like other prime ministers before her, but on a larger scale, she has often sought to get her own way by circumventing the cabinet, by bringing public pressure to bear on it from outside and even by semi-publicly opposing the policies of her own ministers. . . .

As time went on, she chose to work more and more frequently

through small groups of ministers—if need be, augmented by officials and other advisers—rather than through formal meetings of the cabinet and its committees.

Whatever the issue or forum, Thatcher is a prime minister who characteristically reaches out for decisions. She does not just wait for them to come to her. To be sure, she prefers to delegate when she can be certain that the consequences of the delegation will be to her liking; but, since delegating invariably means losing some element of control, her premiership has been marked—as was Harold Wilson's first term to a lesser extent—by a tendency for decisions on small matters as well as large to be pulled into Number 10. Ministers are reluctant to consult her too frequently because, if they do, they are liable to be accused of not being on top of their job; but, equally, they are reluctant not to consult her for fear of doing the wrong thing, incurring her wrath and possibly finding themselves countermanded. Sir Michael Edwardes, the former chairman of British Leyland, contrasts in his memoirs the freedom of action that James Callaghan gave to his industry secretary, Eric Varley, with Margaret Thatcher's insistence that her industry secretaries consult her about almost every detail (Edwardes 1983, ch. 11). . . . Thatcher, unlike most prime ministers, is not seen in Whitehall as a somewhat remote figure. Her presence is all-pervasive.

Another corollary of her desire to dominate her government, and of her preference for doing so through contact with—and judgements upon—individuals, is her concern, unusual amongst prime ministers, with senior appointments in the civil service. There exists in Whitehall a Senior Appointments Selection Committee consisting of the head of the Home Civil Service and a number of other senior permanent secretaries; and the normal practice has been for most of this committee's recommendations to be accepted by the prime minister of the day without question, or at least without much in the way of active involvement—this despite the fact that appointments at permanent secretary and deputy secretary level are among the few appointments (ministers apart) that the prime minister can make on his or her own authority, without having to consult colleagues. Thatcher, by contrast, determined from the moment she arrived in Number 10 to interest herself in the selection of top civil servants, to make her own enquiries about candidates for promotion and to be prepared to question, even on occasion to reject, the SASC's recommendations. She has shown a similar interest in appointments to the chairmanships of nationalised industries. She undoubtedly shows a marked preference for people who, temperamentally at least, are like her: hardworking, tough-minded and assertive. There is less agreement in Whitehall about how far she also leans towards officials who share her free-market, monetarist economic views (Greenaway 1984).

Thatcher thus reaches out for decisions; she reaches out for people. She also reaches out for ideas. Although she has chosen not to surround herself in Downing Street with a close circle of personal advisers, she partially offsets this lack in a highly personal way, one that would have been inconceivable in the time of Callaghan, Wilson, Heath, Home or even Macmillan. She encourages the existence of, and participates actively in, what amounts to a higgledy piggledy on-going academic seminar on the theory and practice of modern conservatism. . . . As one [participant] said:

> The prime minister plays with ideas as though they were ping-pong balls. She just likes to knock them about a bit. It makes her feel relaxed (quoted in Stothard 1983, 10).

It is striking how many members of the Thatcher seminar resemble both her and a considerable proportion of her cabinet in not being members of the old Tory establishment, in being outsiders, "marginal" people, socially or intellectually and sometimes both. Many, like her, are lower middle-class or working-class in their social origins. A considerable number are converts to the Tory party from the more or less extreme left. . . . Most of the converts, however, although they have ceased to be socialists, have not ceased to be radicals. Typically they have exchanged one set of absolutes and certainties for another. Their sense of their own minority status, and of still being "against the system," accords well with Thatcher's own self-image as someone who stands outside both the old economic system and the old system of ideas the better to change them both.

Presentation of Self, Uses of Self

Prime ministers vary considerably in how far they seek consciously to project an image of themselves and in how far they consciously use their own personalities as a means of achieving their political objectives. Winston Churchill and Harold Macmillan were highly self-conscious, self-projecting politicians; Clement Attlee and Sir Alec Douglas-Home in their different ways represented the other extreme of unselfconsciousness, almost insouciance. Margaret Thatcher is firmly in the Churchill–Macmillan mould. "She is," said an official who worked under her at the DES, "an actress. . . . She is very conscious of the impression she is making" (Wapshott and Brock 1983, 85). That being so, it is important to see how she uses her personality, and to what ends.

One element in her style will be evident to anyone in Britain who has ever switched on a television set: Thatcher seeks to command partly by appearing to be in command. Her hair is permed, her clothes are neat, her make-up is carefully applied; and her manner is every bit as unruffled as her appearance. She controls her gestures, regulates her smile, adjusts the timbre and pitch of her voice. She is careful to appear emotional only when she wants to appear emotional and to appear cool and collected when, far more often, that is how she wants to appear. Moreover, the same self-control and attention to detail that are lavished on her personal appearance are also lavished on her public speeches and her appearances in parliament. Hours are devoted to briefing her for prime minister's question time, and time spent under the hair-drier is typically time spent polishing each phrase and paragraph of a speech to be delivered three weeks hence. Little of this, if any, is the product of vanity. It results from the belief that, if one is to control others, one must first exercise self-control. The iron lady is, above all, iron with herself. Nor, it should be added, is Thatcher's concern with "presentation of self" peculiarly feminine. Macmillan, to take only one example, conducted himself in almost exactly the same way (though the details of his personal style were, of course, different).

Her hair-dos and her way with television interviewers are public property. Equally important are the ways she uses herself in private. To the public at large, she often appears cold, mannered, slightly inhuman; a newspaper columnist once said that she always looked as though she were putting on a sympathetic air in order to break the news to someone that their pet cat was dead (Junor 1983, 200). In private, however, her consciousness of others and consideration for them account in part for her political success. Shortly after the 1979 election, a private secretary who had worked for Callaghan at Number 10 and was now working for Thatcher was asked which of them he preferred as his boss. "Thatcher," he replied, "by a wide margin. Jim always thought you had absolutely nothing to do in life except work for him. Mrs. Thatcher never forgets that you have a wife who may be expecting you home for dinner" (Private information). In remembering people's names (and their spouse's and children's), in remembering what was on their mind the last time she talked to them and in being willing to take time to listen to their troubles, Thatcher is the antithesis of Heath. Her ability to relax people, to make them feel that they matter to her, not only endears her to Conservatives in the country; it also comes through in films of her visits to shopping centres and factories. She seems to care for others. . . .

Thatcher has also made a point, as we remarked earlier, of being a good listener. Before campaigning for the leadership of her party, she spent little time mixing with her fellow Conservative members of parliament. Ever since then, she has gone out of her way to be accessible—in her room at the House, in the members' dining room, in the division lobby. One of her boasts is that she has never refused a private meeting with a Conservative backbencher, however trivial-seeming the purpose of the discussion. Edward du Cann, the chairman of the backbench 1922 Committee, similarly says that ever since she became prime minister, he has been able to get through to her more or less whenever he wants, even at short notice. Since her time as prime minister is limited, her main conduit to and from the back benches, apart from the 1922 Committee, is —and has to be—her parliamentary private secretary, Ian Gow, who served during her first term, was often dismissed as being the prime minister's personal spy, a sort of political "supergrass." Such allegations, however, missed the point. Gow remained useful to her not only, or even mainly, because he passed on to her items of information that MPs did not want her to hear, but precisely because he kept her in touch with what they did want her to hear. If he had ever been thought to be merely a spy, his usefulness to the prime minister, even as a spy, would have ceased.

If Thatcher is a prodigious listener, she is also a prodigious worker. Probably few prime ministers have put in more hours. Her working day starts at 6.30 . . . and does not end until 1 or sometimes 2 o'clock the next morning. She works on holiday as well as at Number 10 or Chequers. She enjoys working and, by all accounts, is apt to become bored when not working. Nevertheless, the main purpose of her industry, as with almost everything else she does, is political. She wishes to bring about great changes in British society, changes that are often not welcome to others, including many in her own party and government. If she is to persuade others, if she is to goad them into action, if she is to catch them out doing things that she does not want them to do, then she must know their business almost as well as her own. And, since she is only one individual, whereas her cabinet contains fourteen departmental ministers, she has to work harder than any of them. She operates on the principle: "Get on top of the facts or they will get on top of you. Get on top of your ministers' facts or your ministers will get on top of you." Being on top of the facts means that she can deal with her ministers on equal terms, even on strictly departmental issues; it also means that her ministers are unusually attentive to the prime minister's wishes and unusually reluctant to try to put things past her.

Thatcher is, necessarily given her ambitions, a quick and eager learner. Conscious when she became leader of the opposition of her ignorance of foreign affairs (and conscious that others were conscious of it), she took the trouble to visit in the space of four years: France, West Germany, the Netherlands, Belgium, Italy, Switzerland, Finland, Rumania, Egypt, Iran, Syria, Israel, the United States, Canada, Pakistan, Singapore, New Zealand, Australia, India, China, Japan, Yugoslavia and Spain. She also visited hundreds of factories and business premises, closely questioning managers and shopfloor workers about everything from the details of production processes and stock control to how they were coping, or failing to cope, with foreign competition. By the end of these four years, Thatcher could still be accused of lacking real experience, but not of lacking knowledge. Her curiosity and her keenness as an auto-didact remain among her most conspicuous characteristics.

To those whom she likes and trusts, the prime minister is, as we have seen, considerate and solicitous. She is a loyal person and inspires great loyalty in those close to her. But to strangers, or people she has reason to dislike or distrust, she frequently shows another side of her personality. She clearly makes use of fear as a conscious weapon in her armoury of command. Carefully controlled displays of anger and disdain, together with her own superordinate position as party leader and prime minister, are used to wrong-foot ministers and civil servants, to bully them, on occasion to humiliate them. In this respect, as in no other, her leadership style is faintly reminiscent of Lyndon Johnson's. Few ministers and civil servants are prepared to admit that they are afraid of the prime minister; they prefer to describe themselves as being sometimes "a little nervous" in her presence. But fear is the word and the concept used by most onlookers. . . . She can inspire devotion but she also has an unusually large number of enemies.

Her conscious use of fear as a weapon is allied—another faint echo of Lyndon Johnson—to a disposition to see the political world as being divided into friends and enemies, goodies and baddies, the baddies, in terms of her role as Conservative leader and prime minister, being almost entirely members of her own party (together with sluggish or recalcitrant civil servants). This disposition permeates the language of both her and her advisers. Her supporters are "on my side," "our people"; her critics are "wet," "unreliable," "the enemy" or, when tempers are running especially high, "reptiles." That this Manichaean disposition exists is not in doubt. Whether it adversely affects her judgment is disputed.

What is not in dispute is that, Manichaeism apart, Thatcher has probably been more concerned than any other postwar prime minister with promoting her own supporters inside the government and with ensuring that the departments of government that matter to her—principally the economic departments—are manned exclusively by those who share her views. She told Kenneth Harris of the *Observer* (February 29) before the 1979 election that she wanted in her cabinet "only the people who wanted to go in the direction in which every instinct tells me we have to go"; she wanted hers to be "a conviction government.". . .

Previous prime ministers have used ministerial appointments to bring on talent, to broaden their basis of support in their party, to protect their political position, to strengthen their government in the eyes of the general public. Thatcher is unusual, possibly unique, in her single-minded use of appointments to promote policy ends. The Thatcher government is, by design, *her* government. Her decisions reflect equally her determination to lead and her people-centred approach to the business of government.

Means to Ends: Match or Mismatch?

Margaret Thatcher's is a formidable personality, and hers is a distinctive prime ministerial style. No one in 10 Downing Street before has been quite like her: no one has operated before in quite the way that she does. It is important therefore to emphasise that both her personality and her style are politically neutral. For a politician, Thatcher arouses unusually strong emotions, of admiration bordering on adoration on the right, of animosity sometimes approaching hatred on the left. But the real focus of contention is, or ought to be, not her person but her policies. If someone with her personality and style were the leader of a left-wing government, pursuing left-wing policies with the same single-mindedness and determination, qualities that seem in her vices would instead seem virtues, and "iron lady" would be a term of praise rather than abuse. Not least for that reason, Margaret Thatcher deserves to be judged on professional as well as partisan grounds. Are *her* means, to repeat the question asked at the outset, well adapted to *her* ends?

One way to approach the question is to run a "thought experiment"—to ask what the policies of a Conservative government elected in 1979 would have been like if the prime minister had not been Thatcher but one of the other leading contenders for the Tory leadership in 1975, William Whitelaw, James Prior or Sir Geoffrey Howe. Merely to ask this question, given everything that is known of these three men, is already to answer it. A Conservative government led by any of them would have been a very different government, in its policies as well as its style and rhetoric. Such a government would almost certainly have maintained a quasi-corporatist relationship with the trade unions instead of largely excluding them from economic policymaking. It would probably not have pressed nearly so hard or fast with union-curbing legislation as did the Thatcher government following the 1983 election. It might well have cut the highest marginal rates of income tax, but it would probably not have moved nearly so swiftly to shift the burden of taxation from direct (mainly income tax) to indirect (mainly VAT). A Whitelaw, Prior or Howe government would almost certainly not have built up the Thatcher government's massive programme for the privatisation of state-owned industry. It might well not have fought the Falklands war in the same way, or possibly at all. It would have been far more tempted than was the Thatcher government during the depths of the recession in 1980–81 to reflate the economy in order to reduce unemployment, even at the risk of some increase in the rate of inflation. "The lady," said Thatcher in a famous speech, "is not for turning." Given their outlooks and temperaments, any of the other three probably would have been.

The Thatcher government, in short, is not just any Tory government of the 1980s; it is different. But does the fact that it is different stem from the way in which Margaret Thatcher does the job of being prime minister, from her determination to lead, her respect for power, her people-centredness, her presentation of self, her uses of self? Again, merely to ask the question is to answer it. Given Thatcher's minority position on economic and industrial issues within her own government, it is inconceivable that she could have bent the administration to her will as far as she did without leading from the front, without reaching out for decisions, without carefully calculating ministerial appointments, without bullying people, without working all hours of the day and night. Her personal style has been essential to the achievement—in so far as they have been achieved—of her personal ends. "The Thatcher government" is not just a conventional phrase; it captures a central political reality. Whether Thatcher's policies are good or bad for Britain, whether they will actually bring about the social and economic transformation that she desires, is, of course, a different question. . . .

Has Thatcher in her first period of office fundamentally changed the office of prime minister? Will she bequeath to her successors an office significantly different from the one that she inherited from Callaghan? Up to a point, the answer to these questions is "no.". . . The British constitution and the imperatives of party leadership in the British system mean that the office of prime minister evolves only slowly and that it is probably beyond the capacity of any one holder of the office to change it both radically and permanently. . . . The job can be done in different ways. Thatcher has developed a new way. But the job itself has not greatly changed.

But it would be a serious mistake just to leave it at that because, whatever happens during the remainder of her time in Downing Street, Thatcher will bequeath to her successors two important legacies. The first is simply a powerful example. We now know what we did not know before: that the job of prime minister can be done in Thatcher's way. The repertory of available prime ministerial styles has been extended. Politicians of the future will read biographies of Thatcher, just as they now read biographies of Lloyd George and Winston Churchill, and they will reckon that they can learn a thing or two. . . .

Thatcher's second legacy is more subtle and could easily be overlooked. The great weakness in the British prime ministerial office—as compared with, say, the American or French presidencies—is that there are so few decisions that a prime minister can take on his or her own authority; the prime minister has few statutes to administer, no department of his or her own. But one of the great strengths in the British office lies in the fact that the outer limits of its authority are so ill-defined. It is open to a determined prime minister to take more and more decisions and to defy other members of the cabinet to say that he or she has no right to take these decisions. This is precisely what Thatcher has been doing, in extending her surveillance of senior civil service appointments, in working increasingly through small groups of ministers rather than through the cabinet and cabinet committees, in making it clear to her colleagues that she expects to be consulted about virtually the whole range of ministerial activity. She has been pushing out the frontiers of her authority ever since she took office in 1979; she may well continue to do so in the future. And it would take a brave, determined, powerful and well-organized set of ministers under her to tell her to stop. Who will say that the rules have been broken when, first, there are no hard and fast rules and when, second, the alleged breaker of the rules is one's own boss on whom one's political future is likely to depend? Margaret Thatcher's example will be important in the future not least because it will make it clear to her successors that the job of prime minister can be an even bigger one than had previously been supposed. It will be up to them to decide whether they want to, and are politically in a position to, follow the example that Thatcher has set.

17

Congressional Leadership Style: The Johnson Treatment

Rowland Evans, Jr. and Robert Novak

On the steamy Washington summer morning of Saturday, July 2, 1955, Senate Majority Leader Lyndon B. Johnson sent word to the Senate press gallery that he would see the press immediately in his new "second" office on the top floor of the Capitol. Commandeered from the Senate-House Economic Committee, headed by Senator Paul Douglas of Illinois, who was now suffering for his feud with his party's leader, this two-room suite had become the Majority Leader's office. In the outer office were secretaries and filing cabinets, but the inner office was where the real business was conducted in an atmosphere of leather chairs and couches, tinkling chandeliers and readily accessible liquor cabinets. It was a corner office, and the view was magnificent, looking south to well-tended public lawns and fountains and looking west down the Mall to the Washington Monument and Lincoln Memorial.

The reporters braced themselves for what was coming: a hymn of praise to the accomplishments of the first session of the 84th Congress, now drawing to a close after six months.

From *Lyndon B. Johnson: The Exercise of Power*, by Rowland Evans, Jr. and Robert Novak (New York: New American Library, 1966), pp. 95–117. Copyright © 1966 by Rowland Evans, Jr. and Robert Novak. Reprinted by arrangement with New American Library, a division of Penguin Books USA, Inc.

These sessions of self-congratulation with reporters had become commonplace. The McCarthy censure vote the previous December had been only the prelude to the emergence of Lyndon Johnson as master magician of the Senate when, in January, 1955, he became Majority Leader of the new and narrowly Democratic Senate. At forty-six, he was the youngest Majority Leader in the chamber's history.

In those six months he had justifiably gained the reputation of the young genius who tamed the turbulent Senate for the first time since the Court-packing fight of 1937. And now, with Congress ready to adjourn for the year, newspapers and magazines were spotted with stories further enriching Johnson's new national reputation. . . .

The handful of Senate reporters working that Saturday morning filed into his office to confront a man showing the beginnings of an unmistakable middle-aged paunch. But even at two hundred and twenty pounds, the six-foot-three Johnson could still pass as the lean Texan— hard in the chest and shoulders, more angular than fleshy in the face. His full black hair was brushed back slick and close to the scalp, and he dressed like a riverboat gambler: dark silk suit, monogrammed shirt, French cuffs and those long-pointed collars.

As he faced the press on July 2, Lyndon Johnson was bone-weary from six frenetic months of eighteen-hour days. Blowing out great lungfuls of smoke in steamy jets, chain-smoker Johnson made no effort to conceal his irritation with the reporters' singular lack of perception. In slow, weary phrases, filled with pauses, he repeated the list of the Senate's 1955 accomplishments: extension of the Reciprocal Trade Agreements Act, federal aid for highway construction, Upper Colorado River Bill, increase of minimum wage to one dollar an hour, increase of foreign aid appropriations over the President's request. Continuing his slow monologue, Johnson then briefly reviewed the few bills in committee that might yet be considered on the Senate floor in the little time remaining for the session.

John Chadwick, a soft-spoken, veteran reporter for the Associated Press, interrupted the soliloquy with a question. What about Eisenhower's bill to soften the restrictive McCarran-Walter Immigration and Nationality Act and allow more refugees to enter the United States? Chadwick had touched a sore point with Johnson. James Eastland of Mississippi, chairman of the Senate Judiciary Committee and Johnson's good friend, was a foe of liberalized immigration and had no intention of letting the bill out of his committee. Besides, Johnson himself had been a supporter of the McCarran-Walter Act. Coldly, he informed Chadwick that he could scarcely influence a bill until it was out of committee, and the refugee bill was in the province of the Judiciary Committee.

Chadwick persisted. With unassailable logic, he pointed out that

Johnson had just finished talking about other bills still in committee and not yet on the Senate floor. Without warning, the six months of hyperactivity and tension boiled over in Johnson, and he exploded in unrestrained invective against Chadwick. For Johnson, that sudden loss of self-control in public was unprecedented. So severe was the tongue-lashing that other reporters rose to defend Chadwick. The press conference came to an abrupt and embarrassing end, with the Majority Leader in an angry mood. It was a signal that he had strained his physical resources to a dangerous degree. . . .

The Majority Leader's limousine, chauffeured by Norman Edwards, had barely crossed the Potomac River on the hour-long drive when Johnson complained of the heat (though the air conditioner was going full blast) and of feeling sick to his stomach. Stopping at a gasoline station, Johnson gulped an ice-cold Coke but only felt more nauseated. He tried to vomit but couldn't. On arriving at the Brown estate, he turned aside a suggestion that what he needed was a good, cold swim in the Brown pool and went to a downstairs bedroom to rest. Senator Clinton Anderson of New Mexico, another weekend guest, was worried about him.

"My arms are heavy, and I feel like somebody's sitting on my chest," Johnson told Anderson. Anderson, who had weathered almost every disease known to medical science, including a heart attack, professionally ran his fingers down Johnson's chest to locate the source of pain. A second later he announced: "Lyndon, you're having a coronary."

Johnson was furious. A heart attack! Proud of his good health and strong physical constitution, Johnson simply could not believe he was a heart attack victim. Surely, it was only a severe bellyache. And the timing of the heart attack—if indeed Anderson was right in his diagnosis—couldn't have been worse: on the eve of the presidential trial balloon in Sunday's *Washington Post*.

Anderson made Johnson lie down. Host Brown came to help. Johnson started to light a cigarette. "Don't do that," cautioned Anderson. Johnson settled instead for a belt of Scotch. The pain subsided, then returned. Anderson told Brown: "You'd better call a doctor."

"Now, Clint," Brown said, "Lyndon doesn't want us to do that."

"How will you feel tomorrow when you read those big, black headlines saying that Lyndon Johnson died in George Brown's house without a doctor?"

When the doctor arrived, he correctly diagnosed a coronary occlusion. Pointing to Anderson, Johnson wisecracked: "The best diagnostician I know just told me that. Tell me something new." The doctor sent for an ambulance. Johnson again protested; he wanted to be driven back to Washington in his limousine. Nonsense, said Anderson, Brown, and the doctor. In a matter of minutes the still-protesting Johnson climbed into the ambulance.

He was rushed to Bethesda Naval Hospital, in the Maryland suburbs of Washington. Lady Bird Johnson, who had been at their home in Washington, was waiting at the hospital. So was Walter Jenkins, Johnson's faithful administrative assistant, note pad in hand. An expert at shorthand, Jenkins quickly recorded Johnson's instructions.

Johnson was wheeled into the high-speed elevator and taken up to the seventeenth floor. He was still able to banter. Remembering that Scogna, an exclusive Washington tailor, was making two suits for him, one brown, one blue, he told Lady Bird Johnson: "Tell Scogna to go ahead with the blue. I'll need it whichever way it goes." And then Johnson went into deep shock—and into the battle for his life.

Only when the President of the United States suffered a heart attack a few months later in September, 1955, would the shockwaves travel faster or penetrate more deeply than they did on that Saturday evening when the news of Johnson's seizure was announced. The intense concern, bannered in headlines from one side of the country to the other, was no conventional reaction to the sudden illness of a public figure. It went far deeper. It was a practical concern over the fate of the Senate, and of the entire Democratic Congress, without Lyndon Johnson.

In the White House, President Eisenhower made anxious inquiries. Eisenhower, driving to Bethesda on July 15 to spend fifteen minutes with the Senator, was one of Johnson's first visitors. On July 30 Eisenhower dispatched Vice-President Nixon to give Johnson a one-hour briefing on foreign affairs. And the Senate, as though reeling from a blow, found itself unable to proceed as before. Without Johnson driving it from one bill to the next, the Senate quickly reverted to its accustomed languor. The adjournment, confidently expected within a couple of weeks, was pushed back to August 2.

Yet Lyndon Johnson had been serving just six months in a post that for nearly two decades had enjoyed little prestige and even less power. Why, then, was the illness of the new Majority Leader treated as a national calamity?

Johnson made a remarkable recovery from his heart attack, medically designated as "moderately severe." Once out of the oxygen tent, he was soon trying to run the Senate by remote control from Bethesda—and outflanking Republicans. On July 21, during the Summit Conference in Geneva (which Johnson had helped promote), Assistant Secretary of State Thruston Morton, congressional liaison man for the State Department, went to his fellow Kentuckian, Acting Majority Leader Earle Clements, for advice. Would Johnson like a briefing on Eisenhower's forthcoming "Open Skies" proposal (to permit worldwide aerial inspection) so that he could make a statement on it? Or was he still too sick to see Morton? Clements telephoned Lady Bird Johnson and asked her. Knowing how isolated her husband felt at Bethesda, Mrs. Johnson got the doctor's approval and told Clements: yes, by all means send Morton out.

After the briefing by Morton, Johnson immediately dictated a lengthy statement applauding Eisenhower's Open Skies proposal. He instructed Clements to read it to the Senate in Johnson's name the instant Eisenhower formally made his proposal in Geneva. As a result, the hospitalized Johnson's statement was the first by any congressional figure. Senator William Knowland, the Minority Leader, was beaten to the punch, and Johnson again captured the headlines.

On August 7, Johnson's doctors allowed him to leave the hospital and go home to 4921 Thirtieth Place in northwest Washington. There, propped up in a huge leather chair with a reclining back, Johnson began to receive his friends, gradually expanding his circle to include a few reporters.

In each case the ritual was the same. He produced doctors' reports showing to the ounce his weight that morning, the exact calorie intake, meal by meal, the number of trips he was allowed from bed to chair, his precise time for napping in the afternoon and for going to sleep at night, his cardiogram. Johnson was organizing himself for the long pull back to complete health. And by early autumn, having left Washington for his ranch in Texas and the final stage of recuperation, Johnson left no doubt in anyone's mind that he would be back in the Senate when the second session of the 84th Congress convened in January.

But Johnson's recuperation was not an easy one. His father had died of a heart attack in his early sixties, and Johnson, when he was tired and depressed, used to comment that a similar fate probably awaited him. In the post-heart-attack depression that always afflicts a coronary victim, he sometimes mused aloud about retiring from politics at the end of his term in 1960. When a British reporter naïvely took the rumors of a Johnson retirement seriously and wrote about it, the British Foreign Office panicked and sent an urgent cable to its embassy in Washington asking for verification or denial.

In fact, Johnson's heart attack, far from shortening his political life, lengthened it. He was forced into a new way of life. He stopped smoking. He was under strict orders to eat a hot lunch—and at *lunch*time—not a cold hamburger at four o'clock. He counted his calories, reduced his consumption of Scotch, reduced his weight by thirty-five pounds, and flew to the LBJ Ranch for regular vacations. And the political impact of his heart attack was muted by President Eisenhower's own severe coronary thrombosis in September and re-election a year later.

It remains remarkable, however, that the illness of a Senate Majority Leader could have caused so much concern. The explanation lies in a parliamentary phenomenon known as the Johnson System.

The new Senate force *implicit* in Johnson's two years as Minority Leader (culminating in McCarthy's censure) became *explicit* when Johnson took over as Majority Leader, with narrow Democratic control of the Senate, after the 1954 elections. George A. Smathers, the debonair young Senator from Florida (who was only dimly aware of Johnson's presence when they served together in the House), years later described Johnson's presence in the Senate as "a great, overpowering thunderstorm that consumed you as it closed in around you." Bryce Harlow, who twice had turned down job offers from Johnson and by now was President Eisenhower's chief congressional lobbyist, perceived in Majority Leader Johnson "a new hauteur" that made him scarcely recognizable to Harlow and other old friends in the House a decade before. Charles Watkins, the sage parliamentarian of the Senate, watched a new force at work in the Senate. Not long after Johnson became Majority Leader, Watkins remarked: "Lyndon's passed bills in a few days that I thought would take weeks. He does more buttonholing and going around than anyone I've ever seen."

Smathers, Harlow, and Watkins each was describing in his own way the Johnson System by which the young Senator from Texas stretched the limits of the Majority Leader's inherently meager power to unimagined boundaries.

The informal directorate of the Senate, headed by Richard B. Russell, insensibly yielded operational control and power to Johnson. It was a remarkable surrender considering that the power ratio of the Senate—evenly divided between Republicans and Democrats, ideologically weighted in favor of the conservatives—was unchanged from the earlier postwar years and was not to be altered until the 1958 elections. When Smathers, Harlow, and Watkins—and many others as well—described the momentous changes of the Senate in terms of Lyndon Johnson's personality, they reported the surprising truth. For the Johnson System was a highly personalized, intensive system of Senate rule adaptable to no successor. Because it involved so little institutional change, the Johnson System vanished overnight once Lyndon B. Johnson himself left the Senate. It was as though it had never existed.

Through most of its history, the Senate had been a cockpit of debaters—Websters and Calhouns, La Follettes and Tafts. Only twice before Johnson's rule had a Majority Leader achieved real power and control. The first occasion was a two-year reign by the imperious Republican aristocrat, Nelson W. Aldrich of Rhode Island, in 1908 and 1909. Under Aldrich, the majority leadership reached its peak of institutional authority. Aldrich had sole power to name all members of standing committees—a power destined for short life in a feudal-like institution whose members possessed baronial equality. Not until the long tenure of Democrat Joseph Robinson of Arkansas—Minority Leader from 1923 to 1928 and Majority Leader from 1928 to 1937—was the Senate again brought under tight control. Robinson utilized his personal authority, born of fourteen years as party floor leader, to compensate for his lack of institutionalized power.

Lacking both Aldrich's institutional power and Robinson's long tenure, Johnson had to concoct his own System. Highly personalized and instinctive as it was, the Johnson System stemmed from no grand master-plan or tightly organized chart. Simply stated, the System can be broken down into two interlocking components: the Johnson Network and the Johnson Procedure. The Network was the source of Johnson's power, the tool essential to put into effect the Procedure that enabled one man to tame the Senate and bring it under control for the first time in eighteen years.

J. Allen Frear, a Delaware farmboy who became a successful smalltown, pint-sized banker in Dover, Delaware, was elected to the United States Senate in 1948 and served two terms there before his defeat in 1960. Obscured by his luminous fellow Democrats in the Class of '48, Frear's trademark was his piercing, high-pitched response to Senate roll calls (much to the amusement of the galleries). Otherwise, he was invisible. Nevertheless, this pleasant little nobody became an important link in the Johnson Network.

At heart a conservative Democrat, Frear generally voted the conservative position—unless Lyndon Johnson wanted him to vote otherwise. Almost without exception, Frear's vote—or non-vote—was Johnson's for the asking, a fact abundantly clear to the astonished gallery in 1959 during the debate on a tax bill. Johnson was supporting an amendment to repeal special tax advantages for dividend income put into law by the Republican-controlled Congress of 1954. In a rare miscalculation, Johnson had miscounted the vote and when the roll call was completed, he found himself beaten by a single vote, 41 to 40. Frear had shrieked "no" on the amendment. Unsolicited by Johnson, he voted as a Delaware conservative. But now Johnson shouted across the Senate floor to Frear: "Change your vote!" Surprised, almost stunned by the command, Frear hesitated. Johnson shouted again, "Change your vote!" Frear did, and the amendment carried.

Indispensable to the Johnson System were generous rewards for consistent good conduct. While distinguished economist Paul Douglas spent years angrily and anxiously waiting for a seat on the tax-writing Finance Committee, Frear went on it quickly (as well as onto the Banking and Currency Committee). Moreover, Johnson did all in his power for Frear's pet bill: a tax-relief measure for Delaware's dominating industry, E. I. Du Pont de Nemours & Company. Du Pont's request was opposed even by the conservative Treasury Department of the Eisenhower Administration.

Most members of the Johnson Network were not so faithful as Allen Frear. He was the ideal, not a typical, member of the Network—a collection of Republicans and Democrats, Northerners and Southerners, liberals and conservatives, great figures and mediocrities. In varying degree, Johnson could count on them all for help.

At the core of the Johnson Network were his peers—Senate grandees to whom he turned more for advice than for votes. Richard Russell, of course; Clinton Anderson; Styles Bridges, the Senate's senior Republican; and—one to whom he turned far more often than most realized—his old seat-mate from the Class of '48, Robert S. Kerr. Sometimes unsure of himself on the fine points of complex bills, Johnson often picked Kerr's retentive brain. Once when White House officials traveled secretly to Capitol Hill to give Johnson a confidential advance peek at a new Eisenhower farm bill, they were taken aback to find Kerr waiting for them with Johnson.

Essential to the Johnson Network was the informal, uncoordinated system of lieutenants that he established soon after becoming Majority Leader. Senator Earle Clements of Kentucky—now the Majority Whip—was general handyman and assistant to Johnson and was still able to move moderately well among all factions of Senate Democrats (though he had become increasingly distrusted by the liberals). Taking up that slack with the liberals was Senator Hubert Humphrey of Minnesota. By 1955, though the general public and even much of the Senate failed to realize it, the one-time stereotype of ADA-style liberalism had become a full-fledged lieutenant of Lyndon Johnson. They still disagreed about many matters, just as Russell and Johnson often disagreed. But as much as Russell, though less openly, Humphrey was a Johnson man.

The most important of Johnson's lieutenants in 1955 was no Senator at all. Bobby G. Baker, now twenty-six, had been promoted to Secretary of the Senate Majority when the Democrats regained control in 1955, approved routinely by the Senate Democratic caucus on the Majority Leader's recommendation. Baker promptly remade that job to fit his own specifications, just as Johnson was remaking the majority leadership to fit his. Thus, a routine housekeeping sinecure became in Baker's hands—and with Johnson's blessing—a position of great authority. Mistakenly shrugged off for years by many Senators as a cloakroom chatterbox, Baker now began to eclipse Senator Clements himself as Johnson's top assistant. When Johnson was running the Senate from the Bethesda hospital bed after his heart attack, he relayed his instructions through Bobby Baker. The bouncy, ingratiating—and immensely able—young man from Pickens, South Carolina, came to be called "the ninety-seventh Senator" and "Lyndon, Jr."

When Clements was defeated by the Republican sweep in Kentucky in 1956, Johnson and Baker together cooked up a scheme intended to give further political substance to the system of lieutenants. Looking ahead to the civil rights fight certainly looming in 1957, Johnson and Baker agreed that the new whip should be a bona fide Southerner who would agree to a moderate civil rights bill. The only Senator who fit that description was Florida's handsome George Smathers, who was moving closer to Johnson in 1956. Smathers (who had earned the sobriquet "Gorgeous George") had informally filled in for Clements so that Clements could return to Kentucky to mend his fences in a futile effort to save himself in the 1956 election.

True, Johnson and Smathers as leader and whip would place two sons of the Confederacy in the Senate's two top Democratic leadership posts. But Johnson had a countervailing move. The third, and wholly honorific, position in the Senate's Democratic hierarchy, Secretary of the Conference (caucus), would go to Hubert Humphrey. Thus Humphrey would become a working member of the Democratic leadership, not only strengthening his tie to Johnson but giving the liberals their first man on the leadership ladder.

After the 1956 elections and Clements' defeat, Johnson summoned Smathers to a hotel suite in Washington (after first clearing his actions with the traveling Russell by long-distance telephone to Spain), and offered him the whip's job. Worried about the insatiable demands on his life inherent in getting that close to Johnson, Smathers did not flatly agree. But Baker, who had been urging Smathers for whip, was sure he could be persuaded and that the Senate Democratic caucus would approve him in January despite the misgivings the liberals would surely harbor. Moreover, Baker advised Johnson to disregard his old New Deal friends, who pleaded with him not to name Smathers. Though Smathers was a moderate by Southern standards, they simply could not forgive him for what they regarded as McCarthyite tactics against New Deal Senator Claude Pepper, unseated by Smathers in the bitter Florida Democratic primary of 1950.

The anti-Smathers opposition grew too influential for even Baker to overcome when Sam Rayburn joined it. The Speaker heartily disliked Smathers for his campaign against Pepper, and argued vigorously against appointing him whip. The dispute reached a climax on an airplane that both Johnson and Rayburn were taking to Texas. Before the plane left the gate at Washington's National Airport, Rayburn flatly informed Johnson that he could not appoint Smathers. Accordingly, Johnson left the plane and drove back into town to inform Smathers that the offer was withdrawn.

That unhappy episode dulled Johnson's enthusiasm for picking Clements' successor. There was one desultory conversation with Humphrey about becoming whip, but both knew that Russell and his Southerners would never accept Humphrey on the eve of the twentieth-century's greatest civil rights fight. By process of elimination, Johnson finally selected Mike Mansfield of Montana, a devoutly religious former professor of Oriental history who was more interested in the intrigues of Southeast Asia than those of the Senate cloakroom. With no thirst for power, Mansfield accepted only after much urging. He never became a genuine lieutenant of the Johnson Network in the way that Clements had been. He helped Johnson with all the routine chores, but stayed at arm's length from the center of Johnson operations.

With Mansfield as whip, it would have been hard to sell Humphrey to the South as Conference Secretary. Instead, the job went to ailing Senator Thomas Hennings of Missouri, assuring that the post would remain largely honorific. The failure of a strong Johnson-Smathers-Humphrey leadership team to emerge in 1957 had an unexpected result. It greatly enhanced Bobby Baker's position as Johnson's Number One assistant and drew him still closer to the Majority Leader.

But the Johnson Network was not so much a system of lieutenants as of personal alliances that transcended partisan, ideological, and geographic lines. Johnson slowly built up a cadre of supporters who would vote for LBJ—even, on occasion, against their ideology, their conscience, and their political self-interest, depending on the issue and the Senator. . . . With other, less conspicuous members of the Network, they made up perhaps one-quarter of the Senate—more than enough to provide the balance of power on most issues.

To build his Network, Johnson stretched the meager power resources of the Majority Leader to the outer limit. The mightiest of these was his influence over committee assignments. Still, it was not comparable to the absolute power enjoyed by Nelson Aldrich a half century before. As chairman of the Democratic Steering Committee, Johnson steadily widened the breach in rigid seniority rules, working delicately with a surgical scalpel, not a stick of dynamite.

In January, 1955, his ally and adviser, Clinton Anderson, pressed his claim for an overdue assignment on either Foreign Relations or Finance. Each committee had one vacancy. But former Vice-President Alben Barkley, who had just returned to the Senate as a "freshman" from Kentucky in the 1954 elections, asked for the Finance Committee—a request that could scarcely be denied. A further complication was the still unresolved problem of Wayne Morse, the Oregon maverick who had bolted the Republican party in the 1952 campaign and, after two years in the political wilderness as an "Independent," now joined the Democratic caucus in 1955. Morse's decision was vital to Johnson. It provided him with the narrow one-vote margin he needed to cross the bridge, incalculably important in terms of power, from Minority Leader to Majority Leader. Thus, it was incumbent upon Johnson to give Morse a good committee assignment, and Morse wanted Foreign Relations.

Johnson duly explained these facts of life to Anderson, who agreed not to insist (as he well could have) on either Finance or Foreign Relations. But Johnson remembered his old friend's personal loyalty and, on a 1956 speaking engagement in New Mexico, he publicly—and unexpectedly—promised that Clint Anderson would become the next chairman of the Joint Atomic Energy Committee. That post, because of New Mexico's Los Alamos atomic installation, would solidly enhance Anderson's prestige. To make good his promise, Johnson was required to jump Anderson over none other than Richard Russell, who outranked Anderson on the joint committee.

The Foreign Relations maneuvers temporarily drew the sharp-tongued Morse to Johnson, in sharp contrast to a year earlier. In January, 1954, Morse had told an ADA Roosevelt Day Dinner in Texas: "Johnson has the most reactionary record in the Senate. Look at his voting record. If he should ever have a liberal idea, he would have a brain hemorrhage. . . ." But a little more than a year later, ensconced on the Foreign Relations Committee, Morse gently confided to the Senate: "During the past year, I have been the beneficiary of one kindness after another from Lyndon Johnson. I consider him not only a great statesman but a good man."

And as chairman of the Joint Atomic Energy Committee, Anderson was even more pleased than he would have been on Foreign Relations. The only grumbling over Johnson's ingenious shuffling came from Russell, who had not agreed in advance to step aside for Anderson. But the grumbling was private and soft, not public and bitter. Lyndon Johnson could count on Dick Russell not to make a public fuss about such matters.

Two years later, Anderson was the center of far more devious committee maneuvers by Johnson. After the presidential election of 1956, Estes Kefauver of Tennessee and John F. Kennedy of Massachusetts, who had competed on the National Convention floor at Chicago for the vice-presidential nomination the previous summer, were competing again— this time for a single vacancy on Foreign Relations. Johnson, who had backed Kennedy against Kefauver at Chicago, was now trying to bring Kennedy closer to his orbit. He was determined to have the vacancy go to Kennedy over Johnson's old foe, Kefauver. But how to get around Kefauver's four-year seniority bulge over Kennedy? In December, 1956, long before Congress convened, Johnson telephoned Anderson with a most curious question: "How are you getting along with your campaign for the Foreign Relations Committee?"

Anderson was puzzled. Could Johnson have forgotten that his "campaign" had ended two years earlier? But Johnson persisted.

"This may be your chance," he said.

Before Anderson could reply that he had his hands full as chairman of Atomic Energy, Johnson rushed on.

"You have seniority now over Jack Kennedy," Johnson explained. "But if you don't claim it, Estes Kefauver may get there first."

Johnson's ploy suddenly came through to Anderson. Both Anderson and Kefauver were members of the Class of '48, and therefore had equal seniority. If they both applied for the one vacancy on the Foreign Relations Committee, Johnson could throw up his hands in the Steering Committee, declare a standoff—and give the vacancy to Kennedy. Anderson went along with this neat strategy, and Kennedy was given the seat, just as Johnson wanted.

Johnson's use of power to influence committee assignments cut both ways. "Good" liberals, such as Humphrey, could be prematurely boosted into the Foreign Relations Committee, and a "bad" liberal, such as Kefauver, could be made to cool his heels for years. A "bad" liberal such as Paul Douglas could be barred from the Finance Committee for eight long years, while five fellow members of the Class of '48 (Kerr, Long, Frear, Anderson and Johnson himself) and one from the Class of '50 (Smathers) were finding places there. Senators who dared to function too far outside the Johnson Network waited long to get inside the prestige committees.

In these clandestine committee maneuvers, Johnson seldom exposed his hand. But in the routine committee shifts, he enjoyed wringing out the last drop of credit. One evening in early January, 1955, shortly after the committee assignments for the 84th Congress had been settled and announced, Johnson invited a couple of friends into his Majority Leader's office in the corner of the Capitol for a political bull session over Scotch and sodas. Nothing relaxed him more than these feet-up, hair-down chats. They invariably lasted well into the night and they invariably ended in long, often hilarious LBJ monologues, full of ribald yarns and racy mimicry.

Suddenly, he interrupted himself. "My God," he said, "I forgot to call Senator Stennis and congratulate him." Stennis had been valuable to Johnson a month earlier in the McCarthy censure fight, and now had just landed a coveted seat on the Appropriations Committee—thanks to Lyndon Johnson. Johnson reached over, cradled the phone between his shoulder and chin, and dialed.

Mrs. Stennis answered the phone, and the conversation commenced. "Ma'm, this is Lyndon Johnson, is your husband there? . . . He isn't? . . . Well, I must tell you, Ma'm, how proud I am of your husband and how proud the Senate is, and you tell him that when he gets home.

The Senate paid him a great honor today. The Senate elected your husband to the Appropriations Committee. That's one of the most powerful committees in the whole Senate and a great honor for your husband. I'm so proud of John. He's a great American. And I know you're proud of him, too. He's one of my finest Senators. . . ." Accompanying this monologue were nods and winks in the direction of Johnson's fascinated audience.

Johnson went on to tell Mrs. Stennis how the Steering Committee had selected her husband unanimously for the Appropriations spot and how the full Senate had unanimously concurred, but implicitly he was belaboring the obvious—that it wasn't the Steering Committee or the full Senate that really was responsible. It was LBJ.

Johnson quietly commandeered other bits and pieces of Senate patronage that previous Majority Leaders ignored. To cement his budding alliance with Senator Margaret Chase Smith, for instance, he arranged for a special staff member of the Senate Armed Services Committee to be appointed by her and to be responsible to her alone, even though she was a Republican on the Democratic-controlled committee, and only fourth-ranking Republican at that.

Although in the past, office space for Senators, a source of sometimes intense competition, had been distributed by strict seniority as a routine housekeeping chore of the Senate's Sergeant-at-Arms, Johnson quickly perceived its value as a weapon of influence and fitted it into his growing system of rewards and punishments. When Paul Douglas lost that top-floor Capitol office to Johnson in 1955, the Senate took notice. It was a dramatic sign of the consequences of a lack of rapport with the Majority Leader. Johnson skillfully exploited the gleaming New Senate Office Building in 1958, with its spanking new suites, as an inducement for help on the floor. Senator Mike Monroney of Oklahoma, sometimes troublesome for Johnson, was brought into line on one bill with the award of a handsome corner suite that Johnson knew Monroney coveted.

Johnson also kept his ears open to discover which Senator—or Senator's wife—was really anxious to go on which senatorial junket abroad. At a cocktail party early in 1957, Johnson was chatting with the wife of Frank Church, the young, newly elected liberal Democrat from Idaho. Mrs. Church innocently revealed that she had always wanted to see South America. Knowing that Frank Church might become a valuable addition to the Johnson Network, the Majority Leader saw to it that he was named to the very next delegation of Senators to visit South America.

Even before that, however, Frank Church had reason to be grateful to Lyndon Johnson. Bitterly opposed by the Idaho Power Company and other private-power interests because of his public-power stand, Church was hard-pressed for funds in his 1956 campaign for the Senate. He sent an S.O.S. to the Senate Democratic Campaign Committee in Washington. Senator Smathers, chairman of the Campaign Committee, was dubious about pouring money into what seemed a hopeless cause in a small Mountain State. But Johnson and Bobby Baker argued Church's cause, and their wishes prevailed.

De facto control of the Campaign Committee's funds was one of Johnson's least obvious but most effective tools in building his Network. He controlled the distribution of committee funds through both its chairman—first Earle Clements and later George Smathers—and through its secretary, Bobby Baker. More often than not, the requests for campaign funds were routinely made to Baker, and the money was physically distributed by him. Johnson further tightened his control when Clements was named the committee's executive director after his Senate defeat in 1956. Johnson got the most out of the committee's limited funds (at that time a mere four hundred thousand dollars) by shrewdly distributing them where they would do the most work. In the small Mountain States like Idaho, a ten-thousand-dollar contribution could change the course of an election. But in New York or Pennsylvania, ten thousand dollars was the merest drop in the bucket. Johnson and Baker tried to reduce contributions to Democrats in the industrial Northeast to the minimum. Since Senators seldom bite the hand that finances them, these Westerners were naturally drawn into the Johnson Network, while the Eastern liberals tended to remain outside.

But this ingenious stretching of the Majority Leader's limited stock of patronage could not by itself explain the brilliant success of the Johnson Network. The extra, indeed the dominant, ingredient was Johnson's overwhelming personality, reflected in what came to be known as "The Treatment."

The Treatment could last ten minutes or four hours. It came, enveloping its target, at the LBJ Ranch swimming pool, in one of LBJ's offices, in the Senate cloakroom, on the floor of the Senate itself—wherever Johnson might find a fellow Senator within his reach. Its tone could be supplication, accusation, cajolery, exuberance, scorn, tears, complaint, the hint of threat. It was all of these together. It ran the gamut of human emotions. Its velocity was breathtaking, and it was all in one direction. Interjections from the target were rare. Johnson anticipated them before they could be spoken. He moved in close, his face a scant millimeter from his target, his eyes widening and narrowing, his eyebrows rising and falling. From his pockets poured clippings, memos, statistics. Mimicry, humor, and the genius of analogy made The Treatment an almost hypnotic experience and rendered the target stunned and helpless.

In 1957, when Johnson was courting the non-Senate Eastern liberal establishment, he summoned historian and liberal theoretician Arthur Schlesinger, Jr., down from his classroom at Harvard. Wary at the prospect of his first prolonged meeting with Johnson (whom he suspected of disdaining the liberal cause), Schlesinger had in his mind a long list of questions to ask Johnson. Never known for shyness, Schlesinger was nevertheless on his guard when he entered Johnson's Capitol office and sat in front of the great man's desk.

The Treatment began immediately: a brilliant, capsule characterization of every Democratic Senator: his strengths and failings, where he fit into the political spectrum; how far he could be pushed, how far pulled; his hates, his loves. And who (he asked Schlesinger) must oversee all these prima donnas, put them to work, knit them together, know when to tickle this one's vanity, inquire of that one's health, remember this one's five o'clock nip of Scotch, that one's nagging wife? Who must find the hidden legislative path between the South and the North, the public power men and the private power men, the farmers' men and the unions' men, the bomber-boys and the peace lovers, the eggheads and the fatheads? Nobody but Lyndon Johnson.

Imagine a football team (Johnson hurried on) and I'm the coach, and I'm also the quarterback. I have to call the signals, and I have to center the ball, run the ball, pass the ball. I'm the blocker (he rose out of his chair and threw an imaginary block). I'm the tackler (he crouched and tackled). I'm the passer (he heaved a mighty pass). I have to catch the pass (he reached and caught the pass).

Schlesinger was sitting on the edge of his chair, both fascinated and amused. Here was a view of the Senate he had never seen before.

Johnson next ticked off all the bills he had passed that year, how he'd gotten Dick Russell on this one, Bob Kerr on that one, Hubert Humphrey on another. He reached into his desk drawer and out came the voting record of New Jersey's Clifford Case, a liberal Republican. You liberals, he told Schlesinger, are always talking about my record. You wouldn't question Cliff Case's record, would you? And he ran down the list and compared it to his voting record. Whatever Johnson had on those two lists, he came out with a record more liberal than Case's.

Johnson had anticipated and answered all of Schlesinger's questions. The leader rolled on, reiterating a theme common to The Treatment of that time. He'd had his heart attack, he said, and he knew he'd never be President. He wasn't made for the presidency. If only the Good Lord would just give him enough time to do a few more things in the Senate. Then he'd go back to Texas. That's where he belonged.

Breathless now, ninety minutes later, Schlesinger said good-by and groped his way out of Johnson's office. Eight years later, he was to record his impressions. Johnson had been "a good deal more attractive, more subtle, and more formidable than I expected." And, he might have added, vastly more entertaining.

The Treatment was designed for a single target or, at most an audience of three or four. In large groups, what was witty sounded crude, what was expansive became arrogant. It was inevitable, then, that when Johnson allowed The Treatment to dominate his "press conferences" a sour note entered his relations with the press. Reporters en masse didn't like being on the receiving end of The Treatment. Johnson's failure to understand that annoyed the press, which in turn made Johnson increasingly wary and suspicious. Unable to tame the press as he tamed so many Senators, he foolishly took offense at routine questions, and was quick to find a double meaning in the most innocent point raised by a reporter. Although Senate reporters and Washington's top columnists were captivated in their *private* sessions with Johnson in his office or at the LBJ Ranch, his press conferences were fiascoes. They simply could not be harnessed to The Treatment.

One additional bit of Johnson glue held his Network together. Whenever a seventy-five-cent cigar came his way, Johnson would not forget to stick it in his pocket and save it for Senator Carl Hayden of Arizona, a notorious cigar-chomper and chairman of the Senate Appropriations Committee. When William Knowland became a grandfather for the fourth time, Johnson took the floor of the Senate to make the event a historical footnote in the *Congressional Record*. When the wife of Felton (Skeeter) Johnston, a veteran Senate employee who became Secretary of the Senate in 1955, went to the hospital for major surgery, Lyndon Johnson offered to help pay the bill. These small favors and courtesies were elaborately planned by Johnson and graciously carried out. They built Johnson a bottomless reservoir of good will.

Johnson's meticulous attention to such details predated his Senate leadership. In 1952, Westwood, the only daughter of Virginia's Senator Harry Byrd, met a tragic death. Johnson drove from Washington to Winchester, Virginia, for the funeral. As Johnson told the story in 1955, he was amazed to discover that he was the only Senator present. The courtly old Virginian was deeply touched. When Johnson sought Byrd's vote on a labor issue years later, it was Byrd who recalled the funeral and gave Johnson his vote.

While constructing his elaborate Network, the Majority Leader was also building the largest staff ever assembled by a single Senator. Each of the many hats worn by Johnson—Senator from Texas, Senate Majority Leader, chairman of the Democratic Policy Committee, chairman of the Democratic Conference, chairman of the Democratic Steering Committee, chairman of the Defense Preparedness Subcommittee, chairman of the Appropriations Subcommittee on the State, Commerce and Justice Departments, and (after 1958) chairman of the new Space Committee—each of these hats entitled him to government-paid employees.

Despite the size of this little bureaucracy, the weakest element in the Johnson System was his staff. Throughout his Senate career, he maintained a stable, highly successful relationship with only two staff aides: Walter Jenkins and Bobby Baker.

Jenkins joined Johnson in 1939 fresh from the University of Texas, and except for an unsuccessful race for Congress in a special Texas election in September, 1951, stayed for twenty-five years. He became Johnson's invaluable first assistant, the steadiest rock on the staff. Jenkins ruled the "Texas office" (Johnson's suite in the Senate Office Building, devoted to Texas affairs, which Johnson seldom visited), but was given highly confidential duties that ranged far afield. He was general office manager, personnel chief, private secretary, shorthand stenographer, and errand boy. Johnson rattled off daily chores, from trivial to top secret, and the uncomplaining, unsmiling Jenkins would jot them down in shorthand and get them accomplished, Privy to every scheme in Johnson's brain, Walter Jenkins never complained about his sixteen-hour days, the abuse the Senator would sometimes fling out to relieve his own tension, or the assignment of the most menial chores. The single clue to the suppressed emotional turbulence inside this devoted poker-faced servant were periodic attacks of a skin rash.

Johnson's other staff intimate was Jenkins' antithesis. Bobby Baker was a natural-born politician who wore his moods on his face: he was gregarious, glad-handing, gossipy, and smart as a fox. If Jenkins would have lost his right arm before revealing a secret Johnson scheme, Baker gloried in passing juicy tidbits to his friends in the Senate and among the press, not to damage but to advance the Majority Leader's objective.

Moreover, the Johnson-Baker relationship was altered subtly by the fact that Baker was technically an employee not of Johnson himself but of all the Democratic Senators. This partially explained why there was about Baker none of the hangdog look of the discreet servant that distinguished Walter Jenkins and most of Johnson's own staff. Baker talked out on his own and on occasion even talked back to Johnson, as one day when Johnson halted a reporter in the reception room just off the Senate floor and upbraided him about a story published that morning. Baker listened for a moment, then interrupted. "Now, Senator, that's silly," he said. "You shouldn't say that. That was a damn good story and you ought to appreciate it." To most members of Johnson's regular staff, talk like that was beyond imagining.

Staff became a deepening problem for Johnson. A select band of informal advisers—James Rowe, Donald Cook, Horace Busby—simply declined to serve him on a permanent basis. They knew all too well that Johnson staffers were literally on call around-the-clock. A private life was out of the question. Johnson spent every waking moment on politics and government and demanded no less from his staff.

But unwillingness to serve Johnson stemmed from more than mere hours of work. Johnson had an unfortunate tendency to waste talent, to assign highly priced and highly educated assistants to menial chores. By 1956, Gerald Siegel was overburdened as counsel of the Democratic Policy Committee and badly needed help. With Johnson's approval, he found and hired an exceptional young lawyer from East Texas named Harry McPherson. McPherson wanted to be a poet, but the McCarthy era so outraged him that he switched to the law to fight McCarthyism. McPherson was an idealist and a humanist with imaginative, sensitive intelligence and a quiet competence.

When he arrived in Washington in the spring of 1956, Johnson was in the midst of an ambitious but incredible project to send a letter of congratulation to every high school graduate in the state of Texas that June. McPherson's first job for his new boss in Washington was to man a bank of robot-typewriters, typing out one address after another manually and then feeding in the tape of a form letter, night after night, sending Johnson's congratulations to all the senior class members in Texas. That set a pattern. McPherson's talent was not really tapped by Johnson for a decade, when he was added to the White House staff.

The experience of Lloyd Hand, another young Texan brought to Washington by Johnson in 1957, was somewhat similar. A University of Texas student leader who worked on the 1948 Johnson Senate campaign, Hand came to Johnson's Washington office in 1957 with strong hints of a high position. When he reported for duty, Johnson handed him a couple of books by Winston Churchill. That's how I want my speeches to come out, he told Hand. And Hand went to work writing, but scarcely for Churchillian occasions. Johnson assigned him to reply to Texas constituents who sent their problems to their Senator. He was placed in the "Texas office" under Walter Jenkins and never did have a chance to do the job he was hired to do: write LBJ speeches.

Johnson was a ruthless taskmaster. No one who worked for him escaped entirely the slashing rebukes that, in impatience or fatigue, he administered. Later, he would seek to compensate by acts of kindness. But no one was immune, even though others—Senators or reporters—might be present. During one of those unfortunate "press conferences" in his office, Johnson pulled open his desk drawer to read a memorandum carefully prepared for just that occasion. Halfway through, he discovered to his embarrassment that he was reading the wrong memorandum. Embarrassment quickly became rage. He turned on Gerry Siegel, his efficient legal aide, and loudly berated him for his stupidity. The reporters stared, incredulity in their eyes. Siegel, who deeply admired Johnson, candidly told him later that such outbursts did not hurt Gerald Siegel, but did hurt Lyndon Johnson. Other aides were not so philosophical, however, and even Siegel twice resigned from Johnson's staff to return to private employment during a three-year period.

A dreary pattern marked Johnson's recruitment of his staff. First, ardent wooing of the prospective aide—flattery, appeals to conscience and patriotism, promises of rewarding opportunities for public service. Occasionally this variation of The Treatment spilled over beyond the day that the prospective aide went on the payroll but not for long. More likely, the moment Johnson made his conquest the value of the new aide depreciated. Now that he was bound to Johnson, there was no longer any need to woo him. As inevitable disagreements arose, Johnson invariably became disillusioned with his new acquisition. No one was fired, but middle-level aides recruited with rosy promises of great days ahead were often exiled to drudgery in the "Texas office" under Walter Jenkins' stern eye.

Moreover, internal stresses and rivalries unsettled the Johnson staff in the mid-1950s. A nasty feud developed between Bobby Baker and George Reedy, the affable ex-newspaperman who now held the title of staff director of the Democratic Policy Committee but in fact was an idea man responsible for press relations and speech-writing. Simultaneously, the size of Johnson's overall staff was reaching such proportions that there was a vital need for a chief to pull and hold it together and coordinate the Senator's spreading operations beyond Jenkins' private domain in the "Texas office."

And so in 1956, Johnson laid siege to the man he wanted as chief of staff: James Rowe, Franklin D. Roosevelt's brilliant young aide of the late 1930s who had helped draw Johnson into the New Deal orbit and maintained his friendship for two decades. Johnson asked Rowe to run the staff of the Policy Committee and take charge of policy matters. But Rowe was profitably engaged in a successful Washington law practice with his famous White House colleague of New Deal days, Thomas G. (Tommy the Cork) Corcoran, and he had no desire to return to public life.

Whereupon Johnson set in motion a subtle, implacable campaign of indirection. Tommy Corcoran urgently pressed Rowe to help out Lyndon, for old-time's sake if nothing else. Lyndon needs you, said Corcoran. A third White House insider of the New Deal era, Ben Cohen, telephoned Rowe with the admonition that he was obligated to help Johnson. Then Rowe's wife, Elizabeth, astonished her husband one day with an appeal of her own: give Lyndon Johnson a hand. Feeling like an ingrate with his law partner, his valued old friend, and his wife all pressing on him with the same advice, Rowe succumbed.

He offered to work for Johnson two days a week. Not enough. Four days? No, said Johnson, he wanted Rowe full time, In fact, he went on, Rowe should resign from his law firm. Rowe protested. Johnson, sensing victory, offered personally to call up Rowe's clients to explain. With tears now welling from his eyes, Johnson begged and cajoled. How badly he needed Rowe! Rowe finally surrendered.

The mood changed abruptly. Away went the tears. "Don't forget," Johnson told Rowe, "*I'll* make the decisions."

The Johnson-Rowe friendship was old and strong enough to survive 1956, but Rowe's brief tenure on the Johnson staff was less than entirely happy or successful. He never really did become the boss of the Johnson staff, and in less than a year he was back with his law firm.

Johnson next turned to Colonel Kenneth E. BeLieu, who as chief clerk of the Senate Armed Services Committee had worked closely and amicably with Johnson for the past eight years. A fifteen-year career Army officer with a distinguished battle record who was retired with war wounds (he lost a leg in Korea), BeLieu was now asked by Johnson to put his crumbling staff in order by succeeding Rowe as chief of staff of the Policy Committee. With some misgivings BeLieu accepted—only to find himself without authority and with only minimal contact with Johnson himself. Before the year was over, he returned to the Armed Services Committee.

From then on, Johnson operated without a chief of staff and turned more and more to outside advisers, particularly drawing for advice on an informal three-man board composed of three of Washington's highest priced lawyers—Jim Rowe, Abe Fortas, and Clark Clifford. They met about once a month in Johnson's house. Other Washington veterans of the political scene were also frequently consulted, and the more saga- cious members of the Johnson Network in the Senate—Kerr, Russell, Anderson—were always on tap for advice.

Although this overlapping directorate of unofficial advisers and consultants was not the same as a well-structured staff with sparkling morale, the fact is that the Johnson System, as contrasted to the Johnson staff, was such a smashing success that the lack of a cohesive staff was scarcely noticed. The implications of its absence were to become clear only years later. . . .

At the opening of the 1951 Senate session, when Richard Russell named Lyndon Johnson as floor manager of the universal military train- ing bill (his first major floor assignment), the Senate could justly claim itself to be "the world's greatest deliberative body." The Korean War was raging, and President Truman badly needed passage of the bill to bring the armed forces to full strength. But the Senate took its time, as it had since its earliest days. Debate on the bill—stretching from February 27 to

March 9—had the urgency of a chess game at an exclusive men's club. There was an unhurried discursive tone as the learned Senators— Richard Russell, Wayne Morse, Robert Taft, Henry Cabot Lodge, Herbert Lehman—probed every corner of the bill. The sessions seldom ran beyond six o'clock in the evening, and the chamber was closed over the weekends. Senator Ernest McFarland, the Majority Leader, tried to hurry the Senate along, but he wasn't overly concerned by the languorous pace or the frequency and uncertainty of roll calls on amendments. As floor manager of the bill, Johnson naturally joined in debate, delivering long, rambling speeches. But Johnson did not enter the game with the zest of a Taft or Russell. He seemed impatient with this kind of Senate.

The Senate had always been that way, even in the days of Nelson Aldrich and Joe Robinson. In 1883 the young Woodrow Wilson wrote of the Senate in *Congressional Government:*

> It must be regarded as no inconsiderable addition to the usefulness of the Senate that it enjoys a much greater freedom of discussion than the House can allow itself. It permits itself a good deal of talk in public about what it is doing, and it commonly talks a great deal of sense.

But it would not be hurried, and, without a rule of germaneness, it could not stick to the point, as Senator Lester Hunt of Wyoming perceived in 1952, on the eve of the Johnson System. Hunt complained: "Any state legislature in the United States would make the Senate of the United States look very bad in connection with procedure." Indeed, the "procedure" of the Senate was geared to slow talk, not vital action.

Johnson was quite aware that he could never establish an efficient procedure by modernizing the encrusted Senate rules. His only recourse, then, as the new Majority Leader, was by trial and error, to evolve slowly the Johnson Procedure—along with the Network, the second major component of the Johnson System.

The principal ingredient of the Procedure was flexibility. On any major piece of legislation, never make a commitment as to what will pass; determine in advance what is *possible* under the best of circumstances for the Senate to accept; after making this near-mathematical determination, don't reveal it; keep the leader's intentions carefully masked; then, exploiting the Johnson Network, start rounding up all detachable votes; when all is in readiness, strike quickly and pass the bill with a minimum of debate.

Essential to making the Johnson Procedure work in this fashion was divided government: a Democratic Majority Leader and a Republican President. Freed of obligation to shepherd a White House program through a Democratic Senate (because the White House was in Republican hands), Johnson could hold his own cards and play his own game. Although divided government had come to Washington before, as recently as the Republican 80th Congress of 1947–48 under President Truman, no previous leader in a divided government had had Johnson's political wit. Besides, Johnson genuinely wanted to *pass* bills, not just block everything sent up by the Republican President.

Johnson had another advantage: the Johnson Intelligence System. Unlike his predecessors, Johnson was constantly probing beneath the Senate's bland exterior to discover what the Senate was really thinking. The Intelligence System was a marvel of efficiency. It was also rather frightening. One evening in the late 1950s, Senator Thruston Morton of Kentucky (the Republican who defeated Earle Clements in 1956) dined with seven political reporters at the Metropolitan Club. The meeting was off-the-record. The reporters had been working as a team for several years. All were sworn to secrecy, and there had never been a leak. Morton laid bare some fascinating behind-the-scenes divisions in the Republican party. A few days later, one of the reporters called on Johnson in his Capitol office. Johnson bitterly chided him and the Washington press corps for writing column after column about the divisions in the Democratic party while ignoring internal tensions in the Republican party. To prove his point, Johnson dipped into one of the deep wire baskets on his desk and fished out a memorandum on the "confidential" Morton session—complete in every detail.

The thoroughness of Johnson's Intelligence System worried his fellow Senators, some of whom began to half doubt the security of their own telephone conversations. But Johnson needed no help from electronic eavesdropping. His intelligence had a dazzling multiplicity of sources tucked away in surprising places all over Washington. Bobby Baker and his team of cloakroom attendants were in constant touch and conversation with Senators. Johnson's staff was alert to report what they heard on the floor from other Senators and their staffs. The Johnson Network of friendly Senators kept him informed. Johnson himself was constantly probing and questioning other Senators in the cloakrooms, over late-afternoon drinks, during hamburger lunches in his office: Occasionally aides of other Senators were invited to lunch with the Majority Leader. Immensely flattered, they eagerly volunteered what they—and more important, what their bosses—were thinking.

Speaker Rayburn and the Texas congressional delegation kept Johnson fully informed about what was going on inside the House. Beyond this, moreover, Johnson had loyal friends scattered throughout the government agencies who regularly tipped him on developments.

Johnson took special precautions to maintain a flow of intelligence about the activities of liberal Democrats, his greatest source of trouble in the Senate. Gerry Siegel and later Harry McPherson, his two most liberal staff members, kept lines open to staff members of liberal Senators and sometimes liberal Senators themselves. Robert Oliver, the United Auto Workers staff member from Texas who had maneuvered the CIO behind Johnson in his 1948 campaign and who was now Walter Reuther's chief lobbyist in Washington, was in constant touch with both Johnson and the liberals. But the most important conduit to the liberals was Hubert Humphrey. Johnson had such intimate knowledge of liberal battle plans to reform Rule XXII (the filibuster rule) in January, 1957, that liberals suspected a leak in their own camp. Specifically, they suspected that Humphrey, Bob Oliver, or possibly both were passing word of their secret meetings to the Majority Leader.

The distillation of intelligence was the head count—the report on how each Senator would vote on a given issue. This delicate judgment of each Senator's intentions was entrusted to Bobby Baker, who compiled the famous head counts in their final form. Baker's head counts were an invaluable asset for Johnson not available to labor, to business, to the Republicans, or even to the White House. Baker's invariably precise count not only gave Johnson the odds on a bill, but what votes he had to switch. This enabled Johnson to energize the Network and get a sufficient number of Senators to change their votes, or at least arrange for Network Senators who opposed the Johnson position to linger in the cloakroom while the roll was called. Johnson controlled the speed of the actual roll call by signaling the reading clerk—slowing it down until the Senator with the deciding vote (on Johnson's side, of course) entered the chamber, then speeding it up (by a quick rotary movement of his forefinger) when the votes he needed were in hand.

Very infrequently the Johnson-Baker count would be off by a single tally. Perhaps an anti-Johnson Senator would return unexpectedly from out of town to vote. If that happened, Johnson would flash an S.O.S. to the cloakroom and a Network Senator would emerge, then signal the reading clerk that he wanted to cast his vote and tip the balance to Johnson.

That was the dramatic culmination of the Johnson Procedure. Never had a Majority Leader maintained so precise a check on the preferences and the possibilities of every colleague. But inherent in the Johnson Procedure were basic changes in the daily operation of the Senate, changes emanating from the personality of the Majority Leader and evolving so slowly that they were ignored by the public and scarcely recognized in the Senate itself. Yet they were insensibly transforming the Senate. No longer was it the deliberative body described by Woodrow Wilson in 1883 and found relatively intact when Lyndon Johnson arrived in 1949.

These were the mechanical devices of the Johnson Procedure that transformed the Senate:

Unanimous Consent. This was merely a matter of getting all Senators to agree in advance to debate a bill for a fixed time and then to vote. It had always been used in the Senate, but used sparingly and mostly for minor bills.

Johnson transmogrified this occasional procedural device into a way of life. He applied it to every major bill. And so, gradually, attention and interest deserted the once stately public debate and centered on the cloakroom where Johnson, in nose-to-nose negotiations, hammered out his unanimous consent agreements to limit debate. Sometimes these were extremely complex, containing an intricate maze of provisos and codicils.

Occasionally Johnson forged a unanimous consent agreement adhered to by all interested parties (or so he thought), only to hear one maverick Senator (perhaps emboldened by too many nips from the bottle) shout "no" when the agreement was formally offered, thereby depriving Johnson of his unanimous consent. Angry at being crossed, Johnson would storm into the cloakroom and when the glass door had swung shut, would let himself go with an angry soliloquy against the nonconformist who was well beyond hearing on the Senate floor. Then, composing himself, the glass door would swing open and Johnson would return to the floor, drape his arm around the offender, find the cause for objection (perhaps nothing more than a desire to make an extra two-hour speech), satisfy him—and then propound another unanimous consent request to the Senate. He seldom was turned down twice on one bill.

Thus did Lyndon Johnson revolutionize the Senate, severely modifying its proud heritage of unlimited debate without changing a single rule. Of course, the filibuster was still available as an ultimate weapon. And of course any Senator could block unanimous consent and keep the debate going. In fact, however, few did. Debates grew shorter—and ever less important.

Aborted Quorum Calls. When Johnson first arrived at the Senate, the Majority Leader still followed the ancient practice of demanding that a quorum of Senators (forty-nine out of ninety-six) be on the floor for an important debate. As Majority Leader, Johnson demanded more and more quorum calls—but with a new purpose: to fill gaps in the Johnson schedule. Instead of recessing the Senate for an hour or two as in the past, Johnson would ask for a quorum call and wait, sometimes for close to an hour, while the reading clerk droned slowly through the names. Then, when Johnson was ready for the Senate to resume, he would suspend the calling of the roll. These aborted quorum calls held the Senate in suspended animation while Johnson worked out his deals in the cloakroom. Soon, nobody answered the quorum calls. The ever-increasing proportion of the Senate's day spent in meaningless recital of names of Senators who did not bother to answer was a symbol of the decay of Senate debate under the Johnson Procedure.

Night Sessions. In the 1920s, the Senate recessed for luncheon and then returned in the afternoon for more debate. That leisurely practice ended long before Johnson's arrival. But before the Johnson Procedure was instituted, the Senate session was a civilized twelve noon to five o'clock, except under extraordinary conditions.

Johnson changed that. When a debate neared completion, he drove the Senate into night session—beyond nine o'clock, to eleven, to midnight. Late hours, he shrewdly calculated, dulled the desire for debate. With senatorial brains addled by fatigue and generous libations poured in anterooms, combativeness diminished. The Senator who was ready to fight Johnson at three o'clock on this line until the snows came was only too ready by midnight to accept a unanimous consent agreement—*any* unanimous consent agreement—if only he could go home to bed. By driving the Senate into night sessions, the Johnson Procedure further reduced and deadened debate.

Stop-and-Go. Born of necessity after his heart attack, this technique became a positive asset to Johnson. Because doctor's order's called for Johnson to make frequent rest trips back to the LBJ Ranch, he compressed packets of complex legislation into a single week or so, then let the Senate limp along with little or no business (under the loose guidance of the Majority Whip). As the years passed, Johnson out of choice began to legislate in bursts of activity followed by spells of torpor—even when he was not home in Texas.

In 1959, Johnson brought this technique to perfection. He drove the Senate into passing important bills on January 5 and 6 during two long sessions. Next followed a lull to March 11 in which the Senate was virtually inoperative. Johnson then harassed the Senate to overtime work and passed four bills between March 11 and 23. Two bills were passed in April, two in late May and then quiet, until a frenetic burst of activity between June 25 and July 9 brought the Senate to the point of exhaustion with the passage of four major bills. Again a long pause, then the frenzied session-end burst of activity with five bills passed between September 5 and 14.

Stop-and-go was the twin sister of the night session. Exhausted by the numbing consideration of one bill after another in a short time span, the Senate was infinitely more pliable and at the mercy of Johnson's debate-limiting, unanimous-consent agreements. It was another nail in the coffin of debate.

The techniques employed by Johnson weakened, very nearly destroyed, the Senate as a debating society. But in place of a debating society, Johnson did not substitute a parliamentary body that functioned with a comprehensive set of rules, such as the House of Representatives or the British House of Commons. For the Senate functioned under Johnson only because of the Johnson System—the Network and the Procedure, both so attuned to one man's genius they had no chance to survive him.

Johnson's Senate procedure was a natural extension of Johnson's personality. Because he was no orator, his genius was not to sway men's minds in forensic debate. Besides, he thought it a waste of time. He knew that Senators seldom revealed their inner nature in public talk, and discovering that inner nature was at the core of the Johnson System. With rare exceptions, the Senate's important work was done in bilateral negotiations, with a premium on secrecy.

But when it came to those rare exceptions when Johnson wanted a single major speech to administer the coup de grace to his opposition, he was a master at setting the stage on the floor of the Senate and at squeezing out the last drop of drama.

Thus, as the annual debate on foreign aid droned to a conclusion and Eisenhower dispatched urgent messages . . . to hold the line, Johnson carefully staged a debate-closing speech for the bill by the chairman of the Foreign Relations Committee, elder statesman Walter George, whose resonant voice gave off the vibrant timbre of a cathedral organ.

Lesser Senators prepared the way for the chairman's final appeal. As the last of the second-stringers rose to his feet, Johnson sent another Senator into the cloakroom to alert George. Johnson's agent led the old man across the hall to the comfortable quarters of the Secretary of the Senate and poured him a glass of a particular fine old wine that George fancied. Allowing time for George to sip his wine, Johnson finally crossed into the office of the Secretary himself and led George back into the chamber. The Senate quickly filled up—because Johnson had passed the word he wanted a full attendance. Relaxed and lubricated, George spoke for the better part of an hour, excoriating the small minds who opposed the foreign aid bill—his arms pumping the air, his magnificent voice filling the farthest reaches of the chamber. The moment the old man stopped, Johnson signaled to the reading clerk and the roll was called on the foreign aid bill, the conclusion foregone.

The George performance was out of the old pre-Johnson Senate, now becoming extinct, smothered by the Johnson System. Johnson himself seldom attempted a major speech. Instead, he read brief statements from a typewritten sheet of paper, often mumbling inaudibly into his chest.

Just as Thomas Jefferson was a strong President who weakened the presidency as an institution, so did Lyndon Johnson tame the Senate and make it work for him but leave it a weaker institution than he found it. . . .

Under the Johnson System, the Senate enjoyed a golden era. And the full fruition of the System came in 1957 when it achieved the impossible: the passage of the first civil rights bill since Reconstruction, without a filibuster and without splitting the Democratic party.

SECTION VIII

LINKAGE BETWEEN LEADERS AND FOLLOWERS

Introductory Comment

What is the nature of the linkages between leaders and followers, between representatives and represented? In democratic societies these relationships are vitally important. We have posited that leadership itself is relational, depending crucially upon interactions or interrelationships between leaders and followers. How do leaders affect their followers, shape and channel their values and beliefs, represent their interests, mobilize them to action? By the same token, how do followers influence leaders: determine who they are, what decisions they make, how they will be responsive?

We must recognize at once that ferreting out linkages between leaders and followers is a time-honored enterprise in political analysis, and it involves highly diverse and complex interconnections. Because democratic government is based upon consent, a large part of the political process in democratic societies is devoted to establishing and nurturing linkages between leaders and the mass public. Studying the nature of these linkages is a tall order.

The leitmotif for leader-follower linkages in democratic societies is *elections*. Elections provide leaders and would-be leaders with opportunities to test their political ideas, policy initiatives, and leadership styles in the crucible of public debate and competition. And, elections give followers, the citizenry, chances to influence who the leaders will be, what they will do, and how responsive they can be. Elections are the central mechanism in democracies for holding leaders accountable to the public (Bunce 1981; Lijphart 1984; Powell 1982). At their best free elections are fought between ambitious politicians who have strong desires to run and win, and who are thereby highly responsive to the electorate. And, ideally, elections are hotly competitive, with at least two contenders for the voters' affections. Finally, the ideal electorate is rational, and voters are well-informed. Of course, these conditions are seldom fully met; elections in the real world often present various distortions from the ideal, both in leaders' behavior and followers' responses.

In small groups, leaders and followers can readily be linked together directly. But in larger organizations the linkages cannot be merely direct; the connections between leaders and followers are crowded with mediate groups and institutions. These formal and informal *intermediaries* link leaders and followers by, above all, providing channels through which the needs, demands, or preferences of followers can be communicated to leaders. In general, intermediaries may include a very wide variety of subleaders, friends, cronies, local supporters, or media purveyors. But in democratic political systems, the most important intermediaries are political parties and interest groups.

Political parties channel the electoral ambitions of leaders, foster the competitive politics required for democratic leadership selection, and permit the interplay of responsiveness and accountability. More often than not, parties also provide a linkage between leaders and followers that is independent of that of the electoral process—through participation in party activities and loyalty to party leaders. Linkage is, indeed, the distinguishing feature of political parties in democratic societies (Lawson 1980).

To one degree or another, democratic societies are characterized by a multiplicity of private interest groups, associations, or organized interests with concerns about public policies. Democracies tend to be pluralistic. Some organized interests may be built into a nation's political party system, just as the trade unions are structurally embraced by the British Labour Party. But many political interest groups are independent of the party system, and may provide autonomous linkages between citizens and leaders. In the United States, a large share of the nexus between organized interests and political leaders is direct—groups mobilize support, conduct grass-roots campaigns, organize political action committees (PACs), and engage in direct lobbying

(Schlozman and Tierney 1986). In European democracies, direct lobbying is less pervasive; interest groups more often work through the political party structure or through the bureaucracy.

Democratic societies are especially known for the pervasiveness of their institutionalized patterns of *political representation* (Birch 1964; Eulau and Wahlke 1978). Representation is ubiquitous in democracies, widely diffused in the structures and processes of electoral, party, and interest group politics (Pennock and Chapman 1968; Pulzer 1975). In this technitronic era of media politics and symbolic appeal, the top leaders of nations have come more than ever to seek and gain special visibility and support as the representatives of the people (Kernell 1986). Equally important is the public bureaucracy, that apotheosis of service delivery and provider of welfare, in the representation of citizens' wants and needs (Aberbach, Putnam, and Rockman, 1981; Katz et al. 1975). But political representation is most powerfully built into parliamentary or legislative politics—in the special relationship between representatives elected to Parliament or Congress and their constituents (Bogdanor 1985).

The direct linkages between representatives and represented have been mapped out in a remarkable number of political systems, ranging from European and North American democracies to democracies of the Third World (Barnes 1977; Cain, Ferejohn, and Fiorina 1987; Clarke et al. 1980; Converse and Pierce 1986; Fenno 1978; Jewell 1982; Kim et al. 1984). Because of the centrality of legislative linkages in democratic societies, we draw upon studies of parliamentary leadership in elections in our choices of readings.

In the first reading, Bruce Cain, John Ferejohn, and Morris Fiorina paint portraits of the "home styles" of British MPs, depicting in rich detail the linkages between representatives and represented in the environment of the parliamentary constituency. They present five distinctive profiles of MPs' home styles, both to indicate the diversity of MPs' interactions with their constituents and to suggest that MPs may reap tangible electoral benefits from their constituency work.

Philip Converse and Roy Pierce, in the second reading, investigate the nature of the representatives' roles in France. How do representatives conceive of the nature of their job in terms of their own judgment about constituency interests, the actual preferences of constituents, and the policy position of their political party? French deputies think of their job as elected representatives largely in terms of party loyalty and discipline. Interestingly, French representatives appear closer to the representative role conceptions of their constituents to the extent they are willing to depart from partisan attachments.

In the final reading, Clive Bean and Anthony Mughan turn to the impact party leaders have on the results of parliamentary elections in Australia and Great Britain. They find that the parliamentary party leaders have marked effects on how voters behave in choosing their representatives. That voters in these two systems choose among party candidates who will represent their constituency partly on the basis of the perceived qualities and effectiveness of the prime ministerial candidates is suggestive of the role of television and other mass media in the politics of nations, and it may indicate the "presidentialization" of politics in European democracies.

Select Bibliography

Bogdanor, V., ed. 1985. *Representatives of the People?* Aldershot, England: Gower.

Cain, B., J. Ferejohn, and M. Fiorina. 1987. *The Personal Vote: Constituency Service and Electoral Independence.* Cambridge, MA: Harvard University Press.

Converse, P. E., and R. Pierce. 1986. *Political Representation in France.* Cambridge, MA: Harvard University Press.

Fenno, R. F., Jr. 1978. *Home Style: House Members in Their Districts.* Boston, MA: Little, Brown.

Kim, C. L., J. D. Barkan, I. Turan, and M. E. Jewell. 1984. *The Legislative Connection: The Politics of Representation in Kenya, Korea, and Turkey.* Durham, NC: Duke University Press.

Patterson, S. C., R. D. Hedlund, and G. R. Boynton. 1975. *Representatives and Represented: Bases of Public Support for the American Legislatures.* New York: Wiley.

18

British MPs in Their Constituencies

Bruce E. Cain, John A. Ferejohn, and Morris P. Fiorina

C urrent American legislative research includes two related lines of inquiry whose emphases differ noticeably from earlier efforts. First, researchers have begun to focus on a variety of legislative activities peripheral to the lawmaking and representational functions stressed by democratic theory. Congressional advertising and constituency service, for example, figure prominently in recent work by Mayhew (1974), Fenno (1978) and Fiorina (1977). In the past, such activities have been designated as mere public relations and errand running, and perhaps for that reason only the most fragmentary treatments of such activities appear in the pre–1974 literature. But increasingly, scholars have come to realize that the constitutional significance of a legislative activity need not agree too closely with its practical (i.e. electoral) importance. The recent work of Parker and Davidson (1979) is quite suggestive on this point. As a possible resolution of Fenno's paradox (Why do we love our congressman but hate our Congress?), Parker and Davidson suggest that the electorate judges Congress as an institution against the constitutional criterion of

"The House Is Not a Home: British MPs in Their Constituencies," *Legislative Studies Quarterly*, 4 (Nov. 1979): 501–523. Copyright © 1979 by the Comparative Legislative Research Center. Reprinted by permission of the Comparative Legislative Research Center, University of Iowa.

legislating effective solutions to national problems, while simultaneously judging congressmen as individuals against the more mundane criteria of providing personal access and a good service bureau.

A second new departure is primarily methodological, though its impetus no doubt stems largely from the one discussed above. As scholars became more sensitive to the variety of activities engaged in by legislators, they began to conceive of constituency influences as something more than correlations between constituency characteristics and roll call votes. And as scholars began to consider actual instances of advertising, constituency service and so forth, they came to the realization that the district might be a more illuminating arena in which to study such behavior than the Washington office. This line of thinking culminates in Fenno's recent *Home Style* (1978), a richly detailed study of how a number of U.S. representatives relate to their districts. . . .

. . .Consider the proposition that legislators pursue individualized constituency strategies in order to insulate themselves against the vagaries of national forces. Given its roots in the electoral incentive, this proposition should have wide applicability, but it appears contradicted by the textbook account of the British situation. The parliamentary system supposedly denies the legislator both the incentive and the opportunity to construct a personal power base even though each member is the sole representative of a geographically distinct constituency. If true, this fact is quite significant; it implies that legislative-electoral institutions can be designed to counteract a strong electoral incentive. For those concerned about the negative side effects of particularized constituency politics in America, a responsible party system like that of Great Britain may be the answer.

How might the British parliamentary system thwart the pursuit of personalized constituency strategies? Perhaps MPs do not think that constituency activities make much difference. Donald Stokes (1975), after decomposing the variance of the party votes in Great Britain and the U.S., argues that the local component is less important in Great Britian than the national one and smaller in magnitude than the local component in America. But then again, Stokes does find a measurable local component, so perhaps the explanation is that MPs are not sufficiently strategic to take advantage of it.

An example of this view is P. G. Richards' (1972, p. 164) comment about MPs and constituency work: "There is a political benefit to be gained from building a reputation for being a 'good constituency man,' but it is quite wrong to suggest that members bestir themselves to deal with the problems of electors out of a shrewd calculation of advantage. . . ." MPs, it seems, are above scrounging for votes. Similarly, Rose and Kavanagh (1972, p. 27) inform us that "The lack of consistent and compulsive concern with winning elections also implies that it is unrealistic to expect elected officials to make policy decisions in accord with the changing whims of voters, or changing figures in opinion polls." So, perhaps the British system works differently from the American because its members are motivated by nobler goals than electoral ones. Perhaps.

A second reason MPs might not actively pursue personal constituency strategies is that such activities are precluded by the resource constraints that members face. Without the staff, research facilities, and the independent power base of committees, MPs lack the means to distinguish themselves. Mayhew (1974, p. 21), for example, writes:

> British MP's lack the resources to set up shop as politicians with bases independent of party. Television time goes to parties rather than to independent politicians. By custom or rule or both, the two parties sharply limit the funds the parliamentary candidates can spend on their campaigns. Once elected, MP's are not supplied the kinds of office resources—staff help, free mailing privileges, and the like—that can be used to achieve public salience. These arguments should not be carried too far . . . But the average backbencher is constrained by lack of resources. It comes as no surprise that individual MP's add little to (or subtract little from) core partisan electoral strength in their constituencies.

Finally, MPs may not work to develop a personal local base because of the opportunity costs entailed by such efforts. Young backbench MPs who aspire to climb the ministerial ladder try to impress party leaders with their legislative work. Diligent constituency effort would divert time and other resources away from that activity. Thus, the British system also differs from the American by establishing a stronger link between legislative work and the attainment of national leadership positions.

To sum up, the conventional wisdom suggests that the alleged differences between British and American legislators stem from some combination of differences in the perceived benefits of constituency service, differences in the resources available to commit to such activity, and differences in the perceived opportunity costs of pursuing locally oriented strategies. These reasons are plausible, but frankly we think that the stylized description of the relations between MPs and their constituencies overstates the difference between the British and American situations. The plain fact is that the office of MP is one which most incumbents wish to keep. And like American congressmen they represent a geographically defined district whose inhabitants control their electoral fates. Subject to the lower level of member resources and the stronger influence of party, we should expect to see a weaker reflection of the kinds of activities performed by American congressmen, at least if those activities are generated by the "electoral connection." If we fail to find indications of electorally based service activity in other systems such as the United Kingdom, it may be a warning that the electoral connection as the explanation of American service activity needs to be augmented by other considerations.

In the summer of 1978 we interviewed MPs about their "home styles." Thirteen of the 18 interviews were conducted in the members' constituencies, and each of these "interviews" lasted from one-half to two days. In other words, there was a degree of participant-observation in the data gathering. The body of this paper describes the home styles of four backbenchers and a sitting cabinet minister. We emphasize that the individuals interviewed are not a representative sample of anything. In fact two of the five profiled were identified beforehand as "good constituency men" by other MPs. . . . Still, we believe that American legislative scholars may find these profiles provocative. Based on the interviews and observations, a number of hypotheses about the nature and extent of constituency service activity in Great Britain are proposed in the final section of the paper. Again, we emphasize that these are hypotheses, not conclusions.

Five Cases of Constituency Strategies

"The Squire"–Sir H.

Sir H. lives in a manor in a largely homogeneous, rural, agricultural community. He is a highly respected and well known figure in the community, so well known in fact, that when we lost our way on our visit to his home and pulled into a gas station in a nearby village, the station attendant not only knew who Sir H. was, but could tell us exactly where he lived. Sir H. himself is in his seventies and has served in Parliament since the mid–fifties. The fact that parliamentary work is a part-time job has enabled him to run a business and serve on the board of directors of several companies while in office. Sir H. believes in the amateur role of the MP and fervently opposes attempts by young members to professionalize the position.

Sir H. is a Conservative whose home style nicely matches the social structure and politics of his constituency. He is the local notable who benevolently oversees the interests of his farming constituency, and his constituents in turn regard him with deference and respect. Sir H. is proud of his community and has worked hard to "keep the character of the constituency from changing" by opposing "relocations of socialists from London" and other proposals that might make it less rural and homogeneous. It is, of course, in Sir H.'s interests to keep the working class component of his constituency from getting too large since his home style would be very much out of place in an urban, industrial environment. At the same time, his efforts to preserve the rural character of the constituency are very much appreciated by his constituents, who are no more eager than Sir H. to see their constituency change.

The rural and homogeneous nature of Sir H.'s constituency influences his home style in various ways. To begin with, its geographical dispersion makes certain strategies for dealing with his constituency less feasible than others. A common method of learning about the complaints and opinions of constituents in Britain is to hold surgeries at designated times during the month. Surgeries provide opportunities for constituents to speak directly with their MPs about the problems they might have. These meetings are usually held at the local Town Hall or constituency party headquarters and usually last one to two hours.

As Sri H. points out, however, surgeries are less effective in rural constituencies, because people have to travel greater distances to attend them. Early in his career, Sir H. tried to institute regular surgeries throughout his constituency, dutifully traveling great distances from village to village. He found only a handful of people at these meetings and rapidly came to the conclusion that the attendance did not warrant the effort. He has not held a formal surgery in many years. Sir H. complains that academics and journalists often seize upon the frequency of surgeries as a crude index of how constituency-oriented a particular MP happens to be. Sir H. believes that this is unfair since it is insensitive to the different demands of rural constituencies such as his own. He claims that he keeps in touch with his constituents just as effectively by mail, personal visits, and phone calls as does an MP in an urban constituency by weekly surgeries.

The nature of Sir H.'s constituency affects his home style in other important ways. Sir H.'s style is similar in some respects to the "person to person" style of Fenno's Congressman A. It is both dictated and made possible by the closely knit structure of the villages that comprise his constituency. The styles of both Congressman A. and Sir H. are very personal, requiring an intimate knowledge of the customs, values and interests of their constituencies. What distinguishes Sir H.'s "person to person" style from that of Congressman A. is the paternalistic role that Sir H. plays in his community. By comparison, Congressman A.'s "presentation of self" to his constituents is his claim to be "one of the boys," not the paternal "squire."

Sir H. has a secretary who helps him with correspondence and arranges speaking engagements, but he personally oversees all communications with his constituents. He gives his secretary very little autonomy in dealing with constituency matters and often responds to letters himself in longhand. We can confirm this fact since his invitation to us to visit his constituency came in the form of a personally handwritten note. Sir H.'s secretary resides in the constituency and knows it very well. Indeed, as Sir H. is quick to point out, a secretary in Westminster would not even be able to address the letters to his constituents since many of the residences in his area are not designated by street names and house numbers.

Sir H.'s "person to person" style is suited to the context of his constituency—i.e., the expectations of a conservative, rural agricultural community. It is also personal in the sense that Sir H. is very comfortable with the role of paternalistic squire. At the same time, his style is strategic, because it is calculated to win and maintain support in the community. Sir H. is very careful to attend to the details of constituency politics. He and his secretary regularly scour the local paper for wedding and death announcements and send out personal notes to the families. Sir H. believes that his constituency work has played a major role in building up the morale of the local party and in helping to make his seat safe. As he explains it, the very fact that a man of his stature in the community takes the time to listen to some average fellow's problems in itself creates good will and electoral reward.

To illustrate his point, he gave us the example of some fellow in a pub complaining to his friends about a problem he has with the government. His mates tell him that he has been wronged and suggest that he see Sir H. So the fellow calls or writes Sr. H. who dutifully sends off a letter to the relevant minister asking the minister to please enquire into the matter, and a note to the constituent informing him of Sr. H.'s actions. The minister writes back a reply—in many cases, unable to help—and Sir H. sends a photocopy of the minister's letter to the constituent. The constituent's problem often does not get solved, says Sir H., but at least the constituent can take the letter with him to the pub, "happy in the knowledge that his case has received attention at the highest levels." Sir H. in return acquires the reputation of being a good constituency man who cares about his constituents.

This anecdote is revealing in two senses. First, it indicates the high esteem that Sir H. enjoys. His mere consideration of the matter is sufficient to please his constituents. Secondly, it is noteworthy that Sir H. would take the time to contact a minister about a constituent's problem. There is, of course, no evidence that such efforts have a measurable positive effect, but it is significant that Sir H. should think so. Community ties, Sr. H. claims, are such that knowledge of a favor for one constituent is communicated by word of mouth to others, reinforcing the support of not only the particular constituent involved, but also that of his friends and his family. The belief that this generates electoral support justifies Sir H.'s substantial investment of time in constituency work, which includes an hour or so every weekday dealing with letters, Monday morning meetings with his staff to go over constituency matters and general political meetings on Friday evenings. Being a good constituency man is consistent with Sir H.'s self-image as the local squire (i.e., his social obligation), but it is also a calculated attempt to secure electoral support. Sir H.'s "person to person" style is no less strategic than Congressman A's.

The context of the community Sir H. represents also shapes the nature of the problems he has to deal with and the focus of his activities in the constituency. Urban MPs report that they get a large number of cases dealing with housing, immigration, and crime, but Sir H. is more likely to hear about pensions, taxes, and farming problems. Sir H. has a very well-defined sense of what does and does not fall into his proper domain of responsibility. In his view, the MP looks after the interests of constituents as they are affected by the national government. Thus, when a civil servant in Westminster, or in some local office, administers the law in an unfair way, the MP should try to bring his influence to bear upon the ministry in order to rectify the situation. Therefore, tax and pension problems fall properly in Sir H.'s domain, but purely local matters such as housing and the decisions of the local council do not. These, he refers to the proper local authority. Sir H. does not try to compete with local officials for power and attention. He comments only that "My relations with local officials are cordial and I command their respect."

Sir H.'s home style involves a fairly high commitment of resources to constituency matters, but it is bounded by a "traditional" view of the MP's responsibilities. Where some of the younger MPs involve themselves in almost every conceivable local issue, Sir H. restricts himself as much as possible to contacting ministers about administrative decisions, raising parliamentary questions, and in some rare instances, promoting private member's bills suggested by problems that arise in his constituency. Constituency politics are both an obligation and a means of helping to build up support, but Sir H. believes that in the end they are subordinate to his role as a national legislator. This, as we shall see, sets Sir H. apart from his younger colleagues.

"The Local Man"-Mr. G.

This MP managed to recapture in 1974 what had been a former Labour seat held by the Conservatives since the fifties. Mr. G. is a highly energetic and articulate man in his thirties, who previously had taught at a polytechnic. He is well-read in political science, and takes its lessons very seriously. He has studied the American political system and personally observed American congressmen in their districts. He believes that British MPs have much to learn from them. He opposes more limited conceptions of the MP's role—such as Sir H.'s—and thinks that this is the home style of the future in Great Britian. Mr. G. is one of a number of young MPs sitting in marginal constituencies whose home styles have become controversial among older members. Sir H. and others like him believe that the trend established by MPs like Mr. G. will lead to the undesirable professionalization of the office and an unnecessary proliferation of expense.

Mr. G's constituency is over 50 percent white and working class, but has substantial middle class and ethnic neighborhoods as well. At one time, this region had been a thriving industrial center, but it has been slowly decaying since the Second World War. Numerous industries have closed, and the population has declined. Traveling through the constituency, we saw several blighted residential areas and abandoned factories. Mr. G. is almost evangelical in his desire to revitalize the area. He speaks bitterly of the political neglect that contributed to the economic and social decline of his constituency: in his eyes, the primary culprits are incompetent and poorly motivated local officials, and he believes that it is his responsibility to prod them into action. It is a bit hard to understand precisely why Mr. G. feels so intensely about this community since he was not born or raised there, although he taught at the nearby polytechnic school. Nonetheless, the fact remains that Mr. G. now sees himself as closely tied to the community.

A second curious and notable aspect of Mr. G. is that while he belongs to the Tribune group—the left of the Labour party—his constituency politics are indistinguishable from the service and locally oriented politics of Fenno's Congressman E. Mr. G. votes with the far left for large scale nationalization, heavy wealth taxes and getting out of the Common Market, but what he really seems to care about are problems in the constituency such as housing. Mr. G. is more interested in building up his position in the community than in national politics. In the few days that we spent with Mr. G., we heard very little about his ideology and a great deal about his constituency. He is very careful not to let the former interfere with the latter.

One incident particularly reinforces this point. Shortly after we arrived in his constituency, Mr. G. took us to a meeting with the head of the local Chamber of Commerce. The president of the local group and the Mayor were major figures in the local Conservative party and had energetically campaigned against Mr. G. during the last election. They frequently competed with Mr. G. for publicity in the local press. As we headed to the meeting, Mr. G. recalled with undisguised glee the time that the Mayor and the president of the local Chamber of Commerce tried to hold a press conference at the opening of a new shopping center in an urban renewal area. Hoping to capture the publicity for themselves, they saw to it that Mr. G. was omitted from the list of invited guests. Mr. G., not to be denied, decided that he would attend anyway, and, although he was not allowed to sit on the podium, he strategically placed himself nearby so that his face appeared the next day in the pictures taken by the local paper. It was a moment of great triumph for Mr. G.

The purpose of this meeting was for Mr. G. to announce to the Chamber of Commerce that he was organizing a jobs fair, and that the Chamber was welcome to set up a booth. Mr. G. had been careful not to invite the Mayor and the Chamber of Commerce to participate until after the initial publicity, complete with his picture, had hit the local press. Mr. G. did not want any confusion about who was responsible for this event. Toward the end of the meeting, discussion wandered, and the Chamber of Commerce official began to criticize at length the Labour government's intervention into Rhodesian affairs. We expected that Mr. G. would leap to his government's defense and that a heated discussion would ensure. Instead, Mr. G. nodded his head in quiet sympathy, finished his coffee, and a few minutes later apologized to his host for the fact that he really had to be moving on since he had another appointment to attend to. National issues and ideology are simply of secondary importance for Mr. G.

Mr. G. is deeply involved in all sorts of community affairs. He holds surgeries every week at two locations for two hours each. He actively solicits cases by advertising his surgeries in the local paper and by walking through the town on weekends and letting people approach him on the street with their problems. As Mr. G. explains, this serves the dual purpose of picking up cases from people who could not attend the surgery as well as making him visible to his constituents. As we walked through the town market and through complexes of council homes, people would come up to Mr. G. to tell him their problems. Mr. G. in each case recorded the person's request in a notebook and promised to get back to them shortly. Some of the people we saw invited Mr. G. in to have a quick cup of coffee while they complained about the vandalism of neighborhood kids or the neglect the local council has shown toward the repair of their homes.

Mr. G.'s willingness to play the social worker seems to know no bounds. He never turns down a case and will go to great lengths to find new ones. Local affairs are not off limits in the sense that they were for Sir H. Mr. G. sees himself as a general ombudsman who fights against the maladministration of local as well as national government. Consequently, Mr. G.'s relations with local officials are far more complex than Sir H.'s. Some local officials—such as those in the Consumer Advice Bureau—are his allies while others—like the Mayor and the Chamber of Commerce—are his chief rivals for attention and influence in the community.

Mr. G.'s typical cases are housing, social security, immigration, and vandalism. The importance of housing derives from the role of the local authorities as the landlords of council housing. Those who come to Mr. G. because they feel that they deserve a better flat, or because they have been denied permission by the local authorities to move, are not likely to be helped by Mr. G. (although he tries) since the housing allocation process was changed a few years ago to a point system with objective criteria for different classifications. Mr. G. is somewhat more successful at prodding repairs out of the local council. The immigration cases are a very important bridge to the immigrant community for Mr. G. He has no trouble developing links with the white, working class community, but the immigrants tend to maintain separate religious and cultural ties. Thus, Mr. G. has to work especially hard to court their favor. On one particular evening, for example, Mr. G took us to a local immigrant bar-brothel where he nonchalantly collected cases and heard complaints while we looked on in slightly embarrassed discomfort.

Mr. G.'s local and service-oriented style is consistent with his personality. He seems indifferent to ministerial ambitions and more interested in his community than in his national stature. It is also partly dictated by the context of his constituency. His is a constituency with serious economic problems, and Mr. G.'s crusade to stop the decay has obvious electoral appeal. His willingness to take up any community cause—individual complaints, the funding of a local football team, the building of a new shopping center, helping the relatives of immigrants to enter the country—fits nicely with the heterogeneity of the constituency. His primary supporters are working class, council house dwellers, but he reaches out for support from diverse groups. Mr. G.'s style is certainly strategic. He has excellent working relations with the local press and writes his own press releases. Mr. G. claims that a recent edition of one of the papers had eleven articles about him in it.

Mr. G. took over a marginal constituency, and a good part of what makes him work so hard is the hope that this will give him a safe seat. Mr. G. feels somewhat bitterly about MPs who neglect their constituencies. A recent issue of the local paper carried his advertisement of weekly surgeries next to an announcement by the neighboring Conservative MP that he would be unable to hold surgeries during the next month since he would be on vacation. When a large number of individuals from this neighboring MP's constituency began to appear at Mr. G.'s surgery, Mr. G. would take their cases but remind each one that the reason their MP was not helping them was that he was in the south of France. He then wrote a letter to the editor of the local paper complaining about his neighbor's neglect of his parliamentary duties. This summed up a great deal about Mr. G. for us: he was altruistic enough not to turn them away, but strategic enough to use it to political advantage.

"The Ambitious Young Man"—Mr. B.

Mr. B. is widely considered to be a bright young prospect in the Labour party. When we mentioned his name, we were told several times that Mr. B. was a man to watch in the future. He was almost certain to be given a ministerial post in the next Labour government and a good bet to become a senior minister in the cabinet eventually. Indeed, Mr. B. is an extremely intelligent, well-read and pleasing person. He was educated at the right schools and spent some time teaching at a prominent English University. His perception of politics is much more analytical than that of Mr. G. or Sir H., and he seems more conscious than they of the long-run trends and implications of parliamentary home style. Like Mr. G., Mr. B. has visited and observed American congressmen, but he is not nearly as enamored of the congressional model as Mr. G. Mr. B. would like to see the staffs of British MPs expanded, but he feels that it is important that this growth not get out of hand the way he believes that it has in the U.S. He reminded us that large staffs are unnecessary in Great Britian since the size of the average British constituency is about one-fifth that of a congressional constituency.

Mr. B. self-consciously steers a course between his local responsibilities and his national aspirations. He realizes that his performance as a backbencher will determine how far and how fast he rises up the ministerial ladder. At the same time, he realizes that he needs to establish a reputation as a good constituency man if he is to retain his seat in the future: Mr. B. is in effect "digging in." He believes that his service work will give him a buffer against changing national tides. His constituency, like that of Mr. G., was very marginal in 1974. In a sense, however, it is even more marginal than Mr. G.'s since Mr. B.'s seat is more naturally Conservative and middle class. He hopes that by taking an interest in local affairs and by doing diligent casework, he can offset any policy disagreements he might have with his constituents.

Mr. B. works hard at his constituency duties. He estimates that he spends about one-third of his time on constituency affairs when Parliament is in session and nearly all of his time between sessions. Mr. B. is quite candid about the future problems raised by his strategy. As Mr. B. rises in the ministerial ranks, there will be less time to devote to constituency matters. His hope is that once established, his early record of constituency service will give him enough credit so that he will not lose his cushion of support when future parliamentary responsibilities cut down the time he can devote to his constituency. Later, if all goes well, Mr. B. will be a minister, and the national publicity and pride factor that goes with the job (i.e., the pride that constituents feel about having an important minister in their seat) will offset the necessarily national allocation of his time and resources. Mr. B.'s hypothesis is that his vulnerability will follow a curvilinear pattern. During his first years in office, diligent constituency work will help to establish local support, but in the beginning stages of his parliamentary career, his vulnerability will increase since he will have neither the time to devote to his constituency affairs nor the national publicity to offset his neglect.

Complicating matters is the basic problem that Mr. B. has no firm idea of what electoral impact his constituency work has, nor how quickly an advantage built upon local work will decay if he must neglect his constituency in the future. At the time we interviewed him, Mr. B. was most interested in the fate of Dr. David Owen, the Labour Minister of Foreign Affairs. Owen was sitting in a marginal seat which, it was rumored, was in grave danger of being lost in the next election because of his prolonged absences from the constituency on foreign policy missions. Party workers in Owen's constituency feared that these absences many have seriously undermined local support for him. Mr.B. felt that Dr. Owen's fate might provide some clue as to the likely success of his strategy.

Mr. B., like Mr. G., does not draw the line of his responsibilities at the national government. Mr. B. willingly takes on local cases like housing, and works very closely with local Labour councillors. He thinks that the growing involvement in local affairs by MPs was caused by the incompetence of local officials; the greater salience of the MP such that people were more likely to turn to him than to less well-known local councillors; and the fact that he and others like him actively solicited cases. As Mr. B. pointed out, the demand for casework and services is endogenously related to supply: by being more open to taking on cases, the MP increases the demands placed upon him by his constituents.

Mr. B.'s home style is strategic in the sense that he sees it as a shortrun tactic that will enable him to achieve his long-run ambition of becoming a minister. It is contextual in the sense that the marginality of the seat forces him to find a way to protect himself against unfavorable national trends. It is somewhat less personal than the home style of either Mr. G. or Sir H.: one suspects that were Mr. B. in a safe seat or were it the case that there was a better way of building an electoral cushion, Mr. B. would abandon constituency work rapidly. Mr. B. does not have Sir H.'s conception of himself as a local squire, nor Mr. G.'s desire to win power in the local community. Mr. B. is dealing with electoral circumstances in the best way that he can. If he succeeds and the curvilinear hypothesis is correct, Mr. B.'s home style will probably change in the future.

"The Issue Man"—Mr. R.

Mr. R. is a committed socialist. Unlike Mr. G., Mr. R. cannot talk about politics without reference to socialist principles. The world is neatly divided into two camps for Mr. R.: there are those who exploit the working class and those who defend it. Mr. R. was one of the few MPs who queried us about our politics: were we sympathetic to the working person's cause or were we typical bourgeois intellectuals? Our properly ambiguous response annoyed him. Recently, Mr. R.'s world has been complicated by the Scottish devolution issue. Mr. R. is a fervent supporter of socialist devolution, meaning devolution that would give greater power to a Scottish working class party. He is scornful of the more heterodox Scottish National Party: devolution without socialist principles, he explains, would be no improvement over the status quo.

Mr. R.'s constituency is a Labour stronghold in a Scottish industrial area. Until recently, Mr. R. was a sponsored MP, which meant that his nomination was controlled by a large union in the constituency. In recent years, he has split with the Labour party over devolution and has lost his affiliation with the sponsoring trade union. He did not plan to stand for Parliament again. Mr. R. sees his constituency in far less personal terms than the other MPs we have looked at so far. His constituency is the "working class" and his role is to protect their interest. After his break with the Labour party, he has come to define his constituency more narrowly as the Scottish working class. Mr. R.'s conception of his constituency is more abstract than personal: it is not based upon individuals for whom he has done favors or with whom he has had personal contacts. He is bound to his constituents by a common link of objective class interest. Mr. R.'s job is to represent that interest even when his constituents are indifferent to it. Many times in our conversation, Mr. R. referred with dismay and a slightly detectable contempt to the inertia of his constituents. Interest in socialist causes has declined, he contends, and the working class has lost its leadership and direction. Bright young workers often lose their interest in socialist causes when they acquire the educational training to become leaders.

Mr. R. allocates his personal resources primarily toward his national responsibilities. When his relations with the sponsoring trade union were good, he tried to establish an informal organization of local party and trade union officials to take some of the burden of local affairs off his shoulders. The services these people provided him were voluntary. Together with one secretary each in the constituency and Westminster, these people acted as filters on most constituency cases, leaving him free to carry out his legislative duties. Select cases would be passed on to him but, in general Mr. R. made it clear that he does not believe in the personal touch. Consequently, the demands placed upon him by his constituency are less than those placed upon the others we have examined so far. Mr. R. holds his surgeries on the last Friday of every month whereas Mr. G. and Mr. B hold them every week. Mr. R. does not usually take phone calls or visits at his home as does Sir H. unless the case is very urgent. Mr. R. was one of the few Labour MPs we interviewed who had serious reservations about interfering in local matters like housing. Mr. R. believes that the proper role of the MP is that of legislator. To the degree that an MP must act as an ombudsman, Mr. R. feels that it should be restricted to protecting against executive directives issued by the civil service. In this sense, Mr. R.'s preferred role is most similar to that of Sir H.

Despite his conception of the proper responsibilities of the MP, Mr. R has had to make concessions to the growing constituency demands upon him. He claims that the "social worker" role of the MP has increased in importance greatly over the last 25 years: in his words, it has come "to assume an importance way out of proportion." While he believes that local affairs like housing lie outside his area of responsibility, he says that his staff used to handle these cases when they were brought in. His staff had very good relations with many of the local officials they had to deal with due to connections through the Labour party and the trade unions. These ties facilitated a speedy response to their requests.

More than the other MPs, Mr. R. cares about the role of the MP as legislator. This is, of course, consistent with his issue orientation. Rather than see staff expanded to meet constituency needs, Mr. R. would prefer to see the research facilities in Parliament improved upon, and every MP provided with a research assistant. The problem with exiting research facilities, from his perspective as a policy-oriented critic of the government, is that it provides you only with information from existing government sources. If one is to be an effective critic, he maintains, one needs independent sources of information. Thus, he says, is especially important in the British situation, because of the high degree of secrecy that surrounds decisions made by the cabinet and the civil service. As Mr. R. puts it, "If the civil service and ministers decide that you should not know about something, you don't have a bloody chance." To be an effective legislator, he believes that MPs need every bit of research assistance they can get.

Mr. R. also argues that making the MP an effective legislator will require making the job full time. The part-time status of MPs, he says, suits the Tory gentlemen who take their legislative duties lightly and make a comfortable living on the side as a company director, business, or professional person. The glorification of the part-time legislator is in his eyes another manifestation of the anti-working class bias of the British government. Mr. R. explains it this way, "I am a toolmaker, and their isn't any factory I know of that has any use for a part-time toolmaker."

Mr. R.'s presentation of self is as a highly principled socialist who is committed to principles and policies of the working class and not to specific individuals or interest groups. He accepts the job of social worker grudgingly, and has tried to build an informal organization around him which would screen him from excessive constituency work and free him to pursue his proper role as legislator. He sees himself as a trustee rather than a delegate. More often than not, he feels that he has to prod his constituents to action rather than respond to their demands. Mr. R.'s national orientation sets him apart from Mr. G. or Mr. B. Younger Labour MPs "have discovered that they can get elected to Parliament on the basis of individual help," and this has caused them to turn from a national to a local orientation. This bothers Mr. R. He blames younger MPs for excessively "looking for the vote" and constituency parties for being too preoccupied with local rather than national issues. At the same time, Mr. R.'s commitment to principles sets him apart from Sir H. Sir H. would not approve of strengthening parliamentary committees nor of opening new sources of information in order to criticize his own party, and he most certainly would not break with his own party over some policy, as Mr. R. has done.

Mr. R.'s home style appears to be dictated by personal taste in the sense that he is a committed ideologue, and, for all his protestations about intellectuals, he is an intellectual in his own right. It is also partly explained by institutional factors in the sense that he represented a trade union sponsored, working class constituency that was sympathetic to his ideology. Since the seat was safe, Mr. R. did not have to build up a personal constituency to buffer himself against national swings. Curiously, then, Mr. R.'s home style is the least strategic of the MPs in our sample. It does not appear that Mr. R is strongly conscious of whether his home style maximizes votes or not. He is almost scornful of those who do preoccupy themselves with winning votes. It is possible, however, that Mr. R.'s lack of interest in the strategic implications of his home style may have been his own undoing.

"The Cabinet Minister"—Mr. S.

Mr. S. is a major figure in the Labour party and has held several key cabinet posts. He has been in Parliament since the end of World War II, and when he reflects on the changes that have taken place in constituency politics since then, he has a hard time distinguishing between changes that are part of a general trend and those that are the result of different stages in his parliamentary career. Mr. S.'s seat is something between safe and marginal: he claims that it is less marginal now than it was when he first took it over, but it is, he emphasizes, by no means absolutely secure. Mr.

S. represents a London constituency, and he things that this has given him an advantage over the years. MPs who represent constituencies a considerable distance away from London must travel long distances to attend to their constituencies. As he points out, after a grueling week in London, the prospect of rushing back to the constituency is not very attractive. It either takes its toll on the MP's personal life, or the MP begins to neglect his constituency. Having his constituency in London, however, has made it easier for Mr. S. to be diligent both as a legislator and as a constituency man. Since Mr. S. resides in the constituency, he is frequently seen about the neighborhood and is able to keep on top of local developments even as he ascends the ministerial ladder.

As his career progressed, Mr. S. tried to shift the focus of his activities to the national scene, and thinks that he has done so fairly successfully. In his early days as a backbencher, Mr. S. spent a great deal of time on constituency work. He believes that this work helped establish his reputation as a good constituency man. As he explains, he got involved in heavy constituency work at the beginning of his career because he had the incentive—his seat was marginal and he needed every vote he could get—and because he had the opportunity. The war had left a "whole host of problems" such as national service status, veteran's compensation, rationing, and the like. In addition, Mr. S. felt that his constituency party expected a high level of involvement on his part in the affairs of the community. In a sense, he argued, what may be more important to the MP is not the prospective gain from good constituency work, but avoiding the negative consequences of not meeting those expectations. The stronger incentive, then, may be that "you can do yourself harm" if you fail to fulfill your duties as a good constituency man. As Mr. S. rose to higher positions in the party, he noticed that demands upon him seemed to slacken some. He is not sure whether this was because of a general trend across all constituencies in that direction as the problems of the war were resolved gradually, or whether this was because people were more hesitant to bring their problems to him as he became a national figure.

Even as a minister, however, Mr. S. tries not to neglect his constituency duties. He recalls quite vividly one day a few years back when he concluded negotiations with Gromyko in Moscow during a Friday afternoon and then flew back to London in time for his Friday night surgery. Still, the pressure of holding a cabinet position force Mr. S. to involve himself less in constituency affairs than he had previously. His ministry duties frequently call him out of the country, and his secretary has come to play an increasingly important role in his casework. She has acquired greater autonomy to deal with constituency matters in his absence. Mr. S. also gets help from local councillors and party officials in his constituency. There is usually a local councillor in attendance at his surgeries to handle the housing cases and purely local matters. By having local officials at his surgeries, Mr. S. demonstrates his interest in the things that often matter to his constituents the most, while he avoids to deal with these problems personally.

Mr. S. believes that there is a "pride factor" working for the MP who becomes a cabinet official. This "pride factor" enables him to have some measure of independence from his constituency: normal complaints diminish and criticism of the government's policies appear more frequently in his mail. At the same time, Mr. S. tries to stay close to his constituency. He has worked with local authorities to fight the closure of a local hospital. When he reads about a fire displacing a family in the constituency, he helps the family to relocate. His constituency chores may have slackened to a day or so a week, but they are not insignificant. His involvement is less than that of Mr. G., Mr. B., or Sir H., but it is greater than that of Mr. R. Mr. S.'s home style is influenced in part by contextual circumstances. His constituency is predominantly working class and he knows that many of his constituents care more about housing, pension checks, and tax problems than they do about the issues he deals with as a minister. Mr. S. is aware of the strategic implications of his constituency work and believes that it helps build up a cushion of 1,000 or so votes above and beyond the votes provided by the "pride factor." This blend of national prominence and local concern has worked well for Mr. S., and it is this sort of mixed strategy that younger, ambitious MPs like Mr. B. look to as an example.

Discussion

The preceding profiles reveal a diversity of orientations to the constituency, a diversity evident in our other interviews as well. We found some MPs who strayed little from the "ideal type" MP characterized in the introduction, while others, like Mr. G., closely resembled some of the congressmen that Fenno writes about in *Home Style*. There is reason to believe, then, that the constituency orientations exhibited by MPs are more varied than conventional wisdom suggests. But even more surprising than the variety is the fact that, in some respects, the MPs we interviewed were nearly unanimous in voicing their departure from the conventional image. We shall discuss several examples of departures drawn from the seventeen "complete" interviews in our pilot study.

First, nearly all of our MPs reported a considerable degree of personal attention to their constituencies. All but one of those interviewed went back to the constituency at least forty times a year. While distances in Great Britain are small compared with those in the United States, the frequency of trips to the constituency compares favorably with that found for House members by Glenn Parker (1979). Furthermore, almost all the MPs we interviewed do a lot of casework. The reported number of "cases" per week runs from 10 to 150 with a mean of 79. All but five MPs report receiving more than 30 new cases each week. The content of these cases varies with the nature of the constituency and probably with the receptiveness of the MP as well, but almost all of the MPs reported receiving complaints about council housing and immigration. Virtually all of the members try to take some action on each case submitted to them, in the belief that constituents appreciate the show of effort even if the complaints are not resolved in their favor. Thirteen of the seventeen MPs interviewed indicated that they maintain some kind of regular contact with local officials and try to work through them to do casework dealing with local issues such as housing. In other words, most of our MPs do not restrict themselves to cases involving the national government. They work on cases relating to local government as well. Some of them even work actively with nongovernmental interests in their constituencies when a case demands it.

All but three of those interviewed reported that they maintain regular surgeries in their constituencies for the express purpose of receiving complaints from constituents. And two of the three who do not engage in this activity (like Sir H.) refrain from it because the rural character of their constituency makes the surgery an inefficient way for the MP to receive complaints from his constituents.

Because almost all of our respondents feel that they are expected to do casework, most of them (13 of 17) favor an increase in staff resources for this purpose. And, of those who do not favor such an increase, two included among their reasons that an increase in staff would induce even more of a constituency orientation than presently exists. Under the present circumstances the limited availability of staff and other resources means that the constituency-oriented MP has to commit his or her own time to the servicing of requests from constituents. This fact, together with the possibility of attaining ministerial status if sufficient talent and expertise is exhibited in legislative matters, seem to be the principal factors that inhibit the rapid development of a more pronounced constituency service orientation by MPs. To the average MP, the opportunity cost of expanding constituency-oriented activities is quite high.

Meager resources and high opportunity costs notwithstanding, the MPs we interviewed report engaging in a considerable amount of constituency-oriented activity. Why? Our interviews suggest that much of this constituency service orientation arises from MP's perceptions that constituency service is electorally beneficial. *All of our respondents believed that, for good or ill, doing well on cases could help protect them from national electoral swings.* Of course, some MPs fail to engage in such activity either because (like Mr. R.) they are located in a fairly safe seat; because they have national reputations sufficient (in their view) to offset such electoral advantages as they could gain from performing the welfare officer's job; or, sometimes, because they find the activity distasteful. No matter, for the present it suffices to say that MPs see constituency service as an electorally beneficial activity, and, mostly for that reason engage in a considerable amount of it, even though the opportunity cost is high given the relatively small amount of resources they control.

While our small, nonrandom sample of interviews should not be made to bear too great a weight, it is useful to give some indication of how actual orientations toward the constituency are related to beliefs about electoral benefits. We asked each of our seventeen MPs to assess the extent to which doing casework was electorally beneficial. While all of them attributed some electoral effects to such activity, there was a distinctive subset who said that the potential payoff was very substantial. . . .

Not surprisingly those who believe that constituency service will have a large effect on their electoral fortune allocate more effort to it. Similar results occur when we relate beliefs about the electoral efficacy of constituency service to a question asking whether or not the MP actively solicits cases or simply reacts to those that arise "naturally." Four of the five MPs who actively solicit cases believe that such activity will yield substantial electoral rewards. The remaining MP indicates that he expects some electoral response. Furthermore, those who expect a substantial electoral benefit are much more likely than others to undertake "local" cases as opposed to restricting their activities to complaints dealing with the national government.

Given what appear to be important differences in the amount of effort devoted to constituency affairs, one might ask whether constituency work really does have a significant impact on the outcome of parliamentary elections. We will try to answer this question properly in future studies, but, for illustrative purposes, compare the experiences of our five MPs in the May 1979 election. Two of them—Mr. G. and Mr. B—stood in the May election while the other three—Mr. S., Mr. R., and Sir H.—were all retiring at the time we interviewed them. Mr. G. won despite the fact that the Liberal candidate pulled out of the race (an event that caused Shirley Williams to lose her seat in another constituency even though she had a previous majority of 9,000). The two-party swing against Mr. G. was 3.5 percent, which was considerably less than the national swing to the Conservatives of 5.2 percent and the regional swing of 6.3 percent. Mr. B. by comparison had one of the most marginal Labour seats in the country—a majority of less than 1 percent—and he was swept out of office in the election. Still, the two-party swing against him was 2.3 percent as compared with a regional swing of 6.6 percent. In short, both of our constituency MPs managed to reduce the swing against them, although with varying consequences.

Equally interesting is what happened to the seats of the retiring MPs. In the case of Mr. S., a swing of 8.1 percent gave his seat to the Conservatives for the first time in the postwar period. To be sure, there have been important demographic changes in the constituency in recent years, but the loss was quite unexpected and remarkable. The effect of not having an incumbent may also be evident in Sir H.'s Conservative seat, which his successor won with a swing of only 5.3 percent, slightly less than the regional swing to the Conservatives of 5.6 percent. Finally, in Mr. R.'s safe Labour seat, his successor managed to produce an 8.9 percent swing to Labour, when Scotland as a whole swung to Labour by only .1 percent. Perhaps this is a vivid indication of the "price" Mr. R. paid for his bad constituency relations.

The hypotheses about the prevalence of constituency service, the motivation for service, and variations in service as a function of political perceptions are strongly suggested by our interviews. In addition we can suggest a number of more tentative hypotheses about similarities and differences between representatives in the United States and the United Kingdom. First, Fenno's (1978) four-fold distinction between geographical, re-election, primary, and personal constituencies seems to have cross-national utility. All of those MPs interviewed had what Fenno called a "geographical, space and place perception of their constituency." Sir H., for example, was very much aware of the rural, homogeneous nature of his constituency, and even believed that it was his duty to protect its distinctive character. Mr. G., to take another example, could easily identify the hostile and friendly neighborhoods in his heterogeneous constituency, and planned his constituency strategies accordingly. Fenno's concept of perceived layers of support may also be relevant in Great Britain. At the most intimate level—the personal constituency— are the MP's agent, secretary, spouse, and devoted friends. The primary constituency usually consists of party activists, local government officials of the same party, and local trade unionists or Chamber of Commerce officers. At the outermost edge is the re-election constituency, often seen in class terms, but for the service-oriented MP it may also include anyone who has benefited from a service.

Our interviews suggest several additional points about Fenno's classification scheme. One is that the personal and primary constituencies, contrary to what one might expect in a political system with disciplined parties, do not always correspond with the local party organization. Mr. G., for instance, built an independent personal organization precisely because he believed the local party to be moribund and inefficacious. Secondly, it appears from Mr. R.'s experience that disagreement with one's primary constituency can be as important to an MP as disagreement with one's re-election constituency. Indeed, an important difference between the American and British cases that needs further exploration is the seemingly greater importance of the primary constituency in Great Britain. This raises the question of whether constituency activity is dictated by activists and others in the primary constituency rather than by the larger re-election constituency. Some have suggested to us that the expectations of the primary constituency may be an important reason for the increasing emphasis on constituency work in recent years in Britain. . . .

Lastly, the cases of Mr. B. and Mr. S. point to a [third] similarity in British and American constituency styles: namely, that representatives in both countries face hard choices about how to allocate their time and resources. Mr. B.'s dilemma—whether to maximize local support or influence in the House—is also evident among the congressmen Fenno interviewed. In his words, "no matter how confident members may be of their ability to pursue their Washington and constituency careers simultaneously, they all recognize the potentiality of conflict and worry about coping with it." Of course, the sensitivity of MPs to this dilemma seems to vary significantly. For Mr. B., Mr. S., and Mr. R., it was quite acute: for Mr. G. and Sir H., it was less so. However, as Fenno found with congressmen, there can be linkage between the home and House styles of MPs. Constituency work can be used to offset the severe policy constraint of belonging to disciplined and increasingly unpopular parties. In the end, the policy constraint was too severe for Mr. B., but the low swing against him suggests that he was partly successful in offsetting national forces.

However tentative we must be about particular hypotheses, our preliminary investigations at least show that the "electoral connection" exists in Great Britain. The House of Commons may not be the MP's true home: MPs seem to spend a great deal of time on constituency matters and believe that these are important. We hope our future studies will reveal more about systematic variations in constituency activities and the effects these have on the decisions of British electors.

19

Representative Roles and Legislative Behavior in France

Philip E. Converse and Roy Pierce

Very different patterns of legislative behavior [are] characteristic of France and the United States. Legislative parties are comparatively incohesive in the U.S. Congress, where party discipline in legislative voting is typically quite weak. On the other hand, in the French National Assembly (as well as most other non-American legislatures for that matter), party discipline in legislative voting is normally strict. These differences in legislative practice ultimately reflect differences in assumptions about representation. In the most general sense, we want to examine how these assumptions work out in practice in the French case, with a view toward determining as precisely as possible just how representative government in France operates. That overriding question is too large to be dealt with adequately here, but we can begin to accumulate elements of the answer by examining some smaller questions that are directly relevant to the larger issue. How do French legislative candidates view the role of the representative, particularly with regard to group discipline in legislative voting? Are variations in conception of the representative role held by the parliamentary elite matched by their constituents' attitudes

Legislative Studies Quarterly, 4 (Nov. 1979): 525–562. Copyright © 1979 by the Comparative Legislative Research Center. Reprinted by permission of the Comparative Legislative Research Center, University of Iowa.

toward the role of the representative? Are French deputies who depart from party discipline more representative of constituency opinion on major issues than those who adhere to strict group discipline? These are the specific questions to which we will direct our attention.

In the first stage of our research design, a proper sample of some 86 *circonscriptions* was drawn, at rates proportional to population size, to represent the 467 continental constituencies sending deputies to the National Assembly. Within each of these sample constituencies, personal interviews were conducted with serious candidates for seats, as well as with a sample of their constituents drawn randomly from the electoral registers. In all, successful interviews were carried out with 2,046 voters shortly after the 1967 election, or an average of some 24 electors per constituency, with quite limited variation around this mean. Similarly, 272 candidates were interviewed from the same districts, for an average of slightly more than 3 per constituency.

After the initial data collection in the spring and summer of 1967, we expected to complete the design simply by monitoring the legislative outputs or roll call votes of our sample of deputies in the National Assembly during the remainder of their terms stretching some five years into the future. However, reality intruded in the form of the May-June popular disturbances over elite unresponsiveness in France, which led to the dissolution of the Assembly and new legislative elections in June of 1968. Given the fact that our 1967 study was focused on the question of elite responsiveness, and that the more specific aspects of policy debate at issue in the uprising (most notably, the question of educational reform and the role of workers in factories) had been covered in the original interview, we decided that we had a rather unique "before-and-after" study in the making and returned to the field in the summer of 1968. We reinterviewed both constituents and their new Assembly delegates in all districts where the elections had produced any turnover in representation, and in a half-sample of the remaining districts that had re-elected the incumbent from the 1967 election. Thus the original design was reconstituted, though with a smaller number of cases, and the roll call behavior of our deputy respondents was monitored for the full ensuing term, ending in March, 1973.

Before entering directly into our subject, it is in order to say a few words about the relationship between the variable that is the focus of our attention—the conception of the representative role—and the practice of party group discipline in voting in the National Assembly. We have made an exhaustive study of voting in the Assembly during the two legislative terms of 1967-1968 and 1968-1973, and the evidence for strict party discipline is massive. At the same time, it is not complete: defections from caucus decisions are registered at the fringes. Moreover, when the total corpus of roll call votes for the six-year period of our inquiry is examined at the individual level, it seems apparent that some deputies feel more free to depart from the postures of their parliamentary groups than others.

To some degree, of course, it would be misleading to consider these variations from person to person as necessarily being "individual differences." There are substantial variations in the completeness of party discipline displayed by the parliamentary groups. We shall unearth traces of evidence that some aspirants to deputy roles may select themselves into membership in various party groupings with an eye toward the degree of party discipline that they as individuals, on prior grounds, would find compatible with their private beliefs as to a proper deputy role. However, it seems likely that most of the self-selection is on quite different grounds, and that variations in observed discipline between groups arise because group norms concerning internal discipline differ in their stringency.

Nonetheless, even within each party grouping there remains a distinct tendency for the rate of defection, faint through it is overall, to show a clustering among certain deputies in a degree that exceeds the expectations set by pure chance variation. Therefore it seems likely that there are not only systematic individual variations in respect for party discipline, but also personal differences in more global conceptions of the role behavior that is proper for the deputy.

Measuring Role Conceptions

We asked all of our elite respondents (including mere aspirants to the role, as well as sitting or former deputies) a number of questions designed to tap variation in role conception. Some of these questions were patterned directly after the legislative role items used by Miller and Stokes (1963). Others were fashioned as supplements to broaden the picture for the French case.

Two sequences of questions, somewhat redundant in content, were posed. Since items involving valued role behaviors are often criticized as being too "hypothetical" when shaped in the abstract, and hence subject to responses that are totally stereotypic or lacking in much realism where the informant's actual behavior is concerned, we were eager to probe the experiential grounding of the responses as far as possible. Items with a strong experiential flavor were easy to compose for respondents who had actually sat as deputies in the Assembly. They could not of course be asked in exactly the same form for other candidates, including new winners, and thus variants in wording were introduced.

The first set of items dealt with the handling of three forms of conflict: between personal feelings or "private conscience" on one hand, and on the other (1) the parliamentary caucus decision; (2) constituency preferences; and (3) the preferences of local party workers. Informants who had ever served as deputies were first asked whether or not they had experienced such a conflict in their legislative voting decisions. Over two-thirds (68 percent) of those with deputy service reported familiarity with the conflict between personal conscience and the party caucus position; and nearly as many (63 percent) reported a conflict between own conscience and the preferences of voters in their constituencies. Far fewer (21 percent) reported any parallel conflict with local party leadership.

A sample of these items in the two variant wordings used, is as follows:

Respondents who had never been deputies	*Respondents who had been deputies*
"Suppose that as deputy you found yourself in the following situation: you wanted to vote in a certain way, but your parliamentary group decided to vote otherwise; what solution would you choose?	"In the Assembly, have you ever found yourself in the following situation: your (parliamentary) group had decided to vote in a certain way, but you yourself wanted to vote otherwise? How have you resolved (would you resolve) such a problem?"

. . . The depth of respect for the parliamentary group decision [appears to be] the primary cue in the decision-making of the individual deputy. This effect is slightly less marked among informants with actual deputy experience than it is for aspirants. This difference, to which we shall return later, is not, however, very large. Yet even among the sitting and former deputies, responses are heavily skewed in favor of the caucus position as determining in such cases of conflict. This is true even where the caucus position is paired against its apparent strongest competitor, the deputy's personal position. And on the other items, which did not involve the caucus explicitly, some of the same flavor shows through, in spite of the difference in question intention. For example, nearly one in five of our informants sidesteps the constituent-conscience conflict item by saying that party discipline would reign in any event. And nearly half of the respondents (more among deputies) sidestep the conflict posed between conscience and the positions of local party leadership, on grounds that more often than not point a finger back to party cues at the national level. For many, these other conflicts are simply not relevant: the main potential conflict is between party caucus and personal position, and even here the party caucus clearly carries the day.

We do not have to read much into the data to conclude that among these four potential sources of cues, the party caucus is a very strong first; personal conscience takes a moderate second place; and cues from constituents or local party leadership run a rather distant third and fourth.

Responses to the second set of questions mainly corroborate these impressions. For these items, respondents were asked to rate the priority that is given (or, for aspirants, that should be given) to four sources of cues external to the self (or "own position") in forming Assembly vote decisions: the parliamentary group caucus position; the position of a "majority of one's voters"; the local-party position; or a desire to support the position of the government. The structured responses offered to these priority questions ran from "absolute priority" through "strong" and "moderate" to "weak" and, finally, "none." Figure 19.1 summarizes these responses comparatively across the four types of consideration, after simple integer scoring has been applied to the five response alternatives and means have been drawn from these scores.

Again, we see that, while our respondents are, on balance, willing to assign at least some priority to all four of these external considerations, the dominant ratings by quite a significant margin are given to the positions of the party caucus. Slightly over 50 percent of all informants accord that group "absolute" priority in decision making, with only 7 percent assigning it weak priority or none at all. The latter proportion is not much greater than the proportion of respondents who either are deputies who do not belong to a party group in the Assembly (*non inscrits*), or candidates who are not members of any party. Barely more than 20 percent of the full elite sample assigns absolute priority to the positions of the local party in their districts, and barely more than 10 percent accords this position of highest influence to the majority positions of their constituents.

Although the differences are not large, informants who have never been deputies give persistently higher priority ratings to all four of these external sources of cues than are assigned by those with deputy experience. It seems clear that deputies view all of these sources of cues with more reserve, and it may not be too much to imagine that they are leaving somewhat more room for the dictates of their own consciences than occurs to aspirants to do.

By far the most disparate set of ratings underlying the group means presented in figure 19.1 occurs in connection with "desire to support the government" as a consideration in voting. The two most frequent responses to this item are the extreme categories of "absolute" priority and no priority at all. Thus the moderate mean shown in the figure is somewhat misleading. It is clear that these particular ratings are entirely situational, with support of the government being very nearly coterminous, in the Assembly sessions between 1967 and 1973, with support of the positions of the Gaullist (UDR) parliamentary group, as government party.

Figure 19.1 Average Priorities Assigned to Each of Four "Considerations" in Forming Assembly Vote Decisions (Elite Sample, 1967)

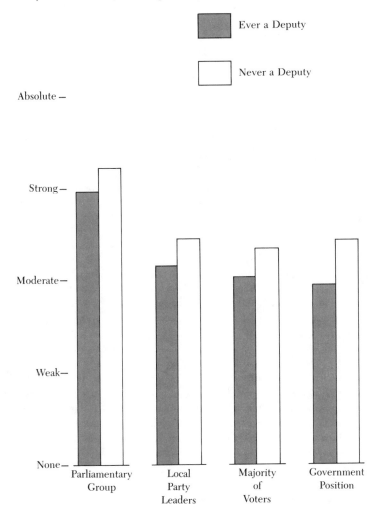

The complete lack of interest in supporting the government *per se* comes from the more determined leftist opposition, largely represented by the Communists and the Federation of the Democratic and Socialist Left (F.G.D.S.). With a leftist government, these roles would almost certainly be as dramatically reversed.

We shall pay little further attention here to these government support ratings. The situational component is so obviously the major source of measured variation, and the ratings so closely aligned with parliamentary group membership along the government-opposition dimension,

Figure 19.2 Schema of Aggregated Representative Role Emphases, France, 1967

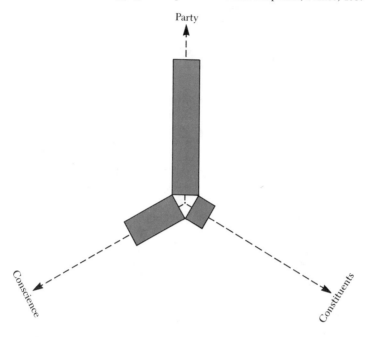

that we can simplify our conceptualizations and analyses by setting this particular item aside.

We will also set aside the local party assessments in moving toward our main working variables defining representative roles. It was of some initial interest to see how our French politicians would rate local party inputs against some of the other possible influences on legislative voting decisions. However, we have found that these potential influences are not accorded much relevance by the actors involved.

Summarizing Representative Role Emphases

Taking the remainder of the data we have presented, and summarizing them in rather schematic fashion in terms of the classic triad of forces bearing on representation—party caucus, personal conscience, and constituency—it would be reasonable to envision the French elite sense of representative responsibilities as looking something like the diagram in figure 19.2, with party entirely dominant, the dictates of personal conscience quite secondary, and constituents a more distant third.

It is important to keep in mind that the design in figure 19.2 is quite deliberately an aggregate summary, and hence dependent in its details upon the particular population or mix of populations being summarized. That is, if we had some reason to exclude from our data those deputies who do not belong to a party group in the Assembly (*non-inscrits*), and candidates running for seats without party membership, the shaded area representing relative sense of responsibility to party discipline would have to be constructed as even more dominant over the other potential responsibilities than already portrayed in the figure. Or again, the preceding data suggest that if figure 19.2 were limited to informants with deputy experience, the weight of the party factor would be slightly weakened in favor of the personal conscience term. In fact, we often will have reason to focus on deputies, setting aside unsuccessful candidates, although we have begun by presenting the full portfolio of data from elite respondents to show how similar the large population of mere aspirants is to the population of deputies. It seems likely that the general contours of these role emphases, if not all the details, represent something reasonably characteristic and durable about French elite political culture where assumptions regarding popular representation in a democratically elected legislature are concerned.

Variations in Role Emphases by Party Group

It is easy to put a finger on a primary source of heterogeneity in these role conceptions that is concealed by the aggregate summary portrayed in figure 19.2. This heterogeneity springs to light vividly when we partition the elite sample by party grouping, whether this is defined as the parliamentary group for current deputies or the party under whose banner the various candidates ran in the election.

The differences from party to party are gaping, and the within-party homogeneity of response patterns is suggestive of strong group norms. The few Centrist (PDM) members show almost a total absorption with the personal conscience term, and some point out that the caucus does not even demand group discipline in voting, an assertion that has a certain amount of truth, although the voting patterns of group members are usually solidary enough to betray what might at least be called substantial intragroup communication and influence. The Républicains Indépendants show some of the same tendencies, although they are less marked. Both of these caucuses were in a way "splinter groups" from the larger, more disciplined factions. The Républicains Indépendants were made up of erstwhile Gaullists who felt it important to be free of the discipline to rubber-stamp government programs that tended to characterize the parent Gaullist caucus. The PDM members were a somewhat heterogenous lot, but tended to be centrist ideologically and hence resistant to giving up the freedom to pick and choose between support and opposition to various government programs, a freedom they would have largely lost if obliged to operate within the discipline of the left or that of the Gaullists. Since resistance to the discipline of the major party groupings was one of the reasons for the existence of both groups, it is not surprising that their own formally constituted caucuses display the weakest norms about discipline, nor that members of both place private conscience ahead of party discipline as well as the preferences of their voters.

Both of these groups were, however, rather small ones. Even in combination, they represented only about 17 percent of the effectives in the 1967-1968 Assembly, and 19 percent in the 1967-1973 period. Therefore they contribute only a modest coloration to the general role emphases summarized for the aggregate of French deputies in figure 19.2. The broadest contours of that diagram are primarily influenced by the three major party groupings, and for all three, party discipline is of primary importance.

The two groups of the left—the Communists and the Federation of the Democratic and Socialist Left—give very similar responses, and here party discipline is supreme. . . The largest grouping, constituted by the Gaullists, is distinct from the left in a lesser emphasis on party discipline, although Gaullists on balance also see party dictates as primary, with conscience secondary, and the preferences of local voters as least important.

The sharp contrasts in role choices from party to party underscore our earlier point that an aggregate summary such as that portrayed in figure 19.2 is dependent on the population included in the data base. If we were to imagine a revised design for a French Assembly in which the PDM and the Républicains Indépendants held a majority, it is clear that the differences in impression would be considerable. However, there is nothing intrinsically misleading about figure 19.2 in its present form, since it accurately reflects the particular admixture of French parties as they stood in the 1967-1968 period. What is considerably more important, it is reasonable to presume that it is at least roughly representative of French parliaments over a much longer period of time, since despite nominal changes, the constellation of a few dominant parties demanding considerable discipline, with splinter groups on the flanks resisting that discipline, has periodically been a feature of the French legislative scene since World War II. This fact, coupled with the strong convergence of role emphases between these deputies and the much larger group of local politicians without any Assembly experience, lead us to suspect that the configuration of role emphases in figure 19.2 tolerably represents an abiding mix of values about representation among French political elites, or at least among that large subset of the political elite that becomes involved in efforts at popular representation.

To judge that these empirically registered emphases deserve to be labelled "French" presumes, however, not only that the responses collected would probably be characteristic of political elites in France over a longer range of time than our immediate study, but also that the patterns displayed are distinctive for French political elites. In other words, if these emphases were about what one would find in interviewing comparable elites in any legislative system, we would simplify matters by dropping the adjective "French" in describing the pattern. There is, however, rather clear evidence that these response patterns are hardly universal.

Some Comparative Reference Points

If party discipline in legislative voting is extremely high in the French National Assembly, it is notoriously low in the United States House of Representatives. Thanks to the initial round of interviewing work carried out by Miller and Stokes (1963) on a sample of U.S. congressmen in 1958, we can profit from parallel representation role data from this contrasting institutional setting.

In some regards, the two bodies of data show uncanny similarities. This is particularly true in the case of the conflict posed between personal opinion and majority opinion in the local district. Some 61 percent of U.S. congressmen report ever having faced such a conflict, while we have seen the figure is 63 percent for French deputies. With regard to the resolution of such conflict, there are minor differences between the two samples in some of the "non-content" categories. Thus, for example, 7 percent of deputies say that such a conflict is impossible, by comparison with 4 percent of the congressmen. Almost 10 percent of congressmen say that they would try to change opinion in their district before voting, while none of those with deputy experience make such a response (although some few candidates do).

If, however, we strip both distributions down to the essential comparisons among the vast majority of these legislators on both sides who are willing to make, although sometimes with qualifications, a clear choice favoring either the district position or the dictates of private conscience, the congressmen show an 86-14 split favoring conscience over voters, as compared with an 85-15 split in the same direction among the French deputies!

Such striking convergences do not, however, hold over all of the representative role items. Since our particular interest at the moment lies in assumptions concerning the party factor, let us turn to those comparisons. The most relevant. . . item is a question which reads: "On most bills that come before the House, how important is it to you whether you vote the way the leadership of your party wants?" This item, which has a

5-point set of response categories, pairs less well with our open-ended item posing conflict between party caucus and personal position, than it does with our structured, 5-point rating item which asks: "In deciding to vote in a certain way, what priority would you generally give to (the position of your parliamentary group)?"

. . . While there are slight differences in wording, both in the root questions and in the response categories, there is no mistaking the two distributions, for they are dramatically different, and in the direction we would conventionally expect. These system differences are the more impressive against the back-drop of responses to the other two terms of the representation triad, where the conflict between voters and conscience is reported as being resolved almost identically between the two political systems. For whatever reasons of political institutions and elite political culture, the sense of responsibility to party as an element in representative role definitions stands in stark contrast between the two countries, and it does not seem rash to imagine that the major differences in the behavioral discipline between the two legislatures are cut from the same cloth. In short, the verbal responses to our items seem to reflect what they should reflect, and with handsome fidelity.

Another parallel study, for which results have been published by Daalder and Rusk (1976) on the same representative role conflict items as we have used, was carried out in the lower house of the Dutch parliament in 1968, and is worth citing as an instance of a system that clearly lies somewhat between the French and American cases, where the party factor is concerned.

Adapting the Daalder-Rusk tabulations to our simplified format, we find that again the responses to the item posing conflict between conscience and the voters are essentially identical to the French and American distributions, at least in their most important particulars. Some 57 percent of Dutch representatives report having experienced such a conflict (as opposed to 61 percent in the United States and 63 percent in France), and the split among content responses as to the resolution of such conflict is 86-14 in favor of conscience (compared with 86-14 in the United States and 85-15 in France). At the same time, responses to the party/conscience conflict are visibly different from those in France and, as best one can guess from less comparable questions, contrast as well with the responses from American congressmen. There is somewhat more frequent report of experience with such conflict in the Netherlands (80 percent compared with 68 percent in France); and the basic split among content responses is 57-43 in favor of *conscience* over party dictates, as compared with the French split of 69-31 in favor of *party fidelity* over conscience.

If we mock up a schematic design like the one presented in figure

19.2, but now restricting our attention to deputies in France and adding somewhat presumptive designs for the sitting legislators in the other two countries, we have the set of contrasts presented in figure 19.3. The only thing the three legislatures depicted have in common is that their members appear to give rather short shrift to majority opinion of voters in their districts in their legislative decision making; and even the implications of this commonality remain clouded at the moment, since one argument for a high degree of party discipline is that it takes the voters into account with the greatest possible fidelity, although at a one-step remove. We can thus reject out of hand any notion that the verbal reports of representative role emphases collected from our French informants are more or less what any set of legislators in any political system would say. More important still, the dramatic Franco-American contrasts in these verbal responses seem to fit admirably with what has long been familiar in "objective" behavioral differences in the voting records of the two national legislatures.

The Individual Stability of Role Responses

Doubts are often expressed as to the "reality" or meaningfulness of responses to items of the type represented by our representative role questions. Most of the doubts cluster around the feeling that they are too hypothetical or abstract. It can be questioned whether in fact there are stable underlying political-value dimensions along which individual legislators actually vary from one another and if there are, whether items like these are able to tap them with adequate reliability. For some investigators, such responses have analytic interest only if it is clear that they tap differences in ingrained values about the democratic process that are rel-

Figure 19.3 Presumptive Patterns of Representative Role Emphases for Legislators in Three Contrasting Political Systems

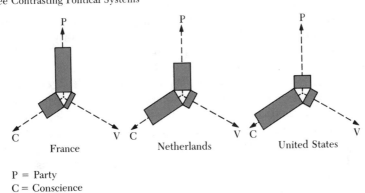

P = Party
C = Conscience
V = Voters

atively "situation-proof." If true value differences are involved, it should be demonstrable that two individuals with opposing assumptions about representative behavior respond to the same situations quite differently; moreover, they should continue to show these characteristic differences in response to a range of relevant choice situations confronted in common over a lengthy period of time.

Up to this point our results have been encouraging in this direction, if less than definitive. After all, we have found marked differences in role emphases offered verbally between legislators in three political systems. And while we have only taken the measures at one point in time, the observed differences in aggregate verbal response lock in so perfectly with behavioral differences (party discipline in legislative voting) that are known to have existed for long periods of time, that it is very hard not to conclude that the distinctiveness of these response patterns from system to system is of comparable vintage and durability. Hence we seem to be tapping differences in abiding system values.

Perhaps more incisively still, we have seen further dramatic differences in response patterns within the French system itself, when we examined role emphases by political party group. . . . Given that moment of individuals from one party group to another in even the intermediate term, while it does occur, is very limited, it would seem necessary to conclude that these role response patterns must be correspondingly stable for individual legislators over time.

However, it is well known that aggregate constancy—even a constancy that is very distinctive for one population relative to others—can also be maintained over long periods of time despite great amounts of individual level fluctuation among population members. Our party members may have no very fixed personal values on these matters, beyond a desire to respect what they see as the norms of their current groups. So they try to report those norms with moderate accuracy; but if their individual responses were tracked over time, they might turn out to fluctuate in a kind of random, Brownian motion around the group norm, so that within-group there would be little or no personal stability at all.

Fortunately, we have some fragments of cross-time data that can throw at least provisional light on this question. Our evidence must be regarded as fragmentary in several senses. After our initial round of interviewing in 1967, we returned to reinterview a subset of departing, remaining, and incoming deputies after the unexpected legislative elections of 1968 that followed in the wake of the May-June disturbances of that year. When we limit our attention to deputies for whom we have double interviews, we have only a very small number of cases (N = 34) with which to work for cross-time estimates, and even these cases are more biased in terms of deputy accessibility than is true of the samples for either year taken alone. Therefore, any estimates we draw from this small deputy panel are much more unstable than most of the descriptive statistics displayed in this article simply because of the small case numbers. We shall try to keep this instability in view of the reader by the device of bracketing the estimates with confidence intervals (at the .05 level).

A second difficulty stems from the fact that some of the cross-time stability estimates that interest us are rather awkward to form if we try to deal with the kind of tripolar representative role variable that is implied by figures 19.2 or 19.3. For many purposes it is useful to have more orderly dimensionalized variables. Therefore we have constructed two major component scales to express the main triad of potential role emphases. The first is a *party discipline* scale, running from no concern about party dictates to exclusive concern, with no attempt made at the low end of the scale to discriminate between legislators emphasizing private conscience and those favoring voters. It is a nine-point scale, based in standard additive fashion on responses to three relevant items within each interview, including the party/conscience and voter/conscience conflict questions, as well as the rating of priority given to the dictates of the party caucus.

The second measure is a bipolar *voter/conscience* scale, capturing the legislator preference between these two possible reference points, while ignoring whatever role he may accord to party dictates, although the purest partisans who give no hint of a choice between voters and conscience naturally fall near the middle of the second scale. This is also a nine-point scale, and is again based additively on the voter/conscience conflict item, supplemented by the priority ratings accorded to voters in the decision equation.

We can evaluate the individual level stability of these two scales, after a lapse of about a year on the average, for barely more than 30 deputies. For the voter/conscience scale the correlation (r) for the two measurements over time is .53 (with a .05 confidence interval ranging from .24 to .74). This is not an exciting magnitude, surely, but enough to suggest a degree of individual level stability that goes beyond what party difference in response would ensure by itself. For the party discipline scale, however, the cross-time correlation is a meager .30 (confidence interval from -.05 to .59). It would seem intuitively that the sharp (and largely constant) party differences, along with lack of much circulation between groups, would be enough to assure individual level correlations at least this high, if not higher.

Closer examination of the paired values underlying the parent cross-time correlation of .30 for the party discipline scale suggested a rather tantalizing property. A considerable majority of the 33 respondents involved, although well-distributed across the nine-point scale, show either exactly the same score in both measurements, or a score differing by only one point. The degree of stability for these cases is impressive. On the other hand, there is a small handfull of cases that show enormous change of $3^{1}/_{2}$ to 5 standard deviations across the scale. It seemed fair to ask whether the few cases of dramatic change on the party discipline scale have other charcteristics in common that set them apart from the informants with stable response patterns.

One of the five cases is rather transparent, as it involves a deputy who shifted between remaining *non-inscrit* in one session and membership in a parliamentary group in the other session. When asked the party questions at the time of group membership, he feels it is his proper role to be a faithful partisan. When he is *non-inscrit*, however, he has no reason to feel he should take a parliamentary group into account. This is an interesting case, as it helps to make clear the fundamental differentiation between what we are calling an abiding personal value, accurate situational measurement, and pure unreliability. Clearly the responses here are situational: the informant is saying what he sees as appropriate role behavior *given* that he is a caucus member, or *given* that he has chosen to remain a non-member.

Proceeding with an effort to understand the sharp contrast between changers and non-changers, on the party discipline scale we formed one hypothesis that seemed reasonable. While all 33 of these respondents were deputies, at least by the time of the second measurement in 1968, a substantial number (N = 13) had just taken seats in the Assembly for the first time at the point of either the first or second interview. We could imagine that this set of new deputies might be only in the early stages of crystallizing a set of personal values concerning the appropriate role of the representative vis-à-vis the parliamentary group. If the role assumptions among these novices were in particular flux, the responses showing remarkable change might be concentrated in this subset.

It is hard to remember an hypothesis as plausible as this that subsequent data have so thunderously disconfirmed. The stability correlation within the set of more experienced deputies (N = 20) recedes to .20 (confidence interval from -.27 to + .68). Among the novices the correlation is .81 (interval from .47 to .94)! Furthermore, despite miniscule case numbers, the difference in these correlation estimates is statistically significant, well within the conventional .05 level.

These findings naturally require some revision of our original surmises, although it is not difficult to construct a plausible scenario, albeit one that is patently *post hoc*, which might account for these results. Although new to the Assembly, all of the novices of the 1967–1968 period were experienced politicians, and many had been aiming for an Assembly seat for a considerable period of time. It would not be surprising if attentive elites of this type were already well schooled before election on role expectations within the Assembly and had already crystallized their own personal responses. While our novices had in fact begun to engage in some legislative decision making by the time of at least the second interview, this "career" had by definition been extremely brief. Therefore it may be tenable to argue that their responses are as extremely stable as they are because the items appropriately tap what are, for them, as yet *untested values*, or assumptions about behavior that have not been forged in the crucible of any substantial experience with the situational pressures of reality.

Given such an interpretation, we would be obliged to set back in time the period in which we thought these responses might be in considerable flux. That flux might be expected to occur after enough experience in the Assembly had accumulated that, for at least some deputies, the demands of reality were forcing change in the naive assumptions with which their Assembly careers had begun. Then at some subsequent time, after the initial values had been adjusted to the constraints of reality, we might expect a return to greater individual level of stability of responses.

We do not have adequate case numbers to partition the data further with results of any satisfying stability. However, the "sophomore" class of deputies that might represent the middle, or flux, phase of our scenario, involves the set of politicians who won their first Assembly seats in the 1962 legislative election, and who were heading into their second term in the 1967–1968 period. There are only eight such cases in our sample of thirty-three. If however we proceed to this new trichotomization of the parent sample, we have the same .81 correlation for freshman deputies; a correlation of .45 among deputies with pre-1962 experience; and, for the suspect set of sophomores lying "between" these oldest and newest groups, a correlation of -.03! Moreover, four of the five cases of dramatic change in scores on the party discipline scale are concentrated among the eight sophomore deputies!

Further spice is added if we ask the same question concerning the phasing of experience with the voter/conscience role preference scale, where the total sample, cross-time correlation was a more satisfying .53. The basic dichotomization here shows a correlation of .16 among freshmen deputies, as opposed to .63 among experienced deputies, or exactly the reverse of the stability contrasts for the party discipline scale. This trend does not quite achieve normal levels of significance (the p-value of a difference is under .15). However, the trend is strong, and in a direction fitting our original, purely intuitive two-stage hypothesis. If we were to credit the difference, we might well rationalize all of these findings in a rather simple way. As we have noted, the question of party discipline is highly salient in the French setting. It would not be surprising if most politicians aspiring to Assembly seats had crystallized some personal values—if largely untested ones—to the dimension in advance. The voter/conscience axis, however, involves issues that would be less likely to be salient in advance of actual occupancy of the representative role. Therefore, novices come to the role with less crystallized attitudes, and our original two-stage surmise remains quite appropriate, despite the fact that a three-stage process of prior crystallization, reality testing, and final firming is necessary to understand the party discipline patterns.

What we have learned in this section is that role preferences concerning party discipline are surely not essentially immutable for all of our French deputies, at least over an interval as crisis laden as the 1967-1968 period. Even this judgment must remain relative. Despite the intervention of the crisis, the data examined remain compatible, for example, with a model in which these role preferences are nearly immutable for most deputies most of the time, but for some few deputies under circumstances of harsh situational constraint, they are subject to dramatic adjustment.

At the same time, we have begun to rule out the possibility that any lion's share of the observed instability in the party discipline responses is due to intrinsic unreliability in the measurement instruments. The case study of the deputy with a status change between being *non-inscrit* and a group member makes clear that at least some of the observed change is situational and real, rather than mere "measurement noise." Similarly, and on a broader front, the ebb and flow of relative stability on the two role preferences scales through the phases of deputy experience seems intelligible enough to suggest that much of what instability is observed in either measure is more decodably "situational" change than it is some endemic defect in the measurement. . . .

Role Preference Statements and Actual Role Behaviors

The ultimate validation of any operational measure requires some demonstration, by independent and external means, that it in fact registers what it purports to measure. For attitudes, values, or other preferences, the ultimate proof of the pudding is often taken to be the degree of fit between verbal responses defining such preferences and the evidence as to actual choice of behavior.

Where responsiveness to the dictates of the party group is concerned, modes of external validation lie very close at hand. After all, the positions of all parliamentary groups vis-à-vis hundreds of roll call votes taken in the Assembly are a matter of public record. Those records of crucial behavior contain the evidence as to which deputies were most doggedly faithful to the positions of their caucuses, and which showed signs of more frequent defection. It is natural to ask how well our party discipline scale predicts of these trends in actual behavior.

Aggregated Behavior Prediction

At the level of aggregation that lies between the complete disaggregation to the individual on one hand, and summaries for the total system on the other, the accuracy of prediction is simply superb. We know from separate observation that there were very large differences, in at least a proportional sense, in the behavioral rates of defection from 1967 to 1973 over the five parliamentary groups. If we partition our informants by parliamentary group membership and take means of the party discipline scale scores within each group, we also find substantial differences. The correlation between the vector of five attitude means and the corresponding vector of five behavioral defection rates is .88, in the anticipated direction.

This is not to say that the norms of these party groups need be seen as perfectly constant. In fact, the Gaullist parliamentary group displayed notably higher rates of defection in member voting patterns during the second period of our study (the 1968-1973 Assembly) than it had in the first period (1967-1968). We hypothesize that this change stemmed from an unusual situational factor: the Gaullists needed almost monolithic internal discipline to carry votes in the evenly divided 1967-1968 Assembly, whereas they could afford remarkable defection rates and still win final outcomes in the second period.

It is therefore of lively interest to note that among the deputies who provided us with two measurements of their party discipline postures, one early in the 1967 session, and the other very early in the 1968-1973 session, there is a slight overall decline in respect for party discipline by the time of the 1968 measure. Virtually all of this decline stems from a rather more brisk decline between the two years within the subset of Gaullist deputies. This minor relative movement indicates not only that group means on attitude predict admirably to subsequent defection behaviors, but also that *changes* in those means predict to group changes in defection behaviors as well, even though the period of prediction stretches some four years after the moment of measurement. . . .

Individual Level Prediction to Behavior

However, all of these assessments remain at an aggregated level, and it is worth continuing the validation procedure down to the level of the individual. In part this is desirable because it is the form in which attitude-behavior correlations are typically cast. In part it is important because there remains a substantial amount of within-party variation in individual scores on the party discipline scale, and it is of interest to know whether such variation, holding group norms constant, continues to seem meaningful.

One explanation is important before proceeding to the data. We have constructed two versions of the behavioral record of defection. The first version is the obvious one: a simple proportion of his total "trials" that the deputy deviated from the discipline of his parliamentary group in casting his roll call vote. But this intuitively obvious measure of the behavioral record concerned us, for the simple reason that some specified topics were subjected to very large numbers of roll call votes, while others were simply represented by a vote or two.

Therefore we constructed a second measure of the behavioral record that would take account of the lack of independence between defections on the same topic. All 445 roll call votes were sorted roughly into one or another of 61 topical categories. The defection score of the particular deputy was calculated as the sum of the proportion of times within each topic area that the deputy defected, given the total number of chances he had to defect for each topic. Thus if the deputy defected once on a topic that only was subjected to two votes, a contribution of .50 was made to his total defection score, as compared with the contribution of .75 that would rise from 12 defections in a topic area voted on 16 times. We shall cite our findings in terms of this "chunked-defection" measure.

There is a whole portfolio of possible test correlations, depending on what attitude predictors are used (1967 report only; 1968 report only; or some combination of the two in the minority of reinterview cases), and what behavioral record is being predicted to (the 1967-1968 session only; the 1968-1973 session only; or the total 1967-1973 record, for the subset of deputies holding seats in both sessions). The version of the test correlation that utilizes all available data most completely is one in which the attitude predictors are basically drawn from the 1967 reports, although they are averaged in with 1968 reports in the limited number of cases where double reports are available, and in a few cases of single interviews, 1968 reports alone are accepted; and in which the behavioral measure is the total chunked-defection record for the whole six-year period from 1967 through 1973. We have an (unweighted) N of 47 cases for this test, which provides a reasonable estimate.

This particular version of the attitude-behavior correlation shows a value of .56. This is the highest value that occurs in the set of possible test correlations, and apparently is at its maximum because of the more extended record of six years and some 445 roll call votes on which to base the behavioral record of defection. The smallest test correlation is .42, a correlation undergirded by more than 60 cases, yet involving only the short behavioral record of 1967-1968 and 87 roll call votes. The other plausible test correlation values are sprinkled between these extremes.

These are quite respectable behavioral validation values, given the purposes for which the role definition responses were collected. They certainly stand out in sharp relief against the initial stability correlation of a mere .30 that we reported earlier for the total party discipline scale taken alone. Two polar ways of looking at that low correlation are, as we have seen, that it either reflects very inadequate measurement reliability, or that the attitudes measured were real enough but subject to high rates of situational change. Neither of these polar interpretations fits with the further validation data at all. If the only reason that the stability was as low as .30, rather than being 1.00, was measurement unreliability, then .30 would be the upper limit for other validation correlations. Or if the value of .30 over a time lapse of a year were due to high and persistent rates of situational change, then one would not expect the behavioral validation correlations to be able to surpass .30 if predicting ahead over the short span of a year; further, if the situational changes were cumulative at the individual level, as would be most plausible to expect, then the longer the span of the prediction beyond a single year, the more the ceiling on the test correlation would deteriorate below .30. Instead, we find the highest test correlation of .56 for the data assembly involving the longest span of prediction.

When all of the empirical facts are put together at the same time, a number of general conclusions about the measurement of these role preferences emerge. One is that while any such measurement involves some error, and while these measures are likely to be less reliable than some, it hard to imagine that their true reliabilities can fall much below .70, given the attitude-behavior correlations along with the fact that there is no reason to expect the true values of those correlations to be perfect in any event.

A related conclusion is that much of the instability reflected in the low stability correlation of .30 is due less to poor measurement than to accurately measured true change in these role preferences. We have already mentioned evidence that respondents whose feelings about party discipline changed *dramatically* between 1967 and 1968 also showed congruent changes in their probabilities of defection. At the same time, the total weight of our evidence makes a very strong presumptive case that the rate of situational change in these role responses was due to the intervening 1968 crisis, at something of a temporal maximum in the period of panel measurement.

Attitude-Behavior Correlations Within Party Groups

Earlier we introduced evidence to suggest that a major source of stability and patterning in party discipline preferences is the diverse party group norms concerning the sacredness of such discipline, ranging from iron discipline on the left to the somewhat more permissive norms on the center and right. Indeed, it would not be implausible to hypothesize that group norms are responsible for *all* of the stability and patterning that exists.

In terms of such a plausible model, we have imagined that within any party group, members might give party discipline responses that varied over time in something like an individual level Brownian motion without much further meaning, around the distinctive central tendency set by the actual group norm. Such a model would be compatible with all of the data that we have presented up to this point. And if such a model pertained, we would not expect any significant attitude-behavior correlations once group norms are held constant, i.e., within a homogeneous set of members of the same party group. In such a case we would be obliged to conclude that once beyond the choice of a party group, no idiosyncratic individual values about the nature of a representative role were involved at all, and that respect for group norms was the total story of these patterns.

The only barrier to a critical test between this model and a rival model in which individual values make some further meaningful input is once again limited case numbers. However, the relative size of the parliamentary groups, particularly after the 1968 election, was extremely disparate. This means that for some parliamentary groups we have passable case numbers, while for others the number of cases is less than five or six, and the computation of a correlation within such a subset is quite pointless.

For the version of the attitude-behavior correlation that produced our central value of .56, we have some 26 cases who were all members of the Gaullist caucus. The attitude-behavior correlation within this subset is .49 in the expected direction. This value is sufficient to reject the null hypothesis of no internal correlation within the Gaullist caucus at the .01 level.

In none of the other groups do we find an absolute correlation as high as in the Gaullist case, and given the fact that case numbers are far fewer in the other parliamentary groups, there is no hope of establishing other significant within-party results. On the other hand, we have inspected the test correlation formed within other groups, and they usually run in the direction expected. In fact, across all of our possible versions of the test correlation, multiplied by within-party correlations formed for all groups that have over five cases, the average correlation runs about .15 in the expected direction. All told, we are content to conclude that the model which posits that group norms account for all of the observed behavior can be safely rejected. Thus it seems that individual values add to the impact of group norms in the patterning of our role preference results. . . .

Implications for Representation

We have now nearly completed our review of mass and elite conceptions of the representative role in France. What remains to be asked is whether the considerable emphasis on party discipline among political elites in France has any particular implications for the character of political representation in France, beyond the obvious corollary that legislative roll call voting in the National Assembly is, over a high diversity of issues, very sharply patterned by caucus bloc. . . .

We are in an excellent position to ask this question because of the way in which the representative role data reported here were imbedded in the broader study of representation. The parent study asked samples of each of the 86 constituencies opinion questions bearing on a considerable number of policy domains including such areas as the distribution of income, public aid for Church schools, union rights, the educational system, European integration, foreign aid, economic development, and the nuclear striking force. Subsequently the record of 445 roll call votes cast by the Assembly seats associated with each of these 86 districts over the period from 1967 to 1973 was ransacked to isolate clusters of votes associated with each of the policy domains tapped by the constituency questionnaire. A summary scaling was constructed within each of these clusters to express relative deputy positions as they varied from one district to another. In a Miller-Stokes vein, the parent study examines the degree of congruence between voter sentiment across districts in these policy domains, and variations in the actual roll call votes cast by their representative in the Assembly.

It is possible to put this portfolio of congruence relationship . . . to work to address the ultimate question of this paper as to the implications of strong party discipline in the National Assembly for the popular representation function in France. We can do so because of a variant that we introduced while coding the roll call votes associated with our 86 districts. The normal or primary coding of roll call votes within each policy domain simply reflects the actual votes cast by the occupant of the district seat. At the same time, however, a secondary coding registered the summary scale score for the district seat that would have pertained had the representative always cast his vote according to the dictates of his party caucus. This "maverick free" coding thus expresses the legislative contribution that would have been associated with the district had party discipline been not just nearly complete, but absolutely complete. One way to ask about the impress of party discipline upon the congruence between district sentiments and representative votes in the parliament is to ask whether such congruence is generally weaker or stronger because of the modest edge of defections from party discipline that do occur.

Differences between scale scores assigned on the basis of votes actually cast, and those assigned on the hypothesis of iron party discipline, are bound to be rather small for the National Assembly. Less than a half-dozen of every one-hundred votes cast in the Assembly represents a departure from the caucus position, and it may surely be asked whether the difference between the actual scaling and the hypothetical party scaling leaves any margin for analytic maneuver at all.

The margin is, in fact, very slight. However it is greater than might appear at first glance because of the way in which roll call votes were selected to be included in the scaling for any given policy domain. In effect, there was a selection away from pure party votes. If in a particular domain, for example, there were ten relevant roll call votes, six of which showed the same configuration of party positions with very minimal defections form discipline, these six votes were considered to be highly redundant and were treated as no more than a single vote. The other four votes which, by construction, produced variant party divisions and larger harvests of within-party defections, were given heavier weight than "natural" relative to the mechanical repetition of the six party votes.

Nonetheless, across a dozen policy domains, the lowest correlation between the two competing vote scalings is .87, and the next lowest .91. The median correlation is .97, and the values rise as high as .995. Fortunately, given the ponderous care devoted to the collation of roll call votes and extreme measures we have taken to verify our manipulations of them, we can consider these competing scales to be essentially error-free, such that a difference between a correlation of 1.00 and a mere .97 has something in it beyond pure measurement noise, and hence is worth the effort to scrutinize. But we surely cannot expect that our congruence correlations, predicting differentially from district sentiment to two such highly correlated dependent variables, can differ from one another in more than trifling degree.

We can at least exploit the fact that we are not limited to a single comparison, but rather can observe general trends in the differences between congruence correlations associated with the two vote scalings over twelve different policy domains and a still larger number of indicators of district sentiment. The choice as to what measure of district sentiment is to be associated with each roll call was made *a priori*, and in most cases produced a multiplicity of potential congruence correlations for each policy domain. Thus, for example, a summary scaling of roll call votes on De Gaulle's nuclear strike force could be meaningfully correlated with district sentiments on a questionnaire item dealing directly with the necessity of such a strike force; but it could be correlated as well with district feelings about the importance of French independence of United States foreign policy; or with district variations in De Gaulle's personal popularity, since he explicitly staked his personal reputation on that controversial policy; or, for that matter, with variations in general left-right district colorations. Thus each pairing of roll call scales can be linked to multiple predictors, and some indicators of district sentiment (most obviously left-right voter positions) were used *a priori* to predict to several roll call scales. Our summary statements about the contrasts between the congruence correlations for votes actually cast, as opposed to the pure party vote scaling, depends on averages of the relevant differences across multiple predictors or, for the predictors themselves, across various policy domains. We also have set aside potential congruence correlations that lie below r = .07, since these seem merely to indicate no particular representation relationship at all, and we are interested in knowing what difference party discipline makes when there is in fact evidence of some kind of representation occurring.

The general trend of the evidence is that *defections from party discipline serve to increase the congruence between district sentiment and representative roll call votes.* The differences are very modest, although we have already seen that there is a severely limited ceiling on such comparisons, and the differences could hardly be more than modest. Nonetheless, in ten of the twelve policy domains surveyed, average correlations between district sentiment predictors and the scales for the actual roll calls containing normal defections run higher than the counterpart correlations where defections are artificially ruled out. Looking at the same matter another way, some sixteen predictor variables figure in one or more congruence correlations that are large enough to be treated as significant. For thirteen of these sixteen predictors, average congruence correlations are higher for the actual votes than for the absolute discipline scales. Thus it seems likely that one major implication of the pressures toward strict party discipline in Assembly voting is to lower the level of congruence between constituent opinion and representative performance.

Conclusion

This finding is of direct relevance for theories of political representation. If one starts with the assumption that the direct expression in legislative decision making of constituency preferences on matters of public policy is the proper goal of representative government, at least for political systems where popular legislative elections take place on a constituency basis, it follows that the deputy must be free to vote on the basis of his estimate of what constituency opinion is on any particular issue whenever he decides that his estimate is more accurate than that of his party caucus. Strict group discipline in legislative voting obviously constitutes an impediment to the fulfillment of that condition and, as we have seen in the French case, would produce some modicum of loss of fidelity of constituency representation.

However, as Pitkin (1967) and others have made clear, political representation is no simple concept, however much it may be necessary to reduce the notion to terms susceptible of empirical examination. The quality of representation is not exhausted in the direct bond between constituency opinion on particular issues and legislative decisions. It would not be unreasonable, for example, to consider that the proper role of the representative is to reflect the opinions only of his electoral supporters. Another obvious alternate conception, which does not obliterate the constituency-legislative output bond, but broadens it, would hold that the critical constituency-level input element of the representative process is not issue opinion per se, but rather perceptions of partisan positions. From this perspective, accuracy in constituency representation would depend not on how closely a deputy mirrored, in his legislative voting, the opinions of his constituents on central issues, but on how well he and his party colleagues matched the expectations of their constituents concerning how they would vote on those issues. Contrary to the theory of representation that emphasizes the necessity for the deputy to be free to vote his perception of constituency opinion, this alternate theory would require that the deputy always maintain group discipline in voting. Viewed in this light, the small loss in representational accuracy that perfect group discipline would have caused in France over the period we have examined might have been more than compensated for by increased predictability in the behavior of all the deputies. This alternate possibility obviously cannot be explored here, although it must eventually be considered. We mention it, however, because we do not wish to convey the notion that what we have presented here is more than a partial examination of the empirical grounding of representative government in France.

20

Voters and Leaders in Australian and British Elections

Clive Bean and Anthony Mughan

Political party leaders are increasingly the centerpiece of the party battle in contemporary liberal democracies. With television's ever more important role in the dissemination of political information and the structuring of political discussion, they are among the principal means by which political parties project themselves and shape their popular images. This is hardly a novel observation in a United States whose constitution militates against party government. It is a development of relatively recent vintage, however, in parliamentary democracies traditionally characterized by strong party government. The tendency to label governments by the name of their leader rather than of the party seems, for example, to have become especially pronounced in Britain since Margaret Thatcher became prime minister in 1979.

In the United States, this "leadership effect" has long been recognized as the strongest force for short-term change in the distribution of the presidential vote. Moreover, it has become stronger since the 1950s (Miller and Miller 1975, 422). But early voting studies in parliamentary

"Leadership Effects in Parliamentary Elections in Australia and Britain," *American Political Science Review* 83 (Dec. 1989): 1165–1179. Copyright © 1989 by the American Political Science Association. Reprinted by permission of the American Political Science Association.

democracies like Australia and Great Britain tended to downplay the independent electoral impact of party leaders, arguing that they were largely indistinguishable from more generalized party images. . . . More recently, though, this conclusion has been revised as party leaders have been shown to have a significant influence on how people vote (Butler and Stokes 1969; Graetz and McAllister 1987; Mughan 1978).

The question that logically suggests itself is, What personal qualities make political leaders an electoral asset for their party? Moreover, are these qualities unique in their electoral effect to particular individuals or can other party leaders expect to reap similar rewards by being perceived to possess them? By showing that presidential candidates are evaluated according to criteria that by and large do not vary from aspirant to aspirant and from election to election, research on the United States suggests an affirmative answer to this second question. Voters would seem to approach an election with a well-defined mental image, or schema, of what a president should be like; and they evaluate candidates against this image. The characteristics of candidates that affect how people vote thus tend to be stable (Kinder et al. 1980).

It is not certain, however, that this characterization of the nature of leadership appeal is generalizable beyond the U.S. presidential system. Previous studies of party leaders in parliamentary systems do not address this issue since they have detailed the content of their images without relating it to voting behavior. But more to the point, prime-ministerial candidates remain more closely identified with party labels than presidential candidates and do not enjoy the same visibility and importance in the electoral process. Popular expectations of what they should be like can thus be expected to be less well developed, and the criteria on which the public judges them more idiosyncratic; that is, to the extent that party leaders are perceived to vary in the qualities they possess, those qualities having an electoral impact should differ from leader to another. In testing this hypothesis, our basic strategy is to maximize the opportunity for idiosyncratic personality characteristics to come to the explanatory fore by comparing two countries, Australia and Great Britain, whose voters differ in their degree of partisan alignment and whose prime ministerial candidates contrast sharply in both their popularity with the electorate and their personality profiles.

Australia and Great Britain

Reflecting a common cultural heritage, the Australian and British party systems have developed along very similar lines and are perhaps best known for being structured by high levels of class voting relative to other Anglo-American democracies (Alford 1963). In more recent years, how-

Table 20.1   [Average] Midterm Popularity Ratings of Party Leaders and
Parties by Country

| Leader or Party | Australia | Britain | | |
		Total	Pre-Falklands	Post-Falklands
Hawke/Thatcher	53	38	31	46
Howard/Foot	33	21	23	18
Labor/Labour	44	33	35	30
Liberal/Conservative	34	36	30	42

Note: These percentage figures are calculated over the months during which Howard and
Foot were the opposition party leaders in their respective countries.

Sources: The British figures are calculated from the Gallup Poll data in David and
Gareth Butler, *British Political Facts, 1900–1985* (London: Macmillan, 1986), 263–64,
and the Australian ones from various issues of the Morgan Gallup Report.

ever, the developmental trajectories of the two-party systems have diverged. In particular, the influence of social class has weakened in British electoral politics and among the consequences has been the emergence of an electorate more responsive to short-term forces and hence more volatile in its voting habits. The Australian party system, in contrast, has remained largely unchanged over this same period. Popular identification with the major antagonists in elections—the Australian Labor party (ALP) on the one hand and the conservative coalition comprising the Liberal and National parties on the other—has changed little over the last two decades or so, the electorate has become no more volatile in its voting habits, and the same three parties continue to dominate the federal vote (Crewe 1985; McAllister and Ascui 1988).

A second pertinent difference between the two countries concerns the popularity of their major party leaders. The elections to be compared are the Australian federal election of July 1987 and the British general election of June 1983. Bob Hawke, the ALP leader, won national office for the first time in March 1983 and and was reelected in December 1984. His British counterpart, the Conservative party's Margaret Thatcher, first became prime minister in May 1979. At the time of the relevant election, both prime ministers had thus been in the public eye as their country's leading political figure for a period of about four years. Both also entered the election facing a new opposition party leader. In 1987, Hawke faced John Howard, who had become the Liberal party leader in September 1985, whereas Michael Foot, having become Labour leader in November 1980, was Thatcher's 1983 opponent.

Table 20.1 summarizes the midterm popularity ratings of these four prime-ministerial candidates. While both incumbent prime ministers enjoyed much the same margin of advantage over their respective opposition party leader, Hawke was substantially more popular with Australians as a whole than was Thatcher with Britons. His superiority in this regard was particularly marked before the Falklands War did so much to boost Thatcher's personal standing in the polls (Norpoth 1987). Even this foreign policy triumph, however, was not enough to close the gap between the two prime ministers. The second, and more telling, measure of Hawke's exceptional popular appear is the size of the lead that he enjoyed over his party. It averaged out at nine percentage points, while Thatcher's was negligible before the Falklands intervention and climbed to only four percentage points after it.

This analysis, then, compares the electoral effect of leadership characteristics in the substantially different contexts of Australia and Britain in the mid-1980s. The two party systems had been moving along divergent paths for over a decade and the incumbent prime ministers not only differed substantially in their level of personal popularity but also headed parties from opposite sides of the political spectrum. Furthermore, and as will become apparent presently, voters attributed very different personality profiles to them. Thus, if party leaders in parliamentary systems are indeed judged by personalized, idiosyncratic criteria, the leadership qualities having an electoral effect should be markedly different in the two countries. Before this hypothesis can be tested, however, various methodological issues need to be considered.

Data and Analytic Methods

The data used in this analysis come from the 1983 British Election Study and the 1987 Australian Election Study. . . .

[We use these data to explain] the vote at the relevant election (in the Australian case, the vote for the House of Representatives), scored 1 for the party in government (Labor in Australia and Conservative in Britain) and 0 for the party in opposition (Liberal-National in Australia and Labour in Britain). Minor parties are coded .5. When party identification enters the analysis as a control variable, it is scored in the same way. The main independent variables comprise a battery of personal characteristics, or qualities, that are commonly thought desirable in political leaders in both countries. In order of their presentation in both survey instruments, these are *caring, determined, shrewd, likable as a person, tough, listens to reason, decisive,* and *sticks to principles.* Respondents were asked which of these qualities, in their opinion, the party leaders possessed, it being emphasized that they should choose as many from the list as they thought appropriate for each leader. Their choices are operationalized as a series of dichotomies, scored 1 whenever the characteristic

Table 20.2   Correlations of Leadership Characteristics by Country

	Australia			Britain		
Leadership Qualities	Hawke with Howard	Hawke with Party Identification	Howard with Party Identification	Thatcher with Foot	Thatcher with Party Identification	Foot with Party Identification
Caring	−.03	.46	.29	−.07	.30	.25
Determined	.12	.18	.15	−.01	.18	.15
Shrewd	−.10	−.20	−.18	.02	.08	−.02
Likable as a person	−.12	.42	.27	−.08	.24	.22
Tough	.12	.12	.02	−.04	.04	.08
Listens to reason	−.14	.46	.35	−.09	.26	.31
Decisive	.09	.22	.16	−.01	.26	.15
Sticks to principles	−.08	.36	.29	−.07	.24	.19
Effective	−.20	.45	.48	−.16	.28	.39

is mentioned and 0 otherwise. An additional characteristic, *effectiveness*, figures in both surveys as a separate question.

A question requiring careful consideration is, Are individual leadership characteristics better operationalized separately or as a combination of perceptions of the opposing leaders? The argument for their separate treatment might be thought strongest in the relatively consensual U.S. political culture; and, to be sure, many studies use separate measures of popular attitudes toward individual presidential candidates. In other studies, by contrast, the Democratic and Republican candidates are treated as opposite sides of the same political coin and their electoral standing is expressed in terms of the net balance of opinion toward them either in the aggregate or decomposed into separate components. In the more adversarial Australian and British political cultures, it might be thought that this second measurement strategy is more appropriate, since their party leaders are more likely to be seen in zero-sum terms. For a respondent to think of Hawke as caring, in other words, would preclude him from assigning the same quality to Howard.

But how party leaders are perceived is ultimately an empirical question, albeit with important substantive implications. Table 20.2 presents data that speak directly to this issue. Columns 1 and 4 display the . . . correlations between prime minister and opposite leader on each leadership quality for Australia and Britain respectively. These correlations suggest that attitudes toward the party leaders are not zero-sum. . . . Far from being perfectly and negatively associated, the perceived qualities of competing leaders turn out hardly to be related at all in either country. Indeed, there are a few instances (three in Australia and one in Britain) where individual respondents show a slight tendency to attribute

the same personal qualities to both major party leaders, making the inter-
correlation of these items positive. Thus, each of the four party leaders
can properly be treated as an electoral force in his or her own right.

There is one potential qualification to this conclusion and it is that
leaders' profiles may be largely a function of respondents' party identification. There is a known tendency for identifiers to view their party's
leader in a favorable light, and it is possible that we have only shown that
negative partisanship does not lead them to view the opposition party
leader in an equally unfavorable light. This being the case, people's identifying with a party could still structure their perception of leaders, making it misleading to treat these perceptions as independent electoral
forces. This fear proves ungrounded, however. Columns 2, 3, 5, and 6 of
table 20.2 detail the simple correlations between partisanship and the
personal characteristics of the party leaders separately. The various qualities can be seen to correlate with party identification to differing degrees
for different leaders. Moreover, they average out in absolute terms at
only .32 for Hawke, .24 for Howard, .21 for Thatcher, and .20 for Foot.
Thus, while the interrelationship cannot be denied, it is nowhere near
strong enough either overall or in individual cases to show perceptions of
leaders' qualities to be artifacts of partisanship, or vice versa.

The personality profiles of prime minister and opposite leader in
Australia and the same profiles in Britain, then, are substantially independent of each other and of those leaders' positions as party leaders. The
questions now addressed concern first the substance, or content, of these
profiles and second, their relationship to voting behavior.

Personality Profiles: Content and Electoral Effect

Examining the distribution of leadership qualities for Hawke, Howard,
Thatcher, and Foot separately [the] dissimilarity both within and between countries [becomes apparent]. Most obviously, there is no group of
characteristics that can be called "winning" or "losing" characteristics.
Insofar as the winners are credited with more leadership qualities on average in each country, they are distinctive only for having the better defined public profile. It is impossible with these data, though, to say
whether this difference is a function of Hawke and Thatcher as individuals or as incumbent prime ministers. The fuller profile of the victorious
leaders, in other words, cannot be taken to suggest a systematic difference between winners and losers; it may represent instead an incumbency effect.

A noteworthy dimension on which Hawke and Thatcher in particular differ from each other is the polarization of their profiles. The British
prime minister is seen as having certain qualities by more than three-

quarters of voters (effectiveness, determination, and toughness) and as having other qualities (listens to reason, caring, and likable as a person) by fewer than one in six of them. Hawke's image, by contrast, is less sharply drawn. He is credited with only one quality (effectiveness) by more than 75 percent of voters; but there is also only one (sticking to principles) that fewer than one in three see in him. Thatcher might, therefore, reasonably be expected to be the more powerful electoral stimulus.

Overall, the differences in the leadership profiles of the four party leaders clearly outweigh the similarities, and this is especially true for the two prime ministers. By any definition, Hawke and Thatcher are exceptionally successful political leaders; and to the extent that their personal qualities influence voting behavior, they [would seem to] have been deemed successful for different reasons. At first glance, this observation supports the hypothesis that leadership appeal in parliamentary systems is unsystematic in the sense of being founded on qualities peculiar to individuals. Yet as compelling as this conclusion may be on the basis of the evidence so far, bear in mind that the distribution of personal qualities and their effect on the vote are two quite different things. It matters little, for example, that Thatcher is widely perceived to be tough if this quality leaves voters unmoved at the polls.

Table 20.3 details how each leadership characteristic is related to party choice in Australia and Britain when the effects of all the others are controlled. The method used is ordinary least squares (OLS) regression analysis . . . , and the cell entries are unstandardized coefficients. Because the predictor variables are scored 0 or 1, the value for each characteristic can be interpreted as the percentage difference (ignoring the decimal point) in the probability of voting for the prime minister's party between those seeing and not seeing that quality in the leader.

We take the equations that exclude party identification first (cols. 1 and 3 of the table). Since the majority of coefficients are statistically significant, their magnitude is more helpful in determining their relative effect on party choice. The principal conclusion is that this effect is far more uniform across leadership characteristics than their varying distribution from leader to leader would have led us to expect. For all four party leaders, their perceived effectiveness is the single strongest influence on voting for their party. The quality of listening to reason also exercises a strong effect across countries as well as leaders. The quality of caring is likewise significant for all four party leaders even if its absolute effect is substantially less powerful for Howard. Sticking to principles is the only other uniformly significant characteristic, but its impact is generally smaller than effectiveness, caring, or listening to reason. These four qualities stand out for the broad uniformity of their impact, but there are one or two others whose influence is more particularized. Most

Table 20.3   The Electoral Effects of Leadership Qualities by Country

Leadership Qualities	Australia		Britain	
Hawke/Thatcher				
Caring	− .14*	.04*	.14*	.05*
Determined	.03	.01	.10*	.04*
Shrewd	− .06*	− .03*	.03*	.02*
Likable as a person	.09*	.03*	.05*	− .01
Tough	.05*	.03*	− .01	− .00
Listens to reason	.12*	.03*	.12*	.05*
Decisive	.03	.01	.16*	.06*
Sticks to principles	.08*	.03*	.13*	.05*
Effective	.29*	.13*	.20*	.09*
Howard/Foot				
Caring	− .05*	.01	− .12*	− .05*
Determined	− .06*	− .02	− .05*	− .01
Shrewd	− .02	− .02	.01	.01
Likable as a person	− .01	− .01	− .05*	− .02
Tough	.03	.01	− .02	− .01
Listens to reason	− .10*	− .05*	− .13*	− .04*
Decisive	− .01	.02	− .09*	− .03
Sticks to principles	− .07*	− .04*	− .06*	− .03*
Effective	− .28*	− .13*	− .22*	− .10*
Party identification	—	.63*	—	.71*
R^2	.52	.72	.46	.76

*$p < .05$.

notable among them is toughness. This has a significant effect on the vote only in the case of Hawke. Indeed, it is the only quality that is important only for one leader.

This evidence suggests that contrary to the original hypothesis, leadership appeal in parliamentary democracies is far from idiosyncratic in character. Despite widely varying distributions across individuals, the characteristics that matter for voters seem surprisingly uniform from one country to the other and from one party leader to another. This conclusion could be premature, however, since voters' perceptions of party leaders are to some degree tied up with their party identification. This is particularly the case for the most influential variable in table 20.3, effectiveness. Its mean correlation with partisanship is .46 in Australia and .34 in Britain. We must therefore control for party identification before reaching any firm conclusion about the nature of leadership appeal (idiosyncratic or otherwise) in parliamentary elections.

Repeating this analysis with party identification included leads to the results reported in the second and fourth columns of table 20.3. The most obvious result of its inclusion is to bring about a substantial and relatively uniform reduction in the predictive power of the individual leadership qualities. This is only to be expected in view of the close relationship between party identification and party choice in Australia and the same in Britain (zero-order correlations of .82 and .85 respectively). The more pertinent observation, though, is that a good number of leadership qualities nonetheless remain important for how people vote. Indeed, the same four characteristics—effectiveness, listening to reason, caring, and sticking to principles—retain their statistical significance and substantive importance across leaders and countries.

Despite its being the quality most closely associated with partisanship, effectiveness remains the greatest electoral asset for a leader, showing a net effect of at least .09 for all four of them; that is, even taking account of their partisanship, voters who see a party's leader as effective are around 10% more likely to vote for that party than those who do not. Moreover, listening to reason and sticking to principles remain significant for all four leaders, and caring is significant for all but Howard. Thus, 4 of 9 characteristics account for 15 (75%) of the instances of significant relationships in columns 2 and 4 of table 20.3. This is not to deny that certain characteristics are personalized rather than uniform in their effect. Determination and decisiveness, for example, are an electoral asset for Thatcher alone, and the same is true of toughness and likability for Hawke. Nonetheless, a perusal of the table indicates that personalized effects are the exception rather than the rule.

A more rigorous examination of the results only serves to reinforce the conclusion of largely uniform effects. For a start, the leadership characteristics make much the same contribution to the overall explanatory power of each equation despite their very different distributions in the two countries. Party identification is slightly more influential in Britain, but the British equation also has a higher R-squared value. By taking the simple correlation between partisanship and the vote (.82 in Australia and .85 in Britain) and subtracting the squared value of each from the appropriate R-squared value in table 20.3, leadership qualities can be seen to contribute between four and five percentage points to the explained variance in each country.

. . . Still stronger evidence of the uniformity of leadership effects [is to be found in] t-statistics testing the hypothesis of a significantly different effect for each personal quality from one leader to the next. A separate bilateral test is performed for each pair of the four party leaders. The questions [these t-statistics] addresses specifically are, first, whether the broad impression of uniformity in the electoral impact of leadership characteristics is sustained when tested more systematically and, second, whether (as table 20.3 might suggest) this uniformity is truer for some characteristics than others. For prime ministers to be perceived as caring, for example, may make people significantly more likely to vote for the party they lead, but is the strength of its impact much the same in the two countries despite Hawke's far greater likelihood of being credited with this quality?

The broad answer to both these questions is affirmative. In the first place, systematic differences across leaders on particular qualities are relatively rare. Less than one quarter of all the t-tests in [this analysis] are significant and in no instance are more than three of the six leadership pairings different on any single quality. Furthermore, there are no substantial differences between any pair of the four leaders on a number of characteristics. This uniformity of effect contrasts starkly with the large variation in the distribution of each leadership quality, the extent of which gave early support to the idiosyncracy hypothesis. Distributional differences, in short, bear little relationship to the size of electoral effect; whether a particular quality is seen in a leader by a small or large proportion of voters, that perception is about equally likely to influence the vote. Thatcher, for example, is not generally perceived as being caring; but when seen in her, this quality is as important as it is for Foot, even though he is credited with it by over three times as many people.

In the second place, this uniformity of effect is especially pronounced for the leadership qualities identified in table 20.3 as having the strongest influence on voting behavior. Three of these four qualities— effectiveness, sticking to principles, and listening to reason—do not differ, in their impact, between any of the leaders. Indeed, these are the only qualities with this distinction. Moreover, with regard to the fourth quality (caring), only for Howard is its effect different; it does not distinguish Hawke, Thatcher, and Foot from each other. Uniformity, then, is characteristic of the leadership qualities that most influence individual voting behavior, and this conclusion provides powerful evidence against the idiosyncracy hypothesis. . . .

Distribution versus Effect: The Electoral Consequences

Two strong conclusions follow from the analysis so far. First, the leadership qualities influencing how individuals vote are remarkably uniform from one leader to the next; second, the precise qualities which have an effect are poorly predicted by their distribution among voters. This is not to say, however, that distribution is an inconsequential electoral consideration in parliamentary—or indeed, presidential—elections. For a leader not to be widely credited with one of the electorally important qualities may be just as damaging to his or her party political fortunes as the widespread attribution of it would be advantageous. Thus, this anal-

Table 20.4 Hypothetical Vote Gains and Losses Attributable to Leadership Qualities

Leadership Qualities	Hawke vs. Howard	Thatcher vs. Foot
Caring	− .05	− 1.67
Determined	.28	.72
Shrewd	.80	− .19
Likable as a person	.13	− .36
Tough	− .28	.37
Listens to reason	.26	− .24
Decisive	− .31	1.47
Sticks to principles	− .24	1.32
Effective	3.74	5.85
Total	4.33	6.57

ysis would be incomplete if it failed to recognize that despite being a poor predictor of their impact on individual voting behavior, variation in the distribution of leadership characteristics can have important consequences for the outcome of elections through its influence on the balance of party votes. The effects of individual characteristics may be quite small in themselves, but variation in the extent to which opposing party leaders are seen to possess them can make their combined impact the difference between victory and defeat in a close election.

The importance of distribution in this respect can be illustrated by means of a hypothetical projection of how the 1987 Australian and 1983 British elections would have turned out had the unsuccessful leaders (Howard and Foot respectively) been perceived to possess the range of leadership qualities in the same proportions as their more successful counterparts, Hawke and Thatcher. In other words, what would have happened in the Australian election had Howard been seen as caring, determined, and so on by the same proportion of voters as was Hawke? We can move toward a tentative answer to this question by subtracting the proportion of voters seeing each quality in Howard from the proportion seeing that quality in Hawke. This gives a measure of Hawke's distributional advantage on each characteristic (or disadvantage in the case of sticking to principles). If this figure is then multiplied by the matching Howard regression coefficient (with the sign reversed) from the second column of table 20.3, the result is an estimate of the number of percentage points by which the Liberal vote would have increased had the same proportion of voters credited Howard with that quality as credited Hawke with it. In other words, it is a measure of Hawke's net worth (relative to Howard), in votes to the ALP.

The results of this procedure, calculated for both the British and the

Australian party leaders, are presented in table 20.4. A positive sign indicates that the particular quality is an electoral asset for the prime minister in each country, and a negative sign that it is an asset for the opposition party leader.

Summing the individual coefficients indicates quite clearly that both Hawke and Thatcher were a substantial electoral asset for their party. If Foot had possessed Thatcher's personality profile, Labour's vote in the 1983 general election would, other things being equal, have been some six to seven percentage points higher than it was. The difference is less stark in the Australian case, but the contrast in Hawke and Howard's personality profiles was still worth some four percentage points in the ALP. Even allowing for the statistical error in these estimates, such differences are considerable, and they point up the nontrivial vote gains that can be made by having the "right" party leader, even in parliamentary elections.

Table 20.4 also highlights the importance of the quality of effectiveness to the definition of the "right" leader. While this quality has much the same effect for all four party leaders, the two opposition parties can be seen to have been seriously disadvantaged by the tendency of voters not to see their leaders as effective. Howard was credited with this quality by 28 percent fewer Australians than Hawke, while Foot had a massive deficit of 61 percent relative to Thatcher. After taking account of the tendency of some of the other characteristics to cancel each other out, the combination of the strength of effectiveness' influence on the vote and its highly skewed distribution means that this one quality accounts for a very large part of the hypothetical vote difference in each country. It alone generated an estimated 5.8 percent vote advantage for the Conservative party in Britain and an estimated 3.7 percent Labor advantage in Australia. These figures suggest that the perceived difference in the effectiveness of Hawke and Howard was sufficient on its own to tilt the outcome of the 1987 federal election in the ALP's favor.

Conclusion

This analysis has been concerned with specifying the nature of leadership effects in parliamentary elections. Its background is the "presidentialization" of politics in this type of political system and the barrage of adverse criticism that has greeted this development. The importance of leaders is not necessarily new. It is quite probable that a number of leaders in the past, such as Menzies in Australia and Churchill in Britain, also symbolized their parties in the public eye. But one obvious and crucial difference between then and now is television and the central role it has come to play in political campaigning and communication. Critics argue that the personalization of the election campaign strategies adopted by political parties, particularly through this medium, trivializes democracy as individuals are encouraged to make their voting decisions on the basis of ill-informed judgments about the idiosyncratic personality characteristics of individuals who rise and fall from the political stage. In the words of one respected Australian journalist: "We are now firmly in the age of polished, packaged politics; image is on a par with intellect; presentation matters as much or more than ideas. . . . The contestants . . . trade simplified, if not simplistic, slogans that will indicate at only the most generalized level the values and priorities on which they differ. . . . The tailor, hairdresser and color consultant will become important political advisors" (Barker 1984).

Our analysis speaks directly to this debate in two respects. In the first place, it confirms that just as with candidates in presidential elections, party leaders can influence the distribution of votes in parliamentary contests. Indeed, Hawke would seem to have been the difference between victory and defeat for his party in 1987. . . . While the same cannot be said for Thatcher in 1983, dealignment and the rise of minor parties in Britain could mean that party leaders will find themselves playing the same pivotal role there on occasion.

In the second place, little support is found for the claim that leadership characteristics affecting the way people vote are idiosyncratic and trivial. We made every effort to ensure that the idiosyncratic prevailed over the systematic in this examination of leadership effects in two countries. The evidence, however, points clearly to the unimportance, by and large, of the idiosyncratic, suggesting instead that prime ministerial candidates are judged against some kind of well-defined schema in the public mind and that they will have a positive electoral impact to the extent that they conform to this mental image of what a leader should be like. Miller, Wattenberg, and Malanchuk (1986) demonstrate this purposive evaluation of political leaders to hold true over time in U.S. presidential elections; we demonstrate it to hold true across countries and leaders in parliamentary elections.

Nor is there much reason to believe that it is the trivial in leaders that appeals to voters. If it were, we would expect the highly personal quality of liability in particular to have had a strong—if not the strongest—effect on voters. As it turns out, however, it is of little importance overall. Instead, perceived effectiveness dominates how voters respond to leaders, and few would deny that this quality is a key ingredient of successful political leadership, especially when viewed from the parliamentary perspective of implementing the manifesto on which the government was elected. Their ability to have demonstrated their effectiveness in office means that other things being equal, incumbent prime ministers go into an election with an advantage over opposition party leaders who have not held the top job before. This advantage is limited, though, since voters who perceive the opposition party leader to be effective are no less likely to vote for his party than are those who see the same quality in the incumbent prime minister. For this apparent incumbency advantage to be neutralized, in other words, the calculus of voting does not have to be reshaped. The challenger faces the less onerous task of matching the incumbent in conveying the image of being likely to be an effective prime minister.

These results indicate, above all, a pressing n⸌ ⸌ to understand better the nature of leadership appeal in democratic political systems, be they parliamentary or presidential. It is not enough to know, for example, that Australians and Britons are particularly likely to be swayed in their voting decision by the perception of leadership effectiveness. There is also the question of what this quality means for voters and whether its meaning is the same from one country to another.

SECTION IX

IMPACT OF
POLITICAL LEADERS

Introductory Comment

The focus on linkage in Section VIII serves as a reminder that leadership is a relational phenomenon; it can occur only in the context of interaction between leaders and followers. This interaction is, of course, not random. Political leaders generally obtain support from would-be followers by promising to use their control of the apparatus of the state to provide them with valued goods and services, which may take a variety of forms, ranging from the relatively intangible, like psychological gratification, to the very tangible, like economic improvement. The important point is that political leaders cannot feel confident about retaining their position indefinitely if their delivery on the promises that brought them to office in the first place fails to satisfy the expectations of followers.

The need for leaders to have an impact on the availability and distribution of goods and services would appear to be nowhere more apparent than in democratic political systems. In exchange for their support at the ballot box, competing political parties offer voters a package of policy promises in particular and governmental competence in general. The institution of regular, free, and competitive elections is the device by which voters express their preference among the compet-

437

ing teams of leaders on offer to them. It is at the same time the means by which the party in government is brought to account for the competence of its performance in office and for its delivery on its campaign promises. Its failure to satisfy erstwhile followers on either or both counts risks vote defections that could lead to its ejection from office.

In view of the centrality of elections to the democratic political process, it is no surprise that a considerable research effort has been spent on gauging the impact of political leaders on the policy outputs of governments. The result is a lively debate the question at the center of which is, Does politics matter? In other words. ꟼoes the ideological complexion of the party or president in office havᴄ an impact on the kinds of policies that democratic governments enact?

The assumption appears to have long been that it clearly mattered. Political parties propagate different ideologies and make different policy commitments in their quest for election to office and it seems inevitable that their desire for reelection would lead them to act on their campaign promises once a mandate to govern had been conferred on them by voters. A number of empirical studies, however, have suggested that this assumption is at least questionable.

Some early doubt was cast on its validity by empirical studies of welfare policy outputs in the American states. The conclusion of these studies was that such outputs were largely unaffected by the identity of the party, Democratic or Republican, that controlled the state government. Their more potent determinant was the level of economic development of the states (Dawson and Robinson 1963; Dye 1966). The same conclusion followed from Cutright's (1965) analysis of 76 nations, which indicated that economic development was more important than political factors in determining social policy outputs. Finally, an analysis of British economic policy under a succession of both Conservative and Labour governments leads to an equally pessimistic conclusion. Insofar as a range of aggregate economic performance measures, like gross domestic product and the level of public expenditure, show a more or less upward trend regardless of which party is in office, Rose (1984) concludes that "something stronger than parties" controls economic policy and thus parties do not in fact "make a difference."

There is also a body of literature that is equally emphatic in its conclusion that leaders do have an impact. It has been convincingly demonstrated, for example, that parties do deliver on a good proportion of the campaign promises their leaders make to win office (Budge, Robertson, and Hearl 1987). Similarly, after an extensive analysis of the policy effects of leadership succession in democratic and socialist societies, Bunce (1981, 223–24) concludes that "new leaders—under socialism and under bourgeois democracy—do matter. . . . [N]ew leaders make a difference in the rhythm of policy change and the types of policies that are advocated."

Examples of both conclusions could be presented endlessly. Neither can be said to be right or wrong, however. A central theme in the study of leadership is that the impact of leaders varies with the situation. The appropriate question, therefore, is not whether leaders have an impact, but under what conditions they have an impact.

To be sure, leaders who are of a certain personality type or who have a certain orientation to their role may be more likely than their opposites to leave their mark on politics. But even activist leaders might find their impact on the policy output of their government seriously undermined by changing circumstances. Equally, a leader might find his political impact greatly enhanced by changes in the political environment. Winston Churchill, for example, would probably not enjoy the reputation that he does had Britain not gone to war with Germany and thereby created a demand for his particular blend of leadership skills and talents that was simply not there in peacetime. Similarly, the question must be asked whether Abraham Lincoln would still be considered America's greatest president had the Civil War somehow been averted.

The selection of readings in this section emphasize the circumstantial character of leadership impact. All three are studies of the U.S. presidency to make this point the more strongly. The first two of them focus narrowly on the short-term policy impact of presidents. Jones shows clearly how a combination of favorable circumstances allowed Ronald Reagan to pass a particularly radical budget in 1981, a budget that laid the foundations for the so-called "Reagan Revolution." These circumstances soon changed, however, and Reagan came nowhere matching this initial legislative success in his remaining seven years in office. The second reading makes much the same argument, but over a longer time period. Writing in the mid-1960s, Wildavsky had examined the success rates of a number of presidents in their dealings with Congress and concluded that the United States had not one but two presidencies, a weak domestic affairs presidency and a strong foreign affairs one. This conclusion came to be part of the conventional wisdom surrounding the presidential office. It does not hold for more recent presidencies, however, and Oldfield and Wildavsky trace the changing circumstances that have eroded presidential autonomy in foreign affairs.

The Kernell reading takes a longer-term perspective on presidential impact. His starting point is the observation that advances in communications technology have allowed modern presidents to seek to mobilize support for their policy initiatives by "going public" and appealing directly to voters "over the heads" of their Washington adversaries. This practice circumvents the bargaining and persuasion that have long been the hallmark of American politics, and Kernell's chapter examines its implications for the way politics is conducted in the federal government.

SELECT BIBLIOGRAPHY

Budge, I., D. Robertson, and D. Hearl, eds. 1987. *Ideology, Strategy and Party Change: Spatial Analyses of Post-War Election Programmes in 19 Countries.* Cambridge: University Press.

Bunce, V. 1981. *Do New Leaders Make a Difference?* Princeton, NJ: Princeton University Press.

Castles, F.G., ed. 1982. *The Impact of Parties: Politics and Policies in Capitalist Democratic States.* Beverly Hills, CA: Sage.

Jackman, R.W. 1975. *Politics and Social Equality: A Comparative Analysis.* New York: Wiley.

Pomper, G.M. 1968. *Elections in America: Control and Influence in Democratic Politics.* New York: Dodd, Mead.

Rose, R. 1984. *Do Parties Make a Difference?* 2d ed. Chatham, NJ: Chatham House.

21

Ronald Reagan's Leadership of Congress

Charles O. Jones

This chapter examines President Reagan's method of, and success in, dealing with Congress. There is perhaps no better indicator of a president's political style than his working relationship with those on Capitol Hill. . . .

This actor liked playing the president. He understood the role better than most, possibly because his occupational training prepared him to do so. The distinction between becoming president and playing the president is an interesting and important one. Reagan himself appeared to make it in an interview in 1986: "Some people become President. I've never thought of it that way. I think the Presidency is an institution over which you have temporary custody and it has to be treated that way. . . . I don't think the Presidency belongs to the individual." Perhaps one starting point in the exercise of power is knowing who you are and where you are.

The 1980 Election: Advantage Reagan

" 'Mandate' was one of the favorite nouns on the election night televison coverage. . . ." (Wolfinger 1985, 292). Those who interpret elections

From *The Reagan Legacy: Promise and Performance*, edited by C. O. Jones (Chatham, NJ: Chatham House Publishers, 1988), pp. 30–59. Reprinted by permission.

search for the message. If a president wins 91 percent of the Electoral College vote, and his party returns with a majority in the Senate for the first time in twenty-six years, it is virtually guaranteed that a "mandate" will be declared to exist. This will occur regardless of the implausibility of the concept in American national elections or solid evidence that, for example, many voters were expressing dissatisfaction with President Carter, not approval of candidate Reagan (Markus 1982, 560).

Reading a mandate into the 1980 election outcomes established policy expectations of President Reagan and provided him with significant political advantages in working with Congress. As it happened, Reagan conveyed a rather strong policy message during the campaign—"an unusually coherent social philosophy," as one analyst put it. (Reichley 1981, 229). Thus, those anxious to declare a mandate did not have to search long and hard for a policy message. During the campaign, Reagan offered a prescription for change and promised to put it into effect once in office. There was none of the ambiguity that came to be identified with the Carter approach. When the pundits declared a mandate to exist, they could then follow that announcement with a clear exposition of what to expect.

Meanwhile, at the other end of Pennsylvania Avenue, House and Senate Republicans returned triumphantly to Washington after the election. In the House, the net increase of thirty-three Republicans was the greatest in a presidential election since 1920. But it was the Senate results that stunned observers. No one called that one in advance. . . .

As it happened, Republican candidates won eight of the nine [Senate] races that were too close to call, five of the seven that were leaning Democratic, and one of eight that were declared safe for the Democrats. The net gain of twelve seats was the second greatest in this century for the Republicans. The fact that the Democratic senatorial candidates as a whole actually outpolled the Republicans was lost, or not discovered, in the short-term rush to declare a Reagan mandate.

Comparison of these results with those of previous Republican landslides in the post-World War II period shows why observers were encouraged to declare a Reagan mandate. In 1952 Eisenhower won impressively, to be sure, but by a lesser percentage in the Electoral College (83 percent). Further, the 1952 race was between nonincumbents; Reagan defeated an incumbent Democratic president (the first to lose since 1888). The Republicans did gain House and Senate majorities in 1952, but the actual gains were less impressive than in 1980: a net increase of twenty-two House seats (33 in 1980) and just one Senate seat (12 in 1980). In his second term, Eisenhower did slightly better in the Electoral College (86 percent) but House Republicans had a net loss of two seats; the number of Senate Republicans did not change. The third landslide for

Republicans belonged to Richard Nixon in 1972. His Electoral College margin (97 percent) surpassed that of Reagan in 1980, but the net gain of House seats gained was small (12), and there was a net loss of two Senate seats. The 1972 election was widely interpreted as a triumph for Nixon, but not for his political party in Congress—in this regard similar to Reagan's 1984 reelection.

Also relevant is the fact that Ronald Reagan ran with his party in 1980, not alongside it. Eisenhower was judged to be above party politics, and publicly he sought to preserve that image. In 1972 Nixon ran more for himself than for his party. Reagan worked at unifying the party at the nominating convention and after. He integrated his campaign effort with that of the national party organization, and he never shied away from appearing with or aiding other candidates. Further, for those who pay attention to such matters (as do most members of Congress), Reagan ran ahead of thirty of thirty-four Senate Republican candidates (counting just the two-party vote). And although he ran behind most successful House Republican candidates in their districts (most presidential candidates do these days), still he did better than President Ford in 1976 in most districts.

The point is that there was more reason than usual in 1980 to interpret the presidential and congressional elections as representing a package deal. The victory for Reagan was decisive, there seemed to be "nontrivial coattail effects," and the policy message was unambiguous. Even the Democrats and liberals detected a conservative tide in the nation. Defeated incumbent Senator Frank Church of Idaho concluded that "the conservatives are in charge now. This is what they wanted and the people have given it to them." There was a receptive mood for giving the president a chance, even though to do so was to invite dramatic change. . . .

Organizing to Take Advantage

President Lyndon B. Johnson observed that "you've got just one year when the [members of Congress] treat you right, and before they start worrying about themselves." He acted on this knowledge and had one of the most productive first years of any president. Ronald Reagan intended to be an activist president too, although in the opposite direction from the one that Johnson took. Therefore, Reagan wanted to act fast, to "hit the ground running," as the phrase has it.

As has been emphasized, the 1980 election and how it was interpreted offered many advantages to the new Reagan administration. As an additional plus, it seemed that members of Congress from both parties were ready for somewhat better treatment by the White House. Presidents Nixon and Carter, in particular, preferred the full length of Penn-

SECTION IX: IMPACT OF POLITICAL LEADERS

sylvania Avenue in distancing themselves from Congress. Neither had very flattering views about the institution or its members.

The Reagan style was very different. Although not from Capitol Hill, Ronald Reagan demonstrated respect for the politics practiced there. Whereas he was unlikely to be as close to the members as either Presidents Johnson or Ford, still he would not make the mistake of distancing himself from Congress in either thought or deed. And as the "great communicator," he understood the need to sell his program to those who would vote on it. James P. Pfiffner (1983, 627) describes how it went in those months between election and inauguration:

> The president-elect held a series of dinners to which he invited members of Congress. With the realization that Democratic votes would be necessary for his legislative agenda he announced that he would retain ex-Senator Mike Mansfield as ambassador to Japan. He took particular care to court House [Speaker] Tip O'Neill who had chafed at perceived slights from the Carter White House. He and his wife were invited to a private dinner at the White House, and he was also invited to the president's small seventieth birthday party. Republican members of Congress were invited to advise the transition teams in the departments. And the President-elect sought the advice of Senators Robert Dole, John Tower, and Strom Thurmond in making his cabinet choices.

Members of Congress loved this attention. . . .

The president also acted quickly in establishing a congressional liaison team and in preparing his program for submission to Congress. A veteran Capitol Hill staff person, Tom Korologos, was called on to assist the President-elect in his preinaugural congressional contacts and to build a White House liaison team that would take over after the inauguration.

Korologos himself did not stay on to manage the team. That task fell to another Hill veteran, Max Friedersdorf. It would be hard to imagine a better choice, given the circumstances. Friedersdorf served on the liaison team for both the Nixon and Ford administrations, and before that he worked for a House member from Indiana for ten years. He also served as chairman of the Federal Election Commission, an agency with many congressional contacts. . . . Whether or not they agreed with Reagan's policy preferences, those on Capitol Hill were reassured that they would be dealing with, in Speaker O'Neill's characterization, "an experienced and savvy team." In fact, O'Neill was impressed with the whole White House staff: "All in all, the Reagan team in 1981 was probably the best-run political operating unit I've ever seen." (O'Neill 1987, 345). No doubt this was in part because the Speaker himself got quite good service, even as a Democrat: "Reagan's aides were never parochial, and despite our many disagreements, they never showed any animosity toward me. On a few occasions, when lower-echelon people tried to block programs for my district, I would call the White House, where Mike Deaver or Jim Baker or somebody else on the president's team would always straighten things out" (O'Neill 1987, 342). Later in the Reagan administration, O'Neill's relationship with Donald Regan was not so amiable.

All presidents must depend heavily on their staffs, but Reagan's style made him more dependent than most. His has been a very public Presidency, yet, compared to other recent presidents, he has a low tolerance for detail. Further, he proposed a difficult, even contentious, agenda for Congress. Thus he needed an able and experienced liaison staff. Friedersdorf [Reagan's chief liaison with Congress] was just the person to provide it. He selected "young-old" people. "I wanted people youthful enough to put up with the long hours and physical demands, yet old enough to be patient and mature." It was an impressive group. The average age was thirty-seven. All the principal lobbyists had experience on Capitol Hill—four in the Senate, four in the House, one in both. In addition, several had experience as interest-group lobbyists or, like Friedersdorf himself, in executive liaison offices.

Given the credentials of those beneath him, it was possible along the way for Friedersdorf to step down and be replaced by another "pro." In fact, turnover in the liaison office was rather high. Kenneth Duberstein, initially chief House lobbyist, took over the top position in 1982. Then M. B. Oglesby, Duberstein's replacement as head of the House liaison team, took over for Duberstein in managing the whole office in 1982. Following the 1984 election, Friedersdorf returned so as to get the second administration off to a good start. Oglesby stayed on with his close friend, so the liaison office more or less had two chiefs. While a suitable arrangement for Friedersdorf and Oglesby, it did not work well on Capitol Hill, and in the fall of 1985 Friedersdorf left once again. Then Oglesby left in early 1986, and William L. Ball III took over. Ball had been managing congressional relations for the Department of State—again, an experienced hand to guide the White House liaison office. In late February 1988, Ball was chosen secretary of the navy. His replacement was Alan M. Kranowitz, who had been directing White House lobbying efforts in the House. . . .

No liaison staff can expect smooth sailing throughout. Staff members act as "point persons" for the president on the Hill, and when it comes to difficult issues, members are unlikely to be cooperative just because the White House lobbyists are experienced and talented. Once the Democrats recaptured control of the Senate and the Iran-*contra* matter broke, the liaison team had its hands full. Fashioning majorities for budgets, domestic priorities, even treaties, and certainly appointments to the Supreme Court would be very difficult. What can be said here is that no more problems were added because of liaison personnel themselves. Apart from the confusion caused by Friedersdorf's returning in 1985, the liaison staff performed ably in coping with deteriorating political conditions.

Finally, the President himself was a tremendous asset for the liaison team. "We had to lasso him to keep him off the Hill" during the first year, according to one close adviser" (Wayne 1982, 50). Members of Congress naturally make comparisons with the immediately preceding occupant of the White House. They found Reagan to be approachable; a willing participant in support of his legislation (if seldom conversant with the details). Relationships with President Carter, even for Democrats, were much more uncertain and distant.

Establishing the Legacy in 1981

Very few presidents can claim legislative triumphs that are truly turning points in domestic policy. In this century, Franklin D. Roosevelt and Lyndon B. Johnson can legitimately make that case. The New Deal and Great Society programs constituted quantum increases in the role of the federal government in social and economic life. In both cases the president and Congress acted quickly to effect a policy shift that was so dramatic as to dominate future agendas. The politics of incrementalism, so characteristic of the American system, was suspended for a short time. We experienced unprecedented policy breakthroughs, unchecked by the normal restraints of separated institutions and intergovernmental divisions.

Ronald Reagan could claim such a breakthrough in 1981. By employing "speed and focus," the White House produced breathtaking legislative successes. Friedersdorf (Wayne 1982, 56–57) was quoted as saying that "we knew we had to get our bills enacted before the Labor Day recess" and that "the president was determined not to clutter up the landscape with extraneous legislation." The Carter legacy of distressingly high interest rates and inflation contributed mightily to determining the policy focus.

> The economy became the first, second, and third objective and Reagan staked his reputation on it. By choosing the economy, he added simplicity to both policy making and the policy process. All social and domestic issues were discussed not in terms of need, equity, or values, but in budget recommendations—how much can be cut back without causing an uproar. (Walker and Reopel 1986, 747)

Alongside the maxim "Establish a focus" is the advisory "Don't come up with other mischiefs." This important lesson was also a product of the recent Carter administration. For in addition to overloading the legislative circuits, President Carter induced ill will on Capitol Hill by asking members to eliminate public works projects from their states and districts. Such "mischiefs" were highly diverting from his other priorities. For Reagan, certain far-right causes could easily cause mischief. As Chief of Staff James Baker noted: "Abortion cuts both ways hard. If you come down one way or the other, you lose some people. Most of the social issues are polarizing" (quoted in Walker and Reopel 1986, 747).

One learns much about the Reagan legacy from this avoidance of mischiefs. The politician uses ideology, but does not lose because of it. Ideology provides policy direction, but not to the exclusion of political success. Presidents who try to satisfy the fringes of their support, whether it be to the right or left, sacrifice support in the middle, where the majority normally resides. The trick is to press policy preferences to a limit beyond which you would lose support, then compromise and declare victory, saving ideological purity for another day.

What was won in 1981, and with what impact? Allen Schick (1982,14) points out that "Ronald Reagan won the battles but lost the budget."

> On four issues he challenged congressional Democrats and obtained the legislation he demanded. The first budget resolution was crafted according to his specifications, as was the reconciliation bill it triggered. The President also emerged victorious in a bidding war over tax legislation. His final triumph came in the closing days of the session when Congress approved a continuing appropriation that satisfied most of his demands.

Schick (1982, 14) concedes that winning the battles may have been more important to President Reagan than losing the budget. "Perhaps the budget was only a cover for his real objectives." Whether that was the case or not . . . the effects were clear enough. First, winning most of the battles in 1981 focused attention on the budget and growing deficits. Those favoring additional government welfare programs were literally made speechless. Those supporting current programs were forced to justify them as never before. Many Republicans, including Stockman, wanted to go much further in dismantling the welfare state. Some such advocates felt betrayed by Reagan. Regardless, the 1981 victories produced a significant agenda shift that altered policy politics in Washington.

Second, the effects of 1981 were not limited to one year. Tax cuts went into effect over a three-year period. Defense expenditures were to increase over several years. And although cuts were made in certain domestic programs, Reagan's 1981 plan for social security adjustments was defeated. This combination of less revenue and a significant boost in defense spending, without fully compensatory reductions in entitlement programs, assured mind-boggling deficits through a first and into a second Reagan term. Subsequent policy conversation would be dominated by the legacy of 1981. . . .

A third effect was simply that it was difficult to judge who had won when the president lost, as he did with increasing frequency after 1981. The game was being played on his field, with his ball—that was the effect of 1981. The Democrats prevented him from scoring, but it is hard to win any game by playing defense only. Further, if the Democrats mounted an offensive (typically in cooperation with congressional Republicans), they might find that the president joined them at the goal line to take the ball across (e.g., as with the 1982 tax increase).

The details of the 1981 triumph on Capitol Hill are as follows:

1. Passage of the Economic Recovery Tax Act, a multiyear package that projected a reduction of nearly $750 billion.
2. Enactment of a budget reconciliation resolution designed to reduce domestic spending by over $35 billion.
3. Approval of a defense plan of nearly $200 billion for 1982, less than the President wanted originally but more than President Carter had proposed.
4. Significant reductions in the Aid to Families with Dependent Children (AFDC) benefits, food stamps, certain antipoverty programs, and other minor welfare benefits.
5. Savings in Medicaid and Medicare programs, but postponement of an overhauling of the social security retirement system.

The first session of the 97th Congress was described as "a great personal triumph for Reagan. Congressional approval of his plan was due largely to his own efforts and strength" (Arieff et al 1981, 2505). Certainly the president played the central role, but his "personal triumph" was accounted for by an extraordinarily effective White House political operation. A strategy was developed and executed for taking advantage of the favorable political conditions.

Since so much of the strategy was centered in the budget, it was understandable that David Stockman, as OMB director, played a key role. A Legislative Strategy Group (LSG), made up of "the inner circle of White House aides," met frequently in Chief of Staff James Baker's corner office in the west wing of the White House. The LSG "wasn't even on the White House organizational chart," but it played a key role in formulating an approach to Congress and, in the process, communicating political signals and policy information among the key players in the White House and on Capitol Hill (Stockman 1986, 4).

Essentially the strategy was designed to capitalize on advantages and be ever attentive to the political situation. How this was done in the first months of the new administration is itself an important part of the Reagan legacy. No doubt other presidents in similar situations will seek to emulate the Reagan strategy. First and foremost, the LSG sought to concentrate congressional and media attention on the budget. The Reagan White House got high marks for setting priorities and for not dissipating its energies. Yet, making the budget a priority is not exactly an oversimplification of the policy world. The budget is very nearly everything. Therefore, the Reagan strategists had the double advantage of a seemingly simple agenda and yet one that was bound to have a significant and comprehensive policy impact.

Second, Congress itself facilitated this concentration by its budget reform of 1974. It would have been very difficult for the president to keep all eyes fixed on the budget had it not been for the new organization and procedures on Capitol Hill. The Congress provided itself with budget committees, a budget office (as a counterpart to the Office of Management and Budget), and a budget resolution (as a counterpart to the executive budget). The media could now follow the action. Further, a so-called budget reconciliation was tried for the first time by the Carter administration in 1980, thus providing a sort of test run for Reagan. The reconciliation process is designed to enforce the budget resolution within congressional committees. Thus it was a perfect tool for the Reagan strategists in forcing Congress to meet its own budget targets.

Third, the LSG knew by instinct and recent experience that mandates are short lived, particularly those that are illusory to begin with. Thus it was important to act fast. Among other things, members returning to their states and districts after the first six months of a new administration get a decent reading of constituents' attitudes. It was unlikely that the domestic budget-cutting portion of the Reagan mandate would hold up well back home.

Fourth, it was essential that the administration display strong unity behind the president's program. This required White House control throughout the departments and agencies; the appearance of agreement and cooperation within the White House itself; and few, if any, leaks from those unhappy with policy decisions. Such unity is always desirable, but it is essential if the president is to command support on Capitol Hill. Coalition building there naturally started with the Republicans. If Reagan could keep his troops in line, then he needed only a few House Democratic votes to get his program enacted. In this crucial first year, overall congressional Republican support was high, and it was phenomenal in regard to votes on major budgetary and economic proposals. House Republicans averaged nearly 98 percent support on seven key votes; Senate Republicans averaged 97 percent support on nine key votes.

In 1981 the Reagan administration created a legacy for itself. "Politics had triumphed," according to Stockman. We experienced one of those rare policy breakthroughs, and its effects reverberated throughout the subsequent years of the president's term. Speaker O'Neill (1987, 345) conceded that "I . . . wasn't prepared for what happened in 1981."

Managing the Legacy—The Subsequent Years

Having directed congressional and media attention to the budget, the White House now had to produce its own plan for reducing the deficit. But the president had conflicting goals. Having just cut taxes, he did not want to turn around and raise them. So that option for deficit reduction was out. He favored further increases in defense expenditures, thus obviating another possible source of deficit reduction. And he was not about to stand alone on social security adjustments, especially with the upcoming 1982 elections. David Stockman even indicates that the president failed to support OMB's effort to make significant cuts in other domestic programs (e.g., farm supports).

As proposed by the administration, the fiscal year (FY) 1983 budget did speak of a deficit reduction plan of $239 billion over three years. The reductions were primarily in what might have been spent if certain cuts were not made. In other words, savings were counted where there was a decrease in the rate of growth. No amount of rhetorical or statistical manipulation could cover up the stark reality of huge imbalances, however. The bottom line was a projected $92 billion deficit for the new fiscal year and abandonment of the plan for a balanced budget in 1984.

For their part, members of Congress were unlikely in an election year to be receptive to President Reagan's proposals. Nor were they anxious to go it alone in cutting domestic programs further or in raising taxes. Yet much of the FY 1983 budget was rewritten on Capitol Hill, and the president was even convinced to approve a tax bill—one primarily designed to close loopholes and prevent tax evasion. Democrats used the deficit to frighten voters about the future of social security, noting that the president's plan for increased defense expenditures and reduced taxes would lead eventually to drastic cuts in retirement and other social welfare programs.

Presidential-congressional politics, as practiced in 1982, essentially became the basic pattern for the remainder of Reagan's term in office. His budget success in 1981 created the conditions for unpleasant confrontations. The president's personal popularity was his principal resource in the struggle to cope with mounting deficits. Meanwhile, congressional

Democrats were emboldened by midterm election successes in 1982 to assert their independence. Unfortunately, they did not have the leadership or the organization to prepare credible alternative proposals. At times, in fact, it seemed that the Senate Republicans were offering the only options to the president's proposals.

. . . Changes in the 98th, 99th, and 100th [Congresses] naturally contributed to different policy responses to the 1981 legacy. Each deserves brief review.

The 98th Congress—The Politics of Avoidance

. . . Political conditions changed rather dramatically following the 1982 congressional elections, for several reasons. First, of course, was the significant increase in the number of House Democrats—from 243 to 269. This change meant that 52 Democrats would now have to defect for the Republicans to win a vote—double the number required in the 97th Congress. Effectively then, the House Democratic leadership was able to resume control over its membership.

Actually the Republican losses in 1982 were somewhat smaller than predicted for the average midterm election. But following the 1980 elections, Democrats were fearful that a realignment might be under way—that, as happened in 1934 for Roosevelt's Democrats, Reagan's Republicans might actually increase their numbers. Therefore the twenty-six-seat increase reassured Democratic leaders that the president's popularity was not fully transferable to congressional Republicans. They were bound to be less deferential to Reagan and more optimistic about recapturing the Senate and the White House in 1984.

Second, the president's own popularity was declining. His Gallup poll rating slipped into the 40s during 1982 and declined further to 35 percent in January 1983. Reagan's economic program was not working in the short run. Although inflation had been cut, unemployment and interest rates remained high, and the national debt continued to soar. Doubt was expressed that the President would even seek reelection.

Third was the inevitable media reaction to any exposed failing of the president. Dick Kirschten (1983, 4) reflected the views of many commentators when he stated:

> The mood in Washington has changed vastly since the heady first months of the Reagan administration, when the President adroitly pulled off a series of startling coups. One no longer hears of a Reagan Revolution or of an emerging Republican majority. Democratic gains in the 1982 elections, while not shattering, nonetheless indicated disenchantment with Reagan's leadership.

The one encouraging result from the 1982 election was that the Republicans retained their Senate majority status for the first time since 1930. Thus the Reagan White House continued to enjoy the advantage of sequence—gaining Senate approval first, then pressuring the House for action.

With one major exception, these political conditions led to a politics of avoidance throughout the 98th Congress. The exception was passage of social security reform. Acting on a bipartisan basis, Congress accepted the recommendations of a National Commission of Social Security Reform. Referred to as "artful work" by Representative Barber B. Conable, Jr. (R-New York and a member of the National Commission), passage of this legislation removed a major negative issue for Reagan in 1984. Democrats pounded away on Republican candidates in 1982 on social security. They would not be able to do so again.

Otherwise, major issues were more or less postponed. Neither the White House nor Congress had the solution to the budget impasse. Deficits continued to mount. The end-of-session reviews in 1983 and 1984 highlighted the separation between the two branches and its consequences.

> 1983: Congress and President Reagan generally kept to their own turf in 1983—each branch going about its business with little involvement from the other side (Granat et al. 1983, 2467).

> 1984: A year of politics and procrastination on Capitol Hill left many members of the 98th Congress disappointed with their track record and a long list of unsolved problems for the new Congress to address (Granat et al 1984, 2699).

Whether resolved or not, however, the 1981 legacy dominated presidential-congressional policy politics in the 98th Congress. The hard facts were that the Reagan agenda would carry through into the 1984 election, forcing Democrats to discuss budget deficits and taxes. Meanwhile, the economy improved steadily during the 98th Congress, and with it the chances that Ronald Reagan would seek a second term.

The 99th Congress: The Politics of Assertiveness

. . . The 1984 contest [was] an "approval election," that is, one in which the voters said yes to an existing government of split-party control (Republicans controlling the White House and Senate, Democrats the House of Representatives). Ronald Reagan won a huge landslide, winning the electoral count of every state but Minnesota (and the District of Columbia). Meanwhile, a large proportion of incumbent representatives and senators were also reelected—95 and 90 percent respectively. Obviously a high return rate of congressional incumbents means relatively little shift in the partisan balance there. In 1984 the Republicans had a net gain of fourteen House seats and a net loss of two Senate seats. In this respect, the 1984 election was not very different from two previous landslide re-elections by Republicans in recent decades—those by Eisenhower in 1956 and Nixon in 1972. In neither case was there a major change in the partisan balance within Congress. Both were approval elections too. . . .

Given the mixed signals of an approval election of this type, it is not surprising that the 99th Congress was more assertive. House Democratic leaders acknowledged the president's popularity but were bound to take more initiative than before. The Republicans were still in the majority in the Senate, but Howard Baker (R-Tennessee) did not seek reelection and the new majority leader, Robert Dole (R-Kansas), was selected in part because of his greater independence from the administration. Then, of course, however popular the President might be, he could not run again.

It was also the case that the second term brought changes in the management of the White House. Donald Regan took over as chief of staff, with James Baker assuming Regan's previous position as secretary of the treasury. Regan's style was better suited to the boardroom than the White House. He had limited tolerance for members of Congress, and would have less with each passing month. Having an antipolitical chief of staff was strangely inapt for a political President. It raised questions about how attentive he was in regard to his own staff operations, questions that resurfaced during the Iran-*contra* hearings.

Finally, the agenda itself encouraged a more assertive posture for Congress. The 1981 legacy continued. There was no escaping the heavy burden of the deficits. Congressional anxiety increased during the 98th Congress and was bound to result in greater initiative in the 99th. The president's budgets were deemed "dead on arrival" by congressional Democrats—a declaration suggesting that they were prepared to provide an alternative. Then foreign and defense policy issues became more and more contentious—for example, sanctions on South Africa, aid to the *contras*, the strategic defense initiative, arms control, the MX missile.

To declare that Congress was more assertive is not to say that Reagan was helpless or that the legislative branch somehow took charge of the government. One of the most sweeping tax-reform bills in history was passed. Other presidents—most recently Carter—campaigned for changes in the tax laws, but Reagan made it a priority for his second term, and presidential-congressional cooperation was achieved beyond the expectation of the most seasoned political observers. Congress publicly announced its limitations in coping with the budget by enacting the Gramm-Rudman-Hollings measure, a procedure for establishing automatic budget cuts should Congress fail to meet designated targets. The procedure did have the effect of focusing even greater attention on deficits, but it turned out not to be a substitute for the hard choices that had to be made.

The 99th Congress closed to very mixed reviews. Yet, under the circumstances, it is hard to imagine what more one could have expected from either end of Pennsylvania Avenue. For his part, despite his overwhelming victory, Reagan was unable to match the accomplishments of his first two years. But he was far from being an incapacitated lame duck. For its part, Congress demonstrated a capacity to produce major legislation despite split-party control between the two chambers. Leadership in both chambers received high marks for their efforts. "The record of the 99th Congress belies early predictions that it would dissolve in partisan rancor (Calmes 1986, 2468). Yet no one believed that we could govern only with Congress. In other words, it all went about as well as could be expected, given what the voters had done in 1984.

The 100th Congress: The Politics of Survival

Presidents who serve two terms are understandably anxious about the second midterm election. There is talk about the "six-year itch," that is, voter dissatisfaction with the president and his party in the sixth year. And there is talk about lame-duck status as a president enters the final two years. Neither phenomenon is an immutable law, but talk is reality too, and it can be unsettling to the president and his advisers.

In 1986 Ronald Reagan accepted the electoral challenge of his status and campaigned heavily for Republican Senate incumbents and challengers. He did so in spite of the conventional wisdom that presidential coattails are threadbare in midterm elections. The results were close to being a disaster. The Democrats recaptured their majority status in the Senate with a net gain of eight seats. Seven Republican incumbents were defeated, and Democrats won two seats held by retiring Senate Republicans. One Republican won a seat previously held by a Democrat.

Presidential success in a campaigning is typically measured by wins and losses. Thus President Reagan lost in his gamble to defy the odds in 1986. Closer examination of the Senate results reveals some interesting developments for understanding future elections, however. The average Democratic percentage in the seven races in which Republican incumbents were defeated was less than 52 percent. The percentage of the two-party vote garnered by all Republican candidates was greater in 1986 than it was in 1980 *when the Republicans had a net gain of twelve Senate seats*. What these results suggest for the longer run is that Senate contests are now highly competitive across the nation. It is entirely possible that the Republicans may recapture control of the Senate again in future elections—a prospect that reflects the growing strength of the party and, possibly, the nationalization of Senate elections.

There was no discernible six-year itch in voting for the House of Representatives. Incumbents were returned at an exceptionally high rate—98.5 percent. The net loss of five House Republicans was the second smallest loss for the president's party in a midterm election in this century and the smallest by far for a minority-party President.

Comparisons with the two most recent Republican presidents to win reelection are instructive. In 1958, the second midterm election for Eisenhower, Republicans had a net loss of forty-seven House seats and thirteen Senate seats. Even with the loss of a Republican majority in the Senate, President Reagan was in a better position than Eisenhower or Ford. . . .

Loss of the Senate forced a change in White House strategy. Appointments requiring confirmation were in jeopardy, majority building for treaties was altered, and the advantage of playing one chamber off against the other was lessened, if not lost altogether. There was also a change in House leadership. Thomas P. O'Neill, Jr., of Massachusetts retired, and a more aggressive Jim Wright of Texas assumed the chair. Determined to establish his own leadership style, as distinct from that of O'Neill, Wright was unlikely to cooperate very often with the administration.

These political developments encouraged a more defensive posture by the White House regardless of what else might occur. In other words, managing the government as a lame-duck minority-party president while working with a Congress controlled by the other party is something less than an ideal formula for success. But there was more. Analysts barely had time to ponder the 1986 election results when it was revealed that the administration had been dealing with Iran in a complicated maneuver involving the release of hostages, arms shipments, and the diversion of profits to the *contras* in Nicaragua. . . .

No doubt having the Watergate debacle in mind, the president acted quickly to manage the Iran-*contra* affair. National Security Council personnel were fired, an independent counsel was requested, an investigating commission was appointed, and a Department of Justice probe was launched. Later Donald Regan, White House chief of staff, was replaced by Howard W. Baker, the former Senate majority leader.

No amount of initiative from the White House was likely to interfere with congressional investigations. Several were announced, and eventually a committee from each house was appointed. These committees agreed on joint hearings to be conducted during the summer. The president was determined to prevent the Iran-*contra* affair from interfering with his agenda. Although he made several moves to control matters, he could not manage it all. It was not an auspicious start for the last two years of his presidency.

In looking ahead to the 100th Congress the forecasters predicted distractions due to the Iran-*contra* imbroglio and confrontations over the budget. In his response to the State of the Union Message, the new Speaker of the House, Jim Wright, stressed an equal partnership between the president and Congress. He then proceeded to outline important areas of disagreement:

> The basic disagreement is not over how much we spend. It's where we spend it—what we get for it—and who pays the bill, ourselves or our children.
>
> The president's newest budget would cut $5.5 billion from the education of our young—and spend that same amount on research just for one new weapon.
>
> It asks more for the Pentagon, more for foreign aid, more for space, more for "star wars," more for the war in Latin America.
>
> But it would cut education, cut the clean water program, cut Medicare and Medicaid, cut what we do for the disadvantaged, and—are you ready for this?—the president's budget would make deep cuts in our commitment to drug enforcement. (Congressional Quarterly Weekly Report, Jan. 31, 1987, 203-5)

The direct confrontations were not long in coming. The president had pocket-vetoed a water-pollution-control bill at the end of the 99th Congress. The bill was quickly passed again by large margins in the House and Senate at the start of the 100th Congress. Reagan vetoed it directly this time, and his action was overridden in both chambers (401–26 in the House, 86–14 in the Senate). In late March, Congress presented him with a highway bill that he opposed. Again he accepted the challenge and vetoed it. And again the veto was overridden—this time by the very narrowest of margins in the Senate (67–33), following active lobbying by the president to sustain his veto.

Although he lost both battles, the president established his own combative posture in the face of the Iran-*contra* distraction. This aggressiveness probably benefited him later in the year when the impact of the hearings had abated. . . His action certainly suited Reagan's determination not to suspend politics as a result of the Iran-*contra* affair or become too protective or defensive.

The events of 1987 consistently threatened presidential leadership. A brief review of some of the more dramatic presidential-congressional conflicts illustrates what a remarkable year it was.

- The joint hearings of the House and Senate Select Committees to investigate the Iran-*contra* affair took place throughout the summer, from 5 May to 6 August. There were forty days of public hearings, four days of closed meetings, thirty-two witnesses, and nearly 10,000 pages of transcripts. Lieutenant Colonel Oliver North was the star witness; his testimony and questioning took up approximately 14 percent of the transcript pages. A highly critical report was issued on 18 November, signed by all fifteen Democrats and three Republicans. Six Republicans issued a minority report.
- Supreme Court Justice Lewis F. Powell retired on 26 June, providing President Reagan with an opportunity to appoint a conservative who would then tip the political balance on certain crucial cases. The president nominated Robert H. Bork on 1 July. Confirmation hearings before the Senate Committee on the Judiciary did not begin until 15 September, thus allowing ample time for those for and against Bork to mount their campaigns. The two weeks of hearings were very nearly as riveting as those of the Iran-*contra* committees. The Bork nomination was then rejected by the Senate. The president's next nominee, Douglas Ginsburg, withdrew following revelations regarding his personal life.
- The stock market took a record tumble on 19 October, followed by demands for presidential-congressional cooperation to reduce the deficits. This major event drew the attention of everyone in official Washington, but revealed again the differences between the president and congressional Democrats for resolving the budget issue. A White House-congressional summit was begun on 27 October, and an accord was finally reached on 20 November. The president was forced by circumstances to accept tax increases.
- Mikhail S. Gorbachev visited the United States 8–10 December to sign a treaty banning intermediate-range nuclear-force missiles (INF) and to discuss outstanding issues between the two nations. Senate approval of the INF treaty was an issue where the president could expect cooperation from the Democrats and criticism from the far-right wing of his own party.

There were many other extraordinary developments that led to conflict between the branches—for example, the involvement of Speaker Wright in seeking to bring peace to Central America, passage of a revised Gramm-Rudman-Hollings procedure, a reinterpretation by the Reagan administration of an agreement with the Soviet Union regarding the testing of antiballistic missile (ABM) weapons, the reflagging and protection of Kuwaiti ships in the Persian Gulf (without the invocation of the War Powers Act). And through it all was the continuing battle over the budget.

By late summer, it was generally conceded that Ronald Reagan was weaker even than previous lame-duck presidents. . . . The argument was made that Reagan had lost control of the agenda, in part because he had not sufficiently reset the issues in the 1984 campaign. . . .

Once again, however, one has to raise the question whether the president's loss of control led to an advantage for the Democrats. Among other things, the 1988 presidential election was in full flower during much of 1987, with a variety of Democrats seeking to win the nomination. Along the way, the front-runner, Gary Hart, withdrew for rather embarrassing reasons. Leadership for the Democrats was something less than well focused.

Regarding domestic affairs, Democratic leaders were still struggling with the 1981 legacy. They found it very difficult to form a new program in the traditional Democratic cast. And where they did take initiatives, as with trade legislation and welfare reform, there was the threat of presidential veto. In foreign policy, it is inherently difficult for Congress to assume leadership if the president fails. Thus, the president was crippled by the Iran-*contra* affair more than congressional Democrats were advantaged. And, in the end, the president recouped much of his status through the summit meeting with Gorbachev and his leadership in arms control.

The end-of-the-year evaluations of Reagan were much more positive. He actually won more *contra* aid and forced Democrats to withdraw certain broadcast regulations in the final appropriations measure. . . .

Prospects for the second session of the 100th Congress were for continued conflict between the two branches. Many of the divisive issues carried over into the election year. Helen Dewar's (1987, A6) description of the end of the first session is a decent portrait for 1988: "Like two muscle-bound wrestlers, Reagan and the Democrats held each other in a clumsy hammerlock to the end. . . ."

As analysts, we do not have the advantage of rerunning presidencies to see how they might have turned out plus or minus this or that event. Thus, much of what we say is relative. Even so, it seems fair to state that President Reagan sustained the events of 1987 about as well as could be expected by a lame-duck Republican president working with a Democratic Congress. He was seriously wounded, if not totally crippled, by several events, but he ended the year fully ambulatory and perhaps even politically strengthened for his final year in office. . . .

Conclusions

In the words of the British scholar Nigel Bowles (1987, 217), "Reagan successfully fused policy prescription with politics." He took advantage of favorable conditions in 1981 to produce "quick and profound policy change." It was the nature of this initial success, however, that he could not expect to realize anything like it again. That is not to say he lacked other triumphs. Enactment of a tax-reform program was a significant and unexpected achievement. Instead, it directs attention to the scope and effects of what occurred in 1981, which were akin to the policy breakthroughs of the Great Society. Ronald Reagan did not reduce government to nearly the same extent as Lyndon Johnson expanded it. But he created the policy conditions for a contractive politics that had never been played before.

Thus, President Reagan leaves a policy and political legacy for Congress and the next president. His 1984 opponent, Walter Mondale, describes the policy legacy for the Democrats this way (quoted in Perry and Shribman 1987, 1):

> Democrats are in a real box. Reagan has practiced the politics of subtraction. He knows the public wants to spend money on the old folks, protecting the environment and aiding education. And he's figured out the only way to stop it is to deny the revenues. No matter how powerful the arguments the Democrats make for the use of government to serve some purpose, the answer must be no.

Of course, the "politics of subtraction" can produce discomfort for legislators of both parties. No elected representative is anxious to cut back programs affecting constituents. Democrats, then, are denied their traditional platform, even as voters appear to support more spending. Republicans are pressured to support their president even when it hurts. Meanwhile, the president's popularity remains relatively high, declining only as an effect of an affair of his own making—Iran-*contra*—and not of the economic and budgetary legacy left for Congress and the nation.

The next president and Congress cannot easily escape the Reagan legacy. They may be able to manage it better without him, however. Presidents who achieve policy breakthroughs are not the best ones to control the subsequent effects. There seems to be a policy trap for the successful president. Being identified with, and committed to, programs for which they receive political credit, they are then ill prepared to propose solutions to the problems these programs create. Perhaps presidents of achievement should be limited to one term!

22

Reconsidering the Two Presidencies

Duane M. Oldfield and Aaron Wildavsky

More than twenty years ago, Aaron Wildavsky (1966) made a claim, in *Trans*-action, that has led to seemingly endless debate.

> The United States has one president, but it has two presidencies; one presidency is for domestic affairs, and the other is concerned with defense and foreign policy. Since World War II, presidents have had much greater success in controlling the nation's defense and foreign policies than in dominating its domestic policies.

Did the "two presidencies" phenomenon ever exist? If so, why did it exist? Has it now departed from the political scene? In 1966 Wildavsky felt confident stating that "in the realm of foreign policy there has not been a single major issue on which presidents, when they were serious and determined, have failed." Today such a claim would be hard to sustain. The Iran/*contra* scandal, exacerbated by the Reagan administrations's frustrating failure to win Congress over to its Central American policies, is a case in point. A reassessment of the two presidencies thesis is in order.

Too often, discussion of the two presidencies is limited to "success rates." Certainly, Wildavsky claimed that presidential success—however

Society, 26 (July-Aug. 1989): 54–59. Reprinted by permission.

measured—was more likely in foreign policy but equally important were the reasons that lay behind this claim. "The Two Presidencies" argued that foreign and domestic policy are shaped in distinct political arenas, marked by quite different political configurations. First, given the international responsibilities assumed by the United States in the aftermath of World War II, foreign policy has come to dominate the president's agenda. The pace of international events is rapid, decisions are irreversible, and success or failure is quickly apparent. Events in obscure corners of the world come to be seen as integral aspects of a global conflict. Therefore presidents devote more and more of their resources to foreign policy questions. Second, foreign policy is largely outside the field of partisan conflict. Unlike the case of domestic policy, the president does not inherit a detailed party program: "Presidents and their parties have no prior policies on Argentina and the Congo." Third, for a variety of reasons, the president's competitors in the foreign policy arena are weak. Relatively few interest groups are active; Congress is deferential; the public is uninformed and unable to provide policy direction. An expanded, expert staff allows the president to challenge the entrenched interests of the military and the State Department.

The overall picture is that of a foreign policy-making process insulated from the pluralistic pressures normally associated with American democracy. The battle of interest groups, parties, and bureaucracies fades into the background. What emerges is a rather apolitical, technical realm of presidential problem-solving: "In foreign affairs . . . he can almost always get support for policies that he believes will protect the nation—but his problem is to find a viable policy." This picture of the foreign policy-making process is evidently wrong today. What went wrong?

The End of Consensus

Various studies cast serious doubt on the conclusions of "The Two Presidencies" outside of the period in which the thesis was proposed. Only Dwight Eisenhower was clearly more successful in foreign policy. Presidents cannot count upon bipartisan support when they find a workable policy. From Richard Nixon's Vietnam policies and Gerald Ford's attempts to intervene in Angola to Ronald Reagan's difficulties gaining support for the *contras* and the Strategic Defense Initiative (SDI), it has become clear that presidential control of foreign policy is not so complete as Wildavsky claimed.

The controversy over Reagan's SDI provides a useful perspective on these issues. One would expect this to be a technical issue. Will the proposed system be effective in combating incoming missiles? How much will it cost? How quickly can it be developed? If, as "The Two Presidencies" claims, foreign policy is a realm of technical problem-solving, the debate over the SDI could be expected to exemplify it.

This is not how the debate has unfolded. Presidential success has not been easy. If the questions involved are technical, we are left to account for the fact that the debate has split neatly along party lines. The SDI became a litmus test for candidates of both parties in the 1988 presidential campaign. When the debate did turn technical it became clear that the executive branch had no monopoly on expertise. The president's arguments for the SDI were subjected to expert criticism from a wide variety of sources.

The most important issue is that of ideological and partisan divisions. Wildavsky used McNamara as an example of a man who "thrives because he performs; he comes up with answers he defends." Yet the sort of "answers" a McNamara provided can be widely accepted only if participants in policy debates are asking the same questions, accepting a similar framework for interpreting the evidence. Shortly after the publication of "The Two Presidencies" it became clear that McNamara's techniques could not overcome ideological divisions over United States policy in Southeast Asia. Nor could the expertise of the Kissinger Commission resolve more recent controversy over Central American policy. Ideological and partisan differences are too intimately involved; different questions are being asked, different evidence cited.

If we look at key foreign policy votes from the Eisenhower through the Carter administrations, we find that a majority of the opposition party supported only Eisenhower more than half the time. After the Eisenhower administration, opposition members' level of support has run below, usually well below, 50 percent for each chamber of Congress in each administration. Party differences on foreign policy remain very large. Leon Halpert's study of House voting patterns under President Reagan comes to a similar conclusion:

The recent characterization of foreign policy as a field engendering greater partisan based controversy and competition is empirically buttressed by our data . . . when partisanship developed on foreign policy matters during these years it evoked the most intense interparty conflict.

When basic agreements concerning the direction of foreign policy break down, bipartisan deference to the president is unlikely to survive. Let us look in more detail at the changes that have undermined the two presidencies thesis.

Two Foreign Policies

"The Two Presidencies" is time and culture bound. It succeeds in showing that the Eisenhower administration had greater support in foreign and defense than in domestic policy, and in explaining why. It fails in that both the patterns of behavior and the reasons for their maintenance did not exist in the decades before or after the 1950s. In addition to being time bound, the thesis is also culturally limited. The shared values that sustained consensus on defense during the 1950s gave way in the late 1960s to different ones with far different results.

Bipartisanship was never complete. Partisan battles over "missile gaps" and the "loss" of China were intense. Wildavsky, in "The Two Presidencies," had little use for the concept of a "cold war consensus." Yet looking back from the perspective of the last twenty years, this consensus appears to have had a bit more reality to it. The breakdown of this consensus has profoundly altered the operation of the two presidencies.

Not only is the president more likely to face opposition, the nature of foreign policy conflicts has changed as well. In the 1950s and early 1960s, partisan battles tended to be about performance, or lack thereof, in pursuit of commonly shared objectives, as in the missile gap debate. Recent years have seen more fundamental disagreement concerning the objectives of American foreign policy.

A persuasive account of these changes is provided by Michael Mandelbaum and William Schneider, in *Eagle Entangled*, edited by Kenneth Oye et al. They argue that Vietnam and détente led to serious divisions within the then dominant internationalist public. Two groups emerged. Liberal internationalists support cooperative endeavors—arms control, giving economic aid to poorer nations, strengthening the United Nations—but put less emphasis on fighting communism. They show little support for the use of force. Conservative internationalists see a much more hostile world environment in which American interests and values must be actively defended. They support a strong military. Less educated and less interested in world affairs, noninternationalists remain suspicious of both cooperative and competitive international commitments. The crucial development is the rise of serious ideological divisions among the active, educated internationalists. For it is with their demands that foreign policymakers must deal.

Mandelbaum and Schneider's data fit into a larger pattern of cultural change affecting both foreign and domestic policy. Whereas, during Eisenhower's time in office, defense and domestic issues were on separate ideological dimensions, so that public officials who disagreed on one would frequently agree on the other, afterward the two spheres of policy became fused along a single ideological dimension. What had to be explained is how and why major issue areas that at one time were fairly separated became fused.

In the Eisenhower era, once the isolationist forces had been defeated, there was widespread agreement on the desirability and efficacy of American national political institutions. There was the slave world with its captive nations; it was bad and dangerous. There was the free world with its liberty loving alliances. It was good. Protecting good against evil was the role of the United States as "the leader of the free world."

Compared to today, the range of national issues in the 1950s was woefully narrow. A liberal was a person who believed in a greater role for the federal government in providing social welfare. A conservative wanted less. Social issues, such as prayer in school and abortion, were unheard of. Civil rights for blacks were on the agenda but not prominent. Environmental issues were discrete entities, not a movement. Foreign policy mattered, but it was not debated on principles that divided the parties.

The presidency of John F. Kennedy proved to be the dividing line. Recall that Kennedy ran on the basis of a stronger defense in which, among other things, the alleged "missile gap" figured prominently. When he told the American people how much he regretted the Bay of Pigs fiasco, Kennedy said it was so awful that he would never speak of it again. Remarkably, from the perspective of the 1980s, he got away with it. Kennedy's relationships with the media were excellent, a phenomenon that used to be standard but has not recurred since. Kennedy may have reduced one barrier in being the first Catholic to become president, but he was not a champion of civil rights. His exhortations to the American people involved reaching the heights of technology (in the space program) or bearing international burdens, not redressing injustices or inequalities at home. America was good; it had only to extend that goodness outward and onward.

The hostile reaction to the war in Vietnam, which began in Kennedy's time and was extended by his successor, Lyndon Johnson, is usually credited with turning many Americans against military intervention abroad and institutions they suspected of deceiving them at home. No doubt the war was a factor. But if the cause was the war, and only or mainly the war, then we cannot explain what happened afterward. For one thing, there was no national consensus on the war, aside from its inefficacy, or on the American use of force in the international arena. At the same time, there was no new massive use of force. Yet that did not stop the mounting criticism of those in authority, a cascade so constant it has begun to seem like a natural condition, the opposite, say, to the "end of ideology" thesis in the 1950s.

The split on foreign policy was intensified by increasing division over domestic policy. Merely to list the major movements that began or became prominent from the late 1960s onward—not only civil rights but women's rights, gay rights, children's rights, animal rights, environmentalism, grey power, and more—is to trace the emerging differences.

Of special interest to us is the fact that these issues do not appear at random but are politically clustered. All of these issues belong to the Democrats in that their party has become the advocate while the Republicans have become the opponents of using government to protect these rights. Even more striking, foreign and domestic issues line up quite nicely, with the Republicans urging more for defense with less for social welfare and "rights" and Democrats willing to do less for defense and more for rights and welfare.

Here we have it: foreign as well as domestic issues now divide the parties; and there are many more issues—social, civil, rights, ecological, defense—to divide the parties. American parties are becoming more ideologically distinct. Conservative southern Democrats are moving toward the Republican party. Liberal Republicans are now an endangered species. While diversity still exists in each party, particularly at the mass level, the parties are slowly edging their way toward internal ideological unity. In Congress, despite earlier academics' fears of weaking party ties, partisan voting is on the rise. In 1987, Congressional Quarterly's measure of party unity voting in the House, reported by Janet Hook in 1988, hit its highest level since such measurements began in 1955. Warren Miller and Kent Jennings, in *Parties in Transition*, document growing ideological differences between the parties' convention delegates. Indeed, each party's activists are more united internally and more distant from each other than at any other period for which data exist.

Cleavages on international issues are coming to reinforce, rather than cut across, domestic cleavages. The Democrats and Republicans have become the parties of, respectively, liberal and conservative internationalism. In the 1950s, the division between internationalists and noninternationalists occurred within each party. Eisenhower had the more isolationist Taft wing of the party to deal with. Many Southern Democrats did not share their northern counterparts' enthusiasm for international commitments. In the mid-1960s and early 1970s a significant change of position took place. Northern Democratic support for defense spending and military foreign aid dropped dramatically. Support for economic foreign aid remained high in keeping with the principles of an emerging liberal internationalism. Republican and southern Democratic support for defense spending and military foreign aid rose dramatically as conservative internationalism emerged among them.

In order to draw implications for the two presidencies thesis from these developments, we must try to specify the dimensions along which contemporary cleavages occur, dimensions that serve to unify the parties against each other so as to wipe out the differences in treatment of foreign and domestic policy that took place during Eisenhower's presidency. If we inquire about which values unite the Democratic party of the 1980s, the answer is straightforward: greater equality of condition. The main purpose of the movements we have discussed is to reduce power differences between blacks and whites, women and men, gays and straights, on and on. It is precisely the influx of feminists and blacks, and the exit of southern Democrats who oppose their views, that has given the activist corps of the Democratic party its special stamp.

The Republican case is equally clear but a bit more complex because they are arrayed along two dimensions, corresponding roughly to economic and social conservatism. In the period from the 1930s through the mid-1960s, to provide a brief historical dimension, the United States could correctly be called a capitalist country, compared to most others, but there were few talented defenders of its legitimating values. Perhaps capitalism was too firmly ensconced to require constant overt justification. In any event, in the 1970s and 1980s there arose a considerable cadre of capitalist intellectuals who provided new designs for public policies from privatization to the flat tax. More animated and self confident than their predecessors, backed by the apparatus of modern economics, they constituted the free market or equal opportunity dimension of Republicanism.

In mentioning modern social movements, we deliberately left out one that informs the contemporary Republican party, Protestant fundamentalism. Believers in patriarchy, sharing hierarchial values, the fundamentalists sought to maintain social distinctions within family and society. Thus they gave the Republican party a second dimension. Social and economic conservatives disagree about governmental efforts to enforce social norms, but they are sufficiently close on a limited economic role for government, including opposition to such measures as affirmative action in hiring and promotion, as well as opposition to international communism, to constitute a viable coalition.

How, we still have to ask, were the domestic and foreign policy concerns joined through these dimensions? Our hypothesis is that the egalitarians who gravitated to the Democratic party viewed defense as taking away from welfare, therefore inegalitarian. In a corresponding manner, they saw the United States as a First World country beating down upon Third World countries, that is, as engaging in inegalitarian behavior abroad. Liberal internationalist policies were to help address these inequalities and to free up resources for use at home.

Republican social and economic conservatives viewed life in the United States much differently. American institutions, to them, were marvelous except that they were not pushed as deeply and as far as they would like. Freer markets and stronger adherence to moral norms would suit them. At home they wanted less government because the underlying institutions were benign. Abroad, they favored a conservative internationalist policy both to protect democratic capitalism and to project its institutions further where they would do even more good.

Dissensus Undermines

How has the rise of ideological and partisan divisions affected the operation of the two presidencies? Let us take a quick look at the political configuration within which foreign policy was made in the 1950s and early 1960s. An internationalist consensus (a belief in the legitimacy of American institutions and the need to extend them) among northern Democrats and the Eisenhower wing of the Republican party led to a situation in which fundamental disagreement over objectives was rare. Internationalism was particularly strong among political elites. "Responsible" opinion among politicians, academics, and the press held that the United States must be willing to uphold its international obligations even if—as in the case of Korea—this was expensive and unpopular. Elites were held to have a duty to stick together so as to educate the public away from its dangerous tendencies toward isolationism. Internationalism was in the public interest.

In such an environment, Wildavsky's description of the two presidencies had some validity to it. Where fundamental disagreement was not present, Congress was often willing to give the president the benefit of the doubt. The president's advantages in terms of access to information, public stature, and ability to take rapid and decisive action all contributed to congressional deference. The executive branch was seen as the bastion of internationalism, while the Congress was viewed as more likely to support irresponsible parochialism. This led to elite support for presidential control of foreign policy. Given the high value placed upon presidential leadership, "responsible" opinion was reluctant to directly attack the president. Although presidents were likely to suffer the consequences if their policies did not succeed, they did have relatively broad discretion to initiate policies they believed necessary.

With the breakdown of consensus, the situation changes. If members of Congress disagree with the basic objectives of a president's foreign policy, deference is much less likely. Expert execution counts for little if the policy is deemed to be fundamentally flawed or immoral, inegalitarian or un-American. Instead of uniting in an attempt to educate the apathetic public (noninternationalists), elites now appeal to that group as a source of support in their wars against each other. As ideological and partisan divisions have come to reinforce each other, prospects for unity erode further. Foreign policy has become more like domestic policy—a realm marked by serious partisan divisions in which the president cannot count on a free ride.

The old system of foreign policymaking was further weakened by a number of additional changes in American political life. The press has grown less deferential in all areas. A more educated and active public is also a more ideological public. Thus ideologically oriented interest groups have come to play a greater role in the process of presidential nomination. There are also more domestic groups with foreign policy agendas, not only Jews on Israel, but blacks on South Africa, Poles on Poland, and more. All these changes have added to the difficulty of keeping foreign policy isolated from public scrutiny and pressure.

From the viewpoint of the 1950s this looks unusual, but perhaps the 1950s are a poor benchmark. Conflict and shared control of foreign policy are normal in the American system. Divided power is, after all, a hallmark of the system the founding fathers devised. We agree with Bert Rockman who writes, in a 1987 issue of *Armed Forces and Society:*

> This relatively rare circumstance [the post-World War II "bipartisan national security consensus"] has since been shrouded in legend as a norm from which America's recent foreign policy-making process has deviated, moving from consensual premises and presidential leadership to conflicting premises and to frequent policy disagreement.
>   The institutional supposition behind this traditional concept of a foreign policy based on consensual premises is one of a virtually exclusive presidentialist approach to American national security policy-making, and one thereby removed from the tugs and pulls and parochial pressures of domestic policy-making. . . . The "repluralization" of national security policy-making, of course, is intimately related to the growth of fundamental disagreement about policy course. But the American system of government also provides considerable opportunities for the opposition to influence policy that are unparalleled.

What Remains?

Twenty years ago, "The Two Presidencies" exaggerated the degree of presidential control over American foreign policy. Given the changes we have discussed, is anything left of the two presidencies?

First, it is important to point out that partisan and ideological divisions do not affect all areas of foreign policy equally. Many positions do not fit neatly into opposing ideological frameworks (the Arab/Israel conflict, for example). Or, as in the case of the Persian Gulf, no side feels that it has a viable solution to the problem. In these situations, the president may be given more leeway to develop an approach of his own.

Second, the fact that foreign policy has become more like domestic policy does not mean that presidents cannot win; they simply must win differently. After all, presidents have been known to prevail on domestic issues. The new environment favors a plebiscitary presidency; public appeals, replace establishment consensus. The president, symbol of the nation and center of media attention, is not without resources in such an environment.

Third, much of the president's power in foreign policy lies outside of the measures of success we have focused upon in this article. Easily measured, success in Congress has been the central concern of the two presidencies literature. Yet the obvious must be stated. The president is commander-in-chief, and this does matter. There is little Congress can do about a Grenada invasion or, for that matter, a decision to initiate nuclear war. Nor can Congress play the president's diplomatic role. It can express its preferences concerning arms control; it may frustrate the president's plans by refusing to further arm the Nicaraguan *contras*; but without presidential action little that is positive can be done.

What Is to Be Done?

In the era of blessed consensus now gone, things were better—or so it is claimed. We would all love consensus . . . around our own values. Reagan called for bipartisan support of his Central American policies; Democrats claim all would have been well had he not been so divisive. Consensus consists of the other side giving in. As the parties divide more neatly, over more issues, the temperature of national politics rises. According to the theory of cross-cutting cleavages, when decision makers agree on some issues while disagreeing on others, they have an incentive to moderate their conflict in order to work together when necessary. When the same people take opposing sides over more and more issues, by contrast, each difference tends to deepen mutual hostility. Nowadays there is a lot more than a "dime's worth of difference" between the major political parties. Disagreement of this sort, combined with the separation of powers, can be a recipe for stalemate.

President Bush began his administration with a call for a return to the politics of consensus. "A new breeze is blowing, and the old bipartisanship must be made new again," he declared in his inaugural address. The honeymoon may last for a while; some of the Reagan era's more divisive foreign policy issues have receded in importance; but, in the long run, we believe that the politics of bipartisanship are unsustainable. The public is more educated and ideological than it used to be, the divisions we have discussed are deeply rooted in the party system. Neither side is likely to give in. Yet dissensus is not necessarily a bad thing. It is desirable that foreign policy be openly and frequently debated. Perhaps contacts with more minds from diverse perspectives would have avoided past blunders. Perhaps the inability to find a publicly acceptable rationale for the growing involvement in Vietnam or for giving arms to "moderates" in Iran should have sent up warning signals. Whatever short-run difficulties it causes, public debate is more likely to lead to a policy that can be supported in the long run. On some issues, such as the intermediate-range nuclear forces (INF) treaty, debate may lead to agreement across party lines. On others we may, for the moment, have to learn to live with disagreement. Attempting to suppress debate with pleas for consensus and presidential discretion cannot hide the reality of ideological division. Nor does it place much faith in our democratic process.

23

The Prospects for Presidential Leadership

Samuel Kernell

No matter whether one arbitrarily designates Richard Nixon or Jimmy Carter as the president who initiated the *routine* practice of going public for his leadership in Washington, data are still insufficient to delineate fully the implications of going public for future politics. And yet, since Nixon was in the White House, regularities in presidential behavior and in others' responses to it, which are at odds with past practices, have begun to reveal how the new order might look. These emerging patterns appear all the more indicative since they are consistent with the model of today's Washington described as individualized pluralism.

Aside from the caution that must attend instant history, the personal character of the office also limits speculation about the future. The presidency affords each occupant the latitude to define the job for himself. In the absence of apprenticeship, the incumbent must lean heavily upon his experience in public life. In important respects, then, presidential leadership will be as varied as the political careers and talents of the politicians who occupy the Oval Office. Could anyone have anticipated in the spring of 1932 the direction in which Franklin Roosevelt would take the presidency?

From *Going Public: New Strategies of Presidential Leadership*, by Samuel Kernell (Washington, DC: Congressional Quarterly Press, 1986), pp. 211–231.

Here again, however, uncertainty is bounded, and one is not completely adrift in trying to chart the future. Some presidents leave their mark on the office. Occasionally, a figure enters the White House whose political intuition eclipses the perspicuity of those who are currently studying the office. His success educates scholars and future presidents alike. Franklin Roosevelt was just such a president. Within a short time after his departure, Roosevelt emerged a paragon, clarifying for many the techniques of bargaining, for others the exercise of charisma, and still for others the inner bearings necessary for success at the job. Because Roosevelt established new standards, his successors have been saddled with comparisons of their performance against his (Leuchtenberg 1985).

Will Ronald Reagan cut such a figure? Will his shadow loom over the next generation of White House occupants? Quite possibly. This is more than idle speculation, for Ronald Reagan has relied on going public for his influence in Washington more heavily and more profitably than did his predecessors. His success has forced others in Washington to reevaluate the way they assess the office. How they adapt to these new assessments will permit, and even encourage, future presidents similarly to go public.

As instructive as Reagan's example may be for his successors, the accuracy of the prognosis for future leadership does not depend wholly on the length of his shadow. Going public is a leadership style consistent with the requirements of a political community that is increasingly susceptible to the centrifugal forces of public opinion. The choice to go public will be inspired less by Reagan's example than by the circumstances of the moment encountered by future presidents. The evolving structure of political relations along the lines described by individualized pluralism will continue to make going public a favored approach to leadership.

Other tendencies are emerging in Washington relations that reflect but also complement, accentuate, and reinforce the strategy of going public. Together they may shortly move community politics to a state even less recognizable to those steeped in the traditions of institutionalized pluralism. Future evolution can be classified into two broad types: the behavior of politicians and the effects on policy.

Adaptive Responses to Presidents Going Public

. . . In recent years the president's reputation has expanded to incorporate information about his capacity and willingness to go public. Working from his reputation, other politicians plan their own strategies to minimize his damage to their designs. Adaptive responses occur at a variety of levels—from posturing on issues to planning careers. Examples of each abound. The following responses are typical in that they tend more toward accommodation than resistance. As a result, expectations of going public routinely become incorporated into relations between presidents and other politicians.

Issue Posturing

When a president goes to the country, he is counting on his prestige to persuade sufficient numbers of citizens to communicate their support of his position to their representatives. Success depends neither on building majority support in the country nor on buffaloing other politicians into believing that he has. All the president need do is convince a sufficient number of politicians that the political cost of resisting his policy is greater than any potential gain.

Intense minorities scare politicians more than inattentive majorities for the good reason that the former will act on their beliefs and the latter will not. Presidents who exhort viewers to contact their members of Congress are trading upon the caution with which politicians greet intense preferences. At times, even when representatives know that their position and not the president's represents majority opinion, they will shy away from openly breaking with him for fear that he may take his case to the people. Such an instance occurred in the spring of 1985 when many House and Senate Democrats expressed reluctance to legislate an end to the financial aid for rebel forces in Nicaragua on the suspicion, as one Democratic leader explained, that President Reagan might make it a major public issue later in the summer. Fearful of being caught on the wrong side of the issue, as they had with Reagan in the past on budget cuts and defense spending, the Democrats ceded to the president greater latitude than they otherwise might have. The ability to go public presents presidents with the opportunity to control policy discussion to an extent unavailable to those who would rely exclusively upon elite negotiation for their leadership.

Strategic Planning

At a more advanced level of strategic calculation, politicians anticipate the president's option to go public as they engage in coalition building. During the first half of 1985, scarcely a week passed in which President Reagan failed to campaign publicly on some issue or at least announce plans to do so soon. Politicians in Washington were therefore continuously reminded that they must anticipate his public appeals as they devise their own strategies.

Weeks before the opening of the 99th Congress, Speaker O'Neill announced that House Democrats would refrain from taking positions on sensitive budget issues until President Reagan had fully briefed the country on his proposals. Despite his high profile throughout the first term, Reagan had rarely assumed the role of point man for unpopular policies—hence, his sobriquet as the "teflon president." In this way, O'Neill hoped to avoid an open confrontation with Reagan, who was basking in the popularity that traditionally follows a landslide reelection, and to give the public an opportunity to examine Reagan's policies without the distraction of partisan rhetoric. According to O'Neill's press secretary, "The speaker doesn't want to get between the president and the people on this."

Later in the spring, as the president's budget limped through congressional deliberations, Senate Majority Leader Robert Dole insisted that the president make a national television appeal before he brought to the Senate floor a compromise budget resolution that none of his colleagues appeared eager to embrace. Without a strong public appeal, Dole assured the administration there would be no way he could persuade even his fellow Republicans to pass it.

In both instances, a presidential appeal had a prominent place in the strategic planning of other leaders. For different reasons, neither O'Neill nor Dole was prepared to proceed without first having Reagan publicly stake out his own position. As other politicians come to expect a president to promote his policies through public relations, he will sometimes find that they will force his hand and seek to exploit his ability to go public.

Redefining the Strategic Repertoire

A third level of strategic planning, which derives at least in part from the president's demonstrated ability to go public, is the way other Washington politicians view their own strategic opportunities at public relations. Increasingly, whether learned independently or from observing the president, politicians throughout Washington are coming to adopt aspects of going public as part of their own repertoire.

Again, recent events offer numerous examples. One of the most striking occurred in late May 1985 when House Ways and Means Committee chair Daniel Rostenkowski followed President Reagan's prime time appeal for public support for tax reform with a national television appeal of his own. What an incongruous sight it must have been for the men and women who served with former Ways and Means chair Wilbur Mills to watch a successor telling the country that with its active support his committee would beat back the "special interests" that would be hard at work to frustrate tax reform.

In adopting much of Reagan's script, Rostenkowski sought to neutralize the president's mandate as well as siphon off a share of whatever credit might be forthcoming were a popular tax reform measure to be enacted. Those close to Rostenkowski offered another reason for his rousing appeal. Speaker O'Neill had announced his retirement and sealed it with a million-dollar contract for his memoirs, and Rostenkowski was planning "an outside" bid for the post. To stand a chance against fellow Democrat James Wright, whose job as majority leader made him heir apparent to the speakership, Rostenkowski was building a record of his ability to represent Congress in its dealings with presidents who go public. This quintessential institutional actor appealed to the country to "write Rosty" not only to promote the Democrats' commitment to tax reform but also to advance his own claim later for the highest leadership position within the House of Representatives.

Rostenkowski's insight was not altogether lost on the man he hoped to succeed. In 1981 Speaker O'Neill hired a new, more publicly active press secretary. Although public relations cut against O'Neill's grain, he faced the dilemma, as observed by one congressional reporter, that "if he had not gone public, there would have been nobody at all to tell the Democratic story." Strategic adaptation of this kind is increasingly common on Capitol Hill. Though on most occasions it does not arise directly in response to the president's initiative, his example nonetheless inspires others to try their hand at going public. House leaders, for example, have complained that junior members no longer toe the party line in hope of favorable committee assignments that might help them get reelected. Instead, according to one of O'Neill's senior staffers, they "go directly to voters via television." Senate Majority Leader Howard Baker agreed: "If you don't let them do anything on the floor, they do it on the steps [of the Capitol]. And somehow there's always a TV camera out there."

As politicians at every level routinely go public, the president's public activities become normal behavior to which others respond when they must but to which they no longer take exception. Furthermore, as other politicians similarly engage in public relations to pursue their own political objectives, public posturing will tend to displace quiet diplomacy as the normal means by which fellow Washingtonians communicate with one another across the institutional boundaries that separate them.

Career Adaptations: Washington Correspondents and Presidential Aspirants

The rise of this new style of presidential leadership appears to have profoundly altered the careers of two groups in Washington: correspondents and presidential aspirants. [I clarify here] the ways in which political careers adapt to the altered circumstances posed by going public as a routine of the modern White House.

During the 1960s and 1970s, the reporting style of Washington correspondents evolved from objective to interpretive journalism. Various reasons have been offered for this reorientation. Certainly, any reporter whose Washington career spanned Johnson's Vietnam credibility gap and Nixon's Watergate would likely say that these events conclusively exposed the deficiencies of objective journalism.

As significant as these events were, other, more structural features of political relations in Washington had begun reworking the professional creed of Washington correspondents by the onset of the Vietnam War. With growing opportunities for news analysis provided by increasing network coverage of the White House, longer evening news programs, and televised news conferences, objective journalism made a hasty retreat. Reporters found themselves describing events their readers had already viewed for themselves. For traditional correspondents whose job it was to report on events in Washington for the readers back home, expanded network television coverage of the White House threatened to leave them without a purpose.

As politicians increasingly employed national media to market policies as well as themselves, objective journalism encountered another problem. Because this creed offers the reporter little latitude for evaluation and interpretation, it is better suited for covering what politicians do than what they say. Reporters found themselves serving as vehicles for the propaganda activities of politicians. Even in reporting what they privately regarded to be partial truths and outright falsehoods, objective journalism required them to play the role of neutral scribes. For some, the credibility gap of Vietnam and the coverage of Watergate posed this dilemma.

Perhaps at no time, however, was the dilemma more sharply felt by the working press in Washington than during Joseph McCarthy's witch hunt in the State Department and the army in the early 1950s. However outlandish were McCarthy's charges in the opinion of many correspondents, they felt obliged to report them in a straightforward manner as news. When privately pressed by these reporters to substantiate his claims, McCarthy would dissimulate and at times as much as admit that he had no proof (Bayley 1981). Yet because these encounters were "off the record," many correspondents were obliged not to report this information to their readers. Some reporters did over time switch to a more evaluative, critical reporting of McCarthy's shenanigans, but one study of press coverage found that efforts to rebut false statements rarely appeared in the wire services and that the other critical stories were significantly less likely to be picked up by other papers around the country.

During the early 1950s, various internal and external mechanisms of the newspaper business were enforcing objective journalism. In the judgment of historians and journalists looking back on the era, the result was that the practice of objective journalism served to broadcast McCarthy's campaign (Rovere 1959).

In mobilizing public opinion to sway events in Washington, McCarthy along with Sen. Estes Kefauver, who conducted televised hearings into wrongdoing within the drug industry, were precursors of the modern politician who goes public. Confronted with going public as a political strategy, objective journalism neither supplies reporters with good copy nor permits them to assess rhetoric against reality. The creed of analysis and interpretation solves both problems.

Because going public is only one part of a broader transformation of community relations, one cannot state precisely the degree to which trends in presidents' public activities . . . contributed to the professional reorientation of Washington correspondents in the 1960s. There is little doubt, however, that this new style of journalism has correspondents balancing presidential rhetoric with independent analysis. One sees it in the insistent questioning at news conferences, in the television and newspaper commentary that follows presidential addresses, and in the coverage of presidents on the evening news. On this last score, one study of network news found that by 1985 the average taped segment of the president speaking lasted only 9 seconds, compared with 44 seconds during the years 1965 to 1972.

The other group whose careers are being redirected in ways that reflect and reinforce the prospects of going public as presidential strategy is the men and women who aspire to hold that office. Reflecting the rise of the national government in public life at home and abroad, the U.S. Senate during the early post-World War II era replaced the states' governorships as the chief source of presidential timber. Senators enjoy resources that few other officeholders can match. Unlike their House colleagues, who are forced by their district's narrower concerns and their chamber's greater number to specialize, senators find that their varied committee responsibilities and the relaxed floor procedures permit them to be reputable and vocal dilettantes on any number of domestic and foreign issues that arise from day to day. The Senate serves as a megaphone with which its members champion policies before a national constituency. Moreover, the Senate is a school for the pluralist arts. When elected to the White House, Lyndon Johnson and John Kennedy—but not Richard Nixon, who served in the Senate only briefly before entering the isolation booth of the vice-presidency—were familiar with, if not expert in, the requirements of a bargaining president (Polsby 1984).

Since the presidential selection reforms and the entry of strong "outsider" contenders for the nomination, the Senate has lost some of its standing as the home of future presidents. This does not mean that it will go the way of the cabinet, which served briefly as the presidency's penultimate office in the early nineteenth century, but it does mean that aspiring politicians will no longer need to find their way to the Senate—or for that matter to Washington—to make a serious run for the White House.

The strategic effects of the biases of the reformed selection system on the 1988 election were already apparent by 1985, winnowing and tailoring candidates to generate party nominees who if elected might well seek to emulate Ronald Reagan's style of leadership. Observers caught a glimpse of these processes in late 1984 when Howard Baker retired early from the Senate after finding his duties as majority leader, and perhaps the "insider" status that comes with it, an encumbrance during his brief and uneventful bid for the Republican presidential nomination in 1980. For much of 1985, three years before the election, private citizen Baker could be found on the circuit of New Hampshire's civic lunches and coffee klatches, which quadrennially provide citizens of that state with their special form of entertainment. While Baker was laying the groundwork for a bid in New Hampshire's early primary, his former Senate Republican colleagues, some of whom also aspire to the presidency, were stuck in Washington grousing with their president and struggling with such unpleasant subjects as the budget deficit, import quotas, and the multiple problems of the American farmer. The same consideration can be seen in the early decision of Arizona governor Bruce Babbitt to forgo a highly promising bid for a vacant Senate seat in 1986 to look for "new challenges," presumably in 1988, and to take lessons in television performance. The ambivalence Gary Hart displayed throughout 1985 about seeking Senate reelection in 1986 also reveals these biases; even were he to win, speculation held that he might hurt his presidential aspirations for 1988. Meanwhile, fellow front-runner for the Democratic nomination Mario Cuomo, safely ensconced as New York's governor, was busy honing his broadcast skills with a weekly half-hour radio show on the state's public radio stations, a monthly call-in show on a Manhattan radio station, a quarterly television call-in show, and every other day a 30-second editorial over Mutual Radio's national network, alternating with Republican candidate Howard Baker.

Finally, individuals who have never held public office, but who do possess the requisite resources—ample television exposure, political action committees, and an established fundraising list—will in the future be considered serious contenders for this pinnacle office of the political career structure. In the fall of 1985, television evangelist Pat Robertson let his presidential aspirations be known. As quixotic as such a bid would have been fifteen years ago, his announcement was greeted in Washington not with derision but with an invitation to speak to the National Press Club and the dutiful regard befitting a plausible contender.

. . . Going public [is] a product of the new Washington and its new breed of presidents. Because the political marketplace is regulated in no small part by anticipation of an adaptation to others' choices, going public has become incorporated generally into the expectations and behavior of Washingtonians. In this way it reinforces and accentuates the community's continued evolution.

Public Policy and Going Public

The implication of public strategies of leadership for policy has been a subject of recurrent interest. So far, I have concentrated mostly upon the deleterious side effects of public activity on bargaining to show that rather than complement, public strategies, when frequently engaged, damage and displace bargaining. Public discussion requires issues to be stylized in ways that frequently reduce choices to black and white alternatives and to principles that are difficult to modify. In part this reflects the rigidifying effect of declaring one's preferences publicly, but it also results from the stylization of issues required to accommodate the limited attention span of the public audience and the brief time spots available on national television. Perhaps more damaging, public discussion tends to harden negotiating positions as both sides posture as much to rally support as to impress the other side. Bargaining and compromise suffer. Even when a stalemate is avoided, the adopted policy may not enjoy the same firm foundation of support had it been enacted by a negotiated consensus. These are some of the unfortunate consequences of making policy in the public arena. Other consequences strike more deeply to the foundation of democratic politics, if not shaking it, at least altering the structure of political relations it supports.

Supply-side Politics

At first glance the perforated borders of individualized pluralism would appear to bode well for democratic politics. After all, should the citizenry's demands not flow more freely into Washington? Weakened leadership and the deterioration of other mechanisms of conformity to the requirements of protocoalitions have made institutions more easily penetrable and have weakened their resistance to poaching by others who compete for the same jurisdiction. As a result, outsiders today are provided with a porous governmental apparatus that contains numerous access points for those who seek to influence policy. Moreover, the increased sensitivity of politicians to public pressure, which follows from these relaxed internal constraints, improves the chances that outsiders will find the necessary institutional sponsorship for their views. A fair reading of these developments might lead one to assume a closer alignment between policies favored in the country and those deliberated in Washington. If so, whatever its ill effects on partisan discussion, individualized pluralism's corruption of the traditionally insular political relations would be a boon to democracy.

The swiftness with which some new issues sweep into present-day Washington and traverse its policy course appears to confirm this assessment. The "flat tax" drive of the late 1970s found eager congressional sponsorship, and under Reagan it emerged in altered form as the core concept of the administration's comprehensive tax reform proposal. An even more impressive example is the alacrity with which Mothers Against Drunk Driving (MADD) won federal legislation in a policy realm that had traditionally been reserved to the states. In 1980, just two years before its legislative triumph, MADD was created by two mothers who had lost children in automobile accidents involving drunken drivers. Enjoying continuous television and press coverage, by 1982 MADD had formed 230 chapters in forty-two states with a quarter of a million members. Because of its inspired grass-roots campaign, the federal government today insists that states have tough drunk driving laws on their books.

In 1983 the savings and loan industry staved off an imminent Internal Revenue Service (IRS) regulation that would have required banks and savings associations to withhold a portion of depositors' interest for taxes. The similar quick success of these bankers is less impressive only because they needed a simple resolution of Congress and did not require the president's signature to a accomplish their goal.

These cases and others like them succeeded by short-circuiting the slow and arduous process by which policy issues have traditionally attracted majority coalitions in Washington. The traditional method consisted of continuous discussions with representatives of those constituencies who would be most affected by the policy and with key governmental participants—most frequently committee and subcommittee chairs and agency heads who would be chiefly responsible for enacting and implementing the program. This involved ongoing reformulation to broaden the policy's political support and to make it administratively feasible. Ultimately, if in this incubation phase the issue succeeded in attracting the right sponsors and sufficient support to give it a reasonable prospect of success (and few did), it would then typically wait in queue for a presidential endorsement, which might provide the necessary impetus to get it enacted.

What allowed the issues described above to circumvent the traditional process was the massive grass-roots campaign generated outside

Washington; by the time representatives of these campaigns approached potential legislative sponsors, many politicians had already begun lining up to support the policy. The savings and loan industry's campaign quickly generated millions of letters and post cards. One senator alone counted 769,000 pieces of constituent mail—almost all of it supporting the industry. By so thoroughly stirring the opinion that flows to members of Congress, many of those promoting special causes find that they can frequently prevail even when their efforts fail to win the endorsement of the president, the relevant agency heads, or committee chairs. The most senior Republican the savings and loan industry could recruit to sponsor its cause was first-term senator Robert Kasten of Wisconsin. A generation earlier, this member's status would have earned him little more than an opportunity to be seen but not heard. By 1983, of course, the Senate had changed, and the opportunities available to a junior member had greatly expanded. Over the opposition of his party's committee and floor leaders, his president, and the Internal Revenue Service, Kasten promoted the cause of the savings and loan industry to a resounding victory on the Senate floor.

Even in the altered circumstances of present-day Washington, Senator Kasten's feat surprised the local cognoscenti. It demonstrated, perhaps better than any other recent event, that great external pressure can be sufficient to induce congressional compliance even without engaging traditional avenues of influence. This is a far cry from the lobbyist's code of "never pressure" under institutionalized pluralism.

Pressure is the essence of public strategies, whether they are engaged by presidents or outside groups. Going public succeeds not by adjusting policy to the mix of preferences represented in Washington but rather by trading on the strategic concerns of elected politicians and, thereby, changing those preferences. When success or failure is decided in the country, institutional leaders are less necessary; even a junior senator can do a splendid job.

If by now the activities of the savings and loan industry and MADD look familiar, they should, because they follow much the same strategic formula President Reagan employed so successfully in 1981 to push massive tax and social spending cuts through Congress. The difference is one only of scale. Whether undertaken by a president seeking to redirect the priorities of the federal government or by two mothers wanting tougher drunk-driving laws, going public has become a frequently preferred approach to coalition building in Washington. On their face, these cases appear to support the improved responsiveness of national political institutions to the citizenry's demands under individualized pluralism.

But is this really what is going on? Are demands flowing more freely into Washington and shaping policy, or rather, are they being created by politicians through inspired mass advertising? One might argue that the distinction does not much matter because the appeals must still strike a responsive chord, or they will be quickly deflated by the public's inattention or even its antipathy. One can support this argument by pointing to the dismal performance of grass-roots lobbying by the Natural Gas Supply Association in 1983. Seeking to decontrol natural gas prices, this organization created a $1 million front called Alliance for Energy Security to drum up a national letter campaign to Congress. A consultant who specialized in targeted mail was retained to mount special pressure on 15 members of Congress whom the gas lobby had designated as vulnerable. Despite enlisting sophisticated technology and an appeal for energy security, the effort failed to generate the desired groundswell of support.

The distinction between the citizenry's continuing demands rooted in life experiences and those of a more ephemeral quality generated by issue entrepreneurs is critical for appreciating the working of modern democracy in a communications age. Do the fixed preferences of the public motivate and direct the strategic activities of politicians, or conversely, do politicians shape the preferences of the public, at least those that are effectively communicated to Washington? To use an analogy from economics, the distinction is between demand-side and supply-side politics. At one time before the media had begun to replace work-related, ethnic, religious, and other voluntary associations as the chief source of civic information, and before political entrepreneurs had the technological wherewithal to mass market ideas through such diverse and specialized media as television and targeted mail, it would have been easy to say that the citizenry's demands are the autonomous force of American politics. Today, however, the answer is less clear. The emergence of mass communications technology gives voice to politicians and organizations who enjoy the financial resources to broadcast commercials to millions of citizens or who have the legitimacy to command similar access via the news media. The president has both.

Except perhaps for the concerted efforts of the Founding Fathers to draft a Constitution that would mitigate transient, "inflamed popular passions," one seldom finds American political thought directed to this matter of supply-side politics. In early democratic theory, representatives served as passive receptacles with whom the citizens could deposit their demands. Later, when under Edmund Burke's influence, students of politics began to view representatives less as delegates and more as fiduciary agents, or trustees, who were to exercise independent judgment, little attention was given to marketing, except as an officeholder defended his policies in a reelection campaign. Even in twentieth-century discussions of party democracy, political parties formulate their programs through close association with mediating organizations that articulate constituency demands, and they adjust their programs to match the preferences of as broad a cross section of the electorate as they can. The idea of campaigning to mobilize public opinion for issues currently before Congress has not so much been condemned by theory as ignored. Such campaigns and the continuing public relations of modern presidents suggest that traditional thinking about the relationship between the representative and the represented needs revision.

Consider the evidence of supply-side politics available in the cases introduced above. Before the efforts of MADD, the savings and loan industry, or the Alliance for Energy Security, one would have had difficulty finding instances of ordinary citizens importuning members of Congress to do something about drunk drivers, to rescind the IRS's plan to withhold interest, or to decontrol natural gas prices. Similarly . . . President Reagan's budget cuts enjoyed majority endorsement only briefly, and that moment came well before he initiated the public campaign for the policy's enactment. On none of those subjects does the issue's sponsor appear to have merely given expression to pent-up or nascent demands. Instead, they (the president included) acted as entrepreneurs creating demands and channeling their expression to Washington. These instances lend support to the recent observation by one member of Congress that "grass-roots lobbying today is a highly sophisticated effort. Just by the sheer mechanics of modern technology, they can often generate what [appears to be] a groundswell of public opinion, when in fact that groundswell does not really exist.

A Variable Agenda and Volatile Outcomes

Individualized pluralism liberates politicians from institutional and party bonds. This has two effects on policy: politicians are freer to choose which issues they wish to sponsor, and the success of those issues depends more heavily upon the talents and fortunes of their sponsor. The first means greater variability in the issues that rise, albeit perhaps temporarily, to the top of the agenda in Washington. The second means that coalition building will be subject to new, extraneous forces and, hence, will be more volatile.

As presidents and aspirants to the office have traditionally tried to expand their electoral support beyond their party's core constituency, a number of political forces have kept them tethered fairly near home. The large role of state parties and mediating organizations in selecting presidential candidates at the party convention meant that these politicians could ill afford to advocate policies too distant from the priorities of the party's base. In Congress, party supplied institutional leadership, which meant that its legislative agenda already enjoyed substantial progress to-

ward the development of a winning coalition. Consequently, policies associated with political parties and their core groups resided comfortably
atop the national agenda. Since the early 1970s, however, presidential
selection reforms and the reduced role of the party in coalition building
have relaxed the parties' influence on presidential policy.

Today's presidents, increasingly outsiders, are freer to choose their
issues than typically were their predecessors. As a consequence, the policy agenda will vary with the incumbent and will do so in ways that cannot be easily predicted by the president's party affiliation (Beck 1982).
This does not mean that presidents will sponsor issues randomly. As individualized pluralism has loosened bonds to party and institution, it had
tightened others. Attentiveness to public opinion, of course, has always
been a chief occupational requirement for those who serve in elective office, but today's politicians are displaying exceptional sensitivity to the
breezes that blow into Washington. Sometimes it shows up in the president's conformity to the perceived moods of the public, but more often it
manifests itself in White House behavior in the way presidents seek to influence other politicians who are equally subject to public opinion and
who have fewer resources at hand with which to mold opinion to their
liking.

There is a compelling rationale for suspecting that the more presidents rest their leadership on going public, the more volatile policy outcomes in Washington will be. The public can be assumed to be more fickle
in its assessments of politicians and policies than will be a stable community of Washington elites, whose business it is to make informed judgment.
As the former becomes more important and the latter less, political relations will be more easily disrupted. Moreover, the effect of the president's
own public standing on his ability to rally public opinion behind his policies exposes policy to extraneous and wholly unrelated events. Whatever
affects the president's standing with the public will alter the prospects for
those policies he sponsors. Sometimes the result may be altogether salu-
tary, as in the boost President Reagan's 1981 budget proposals received after the assassination attempt. But if the president falters, so too will those
policies that depend upon him for their sustenance.

The volatility of modern politics is plainly conveyed in the interpretations Washington politicians and the press give to presidential events.
Two occurrences within a six-week period during the summer of 1985
illustrate the heavy dependence of policy on the public fortunes of its
sponsor. After recouping much of his sagging popularity during late
spring with a forceful national appeal for tax reform, President Reagan
entered June with tax reform the number one issue on Congress's agenda.
Other less politically favorable developments during these weeks, such as
the controversial U.S. support for the contras in Nicaragua, had failed to

register in the news and the public utterances of politicians to the same degree they might have had tax reform not grabbed the headlines. On June 14, however, terrorists hijacked an international airliner and took more than fifty American passengers to Lebanon as hostages. Tax reform faded quickly. During the next weeks, some aides contended that Reagan's presidency hung in the balance. Would this crisis paralyze the administration they way the Iranian hostage crisis had Carter's? Early on, one senior White House official confided to *Washington Post* columnist Lou Cannon that it was fortunate that tax reform would not come up for a vote in Congress until fall. Aside from whatever potential damage the hostage crisis might have on the president's public standing, tax reform had suddenly fallen from public view; and without active public support, it would face tough going in Congress. Then, nearly two weeks into the crisis, as those close to the negotiations realized that the hostages might be released soon, White House aides began voicing brighter prognostications for tax reform. One Reagan aide told Cannon that if the president "were successful in winning the release of the hostages, he would gain in public standing and use his increased popularity to become a more activist president". The next day, before an audience in Illinois, President Reagan returned to the tax issue, stating with renewed enthusiasm that after Congress returned from the summer recess, "I'm heading out to the country—I'm going to campaign all across the nation throughout the fall for tax fairness".

The promise of a "fall offensive" of public appeals was repeated frequently during the next few weeks. But it was turned off again when on July 12 the president was admitted to Bethesda Naval Medical Center to remove a growth from his colon. Next to the president's health, the foremost political question was, if the president is unable to take to the hustings, what becomes of tax reform? Reagan pollster Richard B. Wirthlin cautiously answered one reporter's query by saying that the effect on tax reform depended upon "the speed and completeness of the recovery." Meanwhile, *New York Times* columnist Tom Wicker was speculating that the public sympathy the president's illness could be expected to engender would give his legislative program a new boost. Sen. Pete Wilson sounded a cautionary note on tax reform, however, when during the president's convalescence he told a reporter that the "tax reform is losing rather than gaining momentum [in the country]."

The president gives a prime time address on tax reform, and it immediately soars to the top of the legislative agenda. Within moments, the chair of the House Ways and Means Committee in his own televised address promises action and exhorts the public for demonstrations of support. But when hostages are seized a couple of weeks later, the prospects of tax reform dim. Just as quickly, they brighten when the hostages are

released. Then comes the president's operation and his speedy recuperation, tax reform once again waning and waxing in a two-week period. In
a system such as ours where governing coalitions are formed by independent officeholders rather than by party teams, the personal skills and fortunes of the sponsor have always been a key ingredient in an issue's
chances of success, but with the injection of public opinion into policy
deliberation through grass-roots campaigns and the president's popularity, policy making promises to become more volatile.

The President's Agenda

Whatever their differences in personality—and they were considerable—Theodore Roosevelt and Woodrow Wilson shared one attribute
that shaped their approach to leadership style as much as any other. Both
men were Progressives. This meant that each envisioned a responsive federal government led by an energetic president actively promoting the collective interests of the country over the particular concerns of its political,
geographical and economic subdivisions. Strategically, both men solicited demonstrations of public support for their program. They had to,
since many of their Progressive reforms would strip power and its usu-
fructs from those politicians who would be asked to enact them.

Compared with the access of modern presidents to the airwaves and
to jet transportation, their opportunities to go public were truly modest.
However handicapped, this strategy sometimes held more promise than
did negotiations. When Wilson, as New Jersey's newly elected governor,
was once pressed by reporters to explain how he could possibly hope to
win political reforms from a state legislature dominated by solons loyal to
their party organizations, he replied, "I can talk, can't I?"

Neither president enlisted public strategies casually. The idea of continuous forays into the country to generate public support for their initiatives before Congress was plainly impractical. In their day, the imbalance
between costs imposed by confining technology and benefits limited by
firm institutional resistance would have made frequent public campaigns
foolhardy. Roosevelt and Wilson regarded going public as a strategy appropriate for a limited set of issues. These issues were ones in which traditional bargaining could be expected to fail and for which the president
could legitimately play the role of the national tribune against "the special
interests" entrenched in Congress. By and large, these issues constituted the
Progressive agenda. When these presidents expatiated on political reform,
on the regulation of big business, and, for Roosevelt especially, on conser-
vation, they spoke to the country as well as for it. On more fractious national issues—such as tariff reform, a bloated embodiment of Congress's
particularistic urges—they refrained from enlisting public strategies. One

Roosevelt biographer writes: "Significantly, Roosevelt reserved nearly all his opportunities as president for public persuasion—a bully pulpit, he called the office—for appeals to transcendent national interests and higher standards of personal conduct, rather than redress or justice to particular people or groups" (Cooper 1983, 6). Woodrow Wilson recognized the necessary symbolic distinction when on the subject of regulation he asserted, "The present conflict in this country is not between capital and labor. It is a contest between those few men in whose hands the wealth of the land is concentrated, and the rest of us" (Cooper 1983, 26).

The practices of Roosevelt and Wilson suggest that going public is more serviceable for some issues than for others. A president will enjoy his strongest claim to the public's attention and support when he can present his policies as uprooting unsavory particularism. This theme must be played off a backdrop of an unassailable public interest. For good measure, these appeals should, when possible, exploit Americans' deeply ingrained distrust of politicians. On these rhetorical criteria, the Progressive agenda was a motherlode to Roosevelt and Wilson.

With so many avenues for going public available to modern presidents, one finds them frequently appealing for public support more casually and frequently before the same "special interests" many Progressives held in open contempt. Nonetheless, the president's special legitimacy in going to the people to defend the public interest from private greed remains a powerful force today. Nor have the strategic implications been lost on the White House's recent occupants. Both Presidents Carter and Reagan couched their major legislative proposals as a struggle between public and private interests. When, early in his term, Jimmy Carter began a series of prime time television addresses in behalf of his comprehensive energy program currently before Congress, he did not hesitate to conjure up the threat of rapacious special interests: "We can be sure that all the special interest groups in the country will attack . . . this plan. . . . If they succeed with this approach, then the burden on the ordinary citizen, who is not organized into an interest group, would be crushing. There should be only one test for this plan—whether it will help our country."

During the first five years of President Reagan's tenure he too cloaked his major legislative proposals in the public interest. Although his program differed diametrically from Progressivism in advocating the reduction of federal responsibilities to provide social services and to regulate industry, the imagery fit comfortably in that tradition. . . . The following is an excerpt from his presentation of his tax reform proposal to a national television audience on May 28, 1985:

> The proposal I am putting forth tonight for America's future will free us from the grip of special interests and create a binding commitment to the

only special interest that counts, you, the people who pay America's bills. It will create millions of new jobs for working people and it will replace the politics of envy with a spirit of partnership.

For the rest of the year, Reagan would continue to sound this theme.

The earlier two presidents engaged in public leadership to the degree they could because, despite their different party affiliations, each sought to enact a Progressive agenda over formidable opposition in Congress. What do Presidents Carter and Reagan have in common that has led them to enlist similar rhetorical devices? Certainly, it is not progressivism . . . Their outsider status, [however,] enhanced the credibility of their attacks on special interests. Presidents of this era portray special interests as being entrenched in the bureaucracy that doles out government funds ("puzzle palaces on the Potomac" administering the "social pork barrel") rather than in the party machines that extorted graft and dispensed patronage.

Even more important than their outsider status, these presidents share the modern facility to go public. For its first practitioners, going public was an invention inspired by a policy agenda that would fail if left to the traditional political process. The ends dictated the means. Today, the situation may well be reversed. As modern presidents seek to exploit their strategic advantage in public opinion, they gravitate toward issues that endow them with the strongest claim to represent the "public interest." By its very nature, the policy program of the president's core constituency will be ill suited for the kinds of appeals public strategies require. But no matter: presidents are no longer much beholden to these constituencies. Nor, in the setting of supply-side politics, are their policy options sharply circumscribed by the once great need to choose among policy ideas that had over time already attracted a sizable number of supporters in Washington. The profusion of think tanks, new-styled interest groups, and even the congressional caucuses offer presidents an ample supply of policy ideas from which to choose.

When President Reagan mentioned in his 1984 State of the Union message that he would ask the Treasury Department to examine tax reform, his remark elicited tepid applause befitting its apparent insignificance. Little did the assembled members of Congress and other president watchers realize that by year's end, tax reform would emerge as the centerpiece of his second administration. With it he hoped to establish the Republican party as the new majority party of the country. That one of the principal authors of the Treasury bill had been a colleague of some of the early proponents of the "flat tax" proposal at the Hoover Institution illustrates the new, alternative sources of policy available to modern presidents.

As one looks to the future, the prospect for the continued use of going public as presidential strategy shines bright. The forces of technology and of an evolving political environment that set public campaigning from the White House on its current trajectory have not abated. Moreover, professional self-interest dictates that all participants in Washington's politics take going public into account as they plan their strategies. The president must as he decides which policies he wishes to promote. Would-be presidents must as they groom themselves and tailor their policy appeals for a future bid for the White House. So must White House correspondents as they evaluate the president's performance and as they weigh his rhetoric against their own and others' notions of reality. And so must all who do business with the president and are thereby vulnerable to his public appeals. The strategic adaptations these men and women are making will, as much as its original causes, guarantee that going public will occupy a prominent place in the strategic repertoire of future presidents.

Contributors

James William Anderson is Associate Professor of Clinical Psychology, Northwestern University Medical School.

Clive Bean is Research Fellow, Research School of Social Sciences, Australian National University.

Martin Burch is Senior Lecturer in Government, University of Manchester, England.

James MacGregor Burns is Woodrow Wilson Professor of Government Emeritus, Williams College.

Bruce E. Cain is Professor of Political Science, University of California, Berkeley.

Philip Converse is Director, Center for Advanced Study in the Behavioral Sciences, Palo Alto.

Rowland Evans, Jr. has written the syndicated column *Inside Report* since 1963. He also cohosts, with Robert D. Novak, the weekly CNN television program, *Evans & Novak.*

Richard F. Fenno, Jr. is Kenan Professor of Political Science, University of Rochester.

John A. Ferejohn is Senior Fellow, Hoover Institution, and Professor of Political Science, Stanford University.

Morris P. Fiorina is Professor of Government, Harvard University.

Alexander L. George is Professor of Political Science and Graham H. Stuart Professor of International Relations, Stanford University.

Juliette George is a Senior Scholar, Institute of International Studies, Stanford University.

Fred I. Greenstein is Professor of Politics, Princeton University.

Stanley Hoffmann is Douglas Dillon Professor of the Civilization of France and Chairman of the Center for European Studies, Harvard University.

Hugh Heclo is Clarence J. Robinson Professor of Public Affairs, George Mason University.

Charles O. Jones is Hawkins Professor of Political Science, University of Wisconsin, Madison.

Samuel Kernell is Professor of Political Science, University of California, San Diego.

Chong Lim Kim is Professor of Political Science, University of Iowa.

Anthony King is Professor of Government, University of Essex, England.

Arend Lijphart is Professor of Political Science, University of California, San Diego.

Arthur S. Link is George H. Davis '86 Professor of History, Princeton University.

Michael Moran is Professor of Government, University of Manchester, England.

Anthony Mughan is Professor of Political Science, The Ohio State University.

Richard E. Neustadt is Douglas Dillon Professor of Government, Harvard University.

Pippa Norris is Lecturer in Politics, University of Edinburgh, Scotland.

Robert Novak has written the syndicated column *Inside Report* since 1963. He also cohosts, with Rowland Evans Jr., the weekly CNN television program, *Evans & Novak*.

Duane M. Oldfield is completing his Ph.D. dissertation at the University of California, Berkeley.

Samuel C. Patterson is Professor of Political Science, Ohio State University.

Roy Pierce is Professor of Political Science, University of Michigan.

Donald Searing is Professor of Political Science, University of North Carolina.

Robert C. Tucker is Professor of Politics Emeritus and IBM Professor of International Studies Emeritus, Princeton University.

Edwin A. Weinstein, M.D. is Guest Researcher, Laboratory of Neurosciences, National Institute of Aging, Bethesda, Maryland.

Aaron Wildavsky is Professor of Political Science and Public Policy, University of California, Berkeley.

References

Aberbach, J. D., R. D. Putnam, and B. A. Rockman. 1981. *Bureaucrats and Politicians in Western Democracies.* Cambridge, MA: Harvard University Press.

Ake, C. 1967. *A Theory of Political Integration.* Homewood, IL: Dorsey.

Alexander, F. 1930. "The Neurotic Character." *International Journal of Psychoanalysis* 11:292–311.

Alford, R. R. 1963. *Party and Society: The Anglo-American Democracies.* Chicago, IL: Rand McNally.

Almond, G. A. 1956. "Comparative Political Systems." *Journal of Politics* 18:391–409.

Almond, G. A. 1958. "A Comparative Study of Interest Groups and the Political Process." *American Political Science Review* 52:270–82.

Almond, G. A. 1960. "A Functional Approach to Comparative Politics." In *The Politics of the Developing Areas*, eds., G. A. Almond and J. C. Coleman. Princeton, NJ: Princeton University Press.

Almond, G. A. 1963. "Political Systems and Political Change." *American Behavioral Scientist* 6:3–10.

Almond, G. A., and G. Bingham Powell. 1966. *Comparative Politics: A Developmental Approach.* Boston, MA: Little, Brown.

Almond, G. A., and S. Verba. 1963. *The Civic Culture: Political Attitudes and Democracy in Five Nations.* Princeton, NJ: Princeton University Press.

Amery, L. 1948. *Thoughts on the Constitution.* Oxford: Oxford University Press.

Arieff, I., et al. 1981. "The Year in Congress." *Congressional Quarterly Weekly Report*, December 19.

Aron, R. 1965. *Démocratie et Totalitarisme.* Paris: Gallimard.

Asher, H. B. 1973. "The Learning of Legislative Norms." *American Political Science Review* 67:499–513.

Baerwald, H. H. 1974. *Japan's Parliament.* Cambridge: Cambridge University Press.

Bailey, F. G. 1988. *Humbuggery and Manipulation: The Art of Leadership.* Ithaca, NY: Cornell University Press.

Baker, R. S. 1927. *Woodrow Wilson: Life and Letters*, vol. I. New York: Doubleday, Page.

Barber, J. D. 1968. "Classifying and Predicting Presidential Styles: Two Weak Presidents." *Journal of Social Issues* 24:51–80.

Barber, J. D. 1977. *The Presidential Character: Predicting Performance in the White House*, 2nd ed. Englewood Cliffs, NJ: Prentice-Hall.

Barkan, J. D., and J. J. Okumu, eds. 1979. *Politics and Public Policy in Kenya and Tanzania*. New York: Praeger.

Barker, G. 1984. "Television Blood Sport and the Future of Democracy." *Melbourne Age*, Oct. 20, 13.

Barnes, S. H. 1977. *Representation in Italy*. Chicago, IL: University of Chicago Press.

Bayley, E. R. 1981. *Joe McCarthy and the Press*. Madison: University of Wisconsin Press.

Beck, N. 1982. "Parties, Administrations, and American Macroeconomic Outcomes." *American Political Science Review* 76:83–93.

Beckwith, K. 1990. "Women and Election to National Legislatures: Lessons from France and Italy." Paper presented at the Conference of Europeanists, Washington DC (March).

Beer, S. H. 1965. *British Politics in the Collectivist Age*. New York: Knopf.

Behrens, R. 1980. *The Conservative Party from Heath to Thatcher*. London: Saxon House.

Bell, C. G., and C. M. Price. 1975. *The First Term: A Study of Legislative Socialization*. Beverly Hills, CA: Sage.

Bell, R., D. Edwards, and R. H. Wagner. 1969. *Political Power*. New York: Free Press.

Bentley, A. F. 1955. *The Process of Government: A Study of Social Pressures*, 4th ed. Evanston, IL: Northwestern University Press.

Birch, A. H. 1964. *Representative and Responsible Government*. London: Allen & Unwin.

Blake, R. 1955. *The Unknown Prime Minister*. London: Eyre and Spotiswoode.

Blake, R. 1970. *The Conservative Party from Peel to Churchill*. London: Fontana/Collins.

Blondel, J. 1987. *Political Leadership: Towards a General Analysis*. London: Sage.

Bogdanor, V. 1983. "Conclusions: Electoral Systems and Party Systems." In *Democracy and Elections*, eds. V. Bogdanor and D. Butler. Cambridge: Cambridge University Press.

Bogdanor, V., ed. 1985. *Representatives of the People?* Aldershot, England: Gower.

Bowles, H. 1987. *The White House and Capitol Hill: The Politics of Presidential Persuasion*. Oxford: Clarendon Press.

Bridges, E. L. 1964. *The Treasury*. London: Allen & Unwin.

Brodie, F. M. 1981. *Richard Nixon: The Shaping of His Character*. New York: Norton.

Browning, G. K. 1987. *Women and Politics in the USSR*. London: Wheatsheaf.

Brogan, D. 1964. *American Aspects.* London: Hamish Hamilton.

Bryce, L. 1893. *The American Commonwealth*, vol. 1. London: Macmillan.

Budge, I., D. Robertson, and D. Hearl, eds. 1987. *Ideology, Strategy and Party Change: Spatial Analyses of Post-War Election Programmes in 19 Countries.* Cambridge: Cambridge University Press.

Bunce, V. 1981. *Do New Leaders Make a Difference?* Princeton, NJ: Princeton University Press.

Burke, J. P. 1985. "Political Context and Presidential Influence: A Case Study." *Presidential Studies Quarterly* 15:301-19.

Burns, J. M. 1963. *The Deadlock of Democracy.* Englewood Cliffs, NJ: Prentice-Hall.

Burns, J. M. 1978. *Leadership.* New York: Harper and Row.

Butler, D. E., and G. Butler. 1986. *British Political Facts, 1900-1985.* London: Macmillan.

Butler, D. E., and A. King. 1965. *The British General Election of 1964.* London: Macmillan.

Butler, D. E., and A. King. 1967. *The British General Election of 1966.* London: Macmillan.

Butler, D. E., and D. E. Stokes. 1969. *Political Change in Britain.* London: Macmillan.

Butler, R. A. 1971. *The Art of the Possible.* London: Hamish Hamilton.

Cain, B., J. Ferejohn, and M. Fiorina. 1987. *The Personal Vote: Constituency Service and Electoral Independence.* Cambridge, MA: Harvard University Press.

Calmes, J. 1986. "The 99th Congress: A Mixed Record of Success." *Congressional Quarterly Weekly Report*, October 25.

Campbell, A., P. E. Converse, W. E. Miller, and D. E. Stokes. 1960. *The American Voter.* New York: Wiley.

Campbell, C., and M. J. Wyszomirski, eds. 1991. *Executive Leadership in Anglo-American Systems.* Pittsburgh, PA: University of Pittsburgh Press.

Castles, F. G. 1981. "Female Legislative Representation and the Electoral System." *Politics* 1:21-27.

Charlot, J. 1971. *The Gaullist Phenomenon.* London: Allen & Unwin.

Childs, M. 1958. *Eisenhower: Captive Hero.* New York: Harcourt, Brace.

Churchill, W. S. 1949. *Their Finest Hour.* Boston, MA: Houghton Mifflin.

Churchill, W. S. 1961. *The Gathering Storm.* New York: Bantam Books.

Clarke, H. D., C. Campbell, F. Q. Quo, and A. Goddard, eds. 1980. *Parliament, Policy and Representation.* Toronto: Methuen.

Cocks, G., and T. L. Crosby. 1987. *Psycho/History: Readings in the Method of Psychology, Psychoanalysis, and History.* New Haven, CT: Yale University Press.

Connor, W. 1967. "Self-Determination: The New Phase." *World Politics* 20:30-53.

Converse, P. E., and G. Dupeux. 1962. "Politicization of the Electorate in France and the United States." *Public Opinion Quarterly* 26:1-23.

Converse, P. E., and R. Pierce. 1986. *Political Representation in France.* Cambridge, MA: Harvard University Press.

Cooper, J. M. 1983. *The Warrior and the Priest.* Cambridge, MA: Harvard University Press.

Cornwell, E. E., Jr. 1977. Review, *Wilson Quarterly* 1:68.

Cosgrove, P. 1978. *Margaret Thatcher.* London: Hutchinson.

Cotteret, J. M., and R. Moreau. 1969. *Le Vocabulaire Politique du Général de Gaulle.* Paris: Gallimard.

Crewe, I. 1985. "Great Britain." In *Electoral Change in Western Democracies.* eds. I. Crewe and D. Denver. London: Croom Helm.

Crewe, I., and D. Searing. 1988. "Ideological Change and the British Conservative Party." *American Political Science Review* 82:361–84.

Crotty, W. 1986. *Political Parties in Local Areas.* Knoxville: University of Tennessee Press.

Crozier, M. 1964. *The Bureaucratic Phenomenon.* Chicago: IL: University of Chicago Press.

Cutright, P. 1965. "Political Structure, Economic Development, and National Social Security Programs." *American Journal of Sociology,* 70:537–51.

Daalder, H. 1966. "Parties, Elites, and Political Developments in Western Europe." In *Political Parties and Political Development,* eds. J. LaPalombara and M. Weiner. Princeton, NJ: Princeton University Press.

Daalder, H., and J. G. Rusk. 1976. "Perceptions of Party in the Dutch Parliament." In *Comparative Legislative Behavior: Frontiers of Research,* eds. S. C. Patterson and J. C. Wahlke. New York: Wiley.

Dahl, R. A. 1963. *Modern Political Analysis.* Englewood Cliffs, NJ: Prentice-Hall.

Dahl, R. A. 1966. "Patterns of Opposition." In *Political Oppositions in Western Democracies,* ed. R. A. Dahl. New Haven, CT: Yale University Press.

Dahl, R. A. 1968. "Power." In *International Encyclopedia of the Social Sciences.* New York: Macmillan and Free Press.

Dahrendorf, R. 1967. *Society and Democracy in Germany.* New York: Doubleday.

Dahrendorf, R. 1980. "Effectiveness and Legitimacy: On the 'Governability' of Democracies." *Political Quarterly* 51:393–410.

Dalton, H. 1962. *Memoirs, Vol. 2: High Tide and After.* London: Muller.

Dawson, E., K. Prewitt, and K. S. Dawson. 1977. *Political Socialization.* Boston, MA: Little, Brown.

Dawson, R. E., and J. Robinson. 1963. "Interparty Competition, Economic Variables, and Welfare Policies in the United States." *Journal of Politics* 25:265–289.

Debuyst, F. 1966. *La Fonction Parlementaire en Belgique.* Brussels: Centre de Recherche et d'Informations Socio-Politiques.

Deutsch, K. 1954. *Political Community at the International Level.* New York: Doubleday.

Dewar, H. 1987. "Full Plate of Leftovers Awaits Hill, Reagan in 1988." *Washington Post,* Dec. 23, A6.

di Palma, G. 1977. *Surviving without Governing: The Italian Parties in Parliament.* Berkeley: University of California Press.

Dion, L. 1968. "The Concept of Political Leadership: An Analysis." *Canadian Journal of Political Science* 1:1–17.

Dogan, M., ed. 1975. *The Mandarins of Western Europe.* Beverly Hills, CA: Sage.

Dogan, M., ed. 1989. *Pathways to Power: Selecting Pulers in Pluralist Democracies.* Boudler, CO: Westview Press.

Downs, A. 1957. *An Economic Theory of Democracy.* New York: Harper and Row.

Duverger, M. 1964. "The Development of Democracy in France." In *Democracy in a Changing Society,* ed. H. W. Ehrmann. New York: Praeger.

Dye, T. R. 1966. *Politics, Economics and the Public: Policy Outcomes in the American States.* Chicago: Rand McNally.

Edinger, L. J. 1965. *Kurt Schumacher: A Study in Personality and Political Behavior.* Stanford, CA: Stanford University Press.

Edinger, L. J., ed. 1966. *Political Leadership in Industrialized Societies.* New York: Wiley.

Edwardes, M. 1983. *Back from the Brink: An Apocalyptic Experience.* London: Collins.

Edwards, G. C. 1989. *Leadership at the Margins.* New Haven, CT: Yale University Press.

Eisenhower, D. D. 1948. *Crusade in Europe.* Garden City, NY: Doubleday.

Elms, Alan C. 1976. *Personality in Politics.* New York: Harcourt Brace Jovanovich.

Eltheridge, L. 1978. *A World of Men: The Private Sources of American Foreign Policy.* Cambridge, MA: M.I.T. Press.

Engelmann, F. C. 1962. "Haggling for the Equilibrium: The Renegotiation of the Austrian Coalition, 1959." *American Political Science Review* 56:651–62.

Erikson, E. H. 1969. Review in *New York Review of Books,* February 9, 3–6.

Eulau, H., and J. D. Sprague, 1964. *Lawyers in Politics.* Indianapolis, IN: Bobbs-Merrill.

Eulau, H., and J. C. Wahlke. 1978. *The Politics of Representation.* Beverly Hills, CA: Sage.

Fenichel, O. 1945. *The Psychoanalytic Theory of Neurosis.* New York: Norton.

Fenno, R. F., Jr. 1966. *The Power of the Purse: Appropriations Politics in Congress.* Boston, MA: Little, Brown.

Fenno, R.F., Jr. 1978. *Home Style: House Members in Their Districts.* Boston, MA: Little, Brown.

Field, G. L., and J. Higley. 1980. *Elitism.* London: Routledge & Kegan Paul.

Fiorina, M. P. 1977. *Congress-Keystone of the Washington Establishment.* New Haven, CT: Yale University Press.

Gallagher, M., and M. Marsh, eds. 1988. *Candidate Selection in Comparative Perspective.* London: Sage.

Gardner, J. 1989. *On Leadership.* New York: Free Press.

Gellhoed, E. B. 1979. *Charles E. Wilson and Controversy at the Pentagon, 1953–1956.* Detroit, MI: Wayne State University Press.

George, A. L. 1974. "Assessing Presidential Character." *World Politics* 26:234–82.

George, A. L. and J. L. George. 1956. *Woodrow Wilson and Colonel House: A Personality Study.* New York: John Day Co. (New York: Dover, 1964).

Gerth, H., and C. W. Mills, 1953. *Character and Social Structure.* New York: Harcourt, Brace.

Gerth, H. and C. W. Mills. 1958. *From Max Weber: Essays in Sociology.* New York: Oxford University Press.

Gibb, C. A., 1968. "Leadership." In *Handbook of Social Psychology.*, vol. 4, eds. G. Lindsey and L. Aronson. Reading, MA: Addison-Wesley.

Gibb, C. A., ed. 1969. *Leadership.* Harmondsworth, England: Penguin Books.

Glad, B. 1980. *Jimmy Carter.* New York: Norton.

Gottfried, A. 1962. *Boss Cermak of Chicago: A Study of Political Leadership.* Seattle: University of Washington Press.

Graetz, B., and I. McAllister. 1987. "Popular Evaluations of Party Leaders in the Anglo-American Democracies." In *Political Elites in Anglo-American Democracies*, eds. H. D. Clarke and M. M. Czudnowski. DeKalb: Northern Illinois University Press.

Granat, D., et al. 1983. "Partisanship Dominated Congressional Year." *Congressional Quarterly Weekly Report*, Nov. 26.

Granat, D., et al., 1984. "98th Congress Leaves Thorny Legacy for 99th." *Congressional Quarterly Weekly Report*, Oct. 20.

Greenaway, J. R. 1984. "Bureaucrats under Pressure: The Thatcher Government and the Mandarin Elite." In *Updating British Politics*, ed. L. Robins. London: Politics Association.

Greenstein, F. I. 1969. *Personality and Politics.* Chicago, IL: Markham.

Greenstein, F. I., ed. 1988. *Leadership in the Modern Presidency.* Cambridge, MA: Harvard University Press.

Greenstein, F. I., and M. Lerner, eds. 1971. *A Source Book for the Study of Personality and Politics.* Chicago, IL: Markham.

Griffith, E. S., J. Plamenatz, and J. R. Pennock. 1956. "Cultural Prerequisites to a Successfully Functioning Democracy." *American Political Science Review* 50:101–37.

Griffith, R. 1982. "Dwight D. Eisenhower and the Corporate Commonwealth." *American Historical Review* 87:93–95.

Guttsman, W. L. 1965. *The British Political Elite.* London: MacGibbon & Kee.

Hain, P. 1986. *Proportional Misrepresentation: The Case Against PR in Britain.* London: Wildwood House.

Hargrove, E. C. 1966. *Presidential Leadership: Personality and Political Style.* New York: Wiley.

Hargrove, E. C. 1967. "Popular Leadership in the Anglo-American Democracies." In *Political Leadership in Industrialized Societies*, ed. L. J. Edinger. New York: Wiley.

Hargrove, E. C. 1973. "Presidential Personality and Revisionist Views of the Presidency." *American Journal of Political Science* 17:819–35.

Heath, A. 1981. *Social Mobility.* London: Fontana.

Hennesey, P. 1983. "Shades of a Home Counties Boudicea." *The Times*, May 17.

Hermann, M. G. 1986. "Ingredients of Leadership." In *Political Psychology*, ed. M. G. Hermann. San Francisco, CA: Jossey-Bass.

Hoffmann, S., C. P. Kindleberger, Laurence Wylie, J. R. Pitts, J. P. Duroselle, and F. Goguel. 1963. *In Search of France*. New York: Harper and Row.

Horney, K. 1937. *The Neurotic Personality of Our Time*. New York: Norton.

Horney, K. 1945. *Our Inner Conflicts*. New York: Norton.

Hudson, M. C. 1967. "Lebanon: A Case of Political Underdevelopment." *Journal of Politics* 29:821–37.

Hughes, R. 1962. *The Fox in the Attic*. New York: Harper and Row.

Huntington, S. P. 1968. *Political Order in Changing Societies*. New Haven, CT: Yale University Press.

Janda, K. F. 1972. "Towards the Explication of the Concept of Leadership in Terms of the Concept of Power." In *Political Leadership*, ed. G. Paige. New York: Free Press.

Jenkins, P. 1988. *The Thatcher Revolution*. Cambridge, MA: Harvard University Press.

Jewell, M. E. 1982. *Representation in State Legislatures*. Lexington: University of Kentucky Press.

Johnson, N. 1977. *In Search of the Constitution*. Oxford: Pergamon Press.

Johnson, R. W. 1973. "The British Political Elite, 1955–72." *European Journal of Sociology* 14:35–77.

Jones, B. D., ed. 1989. *Leadership and Politics*. Lawrence: University of Kansas Press.

Jones, C. O., ed. 1988. *The Reagan Legacy*. Chatham, NJ: Chatham House.

Junor, P. 1983. *Margaret Thatcher: Wife, Mother, Politician*. London: Sidgwick & Jackson.

Kalaycioglu, E. 1980. "Why Legislatures Persist in Developing Countries: The Case of Turkey." *Legislative Studies Quarterly* 5:123–40.

Kalleberg, A. L. 1966. "The Logic of Comparison: A Methodological Note on the Comparative Study of Political Systems." *World Politics* 19:69–82.

Kane, J. N., ed. 1968. *Facts about the Presidents*. New York: Wilson.

Katz, D., B. A. Gutek, R. L. Kahn, and E. Barton, 1975. *Bureaucratic Encounters*. Ann Arbor: Institute for Social Research, University of Michigan.

Kavanagh, D. 1987. "Margaret Thatcher: The Mobilizing Style of Prime Minister." In *Political Elites in Anglo-American Democracies*, eds. H. D. Clarke and M. M. Czudnowski. De Kalb: Northern Illinois University Press.

Kearns, D. 1976. *Lyndon Johnson and the American Dream*. New York: Harper and Row.

Keller, S. 1963. *Beyond the Ruling Class: Strategic Elites in Modern Society*. New York: Random House.

Kellerman, B. 1984. *The Political Presidency*. New York: Oxford University Press.

Kellerman, B., ed. 1986. *Political Leadership: A Source Book*. Pittsburgh, PA: University of Pittsburgh Press.

Kelley, S., Jr. 1956. *Professional Public Relations and Political Power.* Baltimore, MD: Johns Hopkins University Press.

Kelley, S., Jr. 1960. *Political Campaigning.* Washington, DC: Brookings Institution.

Kernell, S. 1986. *Going Public: New Strategies of Presidential Leadership.* Washington, DC: Congressional Quarterly Press.

Kerr, H. H. 1981. *Parlement et Société.* Saint-Sapherin: Editions Georgi.

Kim, C. L., J. D. Barkan, I. Turan, and M. E. Jewell. 1984. *The Legislative Connection: The Politics of Representation in Kenya, Korea, and Turkey.* Durham, NC: Duke University Press.

Kim, C. L., and S. Pai. 1981. *Legislative Process in Korea.* Seoul: Seoul National University Press.

Kinder, D. R., M. D. Peters, R. P. Abelson, and S. T. Fiske. 1980. "Presidential Prototypes." *Political Behavior* 2:315–37.

King, A. 1966. "Britain: The Search for Leadership." In *European Politics*, vol. 1, ed. W. G. Andrews. New York: Van Nostrand.

King, A. 1981. "The Rise of the Career Politician in Britain—And its Consequences." *British Journal of Political Science* 11:249–85.

Kircheimer, O. 1957. "The Waning of Opposition in Parliamentary Regimes." *Social Research* 24:127–56.

Kirschten, K. 1983. "President Reagan after Two Years—Bold Actions but Uncertain Results." *National Journal,* Jan.

Koenig, L. 1968. *The Chief Executive.* New York: Harcourt, Brace, and World.

Lasswell, H. D. 1960. *Psychopathology and Politics.* New York: Viking Press.

Lasswell, H. D. 1948. *Power and Personality.* New York: Norton.

Lasswell, H. D., and A. Kaplan. 1950. *Power and Society.* New Haven, CT: Yale University Press.

Lawson, K., ed. 1980. *Political Parties and Linkage: A Comparative Perspective.* New Haven: Yale University Press.

Lehman, E. W. 1969. "Toward a Macrosociology of Power." *American Sociological Review* 34:453–65.

Lehmbruch, G. 1967. "A Non-Competitive Pattern of Conflict Management in Liberal Democracies: The Case of Austria, Switzerland and Lebanon." Presented at the Seventh World Congress of the International Political Association, Brussels.

Leuchtenburg, W. E. 1985. *In the Shadow of FDR.* Ithaca, NY: Cornell University Press.

Lewin, M. 1988. *The Gorbachev Phenomenon.* Berkeley, CA: University of California Press.

Lijphart, A. 1968. *The Politics of Accommodation.* Berkeley, CA: University of California Press.

Lijphart, A. 1984. *Democracies: Patterns of Majoritarian and Consensus Government in Twenty-One Countries.* New Haven, CT: Yale University Press.

Link, A. S. 1947. *Wilson: The Road to the White House.* Princeton, NJ: Princeton University Press.

Link, A. S. 1956. *Wilson: The New Freedom*. Princeton, NJ: Princeton University Press.

Lipset, S. M. 1960. *Political Man: The Social Bases of Politics*. New York: Doubleday.

Lipset, S. M. 1963. *The First New Nation: The United States in Historical and Comparative Perspective*. New York: Basic Books.

Loewenberg, G., and S. C. Patterson. 1979. *Comparing Legislatures*. Boston, MA: Little, Brown.

Lorwin, V. R. 1965. "Constitutionalism and Controlled Violence in the Modern State: The Case of Belgium." Presented at the annual meeting of American Historical Association, San Francisco.

Lorwin, V. R. 1966. "Belgium: Religion, Class, and Language in National Politics." In *Political Oppositions in Western Democracies*, ed. R. A. Dahl. New Haven, CT: Yale University Press.

MacRae, D. 1967. *Parliament, Parties, and Society in France, 1946–1958*. New York: St. Martin's.

Manzella, A. 1977. *Il Parlamento*. Bologna: Societè il Mulino.

Markus, G. B. 1982. "Political Attitudes during an Election Year: A Report on the 1980 NES Panel Study." *American Political Science Review* 76:538–60.

Masters, N. A. 1961. "House Committee Assignments." *American Political Science Review* 55:345–57.

Mayhew, D. 1974. *The Electoral Connection*. New Haven, CT: Yale University Press.

Mazlish, B. 1972. *In Search of Nixon: A Psychohistorical Inquiry*. New York: Harper and Row.

McAllister, Ian, and A. Ascui. 1988. "Voting Patterns." In *Australia Votes: The 1987 Federal Election*. eds. I. McAllister and J. Warhurst. Melbourne: Longman Cheshire.

McClelland, D. C. 1975. *Power: The Inner Experience*. New York: Irvington.

McClosky, H., and A. Brill. 1983. *Dimensions of Tolerance*. New York: Russell Sage.

McFarland, A. S. 1969. *Power and Leadership in Pluralist Societies*. Stanford, CA: Stanford University Press.

Mellors, C. 1978. *The British MP: A Socio-Economic Study of the House of Commons*. London: Saxon House.

Merriam, C. E. 1945. *Systematic Politics*. Chicago, IL: University of Chicago Press.

Michels, R. 1962. *Political Parties*. New York: Free Press.

Middlemas, K. 1979. *Politics in Industrial Society*. London: Deutsch.

Middlemas, K., and J. Barnes. 1969. *Baldwin*. London: Weidenfeld and Nicholson.

Miliband, R. 1973. *Parliamentary Socialism*. 2d ed. London: Merlin Press.

Miller, A. H., and W. H. Miller. 1975. "Issues, Candidates, and Partisan Divisions in the 1972 American Presidential Election." *British Journal of Political Science* 5:393–434.

Miller, A. H., M. P. Wattenberg, and O. Malanchuk. 1986. "Schematic Assessments of Presidential Candidates." *American Political Science Review* 80:521–40.

Miller, W. E., and D. E. Stokes. 1963. "Constituency Influence in Congress." *American Political Science Review* 57:45–46.

Mills, C. W. 1956. *The Power Elite.* New York: Oxford University Press.

Mosca, G. 1939. *The Ruling Class.* New York: McGraw-Hill.

Mughan, A. 1978. "Electoral Change in Britain: The Campaign Reassessed." *British Journal of Political Science* 8:245–53.

Muir, W. K., Jr. 1982. *Legislature: California's School for Politics.* Chicago, IL: University of Chicago Press.

Neustadt, R. E. 1965. "Politicians and Bureaucrats." In *The Congress and America's Future,* ed. D. B. Truman. Englewood Cliffs, NJ: Prentice-Hall.

Noble, T. 1975. *Modern Britain: Structure and Change.* London: Batsford.

Norpoth, H. 1987. "Guns and Butter and Government Popularity in Britain." *American Political Science Review* 81:949–59.

Nordlinger, E. A. 1965. "Democratic Stability and Instability: The French Case." *World Politics* 18:127–57.

Norris, P. 1985. "Women's Legislative Participation in Europe." *West European Politics,* 8:90–101.

O'Neill, T. P., Jr. (with William Novak). 1987. *Man of the House: The Life and Political Memoirs of Speaker Tip O'Neill.* New York: Random House.

Olson, M. 1982. *The Rise and Decline of Nations.* New Haven, CT: Yale University Press.

Ostrogorski, M. 1964. *Democracy and the Organization of Political Parties,* vol. 2. London: Haskell.

Packenham, R. A. 1970. "Legislatures and Political Development." In *Legislatures in Developmental Perspective,* eds. A. Kornberg and L. D. Musolf. Durham, NC: Duke University Press.

Paige, G. D., ed. 1972. *Political Leadership: Readings for an Emerging Field.* New York: Free Press.

Paige, G. D. 1977. *The Scientific Study of Political Leadership.* New York: Free Press.

Park, B. E. 1986. *The Impact of Illness on World Leaders.* Philadelphia: University of Pennsylvania Press.

Parker, G. R., and R. H. Davidson. 1979. "Why Do Americans Love Their Congressman So Much More Than Their Congress?" *Legislative Studies Quarterly* 4:53–62.

Parkin, F. 1971. *Class, Inequality and Political Order.* New York: Praeger.

Parsons, T., ed. 1957. *The Theory of Social and Economic Organization.* Glencoe, IL: Free Press.

Passeron, A. 1966. *De Gaulle Parle, 1962–66.* Paris: Fayard.

Pennock, J. R., and J. W. Chapman, eds. *Representation.* New York: Atherton.

Perry, J. M., and D. Shribman. 1987. "Reagan Era Restored Faith in Government Until Recent Slippage." *Wall Street Journal.* Nov. 31, 1.

Pfiffner, J. 1983. "The Carter-Reagan Transition: Hitting the Ground Running." *Presidential Studies Quarterly* 13:623–45.

Pitkin, H. 1967. *The Concept of Representation*. Berkeley: University of California Press.

Pitts, J. R. 1963. "Continuity and Change in Bourgeois France." In *In Search of France*, ed. Stanley Hoffman. New York: Harper and Row.

Polsby, N. W. 1980. *Community Power and Political Theory*, 2d. ed. New Haven, CT: Yale University Press.

Polsby, N. W. 1984. *Political Innovation in America*. New Haven, CT: Yale University Press.

Powell, G. B., Jr. 1982. *Contemporary Democracies: Participation, Stability, and Violence*. Cambridge, MA: Harvard University Press.

Pulzer, P. G. J. 1975. *Political Representation and Elections in Britain*, 3d ed. London: Allen & Unwin.

Punnett, R. M. 1973. *Front-Bench Opposition*. London: Heinemann.

Putnam, R. D. 1973. *The Beliefs of Politicians*. New Haven, CT: Yale University Press.

Putnam, R. D. 1976. *The Comparative Study of Political Elites*. Englewood Cliffs, NJ: Prentice Hall.

Rae, D., and M. Taylor. 1970. *The Analysis of Political Cleavages*. New Haven, CT: Yale University Press.

Ranney, A. 1965. *Pathways to Parliament*. London: Macmillan.

Reichley, A. J. 1981. "A Change in Direction." In *Setting National Priorities: The 1982 Budget*, ed. J. A. Pechman. Washington, DC: Brookings Institution.

Richards, P. G. 1972. *The Backbenchers*. London: Fletcher.

Riddell, P. 1983. *The Thatcher Government*. Oxford: Martin Robertson.

Riker, W. H. 1962. *The Theory of Political Coalitions*. New Haven, CT: Yale University Press.

Riker, W. H. 1986. *The Art of Political Manipulation*. New Haven, CT: Yale University Press.

Rockman, B. 1984. *The Leadership Question: The Presidency and the American System*. New York: Praeger.

Rogow, A. A. 1963. *James Forrestal: A Study of Personality, Politics, and Policy*. New York: Macmillan.

Rose, A. 1967. *The Power Structure*. New York: Oxford University Press.

Rose, R. 1984. *Do Parties Make a Difference?* 2d ed. Chatham, NJ: Chatham House.

Rose, R. 1983. "Elections and Electoral Systems: Choices and Alternatives" In *Democracy and Elections*, eds. V. Bogdanor and D. Butler. Cambridge: Cambridge University Press.

Rose, R., and D. Kavanagh. 1972. "Campaigning for Parliament." In *The Backbencher and Parliament*, eds. D. Leonard and V. Herman London: Macmillan.

Rose, R., and E. N. Suleiman, eds. 1980. *Presidents and Prime Ministers*. Washington, DC: American Enterprise Institute.

Rovere, R. H. 1959. *Senator Joe McCarthy*. New York: Harcourt, Brace.

Rule, W. 1987. "Electoral Systems, Contextual Factors and Women's Opportunity for Election to Parliament in Twenty-Three Democracies." *Western Political Quarterly*, 40:477–86.

Russell, B. 1938. *Power: A New Social Analysis*. New York: Norton.

Rustow, D. A., ed. 1970. *Philosophers and Kings: Studies in Leadership*. New York: George Braziller.

Schick, A. 1982. "How the Budget Was Won and Lost." In *President and Congress: Assessing Reagan's First Year*, ed. Norman J. Ornstein. Washington, DC: American Enterprise Institute.

Schlesinger, J. A. 1966. *Ambition and Politics: Political Careers in the United States*. Chicago, IL: Rand McNally.

Schlozman, K. L., and J. T. Tierney. 1986. *Organized Interests and American Democracy*. New York: Harper and Row.

Schumpeter, J. A. 1961. *The Theory of Economic Development*. Cambridge, MA: Harvard University Press.

Searing, D. D. 1978. "Measuring Politicians' Values: Administration and Assessment of a Ranking Technique in the British House of Commons." *American Political Science Review* 72:65–79.

Searing, D. D. 1982. "Rules of the Game in Britain: Can the Politicians Be Trusted?" *American Political Science Review* 76:65–79.

Seligman, L. G. 1950. "The Study of Political Leadership." *American Political Science Review* 44:904–15.

Shafer, B. 1988. "Scholarship on Presidential Selection in the United States." *American Political Science Review* 82:955–63.

Sigel, R. S., ed. 1989. *Political Learning in Adulthood*. Chicago, IL: University of Chicago Press.

Simonton, D. 1987. *Why Presidents Succeed: A Political Psychology of Leadership*. New Haven, CT: Yale University Press.

Socrates. 1937. *The Dialogues of Plato*, vol. 1, trans. B. Jowett. New York: Random House.

Sorenson, T. 1963. *Decision-Making in the White House*. New York: Columbia University Press.

Stockman, D. 1968. *The Triumph of Politics: Why the Reagan Revolution Failed*. New York: Harper and Row.

Stogdill, R. M. 1974. *Handbook of Leadership: A Survey of Theory and Research*. New York: Free Press.

Stokes, D. E. 1975. "Parties and the Nationalization of Electoral Forces." In *The American Party Systems*, eds. W. N. Chambers and W. D. Burnham. New York: Oxford University Press.

Stothard, P. 1983. "Who Thinks for Mrs. Thatcher?" *The Times*, Jan. 31.

Suleiman, E. N. 1978. *Elites in French Society*. Princeton, NJ: Princeton University Press.

Truman, D. B. 1951. *The Governmental Process: Political Interests and Public Opinion*. New York: Knopf.

Turner, R. H. 1960. "Sponsored Contest Mobility and the School System." *American Sociological Review* 25:855–67.

Twentieth Century Fund. 1988. *A Heartbeat Away*. New York: Priority Press.

Verba, S. 1965. "Germany: The Remaking of Political Culture." In *Political Culture and Political Development*, eds. M. Weiner and S. Verba. Princeton, NJ: Princeton University Press.

Waddington, C. H. 1966. "The Desire for Material Progress as a World Ordering System." *Daedalus* 95:666–73.

Wahl, N. 1958. "France." In *Patterns of Government*, eds. S. Beer and A. Ulam. New York: Random House.

Wahlke, J. D., H. Eulau, W. Buchanan, and L. C. Ferguson. 1962. *The Legislative System: Explorations in Legislative Behavior*. New York: Wiley.

Walker, W. E., and M. R. Reopel. 1986. "Strategies for Governance: Transitions and Domestic Policy Making." *Presidential Studies Quarterly* 16:734–60.

Walter, J. 1980. *The Leader: A Political Biography of Gough Whitlam*. St. Lucia: University of Queensland Press.

Wapshott, N., and G. Brock. 1983. *Thatcher*. London: Futura.

Waste, R. J., ed. 1986. *Community Power: Directions for Future Research*. Beverly Hills, CA: Sage.

Wayne, S. J. 1982. "Congressional Liaison in the Reagan White House: A Preliminary Assessment of the First Year." In *President and Congress: Assessing Reagan's First Year*, ed. N. J. Ornstein. Washington, DC: American Enterprise Institute.

Weber, M. 1947. *The Theory of Social and Economic Organization*, trans. A. M. Henderson and T. Parsons. New York: Free Press.

Weinstein, E. A. 1981. *Woodrow Wilson: A Medical and Psychological Biography*. Princeton, NJ: Princeton University Press.

Welch, S., and D. T. Studlar. 1983. "The Policy Opinions of British Political Activists." *Political Studies* 21:609–19.

Weller, P. 1985. *First Among Equals: Prime Ministers in Westminster Systems*. Sydney: Allen & Unwin.

White, T. H. 1965. *The Making of the President 1964*. New York: Atheneum.

Whiteley, P. 1981. "Who Are the Labor Activists?" *Political Quarterly* 52:160–70.

Wildavsky, A. 1966. "The Two Presidencies." *Trans-Action* (Dec.): 7–14.

Wildavsky, A. 1989. "A Cultural Theory of Leadership." In *Leadership and Politics*, ed. B. D. Jones. Lawrence: University of Kansas Press.

Williams, P. M. 1964. *Crisis and Compromise: Politics in the Fourth Republic*. Hamden, CT: Archon Books.

Willner, R. A. 1984. *The Spellbinders*. New Haven, CT: Yale University Press.

Wilson, E. 1962. *Shores of Light*. New York: Farrar, Straus and Young.

Wolfinger, R. E. 1985. "Dealignment, Realignment, and Mandates in the 1984 Election." In *The American Elections of 1984*, ed. Austin Ranney. Durham, NC: Duke University Press.

Wright, Q. 1951. "The Nature of Conflict." *Western Political Quarterly* 4:193–209.

Yukl, G. A. 1989. *Leadership in Organizations*. 2d ed. Englewood Cliffs, NJ: Prentice-Hall.

Index